CW01655468

From Quinten Metsijs to Peter Paul Rubens

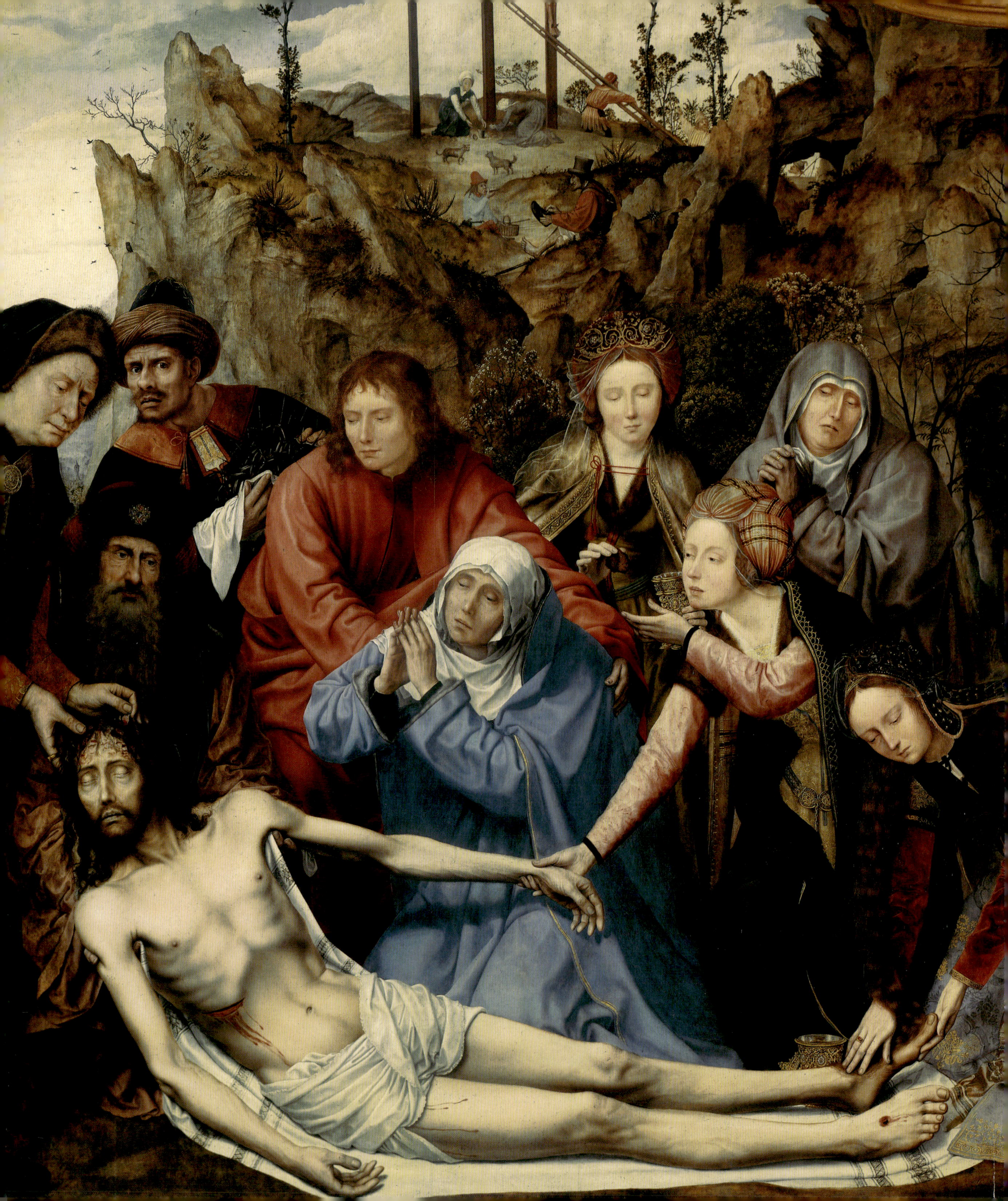

From Quinten Metsijs to Peter Paul Rubens

MASTERPIECES FROM THE ROYAL MUSEUM REUNITED IN THE CATHEDRAL

Under the scientific direction of Dr Ria FABRI and Dr Nico VAN HOUT

With contributions by Willem AERTS
Stef BINST
Claire BAISIER
Bert DEMUNCK
Ria FABRI
Marcel GIELIS
Stefaan GRIETEN
Lars HENDRIKMAN
Valérie HERREMANS
Paul HUVENNE
Madeleine MANDERYCK
Maximiliaan MARTENS
Natasja PEETERS
Prisca VALKENEERS
Carl VAN DE VELDE
Jos VAN DEN NIEUWENHUIZEN
Christine VAN MULDERS
Paul VAN REMOORTERE

DE KATHEDRAAL VZW & BAI PUBLISHERS

This catalogue has been published on the occasion of the exhibition

REUNION · From Quinten Metsijs to Peter Paul Rubens
Masterpieces from the Royal Museum reunited in the Cathedral

Cathedral of Our Lady Antwerp
5 June–15 November 2009

The exhibition has been placed under the High Patronage of Her Majesty The Queen

Contents

Many people know Antoine de Saint-Exupéry as the author *The Little Prince*, but few know that he was also a great thinker. Thus, de Saint-Exupéry pondered on a way of constructing a greater, more spiritual future for mankind, which he symbolically described as a cathedral. 'A rock pile ceases to be a rock pile the moment a single man contemplates it, bearing within him the image of a cathedral,' he said metaphorically in his book *Flight to Arras*.

That a cathedral is so much more than a pile of rocks needs no emphasis. One of the special tasks of the Province is, in fact, the care of the cathedrals of the Dioceses. Thus, the Province of Antwerp is partly responsible for the restoration of Saint Rumbold's Cathedral in Mechelen, *and* for the cathedral of the Diocese of Antwerp, the magnificent Cathedral of Our Lady. At the re-establishment of the Diocese of Antwerp in 1961, the restoration of the cathedral was assigned to the Province, a responsibility which in the French period had been held by the Départements. In 1965, therefore, the Province of Antwerp committed itself to the global restoration of the cathedral, with the exception of the large tower, which falls under the responsibilities of the city.

The major restoration works took place from 1967 to 1993, and since then work has continued on a smaller scale, for which priority is given to the remaining exterior restoration, notably the façades of the nave and transepts, and choir with its buttresses and flying buttresses. Only afterwards, will the rest of the interior be addressed: the ambulatory and the eight radiating chapels. It is through the continuing support of projects such as the Antwerp and Mechelen cathedral restorations that we seek to give a future to our past.

However, the commitment of the Province is broader than the strictly financial perspective; in collaboration with the architect, and in close consultation with the cathedral church fabric, our departments of Infrastructure and Heritage also monitor each project administratively, technically and historically. The non-profit organisation Monumentenwacht Province of Antwerp, too, in collaboration with the cathedral's technical and maintenance teams, serves usefully in the maintenance of the church; the cathedral is, in addition, part of 'The Monumental Churches Antwerp', a non-profit organisation which is also supported by the Province.

Furthermore, an inventory of the art patrimony under the ancien régime was published – under the aegis of the Province – in which the cathedral's impressive artistic treasures from this period were fully discussed. Finally, the present extensive catalogue was also created with the help of the Province, to enable all visitors and enthusiasts to continue enjoying the impressive masterpieces exhibited here, at home.

In the future, too, the Province will continue to care for the cathedral – and also more broadly, for the religious heritage, movable and immovable – for example in advisory commissions concerning conservation, restoration, and security. Furthermore, there are subsidies for the conservation of the church councils' movable patrimony, one of our most successful subsidy systems, which has already made possible the realisation of many important projects. As the provincial council, we continue to take our role as custodians of the heritage seriously, in the cathedral and elsewhere.

Ludo Helsen

Member of the Executive Council
of the Province of Antwerp

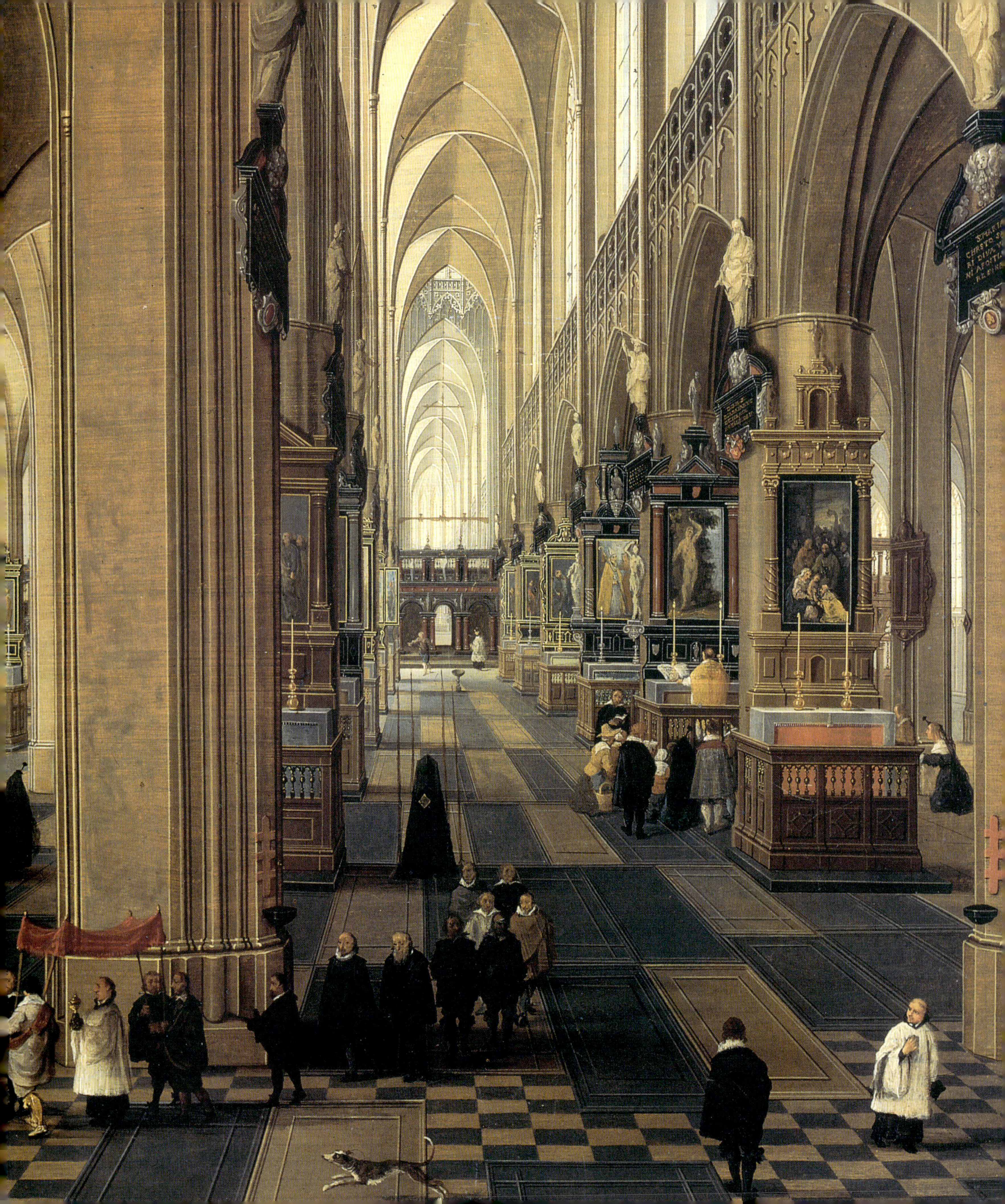

Introduction

PAUL HUVENNE
PAUL VAN REMOORTERE

With the bull *Super Universas* of 12 May 1559, Pope Paul IV decided to establish 14 new dioceses in the Spanish Netherlands. This decision was no coincidence, but a direct consequence of the impressions Emperor Charles and his son, crown prince Philip had gathered during their Joyous Entry to the Netherlands in 1549. They decided to enforce the Counter Reformation movement. Antwerp was allocated an episcopal seat. The Church of Our Lady, which since her establishment in 1124 had fallen under the Bishop of Cambrai (Artois), became a cathedral. Now, 450 years later, we remember this event with the exhibition REUNION: *From Quinten Metsijs to Peter Paul Rubens. Masterpieces from the Royal Museum reunited in the Cathedral.*

From the 16th century onwards, the Antwerp Painting School made its fame and fortune. Artists from far and near came to the Scheldt city to train and to make a living, but especially to paint, since Antwerp was a place of image production par excellence. For a complete understanding of the art of that period it is important to know its context. Today, we often see works of art in a museum environment – but this is far from their original purpose.

They were made for a public domain, which the cathedral pre-eminently was. It was more than a community of worshippers – the whole of society was represented in the church. Fraternities, guilds, and craft, each had their own place. At the beginning of the 17th century there were approximately 40 altars in the cathedral! Each was embellished very beautifully, in honour of God and to the credit of the association it represented. The great fire of 1533, which devastated almost all the church's late-gothic furnishings (among which were more than 50 altars with retables), led to an almost complete refurnishing. The Iconoclastic Fury that raged through the church in 1566, *and* the years of Calvinist rule (1581–1585), both had a decisive impact on the church patrimony.

Nothing, however, was as definitive as the French Revolution. Radical changes occurred during the French invasion and annexation at the end of the 18th century: the diocese, the chapter, the crafts, the fraternities, the militias, and the almoners, were abolished. The church was closed; the furnishings were transferred to Paris, or destined for the Musée Départemental, which was still to be created. Whatever remained was publicly sold. The works of art disappeared from their natural social space and their specific context became that of the 'Beaux-Arts'. In 1815 most of the great masterworks returned from Paris under massive public interest. Some found their way back to the cathedral, which had meanwhile been demoted to a church; others received a new place in the museum. Now, 200 years later, visitors can admire the masterworks from *Quinten Metsijs to Peter Paul Rubens* 'in situ', in their original context, in the impressive cathedral space, for which they were commissioned and designed, where they were displayed and where they functioned for centuries as a religious reference to their commissioners.

To meet again after a long separation is called a *reunion*. We, the cathedral and the museum staff, have attempted to realise nothing more and nothing less with this exhibition. By going back in time, we understand better how these historical objects once had such a fundamental influence. That is why this project is so unique in concept. The choice of the period is easily understood. The reason for this exhibition – the establishment of the Diocese of Antwerp in 1559 – took place in those years.

These ancient artistic treasures may have been reunited, but – and that is how gone by friendships sometimes are – the subtlety and intensity of their mutual relation can no longer be fully understood, as a result of past events. A complete and historical reconstruction is therefore impossible. This is certainly true for a glorious monument like the Cathedral of Our Lady. Today it is a lively episcopal and parish

1
Pieter I Neeffs · *Interior View of the Antwerp Cathedral of Our Lady* · Brussels, Royal Museums of Fine Arts of Belgium

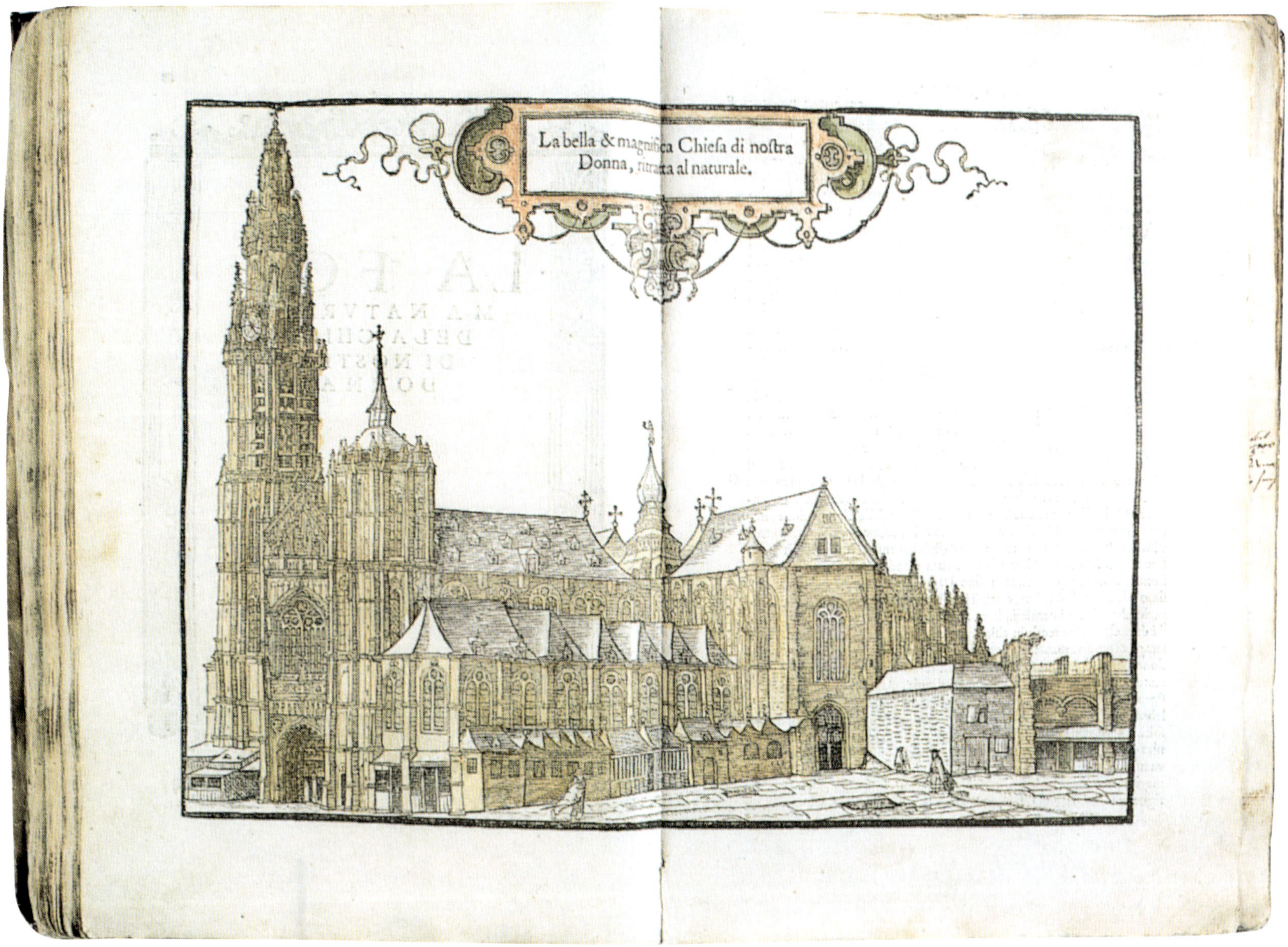

2
Lodovico Guicciardini
Descrittione di tutti i Paesi Bassi
Antwerp, 1581
view of the Cathedral of Our Lady
Antwerp, private collection

church as well as church of choice for many worshippers from a wide area. It has grown to be one of the main cultural-historical sites of the country, which every year receives hundreds of thousands of visitors from home and abroad. Added to this is the complexity of the double identity of the works of art, which are both religious altarpieces and works of national art-historical importance.

Today the cathedral is a monumental, liturgical, and museal site. These different aspects made this exhibition project a challenging undertaking. It was also our wish to integrate the exhibition's works, in the most natural way possible, into the original, sacred atmosphere of the church building. Therefore a high degree of historicity was pursued in the exhibition design. The altarpieces' line-up undoubtedly recalls the atmosphere of the cathedral during the ancien régime, although the works could often not be displayed in their original locations. The changed liturgical customs and – in the specific context of the cathedral – the ongoing restoration of the radiating chapels, made this virtually impossible.

The result is a fascinating exploration. A glimpse of the sacred context of these extraordinary masterworks should inspire and incite the visitor to search for the true relationship between the works of art and their environment, the cathedral. Thus, in the chaplains' sacristy, 16th and 17th century views of the cathedral interior are projected. In the main sacristy, a portrait gallery of the 21 bishops of Antwerp, the 18 bishops of the first diocese, and 3 of the actual diocese, can be visited. In June 2009, a colloquium will be dedicated to the establishment of the new diocese, its first bishop, and the further evolution under the ancien régime, organised by the Provinciale Commissie voor Geschiedenis en het Departement Geschiedenis, Universiteit Antwerpen. All things considered, the diocese had an eventful history. After its establishment in 1559, it would take until 1570 before Sonnius, born Franciscus van de Velde in Son near Eindhoven, was appointed and installed as the first Bishop of Antwerp. The Diocese of Antwerp, together with two other dioceses, was abolished two centuries later by the Concordat of 1801 between Napoleon and Pope Pius VII. Only 160 years later, Antwerp would again be allocated an episcopal seat.

The exhibition itself offers a splendid overview of religious painting from the 16th and 17th centuries by Antwerp masters and their studios. Eight works from the collection of the museum, which could formerly be viewed in the cathedral, and eight works from the actual cathedral patrimony, were brought together by Dr Ria Fabri, the Cathedral Curator, and Dr Nico Van Hout, Curator of the Antwerp Koninklijk Museum voor Schone Kunsten. Together with the exhibition designer Koen Van Synghel, they established the concept for the installation of this exhibition.

The collaboration between the museum and the cathedral was an obvious decision: after the French rule, an important part of the cathedral's artistic patrimony was assigned – by the government of the United Kingdom of the Netherlands – to the predecessor of what would become the prestigious Museum in Antwerp-South.

This is not the first time the Museum and the Cathedral have collaborated. Thus, two triptychs by Hendrik van Balen, whose panels were distributed between the museum and the cathedral, were reunited after a long-term loan and, after restoration, displayed in the cathedral. Furthermore, a 15th century Catalan retable was given as a long-term loan by the Church Council to the Koninklijk Museum, where it received a place next to the Van Eyck and Van der Weyden paintings.

In a parallel exhibition in the more intimate Rockox House, an overview of works commissioned through private patronage from the same period is offered. The Cathedral, the Koninklijk Museum, and several of Antwerp's monumental churches collaborated to realise this project.

The Church Council is grateful to the Flemish government, the Provincial Executive, the City Executive, OCMW Antwerp, and to private sponsors, for the opportunity they were offered to organise this fascinating exhibition.

Finally, on behalf of our colleagues of the Church Council, the Board of the Antwerp Koninklijk Museum voor Schone Kunsten, and the curators, we warmly thank the coordinator An Teyssen and the cathedral staff, led by Christian Devos, for their essential contribution to the realisation of this project.

Dr Paul Huvenne
Administrator-general Koninklijk Museum voor Schone Kunsten Antwerpen

Paul Van Remoortere
Chairman of the Church Council and of the Organising Committee

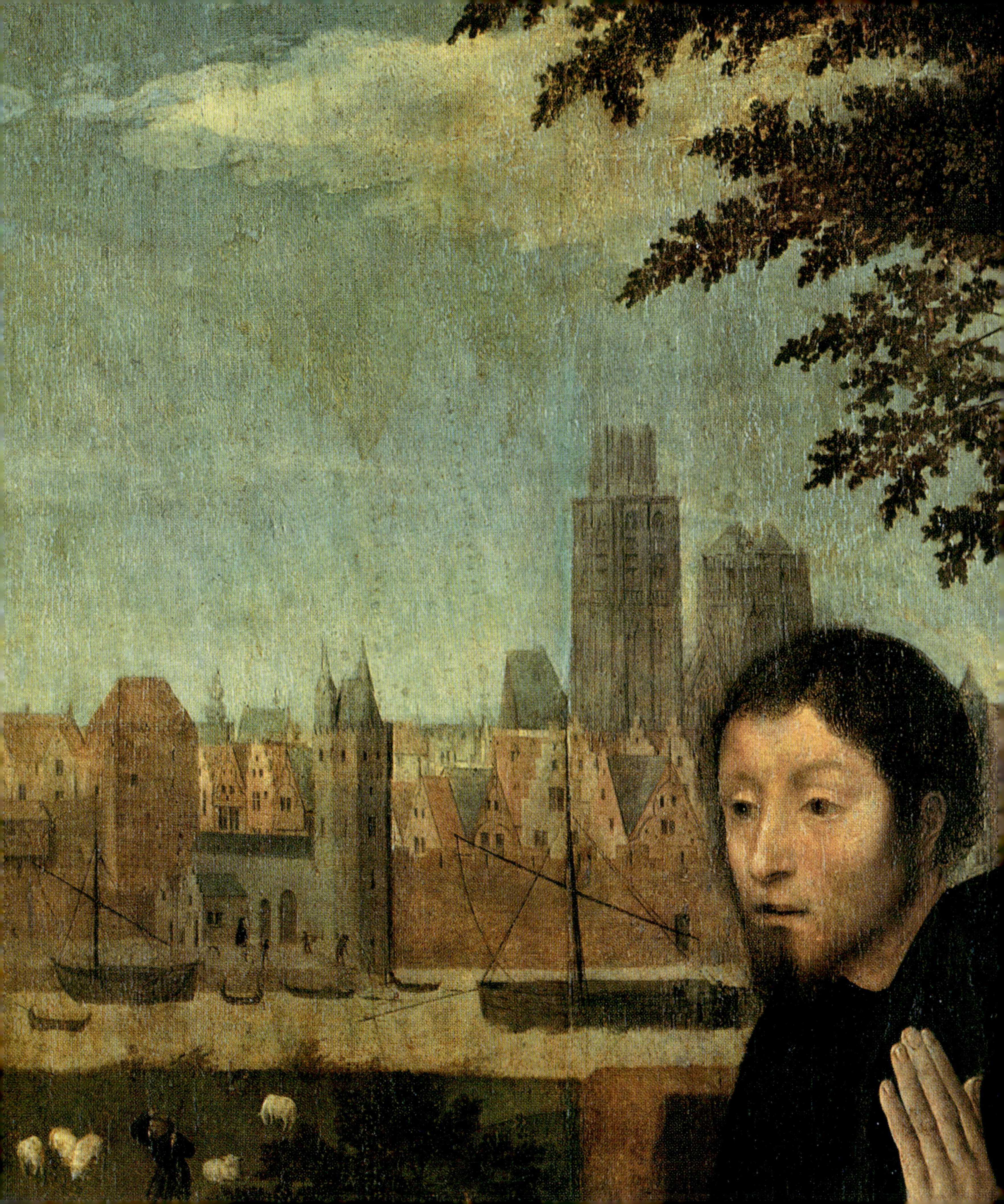

Altars, from chantry to craft

(15th and early 16th centuries)

JOS VAN DEN NIEUWENHUIZEN

In the last quarter of the 15th century the Antwerp crafts were allotted pillars in the nave and aisles of the new Gothic Church of Our Lady, against which they could erect their own altars. In the previous centuries dozens of chantries had been established around altars that were each dedicated to their own saint. Altars needed to be established in the new church, too. Appointing these to the crafts shifted responsibility for their set-up and decoration to them.

Building the Church of Our Lady

From the 12th to the middle of the 14th century the Church of Our Lady was a large Romanesque church building, to which a chapter with a dean and 22 canons was attached. The church was 80 metres long and 42 metres wide. The choir and the transept were built on a cloverleaf pattern with an ambulatory.[1]

In the middle of the 14th century the canons decided to demolish the Romanesque church and build a larger church on the same location. Until 1482, for almost a century and a half, demolishing and building would go hand-in-hand. The works were initiated with the building of three radiating chapels on the south side of the old church. Then the choir of the Romanesque church was gradually demolished and replaced by a new Gothic choir, which was completed c. 1391. At the beginning of the 15th century this new choir with radiating chapels on the north and south sides, in which meanwhile many altars had been erected, was brought into use.

In 1420 the foundations of the north tower were initiated in front of the west façade of the Romanesque church, and in 1430 those of the south tower. Between the new choir and these towers the nave and transept of the old church were preserved; the nave was possibly demolished before 1431. In the period 1455–1469, on the south side of the new church that was yet to be built, a wide side aisle was erected, of which the first two bays were reserved for the Chapel of the Blessed Sacrament and the rest for the parish. After that, until 1478, an equally wide side aisle was built on the north side, of which the first two bays were reserved for the guild of 'Onze-Lieve-Vrouwelof' ('Praise of Our Lady') and the remaining bays were planned to become Chapel of the Holy Cross. The roofs of both chapels were tiled over in 1482.

By c. 1475 the south tower had reached its present height and the north tower its fourth story.

Between the towers, work continued on the west end. In the years 1470 and 1480 the nave was built towards the choir, with two side aisles on each flank, connecting to the two wide side aisles that had already been built. The slate roof of the nave was added c. 1490.

The south transept was built between 1481 and 1492. The sacristy and library were built beside the ambulatory. The north transept followed between 1487 and 1495. The Jerusalem Chapel was built at the east end. The crossing was completed c. 1500. Completing the highest section of the north tower would take until 1520.

Chantries and Altars in the Church of Our Lady

From the 13th to the 16th century dozens of chantries were established in the Church of Our Lady. Chantries were benefices, of which the revenues sufficed to provide for the priest's life maintenance. The priests were obliged to hold a number of Masses each week at one of the altars, and to participate in the offices. The canons appointed the priests.

The two oldest chantries were those of the High Mass, founded in 1227 and 1232. These were followed in 1243 by the foundation of chantries for 'Masses for the Dead' by four priests. From 1274 onwards there was a succession of foundations. In the middle of the 14th century some forty chantries were founded in the Romanesque church around at least eighteen

4
Anonymous
Saint James as a Pilgrim for Antwerp
detail of the Cathedral of Our Lady with unfinished towers · miniature in a Flemish prayer book · c. 1508
The Hague, Museum Meermanno-Westreenianum

1 The story of the building of the church is based on Bungeneers 1993 and Van Langendonck 1993.

3
Anonymous · *Morrison Triptych* · detail of the Church of Our Lady with unfinished towers · c. 1500 · Philadelphia, John G. Johnson Collection

altars.[2] While the choir of the new church was being built, five altars were added, which had possibly also occupied a place in the old church.[3]

All these altars would in time be transferred from the Romanesque church to the new church. On 11 July 1402, Pierre d'Ailly, Bishop of Cambrai, permitted the consecration of the altar of the chapter of Saint Lawrence, two further ones, and some movable altars, by any bishop who would visit Antwerp.[4] These were probably altars that had already been transferred to the new ambulatory. The nine new altars on which chantries were founded in the 15th century were certainly placed in this ambulatory.[5] In the foundation deeds of three of these chantries the altars were explicitly situated there. These were the chantry founded in 1416 on the altar of the Holy Apostle Thomas, Thomas Aquinas, and Thomas of Canterbury,[6] the chantry founded in 1456 on the altar of Saint Cornelius;[7] and the chantry established in 1466 on the altar of Saint George.[8] During the 15th century, altars from the old church were certainly transferred to the new ambulatory.

Some altars may have disappeared, such as those of Saint Giles and Saint Margaret. In 1487 chaplain Egidius Fabri founded a chantry on an altar where three saints were worshipped together: Lambert, Giles, and Margaret. The chantry of Saint Giles had been established in 1295 by canon Hugo van Cnocke. In 1410 its revenues were incorporated into the chanter's choir; the Mass obligations were fulfilled in 1441 on the altar of the 'Kinderbedde' ('Childbed').[9] The chantry of Saint Margaret was also incorporated into the chanter's choir. In 1431 the altar was established in the *'gerfkamer'* (dressingroom for priests) of the church.[10]

An indication of which pillars in the nave were intended to receive which altars from the old church, as well as the altars from the new ambulatory, might be given by the depictions of saints in the bosses of the vaults in the neighbouring side aisles.[11] If so,

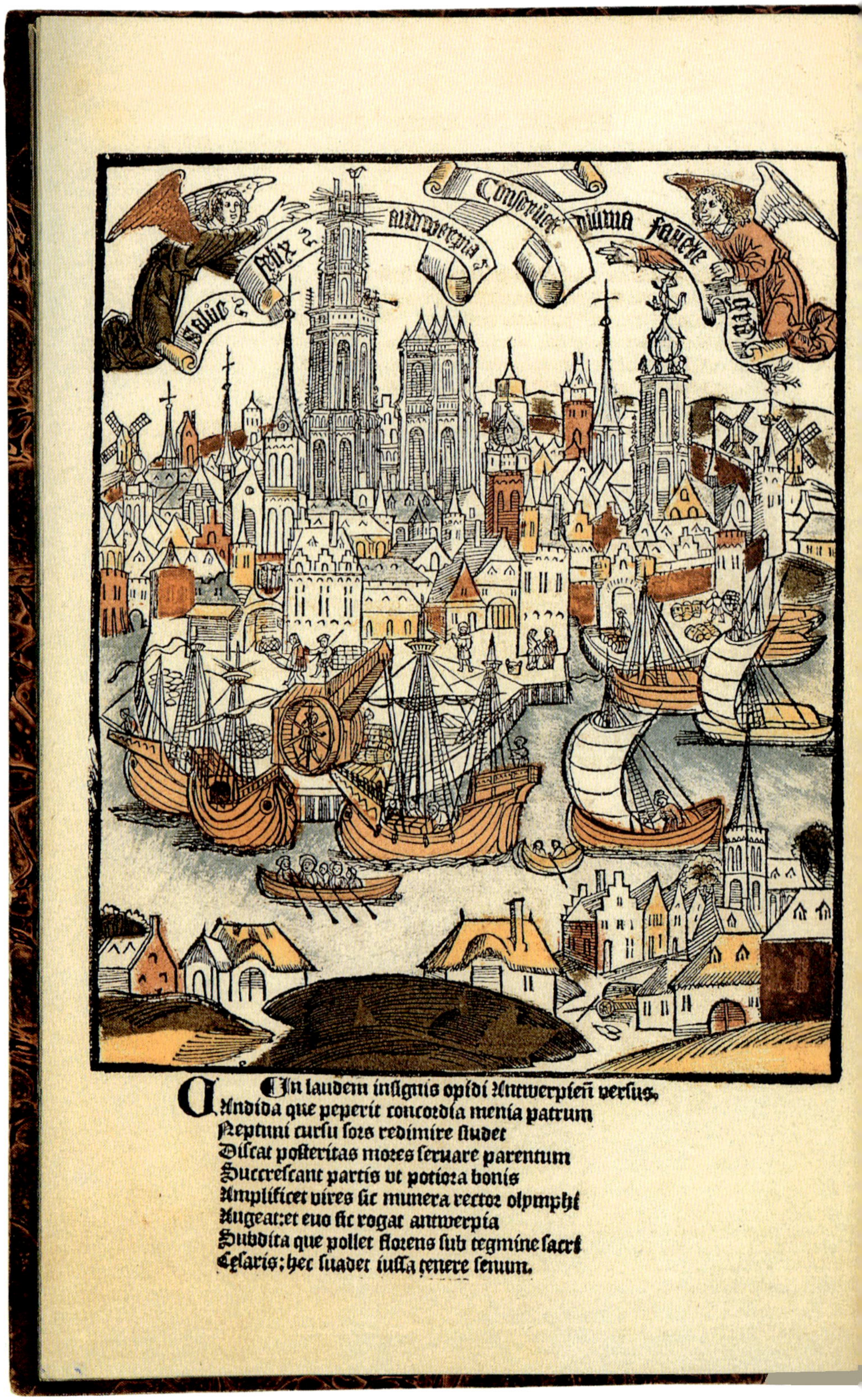

5
Anonymous · *The Roads of Antwerp* · print in Benedictus de Opitiis, *Loeflicke Sanck* · ed. Jan de Geet, Antwerp, c. 1515 · Leuven, University Library

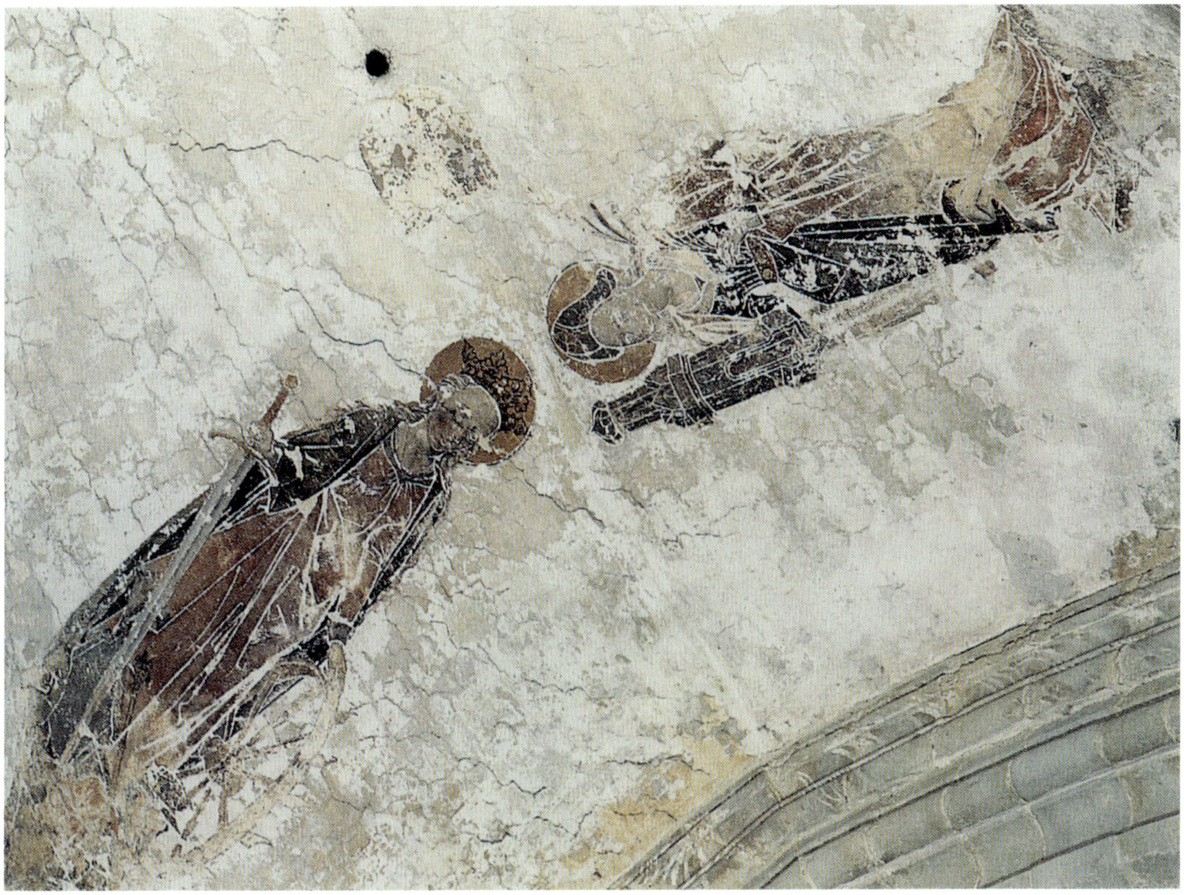

however, this also shows that early assignments were often abandoned. The church accounts of 1472–1473 mention the bosses with Saint Michael and Saint Gummarus in the side aisles, on both flanks of the nave, connecting to the towers. But later, we find Saint Michael's altar (of the Fencers) at one of the crossing pillars, and the altar of Saint Gummarus (of the Woodcutters) in the wide aisle behind the Chapel of our Lady.[12] In 1474–1475, the third pillar on the south flank of the nave became the pillar of the Baker's altar and also the pillar of Saints Peter and Paul.[13] On the boss of the neighbouring bay in the side aisle, however, Saint Nicholas is depicted; Merchants, Bakers and the guild of Saint Nicholas shared the same altar until 1476. This all goes to show that the crafts in the 1470s had quickly become established in the Church of Our Lady.

Craft Altars in place of Chantry Altars

The assignation of altars to crafts relieved the canons and the church fabric of the responsibility for establishing the new altars necessary for the chantries in the new church. Moreover the crafts also took over the burden of decorating the altars. In 1503 the city magistrate allowed the Linen Weavers to levy 8 pounds for the repair of the ornaments of their altar and other expenses.[14] On 3 December 1503 the city magistrate and the Antwerp council allowed the craft of the Old Clothes' Merchants to charge each new member 15 shillings for the maintenance of the altar of Saint Catherine. This would also allow them to pay for their expensive new altar table.[15] On 26 November 1538 the Fishmongers received permission from the city magistrate to charge each member ten shillings for the maintenance of their altar.[16] In 1539 the Merchants even taxed their properties with

2 These altars were consecrated to Saint Catherine (1274), Saint John (1282), the Holy Cross (13th century), Saint Agatha (1288), Our Lady of the New Work (1291), Saint Giles (1295), Saint Laurence (1301), Mary Magdalene (c. 1301), Saints Peter and Paul (before 1302), Saint Barbara (1308), Saint Cecilia (before 1311), Saint Josse (c. 1317), Saint Margaret (before 1323), Childbed (before 1326), Saint Andrew (before 1328), the Holy Trinity (1335), the Eleven Thousand Virgins (before 1339), and Saint Eligius (1346).

3 These were the altars of Our Lady *de Ambra* (1355), Saint James (before 1362), Saint Nicholas (1365), Saint Arnulf (second half of the 14th century), and the Circumcision (1398).

4 KAA, Capsa 14 Capellanorum, litt. F.

5 These were the altars of Saint Blaise (1414), Saint Anne or Salve Regina (1415), Saint Thomas (1416), the Holy Sacrament (1438), Saint Cornelius (1456), Saint Anthony (1460), Saint George (1466), Saint Adrian (1493) and All Saints (1494).

6 KAA, Capsa Testamentorum, Antiqua no. 3 (5).

7 KAA, Capsa 72 Capellanorum, no. 1.

8 KAA, Capsa 68 Capellanorum, no. 1.

9 KAA, Capsa 25 Dominorum, Huysheer no. 5bis.

10 KAA, Capsa 25 Dominorum, Canteman no. 4.

11 The bosses in the church are all illustrated in Grieten & Bungeneers 1996, pp. 45–75, nos. 54–129.

12 See the ordinance of 9 August 1484. SAA, A.4.101: *Privilegieboek van de houtbrekers*, fol. 12 v°–13 r°.

13 Prims 1938–1939, XIII, pp. 301–302.

14 SAA, A.4.202: *Gebonden stukken van de linnenwevers. 1430–1772*, fol. 42–43.

15 SAA, A.4.277: *Gebonden stukken van de oudekleerkopers. 1436–18de eeuw.*

16 16th century copy in SAA, A.4.365: *Gebonden stukken van de visverkopers. 1418–1786*, fol. 346–348.

6
Vault Painting with Saints Barbara and Catherine · second half 15th century · Antwerp, Cathedral of Our Lady

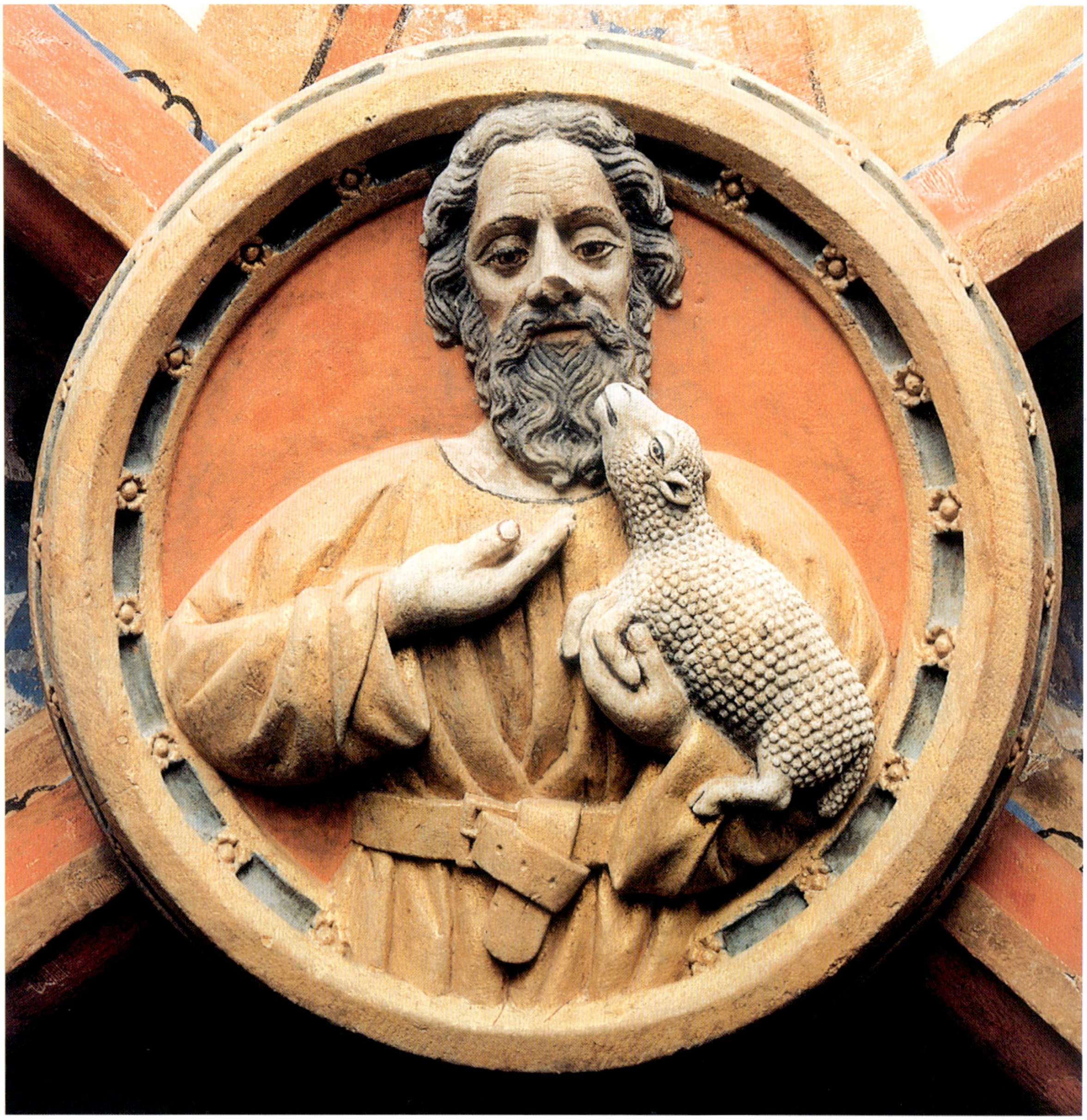

7
Boss with John the Baptist in original polychromy
c. 1400
Antwerp, Cathedral of Our Lady

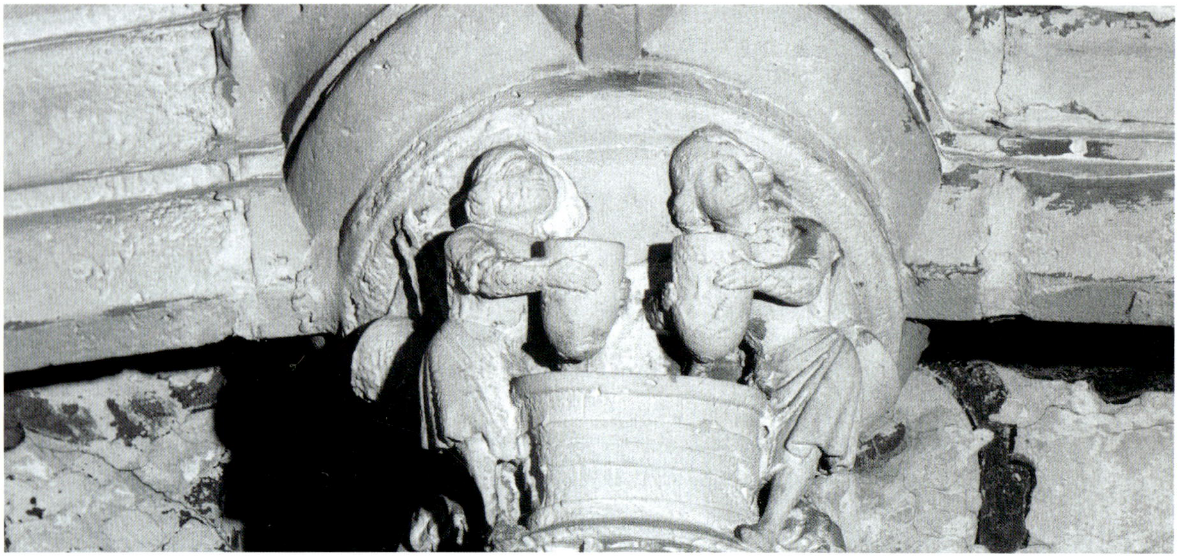

8
Boss of the Brewers' craft
first half 15th century
Antwerp, Cathedral of Our Lady

three interest payments amounting to 90 Carolus guilders for the repair of their altar.[17]

In his seminal article the city archivist Dr. Frans Blockmans has shown that Antwerp crafts were recognised by the authorities as early as 1302.[18] Craftsmen organised themselves in free associations. Already in the first half of the 14th century more than twenty crafts were officially acknowledged. Obtaining an ordinance from the bailiff and council members meant a full legitimatisation in itself.[19] This number increased steadily and the professions regrouped themselves continually. The craftsmen presented themselves in processions in their own livery. Twenty-five crafts took part in the Procession of Our Lady on the Sunday after Ascension in 1399.[20]

Soon they demanded participation in the daily management of the city and the control of city finance. In 1435 Philip the Good authorised twelve delegates from twenty-one crafts to assist the council members. The Shippers, Gardeners, and Merchants, would have a permanent representative each, and nine crafts would, by turns with nine others, depute one representative each. In 1445 this administrative level received a permanent character in 'Monday's Council'.[21] When, later, the 'Broad Council' was created, which decided in matters of general importance, the crafts were part of it, as its fourth fraction after the aldermen, the former-aldermen, and the deans of the citizenry with the wardmasters. In turns twenty-six crafts were represented in this fourth fraction. Sixteen of these twenty-six privileged crafts and five others obtained an altar in the Church of Our Lady: ten in the nave, three in the north side aisle, and eight in the ambulatory.[22]

As long as the building work continued, until 1495, and even afterwards, the allotted places for an altar could be changed. This was certainly the case for the altars of the Dyers, the Drapers, and the Brewers. In the wide northern side aisle with the Chapel of Our Lady, their tools on the bosses indicate the intended place of their altars; but neither the dyers nor the drapers had an altar in the church. On the other hand altars disappeared, like the ones dedicated to Saints Agatha, Andreas, Arnulf, Blaise, Cecilia, Giles, and Laurence, which were housed in the old Romanesque church. Even the altars of Saints George (1466), Adrian (1493) and All Saints (1494), which were still established in the second half of the 15th century, could in the 16th century not be found again in the Church of Our Lady – which became a cathedral in 1559.

In most cases an altar was not allotted directly to a craft, but to the guild in which craftsmen were associated and worshipped their patron saint. Jan Verjuys, the founder of Saint Lambert's altar, and three guild brothers of Saint Lambert's Guild made an agreement on 5 June 1492 with two masters of the Wool Cloth Cutters which allowed the latter to share the use of the altar of Saints Lambert, Giles and Margaret, if they would also share the ornaments. Moreover the wool cloth cutters could worship Saint Francis as their second patron.[23]

The guild of Saint Nicholas maintained the Saint Nicholas altar. The Merchants, Bakers, and Cabinetmakers used it jointly before they received their own altar (see cat. 1). On 21 October 1476, the Bakers, Cabinetmakers, and Coopers passed it on to the Merchants' craft.[24] The guild of Saint Anne, which included the Hosiers, had its altar in the nave of the church until 1487.[25]

The Tailors obtained the altar of Saint Cornelius in the first chapel of the south ambulatory.[26] The Furriers, who worshipped Saint George, were given the altar of Saint Thomas in the ambulatory. The Coopers and Herring Packers obtained the Altar of Trinity in the ambulatory, on which several chantries were established, and on which also Saint Matthias was worshipped.[27] The Herring Packers could also display a statue of Saint Anthony, their patron, there. After the iconoclastic outbreaks both

17 SAA, A.4.246: *Gebonden stukken van de meerseniers. 1429–1780.*
18 Blockmans 1953, pp. 161–201.
19 Prims 1937, pp. 66–74, no. 8.
20 *Oudt register 1336–1439*, pp. 429–433.
21 See Van den Nieuwenhuizen 2000, pp. 467–469.
22 These 21 crafts are in the nave of the church on the south side (the non-privileged are italicised): the coopers (Saint Matthew), the bakers (Saint Aubert), the merchants (Saint Nicholas) and the fishmongers (Saint Philip); in the nave on the north side: *the hosiers* (Saint Anne), the old clothes' merchants (Saint Catherine), the gardeners (Our Lady of the Stake), the smiths (Saint Eligius), the linen weavers (Saints Ambrose and Severus) and the barbers (Cosmas and Damian); against the pillars of the northernmost side aisle: the woodcutters (Saint Gummarus), the cabinetmakers (Saint Joseph) and *the harness makers* (Saint Lucia); in the ambulatory: the cabinetmakers (Saint John), *the painters* (Saint Luke), the furriers (Saint Thomas), *the wine taverners* (Saint Martin), the cobblers (Saint Crispin), the masons (the Four Crowned Martyrs), *the school teachers* (Saint Ambrose) and the tailors (Saint Boniface).
23 SAA, A.4.032: *Privilegieboek van de uitsnijders*, fol. 1 r°–2 r°; Prims 1939, pp. 19–46.
24 Prims 1938–1939, XII, pp. 328–333, no. 52. SAA, A.4.245: *Gebonden stukken van de meerseniers. 1354–1762.*
25 Prims 1938–1939, XIII, pp. 344–349, no. 49.
26 Prims 1938–1939, XII, pp. 334–339, no. 53.
27 Prims 1938–1939, XII, pp. 296–301, no. 47.

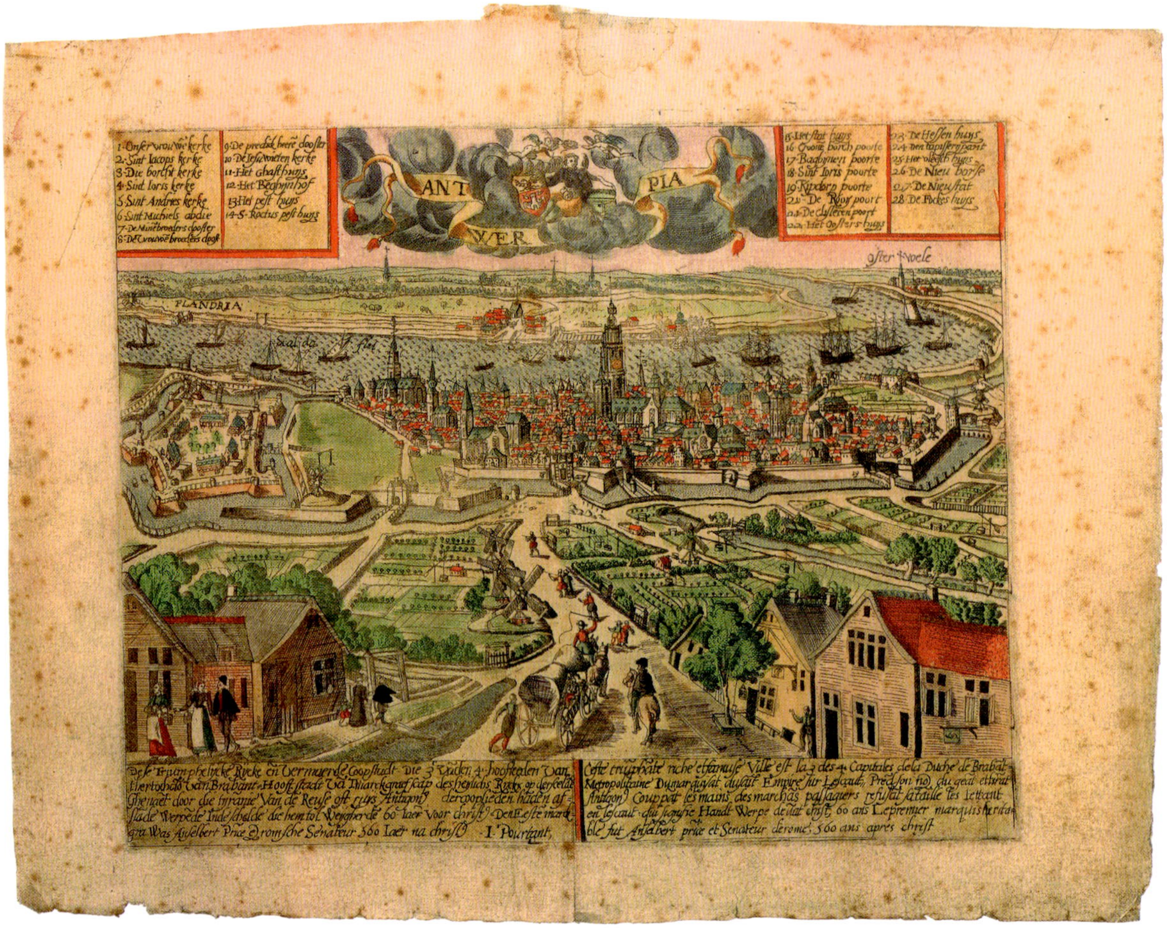

9
I. Pourtant
View of Antwerp
coloured print, 1570
private collection

were allotted the altar of Saint Anne in November 1567.[28] The Gardeners used the altar of Saint Agatha at the end of the 15th century, but later 'Onze-Lieve-Vrouw-op-het-Staakske' (Our Lady on the Branch) was worshipped on their altar in the nave (see cat. 5).[29] The craft of the Barbers asked permission to embellish the altar of Saint Mary Magdalene and perform their services on it. This was allowed on condition that the chaplain of the 'cantuary' (a chantry with a sung Mass) which had been founded on this altar by the Van der Dilf family, would not be disturbed.[30] In January 1530 the Saddlers agreed to care for the altar of the Saints Lucia and Gertrude, which had remained unembellished until then. They had effected this immediately, but the church fire in the night of 5 and 6 October 1533 destroyed everything. They were allotted a new altar opposite the pew of the Holy Ghost. They asked permission from the city magistrate to charge each member 6 Carolus guilders for the repair of the altar.[31] The fifth altar in the north side aisle belonged to the Linen Weavers. After the fire of 1533 a new altar was consecrated on 2 June 1537 by Hugo de Capella, auxiliary bishop of Cambrai, in honour of Our Lady *de Ambra* and the saints Bartholomew, Ambrosias and Severus. Again, after the iconoclastic outbreaks, a new altar was consecrated on 12 July 1568 by Maarten Cuijper, who had succeeded Hugo de Capella as auxiliary bishop.[32]

When chantry altars disappeared, the benefices and Mass obligations still needed to be fulfilled. Chaplains now read the Mass at the altars of the crafts. Thus a bond arose between the crafts and the chaplains; the chaplains became at the same time chaplains for the crafts. They marched with the members of the crafts in the city's many processions, joined in their patron celebrations and participated in the festive meals at these occasions. The deans of the Hosiers' craft even received bequests for Requiem masses their chaplain had to say on the altar of Saint Anne.[33] After the death of a member of the brotherhood of Saint Lambert, which included the Cloth

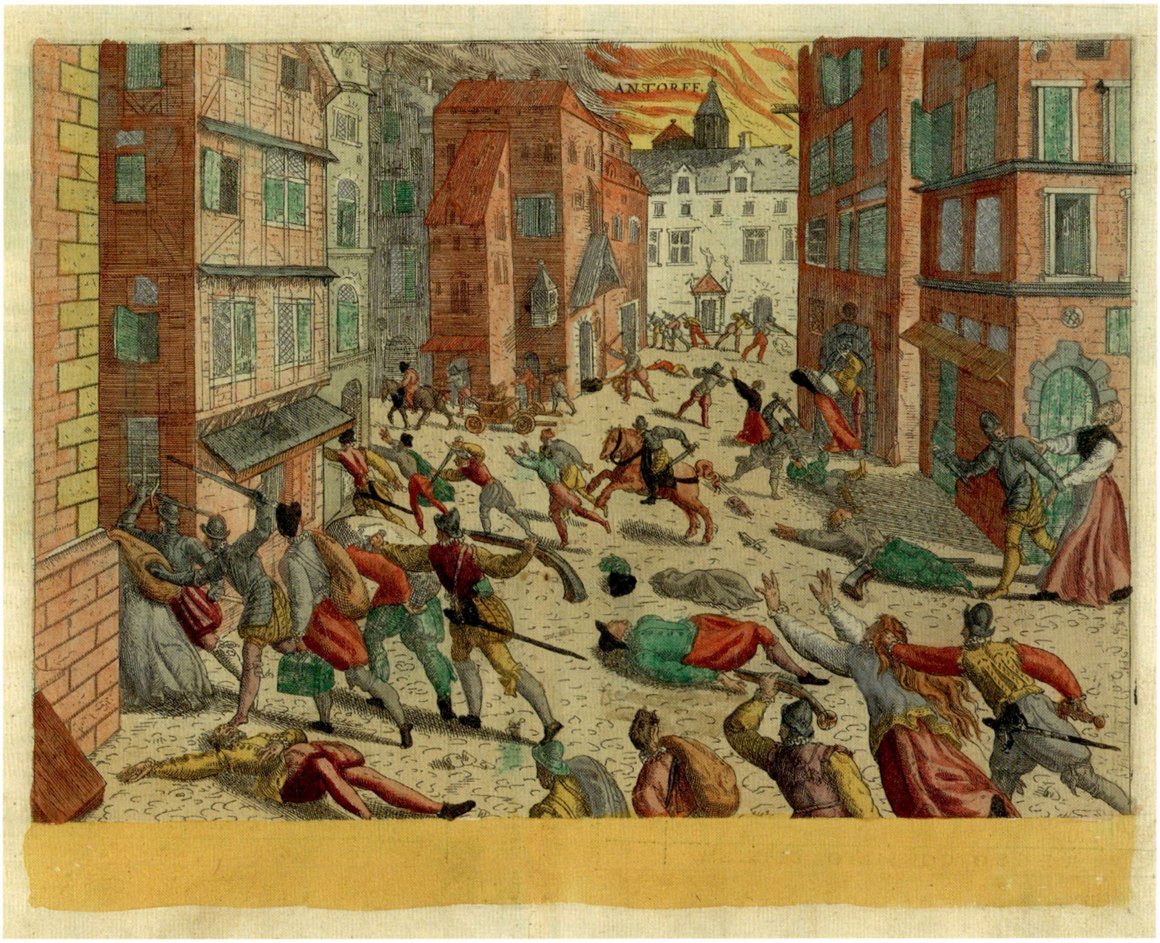

10
Frans Hogenberg
The Spanish Fury of 1576
coloured print · 1586
private collection

Cutters, the chaplain read a *Miserere* and a *De Profundis* for the deceased in the chamber of the craft.[34] In 1568 the Wine Taverners paid a new bonnet and a remuneration of 5 guilders and 12 stivers to chaplain Fynenbuyck.[35]

Prims called the erection of the many chantry altars in the Church of Our Lady 'the altarisation of the offices of the church'.[36] He characterised the moving in of crafts as the evolution from chapter church to 'people's church' and called the church building itself an 'altar barn'.[37]

Little is known about the embellishment of altars in the 16th century. After the fire of 1533 two more events caused ravages in the church. On 20 August 1566 the iconoclastic fury took place. From 19 to 22 June 1581 the church was closed and the altars were removed by the Calvinists. After 1585 the reconstruction and furnishing of altars could start again.[38]

28 SAA, A.4.200: *Gebonden stukken van de haringpakkers. 1525–1670.*
29 Prims 1938–1939, XIII, pp. 337–343, no. 48.
30 Undated piece in SAA, A.4.077: *Gebonden stukken van de barbiers en de chirurgijns. 1454–1787.*
31 SAA, A.4.593: *Privilegieboek van de zadel- en gareelmakers*, fol. 10 r°–11 v°.
32 Deed of 2 June 1537 by Robert van Croy, Bishop of Cambrai, with a back note. SAA, A.4.203: *Bundel losse stukken.*
33 SAA, A.4.049: *Gebonden stukken van de kousenmakers. 1487–1677* (in the back).
34 Ordinance of 4 September 1492. SAA, A.4032: *Privilegieboek van de uitsnijders. 1492–1788*, fol. 3 v°–4 r°.
35 SAA, A.4.590: *Rekening van de wijntaverniers. 1563–1624*, pp. 59 and 67.
36 Prims 1940, p. 27.
37 Prims 1939, p. 30.
38 Vervaet 1976, pp. 197–244.

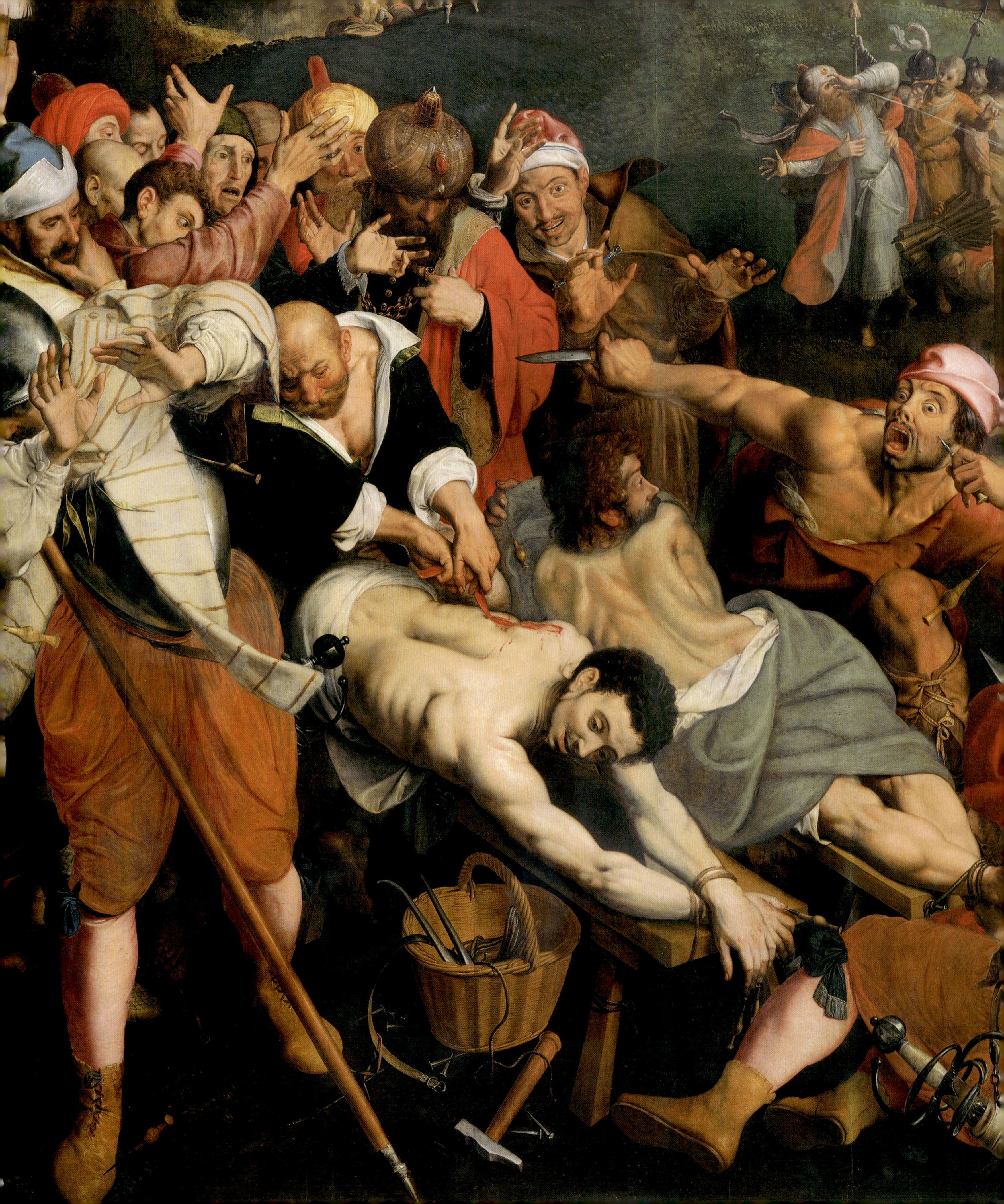

From religious devotion to commercial ambition?

BERT DE MUNCK

Some marginal notes on the religious material culture of the Antwerp crafts in the 16th century

In this essay the investments of the early modern crafts in material religious culture will be situated within, on the one hand, the current research, an on the other hand, 16th century Antwerp. Starting from current knowledge about the crafts as organisations and the developments in the socio-economic and religious climate, we will make marginal comments on the current research and new research questions will be advanced.

Historiographical Development

Historiography and thinking on guilds and crafts have gone through spectacular changes in the last decades. After the abolition of the guilds and crafts in 1795 (in our regions they were liquidated by the French) opinion was roughly divided between two camps. There were those who associated them with obsolete privileges which only hindered the free market and progress. They argued that craft regulations, such as obligatory training periods, master's tests, quality control, prohibition of the use of certain instruments and machines, etc., was intended to segment the market, maintain monopolies and create cartels. The free traffic of goods and the free use of labour were hindered, which was detrimental to the economy and general well-being. On the other hand there were also groups in the 19th century – often with a catholic character – that viewed modernity with mistrust. They regarded the abolished crafts as beacons of order and stability. The strict rules, the compulsory lodging of apprentices at the master's house, the gradual moving up the ladder (in the course of the learning period) from apprentice, to journeyman, to master, and the collective activities, were all regarded as necessary for mental health and social peace. At least until the 19th century, there was a crusade from this quarter to reinstate the guilds and crafts, or institutions were actually founded to replace those bygone organisations (think of the schools of St Luke, or Leuven's Guild of Crafts and Trades).

Today, it is clear that neither of these groups was completely right. As a result of the ill repute of corporatist and hard right conservative ideology and the concomitant anti-democratic (fascist) experiments in the 1930s and 1940s, research into early-modern crafts had come almost entirely to a halt by the middle of the 20th century. From the 1960s and 1970s onwards, however, the historic professional crafts were again approached from a more scientific angle. Since then, research has provided a number of important insights at odds with 19th century thinking. Firstly, it became clear that the norm did not always correspond with reality. Guild and craft regulations were violated – sometimes on a large scale. Masters hired more apprentices or journeymen than was permitted, they fabricated products that did not comply with the required standards, or they lent their hallmarks to craftsmen who had not completed a learning period or a master's exam and who were therefore working illegally. With respect to promotion from apprentice to master, it has become clear that – at least from the 15th century onwards – large numbers of journeymen had no prospect of mastership and were doomed to remain employees their entire lives. Some journeymen were just not interested in mastership because they did not have enough capital to start a business of their own, or would only have themselves registered as apprentices after years of working as unfree journeymen in order save for the mastership (which went hand-in-hand with the payment of an expensive entrance fee).[1]

Over the last ten to twenty years, historians have gone considerably further, and have reviewed the logic behind the standards. Of the training system, it is now said that it may have been advantageous for the production of human capital and that it may even have enabled a technological lead compared to regions where a stipulated training period did not

1 See Lis & Soly 1994; Lis & Soly 1997; Lis et al. 2006; De Munck 2007A.

11
Ambrosius Francken · *Altarpiece of the Shoemakers* · *Martyrdom of Saints Crispin and Crispinian* · centre panel, detail · Antwerp, Koninklijk Museum voor Schone Kunsten

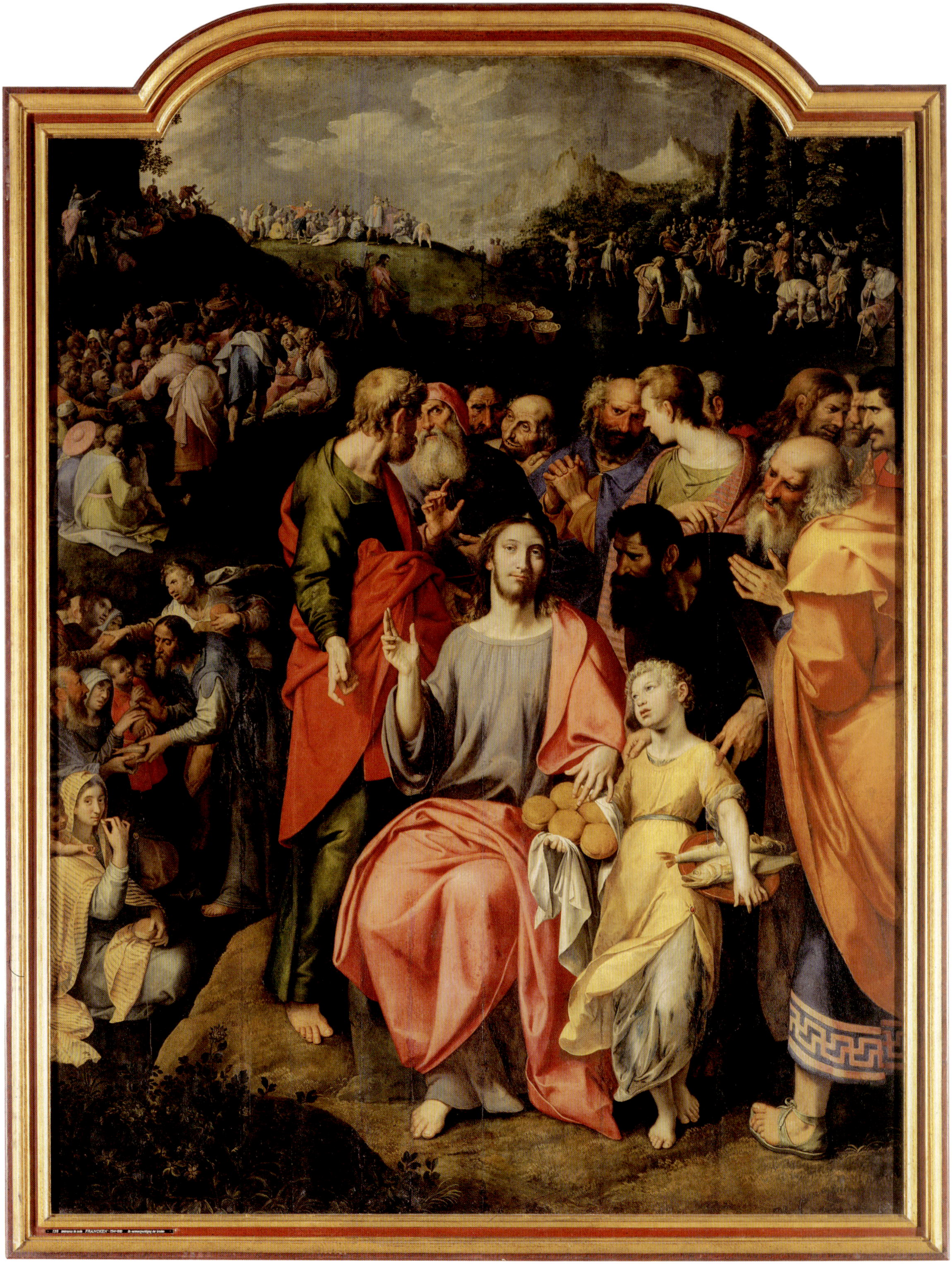
135
FRANCKEN

exist.[2] Concerning quality control and hallmarks, it is assumed today that the crafts improved economic efficiency because they engendered a certain standardisation and market information, causing the market to become more transparent and reducing the transaction cost.[3] The relevance and significance of the crafts is also reviewed from a social and political angle. There is less mention of 'oligarchies' and 'bastions', and the idea that these were by definition tight, closed social groups has been gradually abandoned. Today, the crafts are seen rather as having been flexible networks which – depending on the demographic and economic context – were open or closed. Now, even 'social scientists' see them – along with other social or religious lay organisations – as the cradle of western democracies. The social capital that would have arisen in their midst – in the form of mutual trust and a shared framework of values and standards – would indeed have made well-functioning political institutions and even a well-functioning free market possible.[4]

Historical Change

For a good understanding however, one should beware especially of historical change. It is clear that the crafts of the 18th century were not the same as the revolutionary organisations which in the 13th and 14th centuries fought against the urban patriciate and the central authorities for political recognition. In regard to the first incorporation and recognition of crafts – which were often preceded by full-blown battles such as the Battle of the Spurs – historians speak in terms of 'democratic revolutions', after which the 'mob' claimed its rights and successfully started to participate in political structures. In many Flemish and Brabantian cities crafts not only succeeded in being allowed to elect local administrators, but also in taking direct part in political power. This usually meant that a fixed share of the seats of the aldermen and other elected officials were reserved for representatives of the crafts and guilds. The master craftsmen who held these positions were thus (more or less) democratically elected from the ranks of the masters. In the long run, however, this democratic quality was on the decline. Current research does not always allow us to outline the precise evolution regarding internal democracy (electing one's own leaders, but in any case it is true that the crafts lost power and autonomy as a result of state-forming processes and the increasing power of central authorities (at the expense of the cities). Charles V, among others, is known to have drastically restricted the power of the associations and guilds in the cities under his rule. The best-known local example is the *Concessio Carolina*, by which the Ghent crafts, among others, were denied the right to elect their own administrators in 1540 (these would henceforth be appointed by commissioners).[5]

From a social point of view, too, the crafts underwent far-reaching change. While cities were initially characterised in economic terms by a monocultural cloth trade, the social landscape was determined by significant Weavers' and Fullers' trade crafts. Gradually these massive craft sectors were replaced by a multitude of smaller craft groups which were often quite antagonistic. In those trades the internal cohesion could differ markedly. More generally the social composition of the crafts often underwent great changes. From the start there was a difference between the associations that served the local market, in which most of the master craftsmen were independent, and those that served the export markets, in which the master craftsmen were often dependent on major merchants. The merchants were not only a necessary link for selling the products in distant markets, they often also monopolised the supply of raw materials and even the credit facilities. In these circumstances the masters (weavers) had no control over the production prices or the sales prices, which

2 Epstein 1998.
3 Gustafsson 1987.
4 Putnam 1993.
5 Dambruyne 2006; Jacobs 2000.

12
Ambrosius Francken · *Altarpiece of the Bakers* · *Multiplication of the Loaves* · centre panel · Antwerp, Koninklijk Museum voor Schone Kunsten

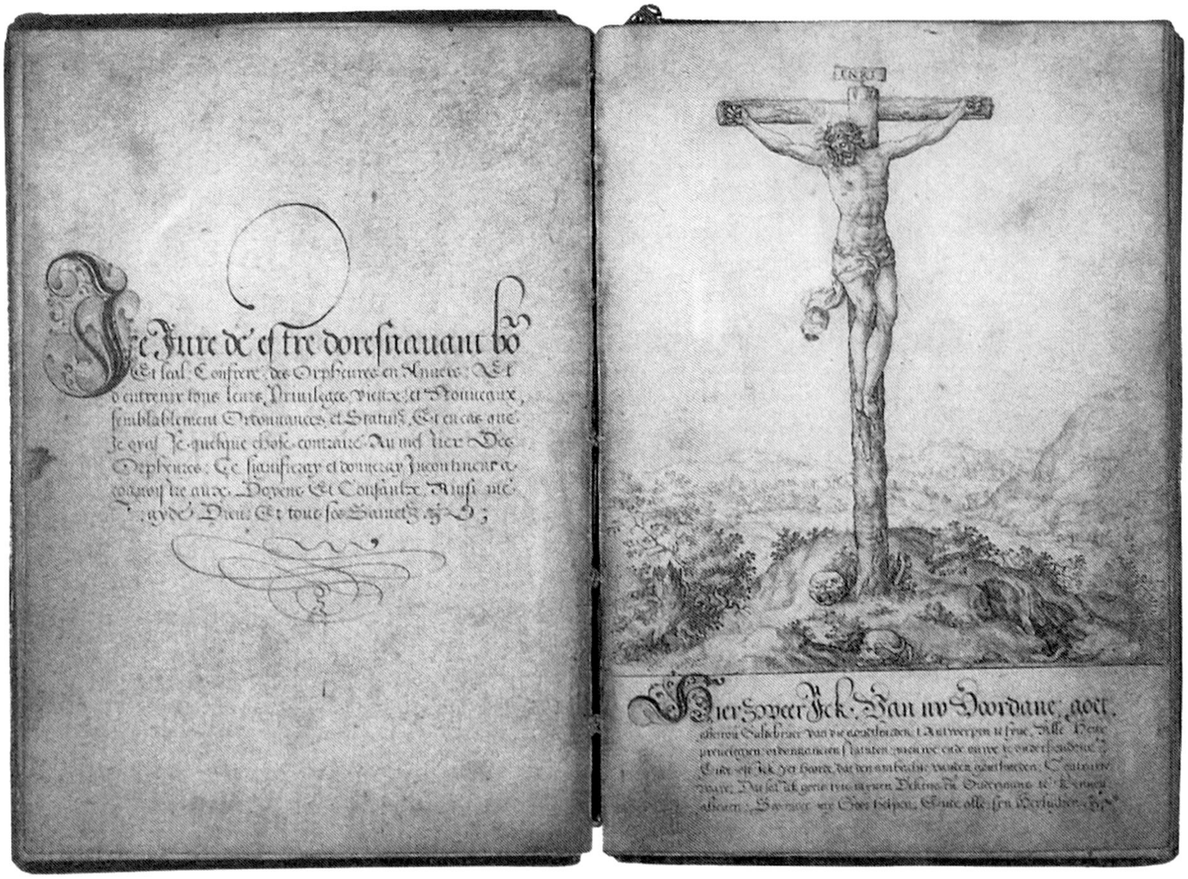

13
Privilege Book of the Goldsmiths
1575 · manuscript and drawing
Antwerp, FelixArchief (City Archives)

over the production prices or the sales prices, which did not necessarily prevent merchants and masters from being effectively equal. That too could change, however. In many sectors a difference arose between major and minor masters, in which the major masters set themselves up as intermediaries between the producers and the merchants and had the minor masters work for them as subcontractors.[6] Meanwhile the gap between journeymen and masters became broader, and women, too, were increasingly excluded from the craft system. While in the late Middle Ages women were still often admitted and there were even exclusively female crafts, during the early-modern period their range of activities was reduced to ever more 'typically female' professions like lacework, spinning, and retail, which were less represented in the association and guild system.

Clearly, these political and socio-economic changes had an influence on the social significance of these associations. It is well-known that they organised many collective activities, such as meals, Masses and the joint participation in processions. But probably not by coincidence, these practices came under pressure at least from the late Middle Ages, as is shown in the increasing number of associations that imposed fines on members who were absent. Finally, in the cultural and religious fields, too, the guilds and crafts underwent great changes, although it must be understood that this history is often less clear, or still waiting to be written. This lack of clarity begins with the rise of crafts, for which there are different theories. One theory argues that they originated from confraternities. In the Frankish and Anglo-Saxon context the terms *gilda* and *gildonia* regularly occur, referring to money and mutual commitments, which were sealed with on oath. These 'oaths' might in turn descend from German 'wergilden', which were established for practicing charity (often called 'caritas') or defending group interests (for example farmers who united to combat theft), etc. To what extent the religious aspect was involved is unclear even at the outset, but gradually these confraternities developed a myriad activities, of which the religious – such as collective devotion practices, the maintenance of an altar, or the burial of deceased members – occupied a central place. In the 14th and 15th centuries, social, cultural, and religious aspects were often very strongly intertwined. Guild brothers annually celebrated their

their elder members in almshouses, etc. In processions and parades they carried their patron saints with them on banners, and collectively bore their deceased members to their grave.

Collective Activities and Religious Practice

For a good understanding of these two phenomena it is important to give due consideration to two elements. Firstly, attention must be paid to the specific juncture at which collective activities arose and (for instance) almshouses or altars were erected. Secondly, it must be accepted that these social-cultural and religious aspects cannot be understood if the economical and political context is treated in the abstract. It goes without saying that medieval and early-modern townspeople – who were mostly first or second generation immigrants – had a strong need to unite. They were less able to rely on family and neighbours in times of stress, or even to maintain simple social contacts and friendships, than they were in the country. Most townspeople were members of one or several associations.[7] Many of these associations had a religious nature, and if they did not, at least part of their activities were religiously inspired. The latter was true of the crafts, which existed side by side with religious confraternities, but in the 14th or 15th century, some craft guilds began to develop from religious confraternities of fellow craftsmen. Initially, these craftsmen had united for the maintenance of an altar or chapel and the worship of their patron saint, but later they began to exercise economic functions – such as the formation of cartels, quality control, the obligatory training period, etc. From the moment they were authorised by the municipal authorities, it is possible to speak of the establishment of a craft. Naturally, these associations did not immediately give up their religious activities. Moreover, even those that did not originate from a religious confraternity cultivated the religious aspect of their association as much as the others. These religious aspects were in turn strongly intertwined with social aspects. The Christian duty to help the needy – *caritas* – steeped poor relief in a religious atmosphere, too – for example, providing a decent funeral for poor 'brothers' and the admission of old members to almshouses and hospitals. Towards the 15th century, all professional associations in Antwerp were simultaneously of a social, economical, and religious nature.

The ethos regarding the religious aspect changed drastically in the late-medieval and early-modern period.[8] In establishing and cultivating religious activities, guilds and crafts in the 15th century followed a more general trend, which persisted until the end of the 16th century. But from the 16th century onwards, dissident voices arose. In the first half of the 16th century the Reformation grew into a fully fledged counter movement and in 1566 and around 1580 iconoclasm broke out, at which point many altars, chapels, and statues that belonged to the guilds and crafts were vandalised. In the 1570s the Calvinists won the battle in different cities, among which was Antwerp, so the craft administrations had to conform to the new doctrine and old 'superstitions' (including the worship of patron saints) had to be abjured – but not for long. In 1585 Antwerp again fell into the hands of the Spanish and the Catholic doctrine was restored – at least in the Southern Netherlands. In the Northern Netherlands the nature of the crafts and guilds would change definitively, as altars and chapels disappeared from the scene (although celebrations for patron saints did not entirely vanish). In the south, master craftsmen were compelled to swear allegiance to the Catholic Church and traditional guild rituals were reinstated. Celebrating a patron saint was permitted again and many altars and chapels were reconstructed. This does not imply that nothing had changed in comparison to the first half of the 16th

6 See for instance Thijs 1987.
7 Lynch 2003; Lynch 2004.
8 Marnef 1996.

century. Under the influence of the Council of Trent, and under the surveillance of the advocates of Catholic Reformation (among whom were the Jesuits), the visual culture of the crafts and guilds was adjusted. Traditionally, in altarpieces and chapel decorations, the patron saint and the legends associated with him or her had been set at the centre. Now, the patron saint sometimes literally disappeared into the margins (the side panels) of the altarpiece. At the centre, a scene from the life of Christ was depicted, for example. A clear example is the altarpiece *Multiplication of the Loaves* (fig. 12), which was painted in 1598 by Ambrosius Francken at commission of the Baker's guild.[9] Often, however, this was not the case and the patron saints and the iconography associated with them reclaimed their place at the centre, as in the *Martyrdom of Saints Crispin and Crispinian* altarpiece (1589), also painted by Ambrosius Francken, for the Cobbler's guild.[10]

In the current state of research it is difficult to estimate what such developments meant for the ordinary craftsmen. For secularised westerners it is in any case hard to understand how important religion was in the daily life of pre-industrial society. We can, for instance, hardly imagine the importance of the patron saint for groups like the crafts and guilds. The patron saint was honoured with an annual feast (the saint's name day), on which a Mass was held and well-attended. As part of that Mass, a eulogy was pronounced – often in close proximity to the image of the patron saint – and the congregants usually received a devotional print with the image of the saint. Even in the worship of the patron saint, the religious could not be separated from other domains of life. The Mass was followed by the annual dinner of the corporation, at which the religious aspect probably quickly moved to the background. At processions and parades the patron saint was proudly carried around on litters in what can be called the 'public space'.

This may suggest that the patron saint had a political function and might, for instance, have enhanced the prestige and supported the political claims of the guild. On the one hand the saint was worshipped in

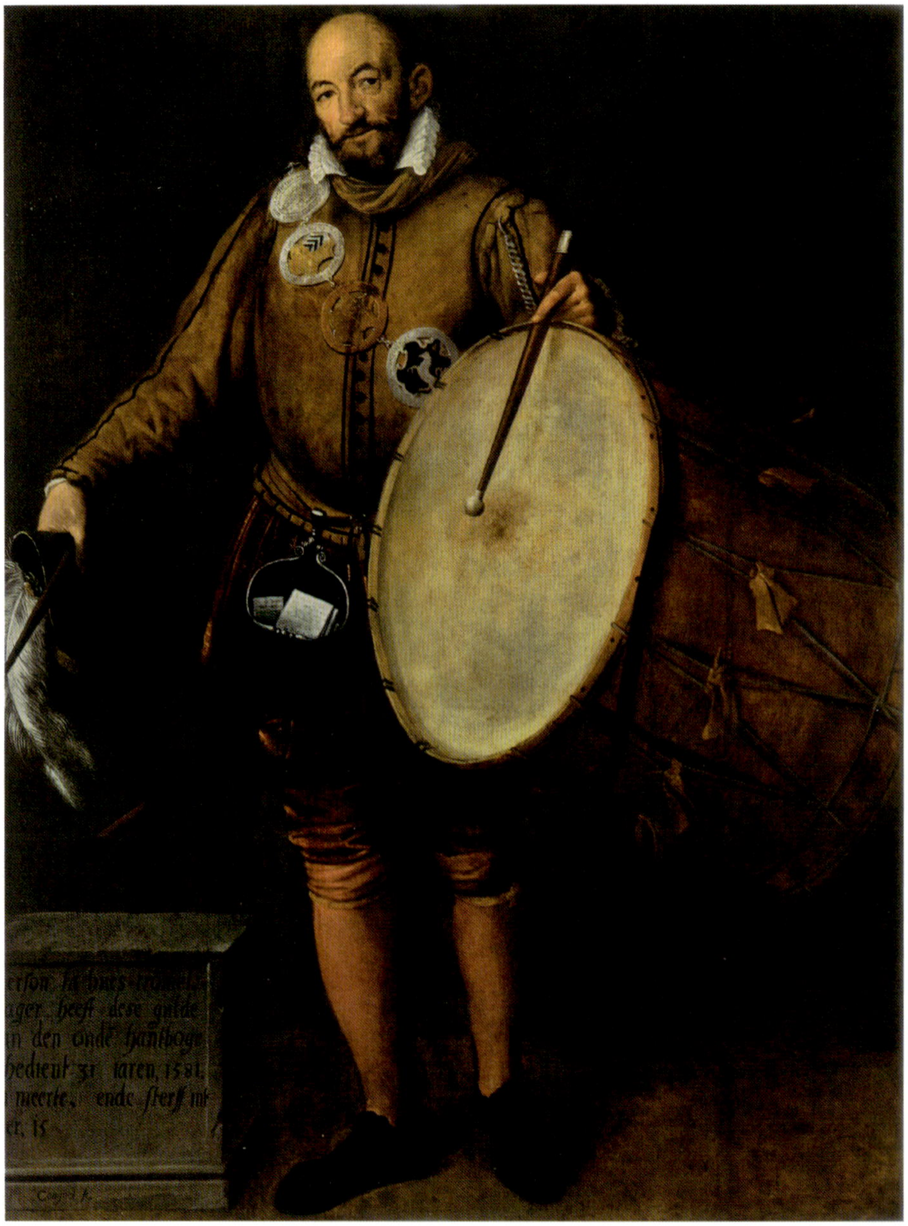

14
Gillis Coignet
The Drummer of the Young Longbow · 1581
Antwerp, Koninklijk Museum voor Schone Kunsten

the hope of receiving something in return, such as protection and help; on the other, the saint was a sort of figurehead that helped the organisation to create a collective identity, to define the contours of the group, and to represent it to the outside world.

Investing in Symbolic Capital

Did it really matter which saint was depicted, and how? Was there a difference whether a scene from the life of the patron was depicted, or a lamentation of Christ? Definitive answers are not possible in the current state of research, but there are indications that form was often more important than content. At first glance the choice of a patron saint was all but arbitrary. Each profession had its own patron and once the choice was made, it was seldom changed. Even journeymen who established their own workshops and therefore distanced themselves from their masters, generally chose the same patron, because they were after all active in the same profession. On the other hand, the original association of a patron and a profession does seem generally to have come into being in an arbitrary way. The iconography of the altarpieces that depicted a patron saint often goes back to the *Legenda Aurea*, a collection of saints' life stories which was compiled by the Italian Dominican Jacobus de Voragine around 1260. In it, Crispin and Crispinian cobbled the shoes of the poor while they preached the Faith, so the link with the Shoemakers was clear.[11] Usually, the association between a craft and a patron saint went back even further and it arose 'incidentally', so to speak. Often the saint in question had practiced the same profession, as the classic example of Saint Joseph, patron saint of Carpenters, illustrates. But the connection is often far-fetched, as in the association of Furriers and Saint Stephen, who was stoned to death and would have appeared in the image culture of the Furrier's craft because Furriers used stones as tools. For the Weavers it was Saint Severus, who had been a weaver himself and had poked out one of the devil's eyes with the point of a shuttle. From that perspective, it is not surprising that Saint Catherine was chosen as patroness of the Old Clothes' Merchants, because she made it possible to present themselves through luxurious (rather than old) clothing.[12]

Of course this does not mean that the altarpiece and iconography did not matter. Association with a saint, who handed out bread or cobbled the shoes of the poor, undoubtedly added prestige to the professional group or guild in question. Moreover, in some depictions the tools of the profession can also be seen, which could have been intended to represent the profession or connected manual work as noble or prestigious[13] – even if this was on the backs of the side panels, as on the altarpiece of the Smiths' craft by Ambrosius Francken (1588) (cat. 7) and the altarpiece for the Bricklayers' craft by Frans Francken the Younger (1624). It must be left to further research to show whether a historical development can be traced that (more or less) tracks the shift in religious sensitivities and iconographical traditions. The first question to ask, then, is whether there existed a profound identification with the patron saint, or whether the depiction of the patron saint and other religious figures and scenes served mainly as an alibi for the depiction of other elements – such as charity, tools of the trade, etc. Or was it simply a case of making a rich impression and upstaging other groups? In my view, it boils down, in every case, to tracing the long-term historical transformations undergone by the individual craft. The material and visual culture of the crafts can only be understood if it is situated in the right context and if the genealogy of certain customs and images is unravelled. In the current state of research, then, a few hypotheses can be advanced concerning the developments that may have been important to the creation and maintenance of altars and chapels.

9 Vervaet 1976, pp. 226–227.
10 Vervaet 1976, pp. 222–223.
11 Vervaet 1976, pp.200, 223.
12 Vervaet 1976, pp. 213, 244.
13 De Munck 2007B; De Munck 2008.

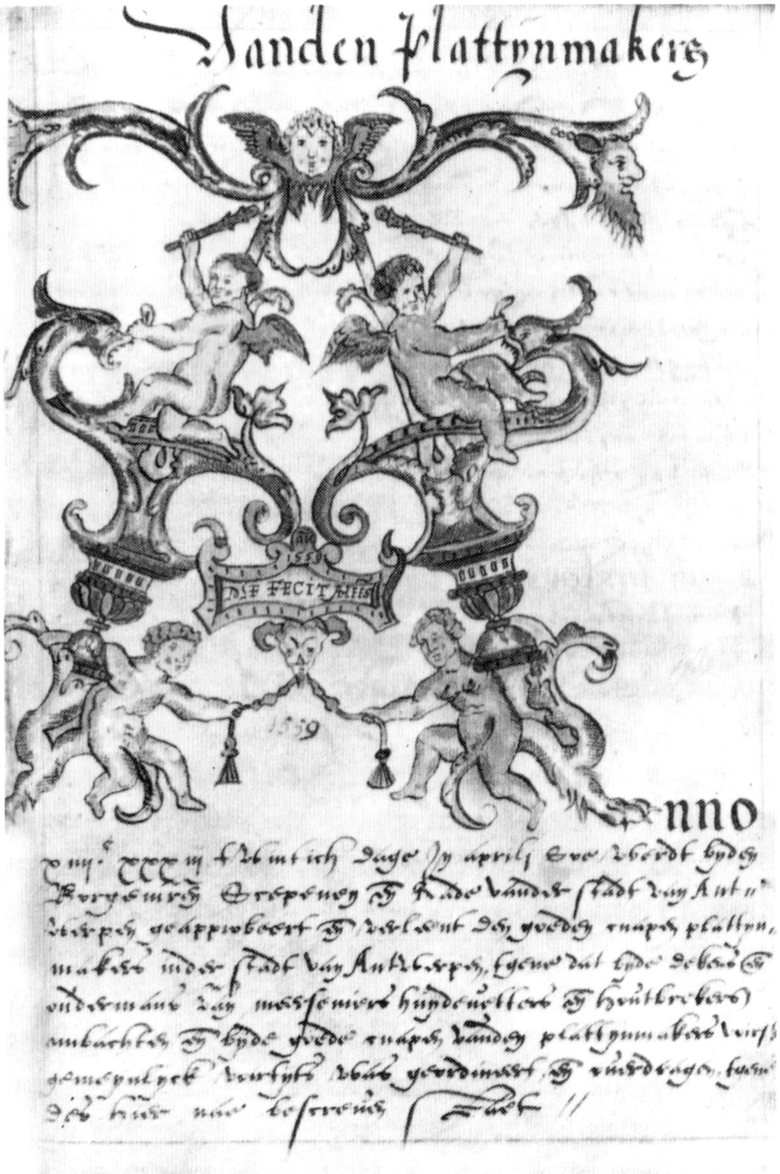
Vanden Plattynmakers

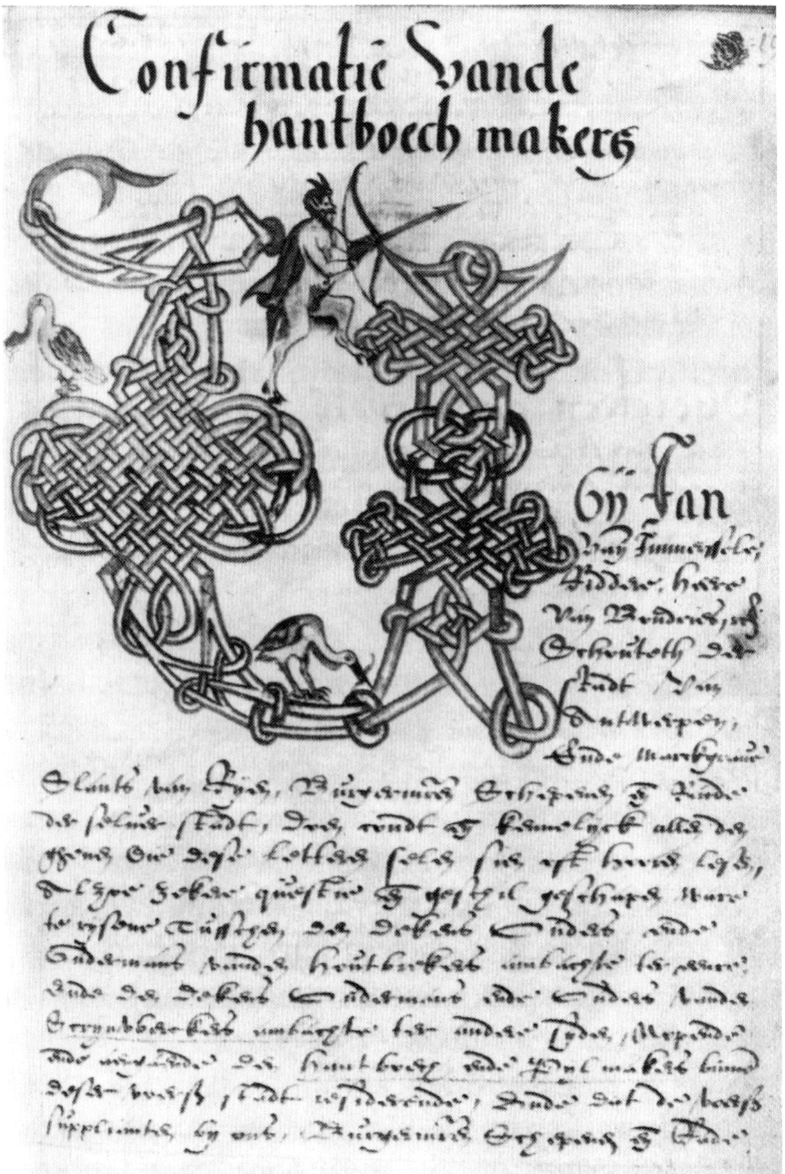
Confirmatie vande hantboech makers

15
Privilege Book of the Woodcutters · initial pages · 1558–1559 · Antwerp, FelixArchief (City Archives)

Firstly, it is possible that outward wealth became more important than internal social cohesion or 'fraternity'.[14] From the 15th century onwards, and increasingly in the 16th century, identification with the guild diminished. Members had to be compelled to be present at collective events such as annual dinners and funerals, and they were fined in the case of absence. The fines increased, too, which indicates that members were often willing to pay them, rather than to be disturbed in their work. The highest fines were imposed for not taking up certain executive mandates by members who were elected against their will. Indeed, many of those mandates were quite time-consuming, and some members were prepared to pay considerable sums of money to evade them. An increasing division between the higher echelons and the grassroots seems to have made it ever more common that certain meals or other activities were reserved to the guild officers only; in other cases women no longer participated. These developments may have had some influence on the material and visual culture of the crafts. As mentioned above, the religious and social aspects were strongly intertwined. Initially the meals – collective social activities par excellence – were even organised in the church and the food was displayed before the altar. Members' meetings or officers' elections, too, could take place before the altar or in the chapel; and even recruiting journeymen could take place there. In the course of the 16th century, the Church was increasingly resistant to this, so that sacred and profane elements were ever more separated.[15]

Secondly, and connected to this, it is possible that crafts evolved from organisations in which fraternity, equality and autonomy were held in high esteem, to commercial structures that were used by different groups in and around the craft (major masters, minor masters, merchants, urban authorities, journeymen) for the realisation of certain goals. As has become clear, the autonomy of the crafts was strongly curtailed by state-forming processes and internal equality was eroded by economic developments because in many sectors there were centralising tendencies at work. In phases of economic acceleration in which commercial capitalism developed ever further – as in 16th century Antwerp – it also became more and more difficult to set out the boundaries determining who could, or could not, become a member. There were, for example, conflicts with major merchants who sought to obtain a mastership in an illegal way so that they could hire apprentices and journeymen themselves. These entered into fictitious apprenticeships (for example with masters who were really working for them) or started to work in partnership in order to use the master's hallmark (while normally only masters who had completed a training period and a master's exam were authorised to use a hallmark). To rectify this, master's tests were prescribed, or it was made obligatory for apprentices to live with their masters.[16] The question is to what extent the universalised prescription of a training period – and possibly even the establishment of crafts and guilds in themselves – were the consequence of an existing pressure from antagonistic relationships resulting from increased mobility. Were the new members increasingly unknown, thus making it ever more difficult to assess to what extent the aspirant-masters really had learned the craft? In any case, 'fraternity' became less, not more, obvious. The rendering of assistance and attendance at funerals and processions, for example, increasingly needed to be codified in regulations during the 15th and 16th centuries.

14 Dambruyne 1997; Dambruyne 2006.
15 Thijs 2006, pp. 162–163
16 De Munck 2007B; De Munck 2008.

It is clear that crafts and guilds were prepared to invest much in their material and religious culture. The almshouses, guild houses, chapels and altars cost a handful of money and caused the crafts and guilds to be heavily indebted from as early as the 16th century. The current state of research does not allow us to enter into detail and sketch precise developments, but it is true in any case that the Antwerp crafts in the middle of the 17th and the first half of the 18th century had to cope with severe financial problems. At that period, they were very busy trying to purge arrears of thousands of guilders. The question of how these debts were created cannot be answered precisely in the current state of research, but the reconstruction of altars after 1566 and 1585 seems to have played an important part in this. From 1585 onwards, the number of new members went down markedly, which caused the revenue from members' fees to diminish. Legal litigation, and the replacement of wooden façades by stone frontals, also contributed to the financial difficulties that hindered the good functioning of the crafts. Since taxing seated members through annual fees and *kaarsgeld* ('candle money', a sort of annual fee) was generally not successful (not least because of the increasing division between the higher echelons and the grassroots), there was no other solution for the crafts and guilds than to increase entrance fees and thus pass on the problems to new members. The Antwerp Shoemakers and Tanners, for instance, were wrestling with debts by the late 15th century, which were at least partly the consequence of expenditure on their chapels and association houses. Around the middle of the 17th century, there was also a need for a new façade for the guild house on Grote Markt (Antwerp's central market place). Its debt already amounted to 2,000 guilders, on which 100 guilders of interest had to be paid every year: roughly a half year's salary. The association saw no other solution than to increase the entrance fee for new members (to 60 guilders) to address this situation.

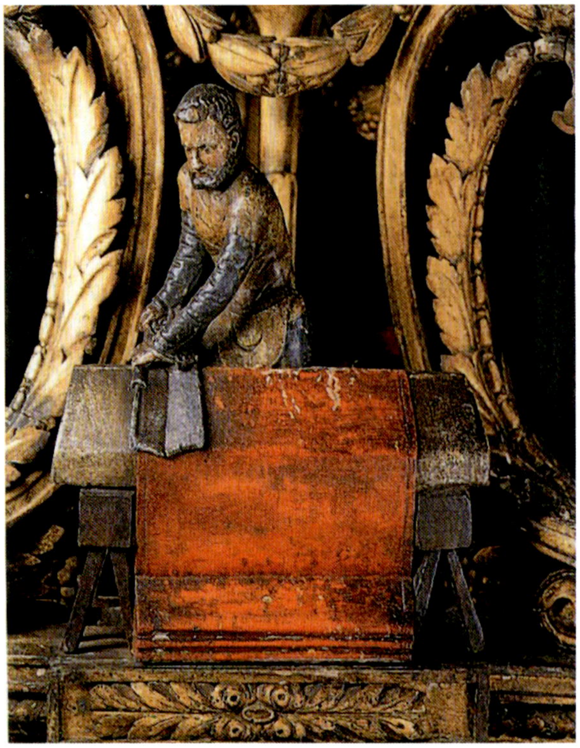

16
Processional Torch of the Drapers
probably 17th century
Antwerp, Vleeshuis Museum

Ultimately, craft and guild entrance fees became so steep that the group effectively became even more elite. Towards the 18th century the fees could amount to hundreds of guilders – a year's salary, say, or even more.[17] Of course, some of these debts were unforeseen and had got out of hand, but this does not prevent their having arisen from well-considered investments in cultural or symbolical capital. Research to these investments might therefore produce insight into the motifs of the craftsmen and their officers. The situation is not straightforward. The work of Alfons Thijs[18] has made it clear that the reconstruction of altars and chapels during the Counter Reformation (now mostly called 'Catholic Reformation') did not necessarily go hand-in-hand with a changing religiosity. Since the work was largely enforced from the top down, it remains unclear to how far it was based on inner religious experience. And even if the crafts and guilds did indeed invest for their own reasons in a religious material culture, it remains unclear what the actual motives were. On the one hand, the interconnection with social factors was so important that it must be asked to what extent the religious aspect expressed social needs. On the other hand, the paintings, sculpture, silverware and marble often conveyed prestige, so that political claims and economic power may well have been the ultimate goal.[19] And all this may have shifted significantly over time, so that roughly the importance of internal social cohesion had yielded to external wealth in the name of power and prestige. In short, we must wait for the first historian or art historian to connect the iconography of the altarpiece with the history of the crafts and guilds.

17 De Munck 2007A, Chapter 2.3.
18 Thijs 1990.
19 Verleysen 2001.

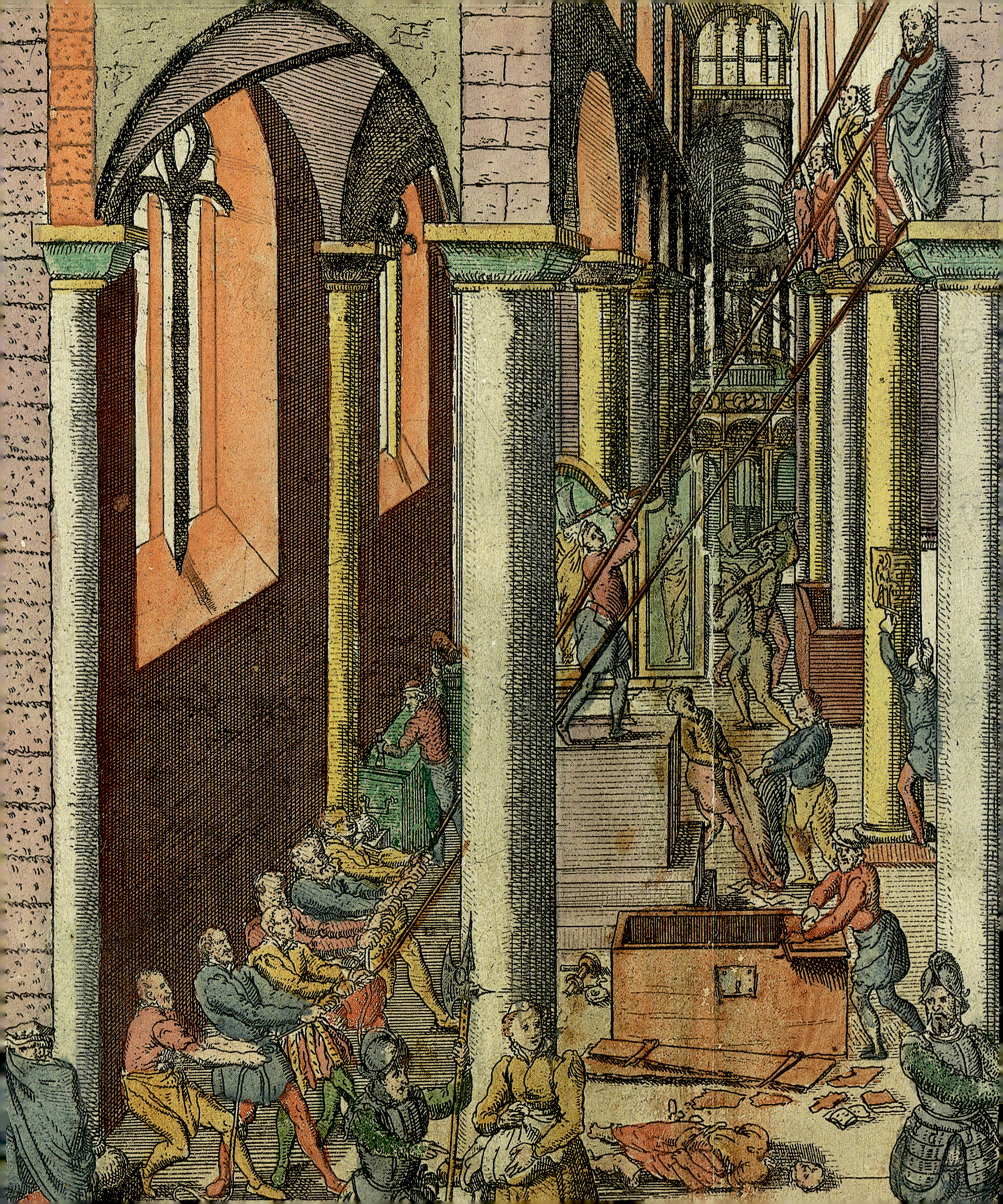

The Triptychs *In Situ*. An Open or Closed World?

RIA FABRI

To impress, to compete and to promote. These were the main aims of the crafts and guilds in the Antwerp Cathedral of Our Lady when they displayed paintings on their altars. There is no question that large triptychs, each more impressive than the last, carried meanings of many sorts.[1] Religious devotion, education of the craftsmen, visualisation of the Roman Catholic faith, and promotion of contemporary religious ideas were the incentives that led to their installation. But there was more.

The cathedral played an important role in the life of its users: not only as a meeting place for the faithful, but also for the same community of interests or professional groups. It was *the* place to be for many inhabitants of Antwerp. The status and legitimacy of crafts were underlined by the presence of an altarpiece in the large cathedral. Moreover, the meetings before the altarpiece enhanced the fellowship of craft brothers even further.

What other function(s) did the painted altarpieces of the Antwerp crafts, guilds, and fraternities have? Or, to put it simply: how were the triptychs used, and how did people experience the altarpieces from 1585 to the middle of the 17th century?[2] Those were the first and basic questions. The answer is not straightforward.

The archival sources are scarce. Crafts' archives, mostly dry records, remain in dusty silence. The summary data need to be patiently gathered from accounts and contracts. Surprisingly enough, ecclesiastical instructions remain neutral when it comes to the effective and daily use of these triptychs.

Research in the *Libri Ordinarii*[3] provides little or no results. Random samples in the *Acta Capituli*[4] are of no help either to obtain an adequate understanding of the possible use of the craft triptychs.[5] Rare so-called verger's books[6] bring some clarity to this complex and little-studied matter, but much meticulousness cannot be expected here either. Descriptions of the cathedral, by Papebrochius or Van der Sanden, or by visitors during the ancien regime do not clarify things much either.. Reliable iconographical sources such as some painted interior views are no more abundant with their information. To obtain visual insight for this maze of questions on the utility and place of the altarpieces, some original drawings could help. Alas, 16th and 17th century ground plans of the cathedral are missing. The lack of information is somewhat compensated by a few 18th century documents. When these floor plans are compared with late 16th and 17th century requests, which sometimes mention the place of a craft altar, then darkness clears up a little.

First some words about the place of the altarpieces. Altar and altarpiece were inseparably attached to each other. A predella was often the link between the two. On an anonymous ground plan, drawn in brown ink and slightly highlighted (fig. 18), surviving in a mid18th century manuscript,[7] the places of the altars are indicated by chapel and by pillar. Added in elegant letters were the names of the saint(s) worshipped at the altars or of the crafts.[8] The altars stood both in the nave and in the ambulatory. All altar constructions in the nave seem to have stood against the pillars perpendicular to the nave or of the side aisles. They were never erected at the back of the pillars. The triptychs of the craft altars were thus seen from the front and visitors walking from the west porch to the east – towards the transept or ambulatory – saw the altarpieces coming towards them as an overwhelming spectacle, at a single glance ...[9]

The ground plan also shows that visitors to the cathedral did not have very much space to manoeuvre between the altarpieces and their altar enclosures or *tuinen*. These enclosures were provided on three sides with a fairly high parapet, sometimes with decorative small columns or balusters below it. A central door gave access to the intimate interior and closed off the

1 Prims 1938–1939, XII, pp 254–339; XIII, pp. 278–447; Marinus 1993, pp. 53, 58; Verleysen 2001, pp.155, 164 sqq.; Timmermans 2008, pp. 188–189.

2 In the fire of 1533, the iconoclastic outbreak of 1566, and the Calvinist rule of 1580–1585, many art works disappeared or were severely damaged. The first phase of repairs that is important for this account occurred from 1585–1586 until c. 1603. On the importance of the re-erections of altars, see Verleysen 2001, p. 154 and Thijs 1990, pp. 92–93, 95, 117.

3 With thanks to Prof. Van Tongeren who allowed me access in his unpublished lecture (Van Tongeren 2009).

4 The documents in KAA, DAA, Acta Capituli, 45 on ceremonies 'resolutio quorundam de breviario et ceremonialis' (1613) give no clarification; neither do the documents in KAA, DAA, Statuten 20, on 'de altaribus corump.ornatu et imaginibus' from fol. 33r° to 92 v°.

5 Works like that by Croegnaert 1921 do not offer the anticipated information.

6 Van Rossem 1876, pp. 109–259.

7 SAA, PK 197: Beschrijvinghe van de cloosters, kerken, autaeren, epitaphien, schilderijen, en beelden ende andere rariteijten in de stadt van Antwerpen, hss, mid 18th century, n.f.

8 Van den Nieuwenhuizen 1993, p. 37.

9 Of course, the high altar always remained within view of the visitors, as was stipulated in *De Instructiones Fabricae et Suppelectis Ecclesiasticae* by C. Borromeus in 1577.

17
Frans Hogenberg · *The Iconoclastic Fury of 1566* · coloured engraving · 1586 · private collection

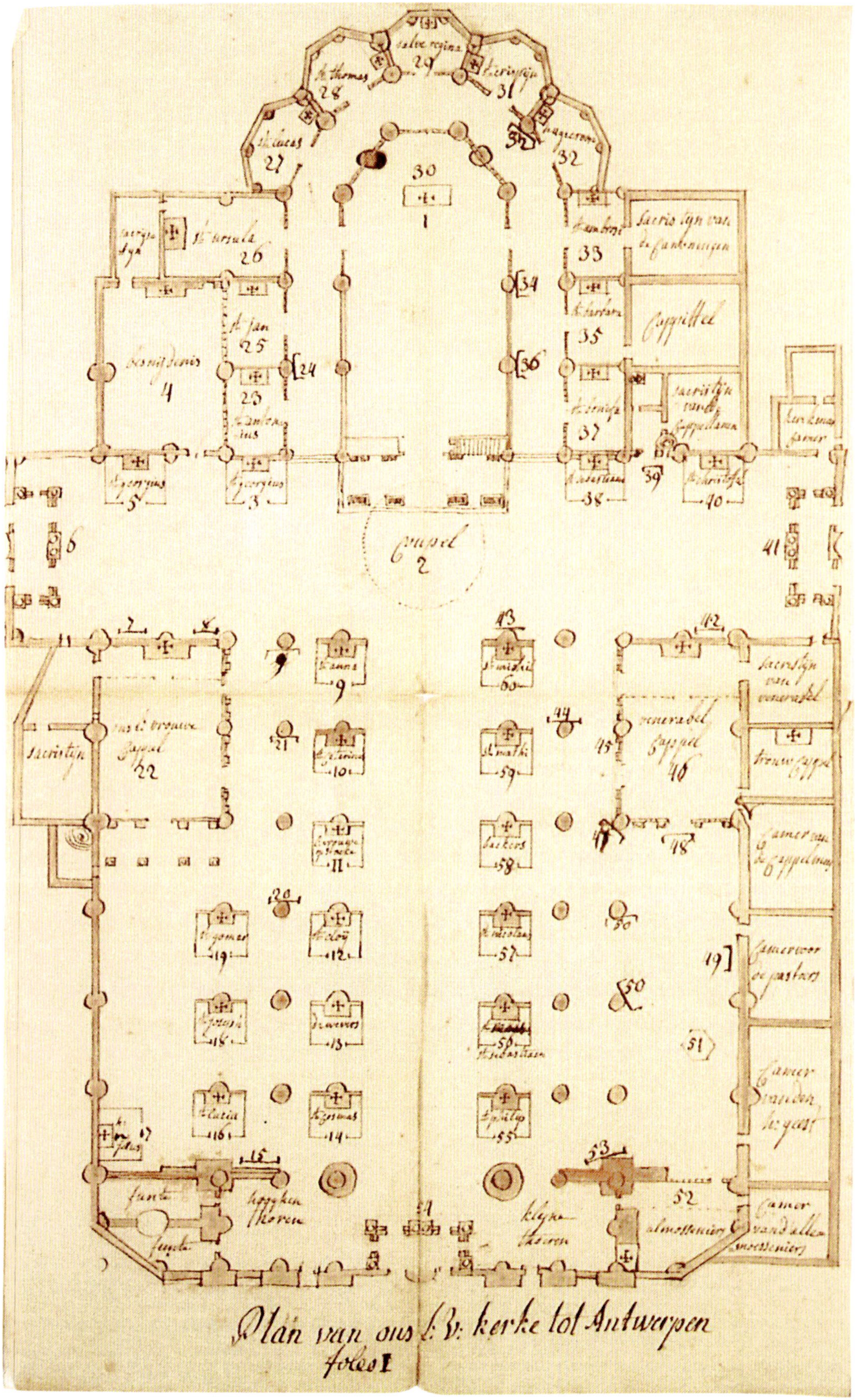

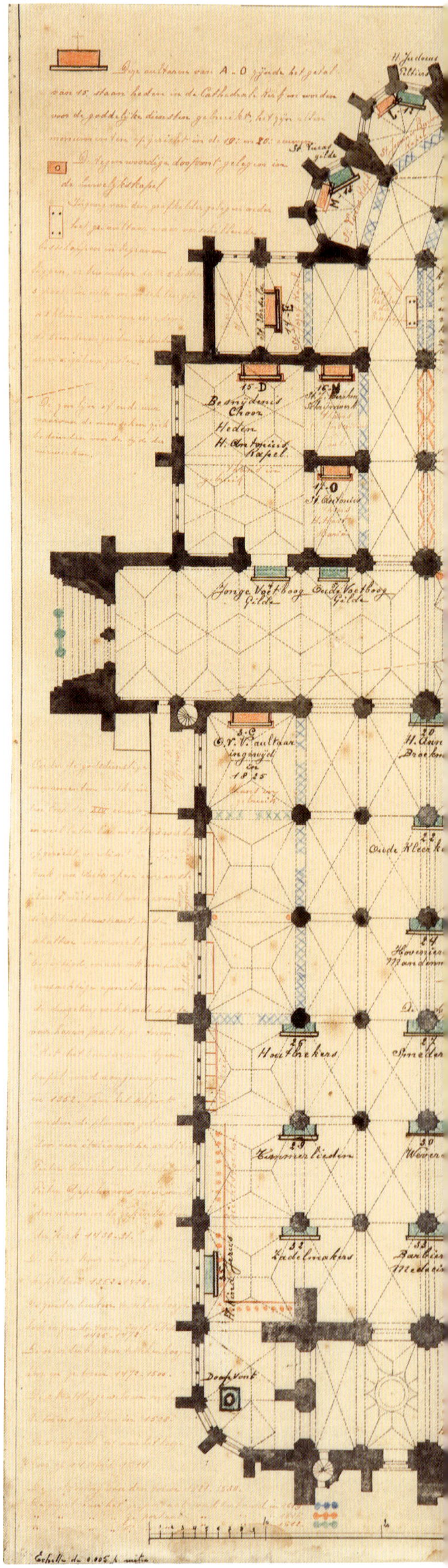

18
Anonymous · *Ground Plan of the Antwerp Cathedral of Our Lady* · mid 18th century · Antwerp, FelixArchief (City Archives)

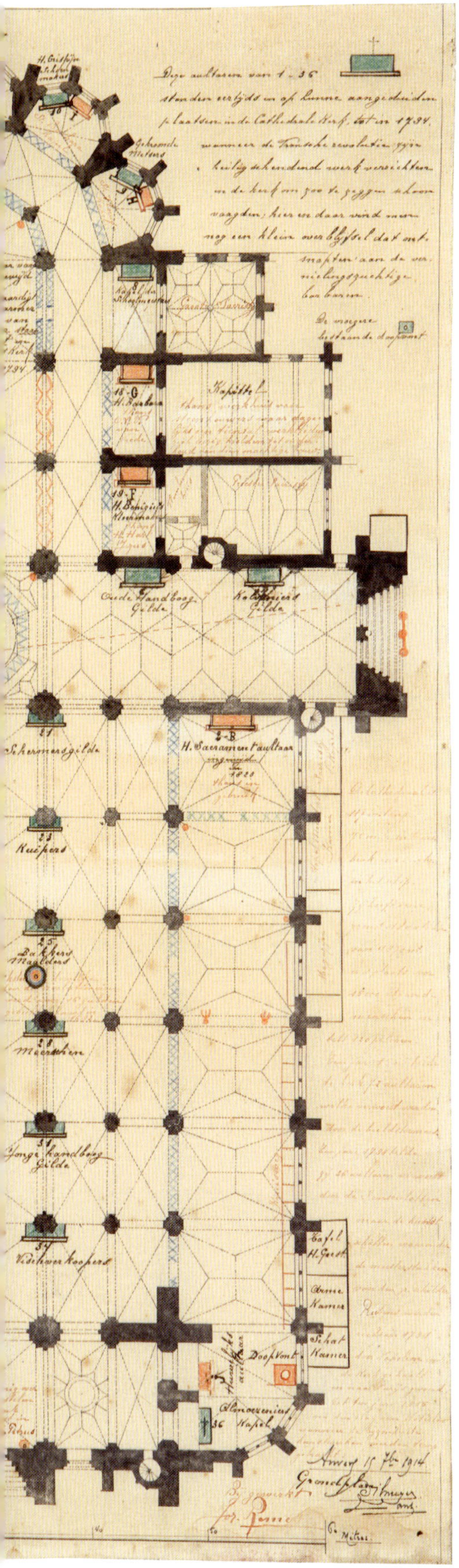

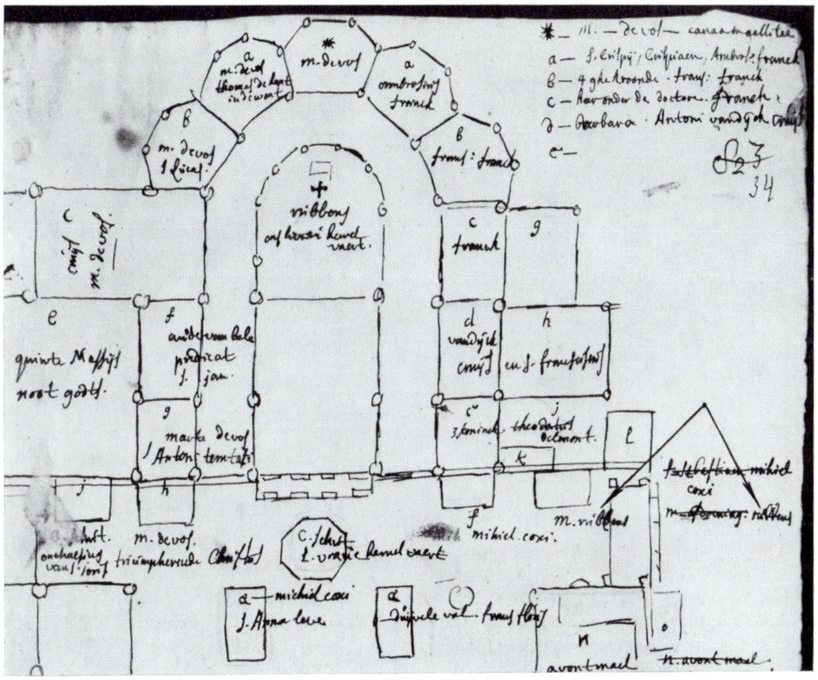

20
Anonymous
Ground Plan of the Antwerp Cathedral of Our Lady · 1703
present whereabouts unknown

space as a *hortus conclusus*. These enclosures, built in wood, metal, or stone, also emphasised the status of the crafts or privileged groups with their arrangement and decoration. To add greater lustre to the whole, the crafts often placed, even in ancient times, as well a historiated boss as vault paintings around their allotted pillar, so that the space was clearly delimited, as in a chapel.[10]

A second ground plan (fig. 20), dating from 1703, gives a better perspective on the presence and effect of the altarpieces.[11] All the paintings of the cathedral are noted with summary title and artist. To map the paintings, the scribe must have walked from pillar to pillar, into the transept and into every chapel in the ambulatory. This document could be useful to reconstruct the exact place of the corporative triptychs and other art objects which were kept in the cathedral in the first years of the 18th century.[12] Of course the placement of the crafts' objects in the cathedral changed, necessarily and regularly, before 1585. Fire, outbreaks of iconoclasm, and the Calvinist rule were the most important causes. In the following years, until the middle of the 17th century, the altarpieces seem steadily to have acquired a more fixed and definitive place, at least partly because a number of altars could be occupied that had become available. But their initial position or internal use was not affected. In this period it remained a must to celebrate, often on a daily basis, masses before the altarpiece.

10 This was the case, among others, for the altars of the Bakers, Brewers, and Merchants, see: Grieten & Bungeneers 1996, p. 236.
11 Van den Nieuwenhuizen 1962A, p. 42.
12 Despite various research efforts, the drawing was not found in either the archives of the cathedral nor Antwerp's city archives. With thanks to J. Van den Nieuwenhuizen and M.J. Marinus.

19
Anonymous · *Copy from 1914 of a late 18th century Ground Plan of the Antwerp Cathedral of Our Lady* · Antwerp, Cathedral of Our Lady, reserve

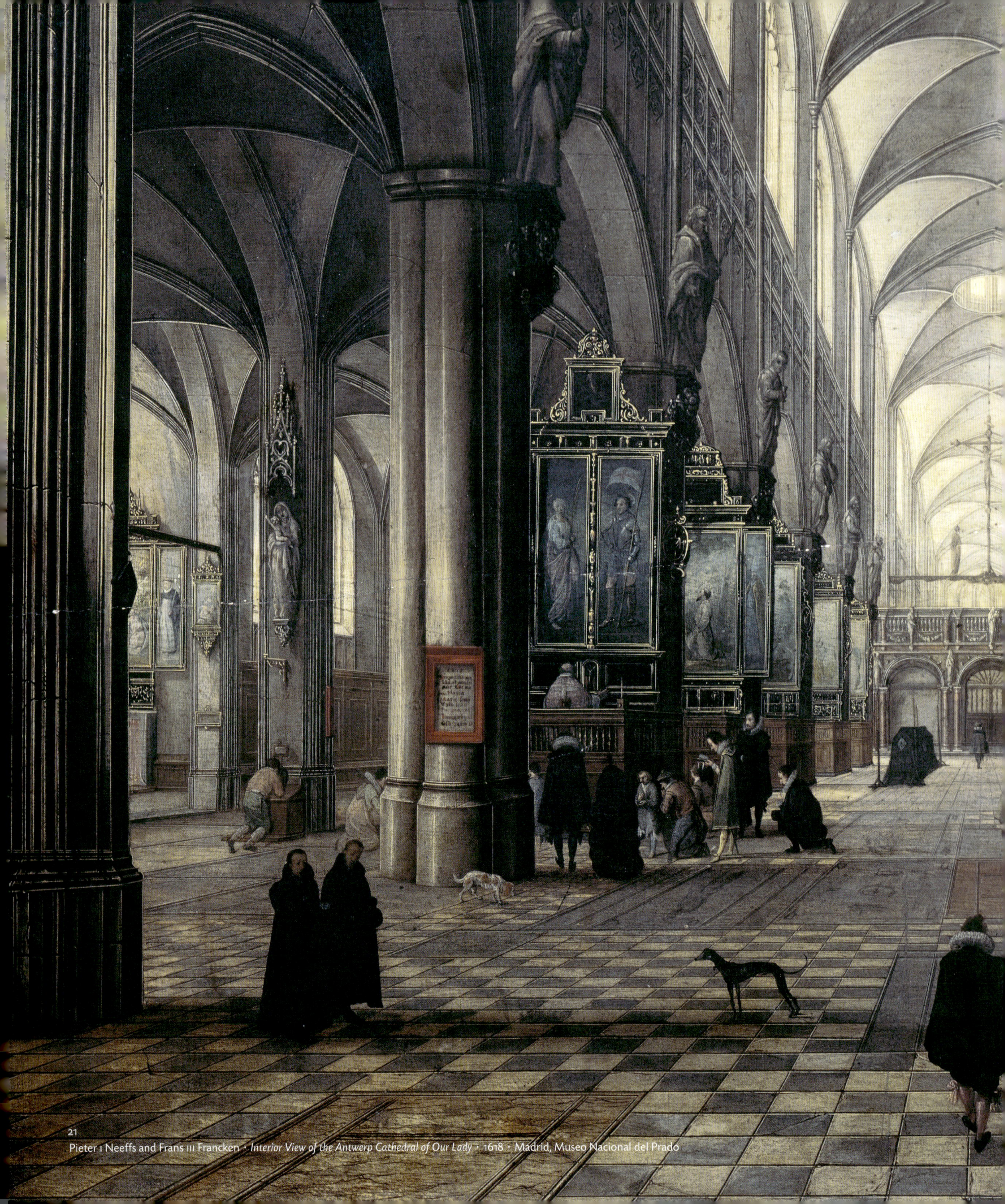

Pieter I Neeffs and Frans III Francken · *Interior View of the Antwerp Cathedral of Our Lady* · 1618 · Madrid, Museo Nacional del Prado

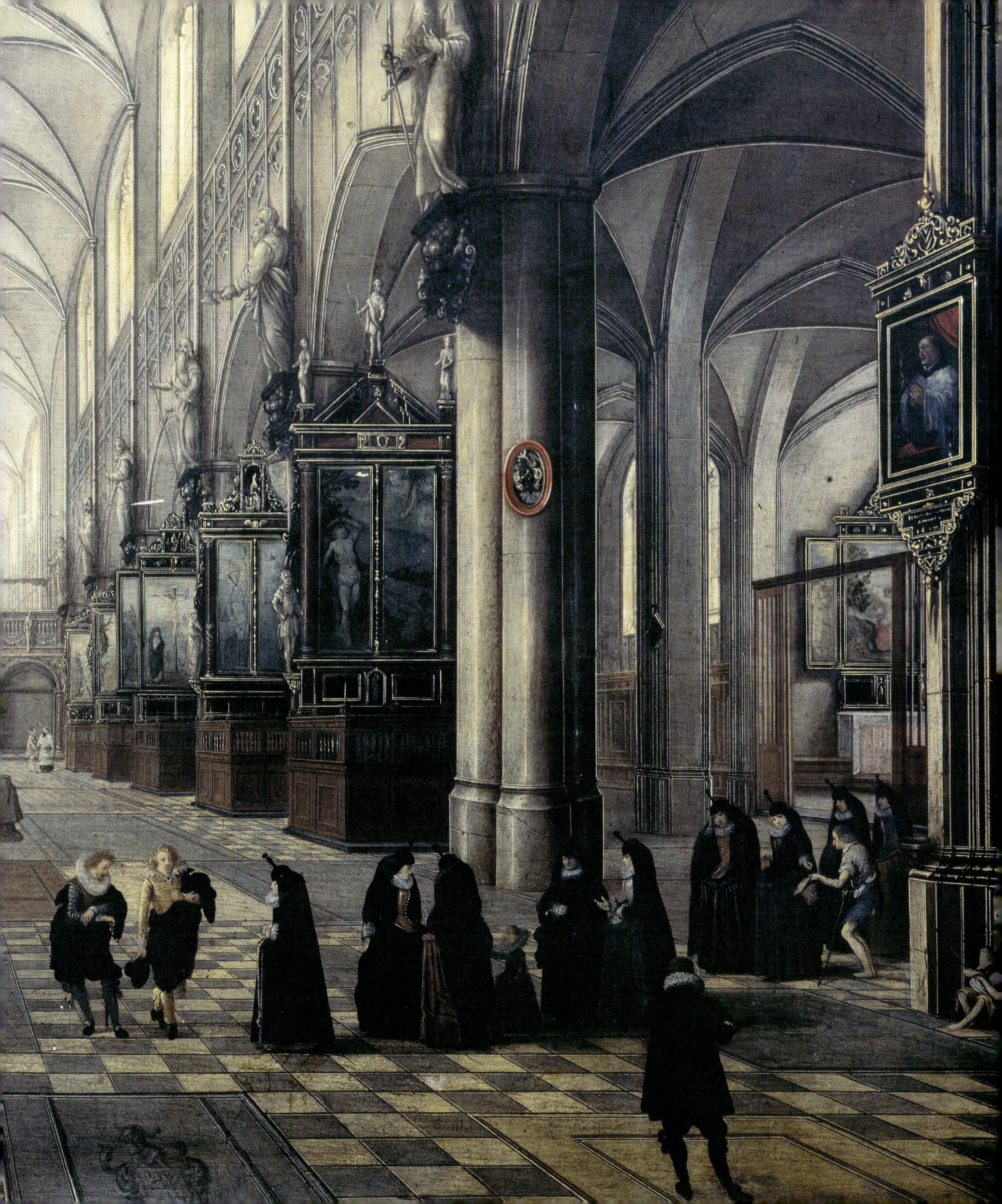

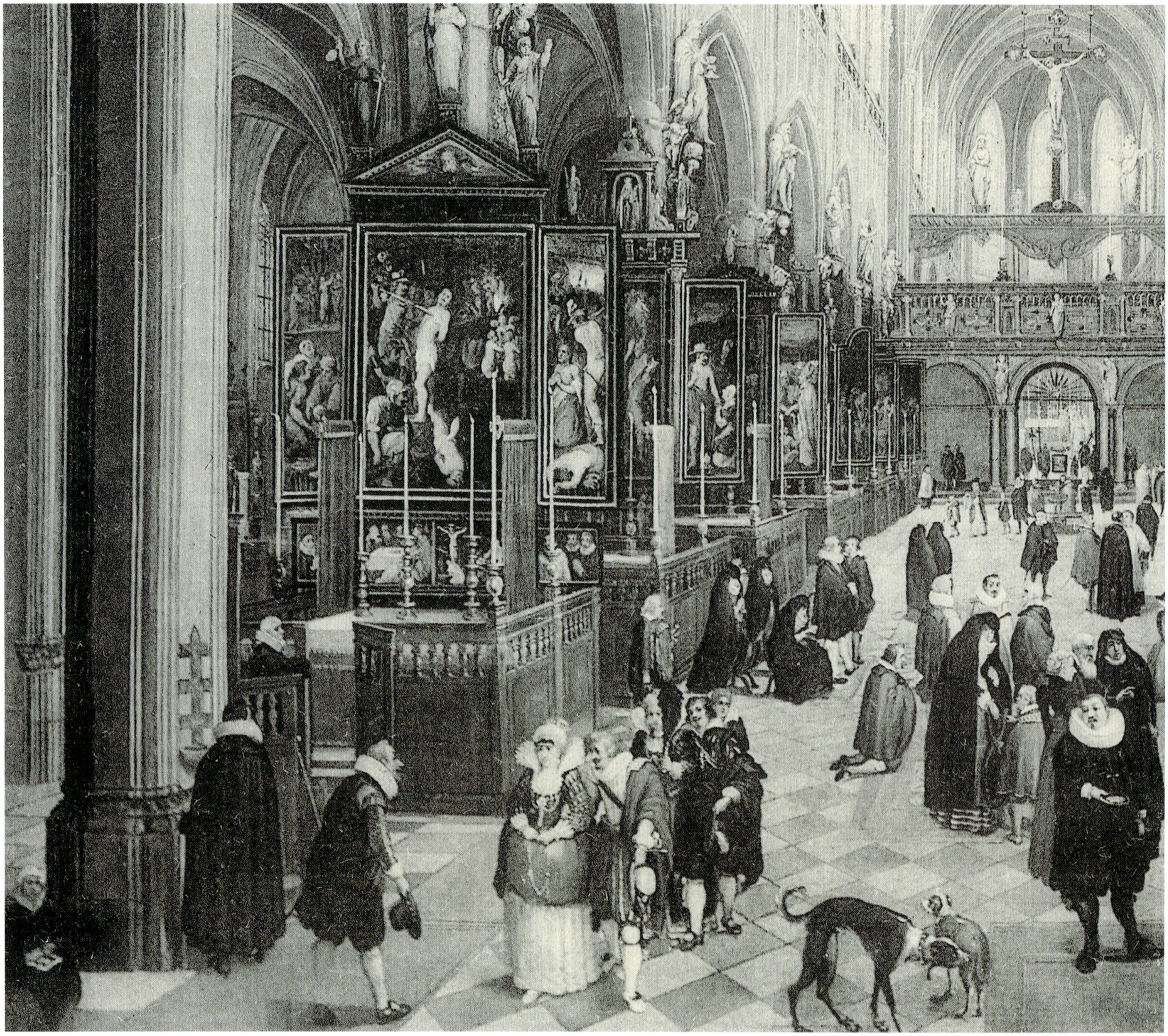

22
Hendrik II van Steenwijck
Interior View of the Antwerp Cathedral of Our Lady
c. 1620, detail
present whereabouts unknown

Particularly informative, finally, is a copy of an 18th century ground plan of the cathedral.[13] On it, the exact location of the altars at the pillars is drawn to scale in blue ink (fig. 19), accompanied by the names of the respective crafts.

It seems clear that there was mutual rivalry between the guilds and crafts to obtain a prestigious place, close to the high altar.[14] Thus the city militias were well represented at the crossing and in the transept. This appears from the positioning of the altars of armed guilds like the Fencers' guild (cat. 3), the Longbowmen, theCrossbowmen, and the Arquebusiers (cat. 11). Powerful organisations like the Guild of Saint Luke, the professional association of artists, painters, sculptors, and other related professions, the craft of the Cabinetmakers with all their affiliates, the Wine Taverners' craft, the guild of the Schoolmasters and the craft of the Tailors each had their own chapel in the ambulatory (cat. 1, 6, 9, 10, 16). Regarding the location of their altars at least, corporations like the Smiths and the Gardeners (cat. 7, 5) could use a central pillar. Carpenters and Woodcutters were allotted a side pillar. The Fraternity of 'Onze-Lieve-Vrouwe-Lof' (Praise of Our Lady) and the Venerable Fraternity of the Blessed Sacrament – two prestigious associations – each had their own chapel, just in front of the north and south transept respectively – thus managing to occupy very important places in the cathedral with their altars and art works (cat. 8, 12).[15] The Almoners, probably through the nature of their activities, were housed in a chapel near the west entrance of the cathedral (cat. 2), where the so called Tables of the Holy Ghost, for poor relief, were situated. All this suggests that zone planning was well established. From these places curacy for the salvation of craft brothers and the deceased was given lustre.[16] In the 16th and 17th century cathedral, too, prestige was a well-known concept.[17]

However, prestige and status were not the only possible motivations. Can the positioning of crafts and their altarpieces after 1585 be seen through Counter-Reformational spectacles? Militias seem to have guarded the high altar, the most important place where the Eucharist was celebrated and the chapter met. The request of the chapter to the militias or armed guilds to occupy precisely those places seems therefore strategic and meaningful, and not merely inspired by financial motives.[18]

Around the choir, were assembled the crafts whose members literally devoted themselves to preaching the faith, like the Schoolmasters for instance. But other crafts, also present, may have been deliberately allotted a spot there. Painters and sculptors, united in the guild of Saint Luke, were called in to preach the faith through the imagery in their art objects. With their artefacts – religious furniture and clothing for the priests and services – cabinetmakers and tailors supported the clergy in the execution of their liturgical tasks.[19]

Triptychs were viewed by 16th and 17th century craftsmen and other – curious people in both open and closed positions. That is apparent from documents, painted interior views, etc. (fig. 21). But when were the triptychs opened and why? Were there strict prescriptions for this?

A handful of craft accounts lift a corner of the veil. The Merchants, a craft to which Shopkeepers and Traders were affiliated in order to conduct business legitimately, repeatedly paid the smith of the craft two guilders per year from 1607 onwards, to open the firmly closed panels of their painted triptych.[20] The account is even more interesting because an annotation also states that the triptych was opened on 'hooghtijden' (high days), namely: Christmas, Easter, Whitsun, and Ascension. However, it does not say how long the panels remained open. Was it some

13 The drawing is kept in the reserve of the cathedral.
14 On the historic changes in the placement of these altars, see Prims 1938–1939, XII, pp. 254–339; XIII, pp. 278–447; Van Brabant 1974, p. 24 sqq.
15 Timmermans 2008, pp. 115–116; Op de Beeck 1978, p. 67; Hermans 1992, pp. 61–64; Grieten & Bungeneers 1996, p. 14.
16 Van de Velde 1993A, p. 198. Verleysen 2001, pp. 166–167, also emphasises that possessing a prestigious altar went hand in hand with the urge for confirmation of the craft as a privileged group.
17 Versluys 2001, p. 166.
18 Van de Velde 1993A, p. 192.
19 For the altars of the Four Crowned Martyrs and the Wine Taverners, arguments can be advanced that might explain their location. The first, for instance, could actively participate in the proclamation of the faith with their architectural work. It is also notable that the privileges of the craft were often incorporated in the iconography of the altarpiece.
20 Geudens 1891B, p. 122 and SAA, GA 4225, n.f.

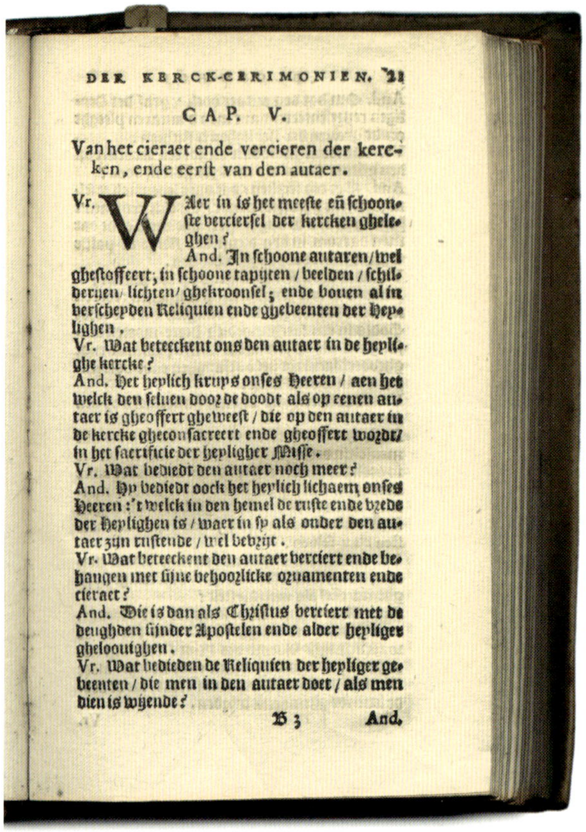

DER KERCK-CERIMONIEN. 21

CAP. V.

Van het cieraet ende vercieren der kercken, ende eerst van den autaer.

Vr. WAer in is het meeste eñ schoonste verciersel der kercken ghelegghen?

And. In schoone autaren/wel ghestoffeert; in schoone tapyten / beelden / schilderyen/ lichten/ ghekroonsel; ende bouen al in verscheyden Reliquien ende ghebeenten der Heylighen.

Vr. Wat beteeckent ons den autaer in de heylighe kercke?

And. Het heylich kruys onses Heeren / aen het welck den seluen door de doodt als op eenen autaer is gheoffert gheweest / die op den autaer in de kercke gheconsacreert ende gheoffert wordt/ in het sacrificie der heyligher Misse.

Vr. Wat bediedt den autaer noch meer?

And. Hy bediedt oock het heylich lichaem onses Heeren: 't welck in den hemel de ruste ende vrede der Heylighen is / waer in sy als onder den autaer zyn rustende / wel bevrijt.

Vr. Wat beteeckent den autaer verciert ende behangen met sijne behoorlicke ornamenten ende cieraet?

And. Die is dan als Christus verciert met de deughden sijnder Apostelen ende alder heyliger gheloovighen.

Vr. Wat bedieden de Reliquien der heyliger gebeenten / die men in den autaer doet / als men dien is wyende?

B 3 And.

23
Johannes David
Den bloemhof der Kerck-Cerimoniën
1622 · detail (p. 21)
Antwerp, Ruusbroec Genootschap

three days after every high feast? Or was a longer period of seven days reserved? Moreover, according to the same text, the panels had to be opened 'als het de dekens zou believen' (whenever 'the deans willed'). Handling the panels was therefore determined by the superiors of each craft, which proves that the devotional act was considered important. But when did the craft deans wish to open the panels? One can only guess. Could a visitor to the cathedral have caught a glimpse of the centre panel of the altarpiece on important occasions like the Joyous Entry of a sovereign, an Episcopal consecration, processions and circumambulations[21], and of course the feast of the craft's patron saint?[22]

Accounts from other crafts and guilds mention that on high days a piece of tapestry was hung 'above the altar and behind the scene'. This happened, for example, with the Schoolmasters in 1570.[23] Did this tapestry add even more glory to the painting? Silk ropes on which hung 'hoeyen' (wreaths) decorated the chapel. All these decorations and the opening of triptychs coincide wonderfully with the customs in the Utrecht verger's book from 1570.[24]

Who doubted that the side panels of the triptychs were firmly closed? In 1588, archives on the triptych of the Schoolmasters' guild mention three different locks:[25] a deadlock on one panel, a spring lock with copper wire pull tag on the other panel, and a lock with a key in the middle. Unfortunately the original framework of this triptych, with a depiction of *Christ Between the Scribes* (cat. 6) was not preserved. In 1710 the Bakers requested a new framework for their altarpiece and 'veranderingen der sleutels' (changes of keys), which again proves that quite some attention was paid to the closing of the triptychs.[26]

Private triptichs, too, were opened on some occasions. Accounts of the church fabric from the late 16th and early 17th century always include an entry for expenses to the verger. For instance, in 1611, and in later years, the verger was compensated for opening and closing the triptych of canon Malapart (Malapert).[27] Furthermore it is noted that the verger carefully turned open the hinges during the four 'high times of the year'.[28] The triptych of Jacob Anthonis was also regularly opened in 1635 and later years, according to the church fabric accounts.[29] Private triptychs were probably partly opened on the same occasions as the altarpieces of the crafts, in view of their function for saying Masses.

Contemporary literature makes clear that displaying the full triptych was not commonplace. Johannes Molanus was worried about safeguarding the ecclesiastic art works against dirt and damage. Did he have the opening and closing of the triptychs in mind? Did he want to protect them against damage, manifold manipulation, and pollution?[30]

In well-known devotional booklets, written by diligent Jesuit fathers, like Johannes David (fig. 23), the use of altarpieces is touched lightly on.[31] Readers can learn that the altar, decorated with paintings, refers to Christ who is embellished with the virtues of his apostles and saints. Following this reasoning the painted patron saints of the crafts, which were often placed above the altar, had to add extra glory to Christ. To the crucifix, the burning candles, the kneelers, and the flowers on the altar, symbolic meanings were given such as the Passion of Christ, the light of love that must be lit, the humbleness with which the Word must be received, and the odour that strengthens the heart.[32] Even the silk ropes and the wreaths, displayed in front of the altar and the painting, were explained. They referred to a resolute and virtuous life which is enriched by good works. Great importance was still attached to the curtains. They symbolised the Throne of God with clouds that opened during consecration. On the other hand they preserved the sacrament against the impudent glances of laymen. Could covering the main scene of the altarpiece be interpreted analogously as an attempt to protect it from the eyes of the uninitiated? The opening of the triptych could then be understood as a special favour for spectators who were only admitted in moments of ultimate excitement on feast days, like a true apotheosis ...

The chaplain and the craftsmen usually had to be satisfied with the depictions of the patron saints on the closed side panels. In these the saints functioned as *memoria in absentia*. A confrontation of all these saints with the craftsmen and guild brothers walking by must have had its charm in the cathedral. It could for example have led to a spiritual dialogue between the painted *exempla* and the craftsman; a spiritual dialogue that may have been inspiring for the well-being of the entire craft organisation or his personal walk of life.

Inside the walls of the cathedral not every craftsman could approach the altar triptych closely. Again from accounts, a hierarchy appears. Deans and aldermen had a key to the altar enclosure in front of the altarpiece. They could take a seat on a wooden pew.[33] Together with the celebrant and the acolyte they were in close contact with the triptych. An aura of exclusive devotion shone around their heads ...

Whether other craftsmen were allowed in the altar enclosure during Mass celebrations on Sundays, on the name day of the patron saint, and other high days, cannot yet be established. The deans, chosen from the free masters of the craft, probably stood in the altar enclosure. According to some ordinances they had to 'appear before the first evangel and hear every Sunday Mass completely out' ('iedere zondagsmis voor het eerste evangelium compareren en die volcomentlijck vuijt horen'), together with the 'busmeesters', deans, and aldermen.[34] It is likely that other craftsmen stood or even kneeled in the altar enclosure. Another question that cannot be answered is where the family members of deceased craft brothers stood and prayed during the Mass for the Dead. Could some of them have sat on a foldable chair?

For guilds and craft organisations which disposed of a full chapel in the ambulatory, the situation was of course entirely different. Apart from the celebrant and the committee members of the corporation several other persons could approach the altar, such as the choristers, among others, as is shown in the Schoolmasters' accounts. On the floor before the altar, 'stroysel' (reeds) could be strewn and often colourful

21 Another indirect proof for the opening of the side panels during the Circumambulation is offered in a sketch by Peter van Lint from c. 1632–1633; see Vlieghe 1979, p. 270.
22 The feast of the patron saint remained an important corporative occasion and all craft members were compelled to be present at the Holy Mass which was held before the altarpiece.
23 SAA, GA 4529, fol.120 r°.
24 Van Rossem 1876, p. 166 ff
25 Prims 1938–1939, XIII, p. 399.
26 SAA, GA 4061, n.f.
27 KAA, Kerkrekeningen, 19, fol. 20 r° and Kerkrekeningen, 21, fol. 41 r°.
28 KAA, Kerkrekeningen, 19, fol. 43 r°.
29 KAA, Kerkrekeningen, 19, fol. 44 v°.
30 Boespflug 1996, p. 91.
31 David 1622A, pp. 26–30.
32 David 1622A, p. 28.
33 SAA, GA 4365 n.g.
34 SAA, PK 757, fol. 125 v°.

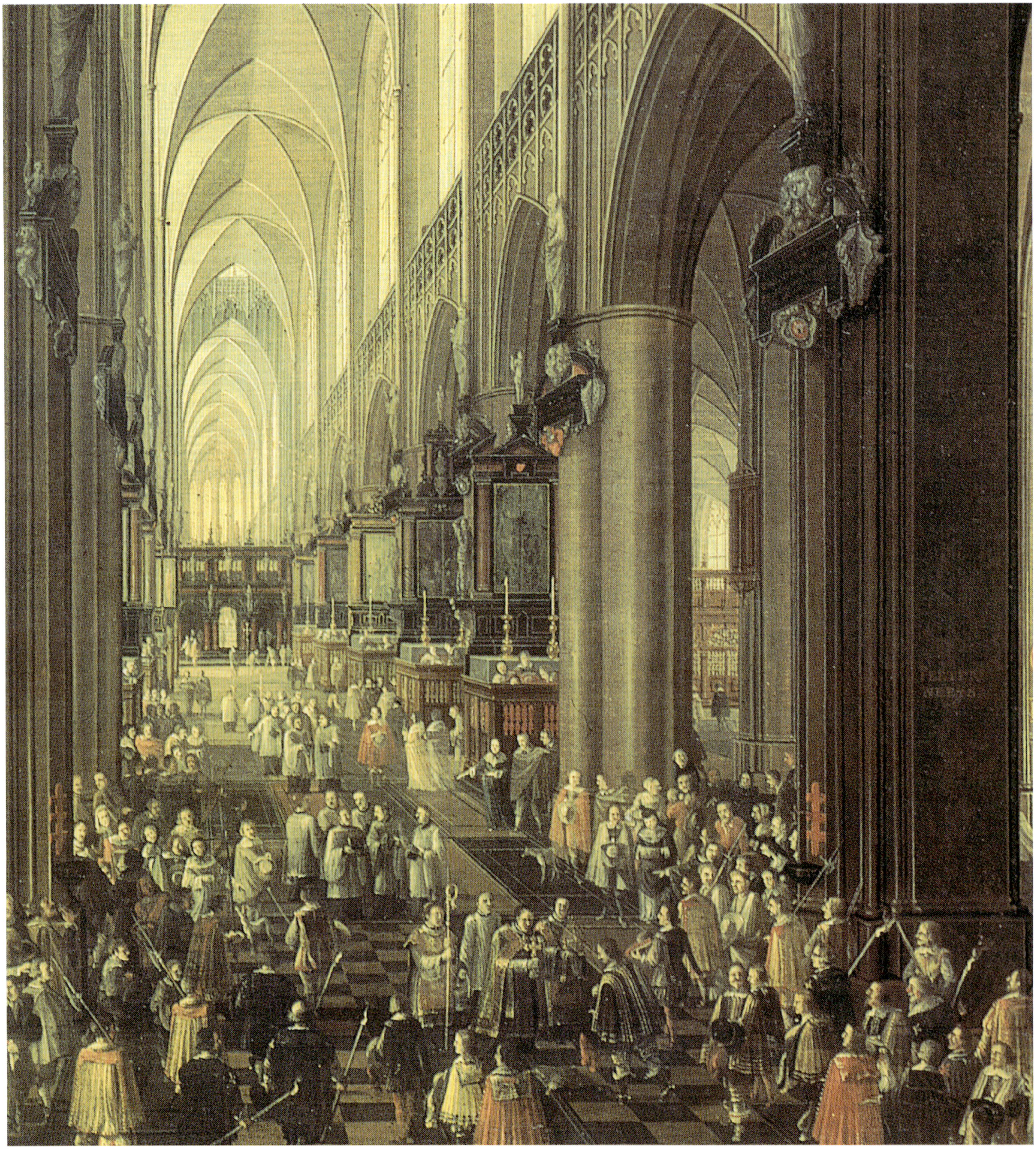

silk flowers were arranged on the altar table in front of the painting.[35]

The light, too, was an important factor in experiencing an art object. The incoming daylight with all its individual properties made the painting come alive. Even while conceiving the composition and determining the colour palette, artists took the natural light sources into account. Candlelight, too, was important. In the crafts' archives – such as those of the Schoolmasters,[36] Cabinetmakers, Gardeners, and Merchants – much attention was paid to the candleholders and candles on the altar. In verger's books very precise instructions were formulated for the arrangement of the candles, which differed according to the service that was held. Of course, candles produced favourable lighting for the painting, which was certainly no superfluous luxury in the gloomy winter months. According to medieval tradition it was also necessary to light the altar until Judgment Day.[37] Sometimes devotional prints were placed near the candles – in processions these were even attached to the candles.[38]

In a first conclusion, it may be said with due caution that the crafts' members were involved in various ways with the altarpiece. It expressed their religious conviction and it was an important element in devotional practice, but it also had important financial implications for the craftsmen. Part of the admission fees went to pay for the painting. Part of the penance money covered the costs of the altar candles etc. Sometimes a craft went into debt. Or real estate was sold to pay for the costs of the altarpiece.[39] On the other hand the craft or guild could save the triptych away for a rainy day. In an emergency, the painting could always be sold or traded.[40]

The social life of the craftsmen partly took place before the altarpiece. Its chronology – the course of the year with its many ecclesiastical feasts, was also indicated by the opened or closed panels of the triptych. In front of their altarpieces, in the cathedral itself, crafts recruited unfree masters. This practice went on until the 16th century, but as a result of disturbances it was moved to the Meir.[41]

There was probably also an emotional bond between the craftsman and the altarpiece. Before these impressive triptychs Masses were held for the salvation of the craftsmen, who were thus assured of a much desired passport to heaven. Probably favours were besought before the triptych at crucial moments, both for the craft and in the personal life of its members. If the altarpiece also affected the craftsmen and incited them to pure devotion, with open or closed panels, its success was complete.

After 1640, many side panels were detached from the triptychs. How the craftsmen then treated their altarpieces is a different story.

35 SAA, GA 4529, fol. 250 r°.
36 SAA, GA 4529, fol. 150 v°.
37 Jezler 2007, p. 25.
38 SAA, GA 4529, fol. 160 v°; see also Van der Stock 1998, p. 117.
39 In 1511 the Cabinetmakers had to sell half of their house 'den Aeren' on Grote Markt to pay for the *Lamentation of Christ* (cat. 1), painted by Quinten Matsijs.
40 Thus the cabinetmakers were considering selling the *Lamentation of Christ* (cat. 1) as early as 1577.
41 Scholliers 1956, p. 295. One can suppose that the custom of distributing the breads and the devotional prints also took place before the altar.

24
Pieter I Neeffs and Bonaventura Peeters · *Interior View of the Antwerp Cathedral of Our Lady* · 1648 · Vienna, Kunsthistorisches Museum

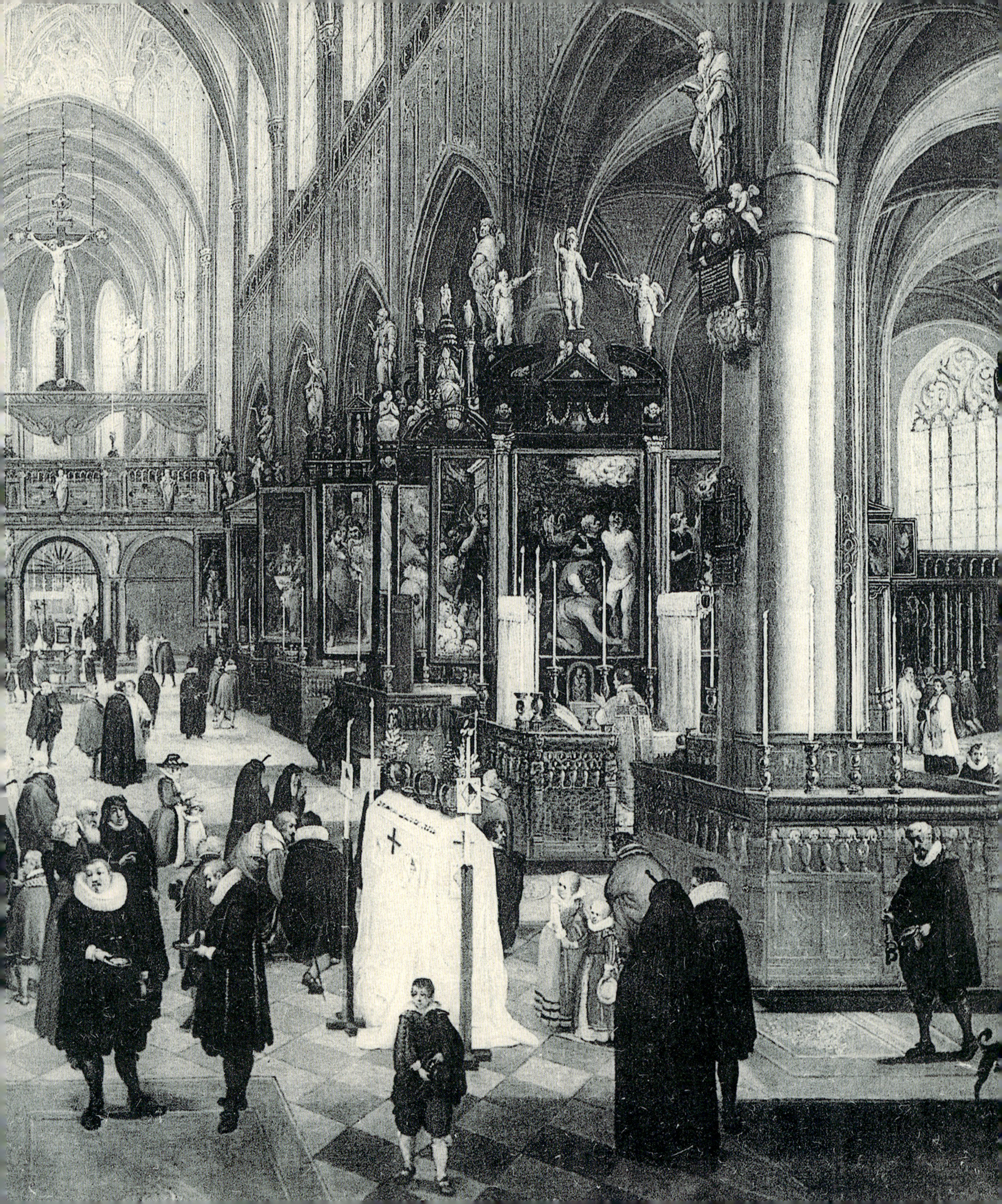

Altars and altar frames in the 17th century

CLAIRE BAISIER
VALÉRIE HERREMANS

In the 17th century numerous altars crowded the Antwerp cathedral. Every pillar in the nave, transept, and ambulatory was allotted to a guild, craft organisation, or fraternity. They were furnished with an altar table, a painted altar piece, statues, and candleholders, and surrounded by a wooden or marble altar enclosure *(tuin)*.

The embellishment of altars has taken very different forms over the centuries.

Apart from applying images to the substructure *(stipes)* of the actual altar table *(mensa)* or on the altar frontal *(antependium)*, the altar table could also be fitted with a *ciborium* or altar baldachin. In contrast to Italy, this was not customary in the Low Countries. Here, the most usual practice was a construction that was not placed above, but behind the altar table and embellished with artistic representations. These 'altar retables'[1] were executed in various materials – such as wood or stone – and in a range of techniques – such as painting, sculpture, and imitation architecture. Not only are most altarpieces no longer on site – most of them are currently also missing the greater part of their structure and framework, which together with the painting formed the entire altar construction. This article aims to clarify the original context.

Diversity

In contrast to today, dozens of altars lined the sacred space of Antwerp cathedral before the French Revolution. Their arrangement is illustrated in over 150 paintings from the 16th and 17th centuries, which give realistic portraits of the cathedral interior.[2] In these interior views, the formal diversity of the many altar decorations is striking. There are many reasons for this diversity. Apart from reflecting the taste and financial scope of the commissioners, these projects were produced over a very broad time span and represent a long-term artistic evolution.

The earliest altarpieces discussed here were created in the first decades of the 16th century (cat. 1, 2). In this period however, Antwerp was particularly renowned for its sculpted, gilded wooden retables, of which only the side panels were painted. The chronicles of the notary Geeraerd Bertryn, Lodovico Guicciardini, and others bear witness to the fact that at the time of the devastating fire in 1533 the church had no fewer than 57 altars, of which many were certainly equipped with sculpted retables.[3] One example that might be mentioned is that in the cathedral's Chapel of our Lady, a work from the renowned Antwerp atelier Wraghe.[4]

Beside these two types of retable, the painted altarpieces and the carved wooden retables with painted side panels, we must imagine a third variant to be admired in a 16th century church interior, namely the alabaster retable – an Italian concept. The retable of Saint Nicholas is an example of this, commissioned from 'cleynsteker' (fine-carver) sculptor Willem van der Borcht (master since 1535)[5] in 1539.[6] The sacrament chapel[7] and the prestigious circumcision chapel (now Saint Anthony's chapel) also possessed stone retables 'as fine as one could find in the country'.[8]

The First Iconoclastic Outbreak (1566) and the Second or 'Silent' Iconoclasm (1581–1585)

The fire of 1533 was not the only disaster that struck the cathedral in the 16th century. In the second half of the century the interior was heavily ravaged no less than twice: first in the iconoclastic outbreak in the summer of 1566, and the second time in the organised clearance during the Calvinist rule in Antwerp. The larger part of the works exhibited here was therefore created only after the second purging of the church interior.

After the Fall of Antwerp (1585) the new catholic city council demanded the immediate repair of the altars and their furnishing. As early as Monday

1 Braun 1924, II, p. 283. The term 'retable' was deduced from words like *retabulum*, *retrotabulum*, *retrotabularium* or *retroaltare*, all of which indicated the position of the object, behind the altar table. Other names are: *reiretaule, retaule, retable* (French), *retablo* (Spanish), *postaltare*, *postautel, reredos*.
2 Baisier 2008.
3 Van Brabant 1974, p. 20.
4 Grieten & Bungeneers 1996, p. 355. Jan Wraghe, son of Gillis Wraghe (master in 1490) who executed the Antwerp retable of the Virgin, may be identified as the contractor of the immense retable of the Dortmund Sankt Petrikirche. Cf. Büttner 2003, p. 65.
5 Rombouts & Van Lerius 1961, p. 124.
6 Grieten & Bungeneers 1996, p. 356.
7 [F.G.V.] 1743, p. 88.
8 *Loc. cit.*

25
Hendrik II van Steenwijck · *Interior View of the Antwerp Cathedral of Our Lady* · c. 1620 · detail · present whereabouts unknown

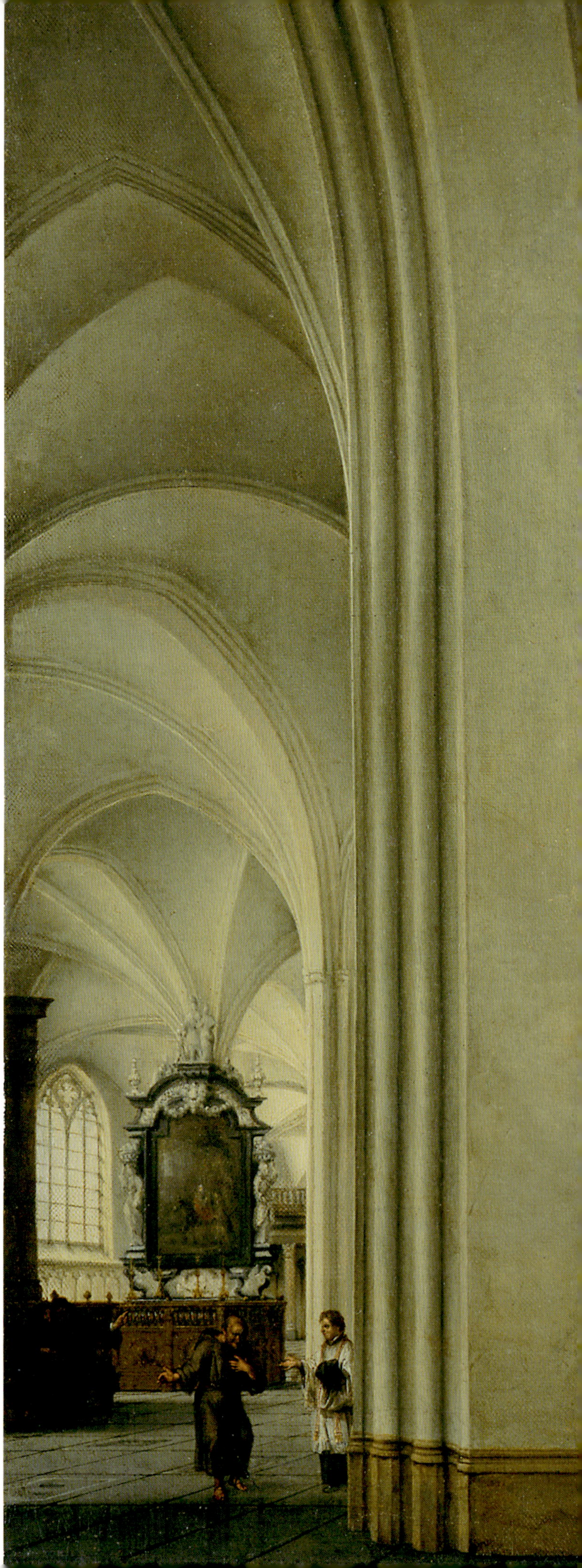

26
Isaak van Nickelen
Interior View of the Antwerp Cathedral of Our Lady
1668 · detail
Cambridge, Fitzwilliam Museum

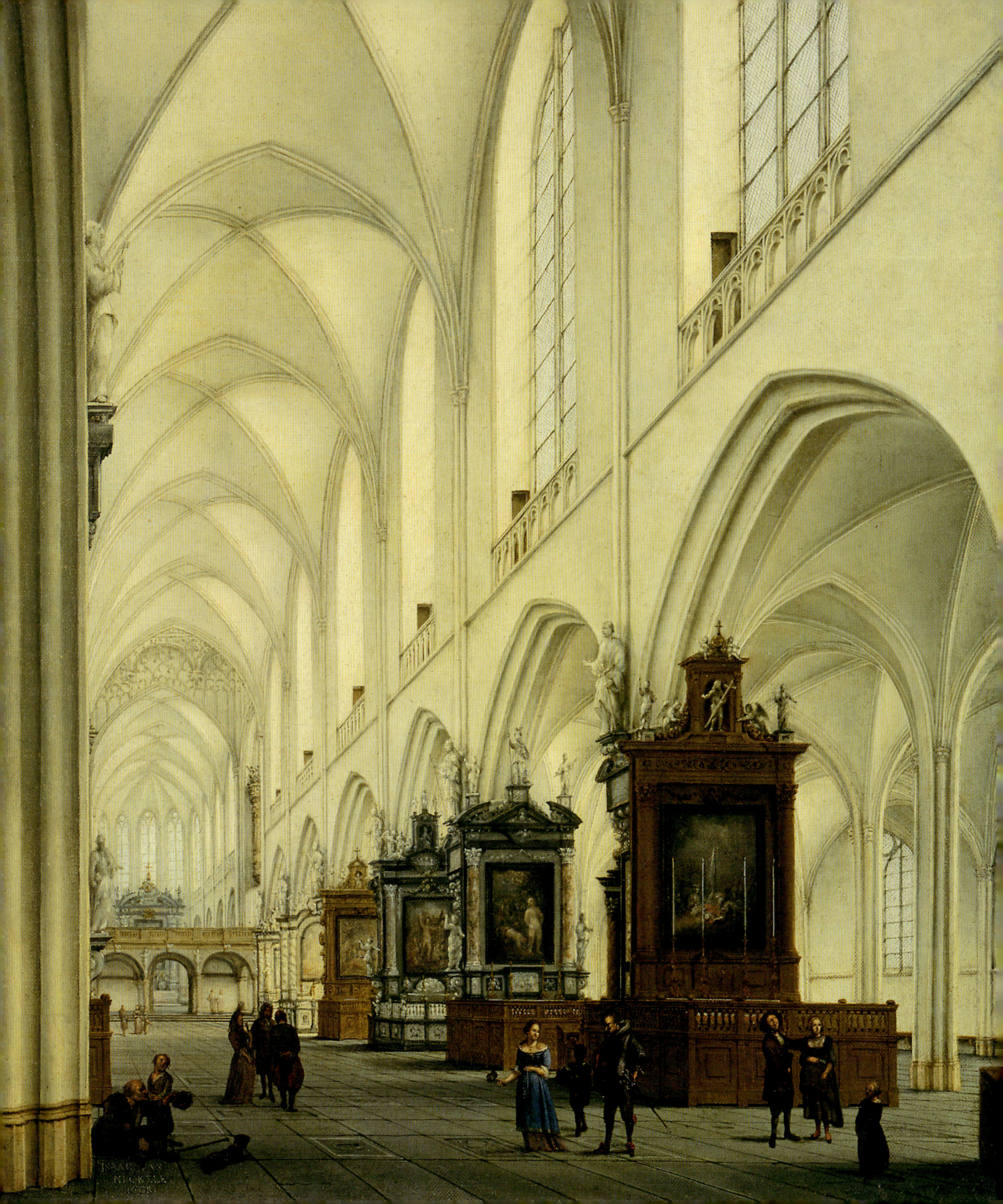

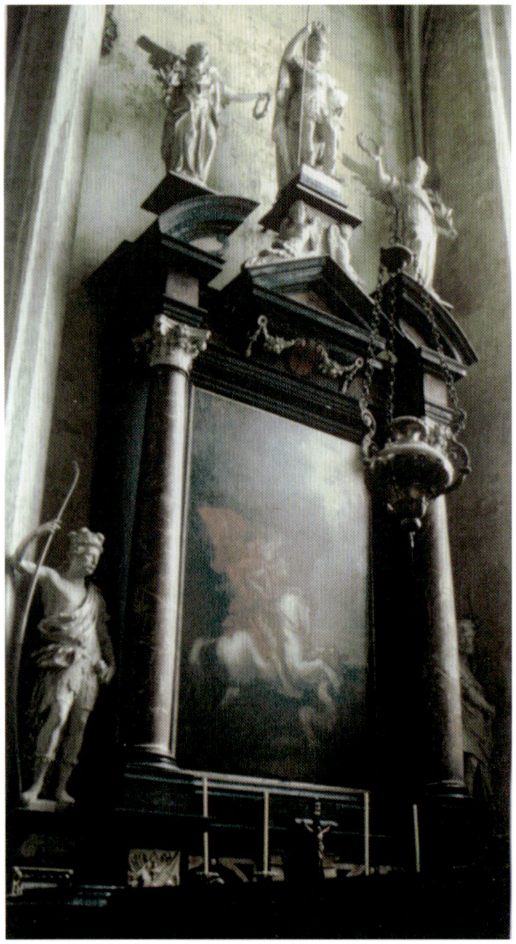

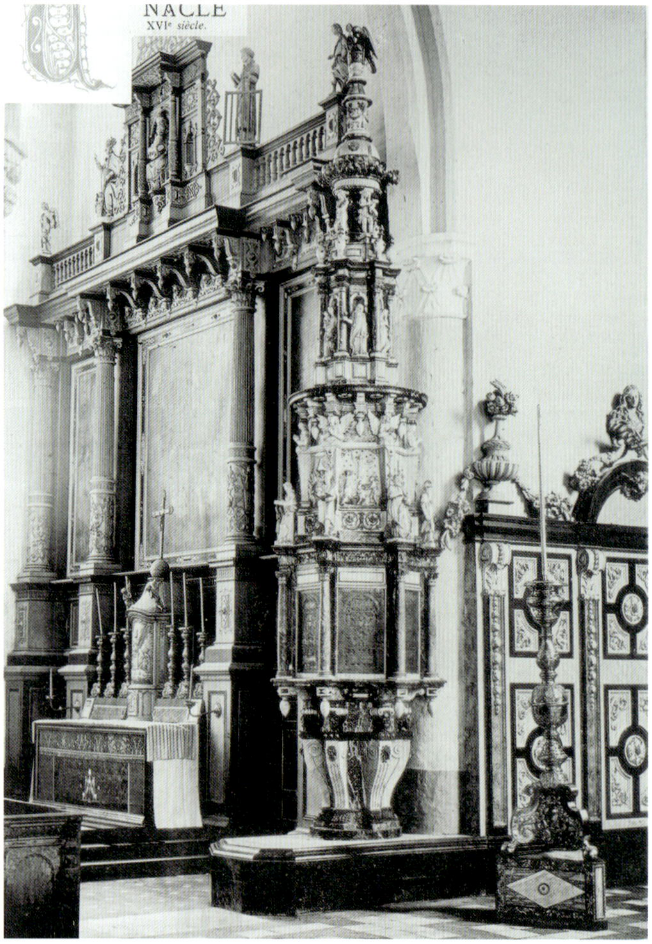

27
Jan and Robrecht de Nole
after a design by Otto van Veen
Altar of the Young Longbowmen's Guild in the Antwerp Cathedral of Our Lady
Antwerp, Saint James' Church

28
Otmaar van Ommen
High Altar of the Church of Our Lady
Nieuwpoort, Church of Our Lady

9 September 1585 – the first day after the resignation of burgomaster Filips van Marnix van Sint-Aldegonde (1540–1598) – it was decided that the vanished and destroyed altars were to be reconstructed or repaired.[9] Few of the guild or craft organisations immediately obeyed this demand. The ecclesiastical – and also the secular – authorities, however, continued to insist on a quick restoration.[10] In 1596 the city council issued a new order.[11]

The chief reasons for this slow response were probably the financial problems of most guilds and crafts resulting from the long-lasting war and inherent economic decline. This also emerges in the pattern of spending for the reconstruction. Re-using old altarpieces and using cheaper wood for the frame were legion.[12] In some cases these were temporary solutions and a new altarpiece was bought, and the wooden frame replaced by a more expensive stone one, as soon as means permitted. This phased restoration to suit all budgets resulted in an even greater range of altar decorations.

Typology

The Altarpiece with a Simple Wooden Frame

The most economical solution was to provide an existing altarpiece with a new frame.[13] This was done for the triptych of the Cabinetmakers' (cat. 1), which was undertaken in 1589–1590 by the atelier of the sculptor Otmaar van Ommen (1539–after 1628).[14] The Arquebusiers, too, initially chose this option, before they ordered a new triptych from Peter Paul Rubens (cat. 11).[15]

Whether out of necessity or not, others bought new altarpieces with simple frames. In 1596 the Wine Taverners ordered a new painted 'table' for their altar from Maerten de Vos (cat. 9).[16] Saint Luke's guild, too, made a deal with de Vos (cat. 10).[17] A drawing of the altar of the Painters' guild clearly illustrates that it was customary to fit the frame of the painting with openwork 'in the manner of the antique' along with crowning sculptures. In some cases, as with the retable of the Barbers' and Surgeons', a painted 'upper part' was also added.[18]

9 Baudouin 1984, pp. 94–95 (off-print); Prims 1938–1939, XIII, pp. 340–341.
10 Thijs 1987, p. 120, note 29; Van Brabant 1974, pp. 47 and 54.
11 Prims 1938–1939, XII, p. 317.
12 Herremans 2007, pp. 257–259.
13 Herremans 2007, pp. 32–33.
14 In 1589–90 Otmaar I van Ommen executed a new frame for the *Lamentation of Christ* triptych on the Cabinetmakers' altar: Van de Velde 1993B, p. 193; Vervaet 1976, p. 205.
15 After the second iconoclastic outbreak, the Arquebusiers' guild initially negotiated the joint building of a new altar with the Soap Boilers. Eventually, however, the Arquebusiers decided to erect their own altar. The painted scenes from the old altar were probably re-used for the new one, which certainly comprised a stone part (substructure?) because a master builder, Niclaes Wyns, was involved. In addition, the retable also contained different pieces of carved wood, because the notes from 1587 mention, 'To Otmer the wood worker all'antica, to repair the scene on the altar, to attach the ornament to it, and to make fireballs with nails'. The new altar was consecrated on Saint Dominic's Day, 4 August 1588. Then, in 1611, a new triptych was ordered with P.P. Rubens – there is no reference to a new altar frame. On 12 September 1612 the centre part was completed, which was already placed in the chapel – the side panels followed in February–March 1614. F. Baudouin published accounts which testify that the brothers de Nole were paid for the stonework of the altar and the altar enclosure. The modest sum of 1,000 guilders indicates that it could not have had a stone retable, but probably a stone altar substructure and sanctuary. Baudouin 1972, p. 79; Grieten & Bungeneers 1996, p. 14; Prims 1938–1939, XII, pp. 305–306.
16 Grieten & Bungeneers 1996, p. 13; Prims 1938–1939, XIII, pp. 429–433.
17 In 1589 a new wooden frame was ordered from Otmaar van Ommen. Grieten & Bungeneers 1996, p. 14; Jansen & Van Herck 1943, pp. 57–107. For an overview of the history of the development, see Peeters 2005.
18 De Poorter 1970, p. 128.

The Wooden 'Renaissance' Portico Altar

Some commissioners were able to invest more in the frame of their altarpieces and chose an (imitation) architectural frame.[19] Again this offered various possibilities, each with a different price tag. The wooden portico was certainly the most cost-effective solution. This construction consisted of architecturally inspired elements like the *edicula,* pillars and capitals, without however respecting the proper architectural proportions. It might be called a piece of furniture, executed in a decorative, architectural formal language. Here, too, openwork 'in the manner of the antique' was often used, applied to the crown piece or to both sides of the construction. The crown piece usually consisted of a niche, flanked by two sculptures. In the niche a third wooden sculpture of modest proportions was displayed. This altar type occurred in the southern Netherlands until ca. 1640.[20]

A well-documented example of this type is the altar of Saint Philip of the Fishmongers. In the early 1620s, when Hendrik II van Steenwijck painted the cathedral interior (fig. 25), the altar enclosure the altar table, and the predella with the three small panels, were already erected against the sixth pillar on the right of the nave. Apparently only the portico and the triptych remained to be moved from the Fishmongers' chapel in the ambulatory. The triptych, whose centre panel showed *The Miraculous Draught of Fishes,* dated from shortly after 1556 and was the work of Hans van Elburcht (cat. 4). It was one of the oldest altarpieces in the cathedral. The left side panel with *Baptism of the Ethiopian Eunuch by Saint Philip* is now in the Boijmans Van Beuningen Museum in Rotterdam (fig. 4c). On the right panel – now in the monastery of the Sisters of Mercy in Saint-Ghislain (Belgium) – *Martyrdom of Saint James the Less* (fig 4b) was painted, with a small circular temple in the background. It seems that both panels had already been removed from the altar in the 17th century, since they are missing in later interior views.[21] Both predella paintings and the vanished small centre panel with Christ on the Cross surrounded by the Virgin, John, and Mary Magdalene would have been added to the altarpiece when the Fishmongers erected a new altar at the end of the 16th century (see cat. 4).

The altar was almost certainly built entirely in wood – the predella and the pedestals perhaps in black jasper. In any case, Van der Sanden noted that 'this old altar in wood or wainscot stands at the first pillar, when one enters at the tower gate on one's right hand'.[22] In the predella two paintings were fitted: on the left *Christ Calling the Apostles James and John* and on the right *Christ Calling the Apostles Peter and Andrew.* At the centre of a niche, rounded at the top, a Calvary was shown. The altarpiece with *The Miraculous Draught of Fishes* was flanked by two fluted columns with square pedestals, richly decorated shafts, and Corinthian capitals. The side panels hinged around the columns, as is still the case with some altars in the Antwerp Saint James' Church. The strongly jutting cornice was decorated with a broad frieze, with dentils and bead-and-reels. The altar crown piece consisted of a high niche in the shape of a small portico with pillars, side volutes, cornice, and serlian motif, with on the inside a standing statue of the Risen Christ with the Cross, blessing the faithful. On small pedestals on each side of the niche there were statues of the apostles Philip and James.

In some cases these portico altars were expanded to three-part constructions which were set up around the three panels of the triptych, as in the high altar for the Church of Our Lady in Nieuwpoort (1595–1597; fig. 28) and Saint John's Church in Mechelen (1610–1619), both by Otmaar van Ommen (1540–after 1617).[23] The altar of the Old Longbowmen's Guild was of this type. From 1590 it stood in the south transept, just beside the entrance to the ambulatory.[24] This portico, too, was ordered from Van Ommen, on 30 January 1591. Because the guild members insisted that it should be built on the model of the altar of Saint George of the

19 Herremans 2007, pp. 33–34.
20 Herremans 2007, p. 104.
21 For example an interior view by Alexander Casteels from the beginning of the 18th century, of which a photograph was preserved in Antwerp's city archive (irretrievable) [Inv. 0117]. Grieten 1997, p. 18.
22 Van der Sanden 1781, PK 171/2: fol. 642.
23 Neither retable survives. The side panels of the triptychs could be rotated through a shaft at the centre of the panel. Herremans 2007, cat. 6, 15.
24 Mensaert 1763, p. 229; Descamps 1769, p. 145; Berbie 1774, p. 11; *Kerken van Antwerpen 1774*, p. 14; Papebrochius 1848, p. 353.

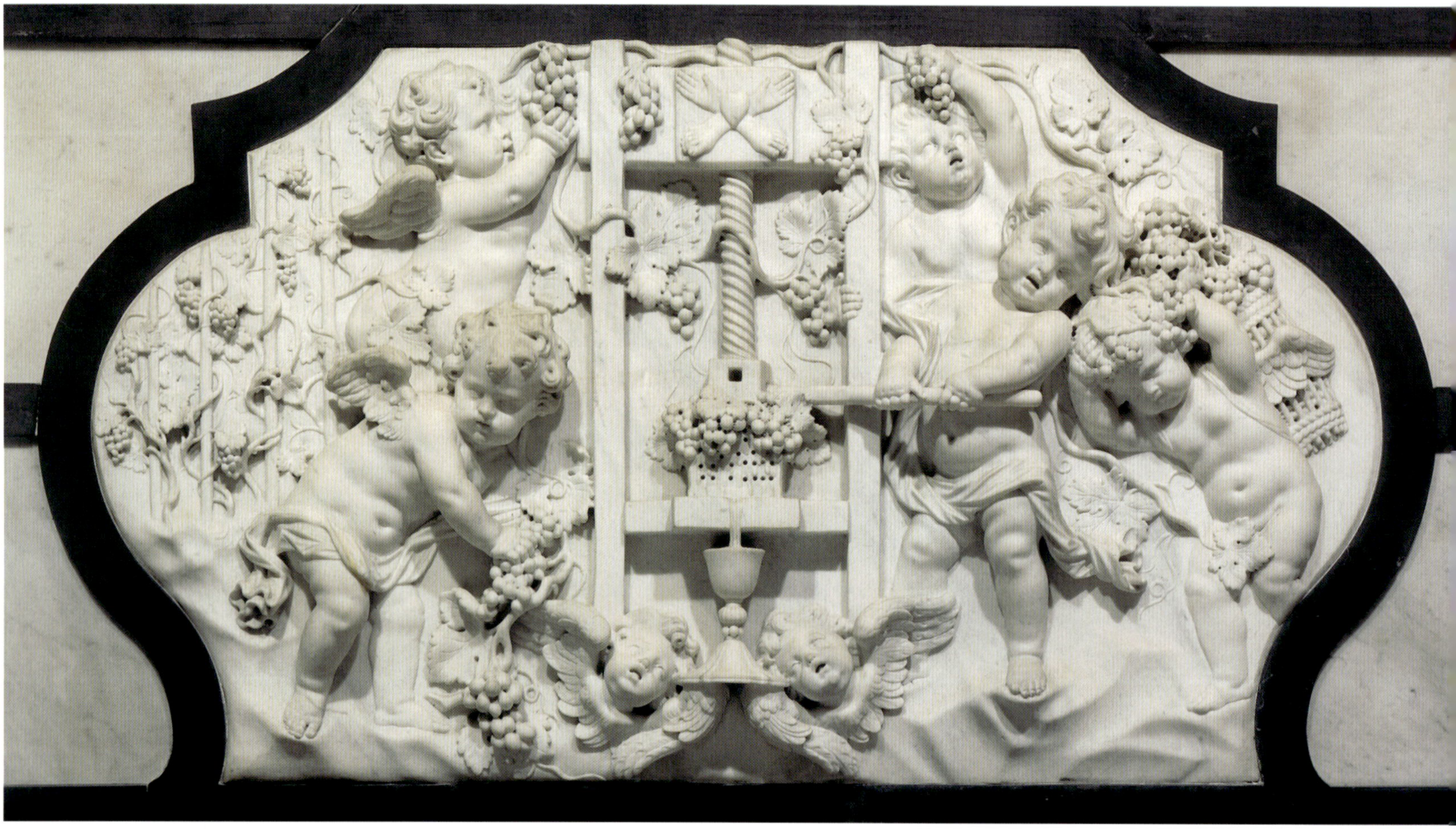

Old Arbalest in the north transept,[25] the whole was crowned with an equestrian statue of Saint Sebastian, although this saint was never depicted in this way according to the customary iconography.[26] Furthermore, as the contract with Van Ommen stipulated, the altar would consist of four columns on pedestals decorated with the emblems of the guild and, on each side of the crowning statue, a pyramid and a candlestick.[27] The construction was to be erected 'on the basis and in the way of the pattern of the Old Arbalest'[28] – in other words: the two altars, each near an entrance to the ambulatory and opposite each other, were formally complementary, which led to symmetry.

An interior view by Batholomeus van Bassen shows the equestrian statue flanked by two standing statues, probably angels. The triptych by Michiel Coxcie (1499–1592), painted in 1575, is presented in a closed position, so only the exterior of the side panels is visible.[29] The original panels by Coxcie disappeared in 1581 and were replaced ca. 1590 by Ambrosius I Francken (1544–1618).[30] Just as on the altarpiece of the Young Longbowmen's Guild the centre panel depicted the martyrdom of Saint Sebastian, but on the side panels other scenes were shown. On the inside, the arrest of Saint Sebastian was displayed to the left, and his death to the right. On the closed panels,

25 Erected in 1590 by cabinetmaker Otmaar van Ommen and sculptor Robrecht Colijns de Nole, see Jansen & Van Herck 1943, p. 44; Van de Velde 1993B, p. 202.
26 SAA, Notarissen, Notary Adriaan De Witte, N 1175 (1591): IX [published in: Van de Velde 1993B, pp. 201–202, 210–211, appendix 1]. Van Brabant 1972, p. 223, no. 38; Van Damme 1985, II, pp. 125–126; Grieten & Bungeneers 1996, p. 15; Herremans, 2007, cat. no. 3.
27 Van de Velde 1993B, pp. 201–202; Grieten & Bungeneers 1996, p. 15.
28 Van de Velde 1993B, pp. 210–211.

29
Artus Quellinus and Ludovicus Willemsens · *Altar of the Coopers, predella* · detail · 1677–1678 · Antwerp, Cathedral of Our Lady

major facts from the life of Saint Sebastian were depicted: to the left the saint who, in prison, urges the brothers Marcus and Marcellinus to go to their death as Christians, and to the right the miraculous healing of the Christian Zoë. The altar was surrounded by an impressive altar enclosure – the first in the church that was not built in wood but marble. This enclosure was constructed almost simultaneously with the altar by the sculptor Rafaël Paludanus and stonemason Jacques Fourmanoir, but in a much richer material: marble, black jasper, alabaster, and bluestone. Here, too, according to the contract from 2 April 1591, the designer had to base himself on the altar enclosure of the Old Arbalest, at least regarding the dimensions.[31] The order for the nine alabaster angel statues shows that the altar enclosure was more than a metre high, which is confirmed by the interior view by Bartholomeus van Bassen.[32]

The Italian Stone 'Renaissance' Retable

Apart from these wooden retables there was also the possibility for more wealthy patrons to have a stone frame erected for their altarpieces, mostly also fitted with stone sculpture. Around the turn of the century (16th to 17th), two stylistic tendencies emerge. The first one continues the aforementioned Italianising tendency in the stone retable architecture of the 16th century.[33] Here – as with the wooden portico altars – (imitation) architectural forms were used, albeit on a monumental scale.

The elevation of the vanished altar of the fraternity of the Blessed Sacrament (1606–1615), a work from the studio of Colijns de Nole,[34] was based on an Italian altar type that dated back to the second half of the 15th century. These are constructions with a three-part elevation, inspired by the antique triumphal arch scheme.[35] The monumental central bay is defined by a round arch. Both side bays are narrower and mostly consist of a range of horizontal registers with niches fitted with sculptures. Examples of this are the retable formerly at the high altar of the church of Santa Maria del Popolo in Rome[36] (Andrea Bregno, ca. 1473) – now in the church sacristy – or the monumental retable of the Piccolomini altar in the Duomo of Siena (Andrea Bregno, Pietro Torrigiani, Michelangelo, from 1480 onwards).

At the centre of the altar of the Fraternity of the Blessed Sacrament the altarpiece by Otto van Veen was displayed, which he had executed as early as 1592 (cat. 8). On each side of this stood the sculptures of Saints Peter and Paul, and above them Moses and Melchizedek. The whole is crowned with a statue of Christ as the Good Shepherd. To the left and right of this were two evangelists each. The top was crowned by a tabernacle and a pelican. Al these sculptures were executed in alabaster.

The Monumental Stone Portico Altar

Even before the end of the 16th century, a second tendency became prominent. The stone portico altar appeared: it was conceived in a contemporary architectural language, in which the legacy of Michelangelo stood at the centre.[37] The use of architectural elements reached a monumental scale and was characterised by some fundamental motifs of post-michelangelian mannerism, like the superposition of columns or breaking through the frame and pediments. This new type of retable set the tone for altar architecture in the 17th and 18th centuries.

The first example of this type, which was trailblazing for the southern Netherlands, is the altar from 1598 of the Young Longbowmen's Guild, at the first pillar on the right of the nave. Yet, not very long before – in 1585, immediately after the Calvinist period – the Young Longbowmen's Guild had had a new altar made by a rather obscure joiner, Heynderic, with a crown piece after a design by Hans Vredeman de Vries.[38] This altar, which was consecrated on 16 December 1586,[39] may have stood in one of the chapels of the ambulatory.[40] On the altar, a triptych

29 Michiel Coxcie, *Martyrdom of Saint Sebastian*, 1575, oil on panel, 267 x 235 cm, Antwerpen, Koninklijk Museum voor Schone Kunsten, inv. 371. Berbie 1756, p. 15; *Kerken van Antwerpen* 1774, p. 14; Prims 1938–1939, XIII, pp. 359–360; Van Brabant 1972, p. 223, no. 38; Freedberg 1976, p. 128; *Catalogue Antwerp 1988*, p. 97; Van de Velde 1993A, pp. 189–190; Van de Velde 1993B, pp. 195–214; Grieten & Bungeneers 1996, pp. 364–365.

30 Ambrosius Francken, left panel with *Saint Sebastian in Prison* and *Diocletian Has Saint Sebastian Captured*, right panel with *The Miraculous Healing of Zoë* and *Martyrdom of Saint Sebastian,* ca. 1590, oil on panel, 283 x 112 cm, Antwerp, Koninklijk Museum voor Schone Kunsten, inv. 151–154. Prims 1938–1939, XIII, pp. 360–361; Antwerp 1946, p. 9, cat. B.3; Freedberg 1976, pp. 128, 130–131, fig. 6–9; Vervaet 1976, pp. 215–217; *Catalogue Antwerp 1988*, pp. 146–147; Van de Velde 1993A, p. 190; Van de Velde 1993B, pp. 201–204; Grieten & Bungeneers 1996, pp. 364–365.

31 SAA, Notarissen, Notary Adriaan De Witte, N 1175 (1591): XXXIV. Published in: Van de Velde 1993B, pp. 202, 211–213, appendix 2.

32 Prims 1938–1939, XIII, p. 362; Duverger 1984–2004, I, pp. 377–378; Duverger 1984–2004, VI, p. 253; Van de Velde 1993A, p. 193; Grieten & Bungeneers 1996, p. 2.

33 Herremans 2007, pp. 34–37.

34 The contract from 27 April 1606 was published in Casteels 1961, pp. 293–296. Herremans 2007, cat. 11.

35 Capretti 1995; Humfrey 1993.

36 De Blaauw 1997; Jürgens 1956, fig 10b.

37 Herremans 2007, pp. 37–38, 142 ff.

38 Vlieghe 1973, p. 343; Grieten & Bungeneers 1996, p. 23.

39 Prims 1938–1939, XIII, p. 326.

40 Prims 1938–1939, XIII, pp. 322–323; Grieten & Bungeneers 1996, p. 13.

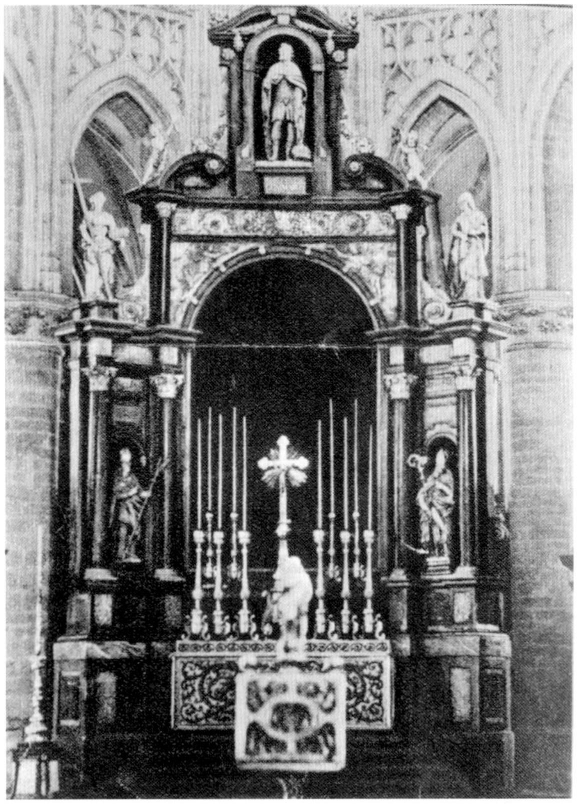

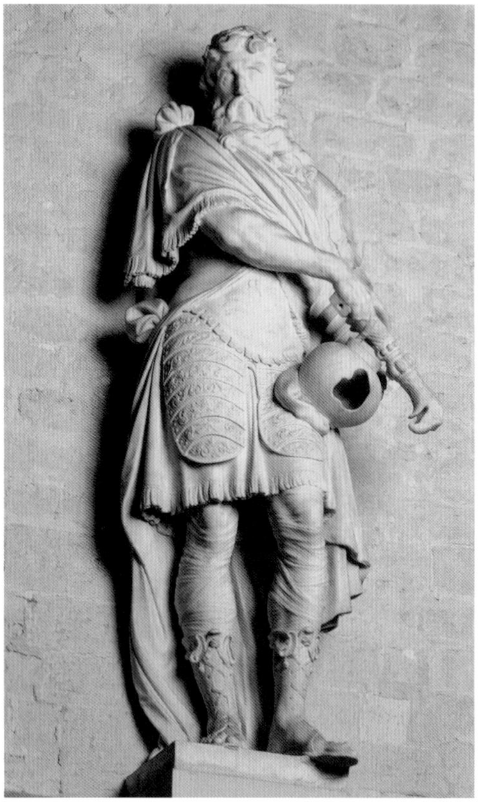

30
Master Heynderic
partly after a design by Hans Vredeman de Vries
Altar of the Young Longbowmen's Guild in the Cathedral of Our Lady, later acquired by the Saint Sebastian's Guild of Lier
Lier, Saint Gummarus' Church

31
Hubert van den Eynde
Gideon
originally from the altar of the Fencers' Guild
after 1650
Antwerp, Cathedral of Our Lady

by Chrispijn van den Broeck (1524–1590/91) was displayed, dating from 1572–1573.[41] The centre panel depicted *The Birth of Christ*, the left side panel *The Holy Sebastian*, and the right side panel *The Holy Dymphna*, the two saints to whom the altar was initially dedicated.[42] Probably the whole seemed rather outdated, because the guild wanted a new altar. The altar, the triptych, and the three small predella paintings, were sold in 1598 to the guild of Saint Sebastian in Lier (near Antwerp) and the next year – paid for by Hendrik or Nicolaas van Varick, margraves of Antwerp – they were displayed in the Church of Saint Gummarus in Lier, where they remain to this day. The original centre panel was replaced by a copy by Adriaen de Bie (1593–1668) after *The Martyrdom of Saint Sebastian* by Coebergher (see below); the side panels are still those by Chrispijn van den Broeck.[43]

The new altar was built in 1598–1599 by the sculptors Robrecht and Jan de Nole after a design by Otto van Veen (1556–1629). The contract with the sculptors – which stipulated among others that the altar was to be constructed in marble and bluestone, and the statues in white Avesnes stone – was signed by both parties on 25 February 1598.[44] To embellish the new altar, a triptych was ordered in 1599 from Wenzel Coebergher (1560–1634) who was living in Rome at that time.[45] This is probably why it was painted on canvas – and not, as was customary, on heavy oak wood panels – to facilitate the transport. Exceptionally, this altar survived the French period; today it stands in the Antwerp Church of Saint James. It was bought, at a public auction of the cathedral furnishings (1798), by a brewer who left it on the site for unknown reasons. As the only remaining altar, it was moved to Chapel of the 'Nood Gods' behind the high choir. However, in 1867, the cathedral's church fabric, in full neogothic flush, sold it to Saint James' Church.[46] There it still stands in the Chapel of Our Lady of Presentation – the sixth chapel on the south side – albeit without the triptych by Coebergher, whose centre panel with *The Martyrdom of Saint Sebastian* is now in the Museum of Fine Arts in Nancy,[47] while the side panels have, alas, vanished.

A comparison between the current condition of the altar in Saint James' Church and that on 17th century interior views of the cathedral reveals only minor differences. The central crowning statue was replaced, but apparently little or nothing was changed in the portico altar itself, nor in the four other freestanding statues on both sides of the portico and on top of the crown piece. All the details of the crown piece are clearly recognisable: the broken pediment,

41 Grieten & Bungeneers 1996, p. 13.
42 Prims 1938–1939, XIII, pp. 322–323; Van de Velde 1993a, pp. 188–189, fig; Grieten & Bungeneers 1996, p. 23.
43 Adriaen De Bie, *Martyrdom of Saint Sebastian*, oil on panel, 193 x 194 cm, Chrispijn Van den Broeck, *Saints Sebastian and Dimphna* (side panels), oil on panel, 183 x 74 cm, and *Adoration of the Magi, Christ among the Scribes, The Baptism of Christ* (predella), 1573, Lier, Saint Gummarus' Church. KIK M50965, B19505. Prims 1938–1939, XIII, p. 326; Vlieghe 1973, pp. 342–346; Grieten & Bungeneers 1996, p. 364. Adriaen de Bie was the father of Cornelis de Bie.
44 Jansen & Van Herck 1943, p. 15, no. 12; Casteels 1961, pp. 108–109, 259–260; Grieten & Bungeneers 1996, pp. 23–24.
45 Wenceslas Coeberger, *Martyrdom of Saint Sebastian*, oil on canvas, 288.5 x 207.5 cm, Nancy, Musée des Beaux-Arts, inv. no. 92. Berbie 1756, p. 7; Casteels 1961, p. 108; Freedberg 1976, p. 135; Dacos & Meijer 1995, pp. 146–147, cat. 60; Grieten & Bungeneers 1996, pp. 23–24, 366–367.
46 Jansen & Van Herck 1943, p. 15 no. 12; Grieten & Bungeneers 1996, pp. 23–24, 366–367.
47 Descamps 1769, p. 141; Vlieghe 1973, p. 344; Van de Velde 1993a, p. 198; Meganck 1998, p. 22; Grieten & Bungeneers 1996, pp. 366–367.

the triangular tympanum with the white cherub's head – and above it a statue of Saint Sebastian on a cubic pedestal, supported by two angel caryatids, and flanked on the side volutes by two large angels with raised arms holding in their hands laurel wreaths in honour of the martyr. Also perfectly executed by the architectural painter is the predella under the altarpiece with at the centre a statuette flanked by pilasters with Ionic capitals and diamond heads, and two panels with a cherub's head in an oval frame.

According to Theodoor Van Lerius, the Saint Sebastian sculpture was replaced at the re-erection of the altar in Saint James' Church in the 19th century by a copy by Jan-Baptist De Vos.[48] The original sculpture was indeed preserved in the cathedral.[49] The opinions of the different authors diverge regarding the authenticity of the four remaining figures, the two angels and the two warrior figures, of which Van Lerius thinks that they are by the hand of Andries Colyns de Nole (1598–1638) and therefore of a later date. Some authors are of the opinion that all five statues of the crown were replaced by the sculptor De Vos.[50] Marguerite Casteels, however, takes the view that all the sculptures were made in the 19th century.[51]

The monumental scale of the 17th century marble altar frames themselves, but especially the addition of an extremely valuable sculpture to the architectural whole, made altar constructions very expensive. Probably price considerations had something to do with the re-use of Frans Floris' splendid altarpiece *The Fall of the Rebel Angels* (cat. 3) in the new portico altar of the Fencers' guild. The guild would have conceived the plan of building a precious altar as early as 1650. The Fencers wished to do business with the very best of contemporary Antwerp sculptors-architects: Hubertus van den Eynde (1594–1662) and Artus II Quellinus (1625–1700). The pricy plans were, however, not finalised before Hubertus' decease in 1661. Eventually, on 12 April 1670, an agreement was closed, for 8,400 guilders, with Artus II Quellinus and Norbertus van den Eynde (1628–1704), the son and successor of Hubertus.[52] The agreement specified a portico with sculpture and an altar enclosure in white Italian marble, black marble, bluestone, and wood.[53] The whole had to be constructed 'following the drawings or models made hereof and shown to the parties present' and finished within two years under penalty of a fine of 50 guilders per month. Incidentally, Quellinus and Van den Eynde did not meet this deadline.

The Fencers' altar was situated at the first pillar to the right of the nave, were it remained until the French period. It was richly provided with sculpture. This made the retable an exceptional spectacle. Life-size marble sculptures were usually not part of the embellishment of a side altar, due to its price – it was easily possible to pay between 500 and 1,100 guilders for a statue.[54] The Fencers' altar, however, was fitted with no fewer than five marble sculptures. The whole was completed with a five-and-a-half Antwerp foot (approximately 1.6 m) high representation of the altar patron, the archangel Michael. To the left and right there were two smaller angels, each five foot (approximately 1.4 m) high. While setting statues of the patron and worshipping angels on top of the portico was still somewhat customary, the huge statues of the Old Testament rulers Gideon and Joshua (6 foot or approximately 1.7 m high) on each side of the portico were definitely not. These high points of 17th century sculpture in the Southern Netherlands are, beside the altarpiece, the only remains from this impressive construction.[55] It has been justly said that they exquisitely express the military leadership from which the members of the prestigious Fencers' guild wanted to take their example.[56] They are also important as monumental testimonies of the cathedral's altars and decorations during the ancien regime.

48 Van Lerius 1855, pp. 11–12.
49 Van Lerius 1871, p. 12; Jansen & Van Herck 1943, pp. 15–16, no. 12. The existence of the original crowning figure was overlooked by Casteels 1961. Grieten & Bungeneers 1996, pp. 23–24, regards this sculpture as a 17th century depiction of Saint Gummarus which crowned the retable after it was re-erected in the then Saint Gummarus Chapel after its dismantlement in 1798. The sculpture is now situated against the exterior wall of the southern transept of the cathedral. It is made of (lime?)stone (KIK. B15890) and is 155 cm tall. The arch and left forearm are missing and the entire work is in a worrisome condition (white stone, height 155 cm, Antwerp, Cathedral of Our Lady, inv. no. 1022).
50 Casteels 1961, p. 109; Grieten & Bungeneers 1996, pp. 23–24.
51 Casteels 1961, loc. cit.
52 Berbie 1756, pp. 9–10; Descamps 1769, p. 142; Van der Sanden 1781, PK 172/2, fol. 563; Grieten & Bungeneers 1996, pp. 464–465.
53 Herremans 2007, cat. 263, contract 4 December 1670.
54 They mostly opted for sculpture of smaller dimensions, executed in wood. Herremans 2007, pp. 252–257.
55 Norbertus van den Eynde, *Gideon*; Artus II Quellinus, *Joshua*, 1670, white marble, height 180 cm, Antwerp, Antwerp, Cathedral of Our Lady, inv. 1026.
56 Grieten & Bungeneers 1996, p. 464.

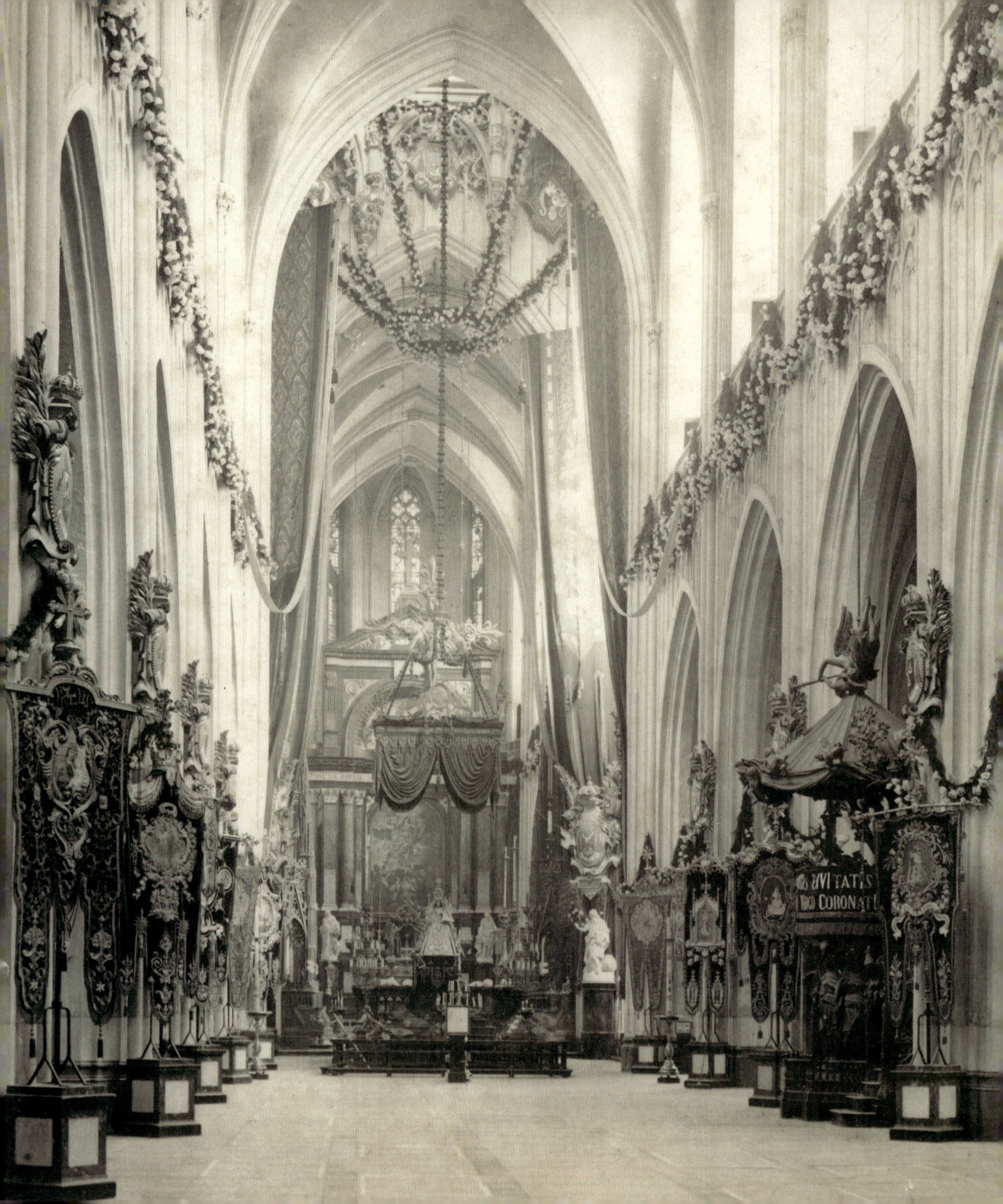

The Cathedral of Our Lady in Antwerp, a Gothic Interior?

Recreating a Medieval Church Interior in the 19th and 20th Centuries

MADELEINE MANDERYCK

The Cathedral of Our Lady in Antwerp, together with St Rumbolds in Mechelen, St Michael & St Gudula in Brussels, St Peter in Leuven, and St John in 's-Hertogenbosch, is one of the most important edifices of Brabantian late Gothic. It is assumed that the building of the present church was commenced with the present choir in 1352. After the north tower was initiated ca. 1420, the completion of the nave and side aisles followed, at which point the older Romanesque church was systematically dismantled. The busiest building years were 1470–1525. At that time the church had about reached its present dimensions. In the 17th century work continued in accordance with the initial Gothic design and the nave received a quadripartite rib vault. The basilical ground plan with its screened-off polygonal ambulatory and radiating chapels, the articulated elevation with slender compound pillars, and the white interior environment with multicoloured accents on the vault bosses characterise Brabantian late Gothic.[1] The design of the interior was determined by the diversity of functions the Church of Our Lady fulfilled at the time. It was primarily a collegiate church to which, from the 12th century onwards, a chapter of canons was attached. The choir was their exclusive domain. Furthermore there were dozens of chantries in the church and numerous chaplains held the daily Masses on the many altars. From the 15th century onwards there were brotherhoods, crafts and guilds, each of which liked to erect their own altar in Antwerp cathedral and see to its embellishment and maintenance. The strong demand for locations for these altars is one explanation for the building of six side aisles on the church, where altars could be erected against the pillars. For a long time, the Cathedral of Our Lady was also the most important parish church of the city and from 1559 to the end of the 18th century the Bishop of Antwerp had his seat there. All these institutions had their well-determined place in the church interior under the 'ancien regime' and provided rich decoration with variegated fittings. However, the closure of the church under the French rule (1794–1815) and the subsequent emptying of the entire interior in 1798 made an irreversible rupture. Indeed, the refurnishing in the 19th century led to a completely different church interior. Everything focussed on the display of Rubens' major works in the choir and transept of the church space, which was almost empty then.

For centuries the appearance of the Cathedral of Our Lady was determined by plentiful religious furniture and an abundance of art works occupying the entire 'furnished zone' of the church.[2] The dozens of altars and sanctuaries set against the many pillars of the church in the transepts and the radiating chapels were striking. As mentioned above, the chantries, guilds, crafts, and brotherhoods – as well as the parish and chapter – had their allotted places. For centuries, the choir and radiating chapels were closed off from the rest of the church by a monumental rood screen which was erected between the crossing pillars. All this time, the choir was exclusively arranged for the canons and the chapter was closed from the rest of the church. The parish, too, had its own 'church inside the church', more precisely in the south aisle, where it had its own altar, pulpit, and organ. Repeated devastations such as the great fire of 1533 and the iconoclastic outbreaks in 1566 and 1581, and indeed the Counter Reformation, lead to the renovation and 'modernisation' of the furniture and art.

Particularly in the 15th and 16th centuries the strikingly furnished interior space was colourfully painted with all sorts of decorative motifs, often on a red or green background.[3] Above it all was an expansive white architectural space, articulated by the high rib vaults. As was customary, all wall surfaces, pillars, and vaults, had been thinly plastered with lime mortar

1 This essay is a shortened version of Manderyck 1999. The summary of the building history is based on Van Brabant 1972, Van Brabant 1974, Aerts 1993, and *Bouwen aan de bouwgeschiedenis 1994*.
2 Aerts 1993; Grieten & Bungeneers 1996.
3 Buyle 1990; Aerts et al. 1990; Van Dijck 1993; Bergmans 1998.

32
Anonymous · *Interior View of the Antwerp Cathedral of Our Lady* · 1894 · Antwerp, Cathedral of Our Lady

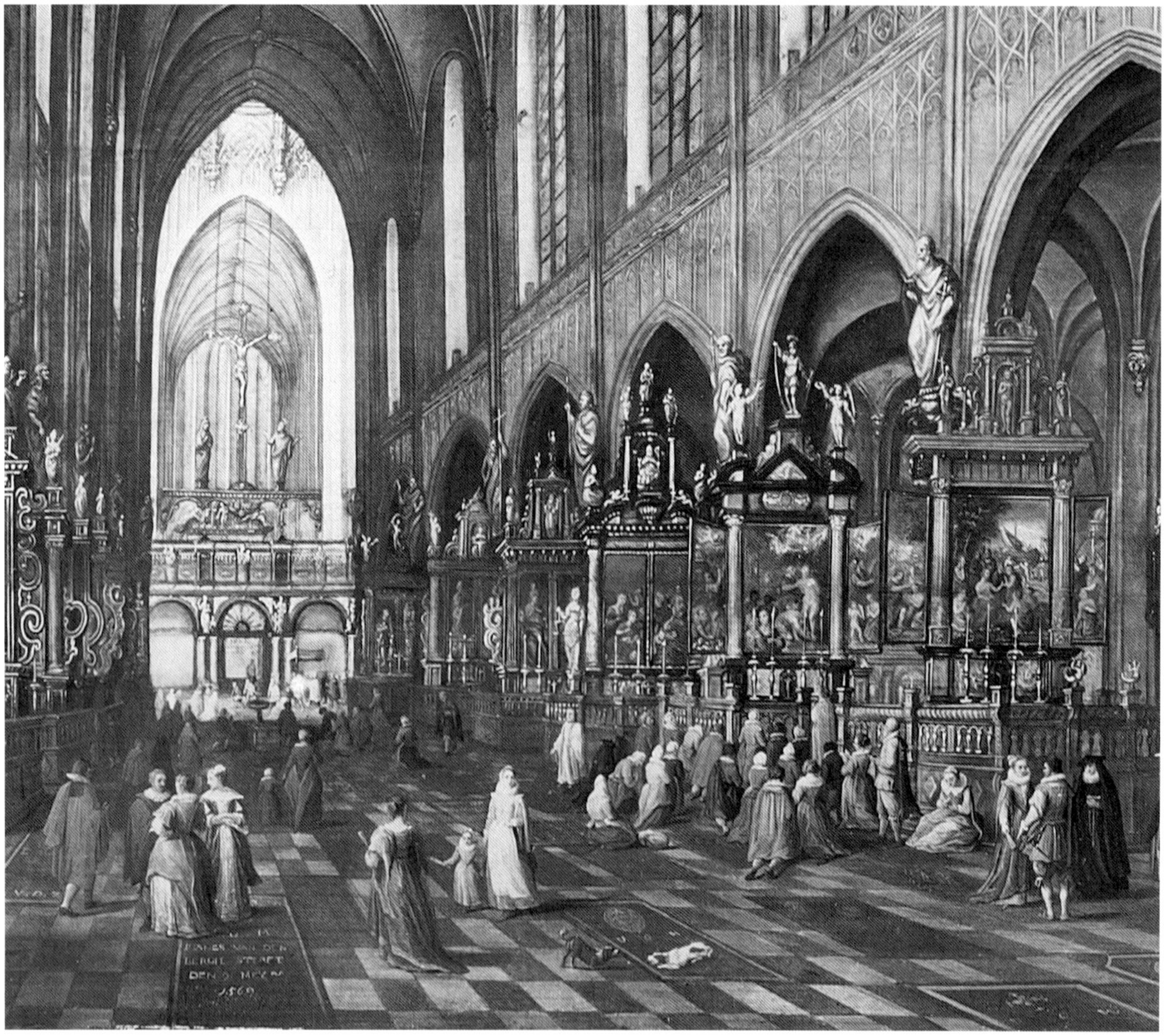

33
Anonymous
Interior View of the Antwerp Cathedral of Our Lady · c. 1631
present whereabouts unknown

and whitewashed from the earliest building stage. No building materials – not even the finely dressed natural stone – were left in view in the medieval church interior. It was a 'dematerialised' transcendent interior space, a preview of Heavenly Jerusalem for the faithful. The sculpted bosses, on the crossing of the vault ribs, had an eye-catching polychromy in strongly contrasting colours, as shown by the surviving 15th century bosses of the choir vaults with their original multicoloured painting (fig. 6–8). The fine stone decorations in the cupola of the crossing tower, dating from the beginning of the 16th century, received black painted outlines. In the 17th century – one generally assumes – the wall decoration became much soberer and in 1695 – although this happened under loud protest – the greater part of the colourful medieval paintings disappeared under a uniform whitewash layer.[4]

The polychromatic muting of the 17th century went hand-in-hand with a more architectural conception of the furniture, as can be seen in different 17th century interior views of the cathedral. In place of the older, rather small retables from the 15th century, there were now monumental Baroque portico altars framed by columns and many sculptural ornaments. Stimulated by the Edict of the Archdukes of 1611 – concerning the restoration of churches – and after the example of the new high altar from 1626 with Rubens' *Assumption of the Virgin*, many new altars were erected, mostly with monumental paintings.[5]

In the course of the 17th century, sculpture gradually began to occupy a more prominent place in the decoration of church interiors. Altars, statues, and epitaphs also received painted outlines (the written sources mention 'grauwen' and 'zwarten' – 'greys' and 'blacks') which caused the sculptures to stand out against the whitewashed walls even as they were integrated into the architectural space. Thus in 1989 – as a result of the preliminary research for the second phase of the interior restoration (1983–1993) – many monumental black outlines were recovered, particularly in the transepts where the archers' guilds had erected their large Baroque altars.[6]

In the 18th century no major interior works were carried out, apart from some four whitewash campaigns. This fitted well with the prevailing classicising style, under which even the last remnants of decorative painting disappeared under a lime layer for the sake of 'uniformiteyt der kercke' ('uniformity of the church interior').[7]

The revolutions and reforms at the end of the 18th century, under Joseph II and particularly in the French period, had major consequences for the cathedral. The building was closed for service and in 1798 it was completely emptied. Many paintings and statues were confiscated to furnish the museums 'for the benefit of the people', while the most important works, including the *Descent from the Cross* (cat. 11), the *Assumption of the Virgin* and the *Lamentation* (cat. 14), all three by the hand of Rubens, as well as *The Fall of the Rebel Angels* by Frans Floris (cat. 3) were sent to the new Musée central des arts in Paris.[8] The remaining possessions disappeared definitively from the church: they were sold or destroyed. However, it was quickly decided not to demolish the Church of Our Lady, as was first intended, but to conserve and repair it, since it represented Antwerp in a special way. A new era had however dawned. The Church of Our Lady was no longer an Episcopal church (or cathedral) and medieval institutions like the chapter and the guilds and crafts, which had once been an integral part of it, remained abolished. It had become an ordinary parish church, for which the church fabric, as a public institution, primarily became responsible – by the Concordat of 1801 – assisted by the city council and city architect.

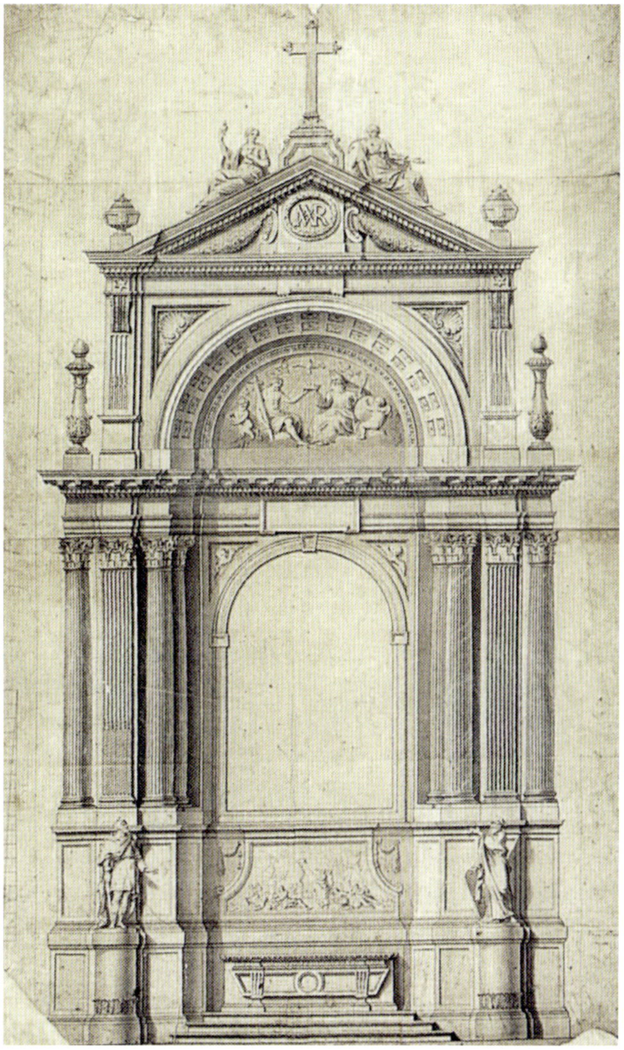

34
Jan Blom
High Altar of the Cathedral
c. 1817–1822 · drawing
Antwerp, Cathedral of Our Lady

The 19th century redecoration constituted an irrefutable rupture with the interior as it had been under the 'ancien regime'.[9] An entirely new concept of church interiors arose, which – necessarily, after the devastations in the revolutionary time – caused a radical solemnisation of the interior. The church must certainly have made a desolate impression at the beginning of the 19th century. The church floor was heavily damaged and filled with debris, and many crypts were broken open. Stripped of furniture and art, the battered building was recognised, for the first time, as a respectable monument of the late Gothic: the impressive architecture, with its rhythm of pillars and vaults, took on its own value, so to speak, and one can safely say that the appreciation of the medieval building, stripped of its rich furnishing, became *the* starting point for the entire redecoration in the 19th century.

4 *De Vlaamsche School 1875*, pp. 104–105.
5 Marinus 1995.
6 *Materieel-wetenschappelijk onderzoek 1989;* Van Dijck 1993.
7 Aerts & De Ceulaer 1993, p. 140.
8 Van der Straelen 1770–1819, IV–VII; Aerts & Grieten 1993, pp. 267–269.
9 Aerts & De Ceulaer 1993; Manderyck 1993.

The impetus for the restoration was given in 1800 when plasterers, on the instructions of the city architect Jan Blom (1748–1828), 'brought' the quadruple drum pillars of the nave 'in their first condition, equal to all other pillars'.[10] The original natural stone compound pillars had been severely damaged in the fire of 1533 and they had simply been plastered over so that altars could be erected against them, as can be seen in 17th century interior views. The reprofiling of the compound pillars was executed in plaster at the beginning of the 19th century and the interior was whitewashed again, a tradition that was maintained in the church throughout the entire 19th century. Repairing the natural stone masonry, which had been heavily damaged by fire, and making it visible again was not considered at that time. The whitewashed and therefore uniformly finished interior attuned well with the neoclassicist ideal of form and use of materials of the 18th and early 19th centuries.

The necessary new fittings arrived piece by piece. Ecclesiastical inheritance from the ancien regime was acquired from abolished churches and monasteries. The eye-catcher was the pulpit which Michiel van der Voort had made in 1713 for St Bernard's Abbey in Hemiksem and which received its place in the church in 1804.[11] The few surviving fittings from before the French rule in the Church of Our Lady were moved. They were arranged disparately and no longer fitted in the new interior which was now conceived as a 'unified space' with one line of view from the entrance porch to the high altar in the choir. A fine example of this is the old Baroque organ, which had remained above the south choir entrance (where a new organ is now set up). It was then considered visually disruptive and received a new place on a neoclassical gallery above the west portal in 1803–1805. Erecting new altars against the columns was of course no longer considered. The guilds and crafts that had used those altars were, after all, abolished. The only altar that had stayed in the cathedral after the French Revolution – that of the Young Longbowmens' guild in the nave – received a less conspicuous place in one of the radiating chapels of the ambulatory.[12]

A major event set the tone definitively for the redecoration of the church interior during the 19th century: in 1815, through the intervention of King Willem, under the Dutch rule (1815–1830), many, but not all, of the paintings that were transferred to France under the French rule, returned to the Netherlands. *The Descent from the Cross*, which was painted in 1611–1614 for the altar of the Arquebusiers' guild in the south transept of the cathedral more or less returned to its old place and the *Assumption of the Virgin* was re-established in its own spot in the choir. Also Rubens' *Lamentation* (cat. 14) and Floris' *Fall of the Rebel Angels* (cat. 5) returned to Antwerp, but not to the cathedral, although they had been removed from it. They now became a permanent part of the collection of the Museum of Fine Arts and in exchange the cathedral acquired Rubens' *Raising of the Cross,* originating from the suppressed church of St Walburgis. The triptych was displayed in the north transept, as a 'counterpart' of the *Descent from the Cross*. Both triptychs were hung above an altar, which connects with their function as altarpieces, but their prominent place in one of the most important churches of the country also gives them an aura of 'major national treasures'. Their striking presence, as eye-catchers in the empty Gothic interior space determined to a large extent the further decoration of the church interior in the 19th century. Although the 17th century had seen an attempt to complete and embellish the interior according to a well-considered programme to obtain an architecturally and artistically perfect whole, it was only in the 19th century that the medieval church interior, characterised by its abundant furniture and art objects, and divided into separate spaces, was irreversibly replaced by an entirely new interior concept, organised as a single unified space with the architecture itself as the

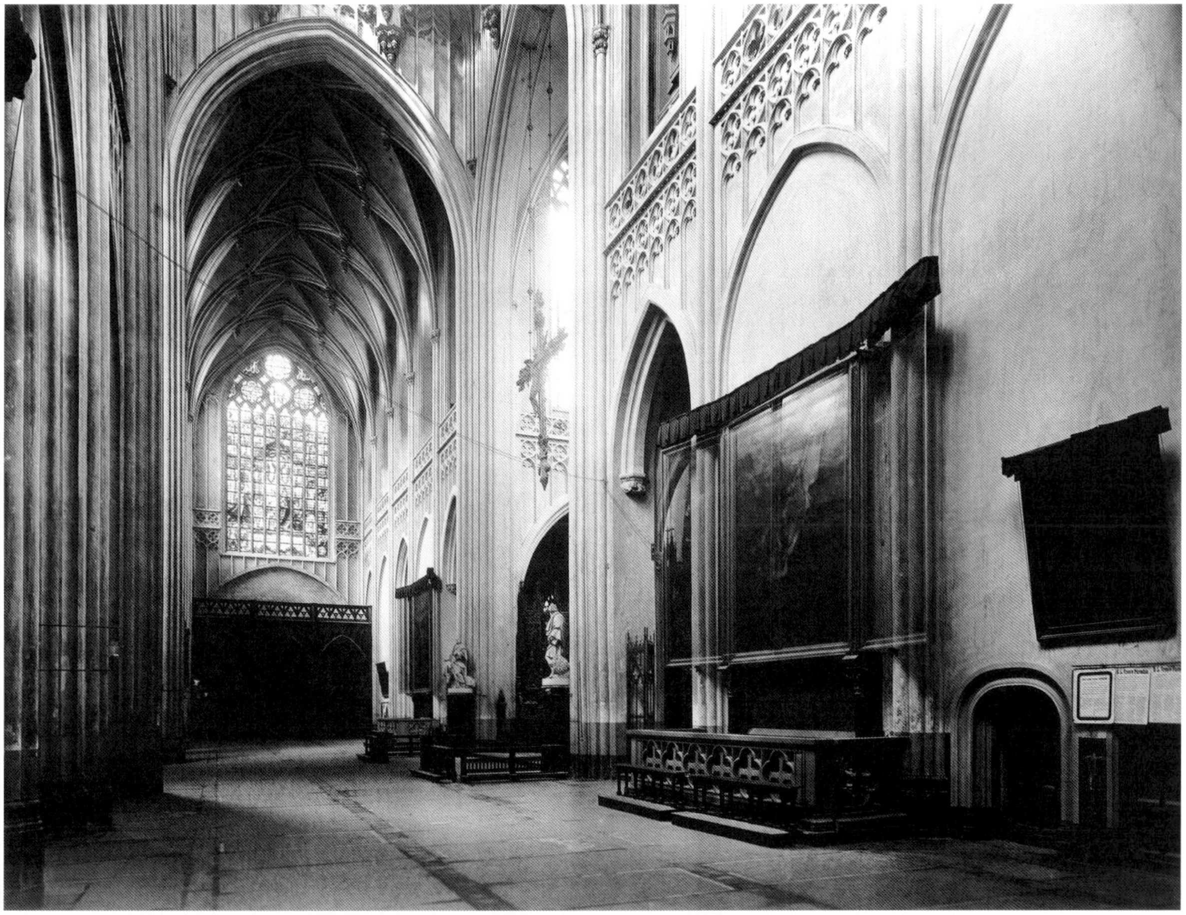

35
Anonymous
Interior View of the Antwerp Cathedral of Our Lady, with Positions of the triptychs by Rubens
c. 1914–1918

starting point. It is safe to say that the empty church interior after the French Revolution and the newly 'discovered' Gothic architecture, along with the three returned Rubens paintings, constituted the starting point for the church interior as we know it today: a pre-eminently 19th century creation, in fact![13]

This was clearly demonstrated with the erection of a new high altar for Rubens' *Assumption of the Virgin* in 1824. Architect Jan Blom designed an excessively big altar which clearly towered over the Rubens triptychs and almost filled the entire apse, in spite of its 16th century stained-glass windows.[14] This new creation in the neoclassical style received much criticism and later (in 1853) F. Mertens and K. Torfs described the main altar as 'the one that they intend to take away for another one, since there exists more taste and good judgement again in the execution of church jewels'.[15]

By 'more taste and good judgement', they undoubtedly referred to the neogothic, which made its appearance quite early in the Antwerp Church of Our Lady. The appreciation of Gothic architecture is also shown in the important repair works which were executed on the great tower from the beginning of the 19th century – under the direction of a succession of city architects, François Verly, Jan Blom, and Pierre Bourla – as well as from the very carefully worked up survey plans that were made of the church at that time.[16]

With the building of the new choir stalls from 1840 onwards, especially, the neogothic style came to dominate the interior. The church council had organised a contest for this project and a jury had awarded the prize to the spectacular design with two pointed towers by the young architect François Durlet (1816–1867), which was considered 'in perfect harmony with the style of the church'. It goes without saying that Durlet was inspired by the Cologne Cathedral. He developed this example in his own very creative 'pointed arch style'. He continued to work on the redecoration of the church interior, and particularly the systematic neogothification, until his death in 1867. The impressive choir stalls were under construction for over forty years and the sculptor Karel Geerts, and later Jan-Baptist De Boeck and

10 Van Brabant 1974, pp. 142–143; De Ceulaer 1993, pp. 143–144.
11 The church fabric and some reinstated fraternities bought back objects, not only belonging the church, but also to many closed monasteries and abbeys in the Antwerp region, see: Baudouin 1993, p. 259; Aerts & Grieten 1993, pp. 267–272.
12 Grieten & Bungeneers 1996, p. 23.
13 Manderyck 1993, pp. 137–139.
14 Aerts & Grieten 1993, p. 274.
15 Mertens & Torfs 1845–1853, VIII, p. 252.
16 Aerts 1994, pp. 84–89. In 1840 Pierre Stoop was awarded the prize for 'Gothic Architecture' with a monumental neogothic design for a new high altar for the cathedral, see *Schone Kunsten in Antwerpen 1976*, pp. 25–26.

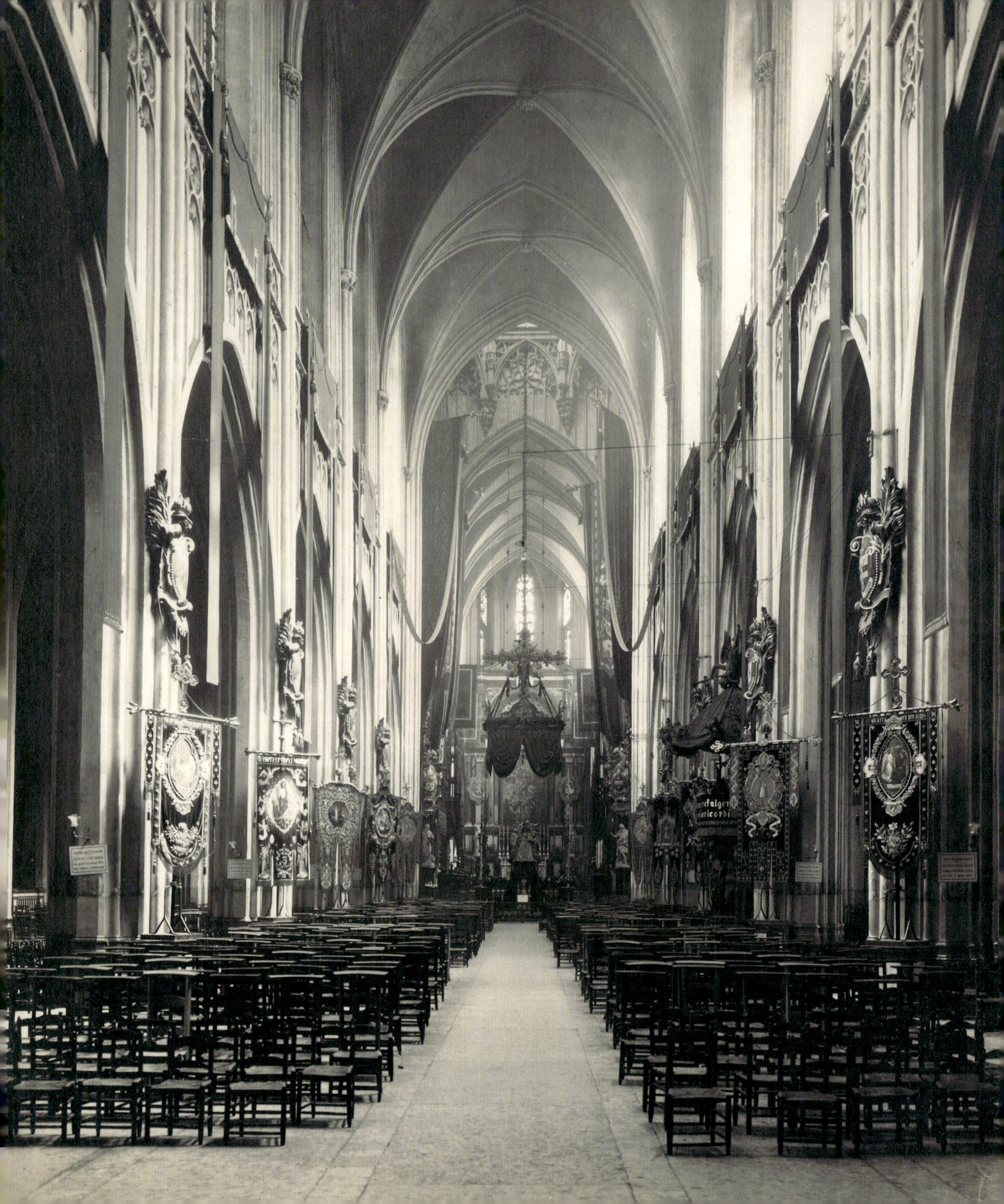

Jan-Baptist Van Wint, delivered the statue series on the theme of *The Lives of Christ and Mary*. The daring tower structures, set centrally as entrances to the stalls, and the rigid ranks of niches with almost endlessly repeated pinnacles and crowded by hundreds of subdued figures, represented the neogothic principles very well. The design of the stalls was clearly medievally inspired, but its monumental measurements were not in the least.[17]

After Durlet's death in 1867, Eugène Gife (1819–1890) continued to the restoration work, while Joseph Schadde (1818–1894) was charged with the interior decoration. Both architects effected a more authentic and archeologically accurate neogothic. The Royal Commission for Monuments played an ever more important role in this, especially after the establishment of the provincial 'Corresponiding Members', several of whose members were closely involved in the interior restoration of the church. Among others, there were also the painter Henri Leys and the city archivist Pierre Génard, who offered their services and performed research on the building history and the previous decoration of the church.[18] Inspired by the rediscovery of numerous ancient wall paintings the tradition of the colourful finish of the interior was revived. Thus, in 1872, the painter Louis Hendrix produced a colourful design for the complete polychrome painting of the choir, a project which had to fit in an 'integrated plan to decorate the entire church'. However, the plan was not executed and the church was simply whitewashed again in 1875 – which provoked much protest because it had become common restoration practice at that time to deplaster church interiors and make the building materials visible. The tradition of painted decoration was almost completely abandoned in the building of new neogothic churches, in favour of ever more 'material polychromy', in which the colourful and texture of the building materials themselves were displayed. This turn in the neogothic style influenced ideas about medieval church interiors to such an extent that it quickly became common restoration practice to adapt old church interiors as well to the renewed insights of neogothic – and therefore, to deplaster. Great influence in this regard came from French building restorers such as Prosper Mérimée and Eugène Viollet-le-Duc who, with the writings of Victor Hugo in hand, took up the battle against 'l'ignoble badigeon' (hideous wall plaster).[19]

After that it was especially the architect Frans Baeckelmans (1827–1896) who, at the end of the 19th century, successfully combined the colourful radiating chapels into a coherent ensemble, with stained-glass windows, furniture, wall decorations, floors, and screens. Thus neogothification had now been applied to the entire building: so, in 1867, the previously moved Baroque altar of the 'Jonge Handboog' archers' guild had to disappear outright from the church and found a place in the church of St James. The neoclassical organ loft of 1803, too, had been replaced by a new one in 1890, a flamboyant neogothic design by Baeckelmans.[20]

The exterior restoration of the Church of Our Lady was demanding ever more attention, and in the 20th century attention focussed on repairs to the façades and roof. Restoration and creation went hand-in-hand here, as can be clearly seen: all roof lines now received openwork parapets instead of simple iron guard rails, the buttresses were embellished with pinnacles, the roof ridge was decorated with stone crocket work – after the example of the Sainte-Chapelle in Paris – and the porches were renewed and provided with statues, all corresponding 'with the cathedral style'.[21]

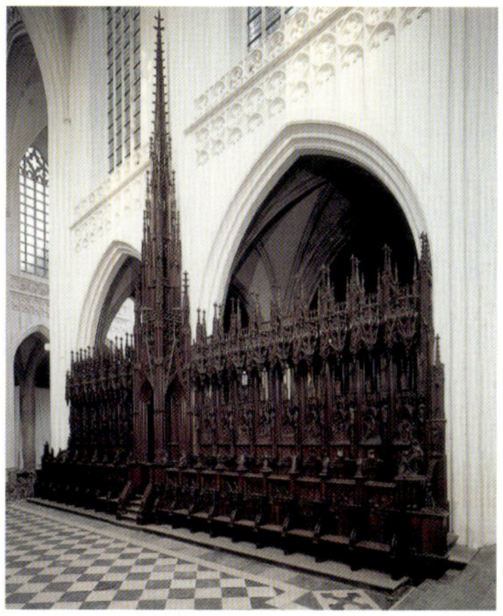

37
François Durlet
Neogothic Choir Stalls
1839–1867
Antwerp, Cathedral of Our Lady

17 Van Gerwen 1977, pp. 23–122 and Van Langendonck 1989.
18 De Ceulaer 1993, pp. 146–147; Stijnen 1998, pp. 119–122.
19 Aerts 1994, p. 88; Meul 1994, p. 16 and *De Vlaamsche School 1875*, pp. 104–105. Bergmans 1996, pp. 28–32. On the deplastering of church interiors in the 19th century, see Bergmans 1998, pp. 107–158.
20 Grieten & Bungeneers 1996, p. 23.
21 De Ceulaer 1993, pp. 146–157

36
Anonymous · *Interior View of the Antwerp Cathedral of Our Lady* · end 19th century · Antwerp, Cathedral of Our Lady

The reinstatement of the Diocese of Antwerp in 1961 brought the interior to attention again. Little had been done since the 19th century and the damp interior gave a neglected impression. More than ever, deplastering of the interior was considered *the* necessary condition for a restoration worthy of a cathedral.[22] The idea was directly founded on the concepts of restoration of canon Raymond Lemaire (1878–1954), a professor at the University of Leuven, whose standard work *La restauration des monuments anciens* from 1938 determined the appearance of many restorations in Belgium until well after World War II. The province council (the commissioner of the works since the recognition of the church as an Episcopal chair) commissioned the restoration to the architects Jozef Stynen (1907–1989) and Guido Derks (1925–2006). In order to keep the cathedral in use the interior works were divided into two phases. From 1973 to 1983 the nave and side aisles were restored, at which time the entire package of plaster layers was pried off with compressed air to make the natural stone visible, after which the stone was sand-blasted. Because of the severe damage to the nave pillars inflicted by the fire in 1533, it was necessary – since the building material was required to be made visible – to replace them with new natural stone. Although it was duly noted that the multiple plaster layers hid valuable ancient paintings and although care was taken about this (even if only mostly for the figurative paintings), we must nowadays deplore the loss of the greater part of the original finish and polychromy on the walls, pillars, and vaults. The remaining paintings on the plastered vaults thus irrevocably lost their coherence and meaning.[23]

In the 1980s art-historical research concerning the colourfulness of medieval church interiors proved in an ever more convincing way the conceptual link between architecture and coloured surfaces: an architectonic use of colour dematerialised medieval churches.[24] As a consequence, among others, of the growing appreciation of the neogothic patrimony the policy was reversed at the restoration of the choir and transept between 1990 and 1993. The option to preserve the entire package of finish layers was supported by extensive historical and material-science research in 1989–1990. Fortunately the plaster layers displayed sufficient adhesion so that they could be finished again with pigmented plaster paint after their cleaning and repair. The original 15th century polychromy of the choir vault keys proved to have survived in excellent condition and was exposed, which caused the authentic medieval appearance to come to the forefront again.

When various altarpieces return to the cathedral today, it will become clear that these art objects have arrived in an entirely different church space than their commissioners intended them for. These fine paintings originally received a place on an altar surrounded by a rich furnishing with a multitude of fittings, statues, textiles, precious metalwork, and other art objects that harmonised with the Gothic interior architecture, which extended above them as a transcendent, lofty white room. As a result of the brutal emptying of the church under French rule, the cathedral interior has a very different appearance today, which is the result of restoration and transformation in the 19th and 20th centuries. The beautiful altarpieces have returned to the building for which they were created, but they are no longer part of a transcendent medieval interior space and its rich decoration.

22 *De Vlaamsche School 1875*, p. 105 and the KCML Archive A/109 note 5 May 1938.
23 Stynen & Derks 1973–1974; *Restauratie 1989*, pp. 25–34; Buyle 1990, pp. 12–24; Bergmans 1996, pp. 275–279.
24 Aerts et al. 1990, pp. 12–37; Manderyck 1996, pp. 197–200; Bergmans 1998, pp. 275–279.

38
Marc Dirkx · *Interior View of the Antwerp Cathedral of Our Lady* · recent photograph

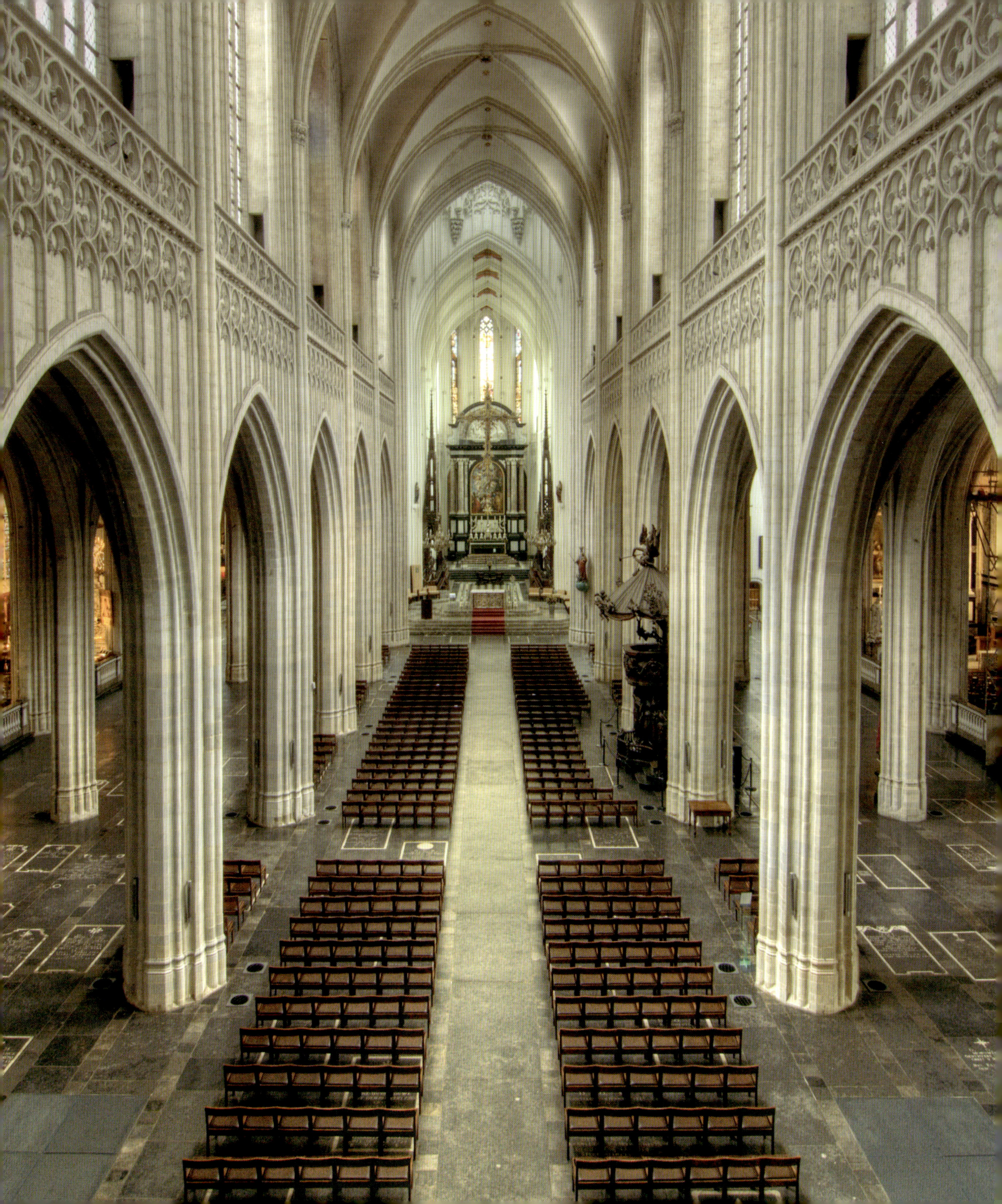

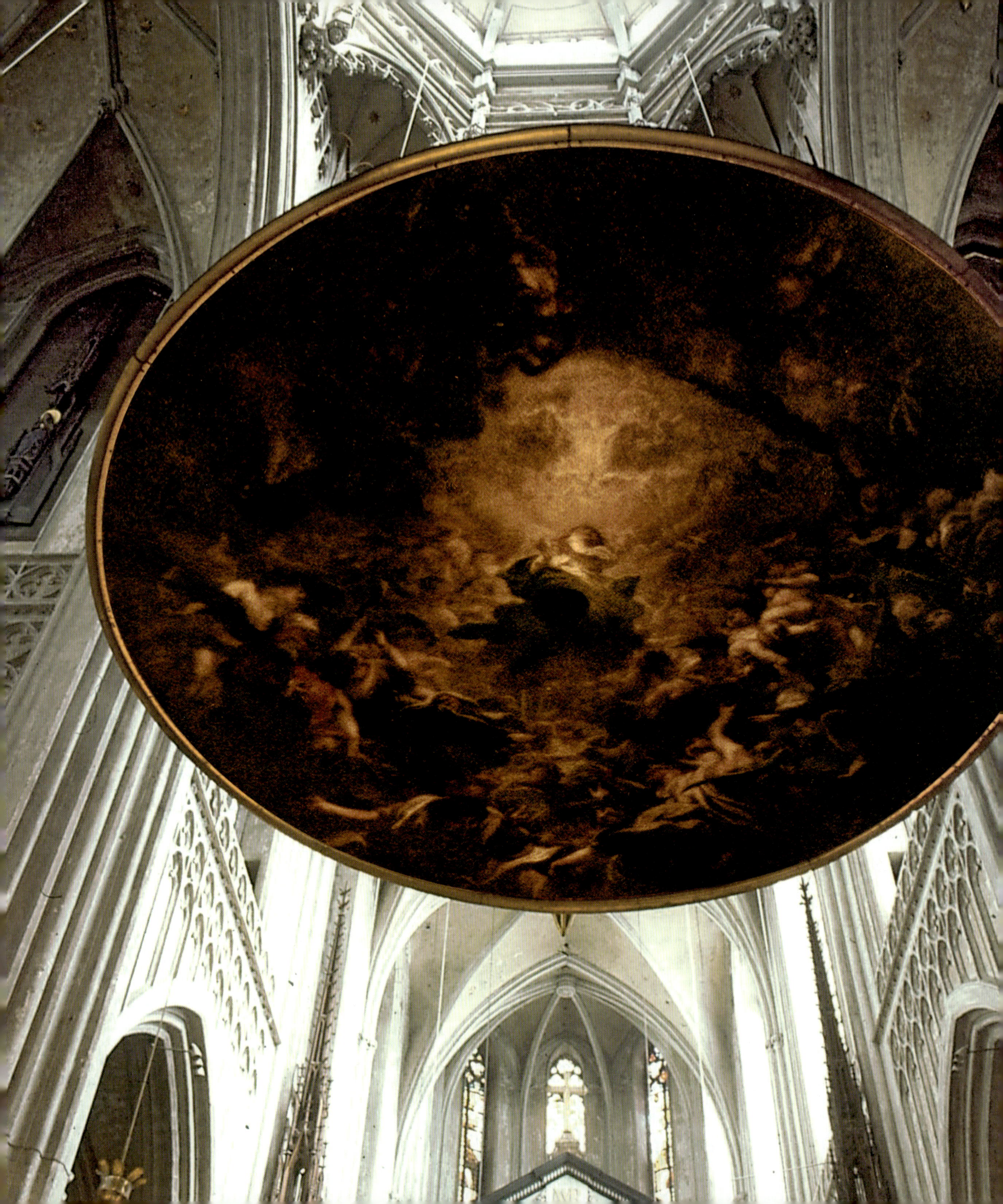

The Restoration of the Cathedral of Our Lady

WILLEM AERTS
STEF BINST

With the reinstatement of the Diocese of Antwerp in 1961 the Church of Our Lady became a cathedral again and the province took on the important responsibility of the monument. In 1965 Antwerp's provincial authorities decided to act as principal for the full restoration of the church. Only the restoration of the great north tower fell outside the authority of the province, for which the city was and is responsible. This massive undertaking was begun in the 1920s and completed in 1990.

Before we look closer into the meaning of some trends and developments in restoration theory and practice for the Cathedral of Our Lady, let us first review the chronology.

After the restoration of the roof (1969–1972), which was an urgent necessity, the interior restoration was initiated, in combination with some accompanying exterior works. First came the nave (1972–1983) and subsequently the transept and choir (1990–1993). Between the two phases a 'linking period' (1984–1989) was included which offered time for archaeological excavations in the transept and chancel and for historical and materials-science research in relation to the further interior restoration. In 1993, when Antwerp was the Cultural Capital of Europe, the cathedral was fully opened to the public again.

The interior of the ambulatory and radiating chapels still needed to be restored at that point. In the course of the next decade some radiating chapels were attended to. On the exterior, the entire façade renovation had to start at that point, with the exception of the small south tower and the west façade which had been taken on together with the north tower (1979–1985).

In 2002, a global status report was compiled pertaining to the remaining work on both the interior and the façade restoration. Based on that overview, the provincial authorities, in consultation with the cathedral church fabric and the Flemish government, drew up a detailed long-range plan, which was subsequently executed. Each year a new phase of the remaining works is commenced. Barring unforeseen circumstances, then, the global restoration of the cathedral should be completed c. 2015, which would bring the total duration of the current extensive campaign to approximately 50 years. After that, and it is to be hoped for several decades, regular maintenance should suffice for the conservation of the building and its exterior. Obviously, maintenance is currently being provided for all the parts that have already been restored.

Attention to maintenance is, in fact, one of the newer developments in the restoration of this largest Gothic church in the Low Countries. The role of the maintenance team of the cathedral and of 'Monumentenwacht' ('Monument Watch') of the province of Antwerp, a provincial non-profit organisation, cannot be underestimated in this regard.

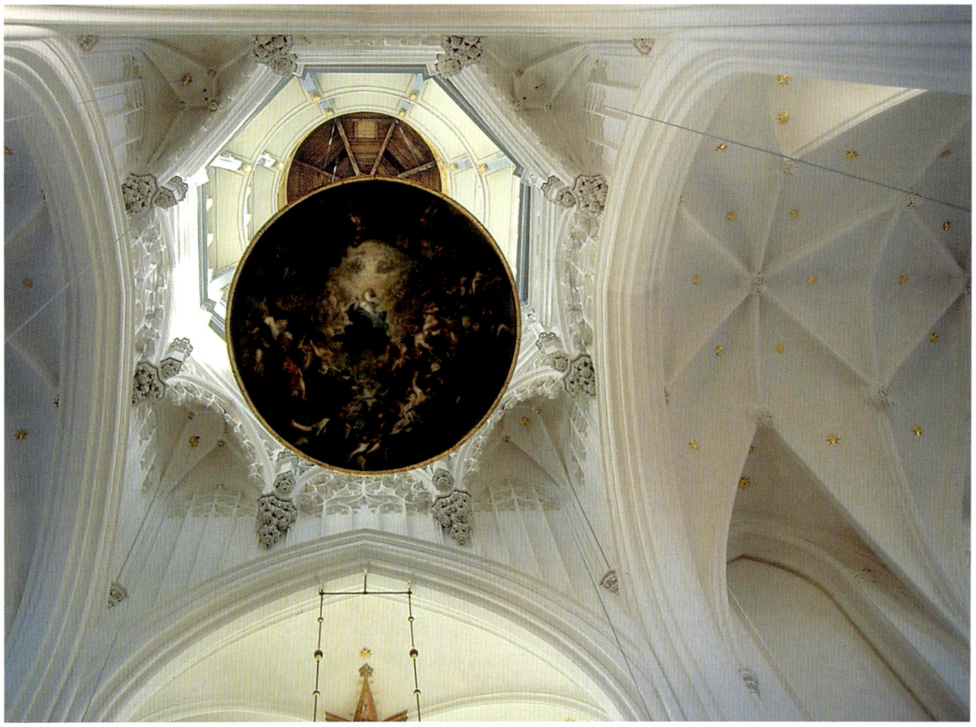

39 – 40
Cathedral of Our Lady, Antwerp, crossing with the dome and the circular painting by Cornelis Schut, *Assumption of the Virgin*, before and after the restoration

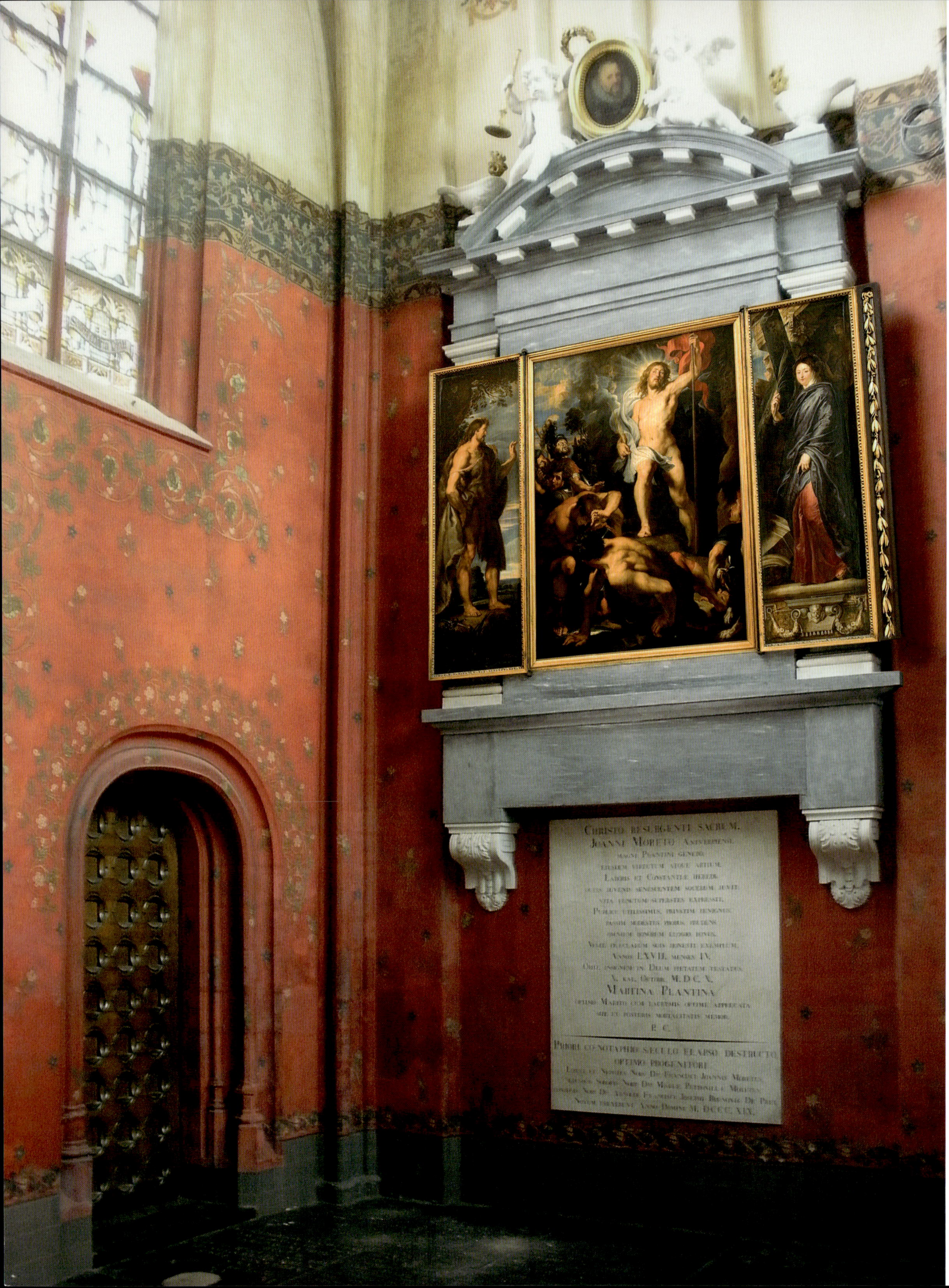

MARTINA PLANTINA
P. C.

Since 1999 the planning and direction of restoration works have been commissioned to a team lead by the architect R. Steenmeijer.

Conservation and Management

It was only logical to start by repairing the roof structure and covering before addressing the interior restoration. Moreover, a fire in 1968 destroyed the roof of Saint-Paul's church, and its artistic treasures barely escaped devastation. For that reason, the repairs to the roofs and south tower (1969–1972) where immediately combined with fire safety work: the renewal of the electrical installation, the installation of fire-proof doors, fire ladders, fire extinguishers and fire hoses, and a new fire fighters' water supply. Furthermore, during the interior restoration, attention focussed increasingly on protection from theft and vandalism. Recently developed understanding and technology lead to a thorough modernisation (with additions where needed) of the installations in 2002–2004.

For the conservation of art objects and religious furniture, climate control is essential. A building of this size and structure can hardly be fully controlled. Nonetheless, an attempt is made to keep the fluctuations in temperature and relative humidity in the interior of the church within acceptable limits. Therefore the optimisation of the present installation has been included in the above-mentioned long-term plan.

Consideration of the light issue is more recent. Abundant natural light is an essential part of the spatial experience in a Gothic church. At the same time, its interior contains art and cult objects which are often exceptionally valuable and that are light-sensitive. It makes sense to keep these objects here. But the cathedral is not a museum. This means that the ideal conditions for the conservation of the art objects will always remain out of reach. Nonetheless, possible ways of limiting the impact of daylight are already being examined. In particular, window filters are being used in an attempt to limit the influx of light.

Cleaning, conserving, and restoring the art objects and furniture, are all part of interior restoration activities but without each of the aforementioned security precautions the risks remain very real for the moveable patrimony. Good and responsible maintenance is therefore a basic necessity. The interiors department of Monument Watch, which was founded by the province of Antwerp, systematically inspects interior elements and movable patrimony. Maintenance is also one of the aspects of the 'disaster plan' that is under preparation. As the managing institution of this legacy, the cathedral must take into account different risks. Fire, theft and vandalism are the most visually obvious risks, but mould and woodworm can also inflict serious damage. The intention of the disaster plan is to control such incidents as far as possible. In consultation with the police and fire department, this plan includes preventive measures, as well as actions and procedures in case of a calamity and a program for damage-limitation afterwards. The ECCE-project ('First Aid at Cultural Inheritance Calamities') comprises 33 heritage management institutions in Antwerp, Mechelen, Leuven and Ghent. One of its initiators was the non-profit organisation 'The Monumental Antwerp Churches', founded at the initiative of the cathedral church fabric, which links the five great historic churches of Antwerp: the cathedral, Charles Borromeo, Saint-Andrew's, Saint-James's and Saint-Paul's. This non-profit organisation is supported by the province and the city.

Interior Restoration

An essential development occurred during the restoration of the interior. In the late 1960s a hard restoration had been instigated, in which the uncovering

41
Neogothic Chapel of Our Lady of Peace with the *Resurrection of Christ* by Peter Paul Rubens

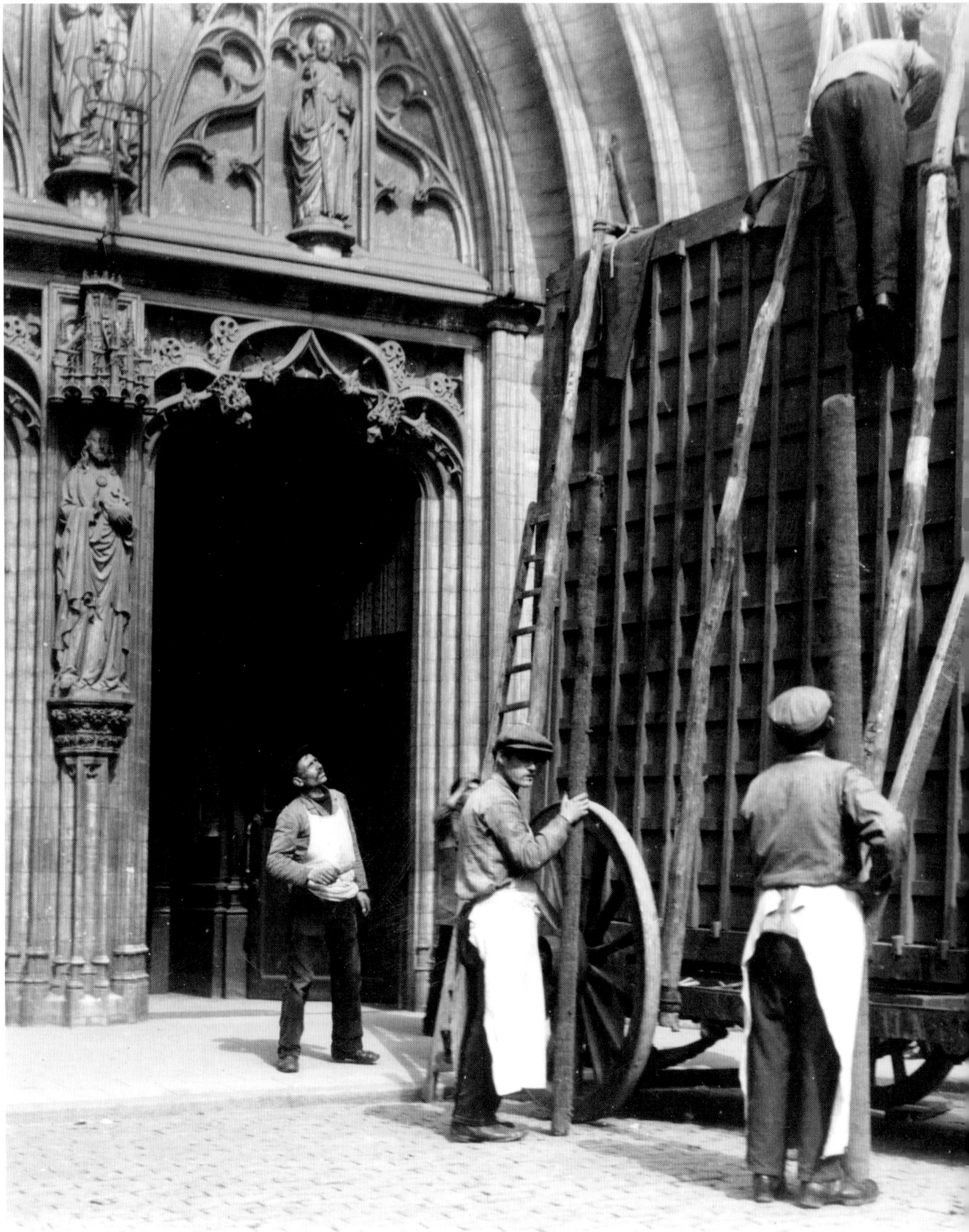

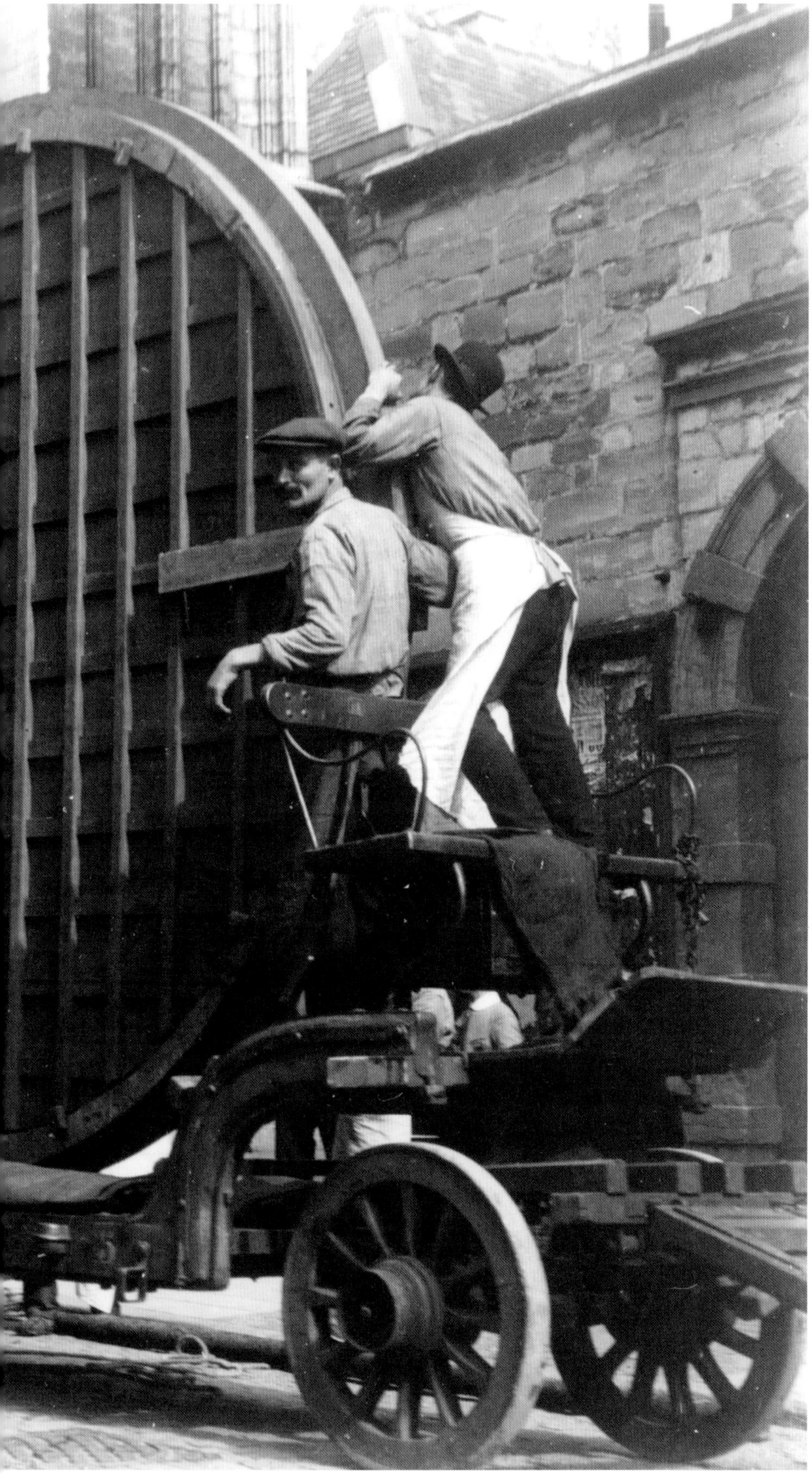

42
Rubens' *Assumption of the Virgin*, the painting on the high altar, is transported from the cathedral to the bombproof cellars of the Koninklijk Museum voor Schone Kunsten · August 1914

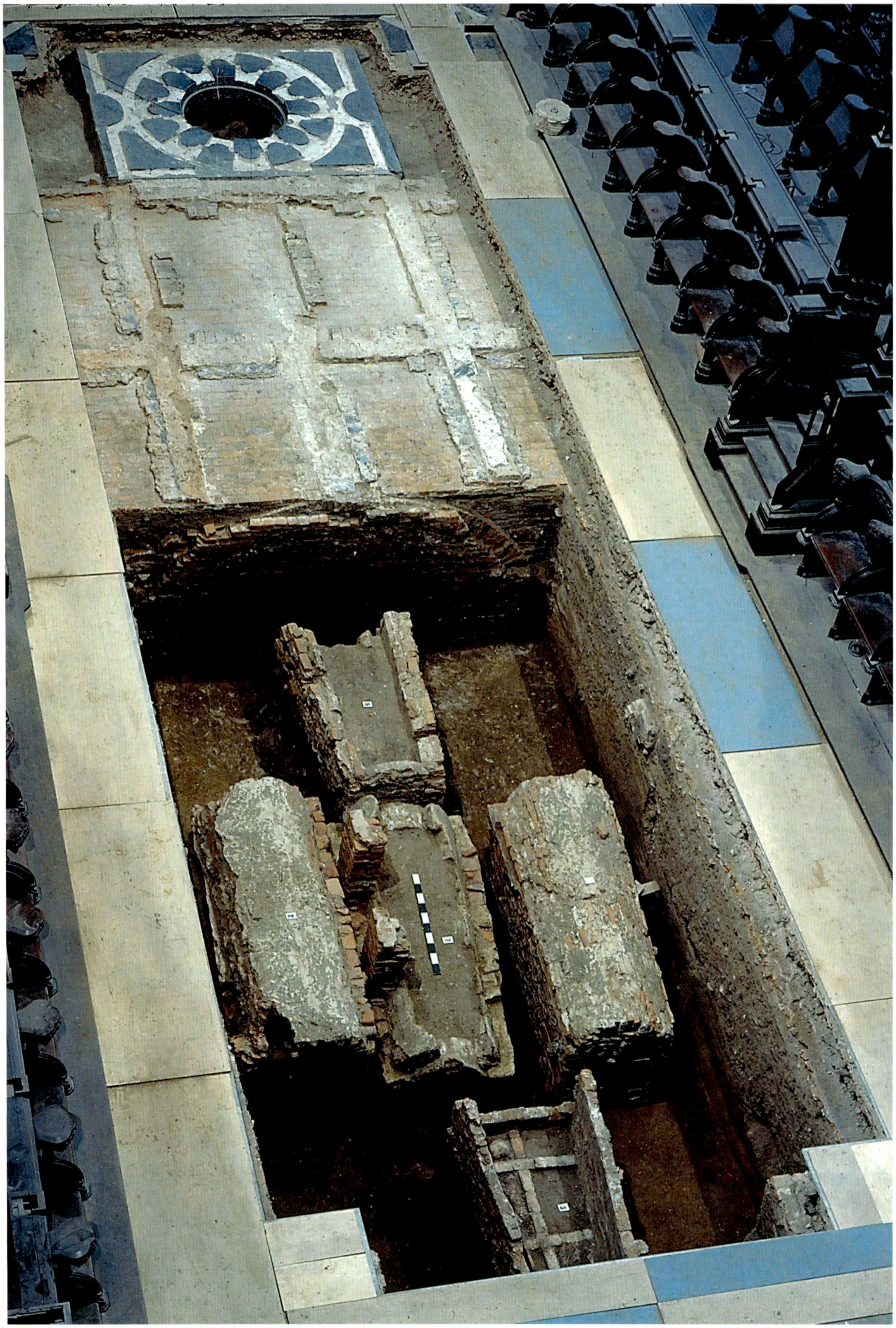

43
Family crypt with sarcophagi in the main choir of the Cathedral of Our Lady, Antwerp

and restoring (if necessary) of the structural members in natural stone was the starting point. In the late 1970s, however, when the repairs to the interior of the nave were in full swing, sounds of criticism were heard on this 'bare stone' policy. In addition to conserving the paintings on the plastered sections of the walls and vaults, the monochrome or polychrome finish of the natural stone pillars, ribs and bosses were a fundamental part of the building and its history. It was becoming evident during these works – as well as in other churches (whether contemporary or earlier, at home or abroad) – that the interiors of Gothic churches received a basic finish when they were built and were colourfully embellished with decorative and figurative paintings. After 1600, this fashion gradually disappeared and the surface was covered with layers of whitewash.

As mentioned above, in the expectation of further interior restoration, time and means were allocated for thorough research. This comprised two components: a historical study of the published, archival and iconographical sources, and an extensive materials-science examination of the finish – whatever its nature – of the walls, pillars and vaults in the transept and the choir. Hundreds of samples were taken to ascertain the nature, composition, chronology, and conservation status of the finishing layers and paintings.

The results of this research confirmed the clues about the earlier finish of the interior and made it possible to formulate an option for this essential aspect of further interior restoration. Only the uppermost layers of soiled and flaking whitewash would be removed and the interior of the transept, crossing, and choir would be whitewashed freshly. The many underlying polychrome paintings, which were found during the investigation, would thus not be scraped off but conserved, and the space would keep an appearance in harmony with those paintings that would be made visible. Some valuable and well-preserved 15th and 16th century paintings would be exposed and restored: the polychromy from around 1400 on the vaults and bosses of the choir, the black background painting from the end of the 15th century on the Gothic stonework of the crossing dome, and a 16th century wall painting in the transept.

For the restoration of the ambulatory, which remains to be done, the same policy will be followed. The situation in the twelve radiating chapels is different: the neo-Gothic finish in the nine chapels (of which six are now restored) is preserved, and in the three remaining chapels, which did not receive a neo-Gothic finish, the desirability and feasibility of a return to the – still extant – 15th and 16th century decorative or figurative finish is being examined.

The decision to undertake the aforementioned research and the choice of restoration options for the transept and choir did not go without discussion, but the visible difference between the approach in the nave and that in the transept and choir shows that the preservation of monuments is itself a product of its time.

Archaeological Research

During the work in the nave, the excavation of canals for climate control led to the discovery of fragments of the foundation of the Romanesque church, brick crypts, and numerous skeletons.

As mentioned above, during the 'linking phase' (1984–1989) systematic excavations were conducted in the transept and choir – that is, prior to the actual restoration work. These provided a wealth of information on burials and burial customs, and proved that at least two churches preceded the current one: a Romanesque church with a tri-conch eastern section from after 1124, and an older, smaller place of worship, probably a basilica from the 11th century. Building an 'archeocrypt' under the choir allowed fragments of the Romanesque church and some painted crypts to remain visible.

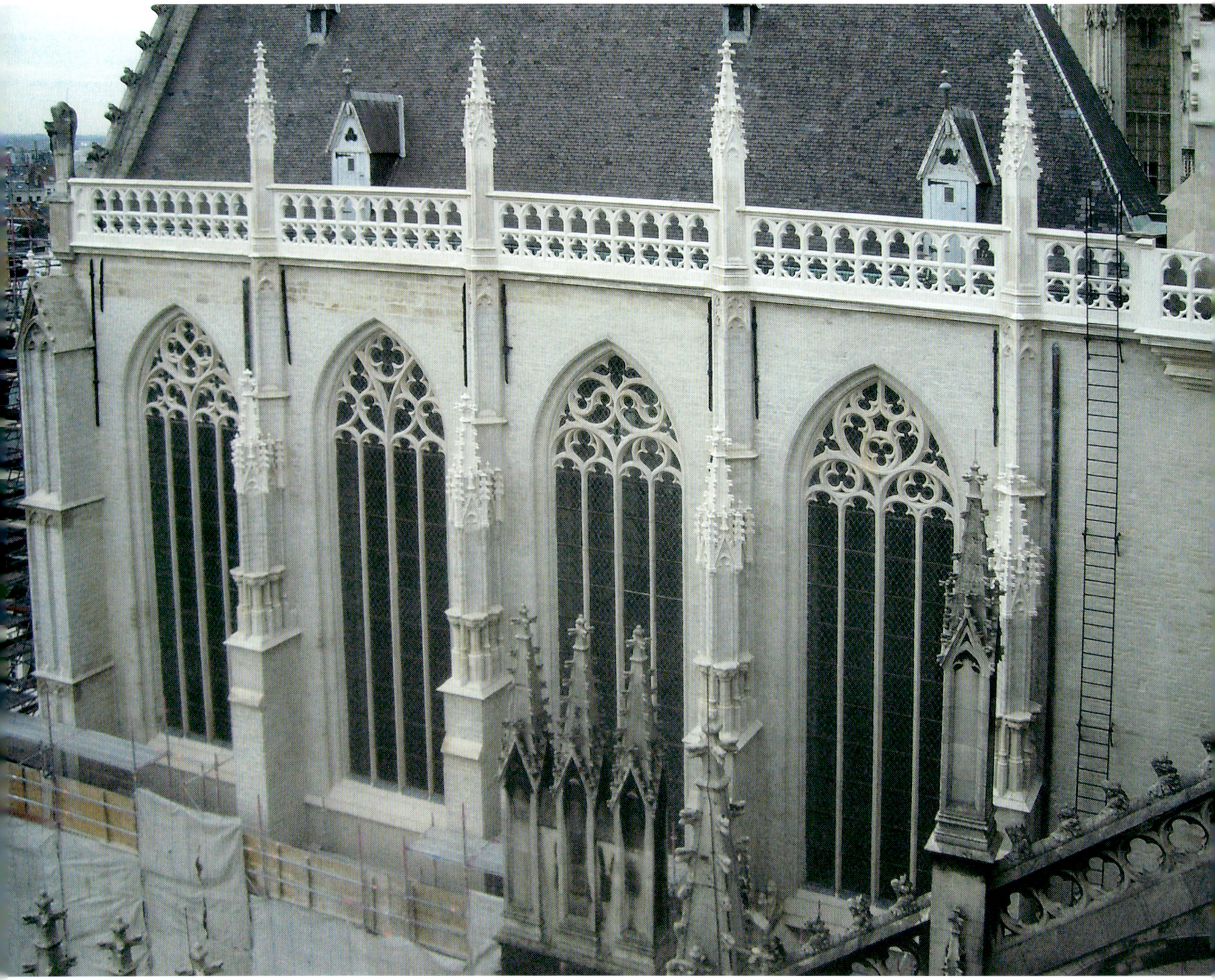

44
Restoration of the exterior, transept with neogothic parapet in artificial stone

Exterior Restoration

Although this is not obvious at first glance, the exterior of the cathedral is a patchwork, both in form and the use of materials. The initial building work lasted more than a century and a half. Moreover, the exterior appearance was changed drastically in restorations from the middle of the 19th century onwards. In the spirit of the 'ideal' (neo)-Gothic church, high parapets were added to the choir, for example. The variety of natural stone used for building, repair, or restoration, differed over time. Twelve different stone varieties have now been identified in Antwerp cathedral. Not all stones were of the same quality or eroded in the same way. At the end of the 19th and the beginning of the 20th century, especially, rather questionable stone types were often used.

For the current restoration all these historical developments are considered fully integral parts of the monument. The intention is neither to reconstruct some (imaginary) 'original condition', nor to erase the traces of time. To the greatest possible extent, the present – more or less eroded – stonework is preserved.

The façades are cleaned: lime encrustation and surface contamination are removed. Thus eroding processes can be slowed down and the magnitude of the damage can be accurately determined. The clean appearance is obviously a bonus.

In places where the damage is limited, but still too considerable to leave untouched, missing parts can be moulded in with repair mortar, which then hardens into artificial stone. Where necessary, stone blocks that are too damaged will be removed completely and replaced by new, traditionally dressed natural stone. For this work, the choice of stone type is determined both by the provenance of the pieces to be replaced and the current availability of suitable stone. For the late 19th century additions, such as the parapets or the ridges, a special policy has been determined. Owing to the original choice of materials they are almost entirely in need of replacement or reconstruction. In formal terms, these are mostly repetitive and stereotypical sculpture work. Therefore, and because of the large quantity of stones to be replaced, they are, in the current restoration, replaced by copies in cast artificial stone. When the repair of the stones is undertaken, the joints will be repaired where needed.

The work over these last decades has not gone unnoticed. In 1993 – when Antwerp was the Cultural Capital of Europe – the restoration of the cathedral received the prestigious Europa Nostra Award, 'for the respectful restoration and conservation of the high and lower tower, the facade and the interior of the church, including the paintings of P.P. Rubens'. More important than this, though, is that, through constant care, this unique piece of legacy also retains a future.

For a bibliographical survey of the restoration issues at Antwerp cathedral, see: Aerts 1993B; Van Leemputten 1993; Oost, Bungeneers, Veeckman, Ervynck & Sorber 1993; Janssens, Marčsik, De Meyere & Hänsch 1993.

CATALOGUE

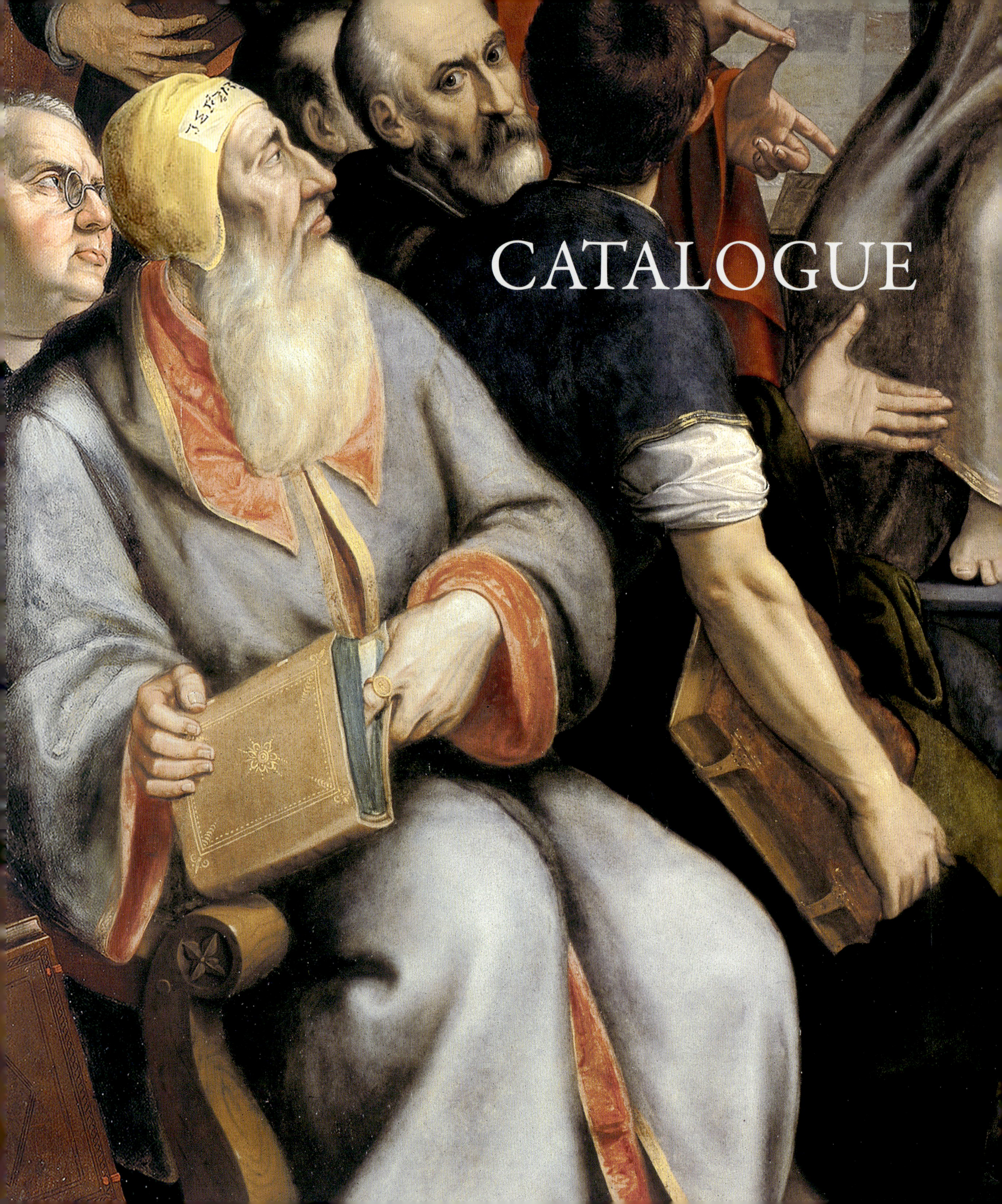

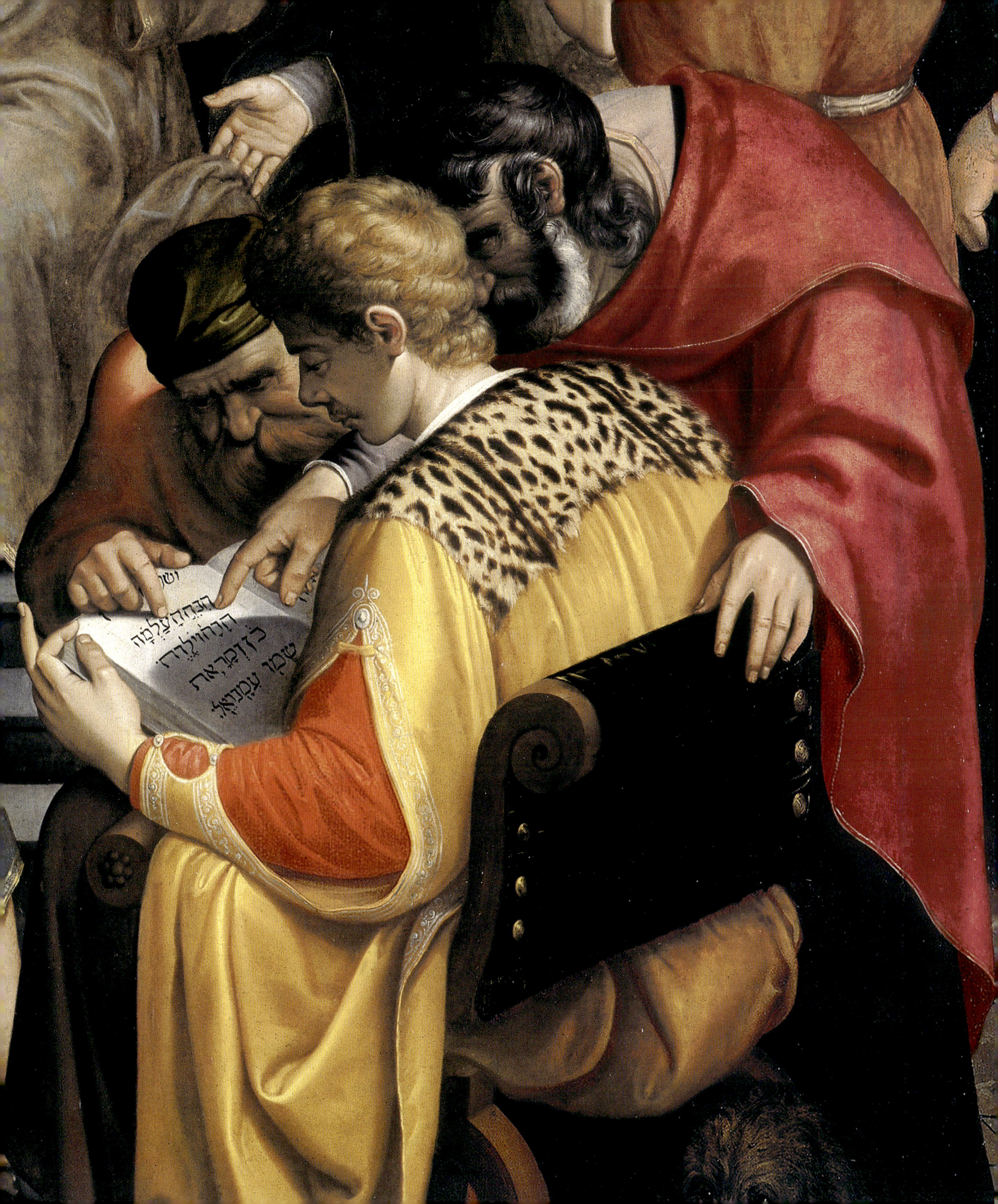
הנה העלמה
הרה וילדת
בן וקראת
שמו עמנואל

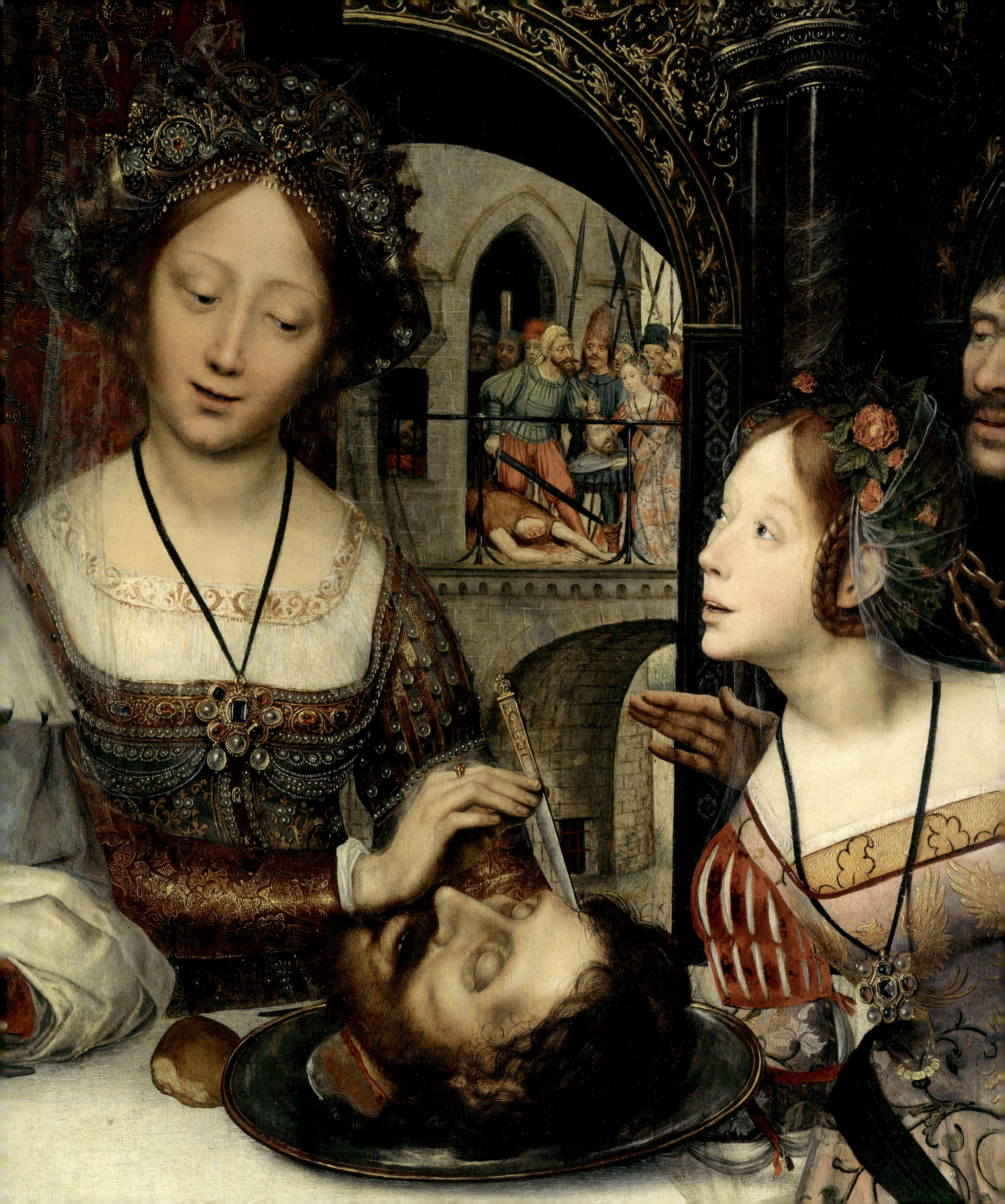

1 Altarpiece of the Cabinetmakers

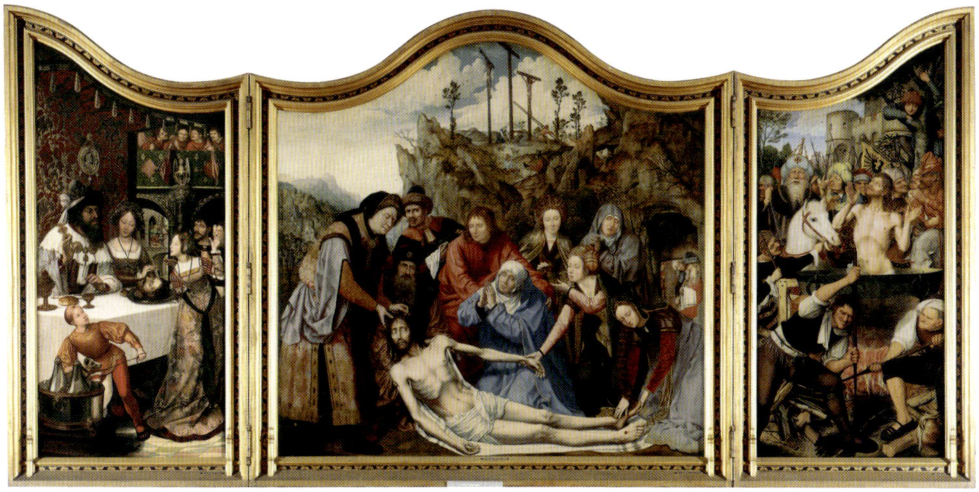

Quinten Metsijs

Louvain c. 1460–Antwerp 1530

The Lamentation

1509–1511

Oil on panel

centre panel: 260 x 263 cm
side panels: 260 x 120 cm

Unsigned

Antwerp, Koninklijk Museum voor Schone Kunsten, inv. 245–249

Provenance: commissioned by the Antwerp Cabinetmakers in 1508; placed on the craft altar in the Antwerp cathedral in 1511; acquired by the city magistrate in 1577 and placed in the States Room in the City Hall; in 1590 transferred to the cathedral and placed on the altar of the Circumcision Chapel; in 1798 transferred to the École Centrale des Deux-Nèthes in the abolished Discalced Monastery; subsequently until 1811 in the Academy in the Exchange building; then in the museum in the former Friars Minor Monastery; foundational holding of the Museum.

Bibliography: *Beschrijvinge 1751*, p. 9 (p. 15)
Mensaert 1763, pp. 239–241
Descamps 1769, pp. 151–152
Kerken van Antwerpen 1774, p. 24
Van Even 1846
Génard 1863, p. 127
Génard 1868, pp. 50–52
Van Even 1870, pp. 381–386
Rooses 1879, pp. 68–80
Van den Branden 1883, pp. 54–66
Hymans 1888, pp. 5–20, 215–223
De Bosschere 1907, pp. 69–83
Brising 1909, pp. 26–31
Friedländer 1924–1937, VII, pp. 15–27, 113
Held 1931, pp. 67, 79 ff.
Prims 1938–1939, XII, p. 297
Roosen-Runge 1940, pp. 125–144
Prims 1951, pp. 162–163
Friedländer 1967–1976, VII, p. 16, 59, no. 1
de Bosque 1975, pp. 101–106
Vervaet 1976, pp. 204–206
Silver 1984, pp. 45–52, 204–205, no. 11
Van de Velde 1993A, p. 179
Grieten & Bungeneers 1996, pp. 362–363:

When the Antwerp Cabinetmakers separated from the Coopers in 1497, they needed a new altarpiece. In the first instance, they turned to the Louvain sculptors Peterceels and Van Kessel. In 1503, the commission was passed to an Antwerp sculptor, but it was ultimately given to Quinten Metsijs, in 1508.[1] The central theme, the *Descent from the Cross*, had been treated earlier by Metsijs for the altar of the Coopers, a work that is lost.[2] The iconography of the panels, both on the interior and exterior, was determined in reference to the Cabinetmakers' patron saints, John the Baptist and John the Evangelist. According to the contract, Metsijs would receive 300 guilders in three instalments for his work, but when it was completed on 26 August 1511, it was decided to convert the payment into a fund for the children from Metsijs' first marriage with Alijt van Tuylt.[3]

The 'bakmakers', who also belonged to the Cabinetmakers' craft, were responsible for the armatures in which carved wooden retables were supported. Around 1500, such retables were one of the most important luxury goods produced in Antwerp. They were in vogue throughout Europe. Wooden retables, sometimes with painted panels, stood on the altars of many guilds and crafts in the Church of Our Lady. It is therefore surprising that it were precisely the Cabinetmakers who chose a completely painted altarpiece. Perhaps this choice was the result of the protracted commission, which eventually (as with the Coopers' altar) fell to Quinten Metsijs.

The later adventures of this masterpiece were certainly dramatic. Only 19 years after its installation, a disastrous fire raged in the church, from which the triptych escaped. In 1566, it was spared the devastation of the Iconoclastic Fury. When Philip II and Elizabeth I of England sought to buy the work in 1577, Maerten de Vos successfully convinced the city council to purchase it for the city. After a short stay in the City Hall it was returned to the cathedral in 1590, and placed on the altar of the Circumcision Chapel, which was then used as a Magistrates' Chapel. In 1798, Willem Herreyns was in his turn able to prevent it being transferred to Paris by French revolutionary troops, as other major works in these regions were; the altarpiece was transferred to the École Centrale des Deux-Nèthes, from where it later joined the collections of the Royal Museum of Fine Arts.[4]

On the centre panel the lifeless body of Christ is presented. He lies on a white shroud surrounded by ten monumental figures. At the centre, his weeping mother kneels, her head slightly bent and her hands folded in prayer. Her blue mantle attracts attention, contrasting vividly with the bright red robe of John, who supports her. To the far left, Joseph of Arimathea, enveloped in rich gold brocade, is holding Christ's head. Beside him kneels the bearded Nicodemus, who supports the Redeemer's body under the arms and thus turns him towards the spectator.

1 According to Prims 1951, pp. 162–163, this refers to the *Retable of Saint Anne* for Louvain; Silver 1984, p. 54, n. 45.
2 Prims 1938–1939, XII, p. 297.
3 Transcription in Génard 1863, p. 127.
4 For more details, see Génard 1868, pp. 50–52; Van den Branden 1883, pp. 61–64, n. 1; Vervaet 1976, p. 205.

Behind them stands a man who watches the scene in terror and holds the crown of thorns with a white cloth. To the right, there are four women. Mary Magdalene, stoops to anoint Christ's feet. Between her and the Virgin, Mary Salome takes Christ's left wrist, while she points to the Virgin, her older half sister. Behind Mary Salome stand Mary Cleophas and an older woman. The former holds a sponge, one of the traditional *arma Christi*; the latter, in an ash grey mantle, folds her hands in prayer, weeping, like the Virgin. The figure group forms a freeze, close to the picture plane. Behind them, Golgotha towers like a fanciful rock mass with three crosses on top. While the thieves are still hanging on the cross, four figures carry out the deposition. One of them leaves the 'place of the skull' with a ladder on his shoulder. To the far right behind the mourning group, three figures prepare the grave. To the left, a deep perspective opens on the city of Jerusalem, set on an atmospheric mountain landscape.

On the interior side panels scenes from the lives of the Antwerp Cabinetmakers' patron saints are depicted. On the left panel, Salome with a graceful turn offers a charger with the severed head of John the Baptist to King Herod and Queen Herodias. Herod watches dubiously and recoils somewhat in horror. With understated pleasure, Herodias pricks the severed head with a knife. In the left foreground, a young servant with a small dog on a leash directs a surprised glance at Salome. To the right, a few people watch; and in the gallery, the court musicians seem surprised and excited by the unusual event. Through an arch opening between Herodias and Salome, the actual execution of John the Baptist can be seen taking place outside.

The right panel shows the torture of John the Evangelist, who is represented in a vat of boiling oil, his hands and eyes raised towards heaven. In the foreground two executioners fan the fire with grim determination. Behind the kettle are a number of horsemen. The one to the left, with an impressive jewelled turban and riding a grey, represents Emperor Domitian. This sovereign, who commanded the execution, looks sideways to his advisor, who raises his finger to emphasise the judgement pronounced by his master. Behind the Evangelist, two fierce figures are deep in conversation while a third sounds a clarion. Yet more malicious figures are seen in the next row behind, while a boy watches the torture scene from a tree. The event takes place outside a city gate; the city wall recedes into the distance.

On the exterior of the panels, John the Baptist stands to the left and John the Evangelist to the right: two sober figures painted in grisaille like two dynamic stone statues against a neutral background. The Baptist points to the Lamb that sits on the book he holds in his left hand. The Evangelist gazes piercingly at the spectator and banishes evil with a blessing gesture over his poisoned cup.[5]

Worshippers generally viewed altarpieces like this *Lamentation* with closed side panels. Only on feast days were they opened and the sober grisailles gave way to the overwhelming colour play of the interior panels. At a time in which visual stimuli were still rare compared with today, the opening of these altarpieces must have been an impressive and festive spectacle. Even more than for other altarpieces, this must have been true of this triptych by Quinten Metsijs, who was already known for his immense visual impact.

The central red-white-blue colour composition, formed by the mantles of John and the Virgin, and Christ's shroud, has already been mentioned. Metsijs defied the artistic imagination in this altarpiece by opposing a great diversity of visual contrasts. A first and striking contrast is the difference in visual structure between the centre panel and the side panels. The composition at the centre is traditional and derived from Rogier van der Weyden's famous *Descent from the Cross* (Madrid, Museo del Prado; fig. 1a). The freeze-like positioning of monumental figures around Christ's dead body close to the picture plane is borrowed directly from the famous example of that 15th century Brussels master. Around the turn of the century, this particular iconographic treatment of the Descent from the Cross was followed so widely and intensely that every spectator must have recognised it at once. This compositional concept consists of enclosing Christ and Mary with massive figures who fill the foreground entirely, with a figure bending forward on the left and on the right – here Joseph of Arimathea at the head and Mary Magdalene at the feet of Christ – who enclose the composition like parentheses. Metsijs' own contribution chiefly consists of determining the dynamic line in the organisation of the figures as a clear ellipse. The course of the oval curve can be easily followed from the figure of Joseph of Arimathea, whose arm connects to Christ's head, continuing through the curve of Christ's body and

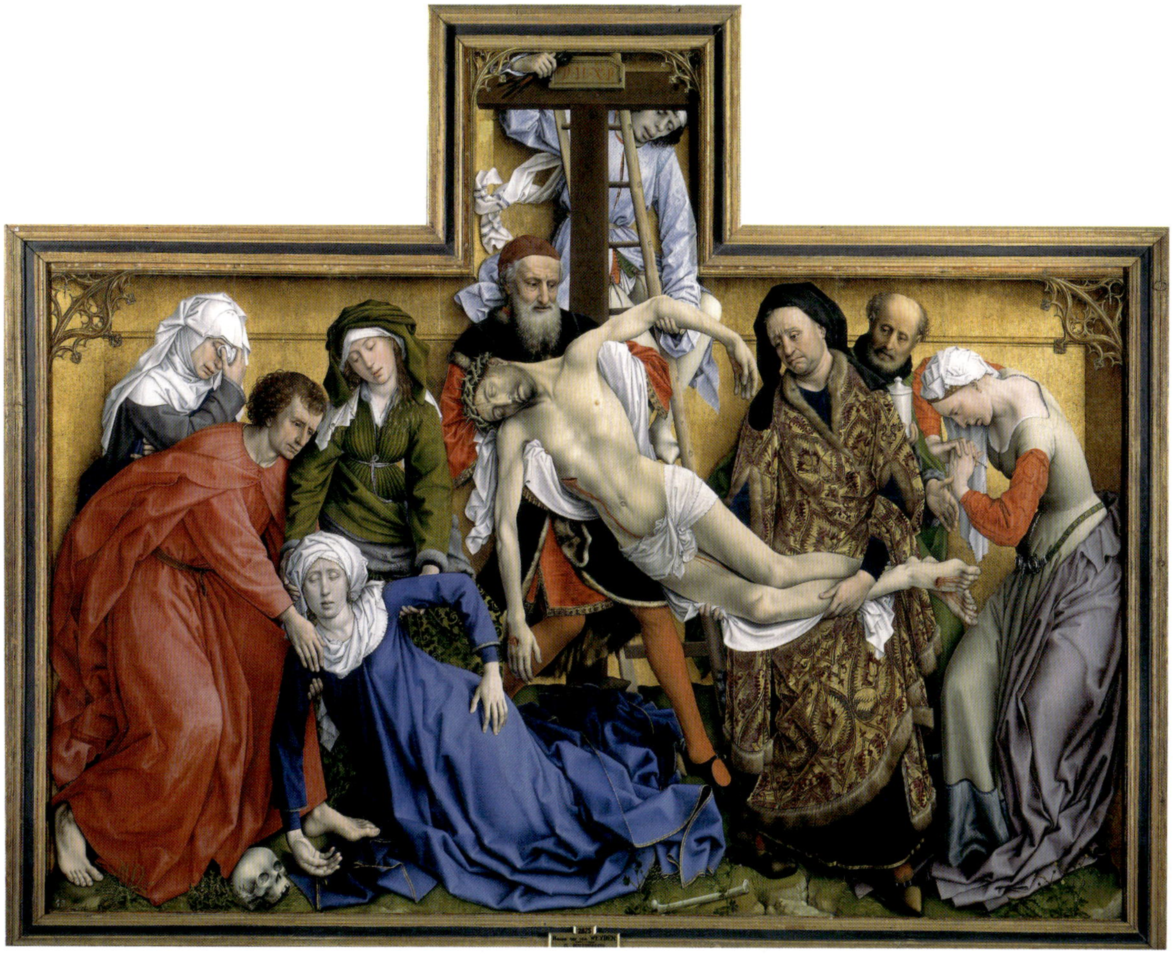

1a
Rogier van der Weyden
The Descent from the Cross
Madrid, Museo Nacional del Prado

the hands and left arm of Mary Magdalene, and returning to a final close through the sequence of heads, placed more or less at the same height. The specific presentation of Christ's body, which is turned by Nicodemus in such a way that it is shown frontally to the spectator, is a strong visual signal that goes along with the individual empathy in the suffering of the Redeemer, propagated by contemporary theologians.[6]

In Van der Weyden's *Descent from the Cross* the figures stand in a narrow, shallow space before a gilded background, which gives the impression they are statues brought to life in a wooden retable niche. Quinten Metsijs, in contrast, sets the lamentation scene before a landscape which recedes in depth. Directly to the right, behind the figures, there is a rock in which Christ's grave is being prepared, in the middle ground the Golgotha mountain top with three crosses and the good and the bad thieves still on the cross, and in the far left distance a masterly representation of the heavenly Jerusalem as a Flemish city, but in a mountainous location. The figure group in the foreground is so monumental that it totally hides the middle ground and is not well integrated with the landscape in the background.

The side panels contrast with the centre panel because they show narrative scenes instead of a monumental devotion scene. It was rightly pointed out that Quinten Metsijs borrowed these compositions from Albrecht Dürer's woodcut, the *Martyrdom of John the Evangelist* from the series of the *Apocalypse* from 1498 (fig. 1b).[7] However, Metsijs did not simply copy

5 For the iconography of this altarpiece, see also the contribution of M. Gielis in this publication.
6 Metsijs' mode of depiction would be copied very soon, for example by the Bruges Master of the Holy Blood (Bruges, Holy Blood Chapel), see Hendrikman 1998, p. 50. Silver emphasises the body of Christ lying on the ground and the head supported by Joseph of Arimathea, motifs he compares with a *Lamentation* attributed to Rogier van der Weyden (The Hague, Mauritshuis) and a *Lamentation Triptych* by the Master of Frankfurt (alias Hendrik van Wueluwe) (Munich, Alte Pinakothek). The author states that it is unclear whether the latter work was created before or after Metsijs' composition; Silver 1984, p. 49.
7 See particularly Silver 1984, p. 45, but first mentioned by Held 1931, pp. 67, 79 ff.

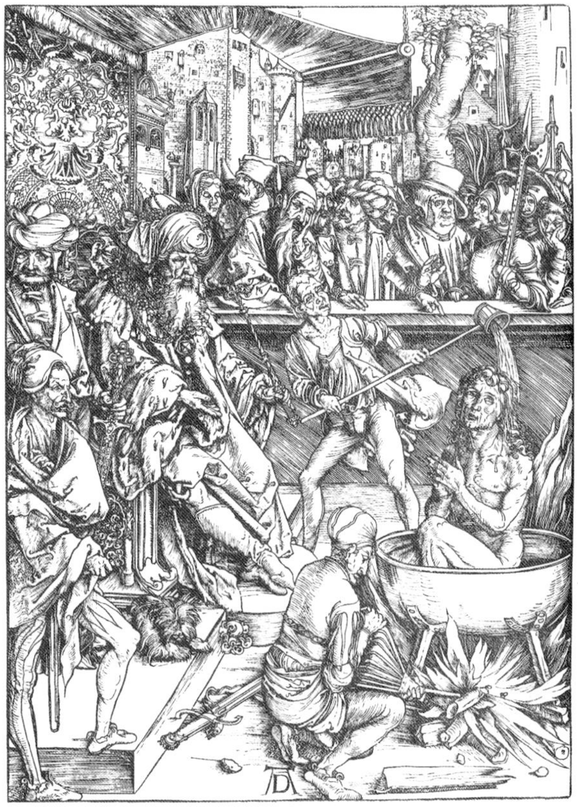

1b
Albrecht Dürer
The martyrdom of John the Evangelist
print from the *Apocalypse* series (1498)

these. He deconstructed the prototype, so to speak, and made new compositions based on the motifs borrowed from the great German master. The pose of the youth who, in the woodcut, pours boiling oil over the saint was used by Metsijs for the page on the left panel, who glances at Salome with astonishment. Emperor Domitian, seated on a throne, is depicted aslant in the composition, just as Herod, who, seated at a slanting table in front of a cloth of honour, inspects the Baptist's head. Domitian's physiognomy and his exotic head covering, moreover, served as a model for the emperor, shown on horseback, on the right panel. The bystanders in the engraving, arranged behind a tribune, recall the row of onlookers behind John the Evangelist, but recur again with Metsijs as the court musicians watching from the tribune on the left panel. Finally, Metsijs also reprised the city gate motif, reversed, in the right panel.

As indicated above, Quinten Metsijs attached great importance to differentiating the individual psychological states of his personages. Thus, all the mourning figures around Christ react in their own way to the dramatic event. The artist expresses maliciousness with ugliness and deformity. The brutal, angry stupidity of the executioners and most of the onlookers around the tortured Evangelist contrasts with the elegant, reserved poses of the sophisticated, exuberantly garbed courtly personages. Metsijs borrowed some caricatured heads from a study sheet with *Grotesque Heads* by Leonardo da Vinci (Windsor Castle).[8] The imperial advisor and the evil man to the right behind John the Evangelist indeed are unmistakably related to the heads on the right and left of da Vinci's sketch, respectively. How the Antwerp painter could have had knowledge of this visual source remains a complete mystery, however. Perhaps Metsijs had contacts with the French court in Fontainebleau, where Leonardo lived at the end of his life. For other Antwerp artists, like Joos van Cleve, two decades later, the transmission of visual models can be explained in this way,[9] but for Quinten Metsijs there is a lack of any written source to support this. We can only establish he had quite thorough knowledge of the work and technique of the great Italian master.[10]

The exceptionally rich garments of the figures in the Cabinetmakers' altarpiece catch the spectator's attention. The green silk dress of Salome with pomegranate motifs and stylised flowers, the gold lamé the page is wearing, and Herodias covered with jewels, undoubtedly display the most precious goods that were then imported through Antwerp harbour, mainly from Italy. Herod and Domitian's exotic head coverings are, as mentioned, influenced by Dürer and situate the scenes in the Near East. Salome, Herodias, and the young women on the centre panel, comply with the ideal of feminine beauty that Metsijs had already displayed with the Virgin's half sisters on the centre panel of the *Retable of Saint Anne* (Brussels, Royal Museums of Fine Arts; fig. 1c). This female type, in fact, became a trademark of Metsijs and strongly contributes to the attraction of his work.

The period in which this *Lamentation* was created, constituted a high point in Metsijs' career. After it, he received several important commissions, which illustrate his international reputation. Between 1507 and 1509 he painted the above-mentioned *Retable of Saint Anne* for the Louvain fraternity of Saint Anne (fig. 1c), which was placed in the fraternity's chapel in Saint Peter's church. In, or shortly after, 1509 the Portuguese Queen Dona Eleonora commissioned him to paint the polyptych of the *Virgin of Sorrows*, destined for the monastery of Madre de Deus in Xabregas – which the queen had founded – outside

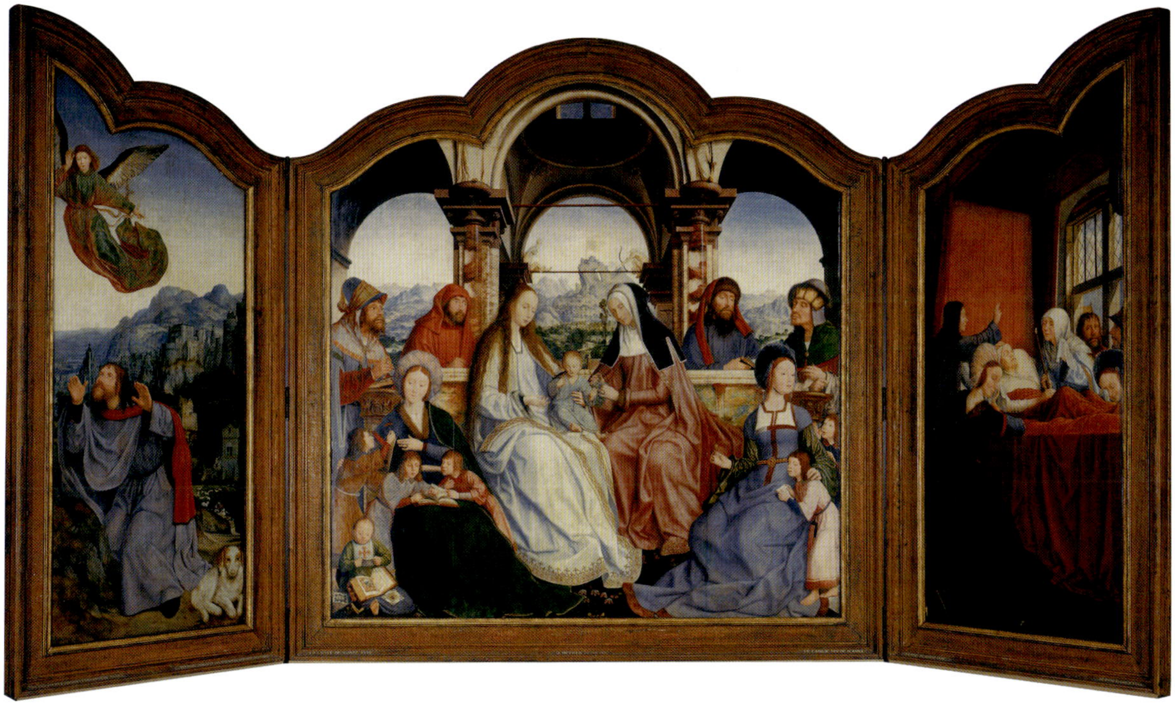

1C
Quinten Metsijs
The Holy Kinship (Saint Anne Altarpiece),
Brussels, Royal Museums of Fine Arts of Belgium

Lisbon. It must be assumed that the commission was given to Metsijs through the agent of the Portuguese crown in Antwerp, João Brandão.[11] The centre panel of that triptych displays the Virgin, seated and in prayer. Her type and her clothing largely match those of the older woman to the right on the centre panel of the Cabinetmakers' altarpiece.

The diverse panels of the Madre de Deus altarpiece show an enormous difference of quality, which indicates that Metsijs' studio took an important share in their execution. The Antwerp Cabinetmakers' altarpiece, on the contrary, appears to be painted entirely by the master himself. It seems logical that Quinten Metsijs gave priority to a work that would be placed in the most prominent church of his home city and would consolidate his fame for the rest of his career. He could not foresee then that his fame would take on almost mythical proportions and that he would be regarded as the founder of the Antwerp Painting School.

MAXIMILIAAN MARTENS

8 Silver 1984, p. 46.
9 Hand 2004, pp. 101–105.
10 Metsijs possibly painted a copy after (or a version of) da Vinci's famous *Saint Anne with the Virgin and Child* (Poznan, Muzeum Naradowe) (de Bosque 1975, pp. 218–221) and applied Leonardesque *sfumato*, a pictorial effect he could obviously not know through prints.
11 Silver 1984, pp. 59–60.

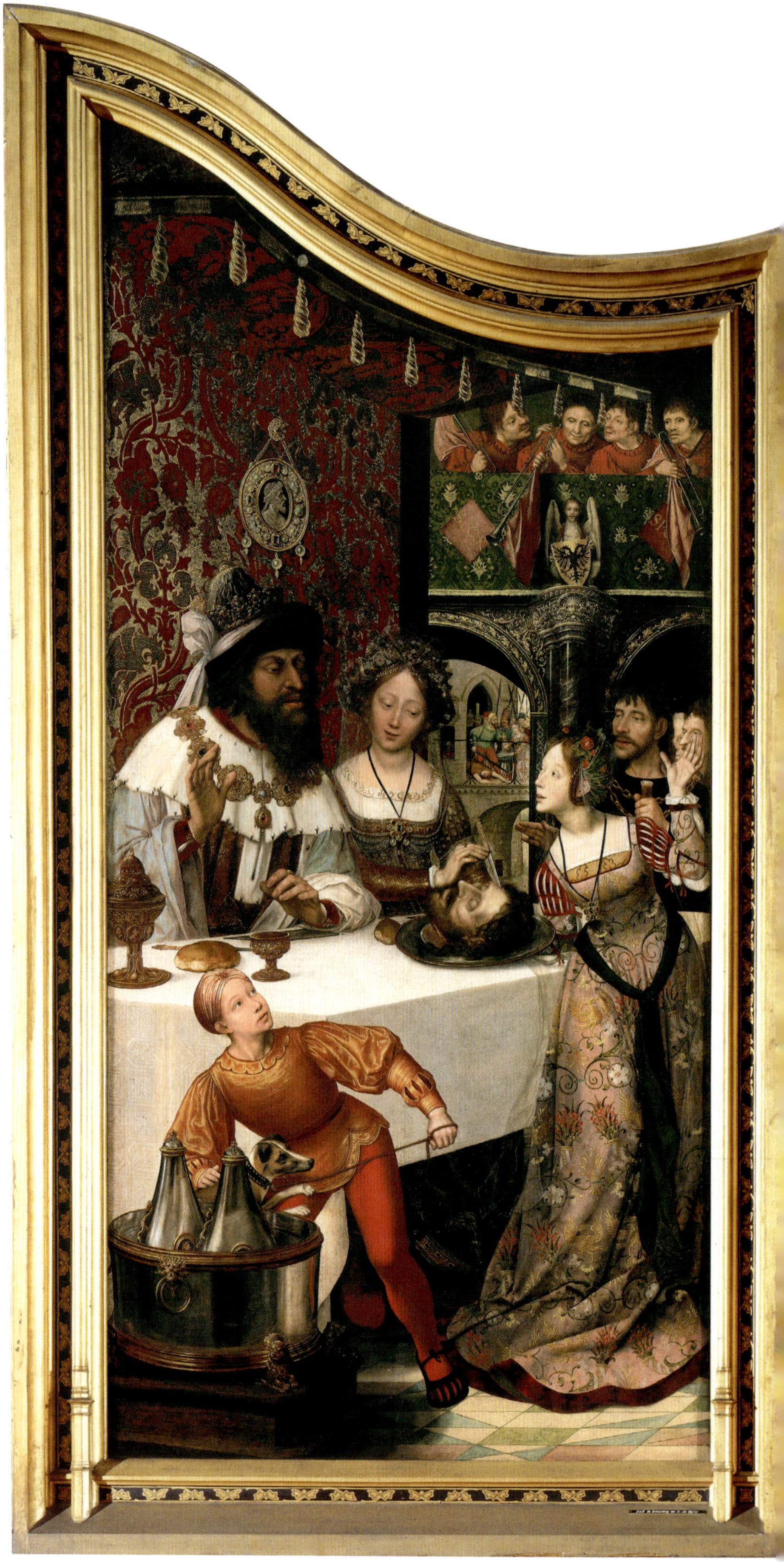

2 Altarpiece of the Almoners of the Table of the Holy Spirit

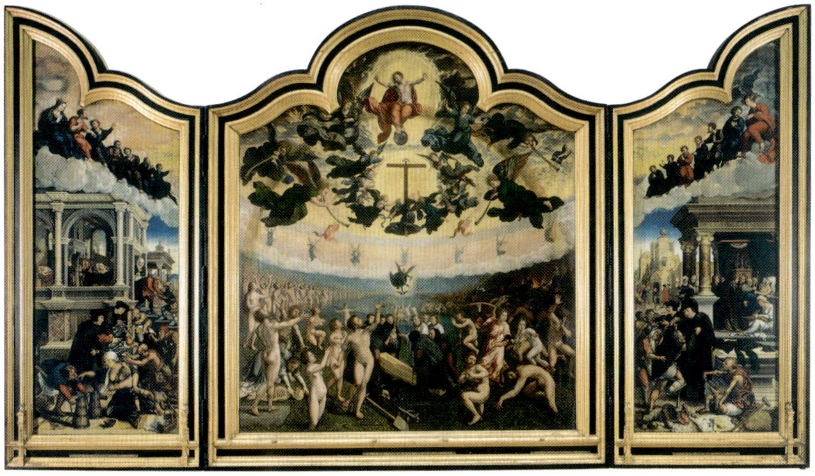

Barend van Orley

Brussels c. 1492–Brussels 1542

The Last Judgement with the Seven Acts of Mercy

c. 1517–1524/25

Oil on panel
centre panel: 248 x 218 cm
side panels: 248 x 94 cm
Unsigned

Antwerp, Koninklijk Museum voor Schone Kunsten, inv. 741–745

Provenance: commissioned by the Almoners to the Table of the Holy Spirit; in 1524–1525 placed on the Almoners' altar in the Antwerp cathedral; in 1794, following the lootings by the commissioners of the French Republic, transferred to the *Knechtjeshuis* (an orphanage for boys); later transferred to the *Maagdenhuis* (an orphanage for girls) and subsequently, in 1877, to Saint Elizabeth's Hospital;[1] on loan to the Museum as a property of the OCMW.[2]

Bibliography: Handwritten catalogues Maagdenhuis 1847, nr. 39 en 1872, no. 21
Van Mander 1604, fol. 211r
Sandrart 1675, pp. 237–238
De Piles 1699 [1725], p. 326
Houbraken 1716, p. 20
Beschrijvinge 1751, p. 1 (p. 11)
Descamps 1769, p. 139
Kerken van Antwerpen 1774, pp. 1–2
Reynolds (1781), p. 29
Schopenhauer 1831, p. 287
Passavant 1833, p. 382
Waagen 1862, p. 293
Van Vloten 1874, p. 70
Geudens 1891A, pp. 126-131
Wauters 1892, p. 40 ff.
Wauters 1902, pp. 18–19, 45
Hoogewerff 1912, pp. 65–66
Winkler 1924, p. 258
Friedländer 1924–1937, VIII, pp. 112–114, 166–167

This triptych of the *Last Judgement with the Seven Acts of Mercy* has a rigidly symmetrical composition. The vertical axis is established by the descending Christ, seated on a rainbow and surrounded by an aura of gold leaf or gold paint. It continues through the Tau cross, the archangel Michael, and in the centre foreground, three priests and seven other figures burying a death body. Horizontally, the composition is divided in half by a cloud bank, extending over the entire width of the work. The heavenly zone on the centre panel is entirely filled with angels. Closest to Christ are angels with a lily and a sword; further outwards are four others with trumpets. The seven angels directly above the cloud bank don't belong to the generally-known iconography of the Last Judgement. There are nonetheless directly borrowed from the Apocalypse.[3] The apostles, the Virgin, and possibly Paul, are shown on the clouds of the side panels.[4] The triptych's bottom register is reserved to the mortals. On each side of the burial the dead resurrect: to the left, the chosen hail Christ's return, and to the right the doomed are led to hell by an angel.[5]

On the interior side panels, Italian Renaissance architecture provides a setting to present the Acts of Mercy. To the left the thirsty are quenched by two almoners of the Table of the Holy Spirit, the homeless are offered shelter, and the hungry are fed by a woman with an apron who stands in the doorway with bread – and whose pose is comparable to customary depictions of Elizabeth. On the right panel the clothing of the naked, again by two almoners, is predominant, while in the middle ground the sick are cared for. Freeing the prisoners, also on the right panel, is a *very* hospitable interpretation of the sixth Act of Mercy: visiting the prisoners. The symmetry of both panels is persevered to the smallest detail, even to the still lifes in the foreground.

The clothes of the crippled beggar in the foreground of the right side panel and the old man in the foreground of the right panel are striking. Each wears an intact red mantle of precious silver brocade, while the others wear obviously worn clothes. Here, it is possibly made clear that fate can hit everybody, rich and poor.[6] This could also be a warning for the almoners, who were part of social elite of Antwerp. The animal's skull beside the well-clothed beggar in

1 A letter from 1877 reveals that this was not straightforward. The centre panel was too large to be taken out of the chapel and a carpenter was needed to adjust the door. Correspondence in Antwerp, OCMW Archives, box 178.

2 'Even the Poor Relief was not spared. Its ecclesiastical existence, its altar with its properties, perished in the general devastation of 1798. Fortunately, some of its art objects survive. One is the splendid triptych by Barend van Orley: *The Last Judgement and the Seven Acts of Mercy*. It is considered one of the best, if not the finest, pieces by that master. Its artistic value is, moreover, nearly inestimable. It was successfully rescued and stored in the Knechtjeshuis. Later, the painting appeared in the chapel of the Maagdenhuis, and finally disappeared from public view until 1885 in a room in Saint Elizabeth's Hospital.' Geudens 1891B.

3 Revelation 8: 6–9: 21. The connection between the Seven Acts of Mercy and the Last Judgement was formulated by Matthew (Matthew 25: 31–46).

4 Farmer 1981, p. 152. The most literal reference to this cloud bank can be found in Matthew (Matthew 24: 30) and Mark (Mark 13: 26).

5 For the iconography of this altarpiece, see also the contribution of M. Gielis in this publication.

6 Suggestion by Prof. Dr. J. Koldeweij, Rijksuniversiteit Nijmegen.

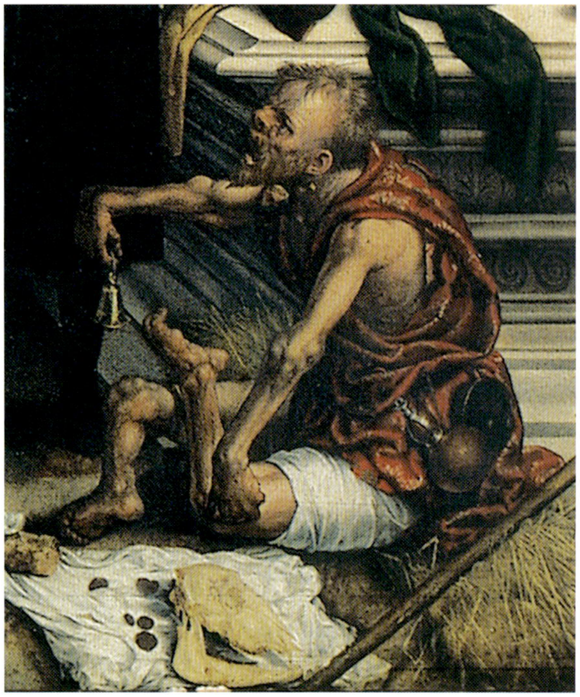

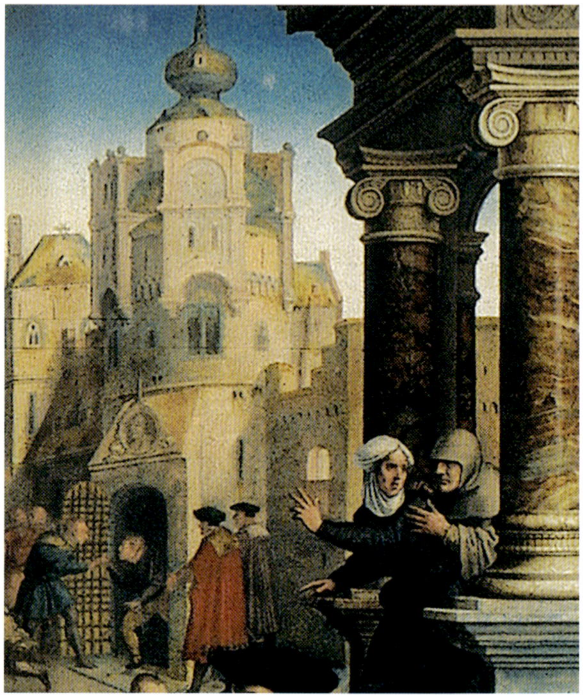

Philippen 1940, pp. 149–166
Lavalleye 1943, p. 47
Von Baldass 1944, p. 178
Dhanens 1948, p. 127
Friedländer 1967–1976, VIII, pp. 69–70, 102
Whinney 1968, p. 142
Cuttler 1968, p. 437
Farmer 1981, pp. 9, 20, 148–155
Dacos 1987, pp. 19–20
Antwerp 1988, pp. 175–176
Van de Velde 1993A, p. 180
Van Mander-Miedema 1994–1999, II, pp. 324–328
Grieten & Bungeneers 1996, p. 363
Hendrikman 2002, pp. 85–87
Ainsworth 2006, pp. 109–112
Hendrikman 2009B

the foreground complicates matters further. If it is a goat's skull, it may indicate man's insincerity.[7] Two of the needy persons on the left panel wear pilgrims' badges: two of these are clearly identifiable. Thus, the crossed small pilgrim's staffs and scallop shells refer to a pilgrimage to Santiago de Compostella, and the John's tray must come from Amiens.[8] The pilgrims are depicted among the Acts of Mercy (feeding, quenching, sheltering), which were of particular importance to them. On the exterior panels, four saints are depicted: to the right Lawrence and Elizabeth of Hungary, and to the left Martin and possibly Jerome or Mark.[9]

Regarding the commission of the *Last Judgement with the Seven Acts of Mercy*, an authentic contract survives.[10] In the undated document it is stipulated by the Almoners that Barend van Orley should complete an altarpiece within four years, counting from next Easter, for a total amount of 100 Flemish pounds 'groot'.[11] This sum has been equated to 600 Rhine guilders,[12] of which van Orley received 100 at the drawing-up of the document – or was at least promised these – for the design, the panels and frames. This money had already been collected by 13 brothers who were deceased by the time of the contract.[13] The second group of brothers, 19 in number, committed themselves to pay 1 Flemish pound 'groot', and on top of that, 2 crowns every year, until the altarpiece should be completed and

7 Goats are a symbol for sinners. LCI, I, col. 314–316.
8 My thanks go to Prof. Dr. J. Koldeweij for the identification of these insignias.
9 All represent one or more of the Acts of Mercy, and are also depicted in this capacity on the anonymous late 15th century *Last Judgement* of the Almoners (Antwerp, Maagdenhuis Museum). Only Mark (as the figure with the book and lion was identified until now) cannot in any way be reconciled with charity. Jerome at least shares the renouncement of (a part of) profane wealth with the almoners. Male saints and prophets who *do* occur on the older piece, Isaiah, Willibrord, Abraham, Ludovic, and Tobias, seem to be irrelevant.
10 Antwerp, OCMW Archives, box 178, file 10. Transcribed and clarified by Geudens 1891A.
11 '[...] that one named master Bernaert living in Brussels, a very excellent and famous master will make this decorated table. If it also pleases the good men for the sum of .c Flemish 'groot' at which price... he would deliver the decorated table within iiij years coming from Eastern [...].' With thanks to Paul de Commer, OCMW archivist, who produced this transcription (in Dutch), which corresponds almost exactly with the transcription Geudens published in 1891.
12 Geudens points out that a guilder is generally appreciated at 28 stivers, and bases the following calculation on it. In the document itself, 100 Flemish 'groot' is explicitly reckoned at 600 Rhine guilders. In modern literature, too, the Rhine and Carolus guilder are customarily equated to 1/6 Flemish 'groot'. Landau & Parshall 1994, p. 370.
13 'Also to pay the prescribed sum of VI c Rhine guilders. To be known that there now lie in the Chamber paid in cash I c guilders that have come from some brothers that have formerly served the poor and that are mentioned below with name and surname, to know from each one 1 Flemish pound 'groot', and the framework (Dutch: 'back') and the patron are paid from this'. This passage does not clarify whether the 100 guilders still had to be paid or were already paid. The Early New Dutch word 'back' (case) can hardly be interpreted differently than as the frame and panel, although it generally indicated the (wooden) framework of a carved retable. In the latter (improbable) case this payment would be referring to an entirely different commission than the *Last Judgement*.

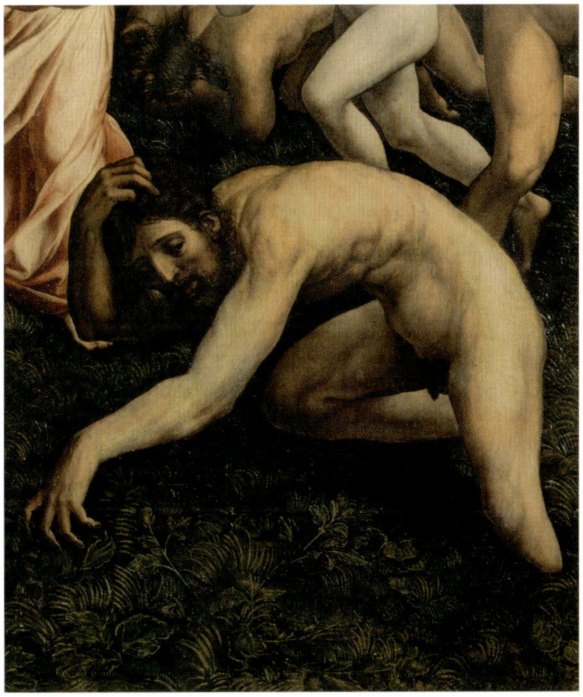

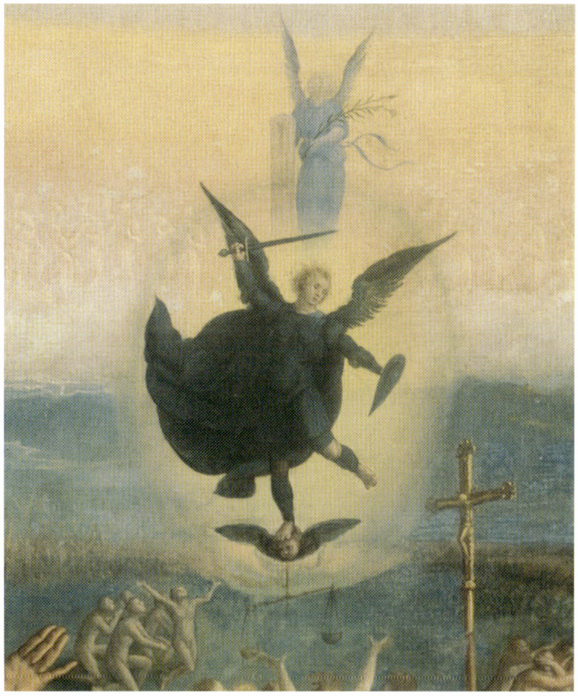

paid for.[14] Finally, they also stipulated that brothers who became members in the future would be liable for the same amount.

The document came about in at least two phases. The list of the deceased brothers mentions the name 'Simon Bisscop', who was sworn in for the year 1517 (on 4 December 1516).[15] In addition it contains a list of 19 names of brothers among whom the last, Andries vand[er] Mast, was sworn in along with Simon Bisscop. Apparently in 1524, this list was supplemented, by a different hand, with three brothers sworn in for the years 1523–24, and in a third hand with five brothers who were probably initially forgotten.[16] Based on this last supplement, the first part of the document (or in any case the running text and the names of the first 32 brothers) can be dated quite accurately to 1517.[17]

Obviously, only brothers who were still alive after the decision to have a large altarpiece made, are mentioned in the document. Only *they* could have put money aside for this purpose. By reference to the brothers who were members of the guild but were not named in the contract, a *terminus post quem* for this decision can be established at 1508. This year corresponds precisely with the 50th birthday of the Table of the Holy Spirit (established 1458).[18] Since the contract says that the altarpiece would be executed by a famous master, work on it didn't start long before the signing of the document in about 1517.[19]

Ever since Carel van Mander mentioned the *Last Judgement* on the Almoners' altar in Antwerp Cathedral in 1604,[20] the triptych has played a central role in the history of reception of Barend van Orley. Van Mander was paraphrased in the biographies by Sandrart (1675),[21] de Piles (1699),[22] Baldinucci (1681–1728),[23] Houbraken (1716)[24] and others, but the triptych itself never enjoyed wide interest.

14 Which crown is meant here, and what its value was, cannot be reconstructed. Geudens uses an average of two guilders and six stivers. Geudens 1891B, p. 134.

15 This part of the document certainly dates from after 4 December 1516. In the text, the list of the deceased is the only one that is explicitly mentioned, and it is reasonable to suppose that these parts were created at the same time.

16 Two for 1518, and one for 1519, 1521, and 1523, respectively. It is certain that the list of names was kept up to date after 1517. At some point the name of Servaes Stollaert (1518) was crossed out, and that of Mechiel Dermoyen (1521) was marked with a cross. The addition of 'de oude' (the elder) to Heynederick Adriaenss (1503), cannot have taken place before the inclusion of 'Heydrick Arieans de jon[g]e' (the younger) (1524).

17 Based on this data, Geudens reaches a dating of 1518, assuming that Simon Bisscop and Andries vander Mast were sworn in on 4 December 1517. Everywhere else, Geudens also supposes that the inscription took place on 4 December (feast of Saint Barbara) before the service year. Geudens 1891A, pp. 128–129.

18 *Antwerp 2002,* p. 3.

19 Barend van Orley probably became a master in 1512, and his quick success would also be due to the commissions he had executed before 1515 for Margaret of Austria. Further biographical data in Van Mander-Miedema 1994–1999, II, pp. 324–328 and Hendrikman 2009B.

20 Van Mander 1604, fol. 211r. Van Mander-Miedema 1994–1999, II, pp. 324–331.

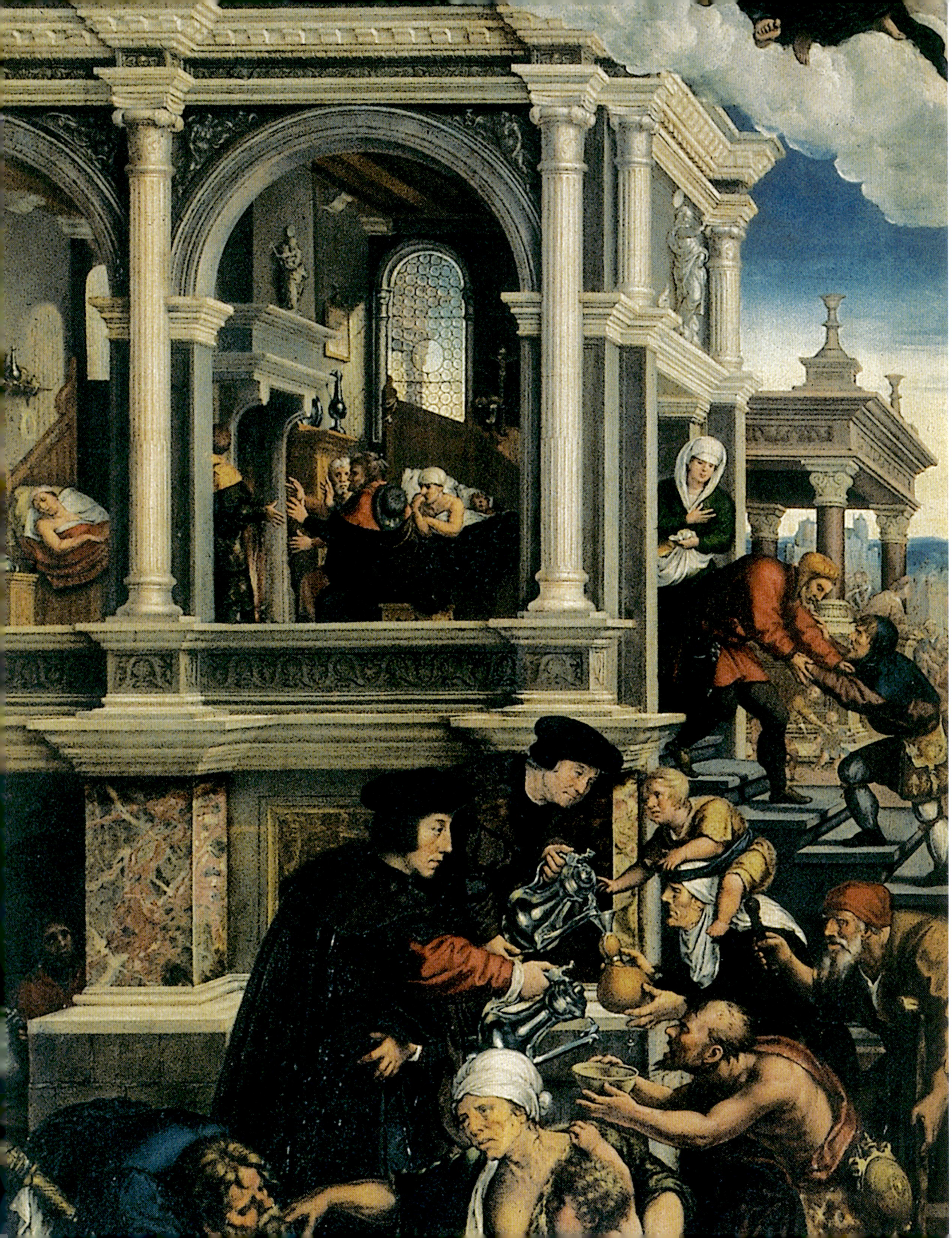

The triptych is mentioned in the first Dutch handwritten travel guide (1751–1753) which specifically focused on visual arts in Flanders and Brabant.[25] On the first page of the manuscript – where the works in Antwerp Cathedral are discussed – the author mentions the 'Last Judgement by Berent van Orleij, who was a disciple of Raphael Urbin'. This supposition was first voiced in the French Academy at the end of the 17th century, by, among others Roger de Piles,[26] and was eagerly repeated after that. Furthermore, the triptych was described in travel books by, among others, Descamps (1769) and Reynolds (1781). The work's obscure whereabouts in the 19th century and its poor conservation condition also caused it to be rarely mentioned or discussed. Johanna Schopenhauer, however, knew it from hearsay. She visited it and was thoroughly disappointed by its bad condition. Apparently the work was so dirty there was hardly anything to sce.[27]

The placement of the apostles in heaven has often suggested the influence of Raphael's *Disputà* (1509) on this *Last Judgement*.[28] The components of the iconography – two groups of six apostles seated in the air, the triumphant Christ surrounded by a rainbow and angels with trumpets, the angelic choirs, and the cross carried by angels – had all been common elements of the Last Judgement iconography for at least 200 years. They can be found, for example, in Giotto's Arena Chapel in Padua (1303–1305), and in van Orley's immediate predecessor Rogier van der Weyden (1443–1451, Beaune, Musée Hôtel-Dieu).[29] Thus the concomitant question is how van Orley could have known the *Disputà*. The first known print of it dates from 1552.[30] Oral tradition is theoretically possible, but impossible to prove. The same goes for the influence of Raphael's tapestry designs for the *Acts of the Apostles*, which were woven in Brussels from 1517 onwards. Dacos, Farmer, and others, point out the similarities between the crippled figure in Raphael's *Healing of the Lame Man* and Orley's equivalent on the right panel of this triptych.[31] The poses of both beggars differ considerably and it was precisely the firm and true-to-life muscle mass of Raphael's figure – a Renaissance aspect par excellence – that was replaced by truly miserable, deformed members in van Orley's work. The often-mentioned, more general, supposition that van Orley's figures are based on thorough study of Raphael's cartoons has never been substantiated. Therefore, van Orley's correct knowledge of human anatomy cannot be attributed to the tapestry cartoons. Furthermore, almost all the depicted figures are entirely clothed.[32] The influence of a tapestry design (1520–1521) by Raphael's pupil Giulio Romano, as recently proposed by Ainsworth,[33] is equally problematic. Not only are the similarities superficial but, more importantly, van Orley's design had probably already been approved by the commissioners in 1517.

For the remarkable Italian Renaissance architecture on the panels, direct examples cannot be found in Raphael's cartoons. Important details, like the Ionic capitals on the right panel and the Corinthian capitals on the left panel, or the fluted columns, do not even occur in Raphael's cartoons. Nonetheless, van Orley must have been informed in one way or another of recent interests in Rome. Especially notably, the building in the left foreground on the left panel shows strong similarities with classical

21 Sandrart 1675, pp. 237–238; Kultermann 1990, pp. 30–31.
22 '[...] When he had a work of importance to make, he first prepared the Panel with Gold Foil and Painted over that, so his Colours preserved clarity and in certain places were added lustre, especially in celestial clarity, as he painted in the Painting of the Last Judgement that is in Antwerp, in the Chapel of the Almoners. [...] and he had the best understanding of the Tapestries the Pope and other Sovereigns of those days had made, after the drawings of Raphael, whose disciple he had been.' de Piles 1699 [1725], p. 326.
23 *Notices of the professors of drawing after Cimabue: since, for which it is proven as such, and for whom the fine arts of painting, sculpture, and architecture, having left behind the rudeness of the Greek way, and the Gothic, they have limited their perfection in those centuries to the Antique way.* id. *Notices of the professors of drawing after Cimabue: since, for which it is proven as such, and for whom the fine arts of painting, sculpture, and architecture having left behind the rudeness of the Greek way, and the Gothic, they have limited their perfection in those centuries to the Antique way: distinct work in centuries, and decades*, Florence 1845–1847. [anastatic reprint, Florence, 1974–1975].
24 Houbraken 1716, p. 20.
25 *Beschrijvinge 1751*, p. 1 (p. 11).
26 Farmer 1981, pp. 10–11; Hendrikman 2002, pp. 73–80.
27 '[...] it was of a reasonably large size, but so dirty and smoked, that is was completely impossible to understand anything of what was displayed [...]'. Schopenhauer 1831, II, p. 287.
28 Baldass 1944, p. 178; Farmer 1981, p. 153; Ainsworth 2006, p. 110.
29 Cuttler also situated the composition in the tradition of van der Weyden and did not appreciate the work more than contemporary depictions of the theme by Jan Provoost and Joos van Cleve. Cuttler 1968, pp. 436–437. Farmer, too, pointed out the similarities with, for example, van der Weyden's conception of the theme, but saw more typological similarities with Raphael. Farmer 1981, pp. 152–154. See also: Hendrikman 2002.
30 Published by Hieronymus Cock. Höper 2001, pp. 371–372.
31 Farmer 1981, p. 165; Dacos 1987, p. 20.
32 For this issue, see Hendrikman 2002, pp. 93–101 and Hendrikman 2009B (with further references).
33 Ainsworth 2006, pp. 109–112.

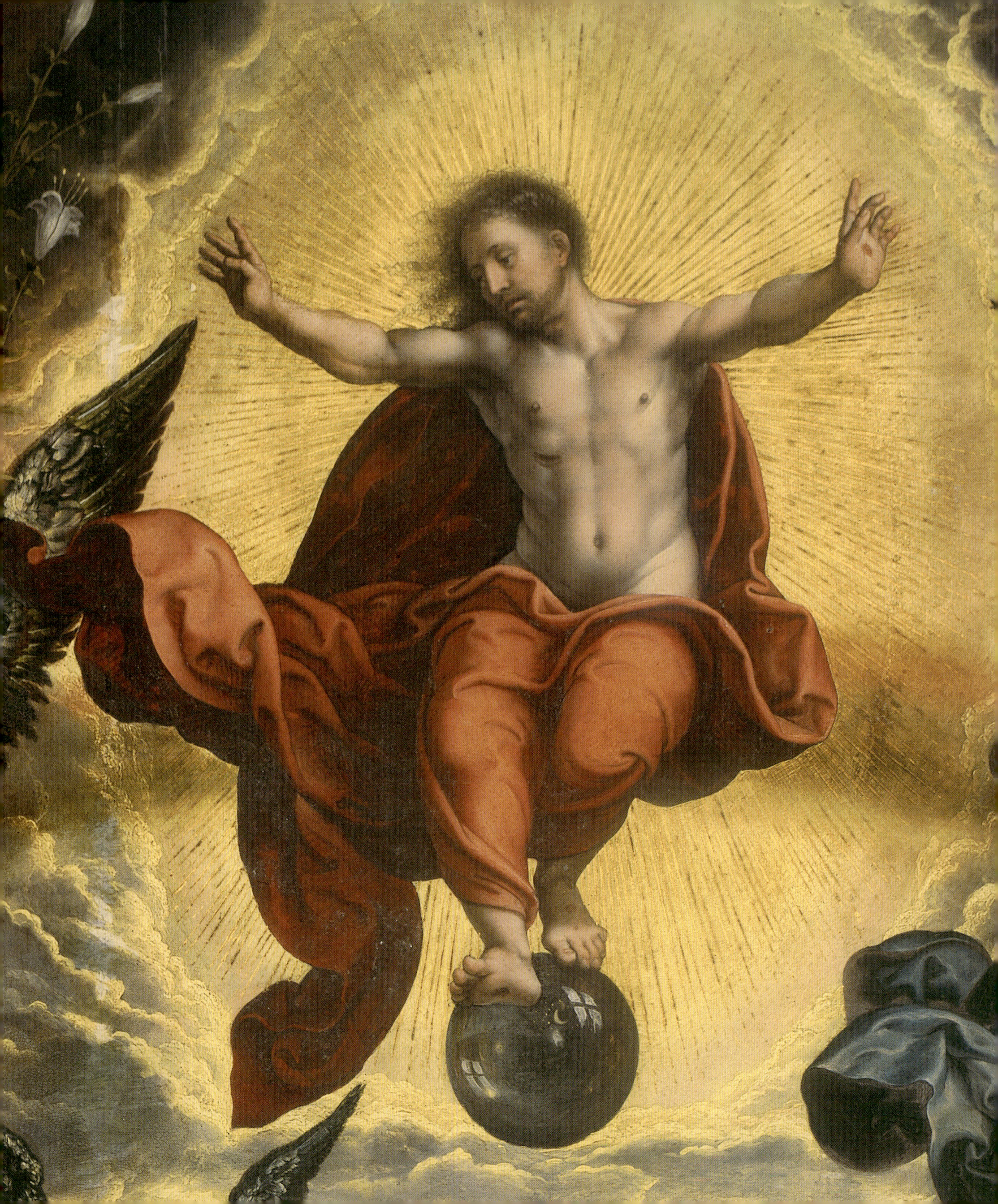

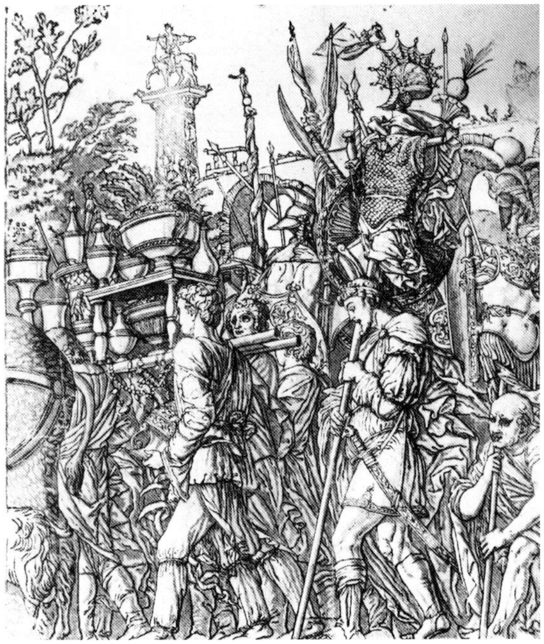

2a
Andrea Mantegna
The Triumphs of Caesar: the armour bearer
engraving

triumphal arches, particularly that of Constantine (312–315). The free-standing columns of the actual construction, the Victories in the spandrels and the remarkable double fluting can also be encountered in this classical edifice. It has not been proven that van Orley ever left Brussels, or that a single print of Constantine's triumphal arch was ever at van Orley's disposal, thus both the direct source and the medium of transmission remain uncertain. We *do* know that van Orley had at his disposal prints of Andrea Mantegna's *Triumphs of Caesar*. The relief behind the almoners on the left panel is directly borrowed from these (fig. 2a).[34]

Despite the prominent place the *Last Judgement with the Seven Acts of Mercy* occupied in Antwerp Cathedral, its influence on other works was minimal. Its closest relative can be found in the Tholen City Hall, in the Netherlands, and was probably not created before the third quarter of the 16th century, despite the inscription giving the year *1524*.[35]

LARS HENDRIKMAN

34 The fragment is copied after the sixth print, the armour bearers.
35 Hendrikman 2009B.

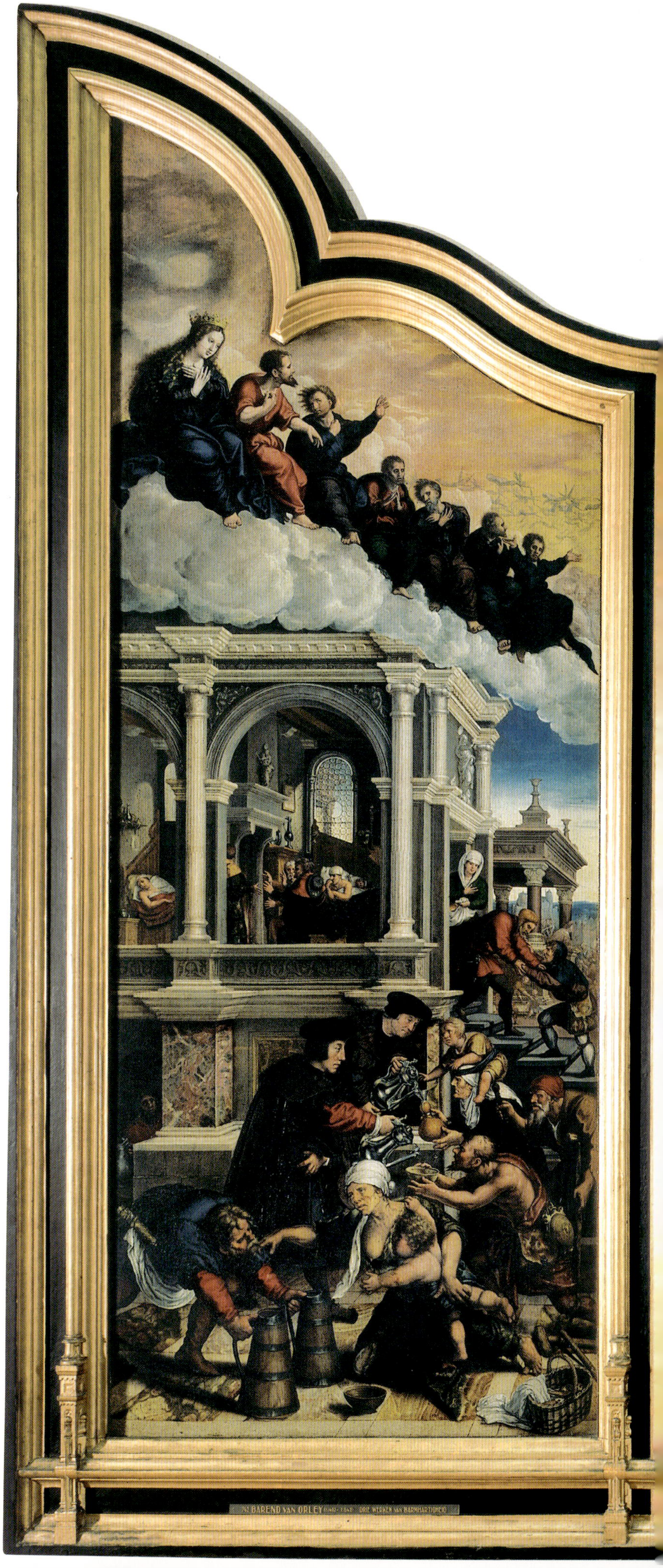
BAREND VAN ORLEY
DRIE WERKEN VAN BARMHARTIGHEID

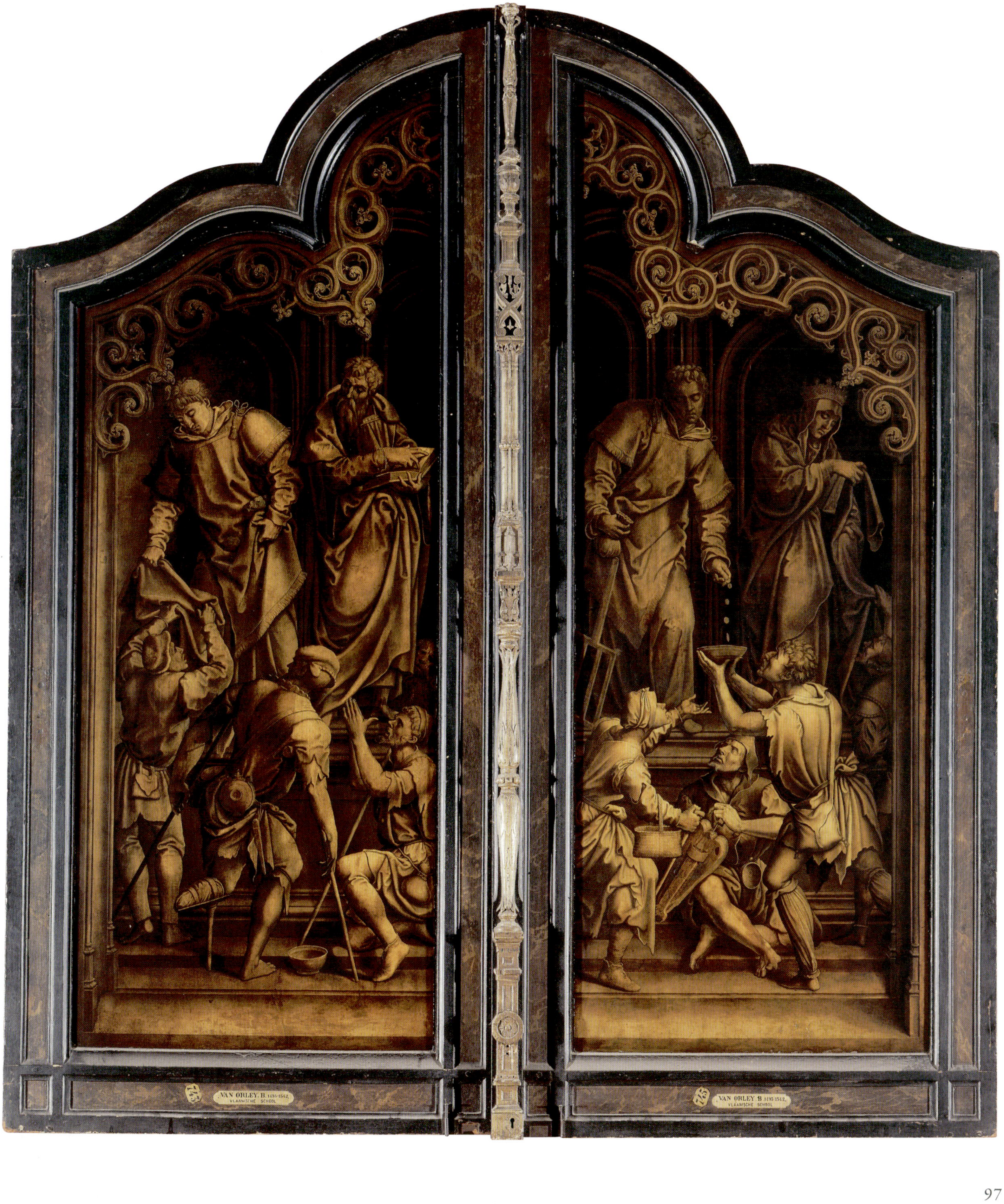
745
VAN ORLEY. B. 1495-1542.
VLAAMSCHE SCHOOL
745
VAN ORLEY. B. 1495-1542.
VLAAMSCHE SCHOOL

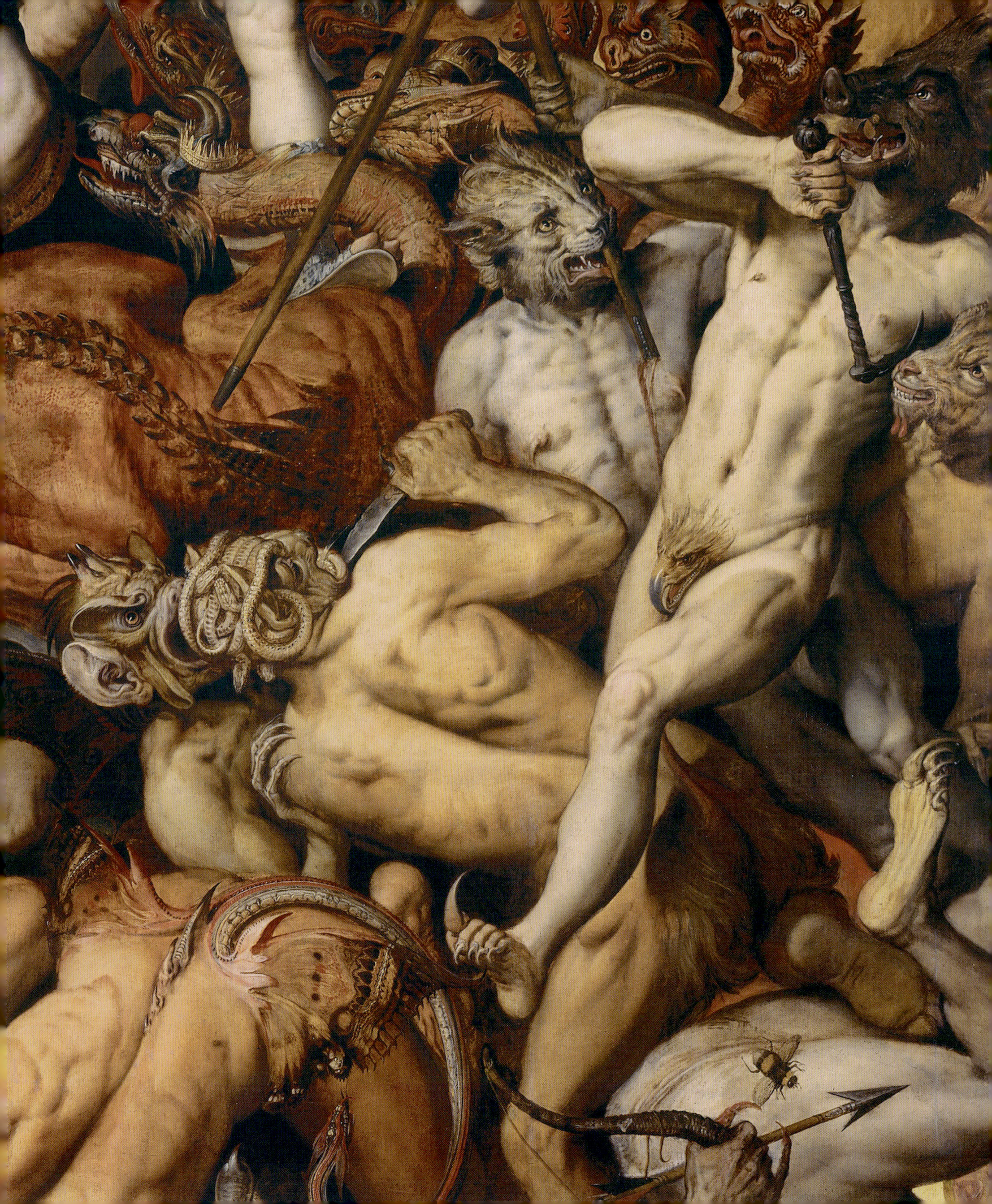

3 Altarpiece of the Fencers

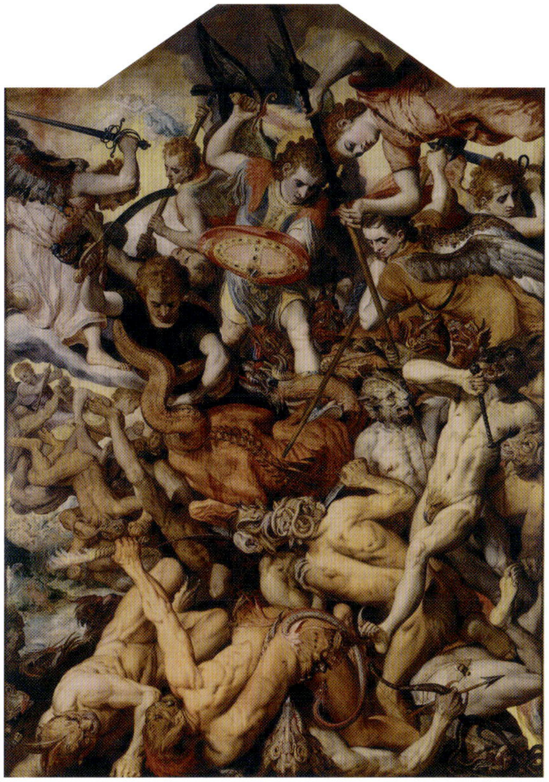

Frans Floris

Antwerp 1519/20–Antwerp 1570

The Fall of the Rebel Angels

1554

Oil on panel, 308 x 220 cm

Signed and dated
in the right bottom *FF.IV.ET F[A] 1554*[1]

Antwerp, Koninklijk Museum voor Schone Kunsten, inv. 112

This painting, undoubtedly the best-known work by Frans Floris, was the centre panel of a triptych that ornamented the altar of the Fencers' guild. The guild was established in 1488 as the third of Antwerp's armed guilds, after the Arbalest and the Longbowmen. Initially it was named 'Archers of the Crown', but later it was usually called 'Guild of the Halberdiers'[2] after the Fencers' favourite weapon, the halberd, a lance with an axe at the top. Initially, the name 'Fencers' would have had nothing to do with the nature of the guild members' armoury, because it referred to their 'protective' role. Differing from the longbow and the arbalest, halberds were not used to shoot with, but were intended for man-to-man fights.

In 1520 the Fencers erected a new altar for their patron, Saint Michael,[3] but nothing more is known about this.

In concordance with what was usual at that time, one can assume that it was more likely a carved wooden retable than a painted triptych. It was probably lost in the fire of 1533. The new altar received a prestigious altarpiece in 1554, for which the guild commissioned Frans Floris, who enjoyed great fame in Antwerp since his brilliant share in the city decorations at the Joyous Entry of Charles V and crown-prince Philip in 1549.[4]

Only the centre panel of Floris' triptych survives. Little is known about the side panels. They disappeared during the 17th century at the latest, although this may actually have happened earlier. We know that the triptych was severely damaged in the Iconoclastic Fury of August 1566. The following year the altar was solemnly reinstated, more splendid than before, as a commemorative inscription from 1567 recalls.[5] Before that, the guild had had Maerten de Vos paint a new altarpiece, but apparently there was dissension among the deans and aldermen about whether they would place the old or the new painting on their altar. An order by Antwerp's city magistrate on 19 September 1567 granted them free choice in this matter.[6] Ultimately, the new painting, by de Vos, was chosen. This is shown in a letter of 14 August 1603,[7] by the merchant-poet Johannes Rademacher (Rotarius) in which he states that Abraham Ortelius

Provenance: commissioned by the Antwerp Fencers' guild; from 1554 to 1566 on the guild altar in the Antwerp Cathedral; damaged during the Iconoclastic Fury (1566); in the Fencers' guild chamber from 1566 to 1585; on the altar of the Fencers' guild in the cathedral from 1585 to 1794; removed from the cathedral by the commissioners of the French Republic and transferred to the Musée Central des Arts in Paris (1794–1815); in 1816 together with Rubens' *Lamentation* (cat. 14) traded against the *Raising of the Cross*, also by Rubens, between the Museum and the Church of Our Lady.

1 Van de Velde 1975A, I, pp. 209–213; II, fig. 26. The A of the monogram is apocryphal.
2 Prims 1938–1939, XIII, p. 384.
3 Ibidem.
4 Van de Velde 1975A, I, pp. 31–32, 159–185, nos. S 7–33.
5 'Athletici Collegii Sodales Urbis praesidio constituti Praefecto F. HENRICO BERCHEMIO Equite Aurato huius anni Consule Primario hanc Aram D. Michaeli Coelestis Militiae Principi sacram picturis statuis his sedilibus caeterisque id genus ornamentis communi sumpto *multo quam antea illustriorem* [the author's italicisation] reddidere anno a Christo nato M.D.LXVII' (Van de Velde 1975A, I, p. 210).
6 Van de Velde 1975A, I, p. 212, note 3.
7 Hessels 1887, p. 782; Van de Velde 1975A, I, p. 212, note 4.

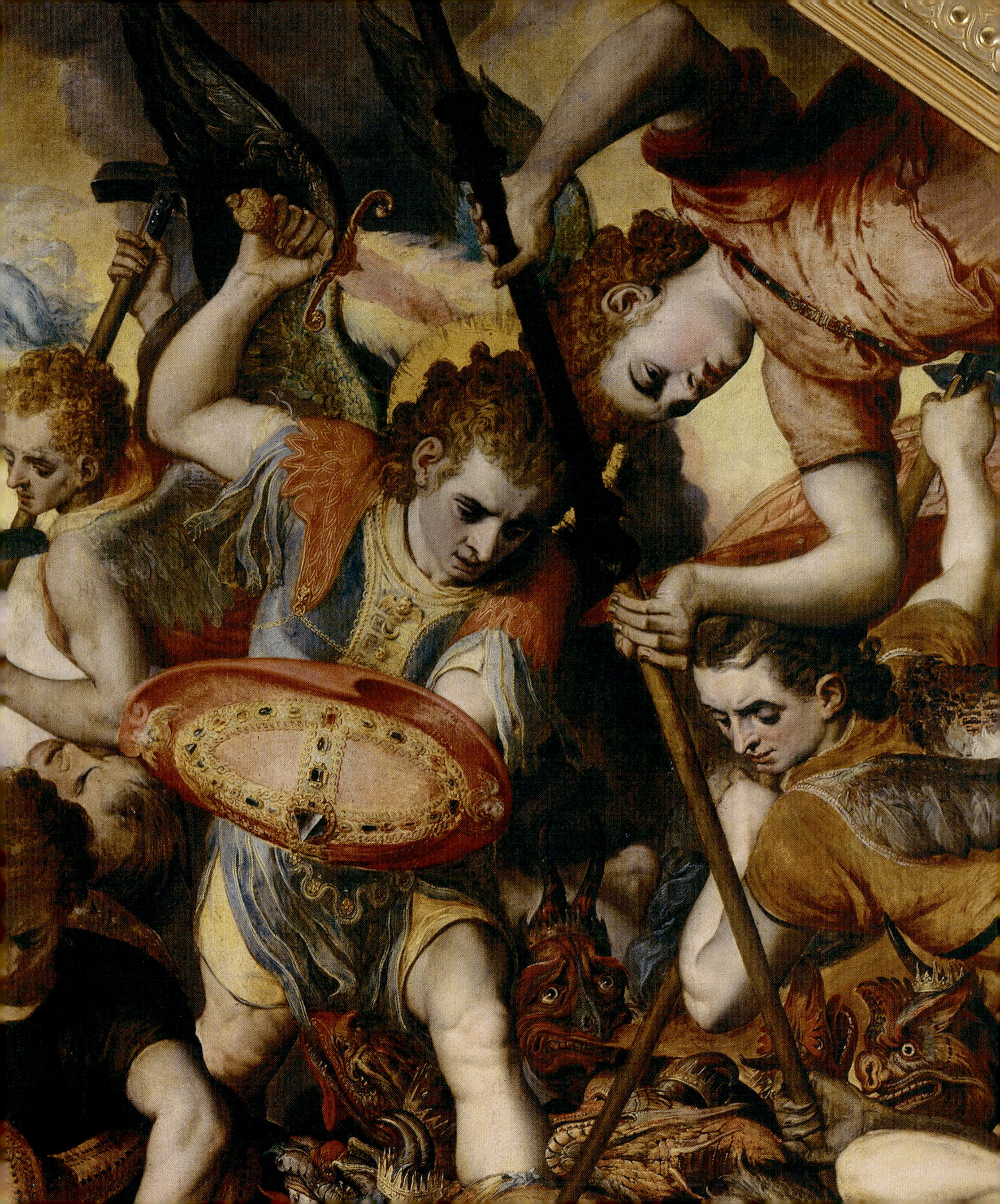

Bibliography: Van Mander 1604, fol. 241
Mensaert 1763, p. 312
Descamps 1769, p. 142
Kerken van Antwerpen 1774, pp. 10–11
Musée Central 1801, p. 51, no. 288
Piot 1883, pp. 18–19, 90, 298, 313, 380–381, 395, 398, 403, 410, 465
Van den Branden 1883, p. 183
Winkler 1924, p. 316
Zuntz 1929, pp. 4–5
Friedländer 1924–1937, XIII, pp. 62–63, 153, no. 129
Sulzberger 1938
Prims 1938–1939, XIII, pp. 384–389
Van den Nieuwenhuizen 1962, pp. 75, 80, 82
Vlieghe 1971, p. 279
Van Brabant 1974, pp. 28, 36, 72, 84, 228
Van de Velde 1975A, pp. 209–213
Vervaet 1976, pp. 207–208
Van de Velde 1993A, pp. 185–186
Grieten & Bungeneers 1996, p. 363

once pointed out to him the Fencers' altar with the painting of *Saint George and the Dragon* by de Vos, to recommend the young painter to him.[8] Ortelius (or Rademacher) was probably mistaken about the subject of the work, confusing the killing of the dragon by Saint George with the killing of the dragon by Saint Michael. The painting by de Vos certainly had Saint Michael, the guild's patron saint, as its subject. An inventory of the Fencers' chamber, made on 21 October 1581, mentions both an altarpiece *with* side panels ('a large scene of Saint Michael with two doors') and one *without* side panels ('a scene of Saint Michael without doors').[9] It may be inferred – although there is no proof – that the first triptych was by de Vos (and had been removed earlier that year at the closing of the church) and that the second painting was the *Fall of the Rebel Angels* by Floris, whose side panels had, therefore, already disappeared in 1566, when the painting sustained great damage in the Iconoclastic Fury.[10] When after 1585 the guild reinstated its altar, it was not de Vos' but Floris' work that was transferred to the cathedral. It remained there until the end of the 18th century. In none of the scarce descriptions of the altarpiece from the 17th century the side panels are mentioned.[11] In a renovation of the altar that took place after 1650, the panel was included in a portico altar, flanked by life-sized marble statues of Joshua and Gideon. Both statues still survive in the cathedral and are attributed to Artus Quellinus the Younger (1625–1670) and Hubert van den Eynde (1594–1661), who are also thought to have been responsible for building the portico altar. It should be noted that the work by Hubertus van den Eynde was only completed after his death by his son Norbertus (1628–1704).[12] The trapezium-shaped enlargement of the panel may have been added to the top during this renovation.

The principal motif of the painting is the battle between the archangel Michael and the rebel angels, as described in the Revelation of John (12, 7–9). With his flaming sword, Michael attacks Satan, the leader of the rebellion, who impotently defends himself with an iron hook. His bestial nature is emphasised by his wild boar's head and the eagle's beak covering his genitals. His followers defend themselves with knives, flaming torches, or longbows. By contrast, the archangel's cohorts use weapons that belong to the Fencers' domain: in the top left we see a rapier and a sabre. The latter could be a practice sword of the katzbalger type.[13] To the left of Michael, an angel thrusts a halberd – the weapon from which the guild derives its customary name – into the flank of the seven-headed dragon; with the same weapon, another angel attacks one of the devils. These weapons are depicted with striking truthfulness, probably at the commissioners' explicit request. To the left, deeper in the background, the painting shows the episodes from the Apocalypse (Revelation 12, 1–6) that preceded the battle. The woman with the crown of twelve stars on her head, standing on the crescent moon, escapes the dragon's threat and is taken to heaven.[14]

The painting's most striking characteristic is its unbridled dynamism, which clearly recalls Michelangelo's *Last Judgement* in the Sistine Chapel. This dynamism is rather the result of the painting's subject matter than of the stylistic development of Frans Floris, who in his other works from this period seeks rather to echo Raphael's *maniera*.[15] Literal copies of Michelangelo's motifs, however, cannot be found. In fact, the *Fall of the Rebel Angels* is at least as much a tribute to Albrecht Dürer's series of woodcuts of the *Apocalypse* (fig. 3a)[16] as it is to Michelangelo's monumental *Last Judgement* fresco. Floris directly copied a number of animals' heads from this,[17] and the entwined bodies in the immediate foreground and the grimness of the fight are also inspired by Dürer. It is clear that with this painting – the largest of all the 16th century altarpieces in the cathedral – the Fencers wanted to make a special impression, particularly in what Ann Woollett has called the 'modern' character

8 'specimen exhibens tum valde spectatum, tabulam altaris gladiatorum in aede Deiparae Virginis, qua tam viué representabatur imago Georgij equitis draconem confodientis, ut esset omnibus admirationj' (see note 7).
9 Prims 1938–1939, XIII, p. 388; Van de Velde 1975A, I, p. 212, note 7. The reverse is also possible, that de Vos' painting was the one without side panels. The letter by Rademacher (see note 8) is not explicit in this regard.
10 Freedberg 1992, p. 55.
11 The side panels are not mentioned, either, in the description of the altarpiece by the Jesuit Carolus Scribanius from 1610, although he explicitly states that he saw the painting: 'At ego video apud vos francisci Floris caeli pugnam' (Held 1996, p. 198; see also p. 179).
12 Baudouin 1993, pp. 234, 398, note 75.
13 Puype & De Gryse 2006, pp. 42, 51. My warm thanks to P. De Gryse and N. Peeters for their help with identifying the weapons.
14 For further data on the iconography, see the contribution of M. Gielis in this publication.
15 Van de Velde 2005, pp. 149–162.
16 Strauss 1980, pp. 157–203, nos. 41–55.
17 Ibidem, pp. 175, 179.

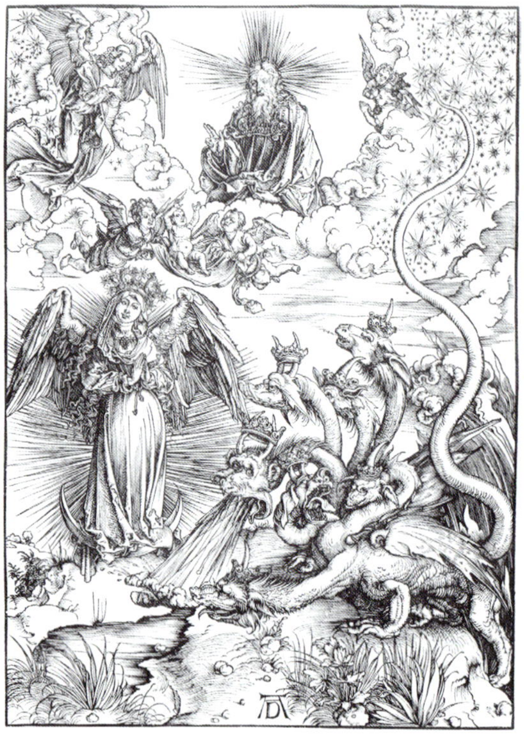

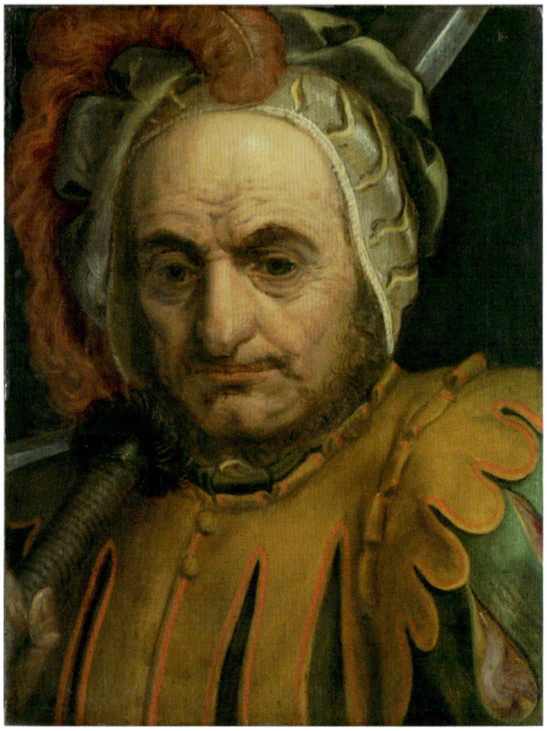

3a
Albrecht Dürer
The Virgin of the Apocalypse
print from the *Apocalypse*

3b
Frans Floris
Head Study of a Man with a Sword
Kassel, Staatliche Gemäldegalerie

of the work.[18] Perhaps this extravagant monumentality was the cause of the controversy in 1567 over Floris' old altarpiece and Maerten de Vos' new one.

As previously mentioned, the side panels of Floris' triptych had already disappeared at an early date. A few 17th century sources describe another aspect of the work, notably that it contained portraits of the guild officials. Carel van Mander mentions in his *Schilderboek* (Book of Painters) from 1604 that on one of the panels the dean of the guild was depicted, with a sword in his hand.[19] The art collector Pieter Stevens (1590–1668) identified two portraits in an annotation of his copy of the *Schilderboek* (Book of Painters): to the left that of Hendrik van Berchem, dean of the guild, and to the right that of Burgomaster van Ursel.[20] Neither van Mander nor Stevens could have seen the panels, so this information must be founded on an oral tradition.

These statements are support by the existence of the *Head Study of a Man with a Sword*, painted by Floris himself, now in the Staatliche Gemäldegalerie in Kassel (fig. 3b).[21] The work shows a man wearing a green jerkin with yellow-brown geers and a yellow bonnet with a red feather on his head. He carries a sword over his shoulder. Its iconography is *so* specific that it is plausible to link this study with one of the side panels of the Fencers' triptych. Weaponry was an important element in the public appearance of the Fencers' guild members. In the guild's statutes from 29 April 1560[22] it may be read that the one hundred able-bodied men who formed the guild corps were required to ensure they were sufficiently armed to fulfil their functions, and moreover that they must present themselves for Processions of the Holy Circumcision and of Our Lady in uniform.

CARL VAN DE VELDE

18 Woollett 2004, pp. 47–49.
19 'In een der deuren hadde hy ghemaeckt den Hooft-man van het Schermers Gildt / met een Slach-sweerdt in de hant / en een bruyne wolck die een aerdighe schaduwe daer in 't werck is brenghende' (In one of the doors he had made the Head-man of the Fencers' Guild / with a Broad-sword in the hand / and a brown cloud which brings a nice shadow into the work) (Van Mander-Miedema 1994–1999, I, p. 223).
20 'Ditto hooftman was Heer (Hendrick) van Berchem, borghemeester tot Antwerpen. Op de rechter syde vanden anderen is den Burghem[eester] van Ursel' (The same headman was Lord (Hendrick) van Berchem, burgomaster of Antwerp. On the right side of the other is the Burgomaster van Ursel) (Briels 1980, p. 212). Lanceloot van Ursel is the only possible identity of 'Burgomaster van Ursel'. He was repeatedly Burgomaster of Antwerp in those years, as was Hendrik van Berchem (Prims 1927–1949, XVI, pp. 198–206; XIX, pp. 289–290).
21 Inv. no. GK 1038. Panel, 47 x 36.5 cm. In the right top, monogram *FFF*; Schnackenburg 1996, I, p. 118; II, pl. 8.
22 SAA (Antwerp City Archives), *Gilden en Ambachten*, no. 4567.

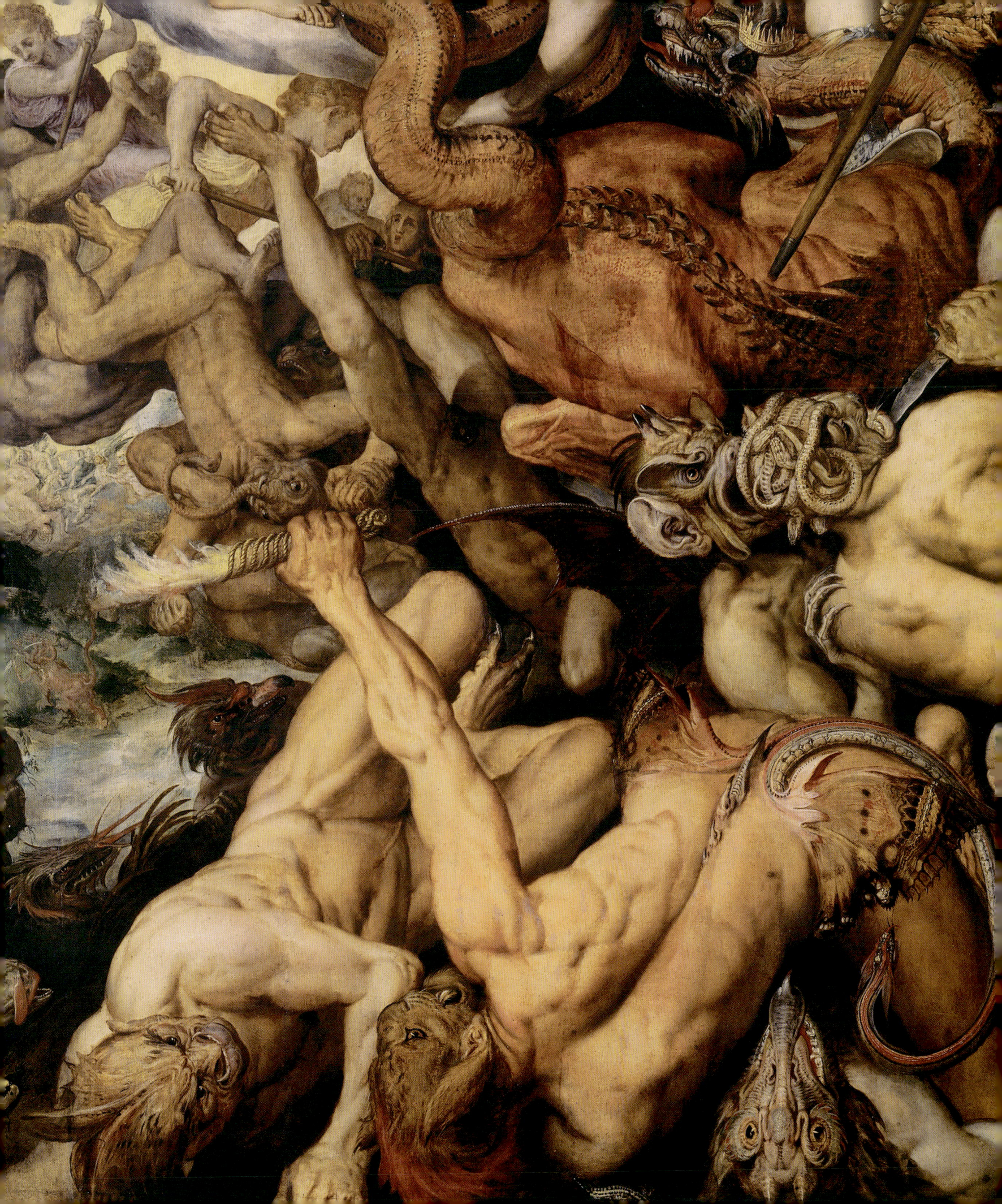

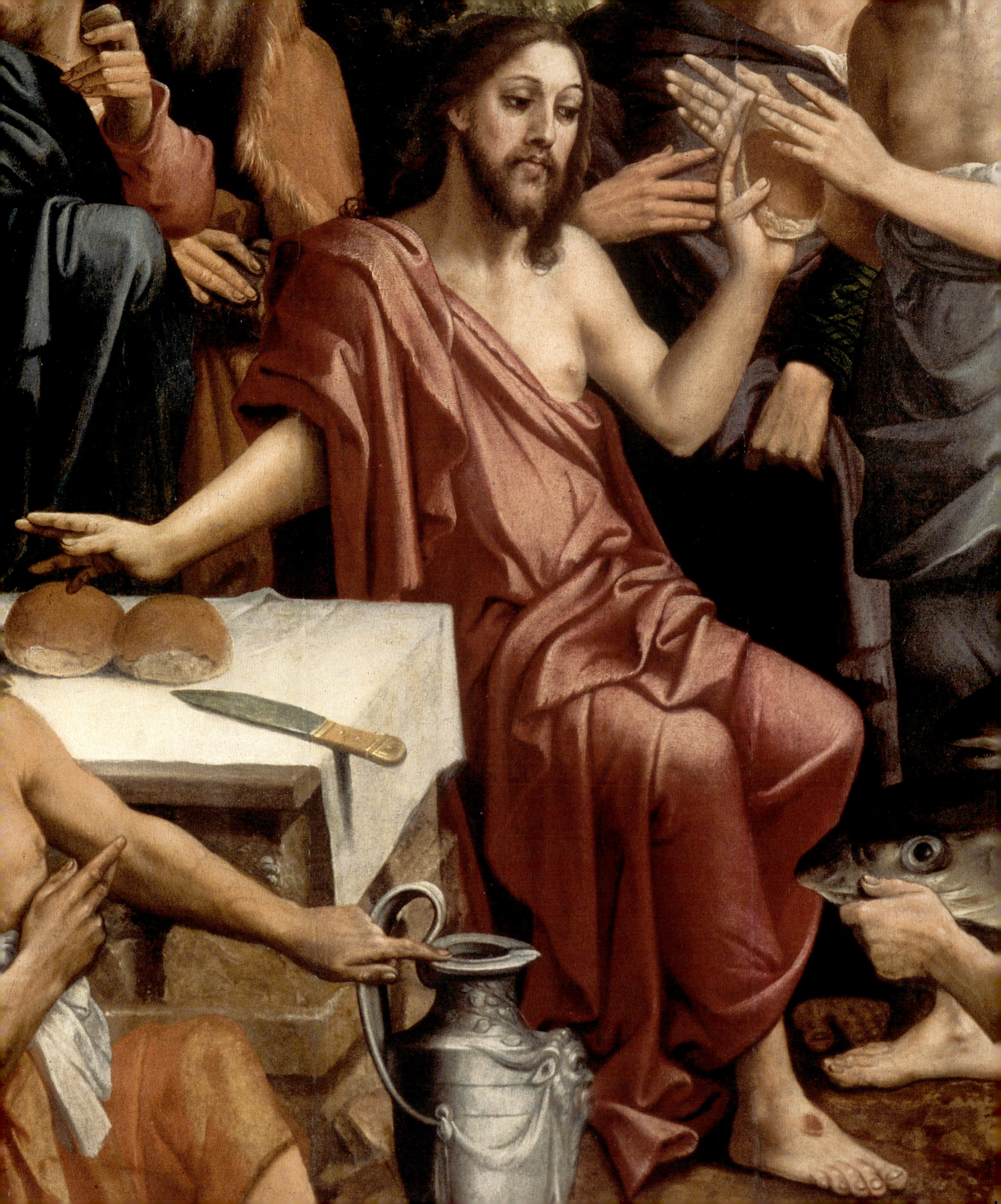

4 Altarpiece of the Fishmongers

Hans van Elburcht

Elburg c. 1500–Antwerp 1571

The Miraculous Draught of Fishes

centre panel

c. 1560

Anonymous

circle of Ambrosius Francken

The Calling of Saints James and John The Miraculous Draught of Fishes

predella

last quarter of the 16th century

Oil on panel
centre panel: 190 x 167 cm
predella scenes: 50 x 69 cm

Unsigned

Antwerp, Cathedral of Our Lady, inv. 925

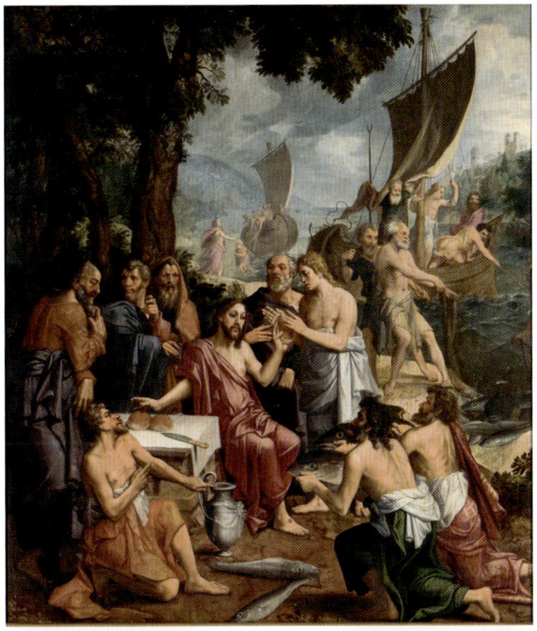

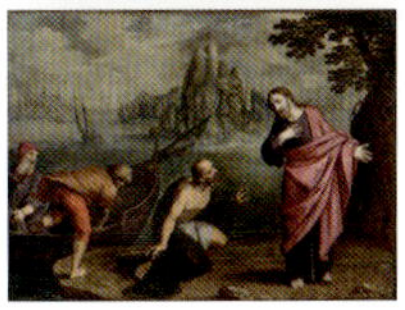

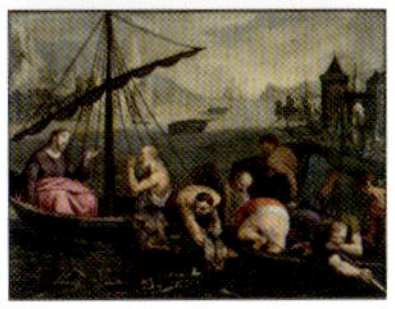

Provenance: c. 1560 commissioned by the Antwerp fishmongers for their altar in the Antwerp cathedral; adapted to the new altar construction at the end of the 16th century; offered and sold as separate lots in an auction of church furniture on 8 November 1798;[1] in 1800 the centre panel and three statues of the altar were restituted;[2] the side panels apparently remained in private hands; in 1841 the centre panel was 'rediscovered' in the cathedral by Th. Van Lerius, the predella panels were in the cathedral archive at that time; thereafter on display in their original context in the cathedral.[3]

Hans van Elburcht was, as his name indicates, from Elburg near Haarlem. In 1535 he moved to Antwerp, where he became a free master in Antwerp's Guild of Saint Luke a year later.[4] He probably worked with Jan Mandyn from 1536 to 1553. This connection may offer an explanation for the affinity of his work with that of Pieter Aertsen, who lodged with Mandyn for a while.[5] According to several witnesses, he collaborated with Frans Floris. In 1540 and 1551, Hanneken der Kynderen and Melsen Salebos respectively joined him as apprentices.[6]

Circa 1560 the Antwerp Fishmongers commissioned *The Miraculous Draught of Fishes* triptych from Hans van Elburcht for their altar in Antwerp cathedral.[7] This work reflects the craft's veneration of its patron saints, Peter (on the centre panel) and Philip and James (on the side panels).[8] The predella scenes, which were painted later and are attributed to an anonymous artist from the circle of Ambrosius Francken, depict the calling of the apostles – who were fishermen, which thus harmonises with the main scene and also refers to the professional activities of the craft members.

The centre panel of the altarpiece illustrates the subsequent scenes of the story of the miraculous draught of fishes, as described in the Gospel of John (John 21: 1–14). The miracle takes place during the appearance of the resurrected Christ before his disciples at Lake Tiberias. The miraculous draught itself is depicted in the background. While the apostles haul the filled nets aboard, Peter walks towards Christ on the lake shore. In the central zone the rich catch is brought ashore under Peter's command. In the foreground Christ and his disciples are seated around a table. The Gospel describes how Jesus called his followers to him after the miraculous draught and asked them to bring along some fish. He broke the bread he had brought with him and gave it to them, together with the fish. Then he appointed Peter as chief shepherd or head of the church. The young beardless disciple to whom Christ offers the bread is John, who would later write the story down.

1 Van der Straelen 1770–1819, VI, p. 295; Delvingt 2002, p. 168.
2 Theunissens 1892, p. 103; Grieten & Bungeneers 1996, p. 378; Delvingt 2002, p. 170.
3 Van Lerius 1841, p. 1841; Delvingt 2002, pp. 170–171.
4 Van Mander 1604, fol. 205a; Rombouts & Van Lerius 1864–1872, I, p. 116.
5 Wescher 1935, pp. 127–128.
6 Rombouts & Van Lerius 1864–1872, I, p. 116.
7 Van Mander 1604, fol. 205a; Descamps 1769, pp. 140–141; Hoogewerff 1941–1942, pp. 445–447; Aerts 1993, p. 37; Lammertse 1994, p. 393; Grieten & Bungeneers 1996, pp. 375–378; Delvingt 2002, pp. 168–183.
8 Prims 1938–1939, XIII, p. 425; Aerts 1993, p. 37. On the position of the altar of the Fishmongers, see Aerts 1993, p. 37, no. 55. Aerts includes an 18th century plan of the cathedral with indication of its altars and their saints (see also pp. 34–35 in this publication). The altar of the Fishmongers was situated at the first pillar on the right of the nave.

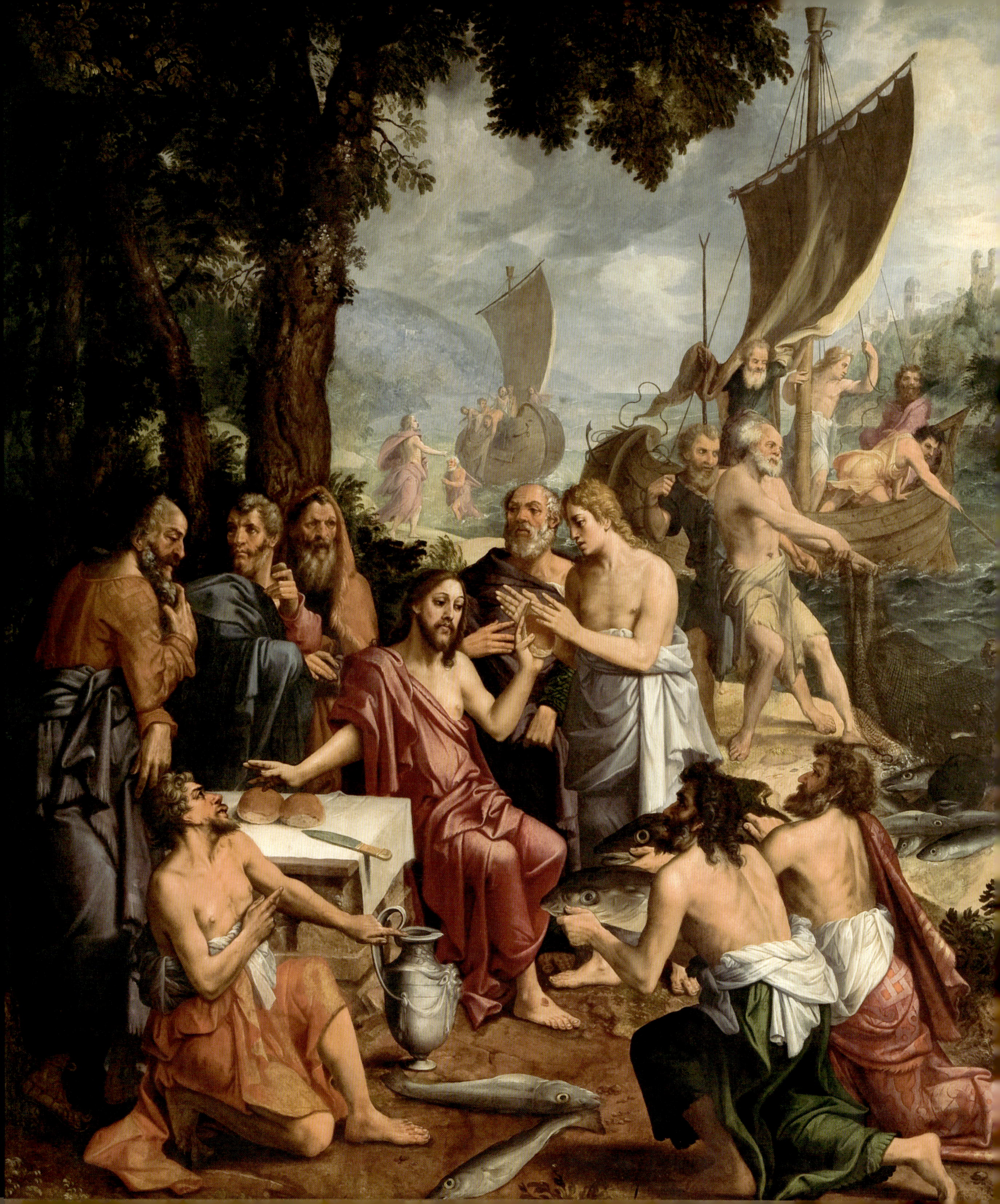

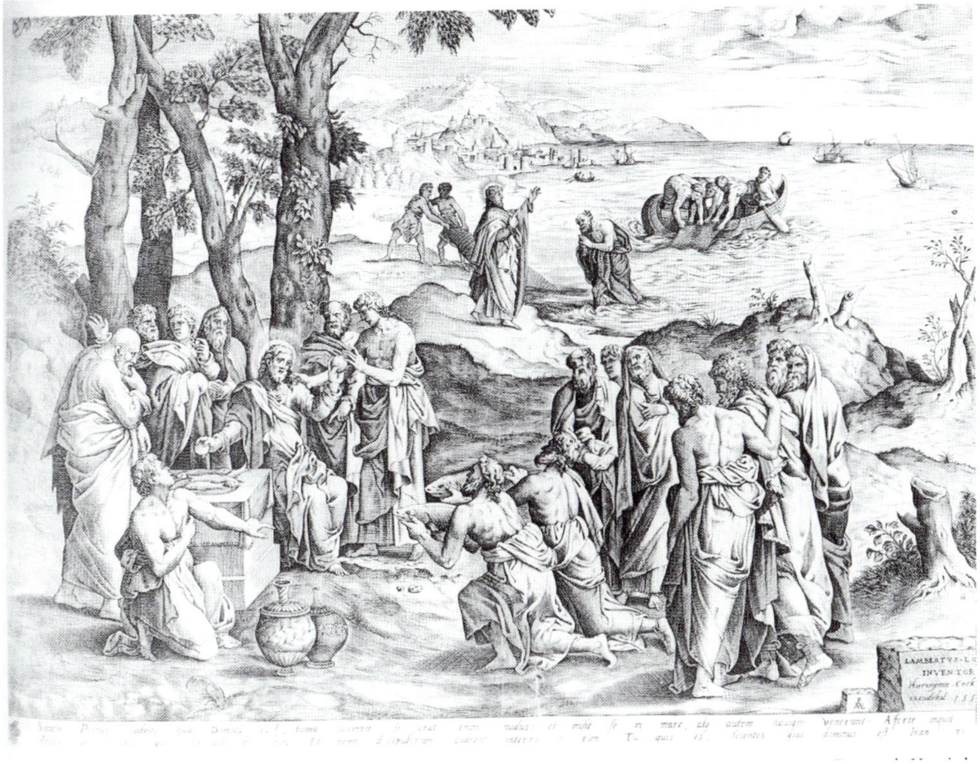

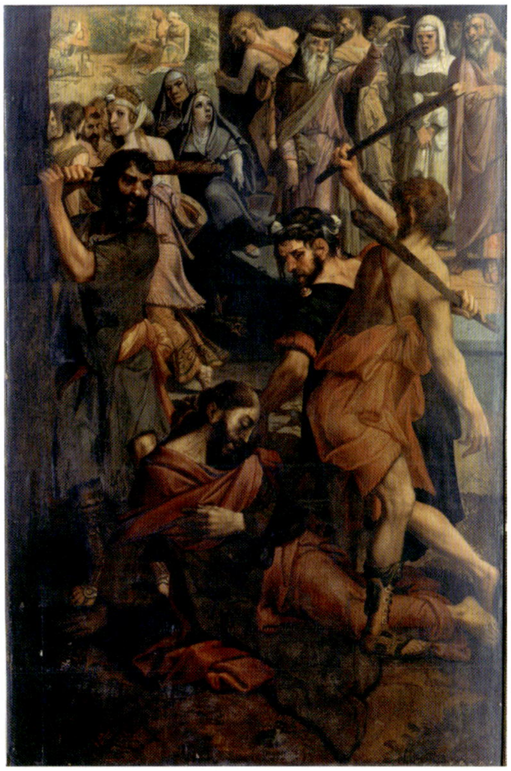

4a
Pieter van der Heyden after Lambert Lombard
The Miraculous Draught of Fishes, print

4b
Hans van Elburcht
Martyrdom of Saint James the Less
Saint-Ghislain, Monastery of the Sisters of Mercy

Bibliography: Van Mander 1604, fol. 205a
Beschrijvinge 1751, p. 2 (p. 11)
Mensaert 1763, pp. 223, 224
Descamps 1769, pp. 140–141
Kerken van Antwerpen 1774, p. 50
Van der Straelen 1770–1819, VI, p. 295
Van Lerius 1841, p. 10
Theunissens 1892, p. 103
Wescher 1935, pp. 127–129
Prims 1938–1939, XIII, pp. 422–423, 425
Hoogewerff 1941–1942, pp. 445–447, 523, 539
Van Herck 1951, p. 42
Genaille 1954, p. 287
Van den Nieuwenhuizen 1957, p. 110
Van Puyvelde 1963, pp. 39–47 (as Adam van Noort?)
Bruyn 1966, pp. 2–12, 39
Van Brabant 1972, pp. 33, 62
Van Brabant 1974, pp. 27, 49, 227
Van de Velde 1993A, p. 186
Lammertse 1994, pp. 390–395, no. 93
Grieten & Bungeneers 1996, pp. 363, 375–378

Hans van Elburcht based his work on a print by Pieter van der Heyden from 1556, after a drawing by Lambert Lombard (fig. 4a).[9] The painting by Van Elburcht was, in its turn, a source of inspiration for a *Miraculous Draught of Fishes* by Joachim Beuckelaer in 1563, now in Los Angeles (J.P. Getty Museum).[10] Both data support the hypothetical dating c. 1560.

The left side panel, now in Rotterdam (Boijmans Van Beuningen Museum; fig. 4c), depicts the *Baptism of the Ethiopian Eunuch by Saint Philip* (Acts 8, 26–40).[11] The painting, formerly attributed to Pieter Aertsen, was attributed to Hans van Elburcht by J. Bruyn in 1966 and identified as a side panel of the *Miraculous Draught*.[12] It is possible that Van Elburcht based it on a lost painting by Aertsen, which is better known through a preliminary drawing attributed to Aertsen in Paris (Institut néerlandais, Foundation Custodia).[13] On the back of the panel, under a uniform grey paint layer, there is a painted portrait of *Saint Philip*.[14] As a consequence of shortening the panel, the saint's head is missing.

The right side panel, currently in Saint-Ghislain (Monastery of the Sisters of Mercy; fig. 4b), displays the *Martyrdom of Saint James the Less* (Jacobus de Voragine, *Legenda Aurea*).[15] Some figures are based on personages from the aforementioned print by Pieter van der Heyden.[16] The verso probably originally held a portrait of *Saint James the Less*, but this is lost because the panel has been planed down.

On two of the surviving predella paintings, scenes of the calling of the first disciples of Jesus are depicted.[17] The small left panel with *The Calling of the*

9 Denhaene 1990, pp. 234–235; Lammertse 1994, p. 393; Delvingt 2002, pp. 175–178.
10 Lammertse 1994, p. 393.
11 In 1938, W.A. Engelbrecht donated the left side panel to the Museum Boijmans Van Beuningen. Amsterdam 1939, no. 128a; Hoogewerff 1941–1942, pp. 523, 539; Genaille 1954, p. 287; Bruyn 1966, pp. 2–40; Braman-Buchan 1975, p. 228, no. 14R; Kloek 1990A, p. 25, n. 25, p. 26, n. 28; Kloek 1990B, p. 145; Boon 1992, p. 6; Lammertse 1994, no. 93, pp. 390–395; Delvingt 2002, pp. 168, 173, 174.
12 Bruyn 1966, p. 4.
13 Kloek 1990B, p. 145; Boon 1992, p. 6; Lammertse 1994, pp. 393–394, fig. c; Delvingt 2002, p. 177. Delvingt discusses the attribution of the drawing to Van Elburcht himself.
14 Lammertse 1994, p. 393.
15 De Bettignies 1867, pp. 221–222; Soil De Moriamé 1931, p. 242; Honnis 1984, p. 177; Tondreau & Huvelle, 1982, pp. 227–228; Delvingt 2002, pp. 167–186.
16 Delvingt 2002, p. 176.
17 Descamps 1769, pp. 140–141.

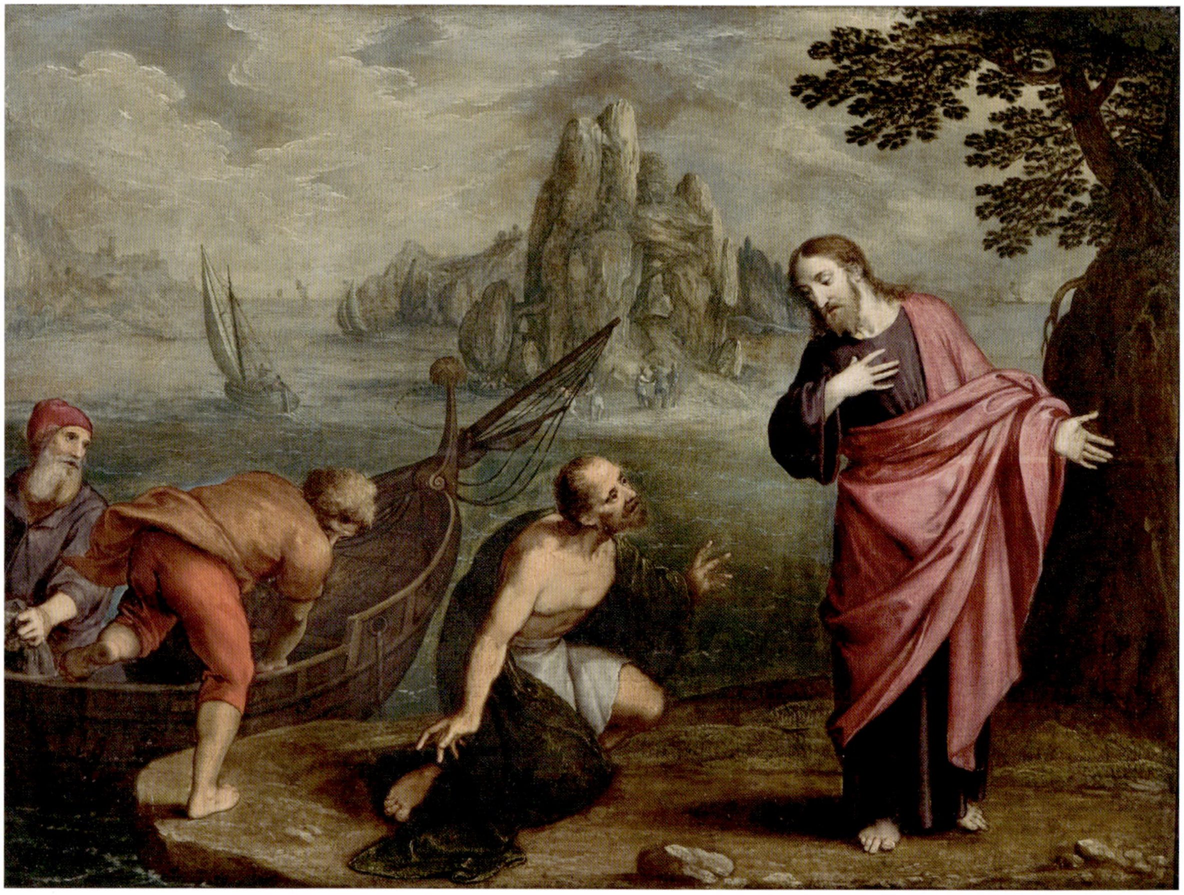

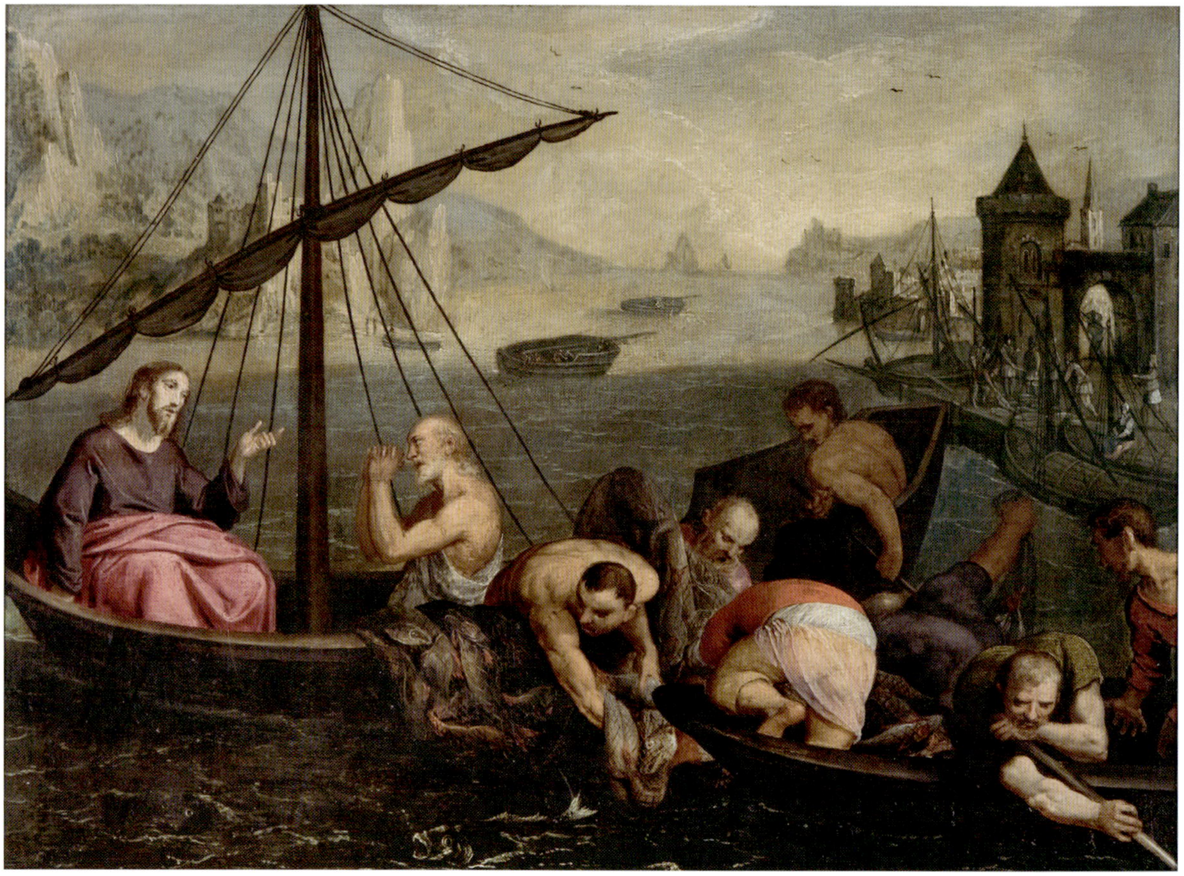

Apostles James and John (Matthew 4: 18–22 and Mark 1: 16–20) shows Christ on the shore of Lake Galilee inviting the two fishermen to become his followers. The small right panel depicts the *Miraculous Draught* from the Gospel of Luke (Luke 5: 1–11). The central predella panel, which is now lost, showed a *Crucifixion with the Virgin, Saint Mary Magdalene and Saint John*.[18]

The various panels of the Fishmongers' altarpiece are related, both in composition and in style.[19] While the main personages in the *Miraculous Draught* are placed in a triangle with Saint Peter at the top, in the *Baptism of the Ethiopian Eunuch by Saint Philip* and the *Martyrdom of Saint James the Less* they are put in a semicircle. The composition was designed on the basis of a detailed drawing; the underdrawing is visible in many places.[20] The figures show similar facial features: large eye sockets, broad eyebrows, and large noses. They move rather awkwardly and their clothing is characterised by a richly decorative hang of folds. The foreground is generally characterised by the use of saturated colours, while in the background pastel colours dominate.

The painting has not preserved its original appearance from c. 1560. Both the centre and side panels were apparently reduced for a renovation of the Fishmongers' altar in the last quarter of the 16th century, to fit them into the new altar construction.[21] Possibly, the anonymous small predella panels date from this renovation phase. The new composition of the altarpiece is visible in an anonymous interior view of the cathedral from c. 1630.[22] On it, we can see how the whole was designed in the form of a portico altar with Corinthian pilasters, a three-part predella, a crown piece with alternating metopes and triglyphs, and on top of the cornice, statues of the patron saints.

CHRISTINE VAN MULDERS

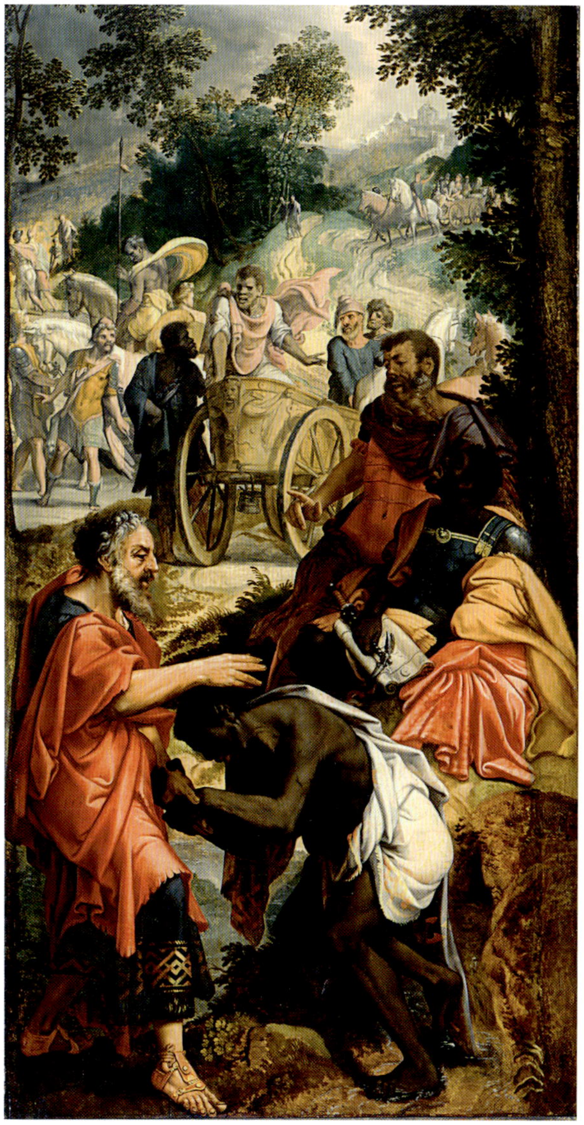

4c
Hans van Elburcht
Baptism of the Ethiopian Eunuch by Saint Philip
Rotterdam, Museum Boijmans Van Beuningen

18 For further data on the iconography, see the contribution of M. Gielis in this publication.
19 Delvingt 2002, p. 174.
20 The underdrawing is visible through infrared detection and in some places with the naked eye. Lammertse 1994, p. 291.
21 Taking into account the intact width of the left and right side panel, it is possible to determine that the centre panel was narrowed by 30 cm. Both the centre panel and side panels were reduced in height by approximately 25 cm, calculated on the basis of the 'decapitation' of the portrait of *Saint Philip* on the back of the left side panel. After the dispersal of the altar in 1789, the right side panel was reduced in height for a second time. Bruyn 1966, p. 5, n. 7; Lammertse 1994, p. 393; Delvingt 2002, p. 173. Delvingt offers a reconstruction of the original altarpiece.
22 Lammertse 1994, p. 292, fig. b; Delvingt 2002, pp. 170, 172, fig. 4.

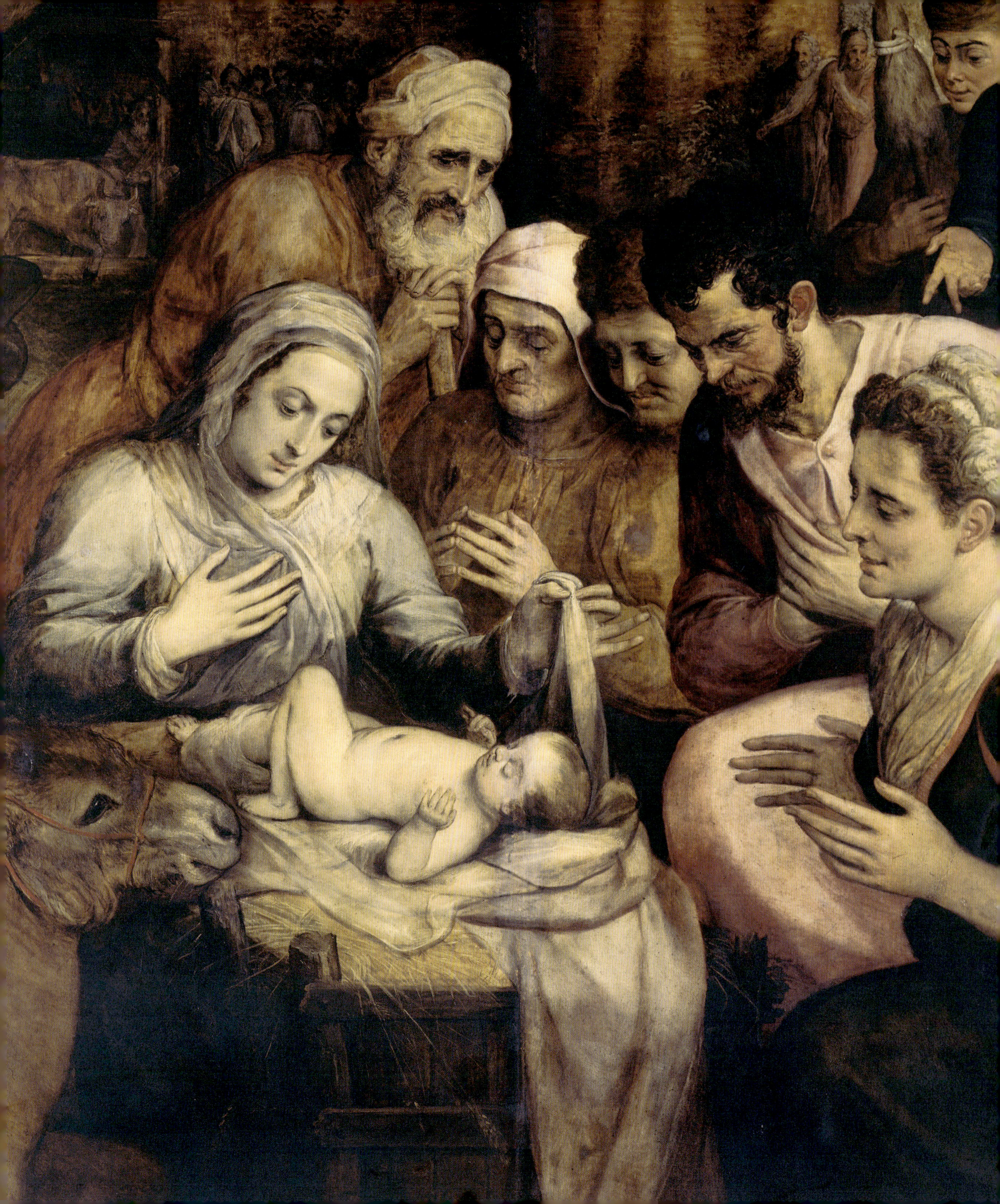

5 Altarpiece of the Gardeners

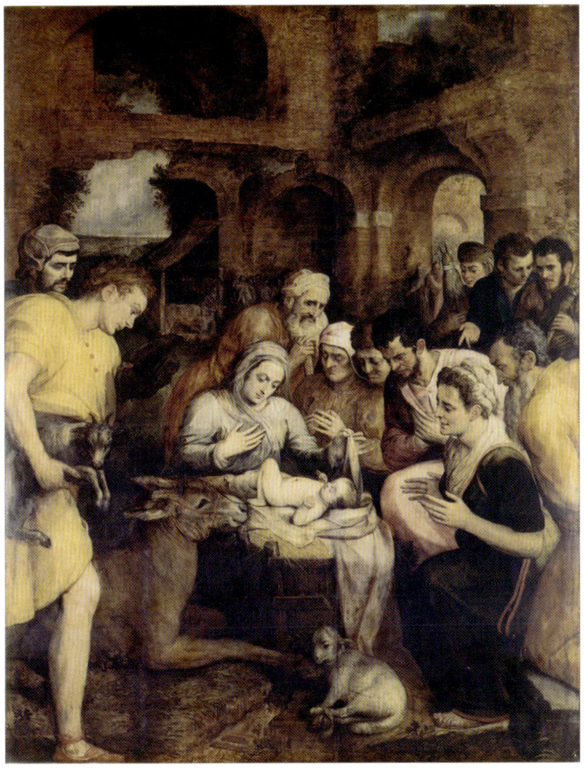

Frans Floris

Antwerp 1519/20–Antwerp 1570

The Adoration of the Shepherds

1568

Oil on panel, 249 x 193 cm

Unsigned

Antwerp, Koninklijk Museum voor Schone Kunsten, inv. 113

Provenance: commissioned by the Antwerp Gardeners' craft; from 1568 to 1581 on the altar of the craft in the Antwerp cathedral; from 1581 to 1585 in the chamber of the craft (?); from 1585 to 1625 placed on the high altar of the cathedral; from 1625 to 1798 returned to the Gardeners' altar; in 1798 transferred to the École Centrale des Deux-Nèthes in the abolished Discalced Monastery; from then until 1811 in the Academy in the Exchange building; thereafter it was in the Museum in the former Friars Minor Monastery; foundational holding of the Museum.

The Antwerp craft of the Gardeners, Fruiterers, and Basket Weavers existed as early as 1431. A document from 1491 confirms that their altar in the Church of Our Lady was dedicated to Saint Agatha. The association of the craft with this saint appears to have come about more or less by coincidence. According to Floris Prims it ended with the destruction of the altar in the fire of 1533. Afterwards – the oldest reference dates from 1537 – the craft services were performed at the Altar of Our Lady on the Branch (Onze-Lieve-Vrouw-op-het-Stoksken), a miraculous statue that was the object of special veneration in the church, particularly in the late 15th century.[1] Interest in this patron seems to have slackened in the 16th century, which might suggest an explanation for the fact that at the resumption of services after the fire of 1533 this altar seems to have been shared with the Gardeners. In 1537 the altar, including the tabernacle with a statue of the Virgin, was renovated by a sculptor. It was profaned during the Iconoclastic Fury of 1566, so a new consecration took place on 15 June 1567.[2] In that same year the renovation of the altar as a whole was begun: craft members were paid by the chapter for woodwork and ironwork, and one of the canons, Thomas du Terne, was willing to have a triptych painted by Frans Floris – the undisputed leader of the Antwerp Painting School at that moment – at his own expense.[3] *The Adoration of the Shepherds,* the subject of the centre panel, was a sort of compromise between Marian devotion and rural life, to which the shepherds referred.

Nothing is known about the side panels of this altarpiece. We only know that it was a triptych, since on 10 September 1568 the painter Dirk van de Velde was paid to decorate the doors and the tabernacle.[4] The altar stood in the church nave at the third pillar in the north transept, surrounded by an altar enclosure. On 30 November 1568, a cabinetmaker was paid to screen off the altar at the back and on both sides.[5] This date may be taken as a *terminus ante quem* for the execution of Floris' painting, which was already

1 Prims 1938–1939, XIII, pp. 337–339.
2 Idem, p. 340.
3 Van de Velde 1975A, I, pp. 325–326.
4 'Item a° lxviii, x september, betaelt Dierick vande Velde, schilder, vande tafel [altar piece] te stofferen van buyten, alst blyckt bij quitantie, vii lb. x sc. Item den selven bet[aald] vanden dueren metten back te stofferen per quitan[tie], i lb. x sc.' (Also a° lxviii, x september, is paid to Dierick vande Velde, painter, for the outside decoration of the table, as is proved by quittance, vii lb. x sc. Furthermore is paid the same for decorating the doors and the tabernacle by quittance, i lb. x sc.) (KAA [Antwerp Cathedral Archives], Accounts, 1567–1568, fol. 38; Van de Velde 1975A, I, p. 462, doc. 58).
5 'Item denselven [Anthoni Boshof] vande tafel achter te schutten, ut patet per quitantie, iii lb. xv sc.' en 'Item bet[aald] Anthoni Boshof vanden outaer van beyde zyden af te schutten, na vuytwysen der celen, ii lb.' (Also the same to [Anthoni Boshof] for screening off the table [altar piece] at the back, as is proved by quittance, iii lb. xv sc.' and 'Also is paid to Anthoni Boshof to board off the altar on both sides, as proves the quittance, ii lb.) (Van de Velde 1975A, I, p. 464, doc. 60).

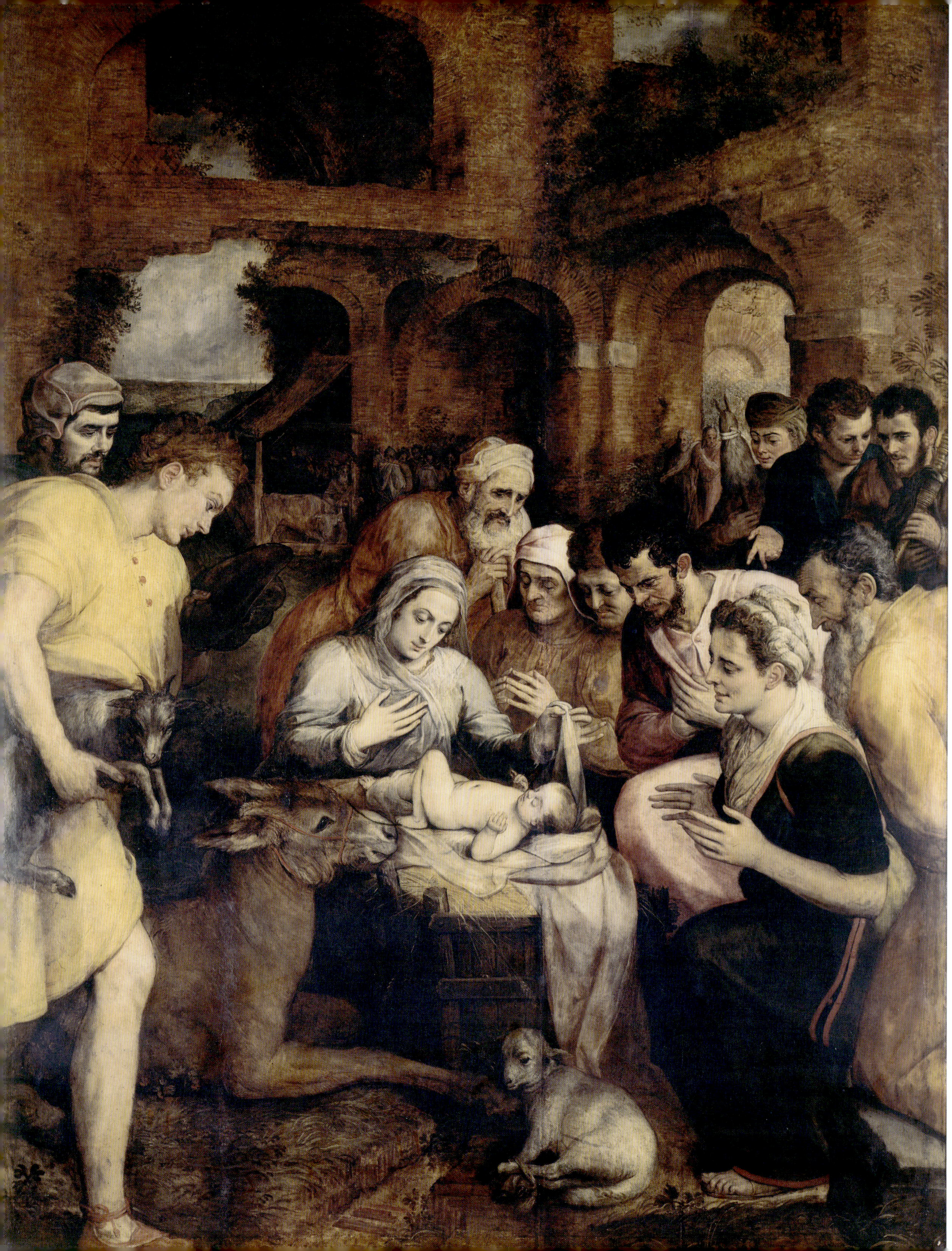

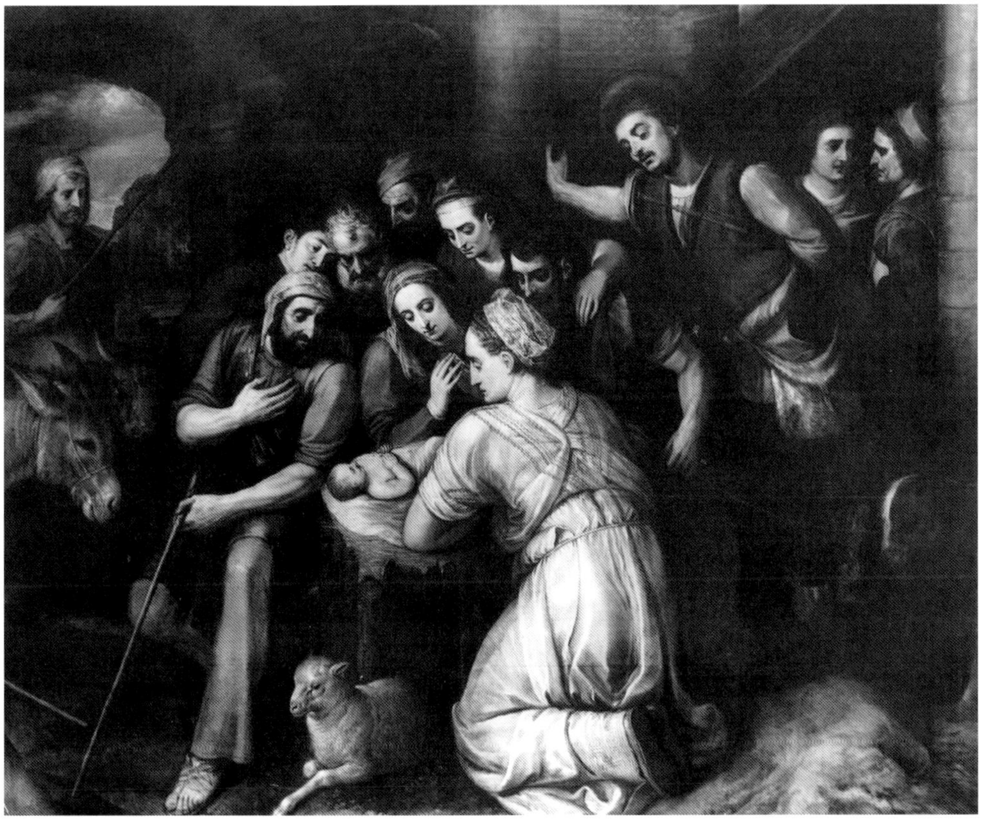

5a
Frans Floris
The Adoration of the Shepherds
Prague, Národní Muzeum

placed on the altar at that time. It can therefore be dated in the years 1567–1568.

In contrast to his earlier *Adoration of the Shepherds* in the Prague Museum[6] (fig. 5a), in which Mary is depicted along with the shepherds in adoration before the Child, here she shows him to a group of common men and women who arrive from different directions. At the left a shepherd offers a small billy goat as a present and in the foreground lies a lamb that was offered by one of the visitors. Other than this, the figures are not explicitly identified as shepherds, as they more clearly were in the earlier painting. In that work, some men have a staff in hand or carry a bag, both of which are obviously shepherds' attributes. In the Antwerp altarpiece the worshippers are younger and older men and women, who express their profound adoration, attracted by the Child in the crib filled with straw. The crib stands in the ruin of a brick building with classical round arches and niches, which emphasises the sacred character of the event.

The painting did not remain long in its original spot. On 22 June the Gardeners asked, together with other guilds and crafts, permission to the city magistrate to clear their altar. Shortly afterwards, the triptych was removed from the cathedral.[7] We can assume that the centre and side panels were transferred to the craft chamber. Then, after the conquest of Antwerp by Alexander Farnese, the guilds and crafts were summoned to reinstate their altars in the cathedral. However, the Gardeners did not use Floris' *Adoration of the Shepherds* for this purpose but a new altarpiece with the *Creation of Adam and Eve*, perhaps because the reference to the Garden of Eden was better suited to their craft. There is almost no information on this new altarpiece. We do not know the artist, or the precise date of its creation, and the work itself disappeared from the church later, when, as will be explained below, Floris' *Adoration of the Shepherds* returned to its old place on the Gardeners' altar.[8]

Meanwhile, Floris' painting was given a new destination. It was placed on the high altar as a replacement of the *Assumption of the Virgin*, a work by the same artist, which had disappeared at the closing of the church in 1581. Floris had painted that triptych between 1561 and 1564 and had delivered a newer version of it in 1567, after the original had been heavily damaged in the Iconoclastic Fury. It is not clear whether he delivered an entirely new work or repaired the old one. One indication in favour of this last supposition may be that the painter, who was paid 100 Brabantian pounds in 1561 for the centre panel of the altarpiece, with an additional 64.5 pounds for the side panels in 1564, received only 27.5 pounds for the new one in 1567.[9]

In 1585 there was apparently an urgent need to repair the high altar of the church. Since there was no painting of the *Assumption of the Virgin* available, it was decided to replace it with the Gardeners' altarpiece. Like the vanished altarpiece, this painting put the Virgin Mary at the centre; it was by the same artist; and since the Gardeners had chosen a different altarpiece, it was available. Of course, the argument

Bibliography: Van Mander 1604, fol. 242
Beschrijvinge 1751, p. 10 (15)
Mensaert 1763, pp. 242, 243
Descamps 1769, p. 152
Kerken van Antwerpen 1774, p. 28
Rooses 1882, p. 69
Philippen 1924, pp. 309, 324, 325
Zuntz 1929, pp. 51–53, 67, 101
Friedländer 1924–1937, XIII, p. 153, no. 13
Prims 1938–1939, XIII, pp. 337–347
Van de Velde 1961
Van Brabant 1974, pp. 39, 68, 219
Van de Velde 1975A, pp. 325–327, no. 187
Vervaet 1976, pp. 209–210
Van de Velde 1993A, p. 188
Grieten & Bungeneers 1996, pp. 363–364

6 Van de Velde 1975A, I, p. 250, no. 107; II, fig. 49.
7 Prims 1938–1939, XIII, p. 340.
8 This painting stood on the Gardeners' altar in the cathedral of Our Lady only until 1626. Shortly before 16 August 1625, the craft regained the original altarpiece by Floris, or at least its centre panel (see below, note 15), and decided to replace it on its altar. The *Creation of Adam and Eve* was removed from the church after the chapter had given permission on 3 April 1626 ('Comparuerunt Magistri altaris Hortulanorum et petierunt sibi restituere picturam quae est de creatione Adami et Evae, nuper ex altari eorum depositam, et placuit dominis ut de gratia capituli illam picturam possint auferre' [KAA (Antwerp Cathedral Archives), Acta Capituli, V, p. 110; Van de Velde 1975A, I, p. 498, doc. 121]). This is the only known document about this painting, which is never mentioned anywhere again afterwards.
9 Van de Velde 1975A, I, pp. 280–282.

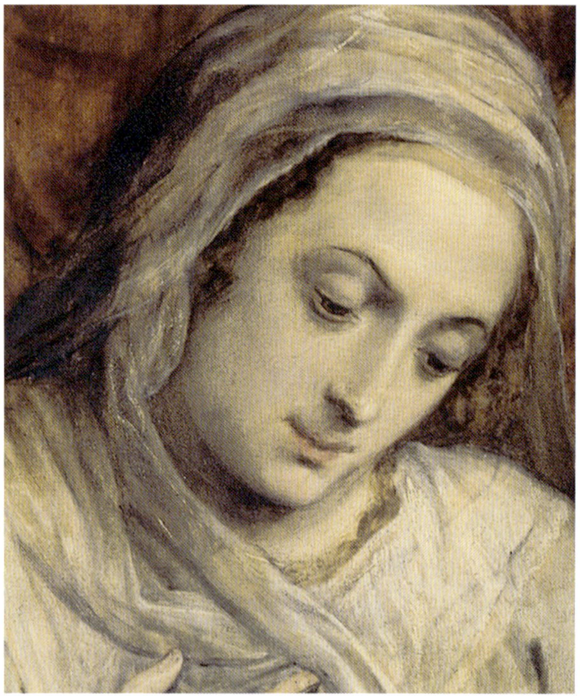

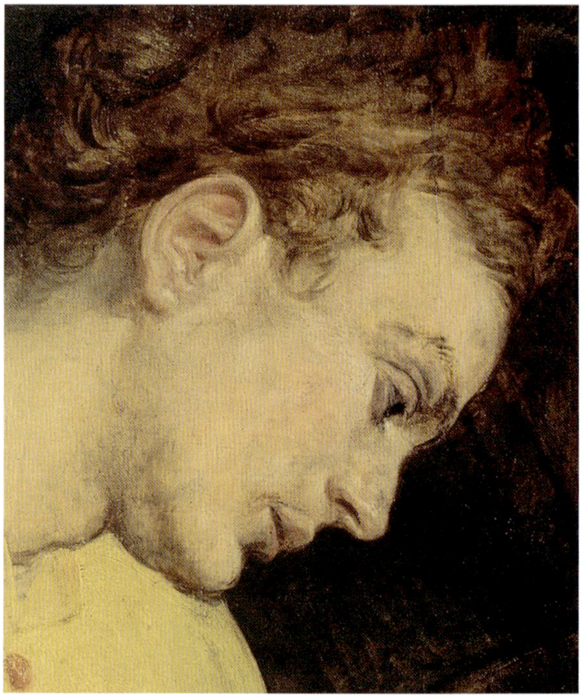

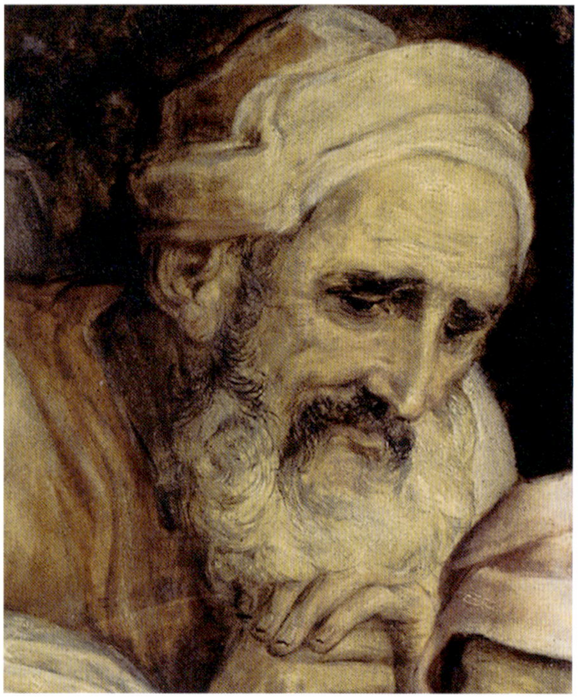

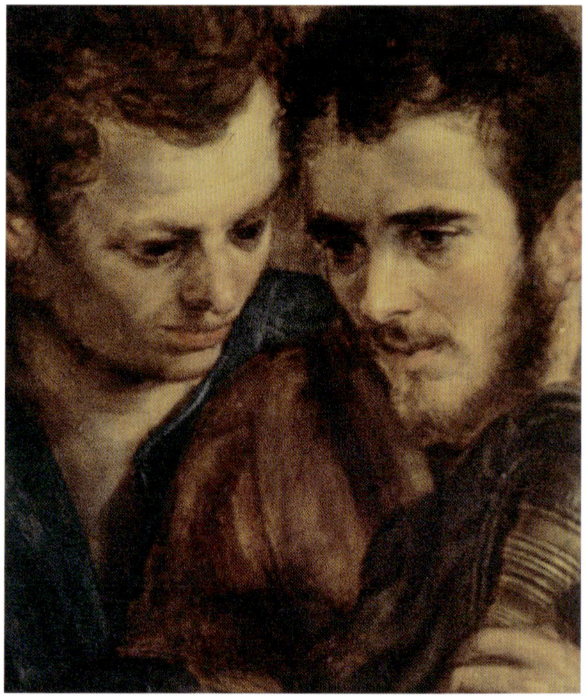

can also be inverted. Perhaps the Gardeners abandoned their work at the request of the chapter and were therefore forced to have a new altarpiece painted. In either case, placing the *Adoration of the Shepherds* on the high altar must have been seen as a temporary measure. Undoubtedly, adaptations were necessary for the new purpose of the painting. Thus, in 1588, the painter Hubert Beda was paid to decorate the predella.[10]

As time advanced, Floris' painting on the high altar must have become an ever more obvious anachronism in comparison to the monumental altarpieces that gradually received places in the cathedral after 1585, such as, for instance, Rubens' *Descent from the Cross* (cat. 11). Initially, the means for a new high altar were lacking, and the *Adoration of the Shepherds* ultimately remained on the high altar for forty years, to the Gardeners' growing dissatisfaction. They attempted to recover their painting repeatedly, every time they were informed that there were established plans for a new high altar. Thus, in 1613, there was a project to have Rubens paint a large triptych, of the same size as the *Raising of the Cross*. On 22 April of the same year, the chapter ordered the dean, the scholastic, and the provisor, to pay a visit to Saint Walburgis' Church to view the new altar which had been erected under its tower in honour of the patron saint Walburga.[11] The Gardeners must have known of these plans, because they addressed an appeal to the chapter to recover their painting. However, the chapter replied that it was not certain the painting actually belonged to the craft, suggesting that it may originally have been paid for with the alms that were collected for Our Lady on the Branch (Onze-Lieve-Vrouw-op-het-Stoksken). This would have to be investigated first.[12] The chapter apparently sought to gain time with its evasive answer. In any case, this first campaign for a new high altar, which had been initiated in 1611, petered out in 1613.[13]

In 1618, *modelli* by Rubens were again presented to the chapter[14] and again the Gardeners filed their request. At this, the chapter, without admitting that the craft was the owner of the painting, announced that the church fabric would provide a new high altar and would allocate the painting concerned to whoever appeared to be the rightful owner.[15] In the end, Floris' *Adoration of the Shepherds* was only restored to the Gardeners in August 1625, when it became clear that Rubens' *Assumption of the Virgin* for the high altar would soon be ready.[16] The *Adoration* was transferred back to the Gardeners' altar and the *Creation of Adam and Eve* disappeared from the church permanently.

In the 17th century virtually all the guild and craft altars were transformed into marble portico altars. That of the Gardeners seems to have been an exception to this. In 1682 the deans asked permission from the chapter to erect a marble altar, but apparently this did not take place. Only between 1776 and 1780 was the wooden altar construction replaced by a marble one.[17]

CARL VAN DE VELDE

10 'Also to Huybrecht Beda, painter, to decorate the foot of the high altar' (KAA [Antwerp Cathedral Archives], Accounts, 1588–1589, fol. 33; Van de Velde 1993, p. 396, note 62).
11 'Deputati sunt cum R° D[omi]no decano, & SQcholasticus et prouisor ad visitandum ecclesiam S. Walburgis et altare quod sub turri extructum est in honorem S. Walburgis' (KAA [Antwerp Cathedral Archives], Acta Capituli, III, p. 207).
12 'Ad lectum libellum supplicem porrectum ex parte Magistrorum Altaris Hortulanorum in ista ecclesia quo petierunt tabulam hactenus in summo altari, pretendentes illam spectare ex donatione rancioscі du Terne, quondam thesaurarii ad altare B. Mariae quod vocant op stocxken in quo ipsi nunc suum servant altaris officium, deputatus est D. Thesaurarius ut desuper se informet cum relatione ad capitulum; D. Trognesius et D. Compostella deposuerunt verisimile esse quod quondam sit depicta ex oblationibus quae ibidem fieri solent in honorem B. Mariae' (KAA [Antwerp Cathedral Archives], Acta Capituli, III, p. 183; Van de Velde 1975A, I, p. 494, doc. 109).
13 Van de Velde 1975B, pp. 250–260.
14 Van de Velde 1975B, p. 260.
15 'Exhibita per Notarium publicaum Supplicatione Hortulanorum petentium suo altari restitui tabulam, quae nunc est in summo altari, pridem eorum altari per D. du Terne concessam et (non concesso quod tabula praefata pertineat ad hortulanos, sed potius ad fabricam Ecclesiae) placuit Ordinari Edituis Ecclesiae ut proximo opere curent fieri novum altare maius; et deinde praefata tabula dimittatur ad opus jus habentium' (KAA [Antwerp Cathedral Archives], Acta Capituli, III, pp. 367–368; Van de Velde 1975A, I, p. 496, doc. 114).
16 'Placuit dominis ut tabula, quae est de Nativitate Domini, Francisci Floris, et nuper deposita est ex summo altari restituatur ad altare hortulanorum, ubi et olim a Domino Thesaurario du Terne donata fuisse asseritur' (KAA [Antwerp Cathedral Archives], Acta Capituli, ff, p. 77; Van de Velde 1975A, I, p. 498, doc. 120).
17 Baudouin 1993, p. 251.

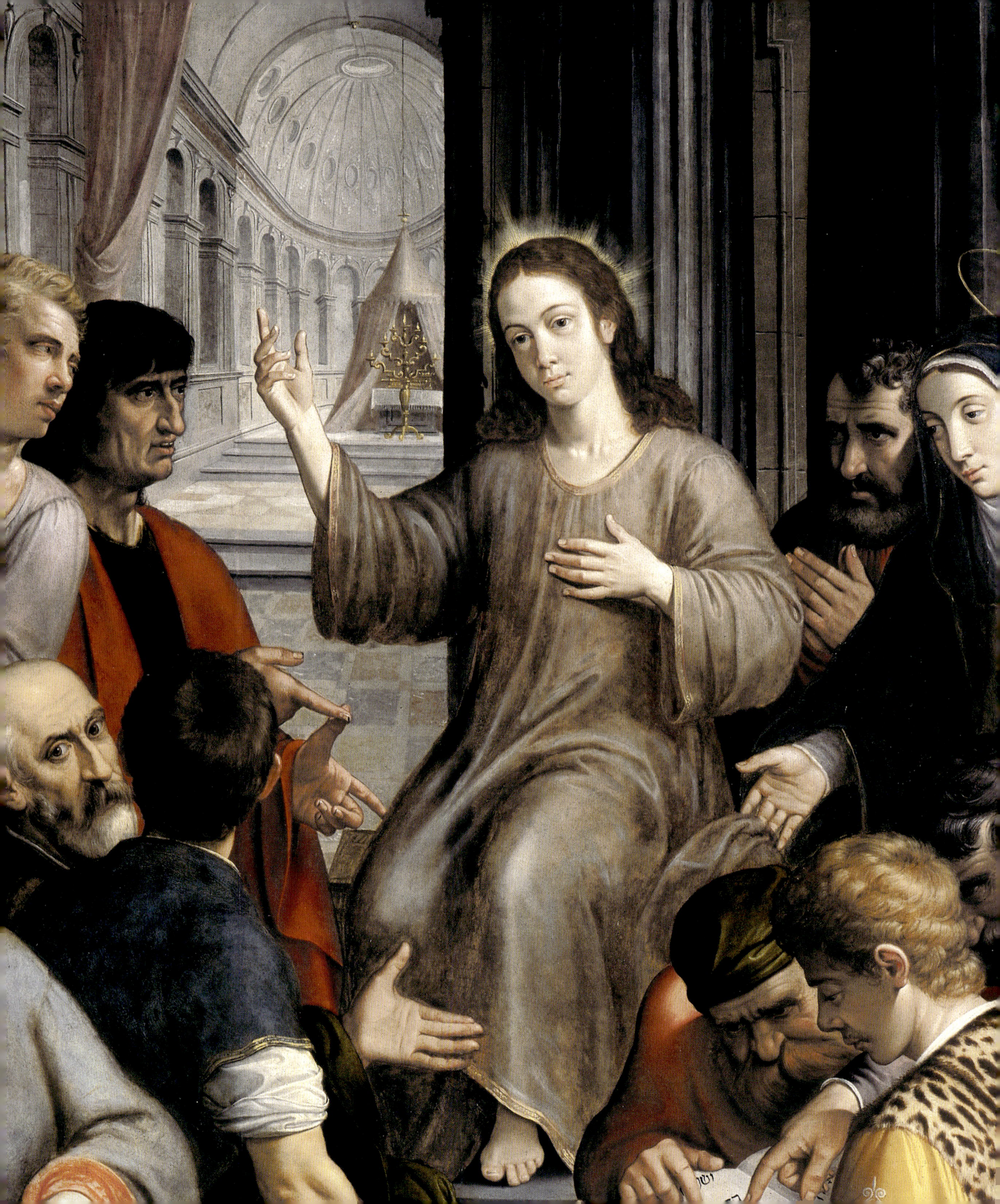

6 Altarpiece of the Schoolmasters and the Soap Boilers

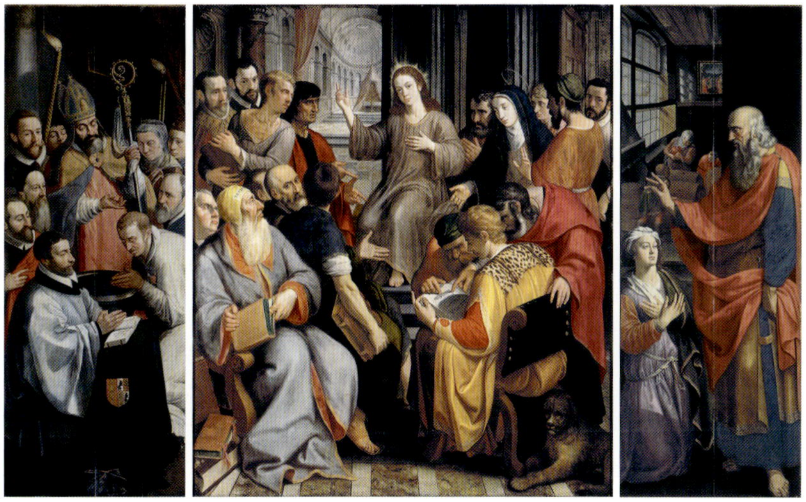

Frans II Francken

Antwerp 1542–Antwerp 1616

Christ among the Scribes

1587

Oil on panel
centre panel: 250 x 220 cm
side panels: 250 x 97 cm

Unsigned;
dated on the exterior left side panel on the book in the hands of Saint Mark: *1587*

Antwerp, Cathedral of Our Lady, inv. 930

Provenance: commissioned by the Schoolmasters' guild and the Soap Boilers' craft for their altar in the Antwerp Cathedral; displayed there in 1587; at the auction of the cathedral's furnishings in 1798 reserved for the École Centrale du Département des Deux-Nèthes; put at the disposal of the church by Prefect d'Herbouville in 1802; thereafter kept in the Cathedral of Our Lady.

Bibliography: *Beschryvinge 1751,* p. 7 (13–14)
Mensaert 1763, p. 235
Descamps 1769, p. 148
Kerken van Antwerpen 1774, p. 19
Van Lerius 1841, p. 18
Van den Branden 1883, pp. 345–347
Poffé 1895, pp. 21–25
Gabriels 1930, pp. 83–88
Leurs & Philippen 1938, p. 49, nos. 82–83, pl. 49
Prims 1938–1939, XIII, pp. 399–408
Van Herck 1951, p. 43
Van den Nieuwenhuizen 1957, pp. 82–83
Van Brabant 1972, pp. 250–251
Van de Velde 1993A, pp. 193–194
Aerts & Grieten 1993, pp. 401–402, note 20
Grieten & Bungeneers 1996, pp. 382–384
Peeters 2000A, cat. F 9

The triptych of *Christ among the Scribes* is the best-known and also one of the best-documented altarpieces by Frans Francken.[1] This artist painted several altarpieces in Antwerp in the late 16th century.[2]

The scholastic dispute between Christ and the scribes takes place in a church. In the background, an elevated choir is visible, and a menorah or seven-armed candleholder for the Ark of the Covenant. Christ, depicted at the centre with Joseph and Mary to his right, is surrounded by scribes who are in fact members of the guild council, such as council member Jacob de Santa Cruz. Protagonists of the Reformation, including Luther, Calvin, and Erasmus, are also recognisable.[3] Frans Francken portrayed himself to the right of the centre panel.[4] On the left panel Saint Ambrosius, church father and patron of the Schoolmasters' guild, is depicted in episcopal robes, and on his head a mitre with his symbol, the beehive. He baptises Saint Augustine, recognisable by the heart with the crossed arrows on his baptismal robe. Canon Reynier van Brakel, a scholastic since 1585 and attached to the chapter, kneels before the saint; his weapon is shown at the side of the prayer desk.[5] Behind Saint Ambrosius stands Saint Monica, mother of Saint Augustine. In the background an altarpiece is visible, screened off by curtains. At a later date Francken added a second self-portrait to the top left of this panel, in which he looks much older than in the portrait on the centre panel. On the right panel, donated by the Soap Boilers, the biblical story of the Miracle of the Flowing Oil is depicted. The prophet Elia helped the widow from Zarephath pay her debts by enabling her to fill a large number of jugs with a small drop of oil. Oil was a basic component of soap; the theme was therefore very suited for the Soap Boilers. In the background of the panel, a painting of *Moses and the Brazen Serpent* is depicted.

The exterior panels of the triptych display the four evangelists, seated around a table which continues over the two panels. The predella, whose subjects are unknown, almost certainly does not survive. The whole was initially crowned with a Salvator Mundi.[6]

The altarpiece is characterised by a fresh and clear palette, in which red and yellow predominate. Although the perspective in the centre and left panels has an unnaturally steep upward slant, the light and colour effect and the display of texture, as in the lion's

1 Peeters 1999A, *passim;* Peeters 2000A, cat. F9.
2 Peeters 2003, pp. 69–91.
3 Van den Branden 1883, p. 347. According to Van den Branden, in addition to Willem Schoyte, dean Willem Fabius and Rombout Verdonck (the future tutor of P.P. Rubens), aldermen Jan Borrekens and Cornelis Hoeck, and three old deans are also depicted, namely Cornelis Phalesius, Jan Desbonnet, and Adriaan Verdonck. In the past, the figures on the centre panel, in whom Protestant reformers were recognised, caused speculation about the theological background of the altarpiece. The presence of portraits of religious and political leaders on altarpieces was not unusual. As early as 1571, Frans Pourbus had painted portraits of Charles V, Philip II, Calvin, and Cardinal Granvelle on his centre panel of *Christ among the Scribes* (Ghent, Saint Bavo's Cathedral; fig. 6a).
4 For Frans Francken's self-portraits, see Peeters 1999B, pp. 80–102.
5 *Verzameling 1856,* I, p. 51; Goetschalckx 1929, pp. 54–56. Reynier van Brakel, scholastic, master in theology and priest-canon of the Cathedral of Our Lady, was therefore actively involved in the design of the altarpiece.
6 For more information on the iconography of the altarpiece, see the contribution of M. Gielis in this publication.

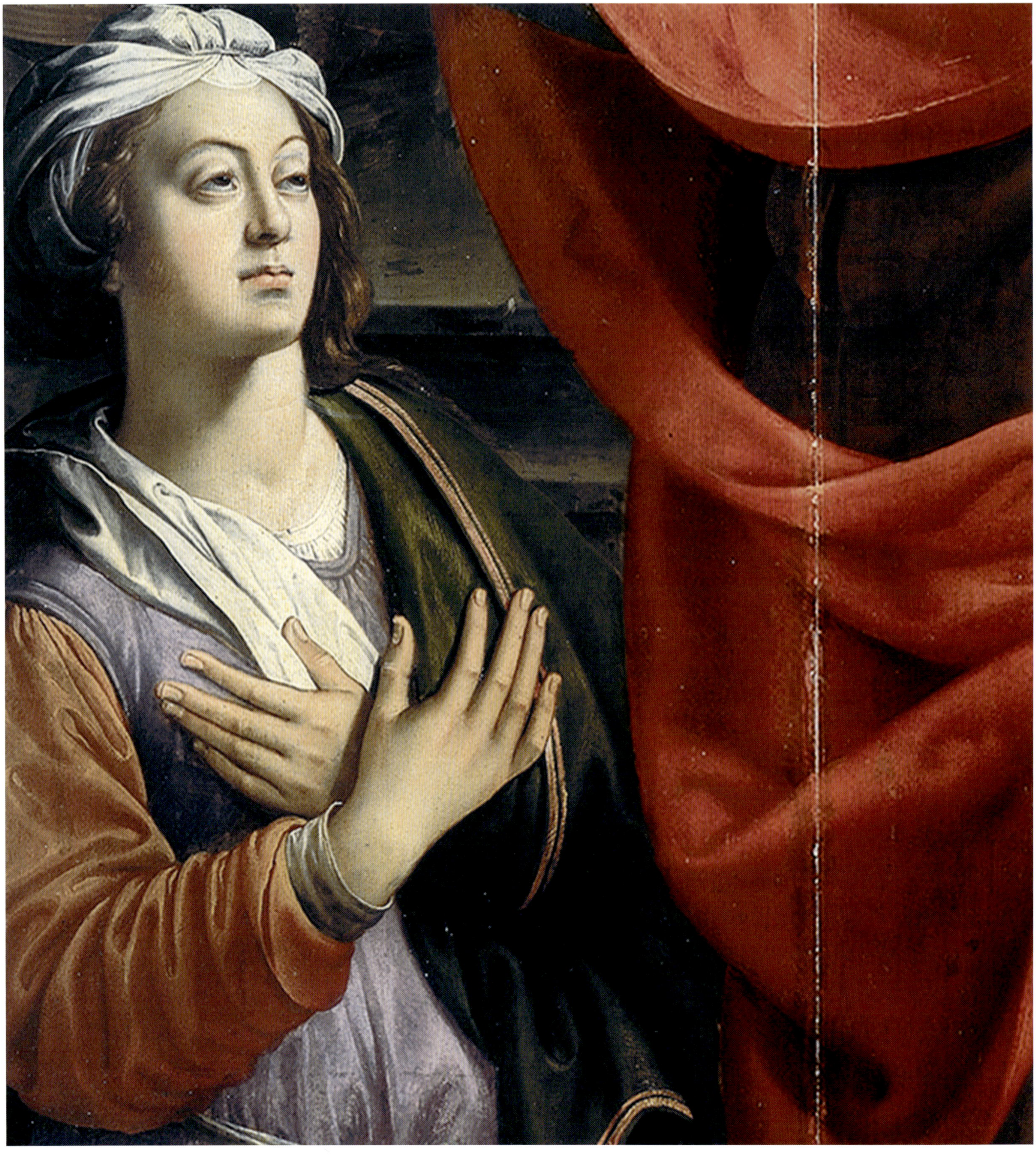

fur, confer a certain virtuosity to the altarpiece. The light, entering the painting from the right, is designed to complement the altarpiece's location in the cathedral. The altar initially stood in the ambulatory to the southeast of the choir, near the sacristy, in fact, and would thus have been illuminated by a southern light descending from the right. The apse in the centre panel of the painting is beautifully reflected by the cathedral's real apse.

The principal donors of the altarpiece were the Schoolmasters (Saint Ambrosius' guild); the Soap Boilers (Saint Gregory's craft) contributed in a more modest way. The history of the commission and execution is amply documented. One 4 March 1586 the first meetings took place. After the restoration of the Catholic regime, the Schoolmasters and the Soap Boilers were among the first to commission a new altarpiece. For that matter, the triptych was the first guild altar erected in the cathedral *after* 1585.[7] That Frans Francken was chosen to paint this altarpiece is due both to his good relations with the many municipal institutions, guilds, and crafts, and his reputation as a painter since the early 1570s.[8]

It is highly unusual that both the altarpiece and the many documents concerning it should survive. The negotiation of the commission, as described in those documents, was probably exemplary for most other commissions.[9] The notarised deeds and contracts, which were drawn up at the meetings, show that the patrons were closely involved in all aspects of the realisation of the altarpiece. On 4 March 1586, the inspectors and altar masters of the Soap Boilers and the deans and aldermen of the Schoolmasters, together with scholastic van Brakel, closed an agreement with Sebastiaan van Halen, joiner and panel maker. Concerning the wooden frame, the contract refers to the woodwork of Saint Sebastian's altar (which no longer exists) of the Young Longbowmen's guild in the Antwerp cathedral, painted by Chrispijn van den Broeck in 1573.[10] The document also refers to the woodwork of the altar of the Friars Minor Church in Ghent, painted by Frans Francken himself.[11] The frieze, however, was to be executed like that of Saint Sebastian's altar of the Old Longbowmen's guild in the cathedral, which was painted by Michiel Coxcie in 1575 (Antwerp, Koninklijk Museum voor Schone Kunsten).[12] Sebastiaan van Halen was required to deliver the panels to the painter before Easter (3 April) 1586.

On 4 March 1586 the deans of the two guilds met with Frans Francken who was to deliver the panel and doors within four months, in good firm paint, for a total price of 240 Carolus guilders. From the contract we can deduce that the painter did not choose the subjects himself – or at least not alone – but that the general concept was developed by Reynier van Brakel. According to the contract, the following subjects were to be included: *Christ among the Scribes* on the central panel; *Eliseus Multiplies the Oil for the Widow from Zarepheth* and *Christ in the House of Martha and Mary* on the panels. On the exteriors, it was originally intended that the four Latin Church Fathers would be depicted. The whole would be crowned with a *Christ as Salvator Mundi* and van Brakel still had to think of subjects for the predella. On 23 April it was decided that the Soap Boilers and the Schoolmasters would share the costs; the Schoolmasters already deposited 200 Carolus guilders.

On 12 July 1586, a new meeting was called: the Schoolmasters had realised that the subject of *Christ in the House of Martha and Mary,* destined for the left panel, in fact referred to the craft association of the Pastry Makers (for whom Saint Martha was patron) with whom they had shared an altar until 1530. It was therefore decided to replace the theme with *Saint Ambrosius Baptising Saint Augustine*. It is not known when it was decided to replace the four Latin Church Fathers who, according to the first contract, were to be depicted on the back of the panels, by the four evangelists, or when the predella and pediment were painted.

Ten days later, the Schoolmasters 'visited' the altarpiece in Francken's studio, at which time the painter was honoured with a gift of wine. Consistent with the contract, he completed the work on 4 August, albeit *with* the depiction of *Christ in the House of Martha and Mary*. Three days later, the deans and aldermen of the Schoolmasters assembled with the

7 Van de Velde 1993B, p. 192.

8 Peeters 1996, pp. 95–100; Peeters 2000B, pp. 72–74; Peeters 2009A.

9 O'Malley 2005, *passim*. For another well-documented altarpiece, see Peeters 2001, pp. 5–34.

10 The backs of the panels are still preserved in Lier, Saint Gummarus' Church; there is also a copy of the centre panel by A. De Bie. See Vlieghe 1973, pp. 342–346.

11 This is probably the triptych with the *Crucifixion with double panels with HH. Francis and Clara* (Ghent, Museum voor Schone Kunsten), see Peeters 2000B; Peeters 2003, *passim*.

12 Vervaet 1976, pp. 215–218; Van de Velde 1993A, p. 194; Van de Velde 1993B, pp. 194–197; Grieten & Bungeneers 1996, pp. 364–365.

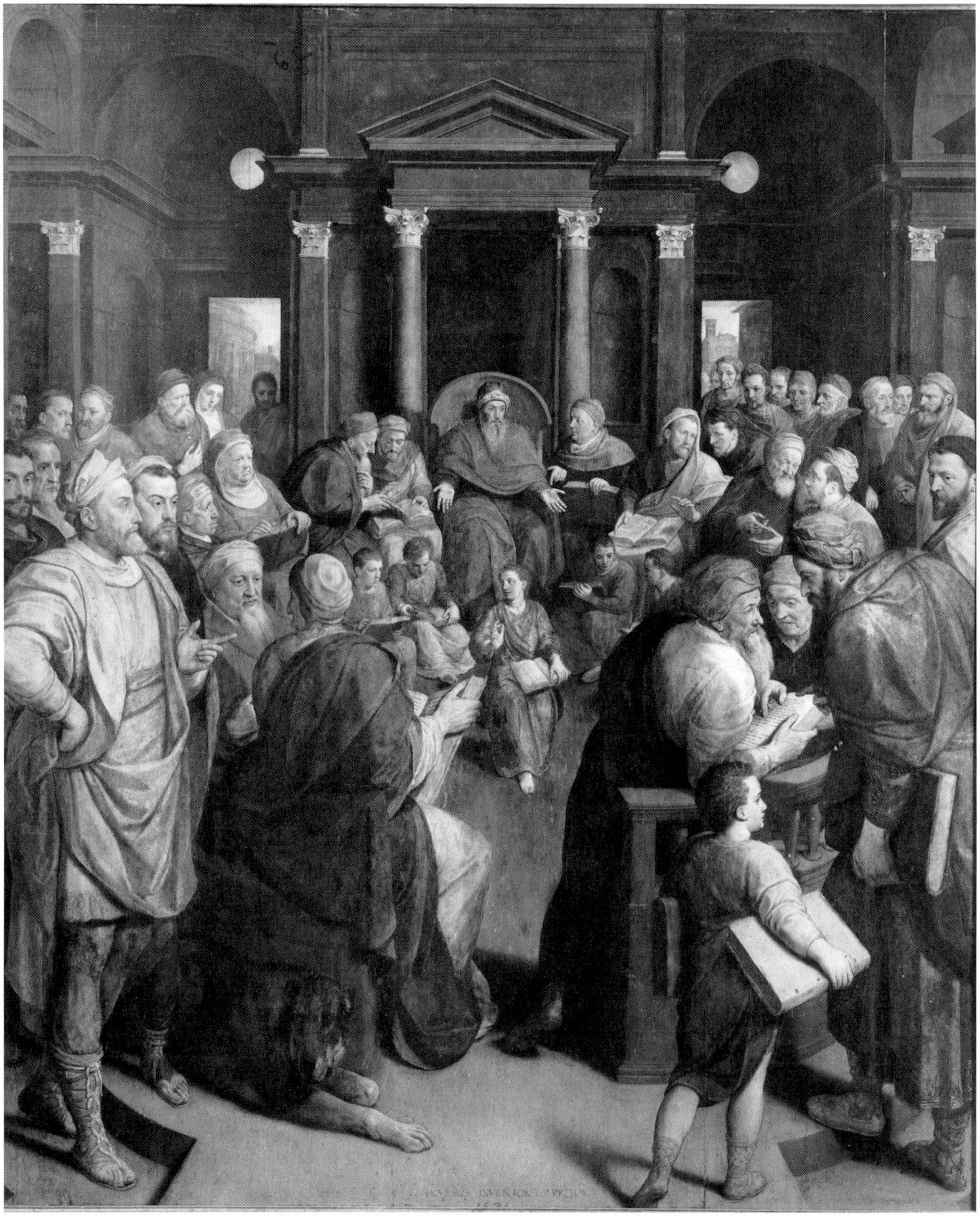

6a
Frans Pourbus
Christ among the Scribes
Ghent, Saint Bavo's Cathedral

commissioners and deans of the Soap Boilers at the house of the scholastic to estimate how and when the alterations, the *staffage*, and finishing, of the altarpiece should be executed. Apparently no new agreement was closed at that date.

On 9 October 1586 there was another meeting at Reynier van Brakel's house and an agreement was reached. For 36 Carolus guilders, Francken would replace the Schoolmasters' panel of Martha and Mary with *Saint Ambrosius Baptising Saint Augustine*. On 19 March 1587 the Schoolmasters and Soap Boilers met again to commission the *staffage* to Filips de Crayer – the father of the well-known 17th century painter Gaspar [13] – and Frans Francken. Twelve Carolus guilders were paid for the *staffage*. Eventually, on 27 March the altarpiece was definitively displayed. The final payment took place at the beginning of April that year: the painter and the woodcarver were respectively paid their outstanding fees of 60 (of the 240) and 70 (of the 120) Carolus guilders.[14]

Between 13 and 16 April Francken added the portrait of Jacob de Santa Cruz to the panel with *Saint Ambrosius Baptising Saint Augustine*. The merchant – and, from 1598, knight – de Santa Cruz exercised important functions in Antwerp's city council.[15] He was supreme church master of Saint James' Church and archdeacon, and was buried in the Schoolmasters' Chapel in the cathedral in 1608. On 16 April, Francken received an extra 36 Carolus guilders, and beer. On 1 July, Sebastiaan van Halen, too, was paid extra for the woodwork he had made in addition to his contract. The altar was finally consecrated mid December 1587.

In 1594–1595 Francken removed a (further unknown) inscription from the painting. In 1601 he gilded and restored the altarpiece for 90 Carolus guilders and painted a second self-portrait on the panel with *Saint Ambrosius Baptising Saint Augustine*.

The Schoolmasters' guild had a standard-setting function as one of the leading players in education and instruction and needed to execute the Tridentine ordinances on Counter-Reformation iconography as closely as possible. Possibly, the altar intended not so much to emphasise the religious polemic between Catholics and Protestants, but rather sought reconciliation and instruction of the Roman-Catholic doctrine. Perhaps this was clarified by the further unknown inscription Francken removed himself in 1594–1595. That the Schoolmasters were very serious about the redecoration of their chapel, is shown for example in the implemented changes, the addition of de Santa Cruz' portrait, and that scholastic's role in the development of an iconography that was as correct as possible.

Francken clearly developed his own style in this altarpiece. The influence of his tutor Frans Floris is less expressly present, and the stereotypical head types, which were initially very characteristic of his oeuvre, had evolved. Yet there remain a few elements which indicate his training with Floris. The evangelists strongly resemble those in the *Adoration of the Magi* (Brussels, Royal Museums of Fine Arts/London, Brompton Oratory), an altarpiece painted in 1571.[16] And in fact, those evangelists were probably based on compositions used in Floris' atelier, as can be seen in a painted copy of Floris' *Four Evangelists* (Antwerp, private collection)[17] and a drawing after Floris with the same theme (London, British Museum).

Frans Francken certainly drew inspiration from an altarpiece by Frans Pourbus, who was once a fellow apprentice of his with Frans Floris, notably his version of *Christ among the Scribes* of 1571 (Ghent, Saint Bavo's Cathedral; fig. 6a). Both show portraits of historic figures: Pourbus in the centre panel of the *Scribes* and on the panel with the *Circumcision*; Francken on the centre panel only. With Frans Francken, the event takes place in the intimacy of a church, as where with Pourbus it is situated in a monumental archaic room. Yet Francken's composition is clearer: Christ is seated on his throne, high above the listeners, whereas with Pourbus he is barely noticeable and almost disappears in the crowd, partly owing to a scribe who sits on the throne instead of Christ, himself.

NATASJA PEETERS

13 Rombouts & Van Lerius 1864–1876, I, pp. 302, 320, 339 and 335; Donnet 1924 (1887), p. 7; De Groote 1967, pp. 245–246. In 1587, schoolmaster Filips de Crayer became free-master in Saint Luke's guild and worked as a calligrapher there.

14 On 6 April they received the last payment. It is not clear whether this was part of the total amount as originally recorded: Frans was paid 112 more Carolus guilders, Sebastiaan van Halen 40 Carolus guilders. For prices, see Peeters 2008B; Peeters 2009B.

15 Ghijs 1988, II, pp. 159–160.

16 He made the triptych together with his brother Hieronymus Francken, see Peeters 1999B, *passim*; Peeters 2009A.

17 Van de Velde 1975A, no. 303.

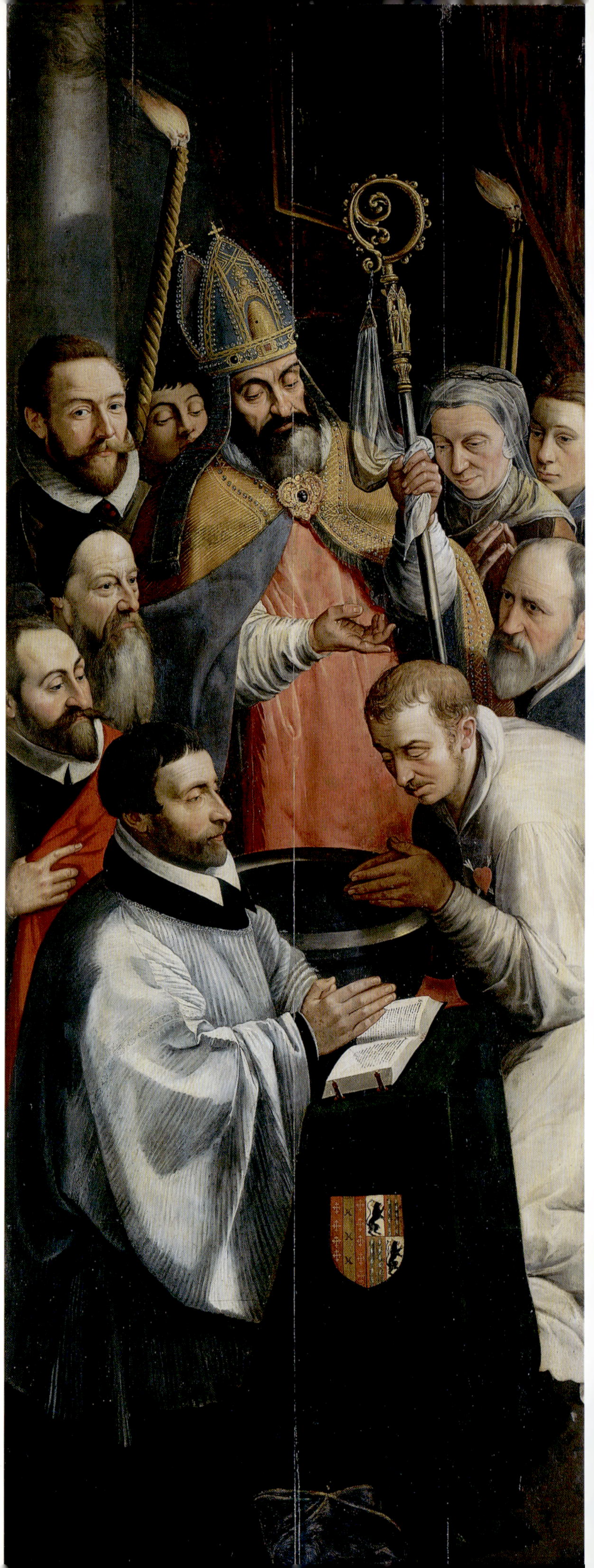

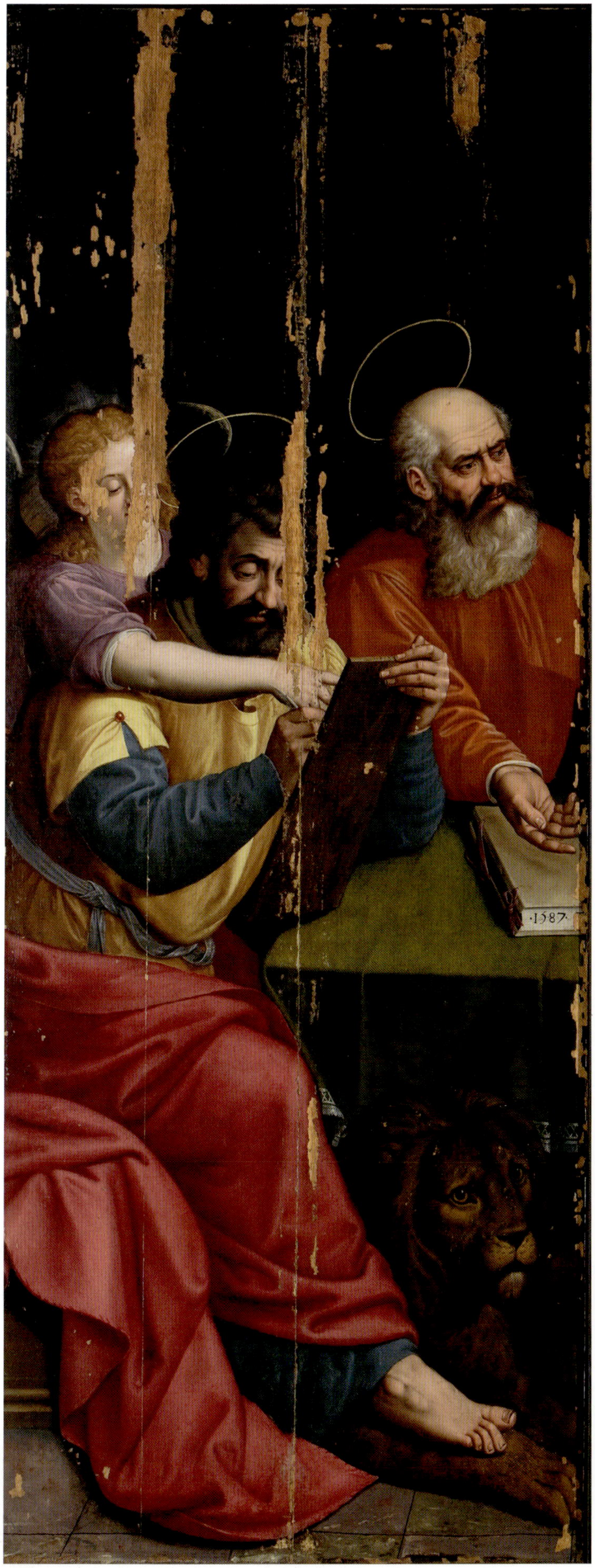
·1587·
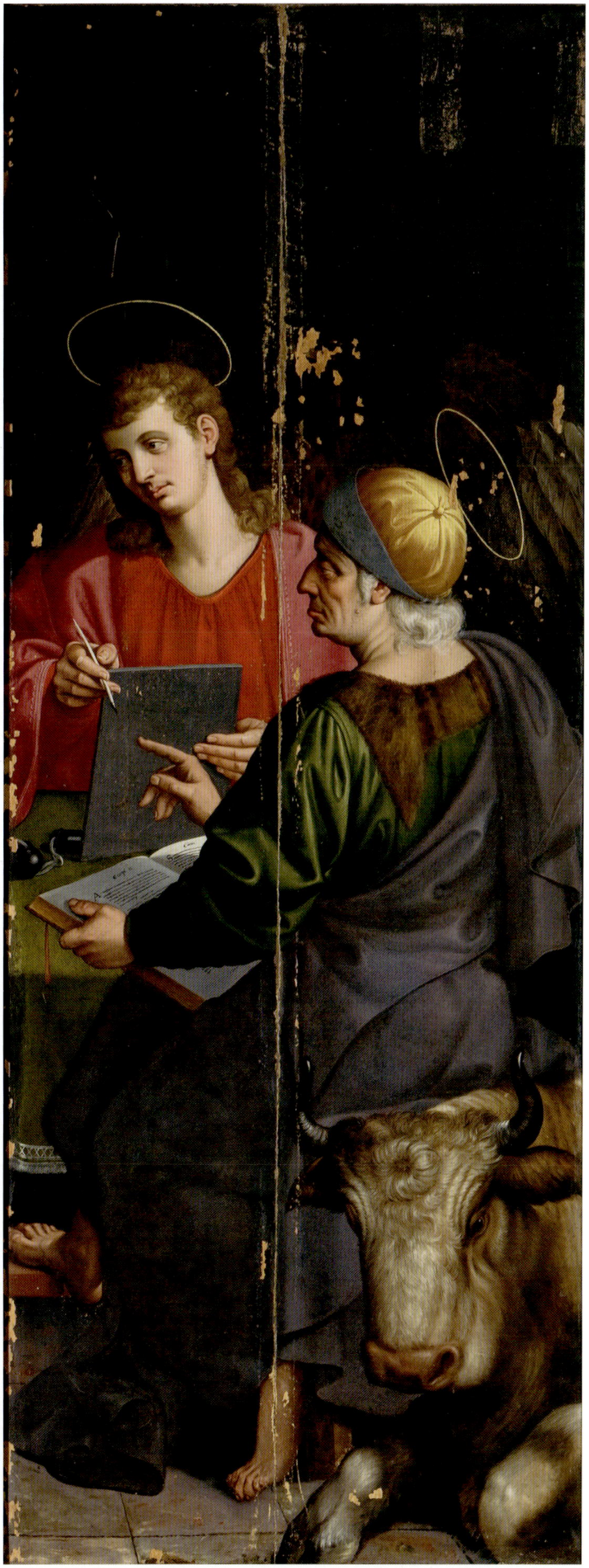

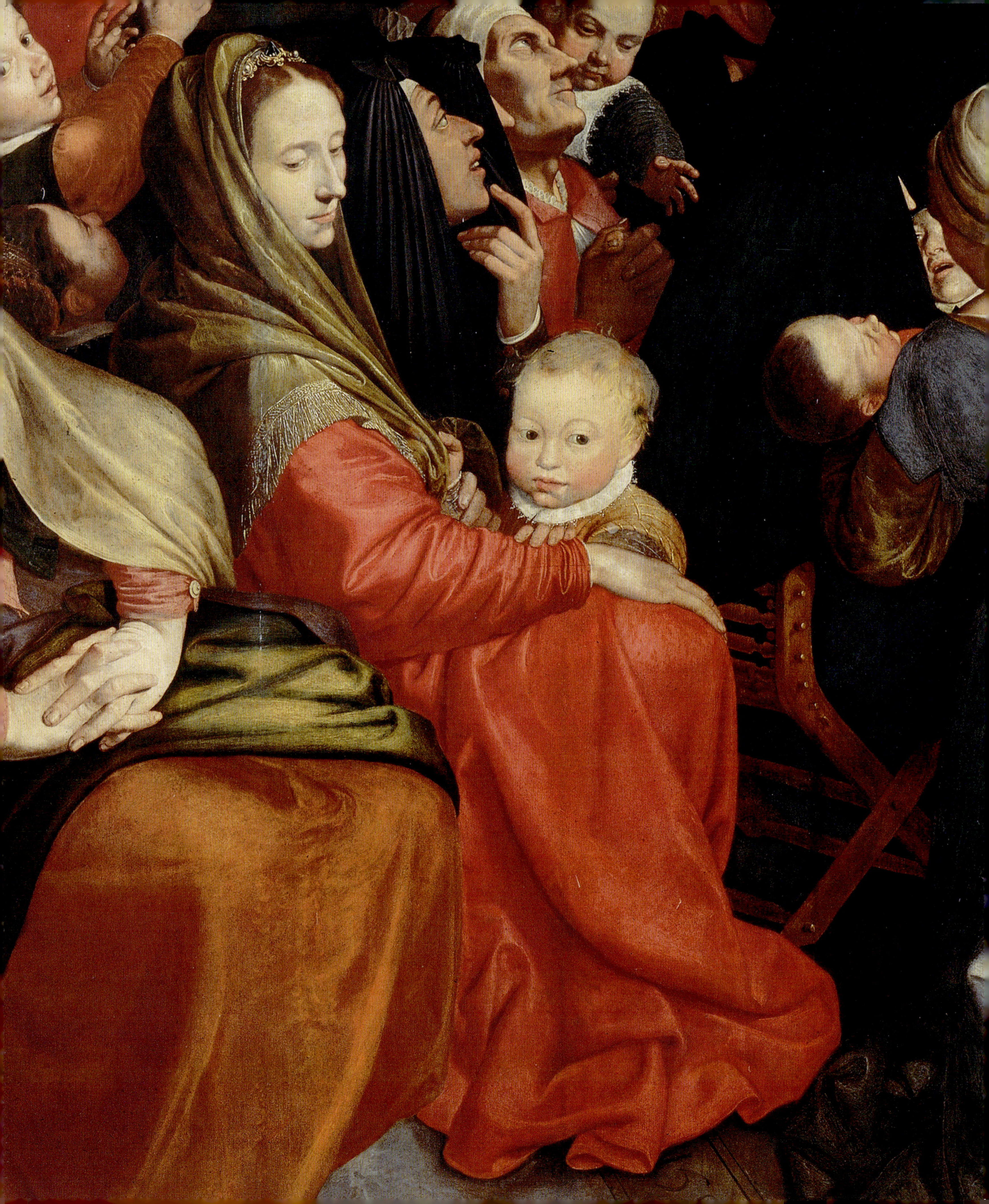

7 Altarpiece of the Smiths

Ambrosius Francken
Herentals 1544–Antwerp 1618

The Preaching of Saint Eligius of Noyon
1588

Oil on panel
centre panel: 250 x 180 cm
side panels: 260 x 89 cm

On the centre panel, the inscription *AGLMB* and on the gravestone: *Hier leet begrave Peeter 1588 (Here lies buried Peeter 1588).*[1] On the back of the right panel, to the left on a band around the torch, the date *1588.*

Unsigned

Antwerp, Koninklijk Museum voor Schone Kunsten, inv. 576–580

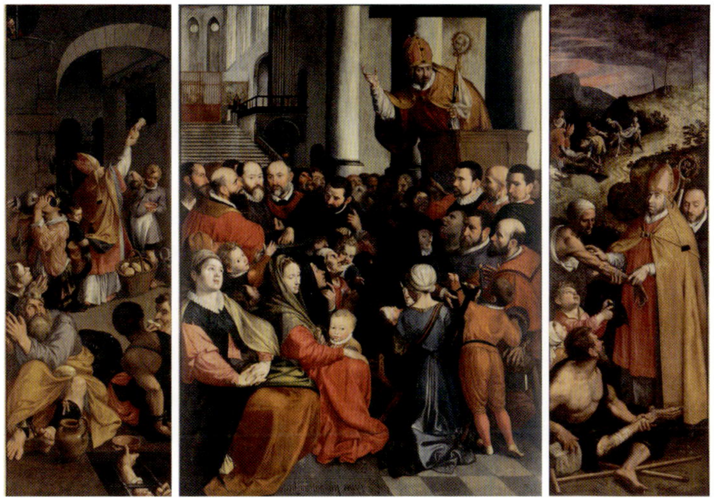

Provenance: commissioned by the Antwerp Smiths' craft; from 1588 to 1798 on the craft altar in the Antwerp cathedral; in 1798 the centre panel was transferred to the École Centrale des Deux-Nèthes in the abolished Discalced Monastery; until 1811 in the Academy of the Exchange building; then in the Museum in the former Friars Minor Monastery; foundational holding of the Museum. The side panels became private property after 1798; until 1853 they were in the collection Antoon Van Camp, Antwerp; in 1856 they were purchased from Fred Schuermans by the Antwerp Koninklijk Museum voor Schone Kunsten.

Bibliography: *Beschrijvinge 1751,* p. 10 (15)
Mensaert 1763, p. 243 (as Frans Pourbus)
Descamps 1769, p. 152
Kerken van Antwerpen 1774, pp. 28–29
Van Lerius 1851, p. 18 (as unknown master)
Gabriëls 1930, pp. 55, 66 (as Hieronymus Francken)
Prims 1938–1939, XIII, pp. 411–414
Freedberg 1972, pp. 224–226
Van Brabant 1974, pp. 49, 84, 219
Vervaet 1976, pp. 219–221
Van de Velde 1993A, p. 194
Grieten & Bungeneers 1996, p. 365
Peeters 1999A, pp. 59–80
Peeters 2000A, cat. A3
Peeters 2003, pp. 69–91
Peeters 2008A

In 1588, Ambrosius Francken (1544/45–1618), one of Antwerp's most famous religious history painters of the late 16th century, painted his first altarpiece for the Antwerp cathedral: the Smiths' altar, showing the *Preaching of Saint Eligius of Noyon* on the centre panel.

The saint, garbed in the episcopal robes, preaches in a church filled with smiths and others who have come to listen. The sober interior clearly resembles that of the Antwerp Saint Walburgis' Church, where the craft had its own chapel before 1585. A panel with a *Crucifixion* and a statue of Saint Eligius is identifiable in the background. The panels of the altarpiece show scenes from the life of the saint taken from the *Vita Eligii*. In the saint's *vita*, the emphasis lays on acts of mercy, which are visually illustrated on the panels. The left panel shows Eligius visiting prisoners. On the right panel he assists the crippled and buries the dead. On the exterior panels, in grisaille, to the left the saint is depicted in his forge and to the right he is consecrated bishop. On the latter panel Eligius is surrounded by colleague-bishops and in the foreground stands an acolyte with a torch. A band around that torch shows the coat of arms of the Smiths' craft and the year *1588.* The small-scale figures of the prefigurations and the narrative scenes in the background on the panel of *Saint Eligius Assisting the Crippled and Burying the Dead* became a characteristic feature of Ambrosius Francken's work over the following years. Through the clear subdivision of the story the work has great didactical value.

Archive documents provide only indirect information on the provenance and realisation of the altarpiece. In 1581, the old altar was removed by order of the Calvinist administration of the craft. As early as 1586, shortly after the catholic restoration, the plan was conceived to erect a new altar. The craft had three chapels, one in the Cathedral, one in Saint Walburgis' Church, and one on Paardenmarkt (Klapdorp). But owing to the lack of financial means, only one of the three chapels could be refurnished.[2] Eventually, it was decided to renovate the chapel in the Cathedral. It was the most prestigious and expressed the privileged status of the craft. In October 1588, the craft raised the entrance fees and diverse smaller works were executed for the altar. The date *1588*, which occurs twice on the altarpiece, confirms its completion.

The composition of the *Episcopal Consecration* recalls Pieter Coecke van Aelst's (vanished) stained-glass window of the *Consecration of Saint Nicholas* for Saint Nicholas' Chapel in the Cathedral (1537), of which a cartoon is kept in the Albertina Museum in Vienna (fig. 7a). It cannot be established whether Ambrosius Francken was influenced by Pieter Coecke van Aelst's composition, because a consecration scene can indeed be painted with only limited variations. The panel with the *Episcopal Consecration of Saint*

1 The letters are difficult to read since they are intertwined. In *Verzameling der Graf- en Gedenkschriften van de provincie Antwerpen* (Antwerp 1856–1887, 6 volumes), no inscription was found that could be connected to this painted inscription, or to the year.
2 Peeters 2005, pp. 239–252, goes more deeply into the issue.

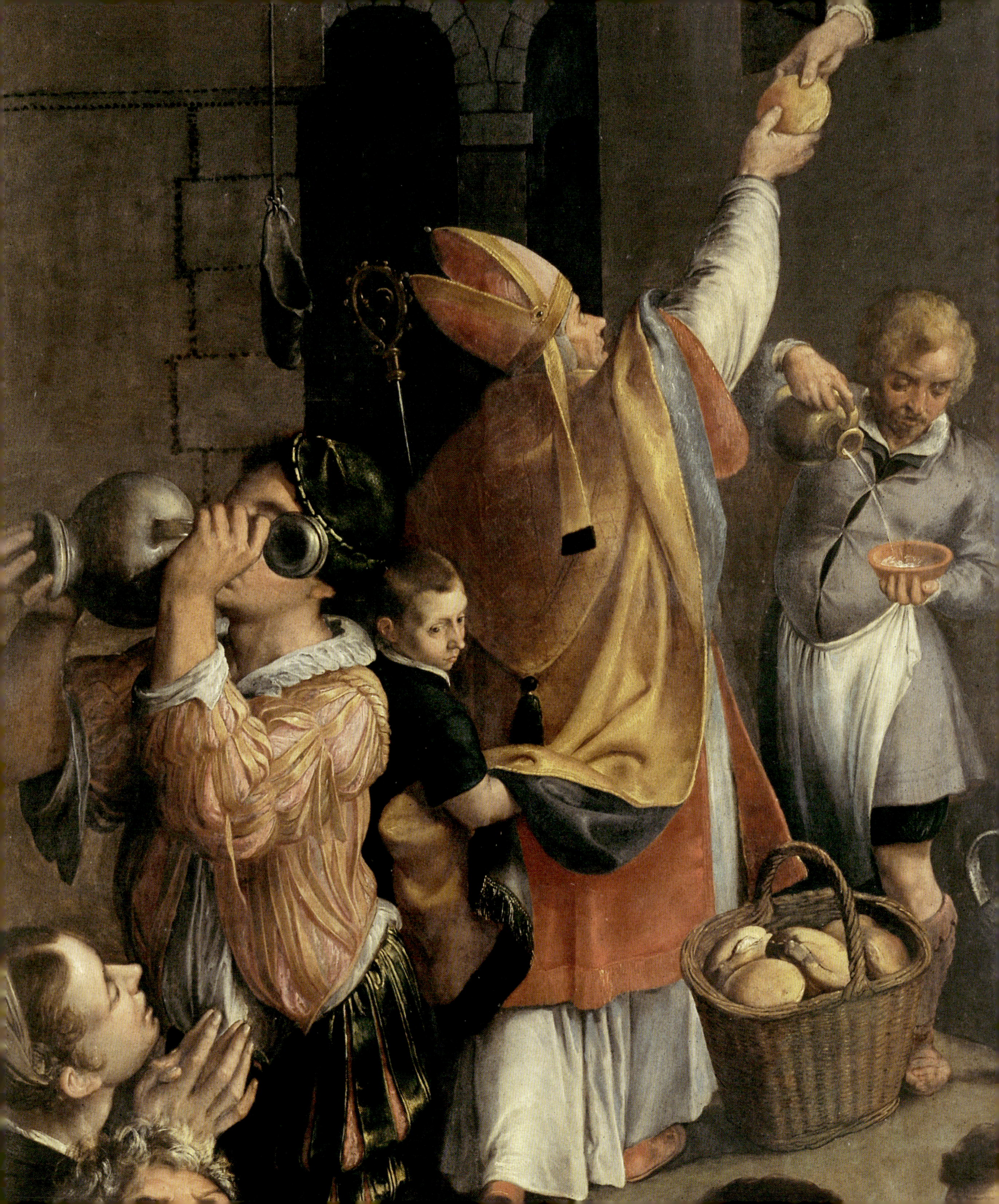

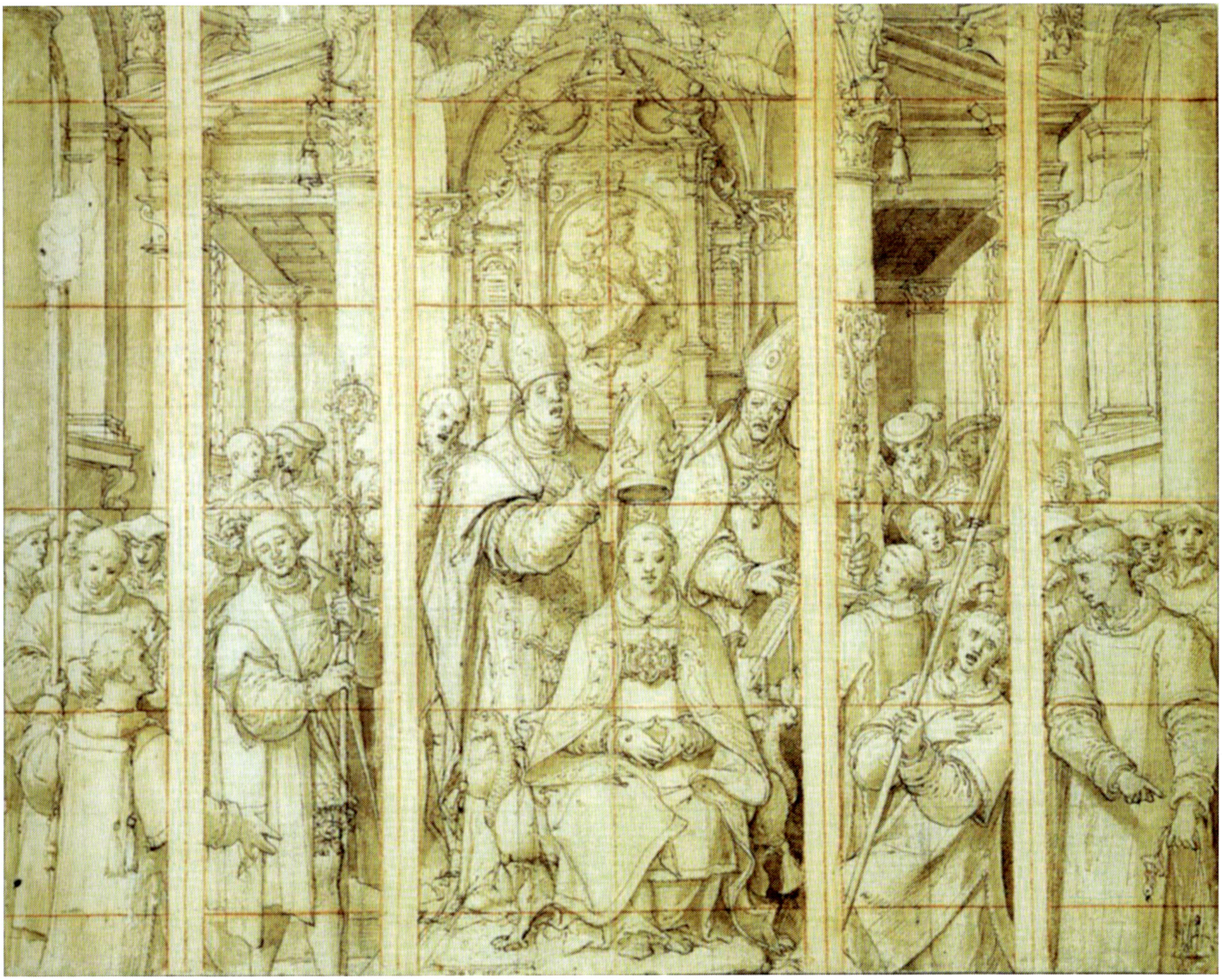

7a
Pieter Coecke van Aelst
Episcopal Consecration of Saint Nicholas
cartoon for a stained-glass window
in Saint Nicholas' Chapel in
the Cathedral of Antwerp (1537)
Vienna, Albertina Museum

Eligius resembles Frans Pourbus' grisaille of the *Episcopal Consecration of Saint Martin* from the series of the *Life of Saint Martin*, painted in 1573–1574 for Saint Martin's Abbey in Tournai (Tournai, Episcopal Seminary; fig. 7b) as well as Pourbus' composition for the centre panel of the altarpiece for Viglius Aytta, *Christ among the Scribes* (1571) (Ghent, Saint Bavo's Cathedral; fig. 6a). Ambrosius Francken and Frans Pourbus had been fellow-apprentices in Frans Floris' atelier. In 1608, Ambrosius re-used the composition himself in the *Episcopal Consecration of Saint Hubert* (Herentals, Saint Waldetrudis' Church; fig. 7c). In the context of the Smiths, the choice of a scene with an episcopal consecration could be connected to the then still recent creation of new dioceses in the Southern Netherlands and the promotion of the Antwerp Church of Our Lady to an episcopal Church or cathedral (1559).

However, none of the preserved archive documents concerning the Smiths' altar mentions the painter's name. The work was recently attributed to Ambrosius Francken by, among others, Van de Velde in 1993 and Grieten & Bungeneers in 1996.[3] Stylistically, the right panel with *Saint Eligius of Noyon Assisting the Crippled and Burying the Dead* strongly recalls the left panel of Ambrosius Francken's *Altar-*

3 Van de Velde 1993A, p. 194; Grieten & Bungeneers 1996, p. 365.

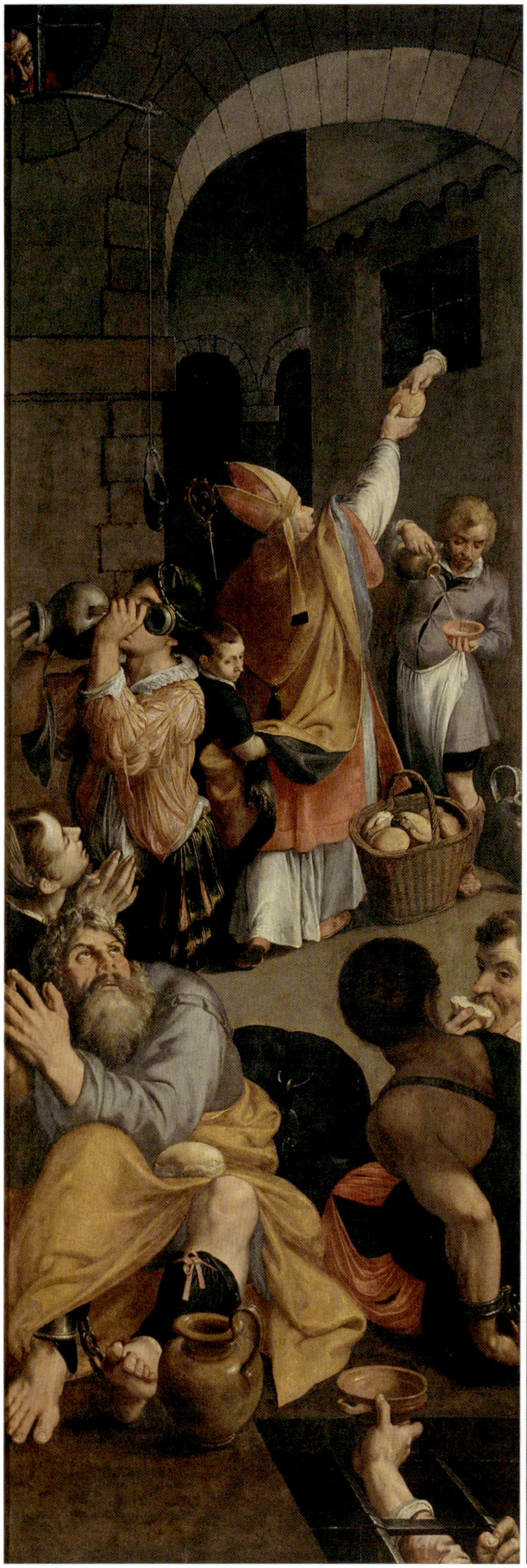
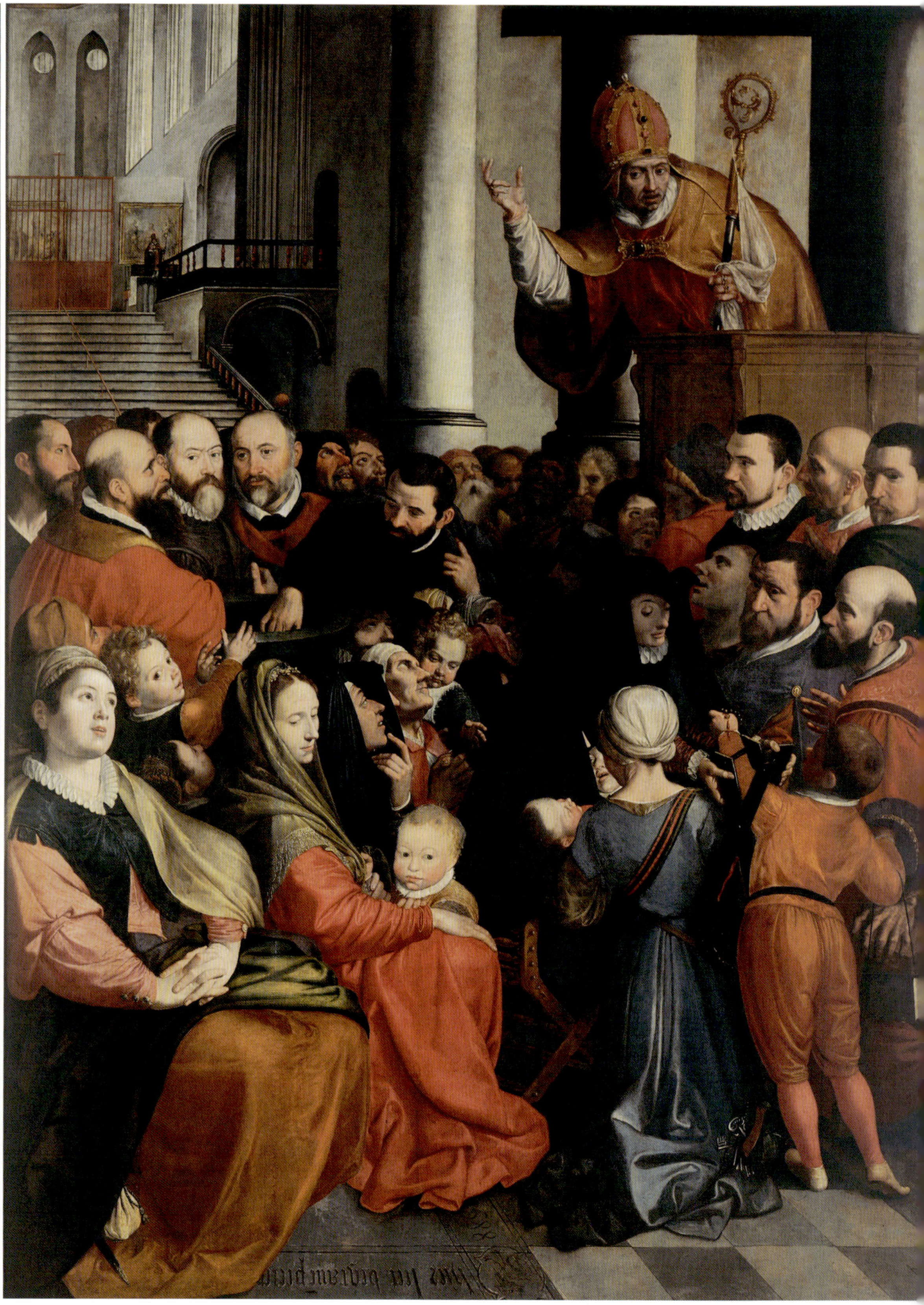

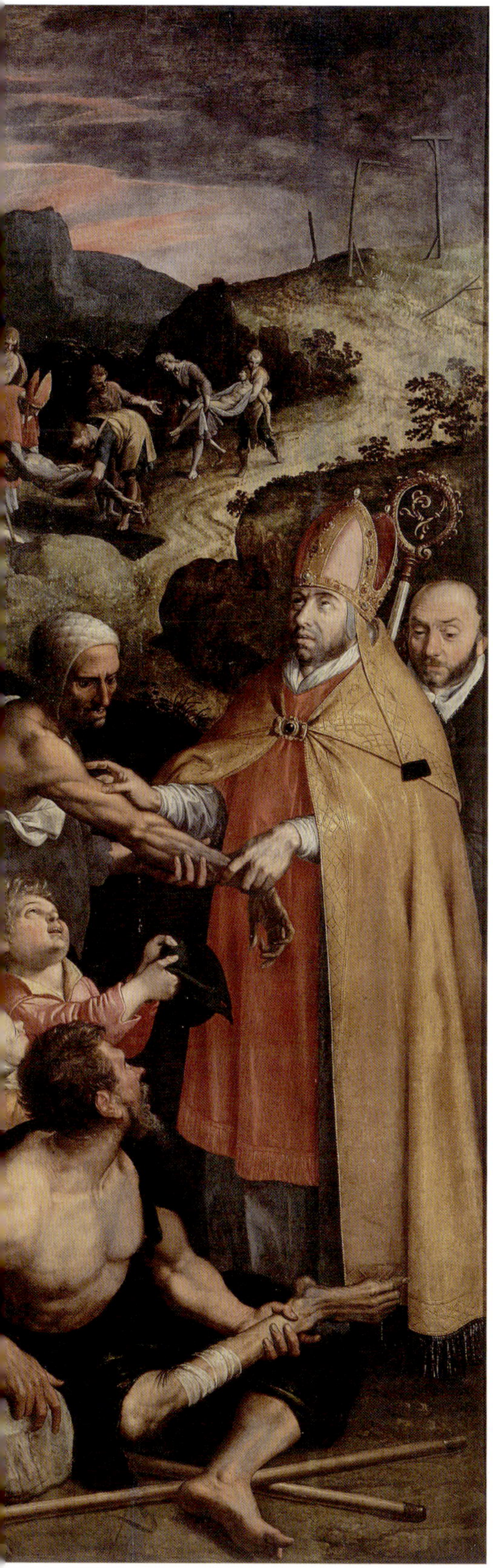

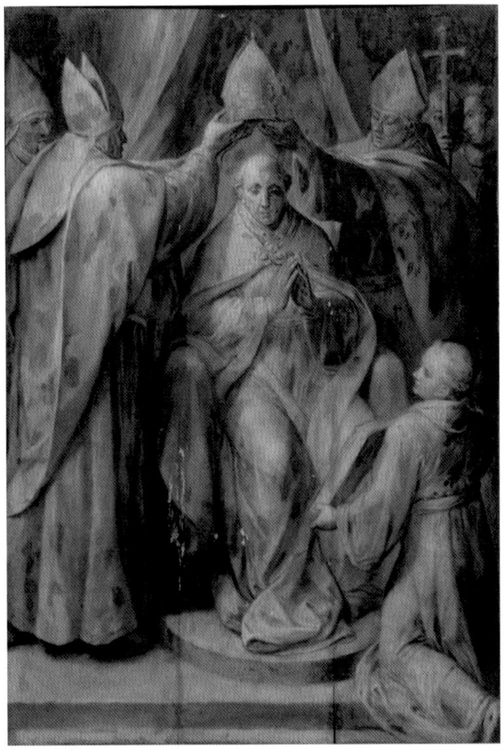

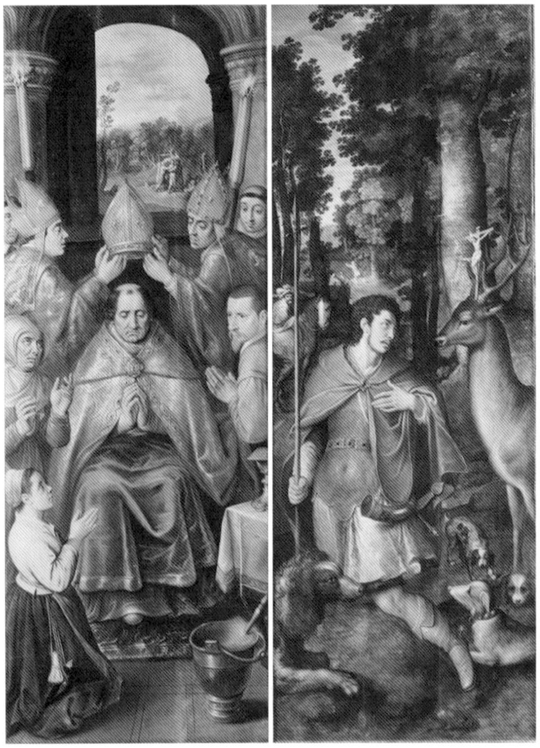

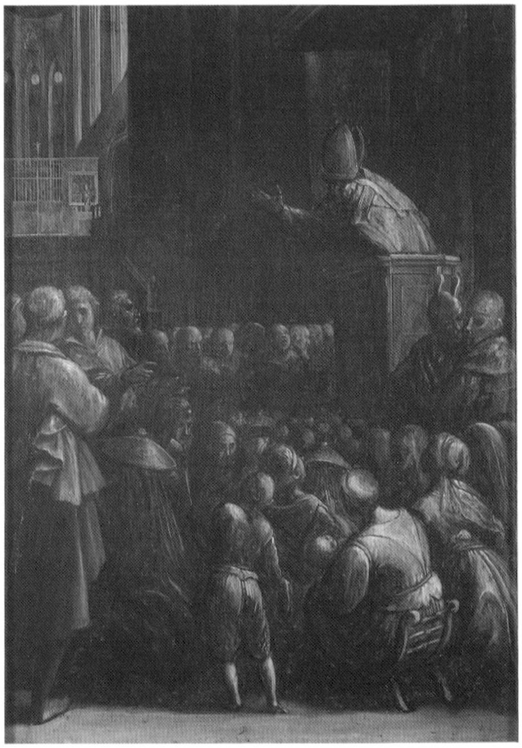

7b
Frans Pourbus
Episcopal Consecration of Saint Martin, grisaille
Tournai, Episcopal Seminary

7c
Ambrosius Francken
Episcopal Consecration of Saint Hubert
Herentals, Saint Waldetrudis' Church

7d
Anonymous
Preaching of Saint Eligius, grisaille
Utrecht, Saint Catherine's Convent

piece of Saints Cosmas and Damian, namely the *Charity of Saints Cosmas and Damian* from 1593 (Antwerp, Koninklijk Museum voor Schone Kunsten),[4] which confirms the attribution.

A small grisaille panel of the *Preaching of Saint Eligius* (Utrecht, Saint Catherine's Convent; fig. 7d)[5] is regarded as the modello for the centre panel of the Smiths' altar. However, the proportions of the modello and those of the large centre panel do not correspond. The portraits that occur on the finished centre panel lack on the grisaille. The figures on the grisaille differ from those on the large panel, but the background is virtually identical. Since the composition of this small grisaille panel does not entirely correspond with that of the finished panel, the question arises whether the work indeed served as a preliminary oil sketch, and whether it is indeed painted by Ambrosius Francken.[6] In my opinion it was made later, by another painter, and with Francken's panel as an example. This hypothesis is supported in the fact that Saint Eligius' altar was very popular and often copied in the 17th century. One might cite, for example, a relatively small painting that Adriaen de Bie made in 1626 for the Smiths' craft of Lier (Lier, Saint Gummarus' Church) and a variant by another, unknown hand (Vienna, formerly the Arenbaum collection).

NATASJA PEETERS

4 Vervaet 1976, pp. 224–225.
5 Panel, 37.5 x 26.5 cm; see Dijkstra *et al.* 2002, pp. 361–362.
6 The research is hampered because of the absence of modelli by his hand. Stylistically, however, the panel fits better in the oeuvres of de Vos or van Veen, both of whom made considerable numbers of modelli. Otto van Veen's modello of *Saint Nicholas Saving the Faithful from Famine* (Amsterdam, Rijksmuseum), executed in grisaille and dating from 1605, shows strong similarities with the modello of *Saint Eligius*.

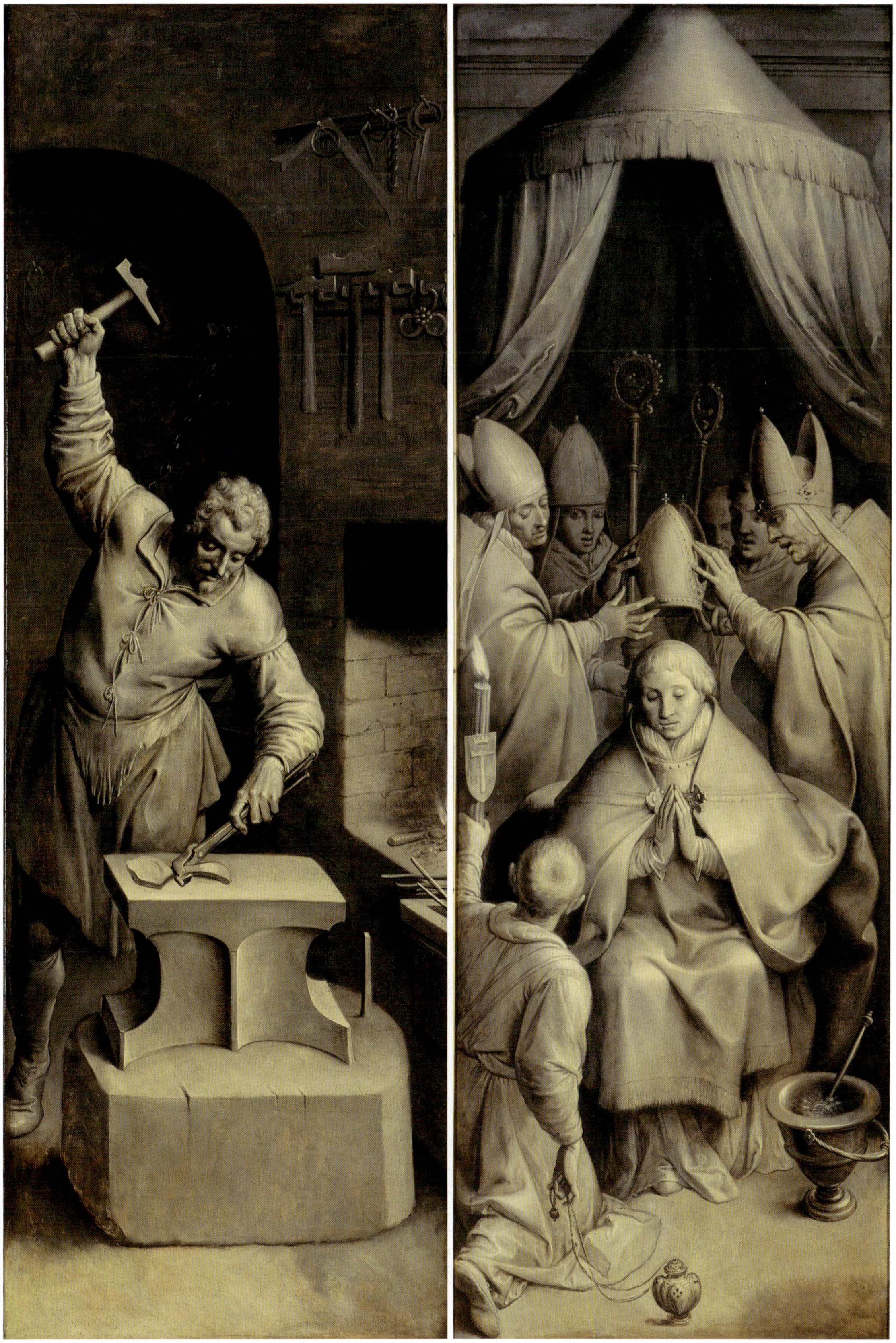

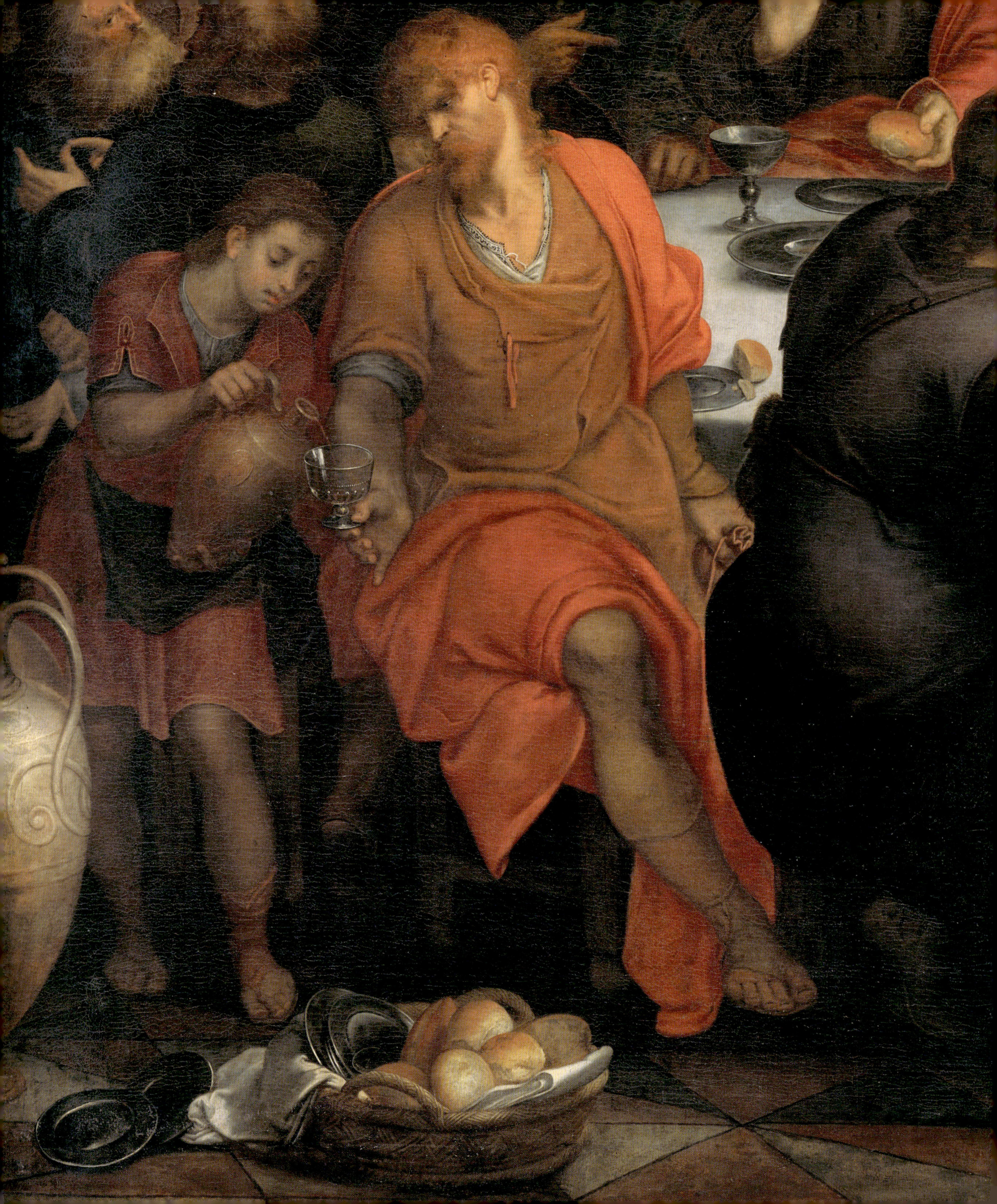

8 Altarpiece of the Fraternity of the Blessed Sacrament

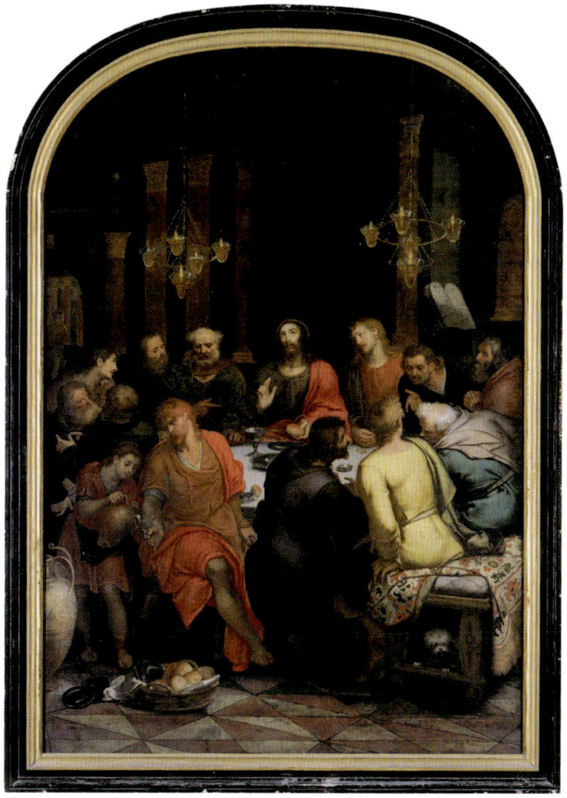

Otto van Veen

Leiden 1556–Brussels 1629

The Last Supper

1592

Oil on canvas, 350 x 247 cm

Unsigned

Antwerp, Cathedral of Our Lady, inv. 931

Provenance: altarpiece of the Chapel of the Fraternity of the Blessed Sacrament (Venerable Chapel); expanded in height and width 1750–1755, to make it fit in the new chapel altar; sold by the Fraternity to the cathedral church fabric in 1828.

Bibliography: *Beschrijvinge 1751,* p. 4 (12)
Mensaert 1763, p. 228
Descamps 1769, p. 143
Kerken van Antwerpen 1774, p. 11
Van Lerius 1841, p. 15
Donnet 1924, p. 7
Leurs & Philippen 1938, p. 50, no. 84, pl. 80
Van Herck 1951, p. 43
Van den Nieuwenhuizen 1957, p. 111
Müller Hofstede 1957, pp. 138–140
Van Brabant 1972, pp. 252–253, no. 139
Van Brabant 1974, p. 225
Van de Velde 1993A, p. 199
Grieten & Bungeneers 1996, pp. 382–384

Otto van Veen, also known by his humanist name Otto Venius, painted several scenes of the Last Supper.[1] Through the surviving sources, we are reasonably well informed about the provenance of this canvas. It was intended for the Chapel of the Blessed Sacrament, or Venerable Chapel, in the Antwerp cathedral, and was probably also commissioned by the Fraternity of the Blessed Sacrament.[2] Bishop Laevinus Torrentius[3] (1556–1628) (fig. 8a) was the mediator of this commission. He recommended the painter to the wardens of the Chapel of the Bessed Sacrament. This is apparent from a letter from Torrentius to Domenicus Lampsonius.[4] The latter was certainly no stranger to van Veen. Lampsonius was a humanist, diplomat, painter, poet, and artists' biographer, and from 1573 to 1575 van Veen's master of apprenticeship. After this, van Veen went to Italy for five years. His visit there would leave a deep impression on his later oeuvre. Although van Veen was born in Leiden, he is considered one of the most important painters in the Southern Netherlands. When he was young, he moved to Antwerp with his family, which remained faithful to the Catholic Church.[5] His catholic conviction is also shown in his attachment to the iconography of the Counter Reformation. In this regard, the theme of the Last Supper is important. Indeed, the Eucharist received a central place in the ideas of the Counter Reformation as established in the Council of Trent (1545–1563). The Last Supper, as a representation of the institution of the Eucharist, was a very suitable subject for an altarpiece of the Fraternity of the Blessed Sacrament.[6] The position of the altar of the Fraternity, just before the south transept, was not without meaning either. There was probably a hierarchical order for the allotment of altar places to guilds, crafts and fraternities.[7]

At the centre of the painting, Christ is depicted amid the apostles. He holds the bread and blesses it. Thus, the moment of the institution of the Eucharist is shown. Some of the disciples pay no attention to the scene, because they are too concerned about the ominous announcement that there is a traitor amongst them. Van Veen has visualised the unfaithful disciple very well. With the purse of silver pieces hidden in his left hand, Judas turns away from the discussion to have his glass filled and thus avoids attracting

1 Otto van Veen's two other versions of the *Last Supper* can be found on the high altar of Saint Peter's Chapel in Herne, and in the Abbey Notre Dame de Soleilmont in Gilly.
2 Grieten & Bungeneers 1996, pp. 384–386.
3 Van Veen painted the bishop's portrait, currently kept in Antwerp's Monastery of the Sisters Terninck (fig. 8a).
4 Letter from Bishop Torrentius to Lampsonius from 29 January 1592.
5 Belkin 1998, p. 26.
6 Other Fraternities of the Holy Sacrament also chose this theme; see Grieten & Bungeneers 1996, p. 386.
7 See Ria Fabri's contribution in this publication.

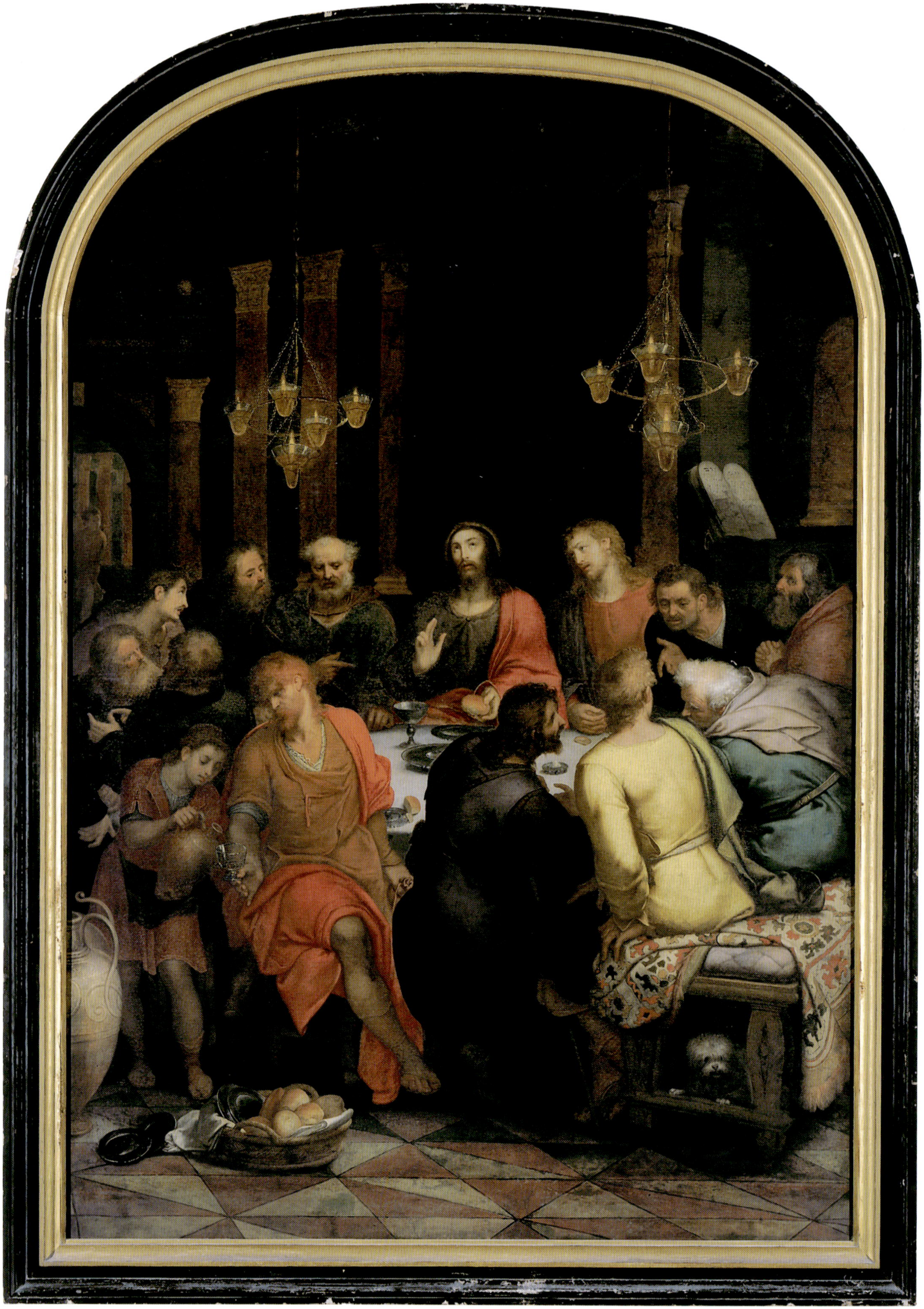

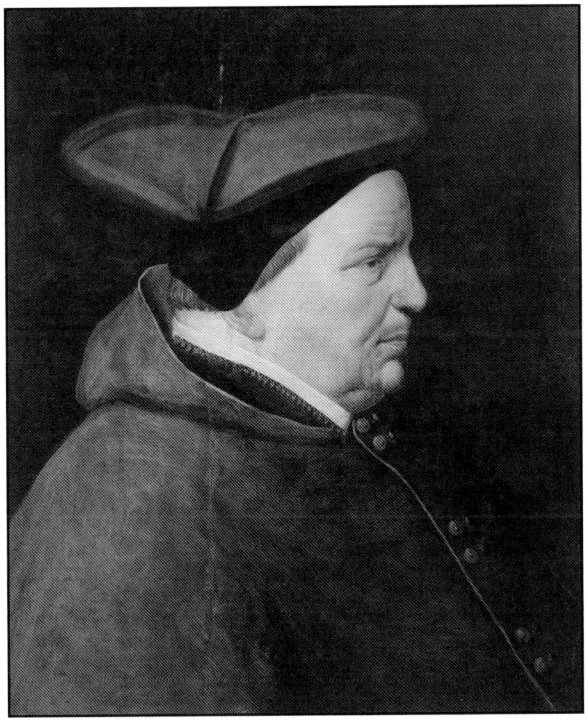

8a
Otto van Veen
Portrait of Laevinius Torrentius
Antwerp, Monastery of the Sisters Terninck

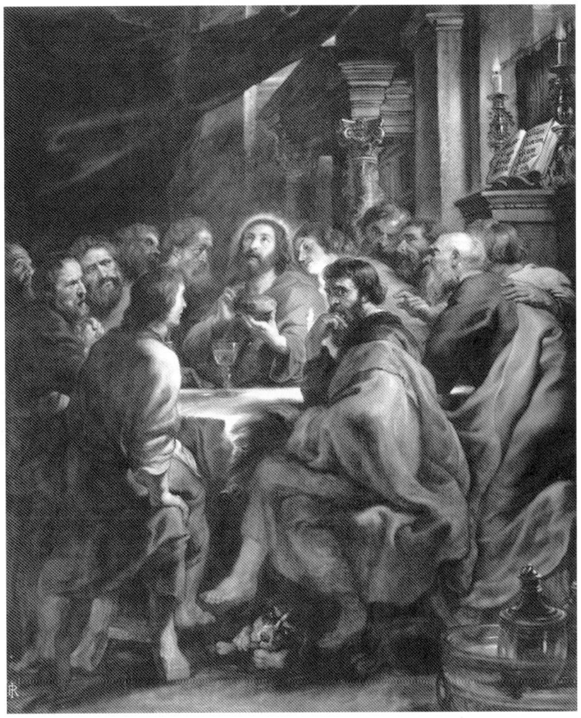

8b
Peter Paul Rubens
The Last Supper
Milan, Pinacoteca Brera

the suspicion of the others. Thus he breaks the unity of the circle of Christ and his apostles physically as well as mentally. The artist placed extra emphasis on the traitor through the expressly sharp facial features, the angry look, and the gingery hair. This physiognomic type recurs in many representations of Judas.[8]

Contrary to what might be expected from the two chandeliers, the room is poorly lit. The Tablets of the Law in the background, however, are emphasised with a subtle light beam. Through the reference to the stone tablets on which the Laws of the Old Testament are inscribed, the New Covenant between God and man, established in the celebration of the Eucharist, gains even greater emphasis. The *chiaroscuro* and the archaising setting indicate Italian influence. Although Italy is never very far away in van Veen's oeuvre, explicit references to Flemish painting can still be found. Thus, the tall wine jug in the left corner, the dog under the bench to the right, and the bread basket in the foreground, are all customary motifs in Flemish painting.[9] The entire scene is bathed in *sfumato*: the contours of the figures blur and seem to dissolve in the surroundings. This may indicate italianising tendencies, but it is not clear whether this was the artist's initial intention. Descamps, who recorded his travels through Flanders and Brabant in 1769, writes about the work, 'The painting by Otto Venius represents the Last Supper: there are great beauties, but it is too dark & has an overuniform effect'.[10] At that moment, the canvas had possibly darkened considerably, a century and a half after its realisation.

In the 17th and 18th centuries, this altarpiece was considered one of the high points of Venius' oeuvre. It was therefore mentioned or discussed by various early historiographers.[11] Thus, in the *Images des divers hommes d'esprit* by Jean Meyssens from 1649, this painting is mentioned under van Veen's portrait.[12] Bellori, too, in his biography of Rubens, referred to the altarpiece of the latter's teacher.[13] Other 18th century sources call van Veen's famous altarpiece as, 'being one of the finest works by this great master'.[14] That the theme itself was also popular is shown in the range of versions, not only by van Veen, but also by his predecessors, contemporaries, and followers.

8 Consider, for example, Pieter Coecke van Aelst, *Last Supper*, Liège, Musée d'Art Moderne et d'Art Contemporain, 1530; Pieter Pourbus, *Last Supper*, Bruges, Groeninge Museum, 1548; Adam van Noort, *Last Supper*, Bernaerts Gallery, first quarter 16th century.
9 Müller-Hofstede 1957, p. 138, note 25.
10 Descamps 1769, p. 143.
11 Grieten & Bungeneers 1996, p. 386.
12 Meyssens 1649, s.l.
13 'Avvenne che trovandosi in Anversa Ottavio Van Veen da Leiden , pittore ... del Principe di Parma, e dopo dell'Arciduca Alberto; ... di cui mano è la Cena del Signore nella Cattedrale della medesima città'. [And thus it happens that he ends up in Antwerp with Otto van Veen van Leiden, painter of the Prince of Parma and later of Archduke Albert, and by whose hand the Last Supper is in the same city.] Bellori 1672, p. 222.
14 Berbie 1774, p. 12.

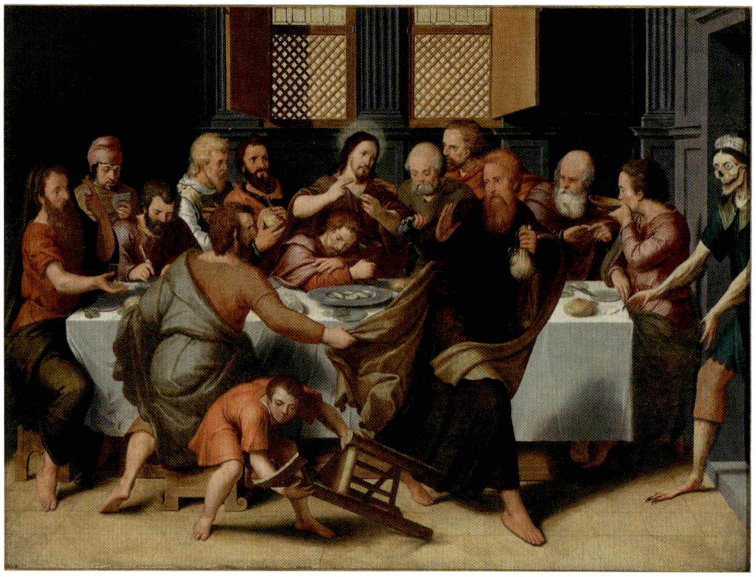

8c
Pieter Pourbus
The Last Supper
Bruges, Groeninge Museum

There was often a conceptual link with the function of the guild, craft, or fraternity, for which the painting was destined. In 1559, Pieter Pourbus painted a *Last Supper*[15] for the Fraternity of the Holy Sacrament of Bruges' Saint Salvator's Cathedral, which is known as the 'Sacra-Fraternity'. Almost simultaneously with van Veen, Ambrosius Francken worked on a *Last Supper* for the Sacrament Altar of Saint George's Church in Antwerp (now in the Koninklijk Museum voor Schone Kunsten in Antwerp).[16] In 1632, van Veen's most talented pupil, Peter Paul Rubens, would paint a *Last Supper* himself. That Venius was an intellectual, a genuine *pictor doctus,* is what attracted the young Rubens to work in his studio.[17] There he started as an apprentice in 1594 or 1595 and did not leave until he became a free-master himself in 1598. Rubens' *Last Supper,* now in the Pinacoteca Brera in Milan (fig. 8b), is based on the work of his teacher, but with Rubens the emphasis manifestly lies on the institution of the Eucharist:[18] the betrayal by Judas was not even included in his representation. Thus, Rubens confirms his role as *the* painter of the Counter Reformation.

PRISCA VALKENEERS

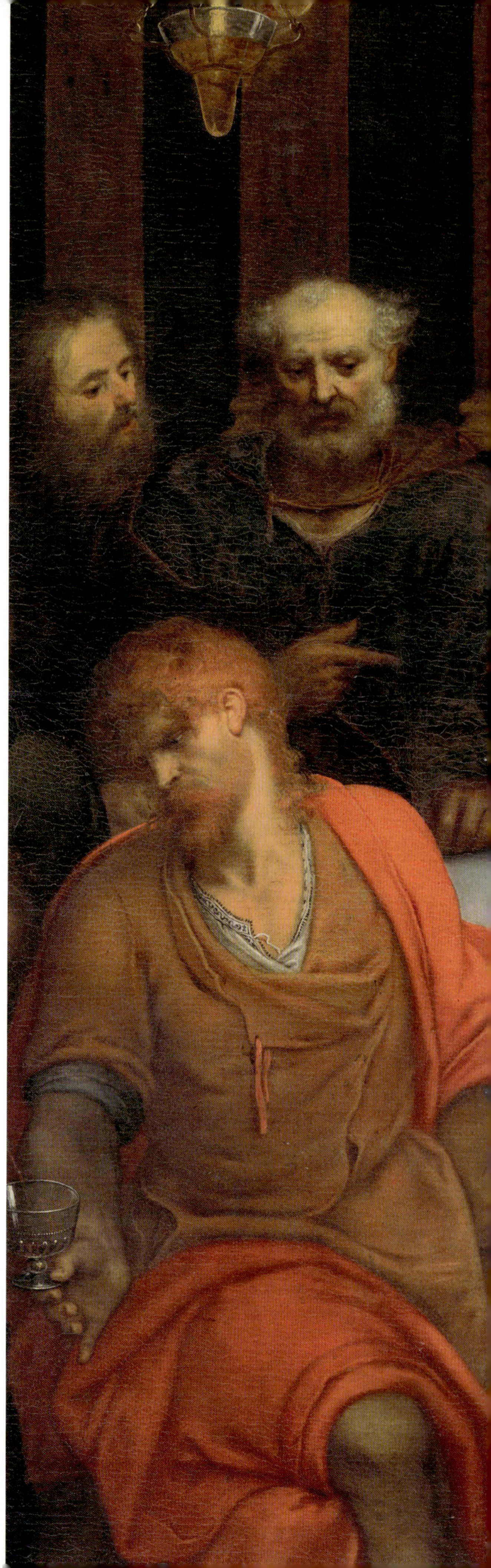

15 Huvenne 1984, pp. 161–166, cat. 6.
16 *Catalogue Antwerp 1988*, p. 142, no. 136.
17 Belkin 1998, p. 27.
18 Judson 2000, pp. 48–52, no. 6, fig. 11.

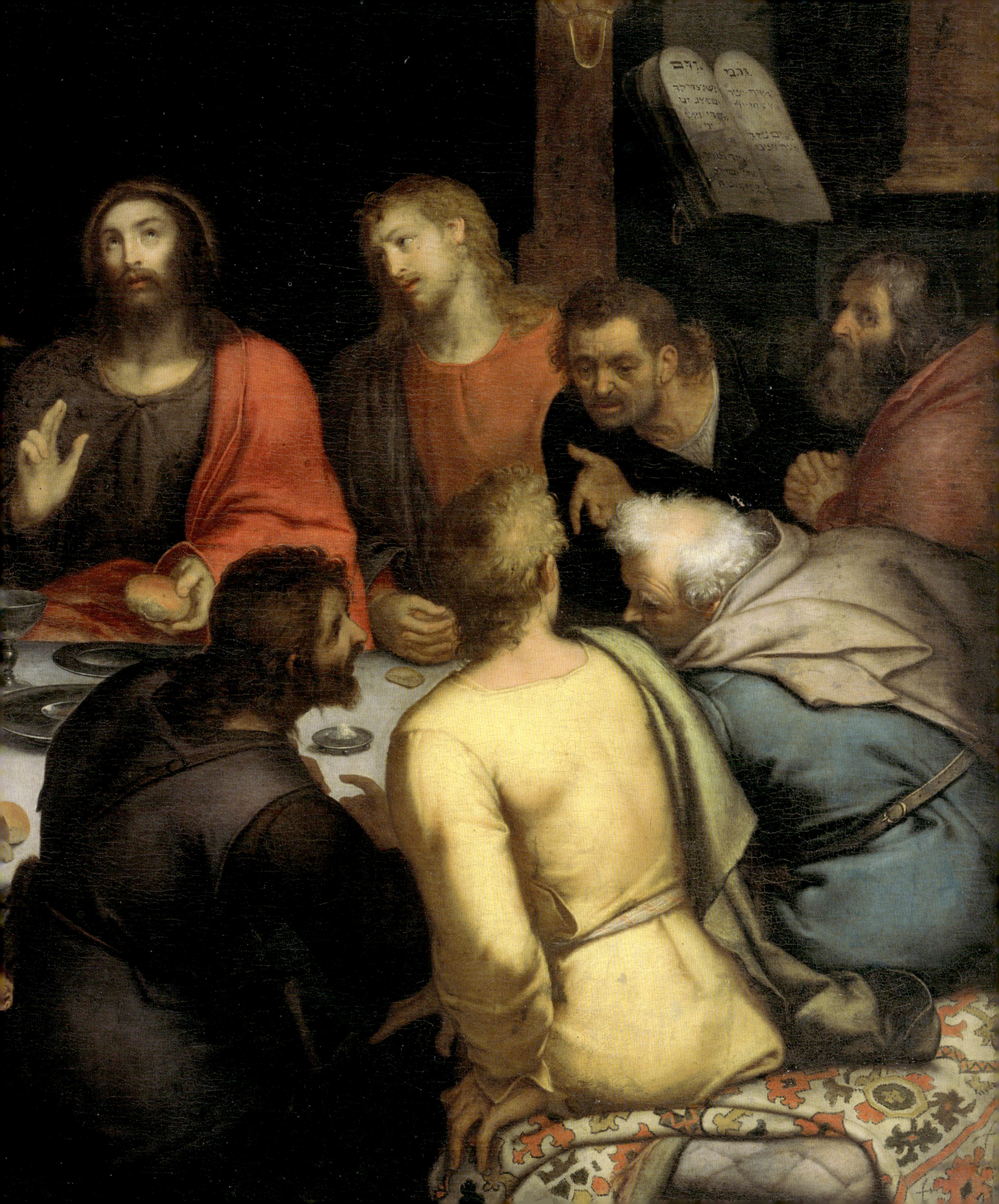

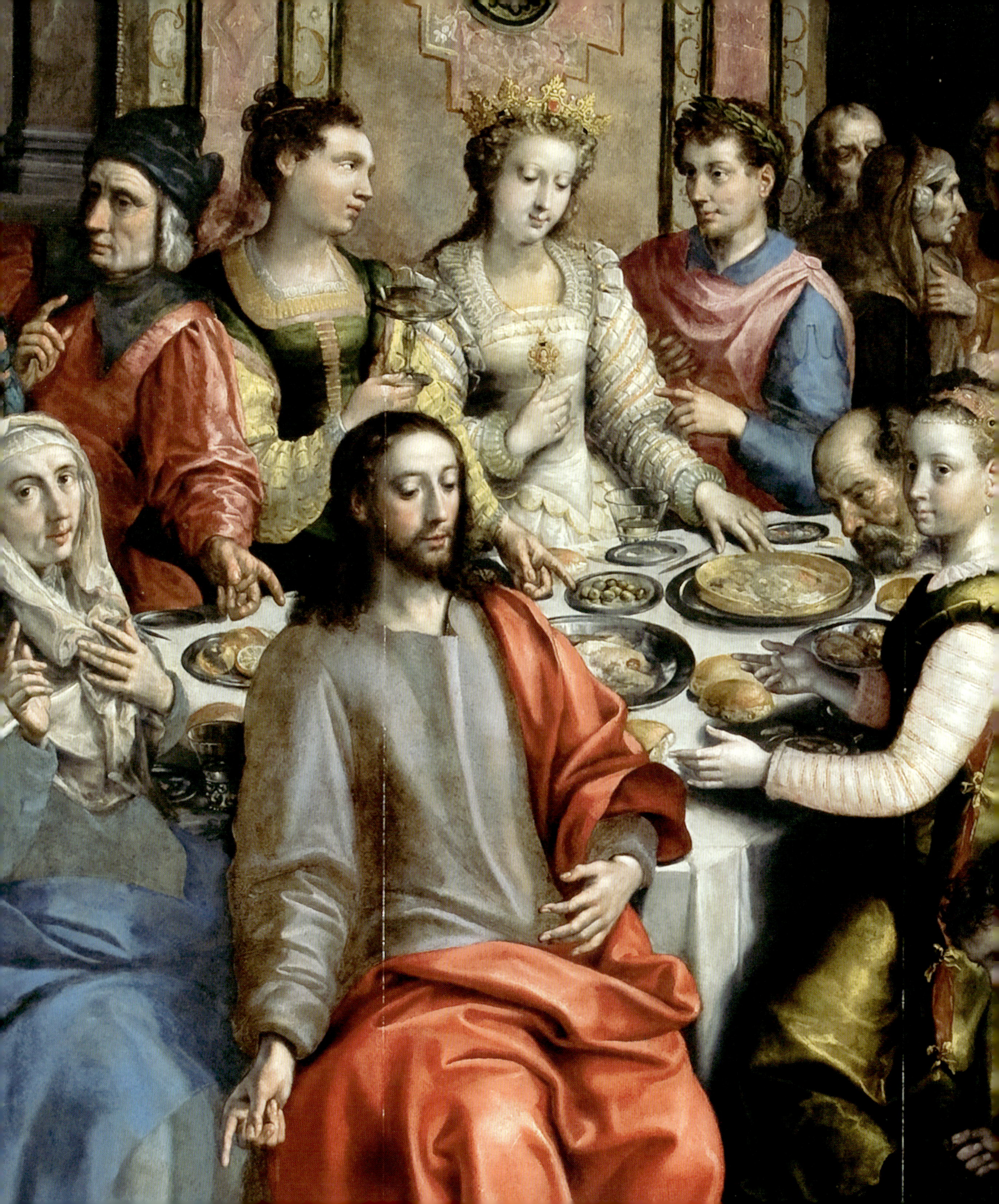

9 Altarpiece of the Wine Taverners

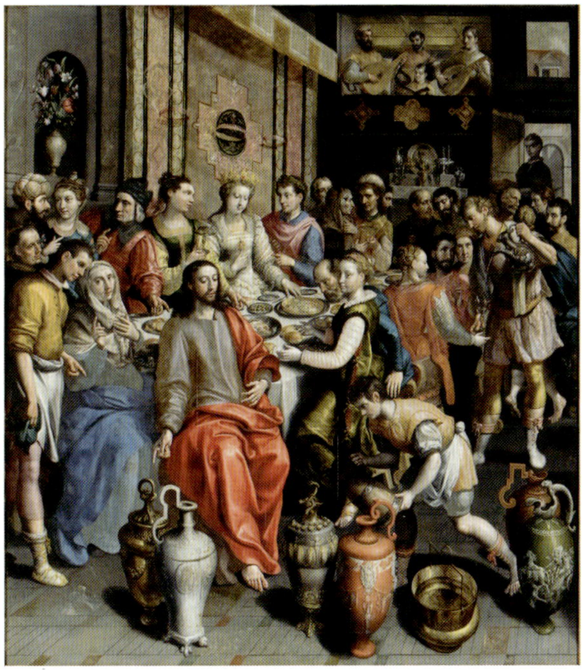

Maerten de Vos

Antwerp 1532–Antwerp 1603

The Wedding at Cana

1597

Oil on panel, 268 x 235 cm

Unsigned

Antwerp, Cathedral of Our Lady, inv. 934

Provenance: commissioned by the Wine Taverners' craft for their altar in the Antwerp cathedral; displayed there in 1597.

Bibliography: *Beschrijvinge 1751,* p. 8 (14)
Mensaert 1763, p. 236
Descamps 1769, p. 149
Kerken van Antwerpen 1774, p. 21
Van Lerius 1841, p. 20
Rooses 1879, pp. 161–162
Van den Branden 1883, p. 222
Leurs & Philippen 1938, pp. 48–49, nos. 79–81, pl. 47
Prims 1938-1939, XIII, pp. 431–433
Van Herck 1951, p. 43
Van den Nieuwenhuizen 1957, pp. 110–111
Van de Velde 1971
Van Brabant 1972, pp. 248–249
Zweite 1980, pp. 212–215, 306–308, no. 8
Van de Velde 1993A, p. 161
Grieten & Bungeneers 1996, pp. 387–389
Peeters 2009C

The wedding guests are seated at a long table in a large room. In the gallery in the back, three lute players and a young singer provide the appropriate musical accompaniment. Maerten de Vos simultaneously depicts different events from the story of the wedding at Cana, as described in the Gospel of John (John 2: 1–11). Jesus, prominently set in the foreground, points at the jug at his feet and urges a servant to fill it with water. To his left, Mary advises another servant to execute Jesus' order. Further on, the master of ceremonies pours wine for a woman, while the other guests around the table discuss the miracle, vividly gesticulating. The bridal couple and the guest of honour to their left – probably the mother of the bride – seem to fail to notice the event, as they blissfully enjoy each other's company.

The story itself is not the only claim to attention – even more is the explicit festive luxury of the scene. The decor is dominated by the baldachin with an oriental tapestry set behind the revellers, but other motifs, too, contribute to a general impression of copious abundance: the valuable vase with flowers in a niche, flanked by marble pilasters, the tapestry against the wall surface below the musicians, the ostentatious display of precious kitchenware with the filled festive fare underneath, generously provided with dishes, glasswork, and tazzas. The company's luxurious clothing, and the refined ladies' hairstyle and jewels are striking. In the foreground the richly decorated jugs catch the eye. They not only enhance the decorative richness of the scene, but also situate the event of the Miracle of Cana, which heralds the public life of Jesus, in the broader perspective of the history of salvation. Indeed, the jugs refer to the six eras of the history of mankind, those of Adam, Noah, Abraham, David, Jeremiah, and Zeus. As Jesus changed the tasteless water into delicious wine, his coming on earth also marked the end of the era of the Old Testament, and ushered the era of Redemption. Another allusion to this is the ascension of the prophet Elijah, depicted on the jug to the far right: this event typologically refers to the Ascension of Jesus himself.

The artist has composed a lush decor in a balanced mix of exotic elements – the oriental tapestry, the turbans of some guests – and the archaic costumes with long tunics, mantles, and sandals, which were traditionally used for staging episodes from the Bible, classical antiquity and mythology, and are here applied to the *dramatis personae* of the story: Jesus and Mary, the servants, and the master of ceremonies. These components were enriched with more contemporary elements – notably the eye-catching clothing of some ladies in the company, such as the bride and the woman who holds out her glass for wine. Such figures refer to the tradition of the rich banquet scenes of the Venetian School at the height of the 16th century, in which – apart from Jacopo Tintoretto – particularly Paolo Veronese set the tone

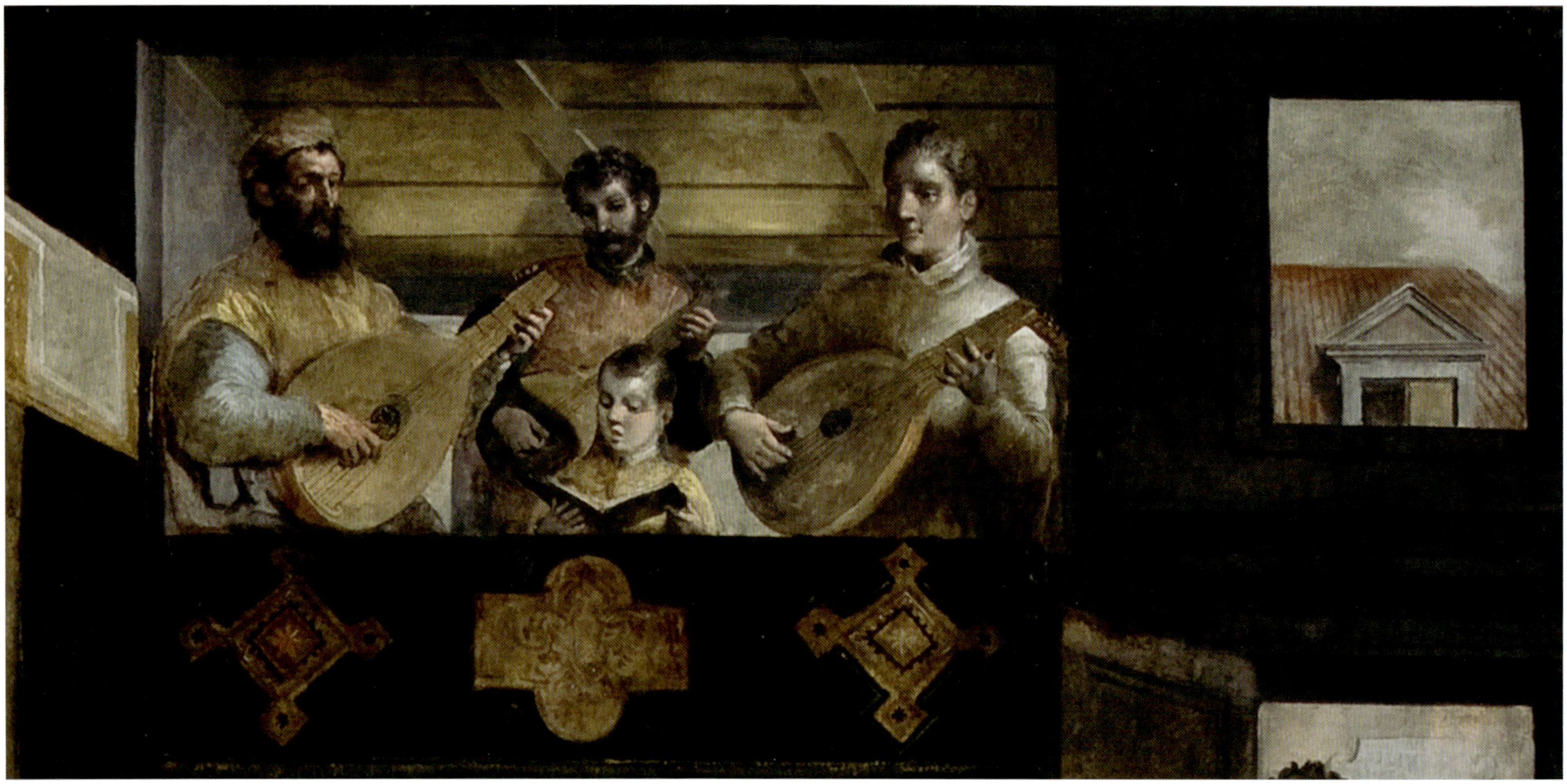

with his *Wedding at Cana,* 1563 (Paris, Musée du Louvre; fig. 9a), as a well-known culminating point.[1] Some men in the company are dressed in contemporary Brabantian bourgeois fashion, such as the figure to the far left behind the servant, and the two guests near the head of the table. These persons are clearly intended as individual portraits, more specifically of the committee members of the Wine Taverners' craft. This kind of incorporation of the painting's commissioners into religious and historical scenes is called a *portrait historié*, a custom with a long tradition, in the altarpieces of guilds, crafts, and fraternities, for example.[2] The older man behind the table, who points at Christ, seems instead to belong (clotheswise) in the early 16th century. Through this wide range of references – oriental, archaising, historic Venetian, contemporary – Maerten de Vos managed to evoke the desired ethos for the depiction of a biblical feast, intensified by the exotic touches and accents of Venetian splendour and elegance, while he also meets the wishes of the portrayed patrons, who are projected into the event. Neither does he fail to use traditional motifs from the local wedding iconography, notably with the crown on the bride's head, and the three small crowns, hung above the bride and her table neighbours.[3]

This visual variety is weakened by the poorly inspired interaction, despite the drama of the depicted miracle. The static effect is mitigated by the dynamic composition, with a viewpoint that shows the room diagonally, in a foreshortened perspective that sweeps the spectator's glance forward, from the head of the table in the left foreground to the open door in the right background, and from the servant entering through it to the distant house across the courtyard. The specialist literature connects this device to the tradition of feast scenes from the Venetian School, or at least to Italian examples,[4] on which de Vos would have drawn, directly or indirectly. In this regard de Vos' Italian journey in 1552 should certainly be mentioned. Carel van Mander specified in his *Schilderboeck* (1604) that the artist also stayed in Venice, and Ridolfi even stated in 1648 that he had been an apprentice and an assistant in Tintoretto's studio there.[5] It has even been suggested that there was a second Italian journey, specifically to explain the alleged Venetian connections in this *Wedding at Cana*.[6] The oeuvre of de Vos indeed contains numerous assimilations and borrowings,[7] but generally the achievements of Italian Renaissance art were in many aspects – theme, style, composition, motif – easily and widely available in the studios of the Southern Netherlands, which makes anecdotal speculation superfluous. Zweite, on the other hand, illustrates that de Vos regularly used the composition scheme coined in Venetian feast scenes, with diagonal space, accelerated perspective, architectural accompaniment with apertures, and decorative personages. Thus, in 1583 he drew a *Wedding at Cana* (Paris, Musée du Louvre, Graphical Arts Department: fig. 9a), but he also handled this concept in other themes.[8]

Although Maerten de Vos knew this tradition at first hand, and though it certainly provided a fertile context for developing the composition of this altarpiece, the artist actually aimed directly at a another iconographical composition that he knew equally well, namely, *Salome Offering the Head of Saint John the Baptist to Herod*, on the left side panel of the altarpiece which Quinten Metsijs had painted in 1508–1511 for the altar of the Cabinetmakers in the Antwerp Church of Our Lady (cat. 1). Just like Maerten de Vos, Metsijs combined a diagonal viewpoint with a feast under a baldachin, a lush decor and a tribune with musicians. The congruence between both scenes is strikingly stronger than that between de Vos' composition and the examples from the Venetian tradition. The primacy of Quinten Metsijs as a source of inspiration in this late 16th century context is hardly surprising. As a prominent representative of the national artistic tradition and a cornerstone of the Antwerp School of painting, he was considered an important cultural and artistic reference. His oeuvre was collected and studied by artists and connoisseurs.[9] An early impulse for this elevated status was the insertion of his portrait in the album *Pictorum aliquot celebrium Germania Inferioris Effigies* (*Portraits of some Celebrated Artists of the Low Countries)* in 1572 by Dominicus Lampsonius.[10] The altarpiece of the Cabinetmakers was a high point in this cult, and when the destitute craft threatened to sell it to Queen Elizabeth I of England in 1577, Maerten de Vos set up a rescue operation. It was purchased by the city council, after which it was first set up in the city hall, and from 1589 onwards in the Chapel of Circumcision (used as a Magistrates' Chapel) in the cathedral.[11] Obviously, de Vos had a far-reaching personal commitment to Metsijs' generally admired triptych. It is not inconceivable that, as homage to the celebrated master, he used the features of Quinten Metsijs for the older man who stands behind the table and points at Christ. In any case, the similarities with his portrait in Lampsonius' album seem unlikely to be coincidental.[12]

The history of the painting is well documented. The Wine Taverners, who had shared an altar with the Coopers since 1586, wished to have a separate altar in the cathedral, as they had previously had. The official separation took place on 12 June 1596, but the first meeting of the commissioners and the artist was organised as early as 26 October 1595 – the contract followed on 28 June 1596. The guild council insisted on the completion of the work for its patron's feast day on 11 November 1596, but not until 16 July 1597 could the members of the Chapter of our Lady – including the choir dean Silvester Pardo – see it at de Vos' studio. On 26 July 1597 it was displayed on the altar. In the final invoice the altarpiece, which cost 500 guilders, was explicitly called 'Wedding at Cana Galilee', which suggests that is was conceived as an isolated painting without side panels. The choice of both the design and the executing artist was made deliberately. The chapter, in accordance with the prescriptions by the Council of Trent, meticulously supervised the theme and its execution. To the commissioners, the subject had to connect with their professional activities. Maerten de Vos, a reputable painter of altarpieces, was an obvious option for them.[13] Of course, the separation from the Coopers also required further investments to furnish the altar space in the central choir chapel appropriately. To that end, de Vos delivered a model for a statue of Saint Martin, the patron saint of the Wine Taverners,

1 See, *inter alia*, *Les noces de Cana de Véronèse*, 1992–1993 (with other examples).
2 There are numerous examples among the altarpieces destined for Antwerp cathedral, and Maerten de Vos himself applied this custom more than once; see Zweite 1980, p. 31 and *passim*.
3 These motifs are found particularly often in country weddings in the 16th century tradition, in which the artist families Bruegel and Verbeeck were active.
4 See Zweite 1980, pp. 212–214 and 307–308.
5 Ridolfi, mentioned by Zweite 1980, p. 22, who is not convinced of this; contrary to Meijer 1999, pp. 137–138.
6 There is no evidence for this, as confirmed in Zweite 1980, p. 26.
7 For example, Zweite 1980, pp. 12–16.
8 Zweite 1980, pp. 213–214 and fig. 226–227. To his examples may also be added the engraving, *The Rich Man and Poor Lazarus* by Crispijn de Passe after Maerten de Vos. See *Paradisus musicus 1977*, p. 48, no. 44 (with fig.).
9 Eisler 1967, p. 50; Silver 1984, p. 2.
10 The edition portrays 23 artists from the Netherlands with a short explanation in verse. See Lampson 1956.
11 Zweite 1980, pp. 24–26.
12 Lampson 1956, pp. 40–41.
13 Vervaet 1976, pp. 212–213, 228–229, 231–232; Grieten & Bungeneers 1996, pp. 360, 365–367.

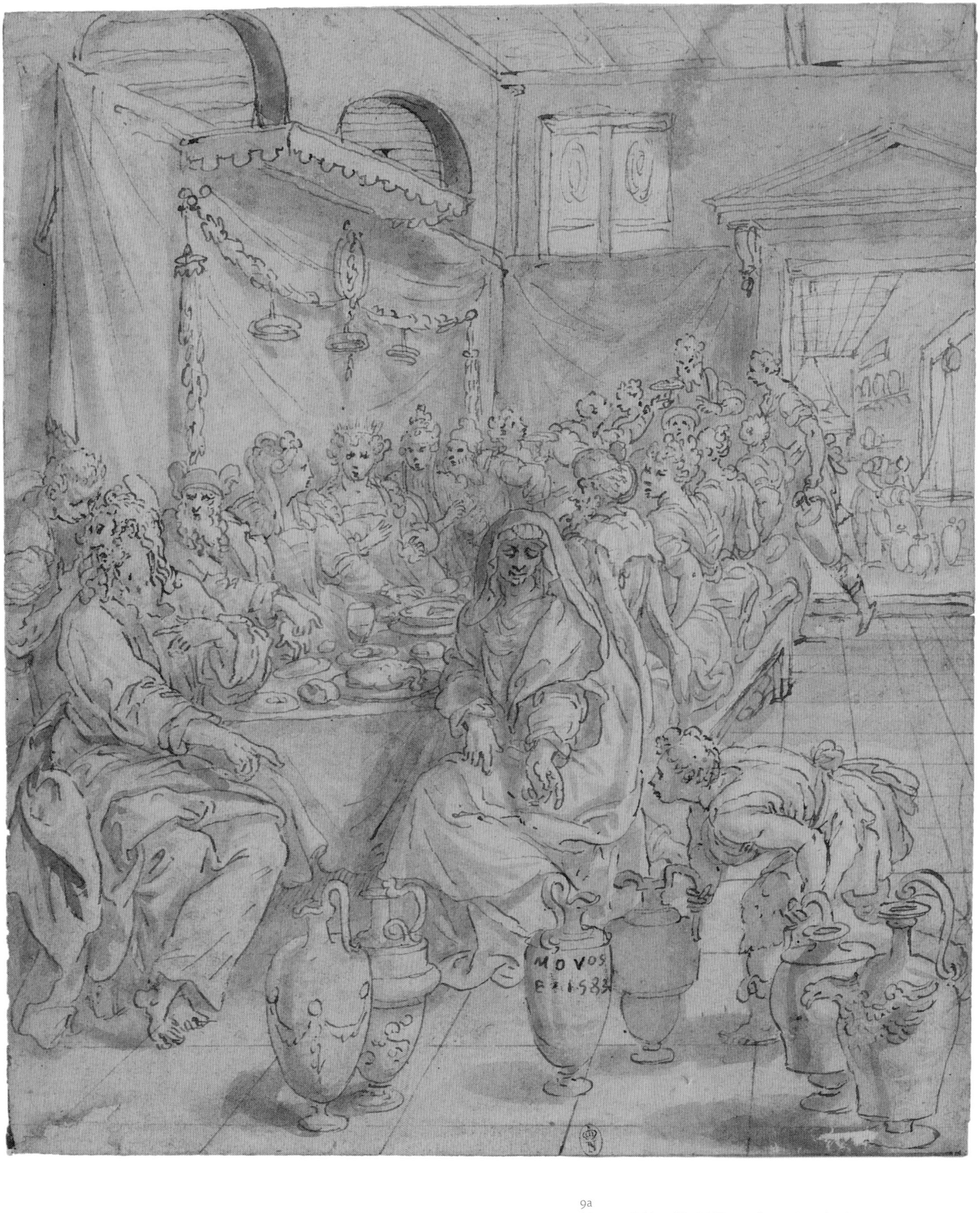

9a
Maerten de Vos · *The Wedding at Cana,* 1583 · drawing · Paris, Musée du Louvre

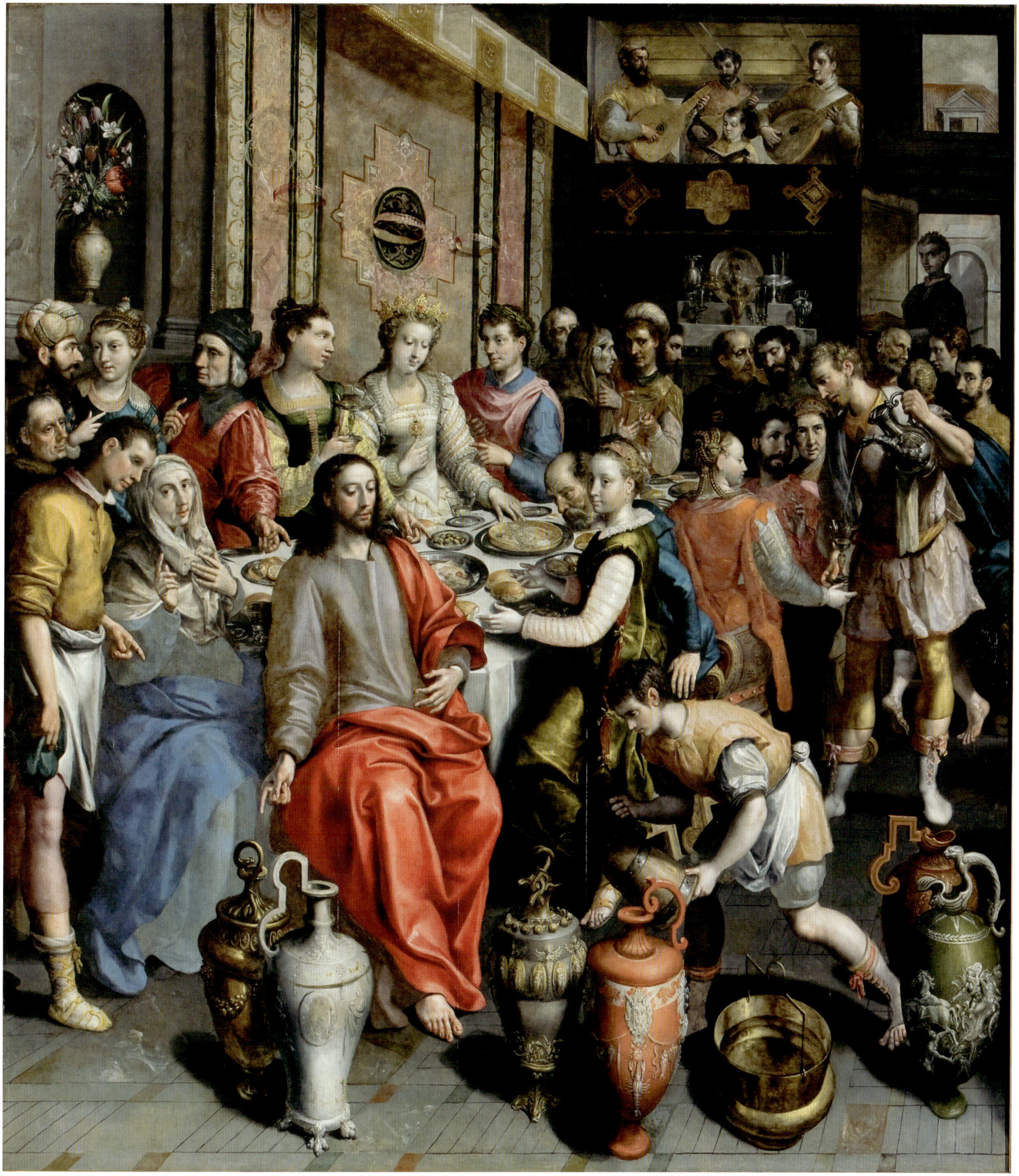

and Artus Claes executed the painted decoration of the chapel itself.[14] In 1597 the craft paid for a 'board upon which Maerten de Vos painted the angels', a *schoreersel*, a flat wooden cut-out decoration of painted angels, which crowned the altar.

Later, in 1618–1619, the guild ordered two large paintings, whose subjects are unknown, from Joos de Momper. Eighteenth century descriptions of the cathedral mention two paintings in the chapel that depicted the stories of Balaam and the Promised Land. The formulation 'two pieces lateral' seems to indicate that these two works did not serve as side panels of the altarpiece but were displayed beside it, against the chapel walls.[15] Although, in 18th century sources, the two works were linked to other names,[16] they might perhaps be identified as the two paintings by Joos de Momper, ordered in 1618–1619. This admired landscape painter would certainly have brought a subject like the Promised Land to a favourable conclusion. It is almost certain that both paintings showed in fact different episodes of the same story: that of Balaam, who predicted the coming of the Messiah and prophesised about the Promised Land. Besides, the story of Balaam can be typologically linked to the Wedding at Cana, the event that heralded the public life of Christ and therefore underlined the importance of the New Testament. Both landscape paintings were called 'very spoilt' as early as 1728.[17]

This *Wedding at Cana* was often copied, more than any other work by de Vos. Most of these paintings have a strongly simplified composition, but nevertheless adopted the characteristic figure groups and motifs.[18]

STEFAAN GRIETEN

9b
Anonymous after Maerten de Vos
The Wedding at Cana
Tournai, Episcopal Seminary

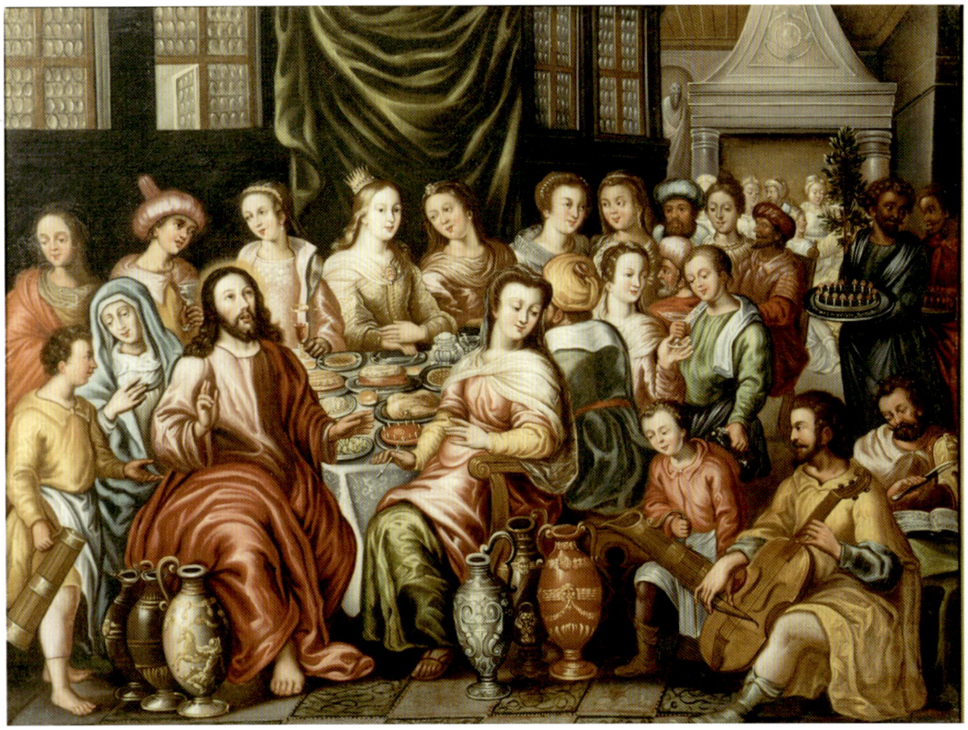

14 Claes also produced the surviving vault painting for the altar area of the Old Longbowmen's Guild, in the first south aisle of the cathedral. Grieten & Bungeneers 1996, p. 239, no. 695.
15 *Kerken van Antwerpen 1774*, p. 21.
16 An anonymous description of the cathedral from 1728 attributes the works to Maerten de Vos, while de Wit and Mols ascribe them to a member of the Francken family *(Kerken van Antwerpen 1774)*.
17 There is no evidence for the claim by Van Lerius 1841, p. 20, that they may have been replaced by copies.
18 See the list in Zweite 1980, p. 308 and the additions in Grieten & Bungeneers 1996, p. 389. The list can be easily extended. A fairly reliable copy in large format in the Kadrioru Kunstimuuseum in Tallinn occupies a special place and is notably relevant in regard to contemporary atelier practice. On this subject, see Peeters 2009c; with thanks to N. Peeters for information about this version.

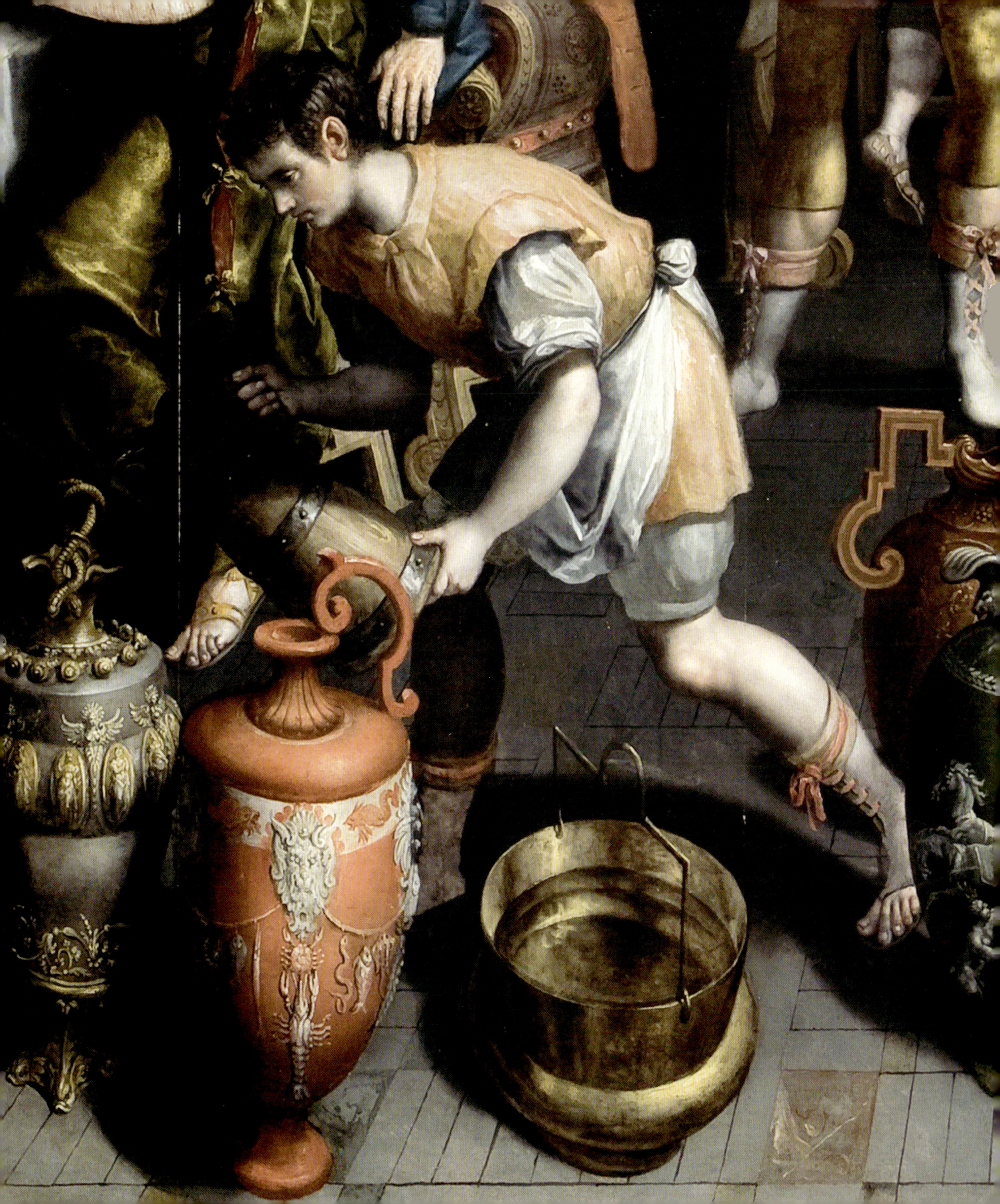

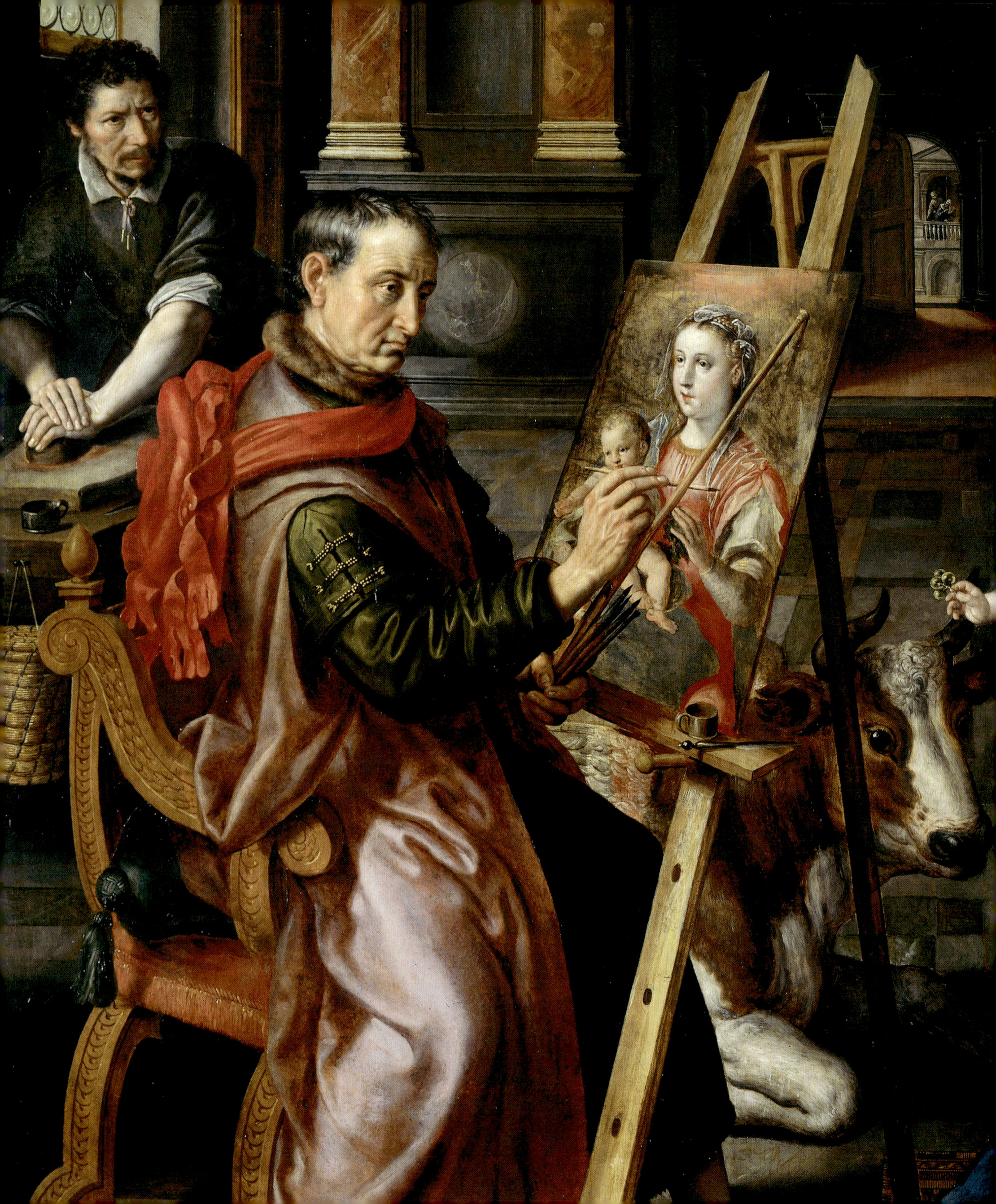

10 Altarpiece of Saint Luke's Guild

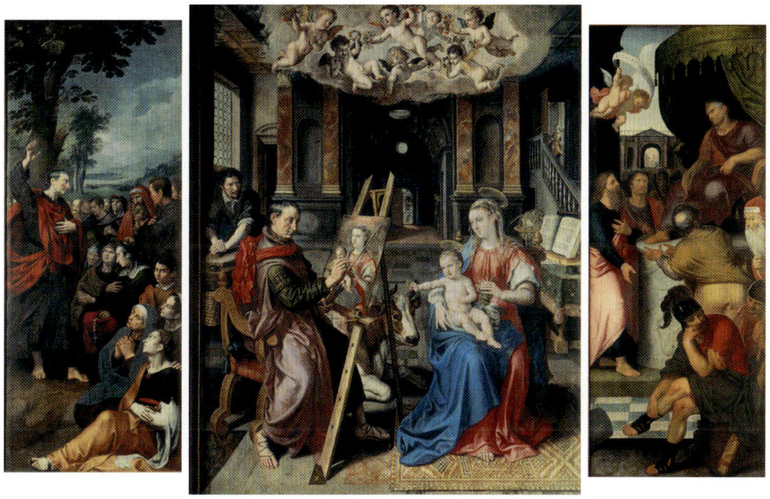

Maerten de Vos
Antwerp 1532–Antwerp 1603
Saint Luke Painting the Virgin Mary
centre panel
1602

Otto van Veen
Leiden 1556–Brussels 1629
Saints Luke and Paul before Emperor Nero
interior right side panel
shortly after 1602

Ambrosius Francken
Herentals 1544–Antwerp 1618
Saint Luke Preaches to the People
interior left side panel
shortly after 1602

Evangelists John and Matthew and **Evangelists Mark and Luke**
exterior side panels
shortly after 1602

Oil on panel
centre panel: 270 x 217 cm
side panels: 253 x 101 cm

Signed and dated on the centre panel, bottom right, on the table-leg:
F.M.D. VOS 1602

Antwerp, Koninklijk Museum voor Schone Kunsten
inv. 88, 274–276 and 484

The legend of the evangelist Luke, who paints the Madonna while she sits for him, only emerged during the 6th century. On its authority, Saint Luke became the patron saint of painters. In the Netherlands, especially, the associated iconography has led to a tradition of numerous depictions – dating back as far as Rogier van der Weyden – and remained vivid for centuries.[1] Maerten de Vos sets the event entirely to the foreground. From behind his easel the saint looks thoughtfully towards Mary. The Virgin, with the Child on her lap, is seated in a chair and turns towards the painter, to whom the Child hands some grapes from the bunch his mother is holding. They are watched by the painter's servant, who grinds pigments at a table behind Saint Luke on the left. The ox, the attribute of the evangelist, sits behind the easel. The cloud of cherubs clearly shows that this is not an ordinary domestic scene.

Maerten de Vos painted this panel in 1602 – it was probably his last work in his long career. Being a prominent painter, he belonged to the select circle of artists who, after Antwerp's reconciliation in 1585, took a large part in the execution of new altarpieces for the churches that had severely suffered in the Iconoclastic Fury (1566) and under the mandatory austerity measures for church interiors under the Calvinist rule (1581). Although the municipal authorities had already urged the guilds, crafts, and fraternities, to provide their altars with altarpieces in 1585, it was precisely Saint Luke's Guild that remained long in default. Only in 1589 did the cabinetmaker and sculptor Otmaer van Ommen deliver the wood for the altarpiece, and later still, in 1598, the then dean Adam van Noort painted the panel without consulting the guild council or ecclesiastical authorities. A complaint in 1600 by the council against van Noort led to the replacement of the panel, after which Maerten de Vos eventually received the commission.[2]

Maerten de Vos had a well-filled career. He was subdean (1571) and dean of the guild (1572), received many prestigious commissions and took a large share in designing city decorations for the Joyous Entry of Archduke Ernst of Austria to Antwerp in 1594 (fig. 10a).[3] However, the commission for this altarpiece differed radically from all others.[4] Its assignment was much more than a financial transaction, and was above all a supreme tribute to de Vos by his guild brothers. Implicitly, they had crowned him the most eminent painter of the corporation, and added his name to a historic line of famous artists in Antwerp's Saint Luke's Guild, such as Quinten Metsijs and Frans Floris. This view, more usually directed towards art of national stature, had already been articulated in the album *Pictorum aliquot*

1 For the iconography of the saint in general, cf. for example Réau 1958, pp. 827–832; Kirschbaum & Braunfels 1968-1976, VIII, col. 448–464. For the iconography of Saint Luke painting the Virgin, see, *inter alia*, Klein 1933; Kraut 1986; and Filedt Kok 2006 (with recent bibliography).
2 For this problematic history see, *inter alia*, Peeters 2005, pp. 243–244 and 247–248.
3 Zweite 1980, p. 24 and 198–199; specifically for the triumphal entry see Doutrepont, 1937.
4 For the history and analysis of the altarpiece, see *inter alia* Vervaet 1976, pp. 231–232; Zweite 1980, pp. 234–235 and 318–320, cat. 103–105; Kraut 1986, pp. 111–121; Peeters 2005 (each with extensive bibliography).

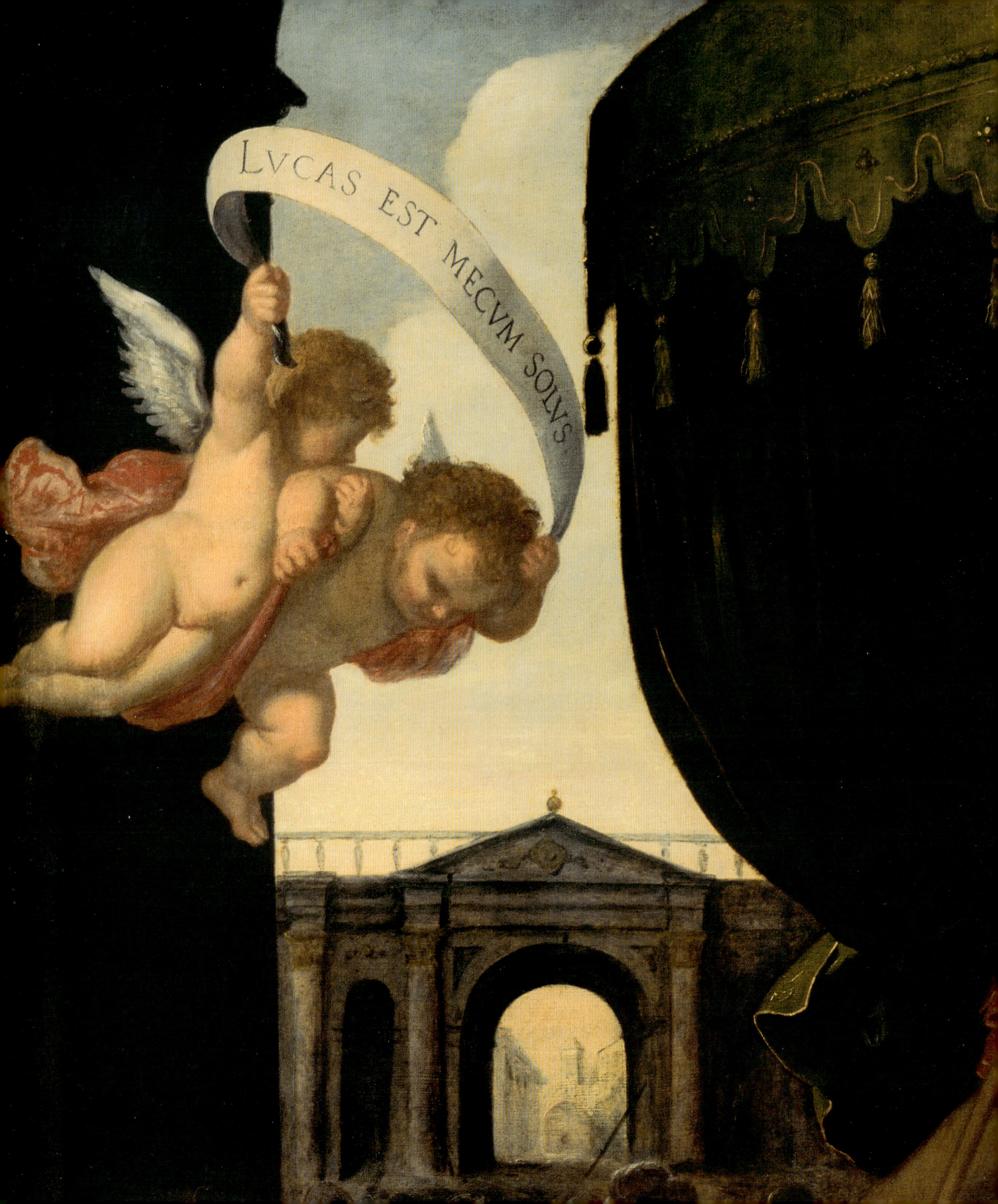
LVCAS EST MECVM SOLVS

Provenance: commissioned by the Antwerp Painters' guild and placed c. 1602 on their altar in the Antwerp cathedral; centre panel transferred in 1798 to the École Centrale du Département des Deux-Nèthes, kept in the abolished Discalced Monastery, 1802 relocated to the Academy in the Exchange building, 1811 passed to the museum in the former Friars Minor Monastery and then to the collection of the Museum of Fine Arts; side panels and predella panels transferred in 1754 to the chamber of Saint Luke's Guild in the Exchange building, where they decorated the wings of the entrance door; after 1811 they were in the museum in the former Friars Minor Monastery, and finally in the collection of the Museum of Fine Arts.

Bibliography: *Beschrijvinge 1751*, p. 8 (14)
Mensaert 1763, p. 234
Descamps 1769, p. 149
Kerken van Antwerpen 1774, pp. 22
Van Lerius 1841, pp. 20–21 (as anonymous)
Van den Branden 1883, p. 255
Piot 1883, p. 81
Dirksen 1914, pp. 88–90
Benesch 1925, pp. 62–63
Klein 1933, pp. 59 sqq.
Prims 1938–1939, XIII, pp. 411–414
Freedberg 1972, pp. 214–215
Van Brabant 1974, pp. 58, 90, 221–222
Vervaet 1976, pp. 231–232
Freedberg 1988, pp. 211–212
Van de Velde 1993A, p. 196
Grieten & Bungeneers 1996, p. 367

celebrium Germania Inferioris Effigies (Portraits of some Celebrated Artists of the Low Countries) from 1572, in which the author Dominicus Lampsonius combined portraits of painters – from Jan van Eyck and Rogier van der Weyden to Frans Floris and Hieronymus Cock – with laudatory poems. In Antwerp, this historic understanding was equally strong, as demonstrated by Maerten de Vos' initiative to prevent Quinten Metsijs' altarpiece for the Cabinetmakers being sold and disappearing abroad in 1577 (see cat. 1).[5] Moreover, the painting de Vos had to produce for Saint Luke's altar was to replace an altarpiece by Quinten Metsijs, which enhanced the prestige of the commission further still.[6] Even in the subject itself, as a theme for an altarpiece of the Painters' craft, ancient considerations on the status, the character, and the possibilities of painting, and on a painter's socio-cultural position, were manifested.[7]

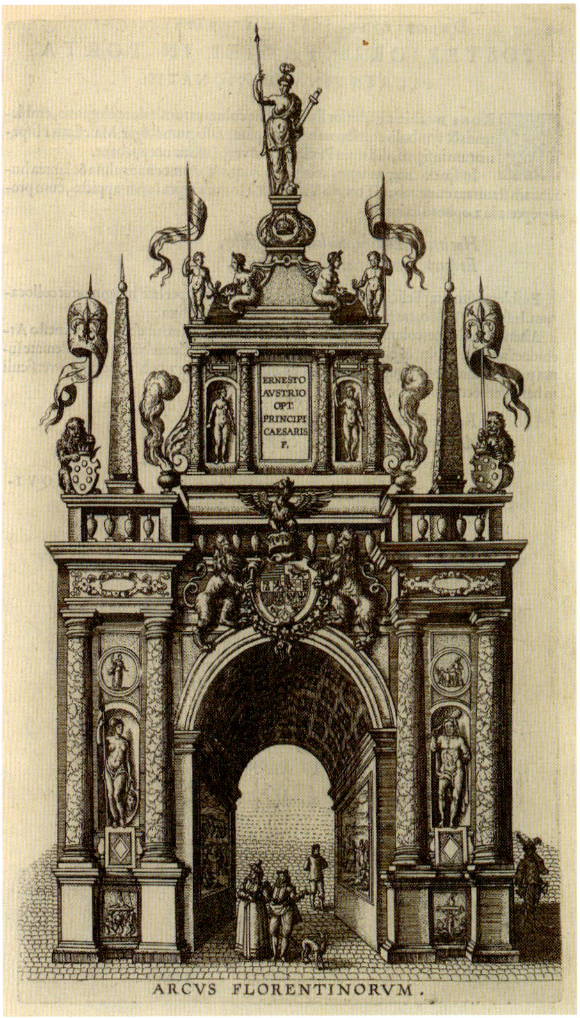

10a
Peter Van der Borcht
Triumphal Arch of the Florentines, copper engraving in Johannes Bochius, *Descriptio publicae gratulationis, spectaculorum et ludorum, in adventu [...] Ernesti archiducis Austriae [...]*
Antwerp, Officina Plantiniana, 1595, p. 101

The honour conferred upon Maerten de Vos therefore went hand-in-hand with a loaded topical and typological programme, and he adapted both the composition and the decorum of the painting to it. The scene of the saint who paints the Virgin with Child is integrated in the age-long tradition of this theme, its explicit place in the foreground included – probably a consciously pursued archaism which recalls paintings on this subject by predecessors such as Rogier van der Weyden and Hugo van der Goes. The saint's clothing combines different emphases. His sandals and mantle characterise him, in a historically authentic way, as a biblical personage, but the more contemporary tabard under his mantle indicates his dignity, while the flat hat with broad ribbons is a pseudo-late-medieval attribute.[8] This combination of historical references articulates Saint Luke, patron of painters, as a comprehensive role model in whom the historical perspective of painting itself is reflected. To this is added the art-theoretical discourse on the unique status of painting as a creative and intellectual force, which is not only capable of depicting nature, but also abstract and supernatural concepts. Because precisely that is happening in this painting: Saint Luke makes a depiction of the Virgin appearing to him. Maerten de Vos directly relates the abstract content of the scene to Antwerp's Saint Luke's Guild, by portraying the servant in the foreground as Abraham Grapheus, the servant and factotum of the corporation.[9] The manual labour he performed in the service of the master painter is answered in the table with celestial globe and books across the room, which express the ideal of the *pictor doctus*.

5 Zweite 1980, pp. 24–26.
6 There is, however, no unambiguous data at hand to reconstruct the history and iconography of this altarpiece by Metsijs. See *inter alia* Silver 1984, pp. 240–241, no. 7; Kraut 1986, pp. 37 et seq.; Peeters 2007, p. 53.
7 Cf. for example Kraut 1986, pp. 11 et seq. and *passim*.
8 This head covering was a well-known motif that evokes, deliberately vaguely, a medieval period. A variant occurs in the engraving with a depiction of Ansegysus and Begga, in the *Ducum Brabantiae Chronica*, published by Jan Baptist Vrients (Antwerp, publisher Jan I Moretus, 1600), as a form of chronological exoticism. See Grieten 1994, pp. 99–104.
9 The identification was already mentioned in the museum catalogue of 1921 and since then has been generally accepted (cf., *inter alia*, Zweite 1980, p. 319; Peeters 2005, p. 248; Peeters 2007, pp. 58–59. The similarities with the portrait of Grapheus by Cornelis de Vos (Koninklijk Museum voor Schone Kunsten, Antwerpen, inv. 104) are indeed striking. The motif of the servant grinding paint occurred from the second half of the 16th century onwards in the iconography of Saint Luke painting the Madonna; cf. Peeters 2007, pp. 55–59.

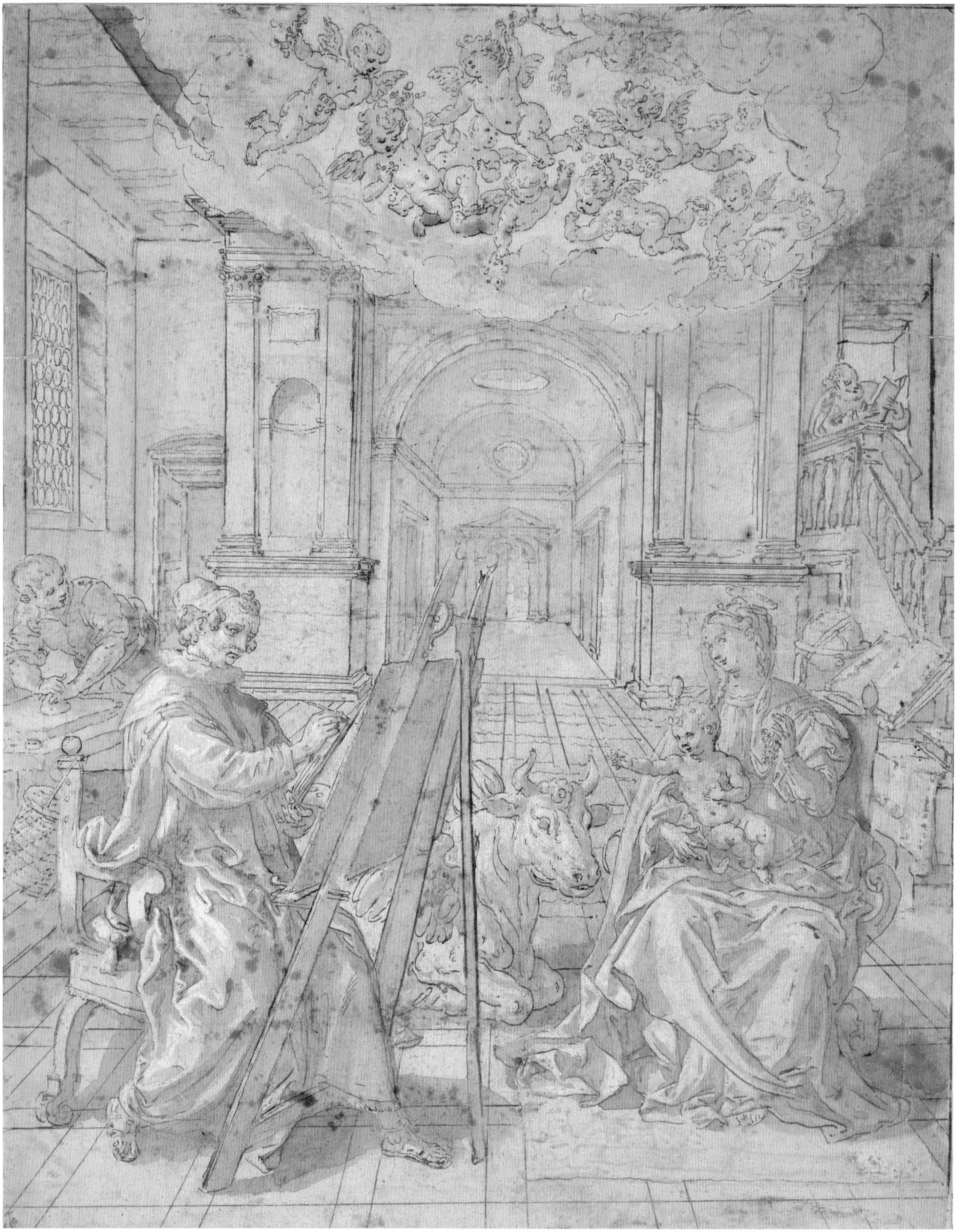

10b
Maerten de Vos · *Saint Luke Paints the Madonna,* 1583 · drawing · Vienna, Albertina Museum

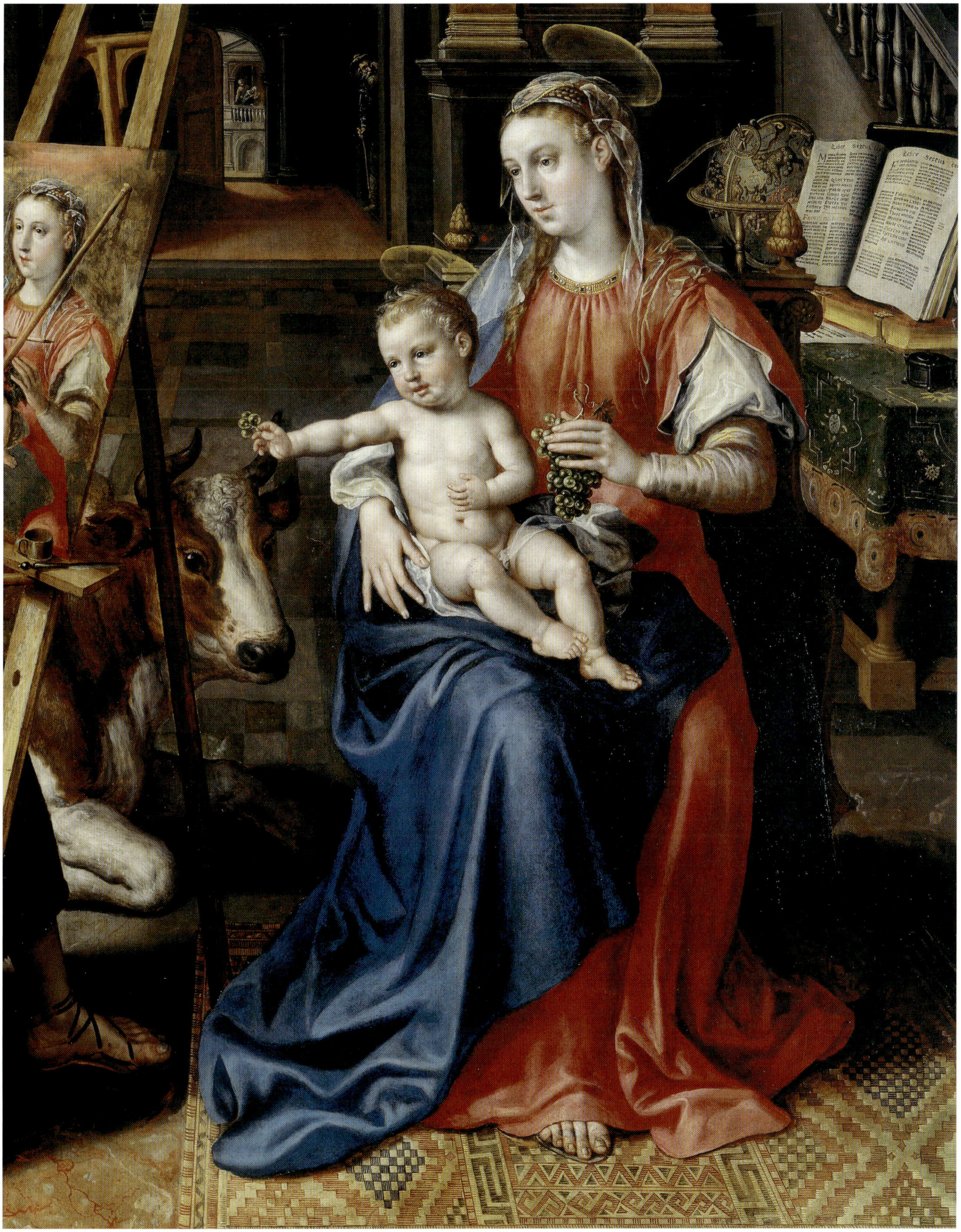

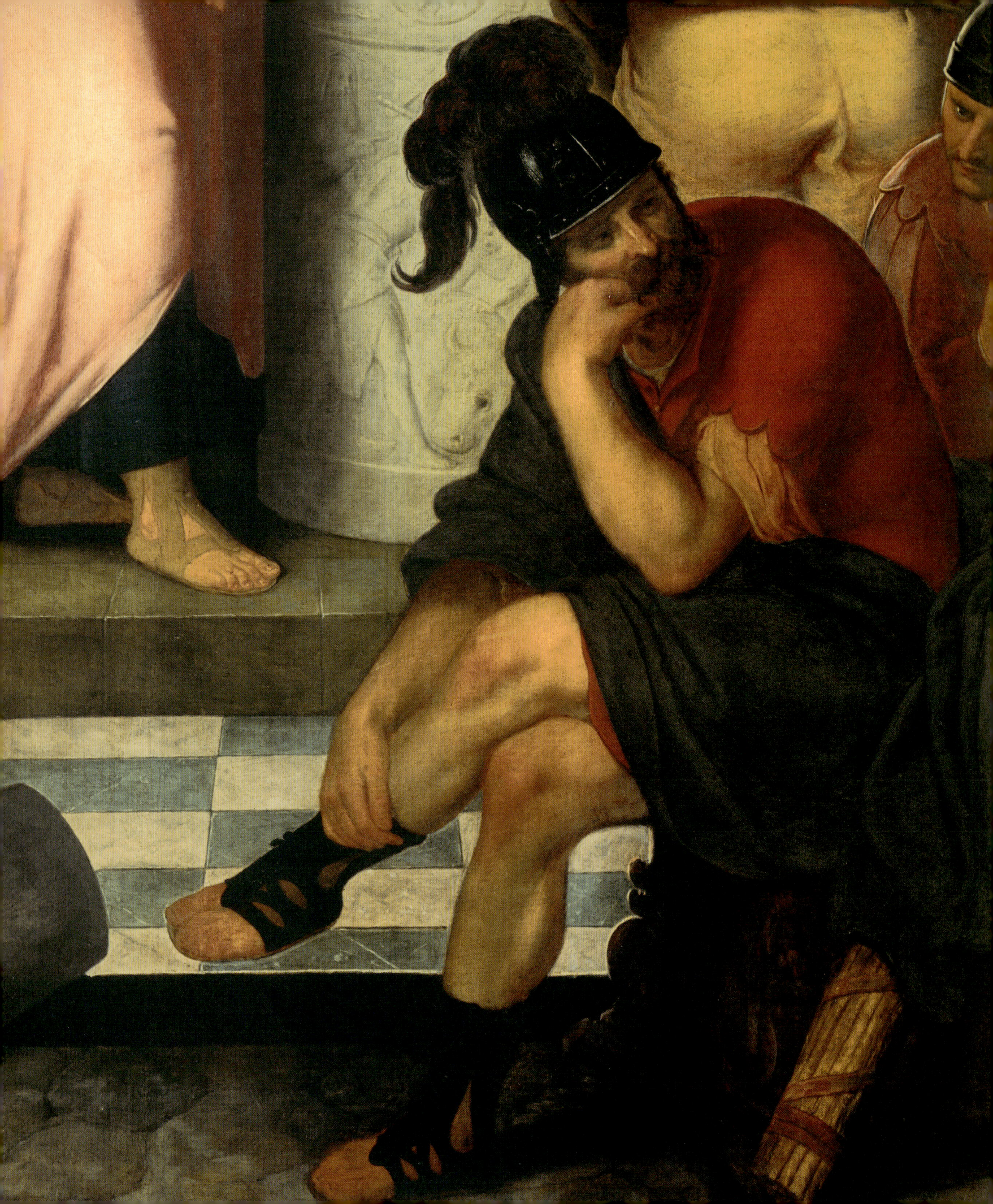

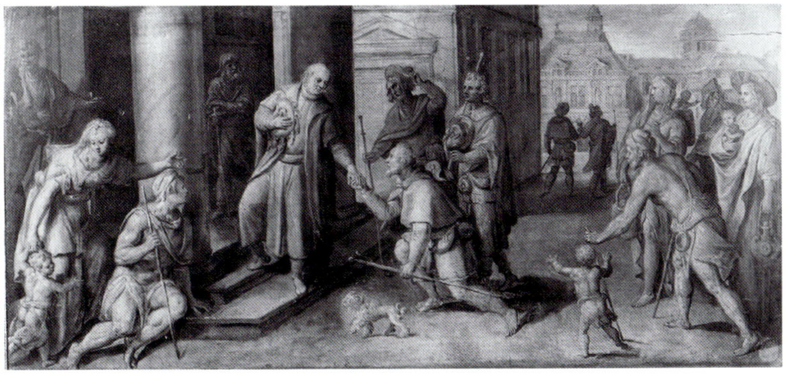

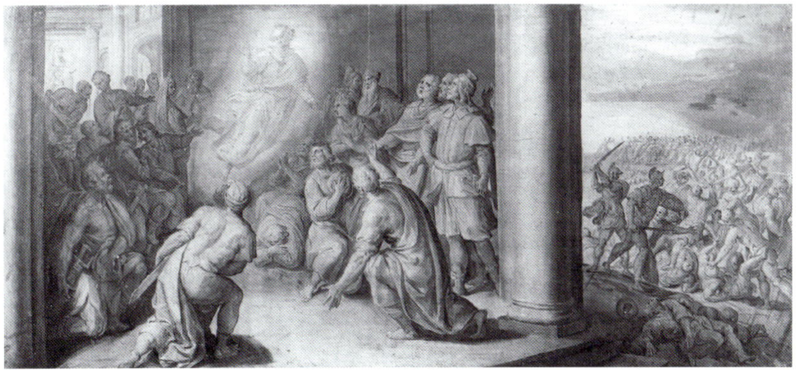

10c
Maerten de Vos
Saint Luke Gives Alms to a Pilgrim
Antwerp, Koninklijk Museum voor Schone Kunsten
(lent to the Vleeshuis Museum)

10d
Maerten de Vos
Saint Luke Appears in the Church of Our Lady in Tripoli
Antwerp, Koninklijk Museum voor Schone Kunsten
(lent to the Vleeshuis Museum)

The room has the impressive dimensions of a visionary palace hall. The building elements, too, evoke this kind of context. Illustrative for this are the marble floor, the coffered ceiling, the background decorated like a theatrical proscenium, the wall niches flanked by pilasters and between them, at the centre of the picture plane, a broad passage with barrel vaulting, which is also coffered and opened through an oculus. To the right, Joseph appears, standing in a doorway. His figure leads our glance even further into the depth, where an open door reveals the balcony of a building in the background, where two women are standing. These figures – as well as the maid who climbs the stairs to Mary's right and looks back before she leaves the scene – enhance the perspectival effect of the architectural setting.[10]

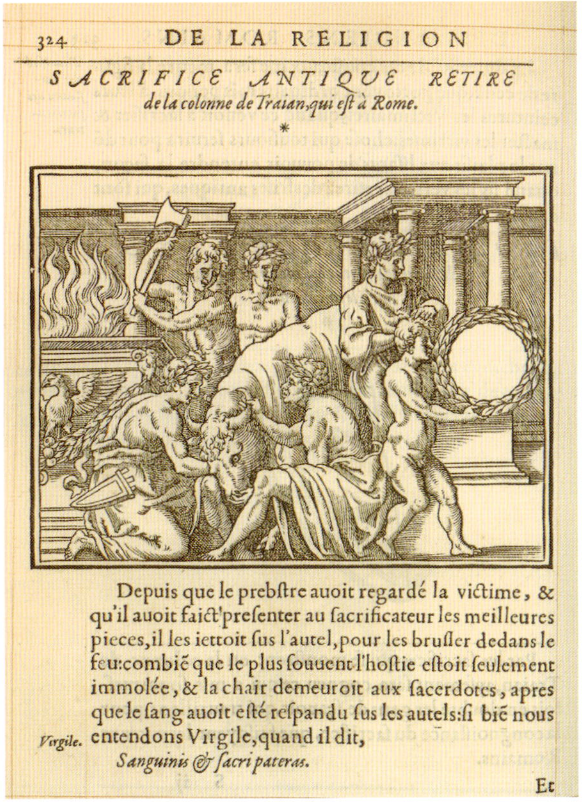
324 DE LA RELIGION
SACRIFICE ANTIQVE RETIRE
de la colonne de Traian, qui eſt à Rome.
*

Depuis que le prebſtre auoit regardé la victime, & qu'il auoit faict'preſenter au ſacrificateur les meilleures pieces, il les iettoit ſus l'autel, pour les bruſler dedans le feu: combiẽ que le plus ſouuent l'hoſtie eſtoit ſeulement immolée, & la chair demeuroit aux ſacerdotes, apres que le ſang auoit eſté reſpandu ſus les autels: ſi biẽ nous entendons Virgile, quand il dit,
Virgile. *Sanguinis & ſacri pateras.*
Et

10e
Sacrifice Scene, woodcut attributed to Pierre Vase in G. Du Choul, *Discours de la religion des anciens Romain,*
Lyon, Guillaume Rouille, 1567, p. 324

This palace-like architecture forms a worthy backdrop for the wonderful and meaningful scene, and also links the painting with the iconographical tradition.[11] While designing it, the artist could draw specifically on his own inventions for city decorations on the occasion of the Joyous Entry of Archduke Ernst of Austria in Antwerp (1594). The images in the commemorative album of city secretary Jan Boghe show numerous parallels with that ephemeral architecture, which de Vos conceived in collaboration with Ambrosius Francken.[12]

A comparison with the preliminary drawing, as identified by Benesch in 1925 (fig. 10b),[13] reveals remarkable changes, notably in the depiction of the personages. On paper, the servant is still typified as a young boy and the saint has no personalised features. In the painting, de Vos brought the *dramatis personae* further forward, which enhances the effect of the understated theatrical rhetoric.[14] The replacement, too, of the emphasised figure of the older man reading by the minor figures in the corridors enhances the theatrical effect.

10 Notably in the Venetian tradition of the second half of the 16th century the motif often occurs and it is not inconceivable that De Vos here drew on the knowledge he acquired during his Italian trip in 1552, which had also taken him to Venice – where he may even have worked as an apprentice in Tintoretto's studio (cf. Meijer 1999, pp. 137–138). However, a more general reception of these inventions, present in the Southern Netherlands should also be taken into account.
11 Kraut 1986, *passim.*
12 Bochius 1595. Pieter van der Borcht delivered the copper engravings. See Antwerp 2005, pp. 110–112. For the triumphal entry of 1594, see Doutrepont 1937; Vandenbroeck 1981. The relation with de Vos' work for these city decorations has already been pointed out by Kraut 1986, p. 114 ff.
13 Pen drawing, 381 x 301 mm. Vienna, Albertina Museum. See Benesch 1925; and also Zweite 1980, p. 235; Kraut 1986, pp. 115–121; Peeters 2005, p. 245.
14 In this respect, Freedberg characterises both this painting and Maerten de Vos' *Wedding at Cana* as 'far more conversational and quieter in tone than his more declamatory earlier works'; see Freedberg 1988, p. 210.

For the central panel of the altarpiece the artist delivered two predella paintings in grisaille.[15] One depicts Saint Luke, who, standing in a porch of a municipal building and surrounded by destitute people, gives alms to a pilgrim (fig. 10c). On the other, Saint Luke appears to a group of worshippers in a church in Tripoli, with the message that God has mobilised the celestial hosts, the apostles, and saints, to break the siege of Antioch by the Turks (fig. 10d). Thereupon the inhabitants of Tripoli speed to Antioch to beat the Turks. The first scene urges the members of Saint Luke's Guild to charity, while the second, a story from the *Legenda Aurea*, receives a contemporary meaning in the light of the then developing Counter Reformation in Antwerp, in which artists were given a substantial role.

This predella was removed c. 1754, when the altar was transformed into a richly ornamented portico altar after the design of the sculptor Gaspar Moens.[16] This drastic innovation also involved the removal of the side panels.[17] These had been executed, after the decease of Maerten de Vos (1603), by Ambrosius Francken and Otto van Veen. Like de Vos, both were reputable masters, and the former had already shown his talent in several altarpieces. Their appointment not only illustrates their reputation, but also indicates that Saint Luke's Guild sought firm guarantees in the field of procedure, execution, and quality.

Ambrosius Francken was responsible for both side panel exteriors and the interior of the left panel, with his depiction of *Saint Luke Preaches to the People*, and Otto van Veen painted the interior of the other panel with *Saints Luke and Paul before Emperor Nero*.[18] Their contributions comply with the Counter Reformation prescription for a clear and biblically accurate iconography. Also entirely in accordance with Counter Reformation thought, the altarpiece, when

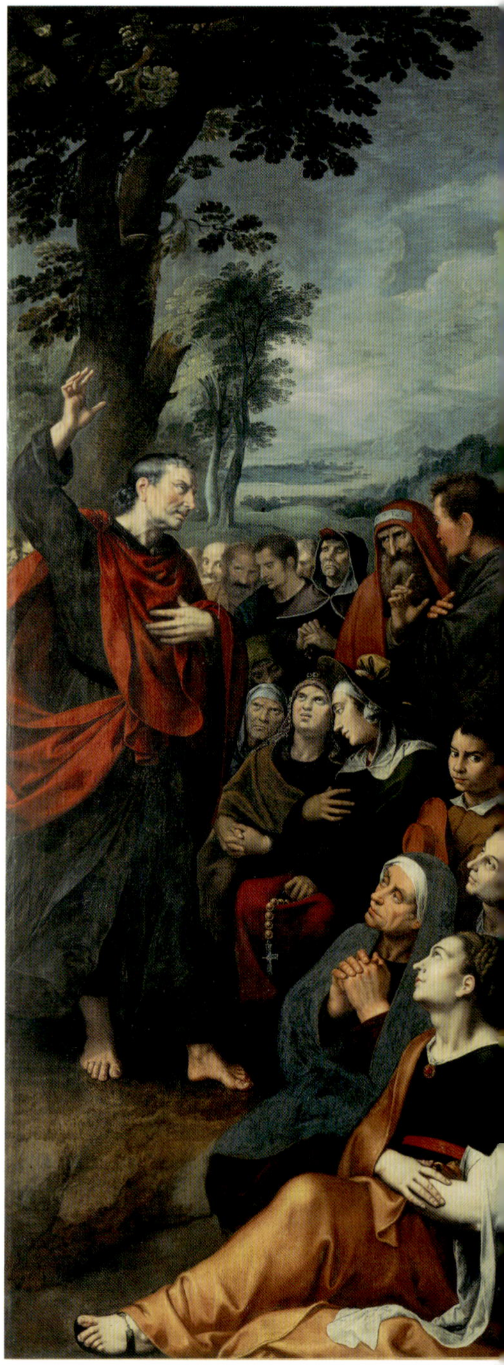

15 Antwerp, Koninklijk Museum voor Schone Kunsten, inv. 101, 102. Zweite 1980, pp. 319–320, nos. 104–105. The difference in width between the central panel of the altarpiece (217 cm) and both predella paintings together (140 cm) supposes a missing and unknown central element, such as a niche with crucifix.

16 Baudouin 1993, p. 251 (ill.); Grieten & Bungeneers 1996, p. 22. The frame, which until some years ago still contained the altarpiece itself and had rounded corner pieces (cf. fig. in Vervaet 1976, p. 230), accords with the design of the frame on Moens' drawing.

17 For another documented case in which the side panels of an altarpiece were transferred from the altar to the craft chamber as a result of a modernisation, see Grieten 1995.

18 For this unusual attribution to two masters, cf. Peeters 2005, pp. 245–246.

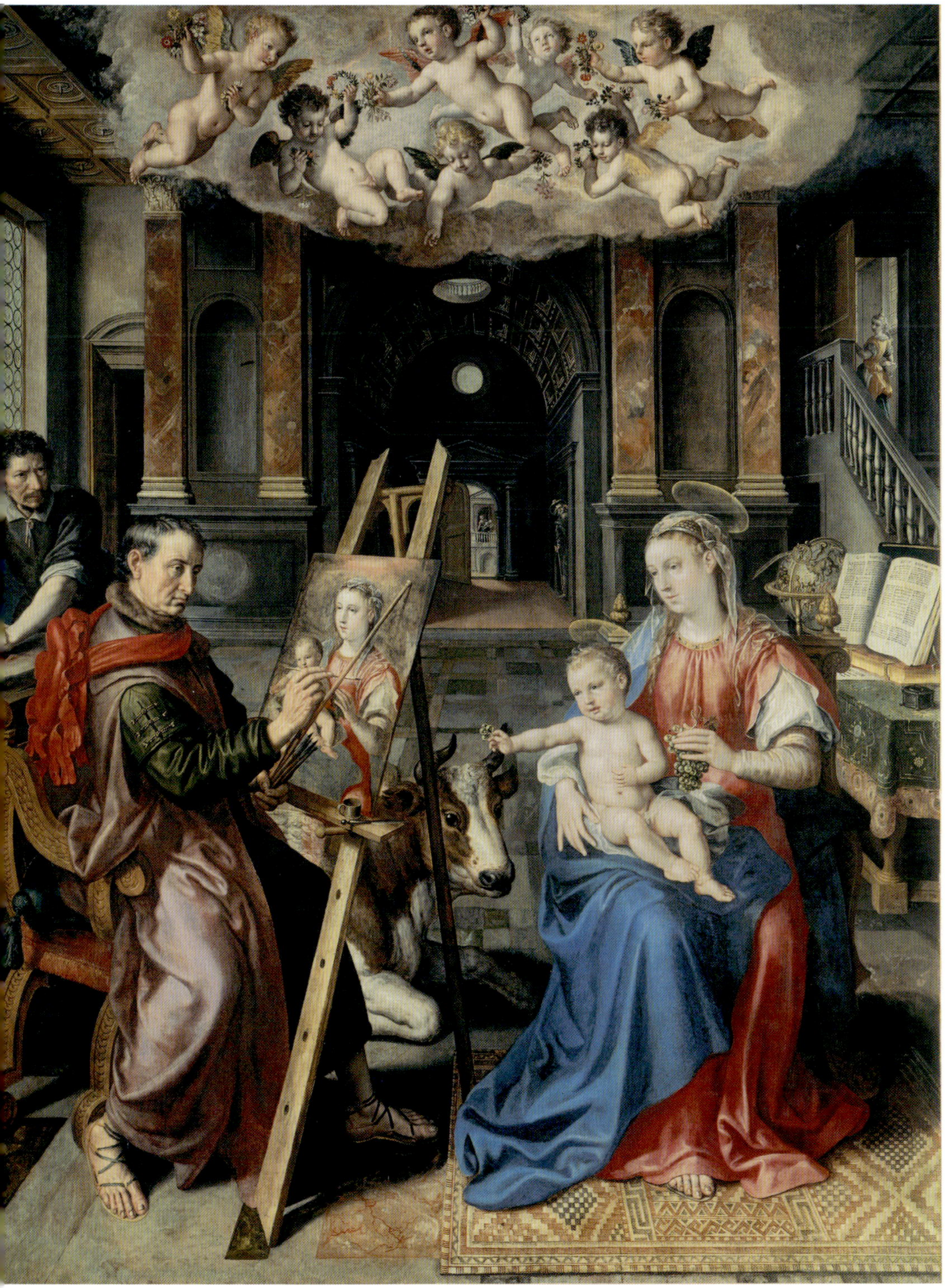

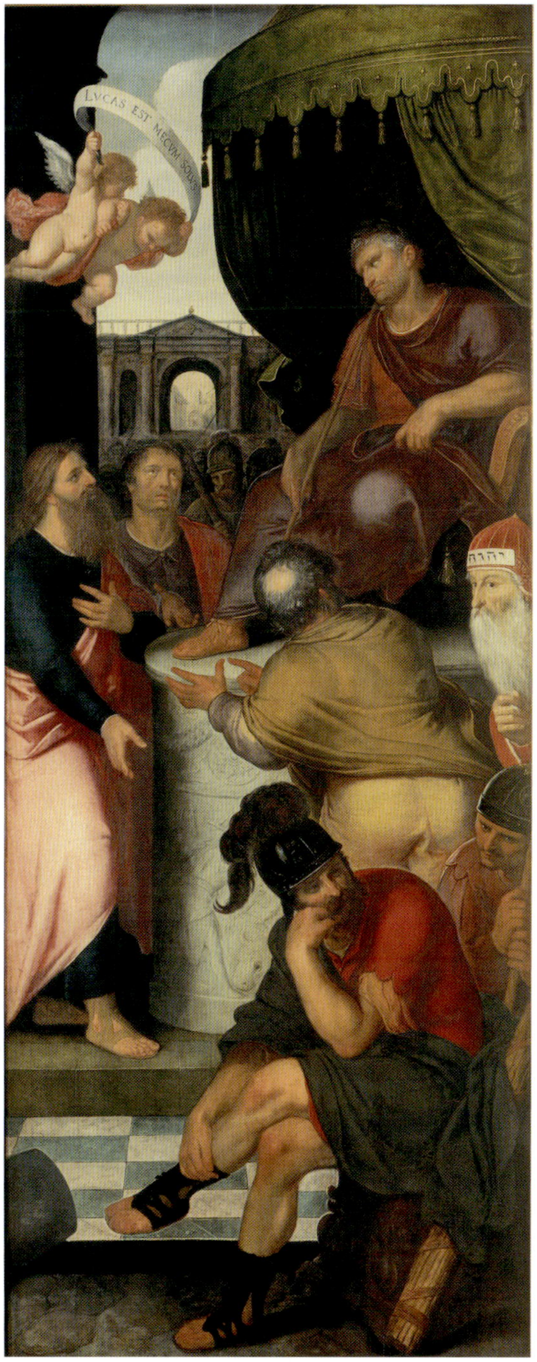
LVCAS EST MECVM SOLVS

closed, displays the four evangelists with their attributes, painted in grisaille: to the left John with the eagle and Matthew with the winged man, to the right Mark with the lion and Luke with the ox. As evangelists they testify, with their books and manuscripts in hand, to the religious content of the altarpiece. In this regard Saint Luke addresses the spectator with a penetrating gaze and a rhetorical arm movement: this is unmistakably a reference to the preaching scene on the panels' interior. In this sense, the preaching of Saint Luke on the left panel illustrates not only the scene from the saint's life, but also emphasises the religious zeal that preaches the Word of God.

The scene by Otto van Veen, too, with *Saints Luke and Paul before Emperor Nero*, expresses one of the core issues of the Counter Reformation call to action. Van Veen, who was elected dean of Saint Luke's Guild in 1602, embodied to a great extent the ideal of the 'learned artist' through his education and erudition. Moreover, he could pride himself on a long stay in Italy and a prestigious trajectory as an artist at different courts in Europe. He used this experience to develop the scene's well-considered presentation.[19] The words '*Lucas est mecum solus*' on the banderole above the heads of the saints, are a quote from the second letter of Paul to Timothy (II Timothy 4:11), which is connected to the Acts of the Apostles, attributed to the evangelist Luke. Paul writes this letter from prison in Rome and urges perseverance in the faith, despite persecution and false doctrine. Saint Paul points directly to the base of the throne, which is decorated with an antique relief showing the ritual slaughter of a bull. This motif seems based on woodcuts of the same subject attributed to Pierre Vase in *Discours de la religion des anciens Romains* (1556) by Guillaume Du Choul (fig. 10e), a successful publication that was widely disseminated in Antwerp's intellectual circles and often used in artists' ateliers as a source of inspiration.[20] In the context of van Veen's painting, the relief refers not only to Saint Luke, whose attribute is an ox, but also on a more general level to the martyrdom of early Christians under the tyranny of Nero and other Roman emperors. Undoubtedly the firmness and selflessness of early Christianity, here depicted by van Veen, was connected, in contemporary opinion, to the challenges with which the Counter Reformation was confronted.

In addition to this solid iconography van Veen also paid attention to a more prosaic reference to the laborious realisation of the entire altarpiece. As demonstrated by Peeters, the year '1589' in the bottom left of the side panel refers to the commission of the painting, and not to its execution.[21]

STEFAAN GRIETEN

19 The composition of this painting is comparable with the *Crucifixion of Saint Andrew* (1597–1599), which was completed some years earlier for the high altar of Saint Andrew's Church in Antwerp: prominent seated figures in the foreground, a background closed off by a Renaissance city gate, and in the middle ground the event, with the holy figure(s) to the left and the Roman commander to the right; the rendering of the top section is visually comparable: a circular baldachin versus a circular temple.

20 For the *Discours*, which also had later editions, see Denhaene 2006, pp. 468–469, no. 119. For applications of this motif in Lambert Lombard's atelier, see Denhaene 1990, pp. 126–127.

21 Peeters 2005, p. 246.

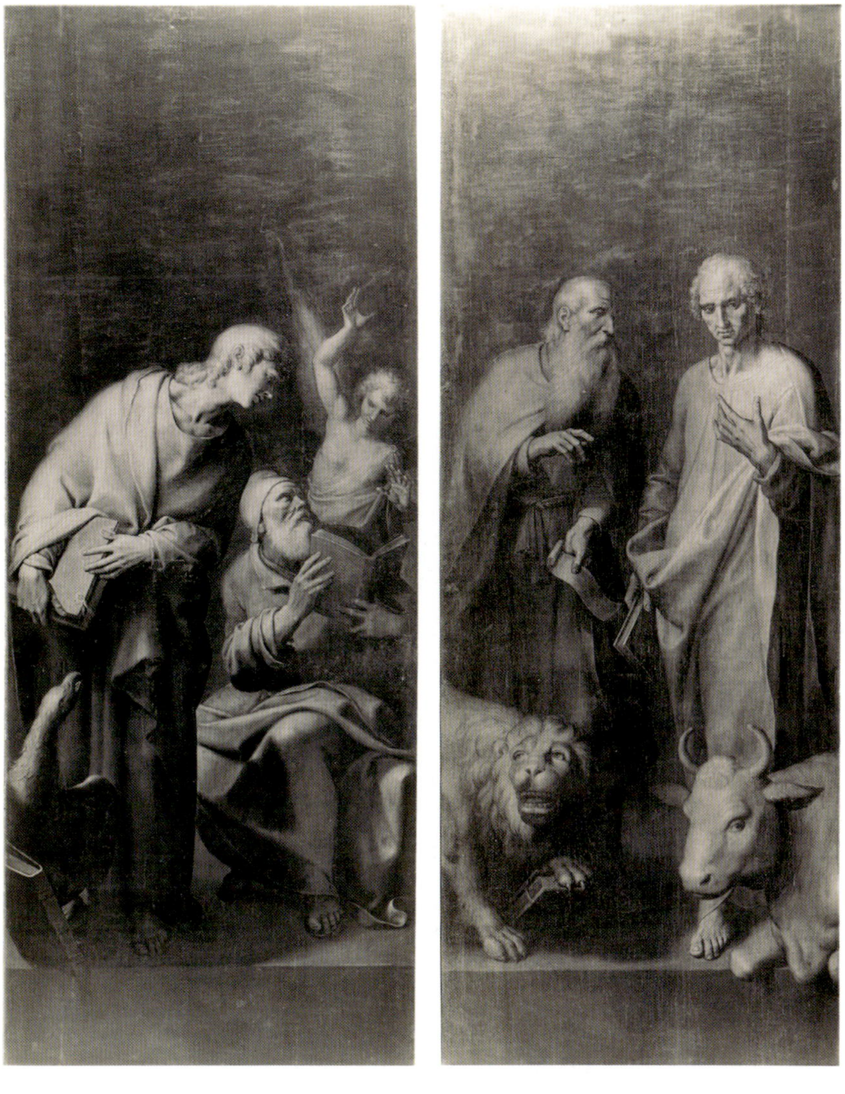

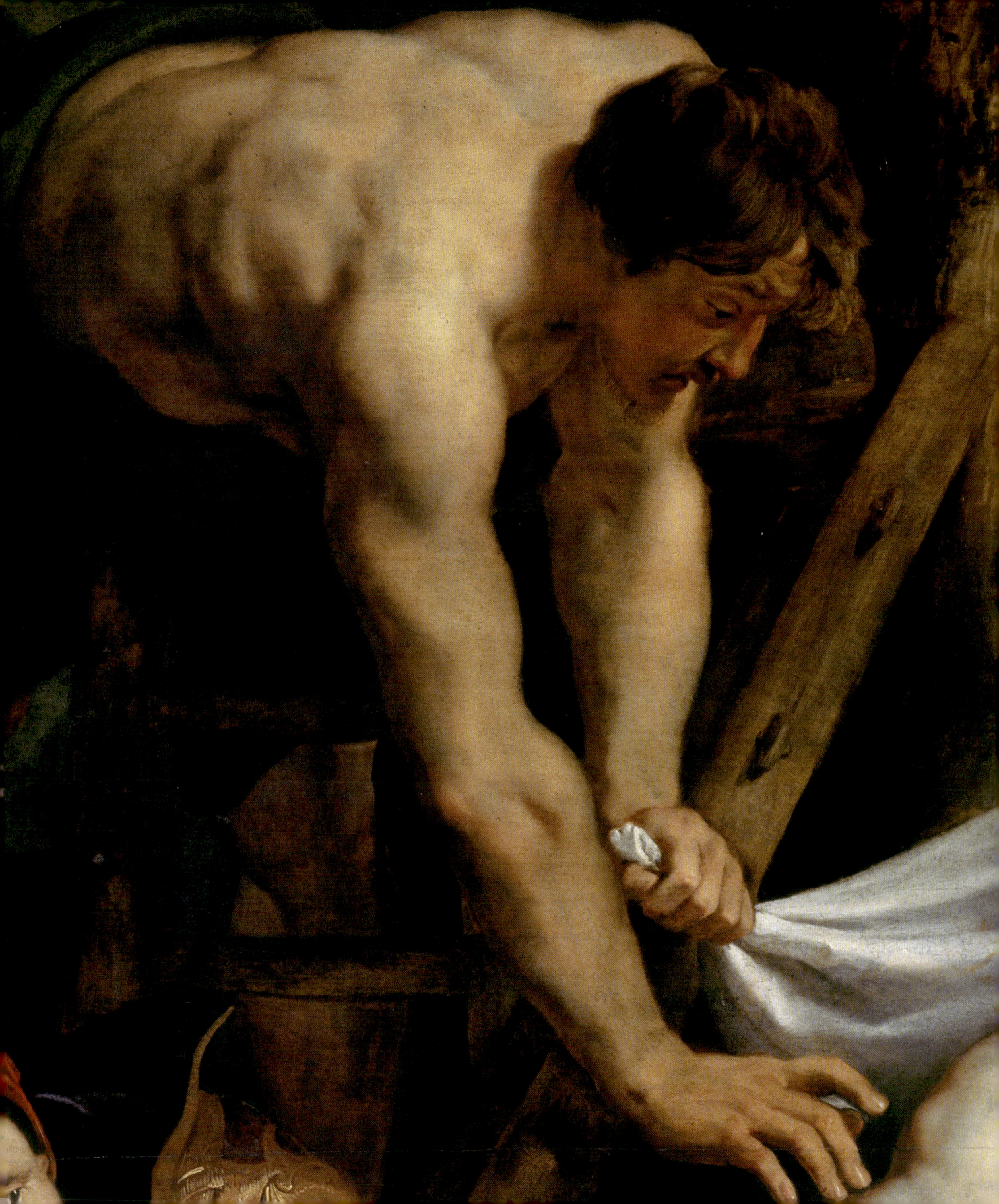

11 Altarpiece of the Arquebusiers

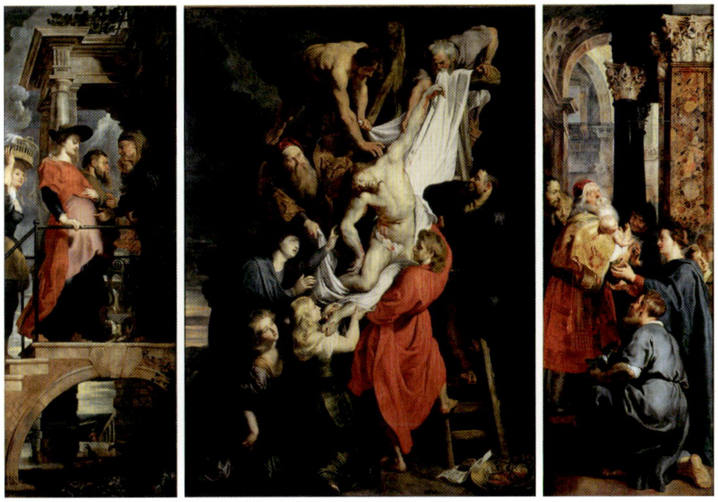

Peter Paul Rubens
Siegen 1577–Antwerp 1640

The Descent from the Cross

1611–1614

Oil on panel
centre panel: 421 x 311 cm
side panels: 421 x 153 cm
Unsigned

Antwerp, Cathedral of Our Lady, inv. 950

Provenance: commissioned by the Antwerp Arquebusiers' guild; placed on the guild altar in the Antwerp cathedral 1611–1614; removed from the cathedral by the commissioners of the French Republic and transferred to the Musée Central des Arts in Paris (1794–1815); restored to the Church of Our Lady 31 May 1816.

Rubens' *Descent from the Cross* still stands as one of the high points – if not *the* high point – of early modern Flemish painting. This masterpiece was painted by Rubens at the commission of the Arquebusiers' guild. After the Fall of Antwerp in 1585, catholic liturgy was restored and one of the new stipulations was that churches and monasteries were to be repaired and refurnished. Guilds and crafts were exhorted to repair or re-erect their altars. The cathedral chapter made such a request to the Arquebusiers' guild more than once, and it remained long unanswered. The Arquebusiers were far from the only ones who were initially in default. Economically, Antwerp was not flourishing – at least in part because of the unremitting war against the North. It would take some time before the tide turned. Two elements were of great importance: the start of the Twelve Years' Truce in 1609 – which guaranteed a more or less durable peace – and Rubens' return from Italy the previous year.[1] The Arquebusiers probably lacked the requisite financial means until then. As a remedy, the city council granted them a number of *wepelaers*. These were new members who, on payment of a large sum, were discharged of further obligations.[2] The means the guild thus acquired could be used to realise the altarpiece.

At a meeting on 7 September 1611,[3] in the presence of Nicolaas Rockox, dean of the guild and 'outside burgomaster' of Antwerp, and of the painter Peter Paul Rubens, an agreement was reached on the execution of the altarpiece. It was undoubtedly at the instigation of Rockox that the commission was consigned to Rubens. Rockox, 'friend and patron'[4] of Rubens, played an important role in Rubens' artistic career. Soon after his return from Italy, the painter was commissioned, through Rockox' agency, to paint *The Adoration of the Magi* (now in the Museo Nacional del Prado in Madrid) for the States Room of the Antwerp city hall.[5] For Rockox' house, Rubens painted the magnificent chimney piece with *Samson and Delilah* (National Gallery, London).[6] The Arquebusiers' guild was one of six armed or sworn guilds in Antwerp.[7] Its altar stood near to the high altar, as did the Fencer's (cat. 3) and the Old Arbalest's altars, among others. The proximity of the armed militias to the high choir is significant. Thus, both guilds and their altarpieces can be attributed a symbolic role as 'protectors of the faith'.[8]

1 Freedberg 1993, p. 133; Baudouin 1978, p. 126.
2 Huvenne 1993, p. 3; Baudouin 1978, p. 122.
3 The contract between Rubens and the Arquebusiers does not survive, but the accounts of the guilds offer a good insight about the developments of the commission. For more details on the archives, see *Inventaris 1925*, pp. 140–141; Baudouin 1977A, pp. 80–87, 97, 368 n. 22–23, 369 n. 57; Glen 1977, pp. 62–87; Grieten & Bungeneers 1996, p. 404.
4 Written by Rubens in a letter on 11 May 1611. On the relationship between Rockox and Rubens, see Baudouin 1977B.
5 See Vergara et al. 2004.
6 d'Hulst-Vandenven 1989, pp. 107–113, no. 31, fig. 72; Belkin 1998, pp. 99–102, 120, 155, 261.
7 *Inventaris 1925*, pp. 140–141.
8 Van den Nieuwenhuizen 1962B, p. 71; see also the contribution of R. Fabri in this publication.

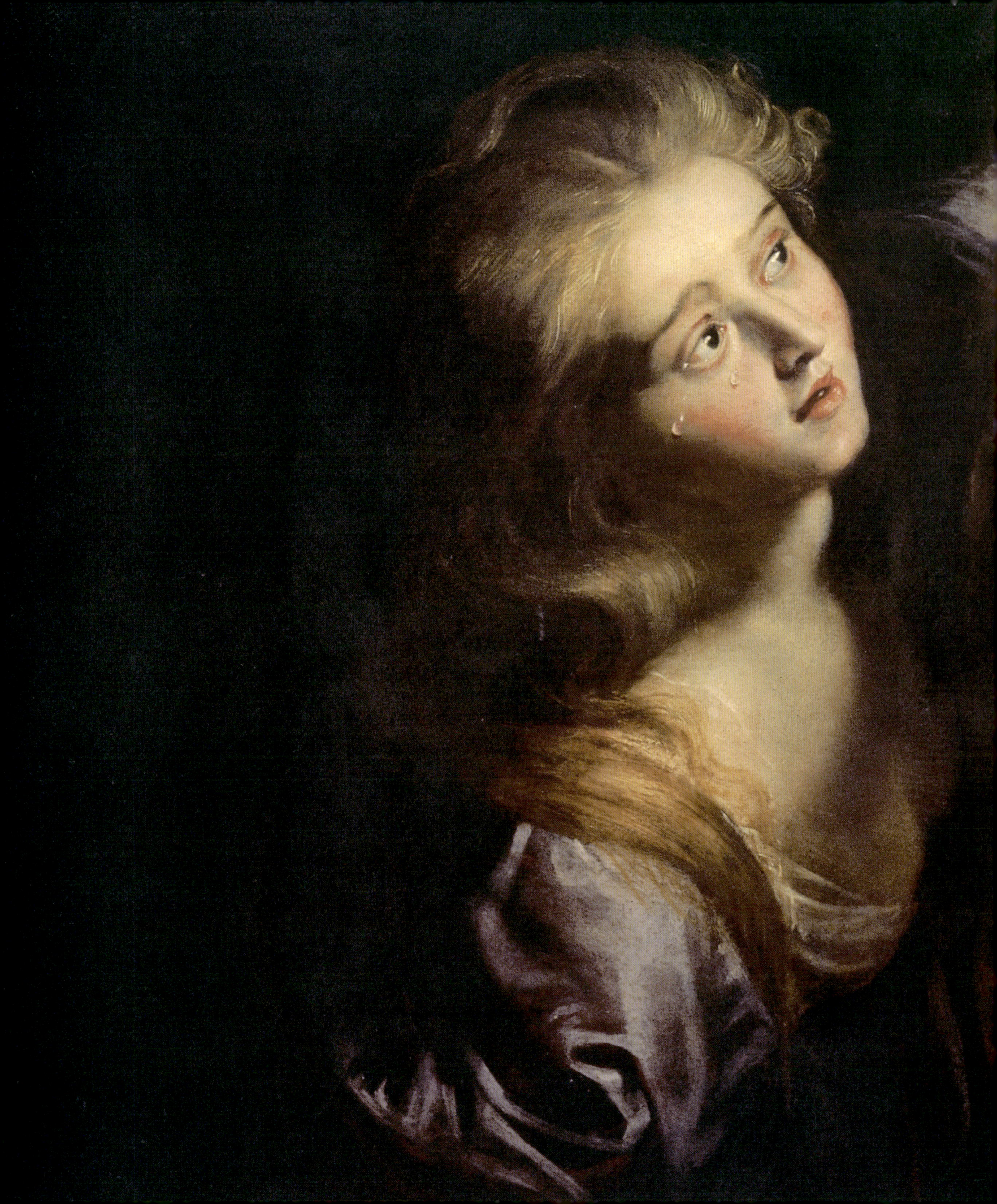

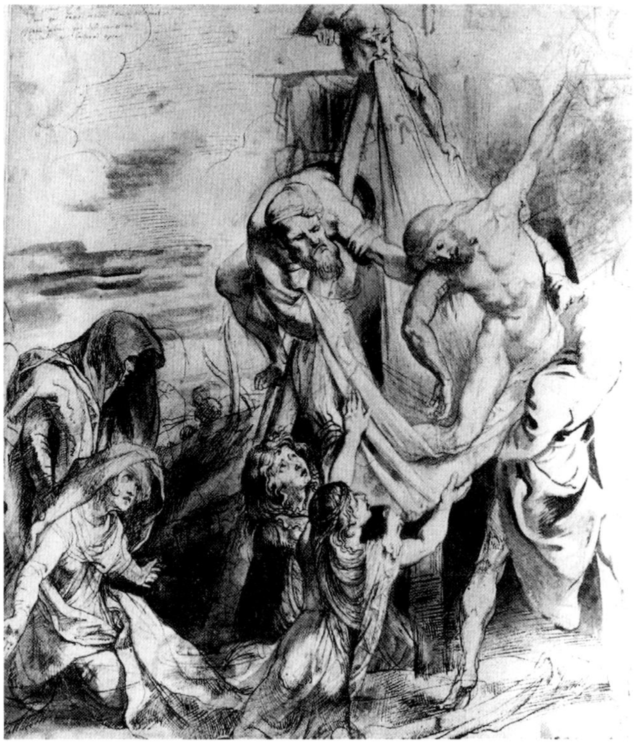

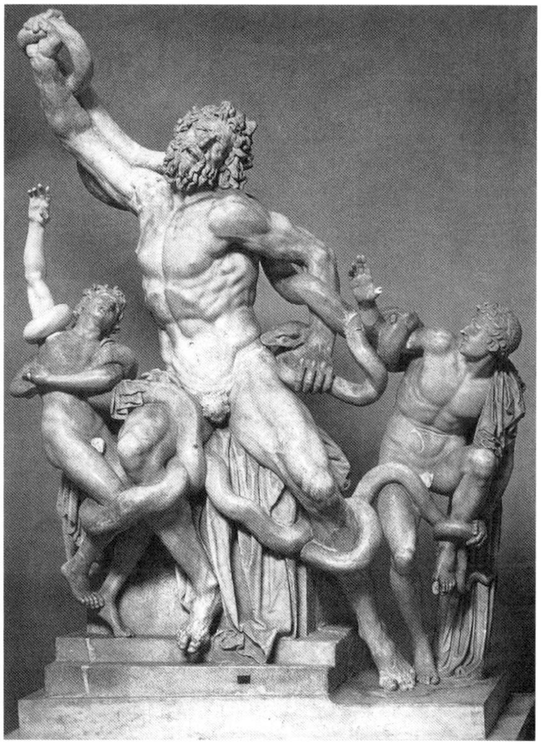

11a
P.P. Rubens
The Descent from the Cross, drawing
Saint Petersburg, Hermitage

11b
Laocoon
Rome, Vatican Museums

Bibliography: *Beschrijvinge 1751*, p. 5 (13)
Mensaert 1763, pp. 229–231
Descamps 1769, p. 145
Kerken van Antwerpen 1774, p. 15
Musée Central 1801, no. 503
Smith 1829–1842, II, pp. 3–5, no. 5
Van Lerius 1841, p. 16
Piot 1883, pp. 18, 19, 314, 392, 418
Rooses 1886–1892, II, pp. 105–123, nos. 307–310
Leurs & Philippen 1938, pp. 51–52, nos. 91–93
Prims 1938–1939, XII, pp. 302–308
Evers 1942, pp. 132–137
Van Herck 1951, p. 43
Van den Nieuwenhuizen 1957, pp. 108–109
Bulletin 1962
Bialostocki 1964
Von Eimen 1968
Martin 1969, pp. IV–XIII, 37, 38, 43, 49, 51, 56, 57, 63–65, 68–70, 73–75, 77–79, 81–85, 87, 88, 90, 91, 101–103, 115 117–130, pl. I–IV, fig. 16–22
Hubala 1971, pp. 64–76
Van Brabant 1972, pp. 269–273
Van Brabant 1974, pp. 104, 152, 161, 162, 223, 224, no. 144
Glen 1977, pp. 62–87
Baudouin 1993, pp. 208–210
Aerts & Grieten 1996, pp. 267, 272
Grieten & Bungeneers 1996, pp. 402–404
Judson 2000, pp. 162–190, nos. 43–46

On 12 September 1612 the centre panel of the altarpiece was installed in the cathedral, in the second bay of the south transept; the side panels came later.[9] Today, this almost unequalled masterpiece can be admired in its original context. Unfortunately, the architectural altar frame was destroyed during the French Revolution.[10]

The theme of the descent from the cross is rooted in Flemish tradition,[11] but Rubens was also clearly influenced by da Volterra, Cigoli, and Barocci, whose works he saw on his Italian trip (1600–1608).[12] Da Volterra, a pupil of Michelangelo, painted a descent from the cross for the church Santissima Trinità dei Monti in Rome (1541). A drawing by Rubens after this fresco, with an inscription that refers to Volterra, is conserved in the Hermitage in Saint Petersburg (fig. 11a).[13] Rubens was never a servile imitator of predecessors of contemporaries – he always chose his own way to develop a composition. He was particularly famous for his ability to unite different elements, and to transform them in a new composition that was totally his own. This becomes apparent in the *Descent from the Cross*. In his pictorial approach, Rubens combined clear line work with intense lighting here. The grey tone of the lifeless body of Christ, in a bright white shroud, vividly contrasts with the dark background of the scene. The figures, arranged in an ellipse around the body, are strongly coloured and are all individually spotlit. This enlivens the spectacle and gives it a third dimension. Breaking through the picture plane is particularly effective in the backward-leaning figure of Saint John in a bright red garment, and also through a magnificently foreshortened helper, at the top left. The deceased Christ appears to weigh almost nothing because of the balanced composition, but the centre of gravity of the body – the pelvis – is still powerfully supported by Saint John. Through the concept of supporting and being supported, Rubens refers to the patron saint of the Arquebusiers, Saint Christopher, in the entire triptych.

Counter Reformation decrees, as enacted in the Council of Trent (1545–1563) and further elaborated in the Third Synod of the Diocese Antwerp in 1610, dictated that the saints' lives could no longer be shown as the main theme of an altarpiece. Theoreticians of the Counter Reformation considered these hagiographies, as described in the *Legenda Aurea* by Jacobus de Voragine, to be too obscure and apocryphal.[14] Christ and the Virgin had to be at the centre of the religious programme of the catholic

9 Jaffé 1958, p. 16.
10 Baudouin 1978, p. 125.
11 As previously depicted by the Master of Flémalle and Rogier van der Weyden, see Judson 2000, p. 167.
12 Huvenne 1993, p. 11; Grieten & Bungeneers 1996, p. 403; Judson 2000, pp. 167–168; Bialostocki 1964, p. 511.
13 Bialostocki 1964, pp. 512, 519.
14 Judson 2000, p. 166.

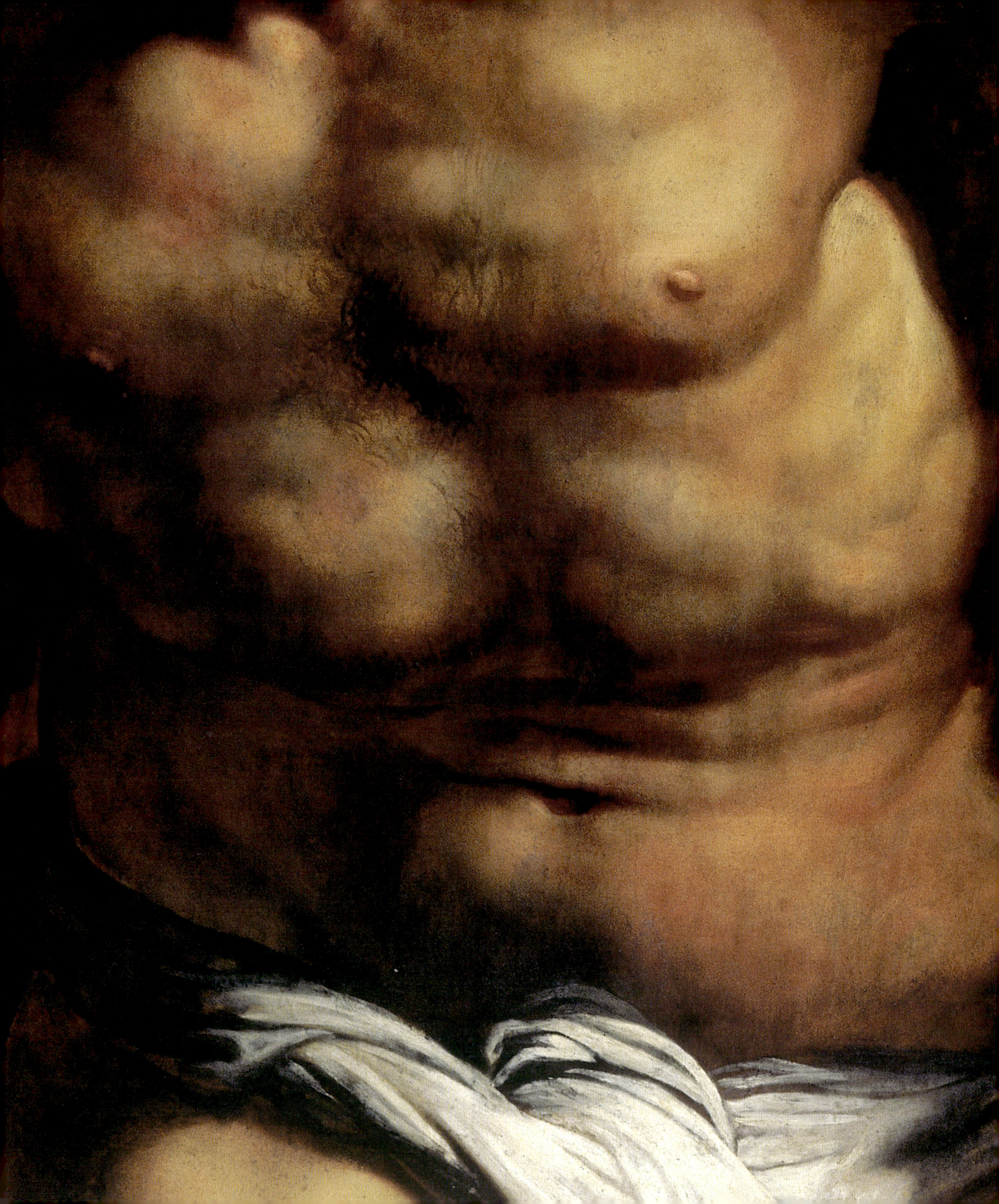

11C
Farnese Hercules
Naples, Museo Archeologico Nazionale

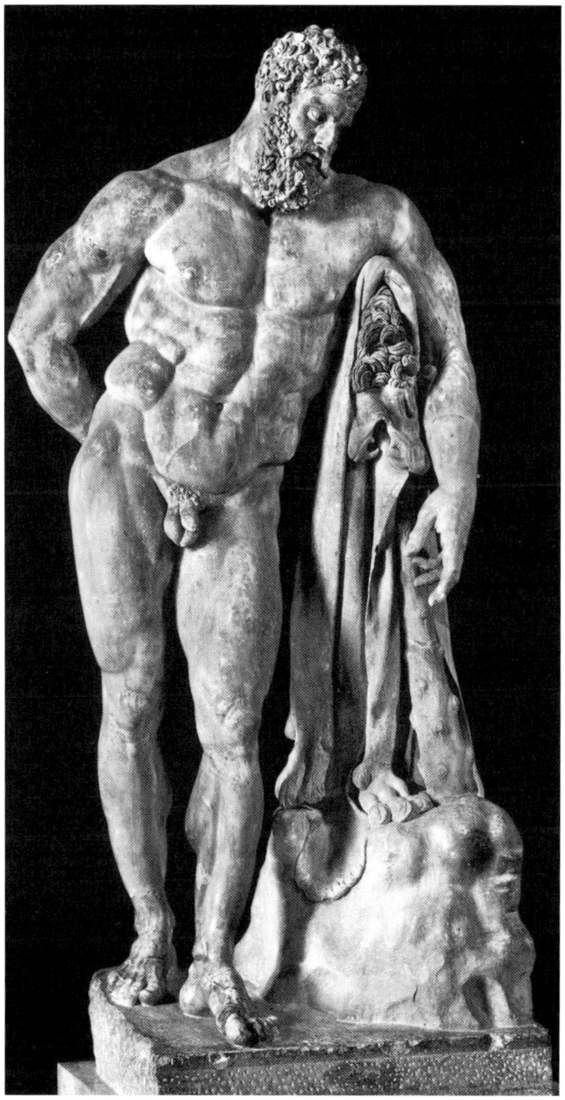

Counter Reformation. Rubens' knowledge of classical languages and his humanist background – and perhaps also his interaction with Rockox and other humanists – enabled him to circumvent this issue in an ingenious manner. The allegory of Christopher (or Christophorus) – which means 'carrier of Christ' – is visualised in all subjects of the triptych. In the left panel Christ is carried by the Virgin, who is pregnant, during her visit to her cousin Elizabeth. The subtle gestures of Elizabeth and Mary, pointing at the mother's womb, are moving references to the long-awaited Messiah. Simeon, a pious old man, had received the message from the Holy Spirit that he would not die before he had beheld the Child. In the right side panel we see him, assisted by the prophetess Anna, at his devotion to Christ in the temple. As described in Luke 2: 23, two turtle doves – here held by Joseph – had to be sacrificed at this joyful event. The man in profile behind Simeon, who watches the scene, is none other than Rubens' friend and commissioner, Nicolaas Rockox. On the left, in its closed position, the triptych shows an imposing Saint Christopher with the Child on his shoulders, and an old man – the hermit – with a lantern. Thus Christopher, the guild's patron saint, was banished to the exterior panels. The staff on which he leans almost seems to collapse under his weight and muscular power. By carrying the Child, Christopher also takes the sins of the world on his shoulders. The hermit – who was Christopher's mentor and had a great influence on him – lights the way for the saint. Christopher was one of the 'Holy Helpers'. Whenever a believer glanced at his image, he or she would be protected against an unforeseen death that day.[15] He was often depicted at the entrance of a church, both in wall paintings and on panels. The armed guilds, in this case the Arquebusiers, probably opted for Saint Christopher as their patron saint for this reason.

For this Saint Christopher, Rubens found inspiration in Antiquity, more precisely with the Farnese *Hercules* (now in the Museo Archeologico Nazionale in Naples; fig. 11c). During his sojourn in Italy he saw this statue in the Farnese collection. Again he did not reprise the sculpture literally, but he adjusted the antique example.[16] Inspiration from Antique motifs can be found for other figures too. The Christ figure is based on the famous *Laocoon* (fig. 11b); Joseph of Arimathea, right at the centre of the ladder, is a variation of the eldest son of Laocoon.[17] Christ's head may be based on a fragment of the Altar of Zeus in Pergamon, which in the 17th century belonged to the collection of the Duke of Arundel. Rubens copied several sculptures in that collection, so this theory seems not entirely implausible.[18]

On 6 March 1614 the two side panels were added and the triptych was complete. It would remain on this spot for almost two centuries, until the French troops had it transferred to Paris in 1794. Amid massive public interest, many of the confiscated paintings – among which were Rubens' famous altarpieces – returned to Antwerp in December 1815.

15 Claes, Claes & Vyncke 2002, p. 136.
16 Baudouin 1977c.
17 Judson 2000, p. 167.
18 Vickers 1981, pp. 140–142.

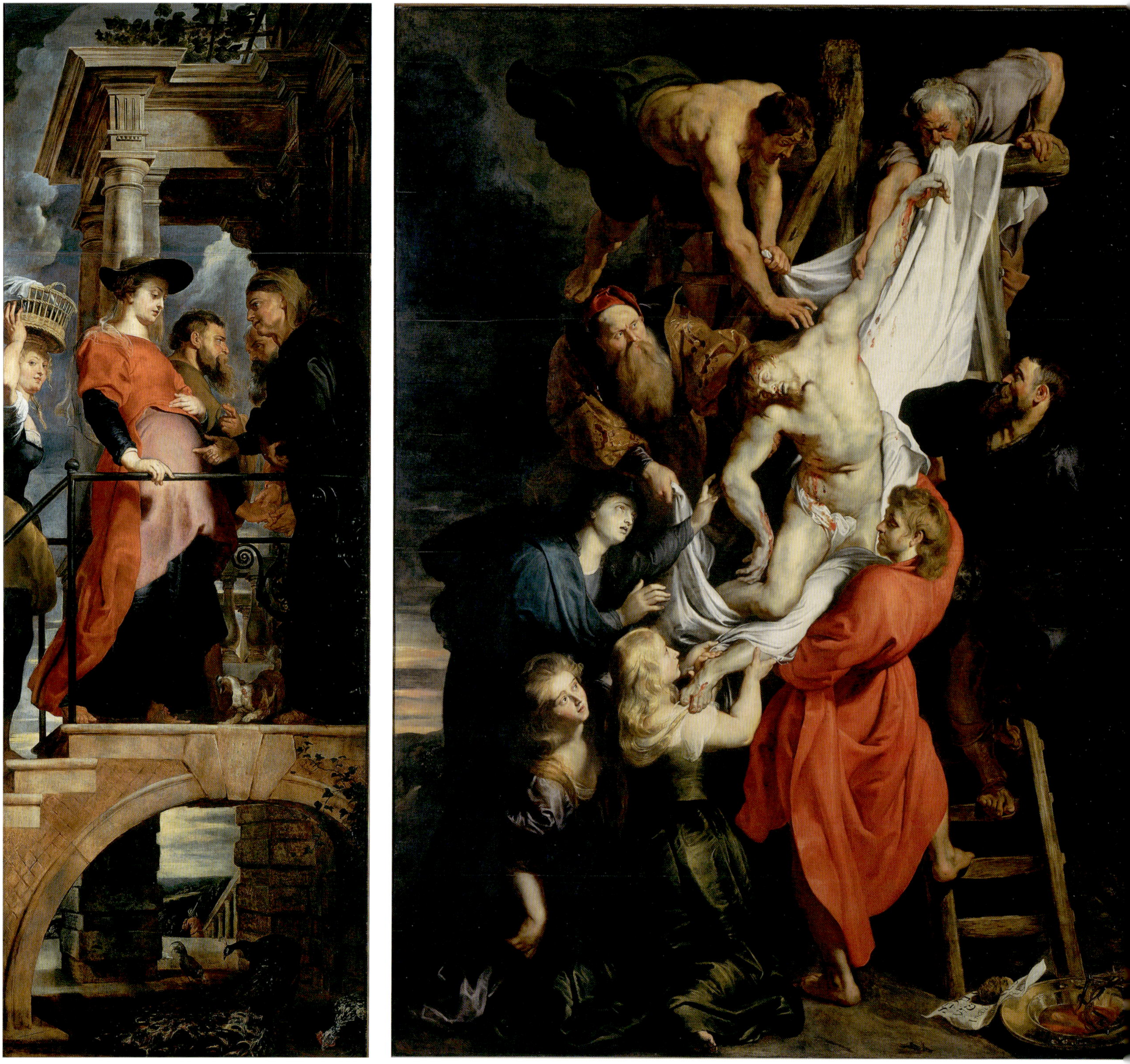

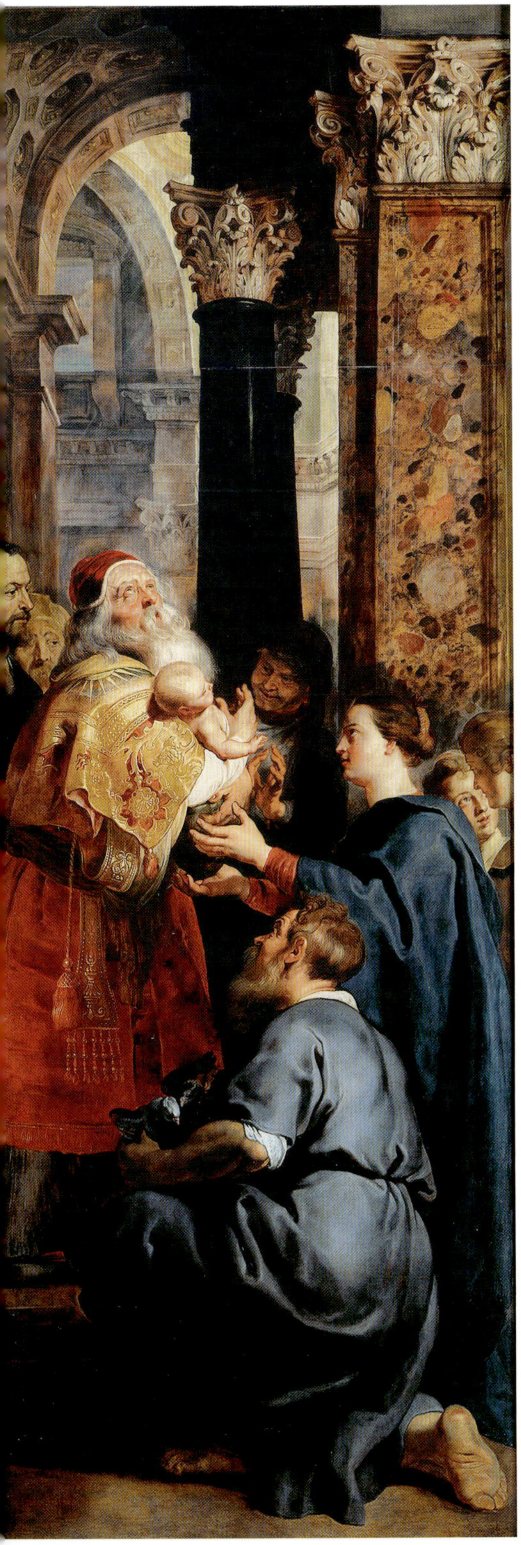

Historic events also determined the future of its iconographic counterpart, *The Raising of the Cross*. This magnificant altarpiece, painted for the church of Saint Walburgis, which had been demolished in the meantime – found a new place in the cathedral. Since 1815 both triptychs can be viewed as pendants.[19]

PAUL HUVENNE

19 Van den Nieuwenhuizen 1962B, pp. 66–83.

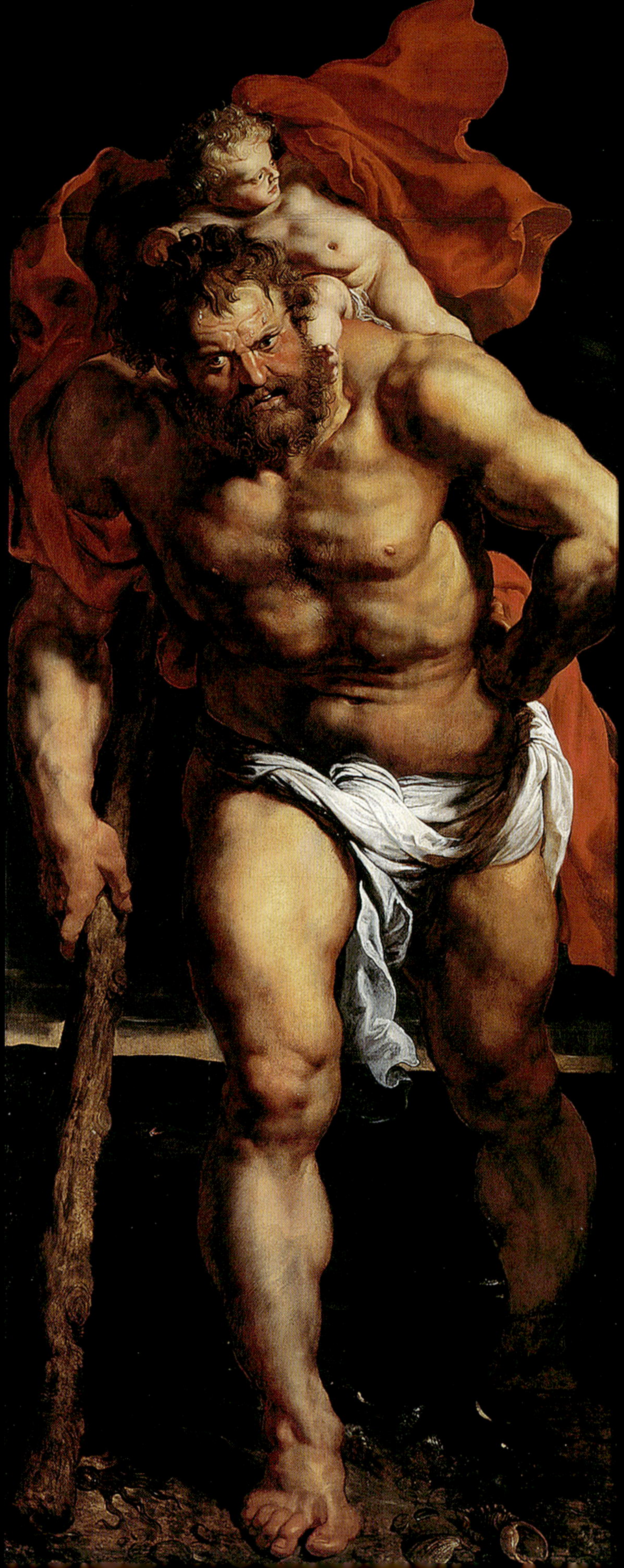

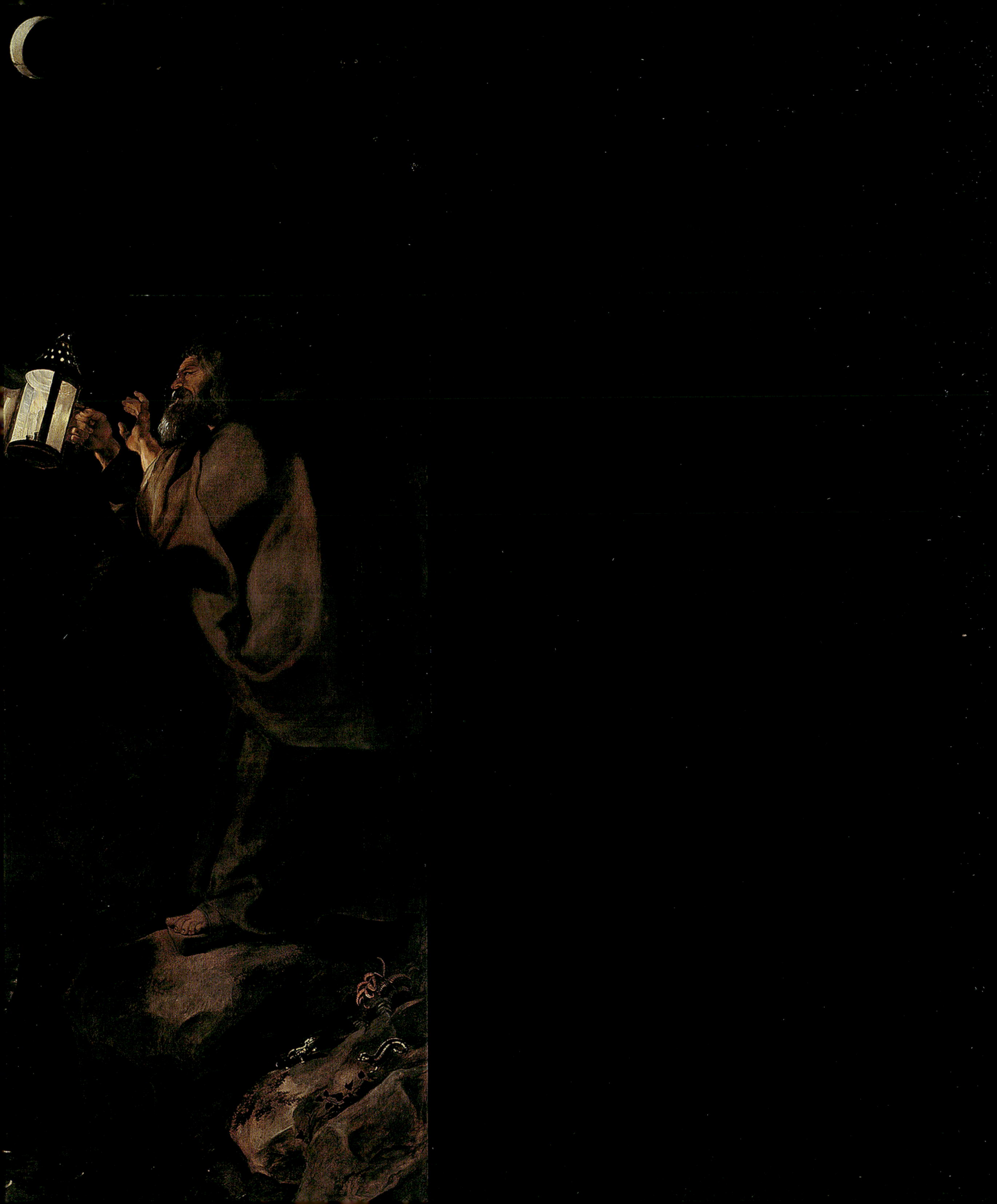

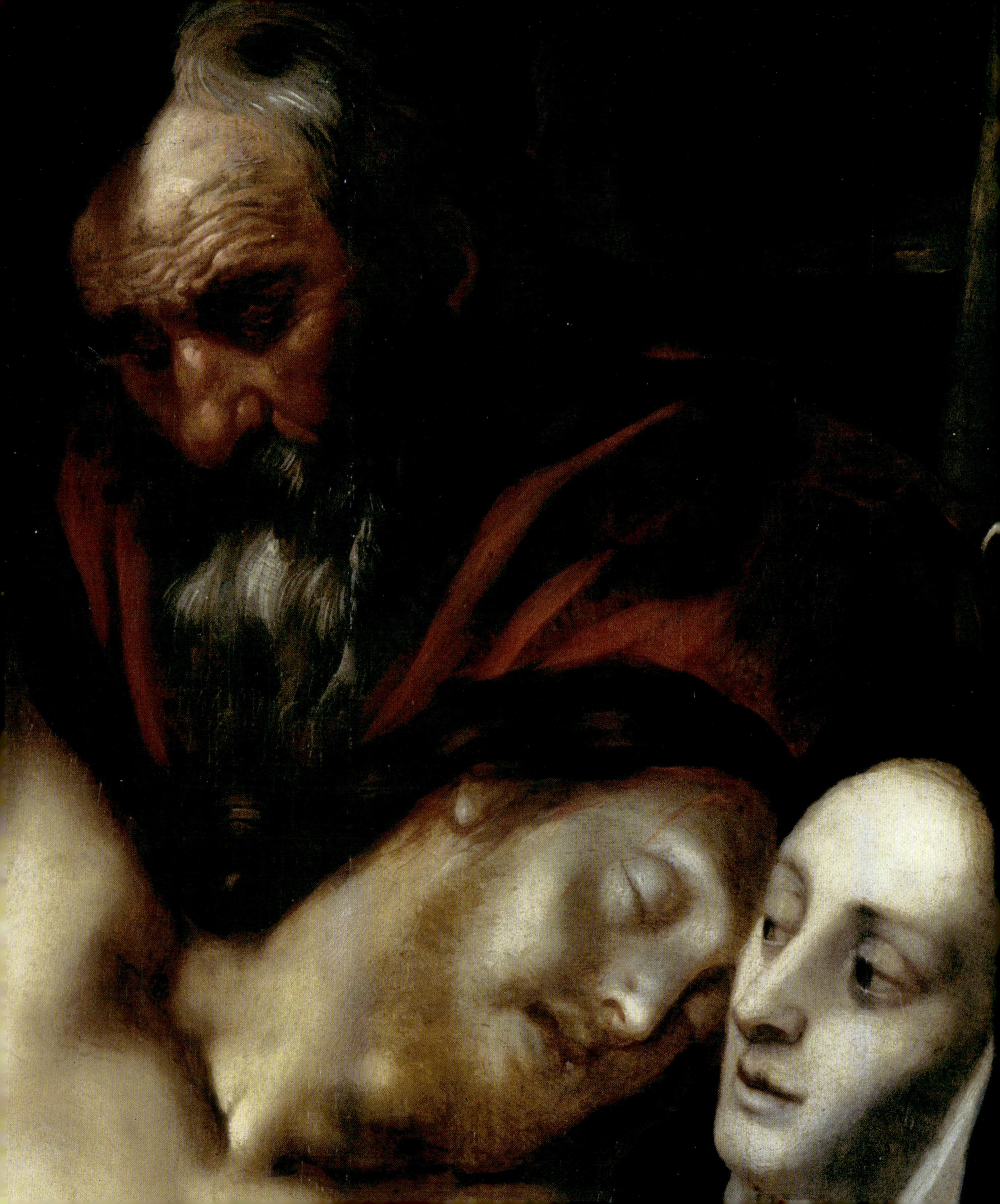

12 Painting of the Chapel of the Blessed Sacrament

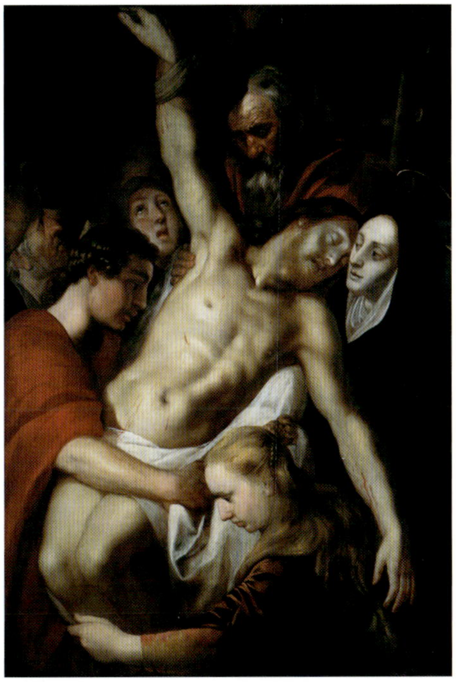

Attributed to Adam van Noort
Antwerp 1562–Antwerp 1641

The Descent from the Cross
After 1610

Oil on panel
138 x 95 cm
Unsigned

Antwerp, Cathedral of Our Lady, inv. 951

The body of Christ, which was taken down from the cross by Nicodemus, is received by the Virgin Mary, John, and Mary Magdalene. At the top right the ladder can be seen still placed against the cross. The two mourning figures in the left background can be identified as Mary Cleophas and Joseph of Arimathea. The dramatic colours and the tense facial expressions suggest that the painting was intended to evoke strong emotions in the spectator, possibly indicating that it was rather intended as a devotional piece for a profane interior than as an altarpiece.

The original destination of the work is unknown. It was first mentioned in *Beschryvinge van alle de Kerken van Antwerpen* by Jacob de Wit (1695–1754)[1] – twice, in fact, probably by mistake. When the Dutch painter – who is known mainly for his drawings (1718) after Rubens' burned ceiling paintings in the Antwerp Jesuit Church,[2] – described the warden's room of the Venerable Chapel in the Cathedral, he mentioned a *Descent from the Cross* against the rood screen, beautifully painted by Adam van Noort.[3] This description could allude to the painting discussed here. But de Wit could also have referred to a painting with the same subject which hung above the entrance door of the church warden's room, which matches the description even better. De Wit also thought that in this *Descent from the Cross*, the Magdalene and the white cloth may have been retouched by Jordaens.[4] In his adaptation from 1774 of de Wit's manuscript,[5] François-Jean-Joseph Mols pointed out that the two entries may have concerned the same painting, because it did not always remain in the same place.[6] That seems to be the case, because later sources combine both data, situating the painting in the Venerable Chapel and attributing it to Adam van Noort.[7]

Nowadays the painting is still conserved in the Venerable Chapel.[8] The classical frame, with its

Provenance: Possibly mentioned in the middle of the 18th century as a work by Adam van Noort in the warden's room of the Chapel of the Blessed Sacrament (Venerable Chapel) and/or in the church warden's room of the Church of Our Lady, Antwerp; since then continually in possession of the church.

Bibliography: *Beschrijvinge 1756*, p. 17
Kerken van Antwerpen 1774, pp. 12, 16–17
Van Lerius 1841, p. 15
Van den Nieuwenhuizen 1957, p. 119
Grieten & Bungeneers 1996, pp. 404–405

1 Brussels, Royal Library, ms. no. 13, 643; published by J. De Bosschere *(Antwerp Churches 1774)*.
2 Martin 1968.
3 'You may also see, in the same Chapel, against the rood screen, a *Descent from the Cross*, beautifully painted by Adam van Noort' (*Kerken van Antwerpen 1774*, p. 12).
4 'In the church warden's room, above the entrance door, is a *Descent from the Cross Saint Joseph*, which is better painted than drawn. Magdalene and the white cloth seem to have been retouched by Jordaens' (*Kerken van Antwerpen 1774*, p. 16).
5 *Kerken van Antwerpen 1774*, p. vii.
6 About the painting attributed to van Noort he noted, 'Compare this note [on the painting attributed to van Noort] with the one the writer names on pa. 26 & verso. The annotation may be appropriate for that one, because it occurs to me that this must be one and the same piece' (*Kerken van Antwerpen 1774*, p. 12); about the second *Descent from the Cross* he observes, 'This piece should be examined, since it has much in common with the one now seen in the Venerable Chapel [*sic*] across the Altar, and it may be the one & same, as in my memory the latter has not always [sic] been placed there' (*Kerken van Antwerpen 1774*, p. 17).
7 'In the same Venerable chapel is a painting against the rood screen being a *Descent from the Cross* painted by Adam van Noort, the first master of P.P. Rubens' (*Kerken van Antwerpen 1774*, p. 12).
8 Grieten & Bungeneers 1996, pp. 404–405, no. 951.

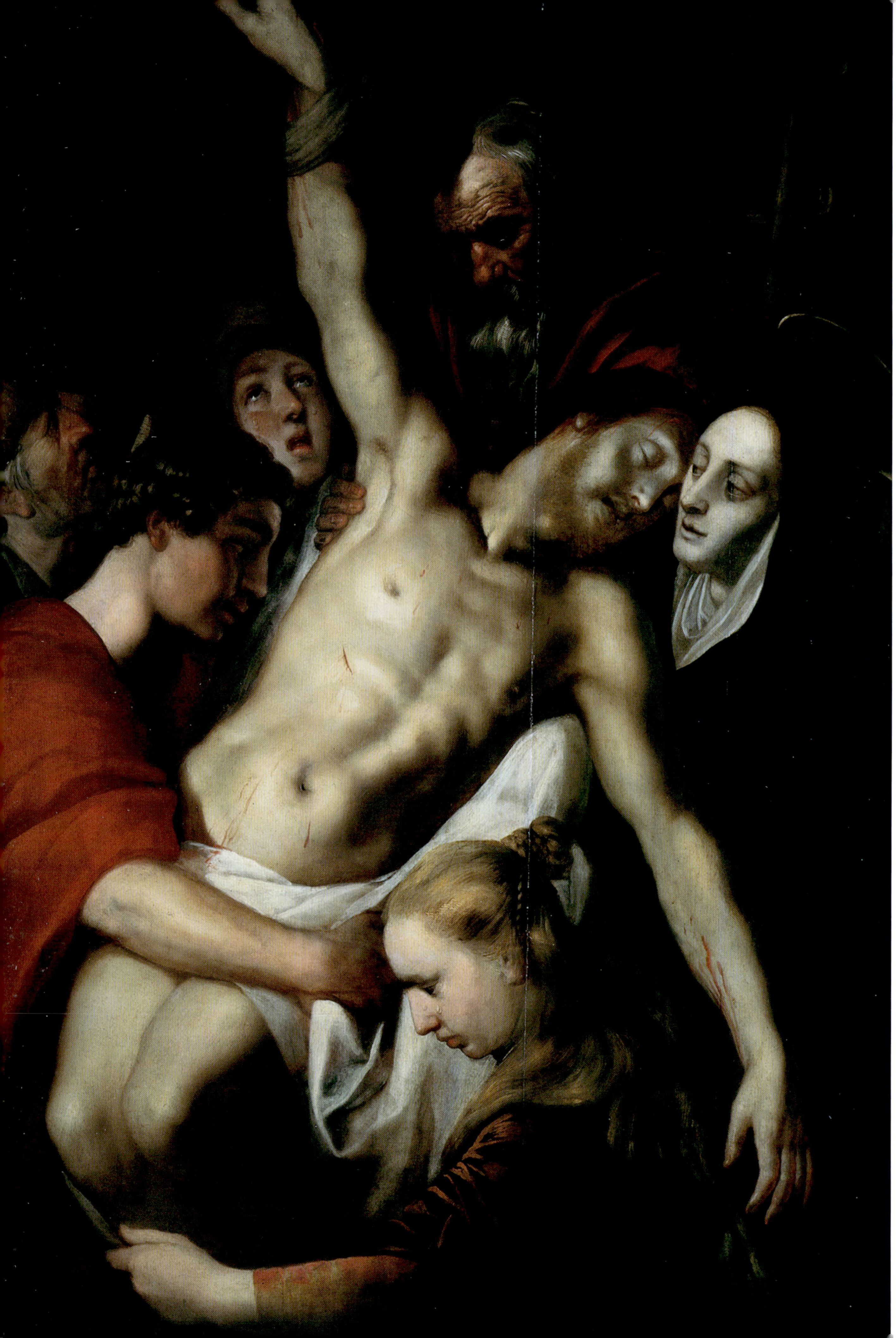

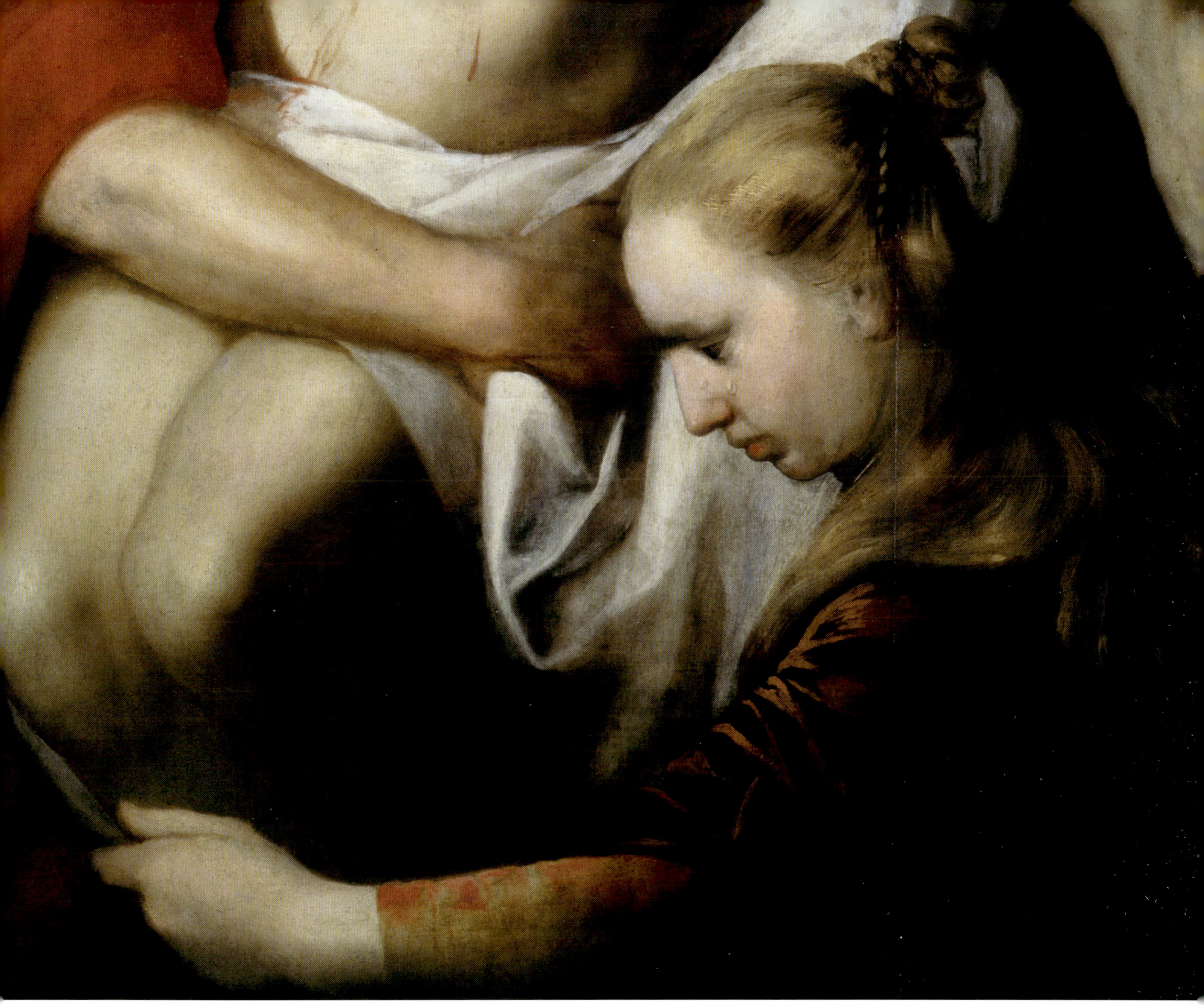

emphasis on the corners with cymatia, triglyphs and rosettes, is clearly more recent than the painting. Furthermore, the fact that the painting did not have a fixed place in the church during the 18th century – see the uncertainty with de Wit and Mols – could indicate that the painting only arrived in the church around that time.

The 18th century attribution to Adam van Noort may refer to a more ancient tradition, but this should be treated with caution owing to the lack of further evidence. In the 18th century, knowledge of Adam van Noort's work could hardly have been comprehensive. Jacob de Wit himself appears to have observed that the painting, or parts of it, recalled Jordaens. It might therefore be argued that this is one of Van Noort's later works, which clearly showed the influence of his pupil and son-in-law Jacob Jordaens. However, this does not make the attribution to van Noort more convincing.

CARL VAN DE VELDE

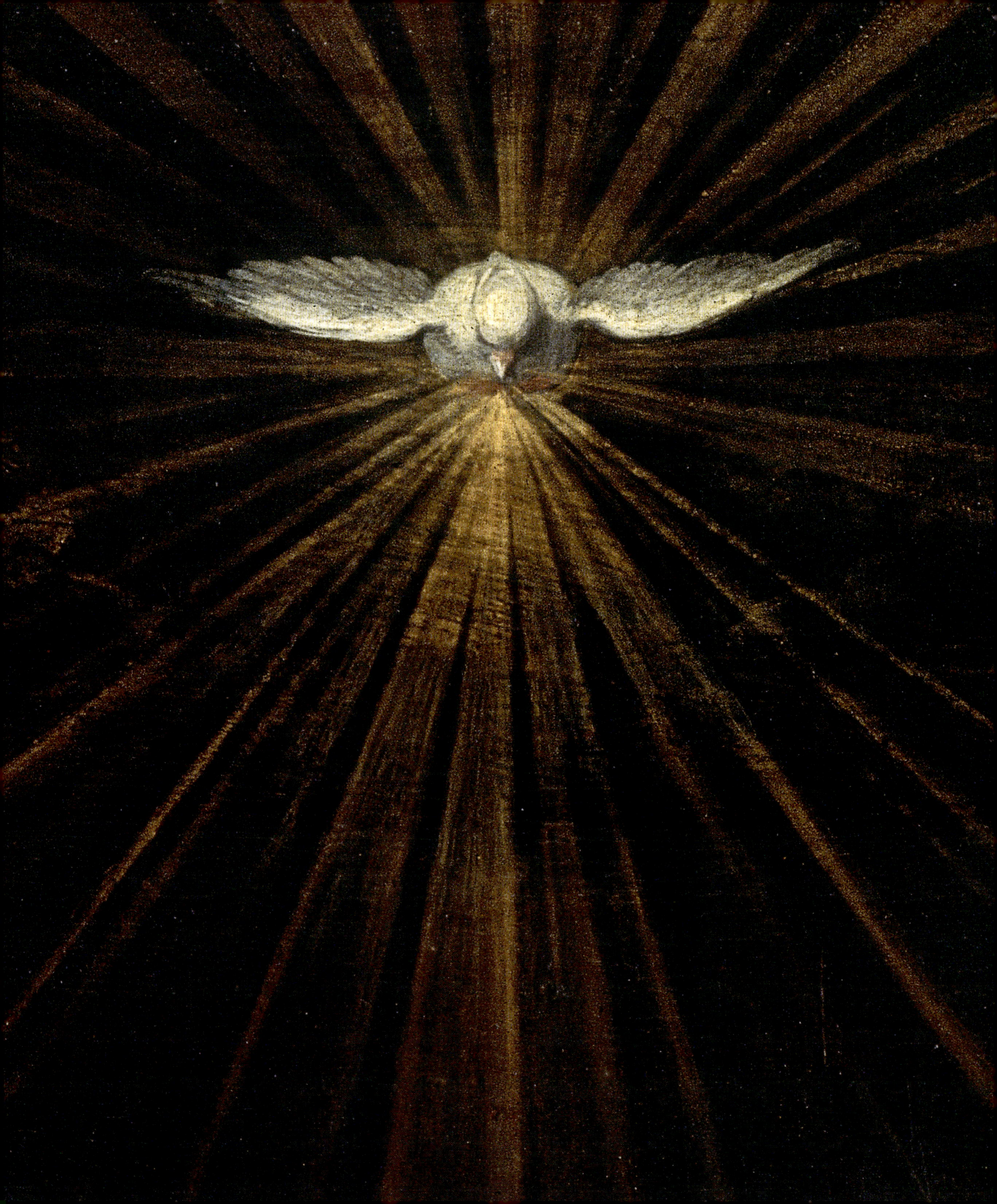

13 Painting for the Almoners of the Table of the Holy Spirit [?]

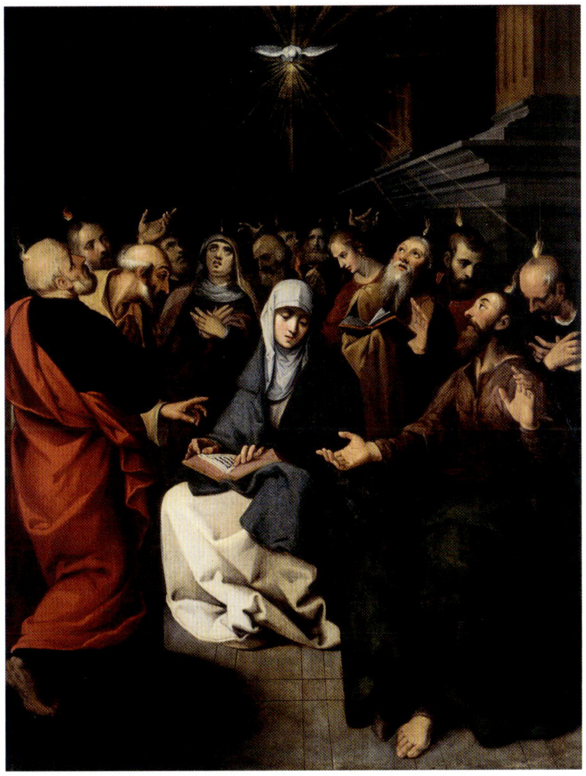

Francken Studio

The Descent of the Holy Spirit

Early 17th century

Oil on panel

125 cm x 102 cm

Unsigned

Antwerp, Cathedral of Our Lady, inv. 952

In a dark, sombre room the Virgin is depicted at the centre as *regina et mater apostolorum* (queen and mother of the apostles), surrounded by the twelve apostles. Her body is entirely enveloped in a grey robe with a wide blue mantle over it. The gathering took place at Whitsun in an upper room in a house in Jerusalem (Acts 1: 3–14). To the right of the indeterminate room, pillars on a marble podium are visible. The scene has a strongly slanting, unnatural perspective. In the foreground the grey tiles catch the eye. Spiritualised and with the Bible open in her hands, the Virgin lowers her eyes. The Holy Spirit, in the appearance of a dove, descends on the company. From its body rays of light fan out. Tongues of fire appear above the heads of all present. The apostles watch the scene with surprise. Gesticulating lively they begin to speak alien languages: they are filled with the Holy Spirit. Of the rear apostles, only the heads, which are almost painted in grisaille, are visible.

This biblical theme (Acts 2: 1–12) is one of the traditional scenes in religious painting. In the Netherlands the *Descent of the Holy Spirit* was painted in a somewhat uninvolved manner in the 16th and 17th centuries. The only exception to this is the monumental triptych by Bernard de Rijckere from 1587, in Saint Martin's Church in Kortrijk (fig. 13a). Versions from the Southern Netherlands often lack life, which is also true of the representations by Otto van Veen in 1612 (Lier, Saint Gummarus' Church), and Cornelis de Vos in 1613 (Nieuwkerken, Church of Our Lady). In Italy, by contrast, the *Descent of the Holy Spirit* is often depicted as an overwhelming apotheosis. In the Southern Netherlands, Peter Paul Rubens, Anthony van Dyck, and Gaspar de Crayer – also under the Italian influence – managed to add a new élan to the traditional composition scheme. Rubens surprisingly situated the scene on a stairway in his print *The Descent of the Holy Spirit* (1627),[1] Van Dyck's *Descent* from 1618/1620 (version Potsdam, Sanssouci) shows a subdued reaction,[2] and the De Crayer (version in Ghent, Saint Michael's Church) is built up asymmetrically.[3]

This *Descent of the Holy Spirit* is certainly based on Albrecht Dürer's woodcut with the same subject, *The Small Passion* from c. 1511 (fig. 13b)[4] and perhaps also on the edition of *The Small Passion* from 1611.

Nothing is known with certainty about the painting's provenance. Perhaps – considering the theme – it was made for the Almoners, or the Masters of the Table of the Holy Spirit. Or it was an epitaph piece, or it belonged to a Fraternity of the Virgin Mary – whether

Provenance: original possession of the cathedral.

Bibliography: Van Lerius 1841, p. 5
Génard 1856, p. 7
Van Herck 1951, p. 51
Van den Nieuwenhuizen 1957, pp. 43–44
Grieten & Bungeneers 1996, p. 405

1 Freedberg 1984, pp. 108–109, no. 27A (copy), fig. 62.
2 Barnes, De Poorter, Millar & Vey 2004, pp. 44–45, no. I, 28.
3 Vlieghe 1972.
4 Bartsch 1980, no. 51. The series was republished in Venice in 1612.

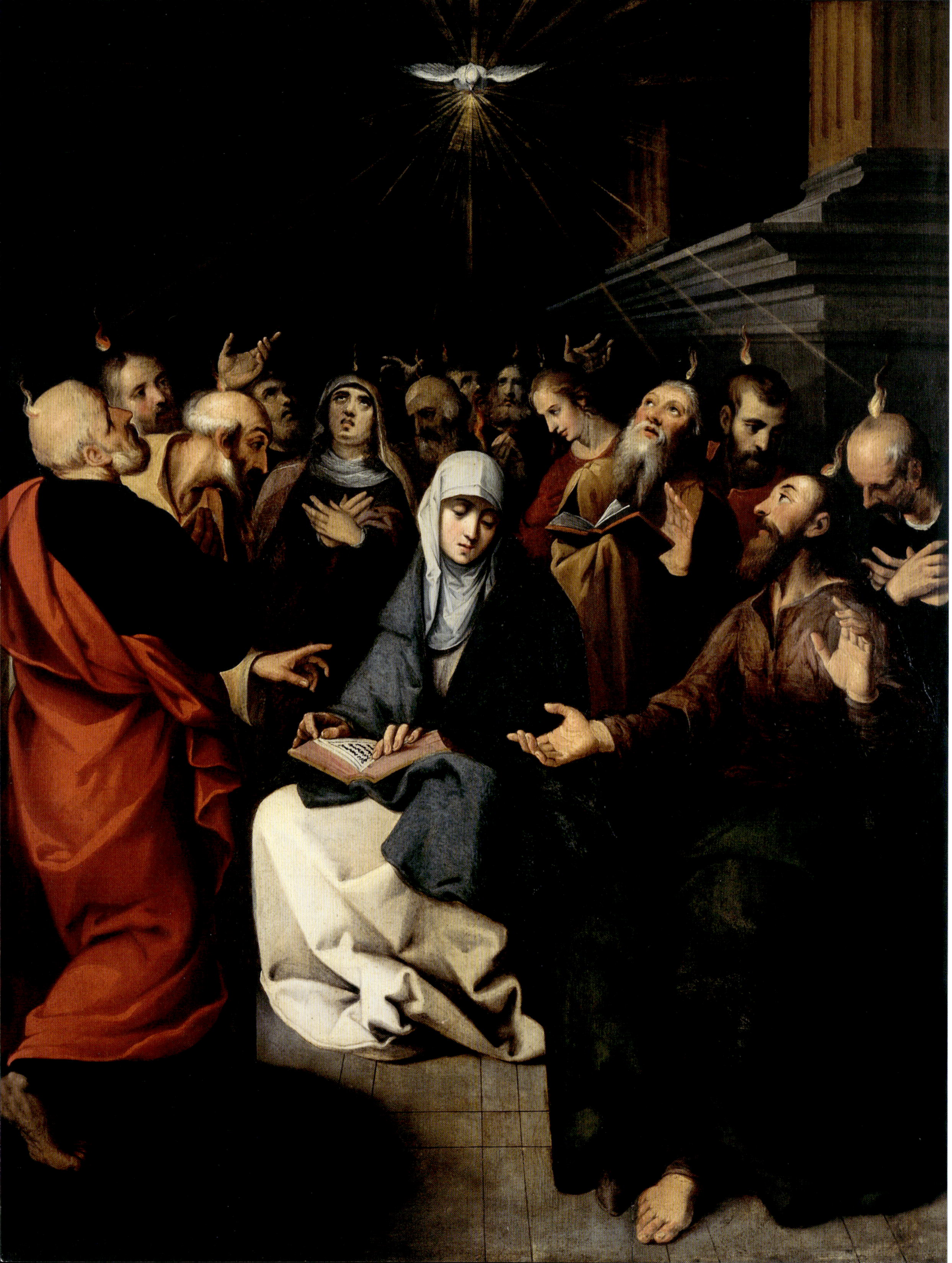

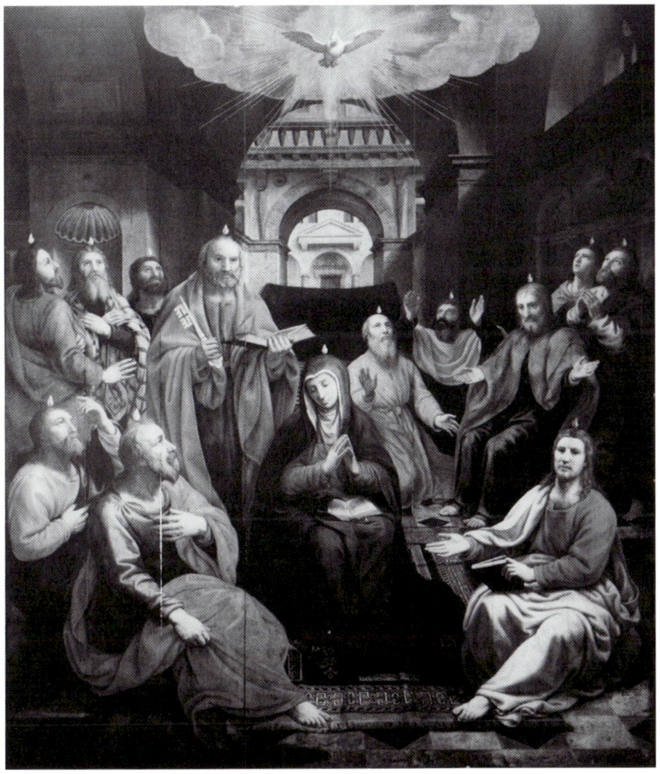

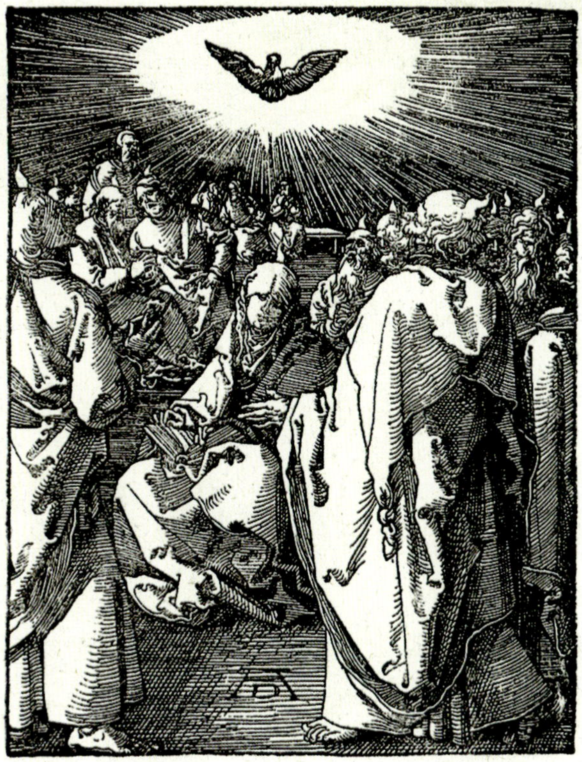

13a
Bernard de Rijckere
The Descent of the Holy Spirit
Kortrijk, Saint Martin's Church

13b
Albrecht Dürer
The Descent of the Holy Spirit
woodcut, from the series *The Small Passion*

or not linked to the cathedral. No references were found on this subject in the cathedral archives.[5]

In the past, the small painting was attributed to Ambrosius Francken by different authors.[6] It was possibly made in the Francken atelier, since it bears resemblances with other works, like *Paul and Barnabas Chosen as Apostles by the Holy Spirit*, the left panel of the *Triptych of the Holy Sacrament*, which Ambrosius Francken painted in 1589–1590 for the sacrament altar of Saint Georges' Church in Antwerp (Antwerp, Koninklijk Museum voor Schone Kunsten);[7] and the *Triptych of the Seven Works of Mercy* from 1609–1610 (Herentals, Saint Waldetrudis' Church).[8] The long-windedness, and the figures and framing, also seem to be related to an *Entombment* (present whereabouts unknown) which may have come from the atelier of Ambrosius Francken.[9]

Judging by the style, the painting probably dates from the beginning of the 17th century. Iconographically, too, it fits in the renewed interest in the Virgin, which was greatly promoted by the Counter Reformation and particularly by the Jesuits and other monastic orders. At the beginning of the 17th century, Mary was seen as a weapon against the Protestants who had minimised her role.[10]

NATASJA PEETERS

5 With thanks to Dr Van den Nieuwenhuizen for this information.
6 It was mentioned in Van Lerius 1841, p. 5. In Génard 1856, p. 7, it was attributed to Ambrosius Francken. It then hung in the chapel that was previously consecrated to Saint Barbara.
7 Inv. 139. *Catalogue Antwerp 1988*, pp. 142–143, no. 139.
8 Peeters 2000A, cat. A 5 and A 24.
9 Panel 102 x 82 cm; Lempertz Cologne 18–19 December 1913.
10 For additional information on the iconography of this painting, see the contribution of M. Gielis in this publication.

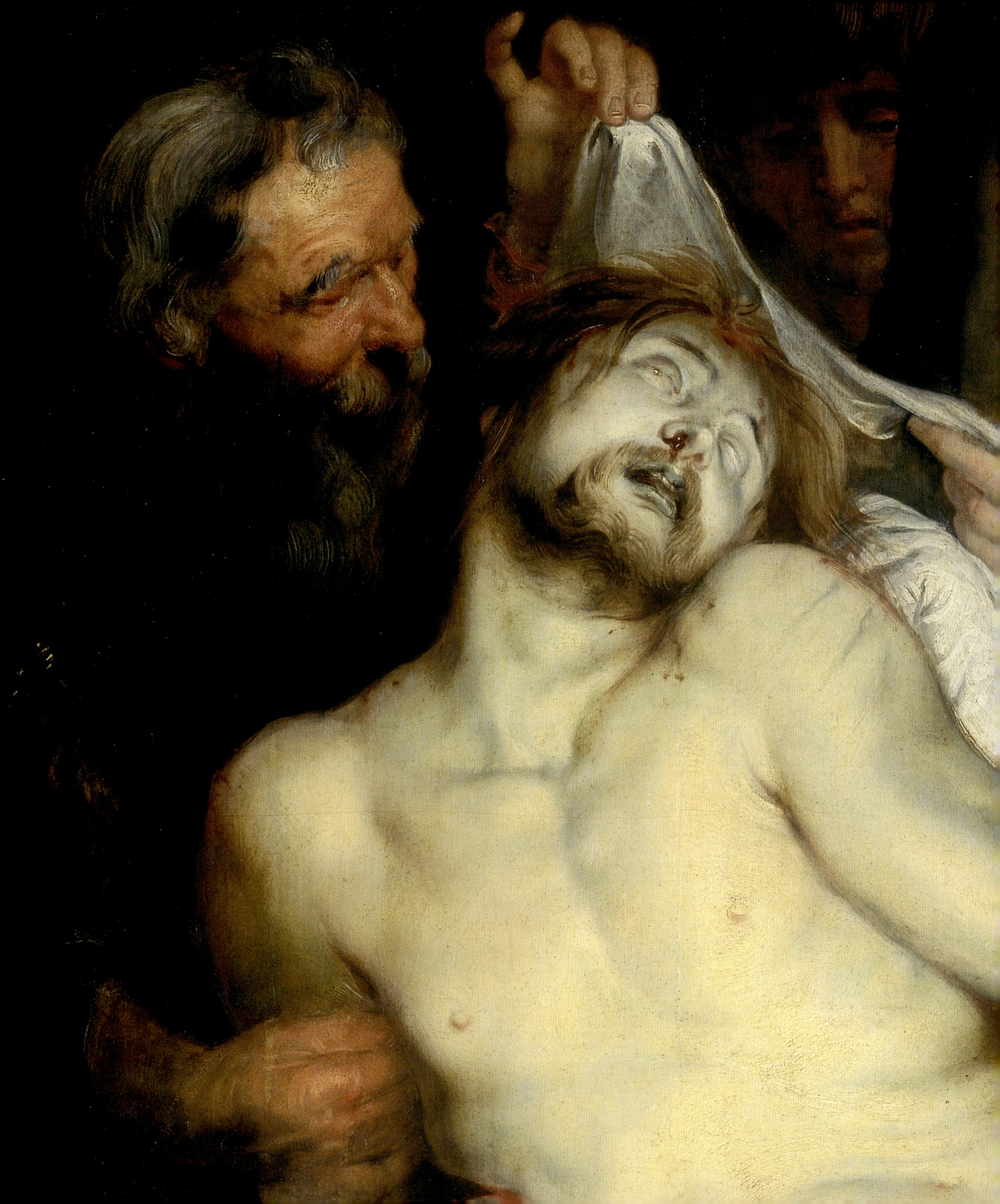

14 Epitaph of Jan Michielsen and Maria Maes

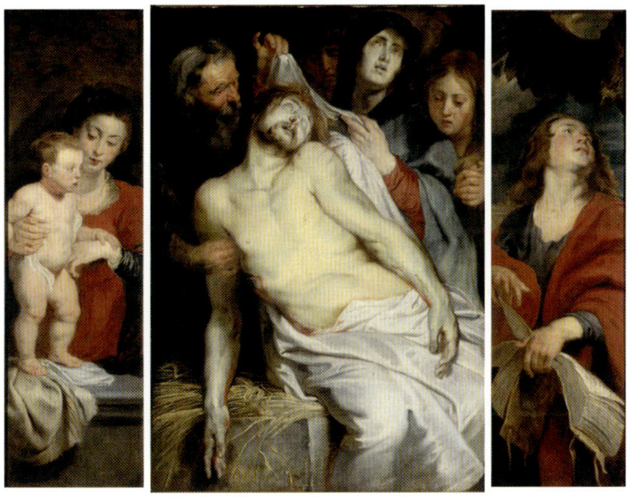

Peter Paul Rubens

Siegen 1577–Antwerp 1640

The Lamentation

1618

Oil on panel
centre panel: 138 x 98 cm
side panels: 136 x 40 cm

Unsigned

Antwerp, Koninklijk Museum voor Schone Kunsten, inv. 300–304

Provenance: Epitaph of Jan Michielsen and Maria Maes; probably displayed in the Antwerp cathedral in 1618; removed from the cathedral by the commissioners of the French Republic and transferred to the Musée Central des Arts in Paris (1794–1815); traded in 1816, together with Floris' *Fall of the Rebel Angels* (cat. 3), against *The Raising of the Cross* by P.P. Rubens, by the Museum and the Church of Our Lady.

Bibliography: *Beschrijvinge 1751*, p. 11 (15–16)
Mensaert 1763, pp. 243, 244
Descamps 1769, p. 154
Kerken van Antwerpen 1774, p. 30
Musée Central 1801, no. 503
Smith 1829–1842, II, pp. 10–11, no. 20
Van Lerius 1841, p. 30
Piot 1883, pp. 18, 19, 73, 314, 392, 418
Rooses 1886–1892, II, pp. 140–143, nos. 307–310
Riegel 1895, pp. 18–22
Van den Nieuwenhuizen 1962B, pp. 80, 82
Eisler 1967, pp. 43–48
Jaffé 1972, pp. 107–114
Glen 1977, pp. 88–96, 244, 245, fig. 30–32
Monballieu 1977, 339, 344, 351, 357
Wuyts 1991, pp. 61–86
Wuyts 1996, pp. 18–23
Grieten & Bungeneers 1996: p. 368
Judson 2000, pp. 222–228, nos. 64–68, fig. 192, 195, 196, 198, 199

The commissioners of this *Lamentation (Le Christ à la paille* or *Christ on the straw),* named after the subject of the centre panel, were the citizens Jan Michielsen (†1617) and his wife Maria Maes (†1633).[1] This triptych was probably commissioned from Rubens shortly after the death of Jan Michielsen.[2] Initially the triptych hung on the fourth pillar of the first north side aisle – as is indicated by a source dating from before the French Revolution.[3]

Being buried in Antwerp Cathedral was an expression of considerable wealth and only the richest citizens could afford it. That Jan Michielsen and Maria Maes also had an epitaph triptych painted by Rubens, confirms their social status. However, the depiction of the humble *Christ on the Straw* stands somewhat in contrast with the wealth of this bourgeois family.

Christ's dead body rests across the stone block, the Stone of Anointment, on which the burial ritual will be performed. Whether apocryphal or not, the Stone of Anointment has been a Christian relic from time immemorial and an important element in the Passion.[4] In this composition, too, the Stone of Anointment is prominently present. Rubens has strikingly visualised the body of the flagellated Christ. The clotted blood in Christ's nostrils, the dried blood on his forearms, the open stab wound in his right flank, and the slashes of the flagellation on his left shoulder, show the suffering of Christ in a moving and realistic manner.[5] The ash-grey skin colour of the lifeless body is reprised in Mary's face – the expression of an extreme form of empathy, and more than that, the identification of a mother's suffering with her son.

Mary raises the shroud and casts her eyes to heaven – the aspect of her dead son is too much for her. To her left an elder (or Joseph of Arimathea?) supports the dead body of Christ. With folded hands, Mary Magdalene looks over the shoulder of the Virgin to the performing of the burial ritual. The shadowy face in the background, beside the Virgin, is that of the apostle John.[6] The Italian influence is visible at the centre of the composition, but as was often the case with Rubens, he interpreted and reprised the composition in a very personal way. The head bent backwards to the left, the half-open mouth, and the pose of Christ's torso, are inspired by the *Laocoon* (fig. 11b). This antique statue had often been copied by Rubens during his stay in Italy.[7] The protagonists, depicted as half-figures, are placed close to the foreground, as in Caravaggio's biblical and allegorical paintings.[8]

On the side panels, not the commissioners themselves, but their patron saints are displayed: the Virgin and Saint John. On the left side panel we see

1 Grieten & Bungeneers 1996, p. 368.
2 Judson 2000, p. 224.
3 'From the Altar of the Woodcutters can be seen on the fourth Pillar an Epitaphy of the Michielsens family, being a Lamentation or a dead Christ on the lap of our Lady, the one door representing our Lady with her child, the other door representing Saint John the Evangelist, and to the outside of the same doors are painted in the way of Raphael two Images of our Lord and of our Lady, all in the best way of Petrus Paulus Rubens.' Berbie 1774A.
4 Wuyts 1991, p. 64.
5 Wuyts 1991, p. 81.
6 Judson 2000, p. 224.
7 Van der Meulen 1994, II, pp. 93–104, nos. 76–93.
8 Judson 2000, p. 224.

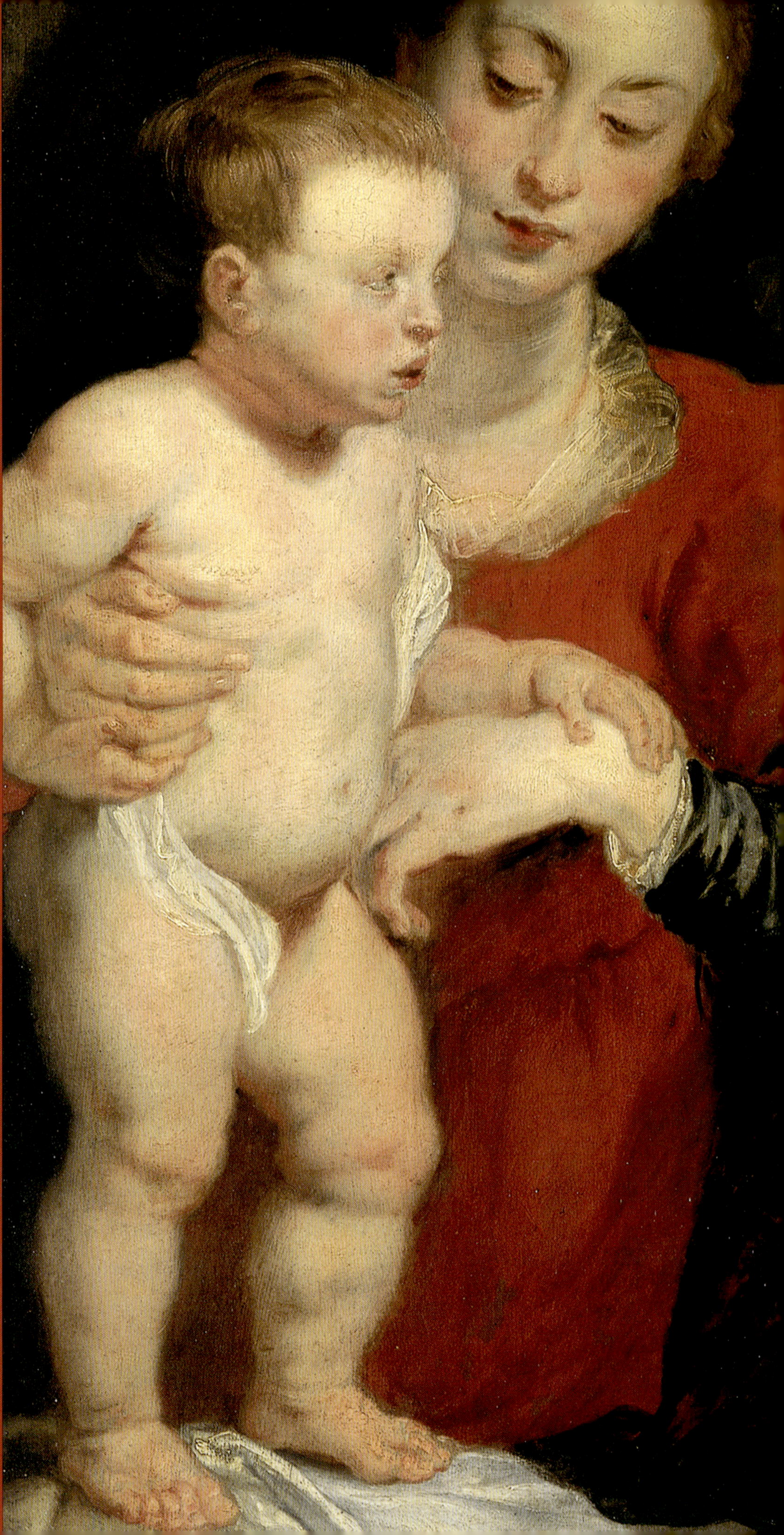

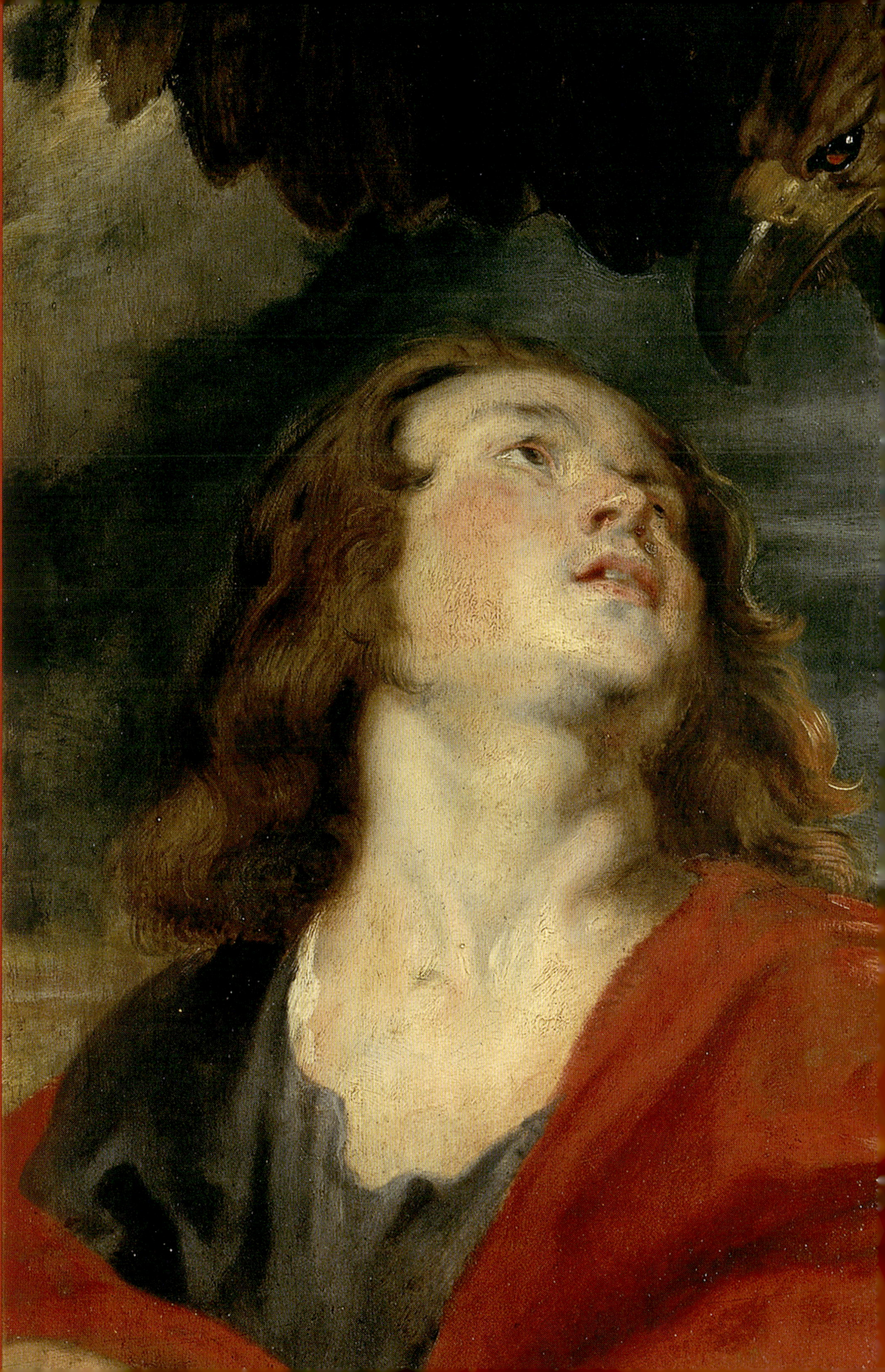

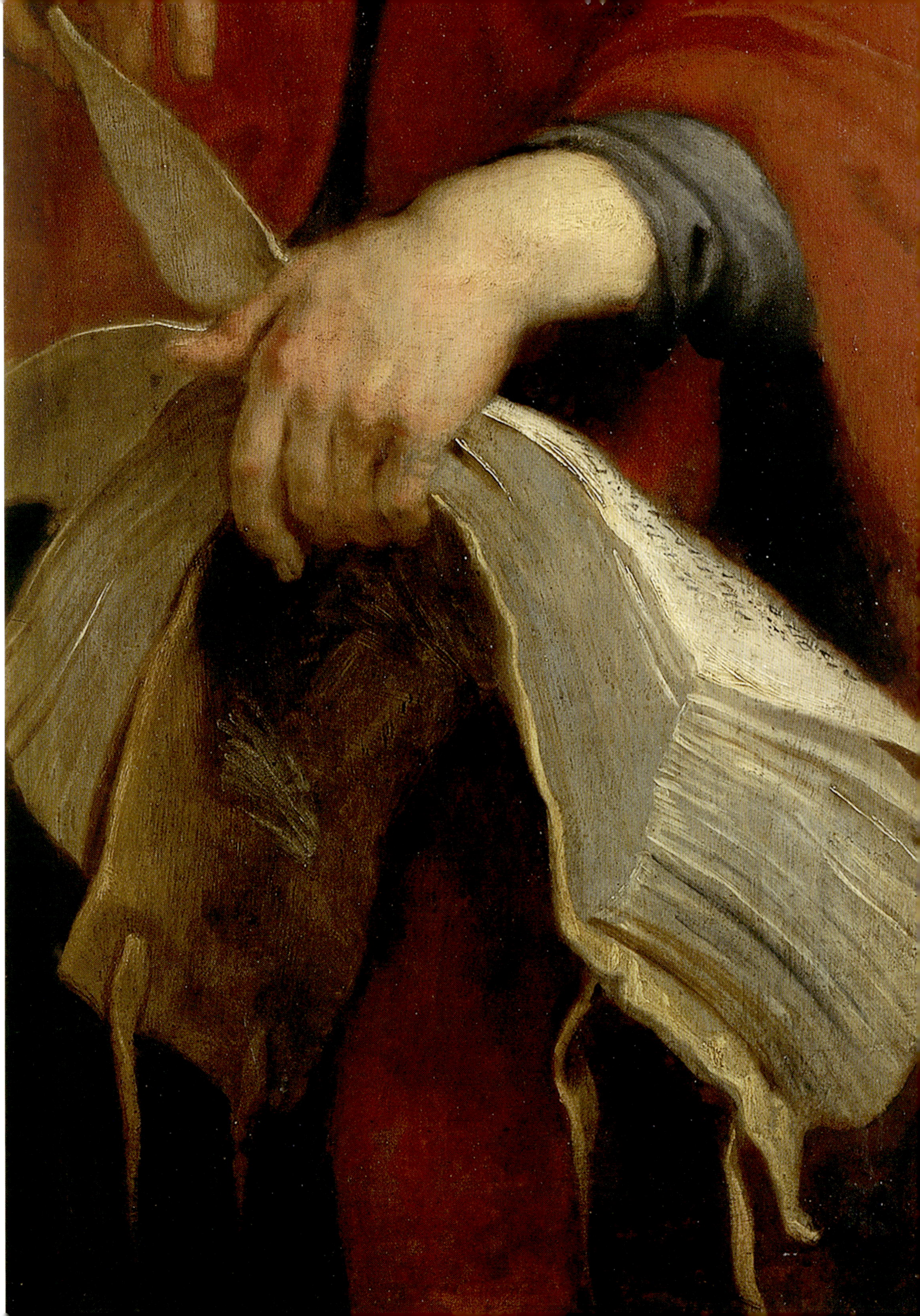

the Virgin, who lovingly holds the Child with her arms around his waste. The Child stands on a stone and looks at the centre panel. On the right panel, John the Evangelist is depicted in three-quarter length with an open book in his hand, with an eagle – his attribute – above his head.[9] The grisailles on the exterior of the panels show Christ with a globe, the *Salvator Mundi*, and the Virgin with Child. These 'grey paintings' were not executed by Rubens himself, but by his atelier staff, probably after a design that was lost.[10] The composition and iconography of the centre panel and side panels attune closely to each other and form a single whole.[11]

There are various opinions about the meaning of this triptych. The scene could be situated in the tradition of the burial rituals. From the Middle Ages onwards, the poor were merely wrapped in a shroud and stretched on straw in the burial pit – Rubens probably knew this custom.[12] In *The Lamentation with Saint Francis* (Brussels, Royal Museums of Fine Arts: fig. 14a)[13] the Messiah is placed on a bundle of straw. 'But the Son of Man has no place to lay his head' (Matthew 8: 20).[14] The stone and the funerary custom would refer to the humility of Christ, although this passage from the Bible is not directly linked to the Passion. According to Wuyts, Rubens – being a competent artist – fulfilled the principal requirement of a history painter, which is truthfulness – depicting an event as it could really have occurred.[15]

While interpreting this work of art we obviously have to take into account its initial function – that of an epitaph – and the specific wishes of the commissioners. It is unusual that they chose not to be depicted themselves on the side panels. An explanation for this can be found in the central theme. In the last station of the Passion, the entombment, in which *all is done*, as was foreseen in God's salvation plan, the hope for resurrection was included. This is very appropriate in the context of a burial piece. The patron saints of the commissioners, the Virgin and Saint John, have their own place within the history of salvation and each refers to the Resurrection. Showing the Virgin with the Child could refer to the incarnation of Christ, as John the Evangelist (the donor's patron saint) described in his winged words, 'And the word was made flesh' (John 1: 1–14) in reference to the gestation of Christ. The incarnation contains all the future suffering of Christ and therefore also the salvation of mankind.[16] The Child, which the Virgin shows to the viewer, stands on the same stone block on which the burial ritual will be performed, and the white cloth around his feet refers to the shroud. Thus, the left panel refers to the suffering on the centre panel. Furthermore, Eisler has directly linked the text of the epitaph,[17] which is only known through an 18th century transcription, with Jan Michielsen and his patron saint, John.[18] According to the popular interpretation of John 21: 22–23, John the Evangelist would never have died: 'Jesus said, "If it should be my will that he wait until I come, what is it to you? Follow me." So the rumour spread among the brothers that this disciple was not going to die'. Combined with the epitaph, this passage offers a remarkable insight about the relationship between the commissioner, the triptych, and its meaning – resurrection and eternal life. The grisaille on the exterior panel, with the *Salvator Mundi*, even refers explicitly to the salvation of mankind, effected through the crucifixion and resurrection. Therefore Christ acts as a mediator between God and man on earth. The other grisaille, with the depiction of the Virgin with the Child, could be a reference to the function of the Virgin as mediator, or intercessor. So this *Lamentation* not only shows Christ's death, but also contains inherent references to the resurrection. This message of hope – the resurrection of Christ and the just who will be admitted to heaven with him – was probably a hopeful thought for Jan Michielsen and Maria Maes, the commissioners of this epitaph.[19]

9 Judson 2000, p. 227.
10 Judson 2000, p. 227.
11 *Catalogue Antwerp 1988*, p. 320.
12 Wuyts 1991, pp. 78–79.
13 Judson 2000, pp. 229–231, no. 70, fig. 204.
14 Wuyts 1996, p. 19.
15 Wuyts 1991, p. 69.
16 Wuyts 1991, pp. 82–83; Wuyts 1996, p. 22.
17 'In honour of God, the All Good, the Supreme. In the grave below lies (but) lies not, is buried (and yet) not buried, him who has been the person of Jan Michielsen, because by the law of fate he has departed from the world (but) not from his wife Maria Maes, lonely in her walk of life and appearance. Surviving himself, he lives on in her heart as if he was alive, and breathes he (on) in his four children. Passer-by, pray for the eternal peace of him who is interred here, and for the (still) long days of life for his surviving consort. He died in the year 1617, on 20 June.' Translated from Latin, see Wuyts 1996, p. 19; Eisler 1967, pp. 58–59.
18 Eisler 1967, p. 59.
19 Wuyts 1991, pp. 83–85; Wuyts 1996, pp. 22–23.

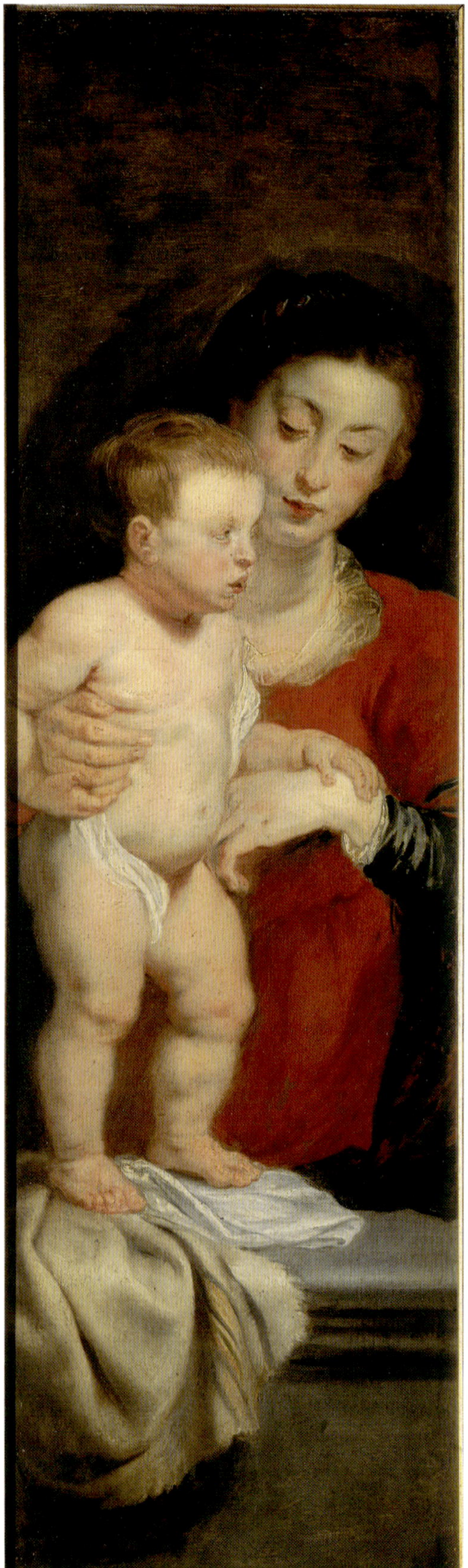

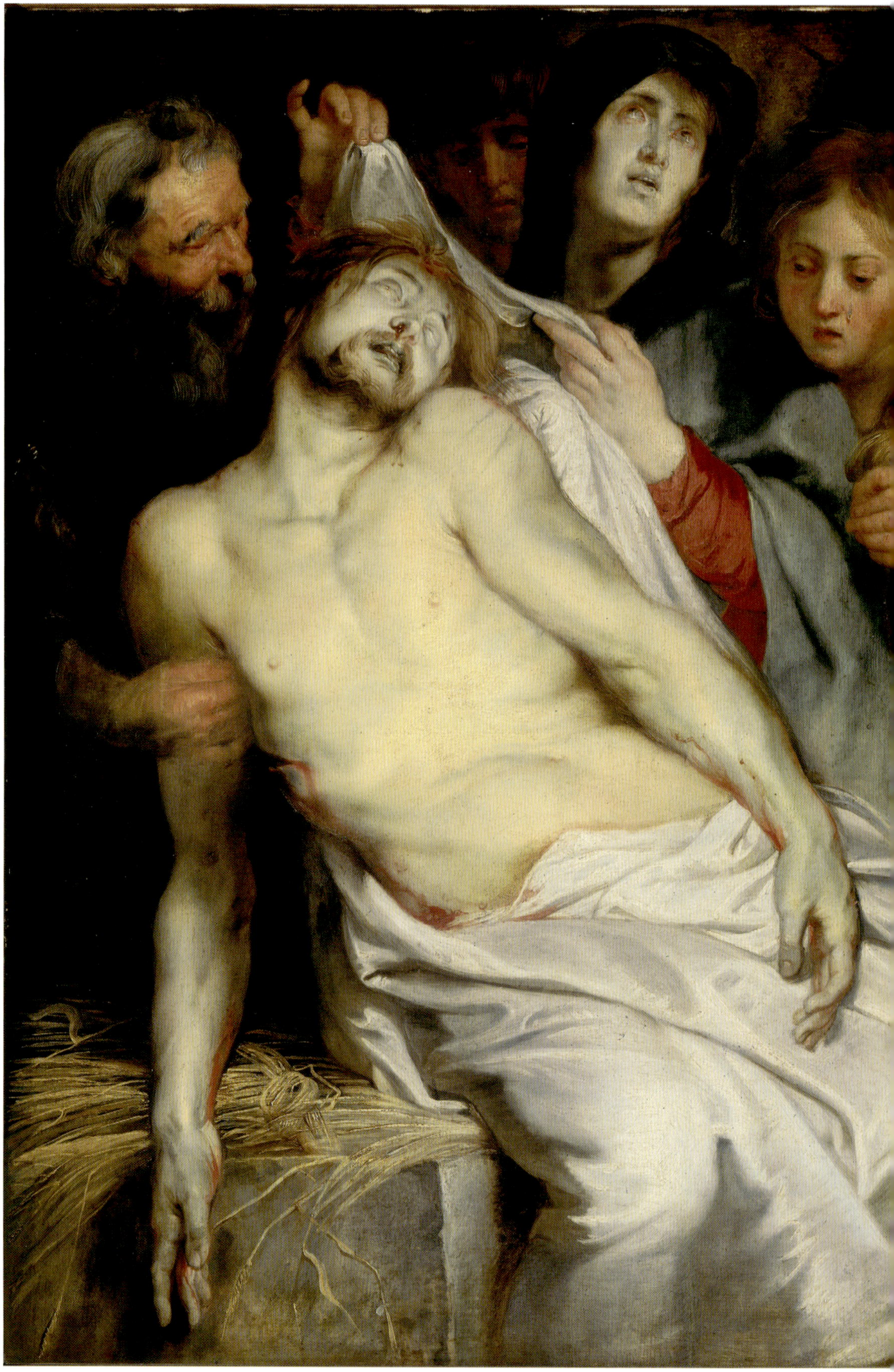

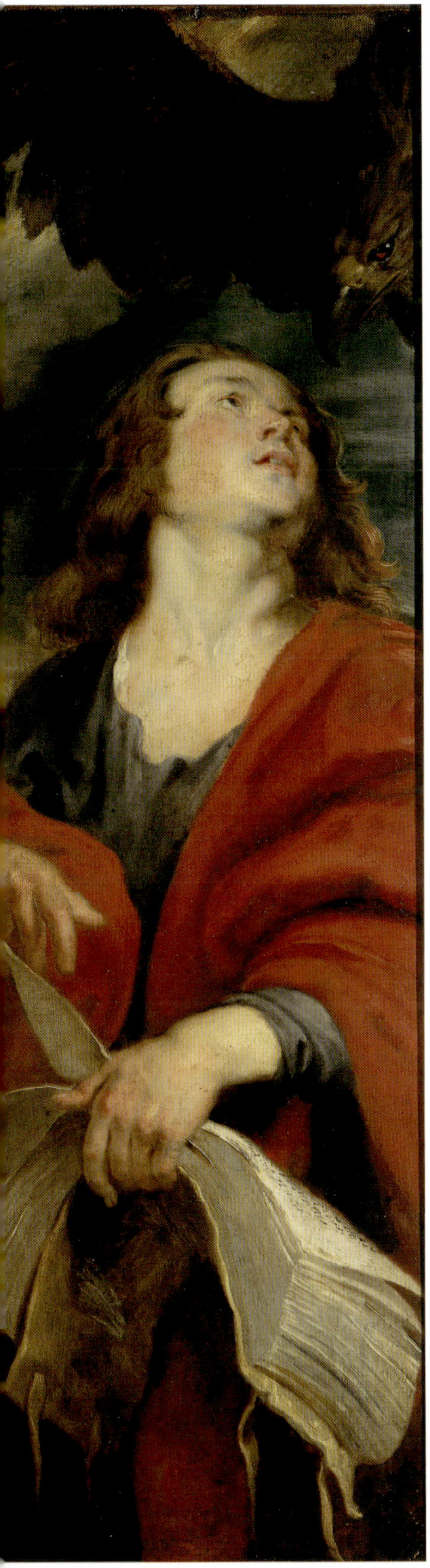

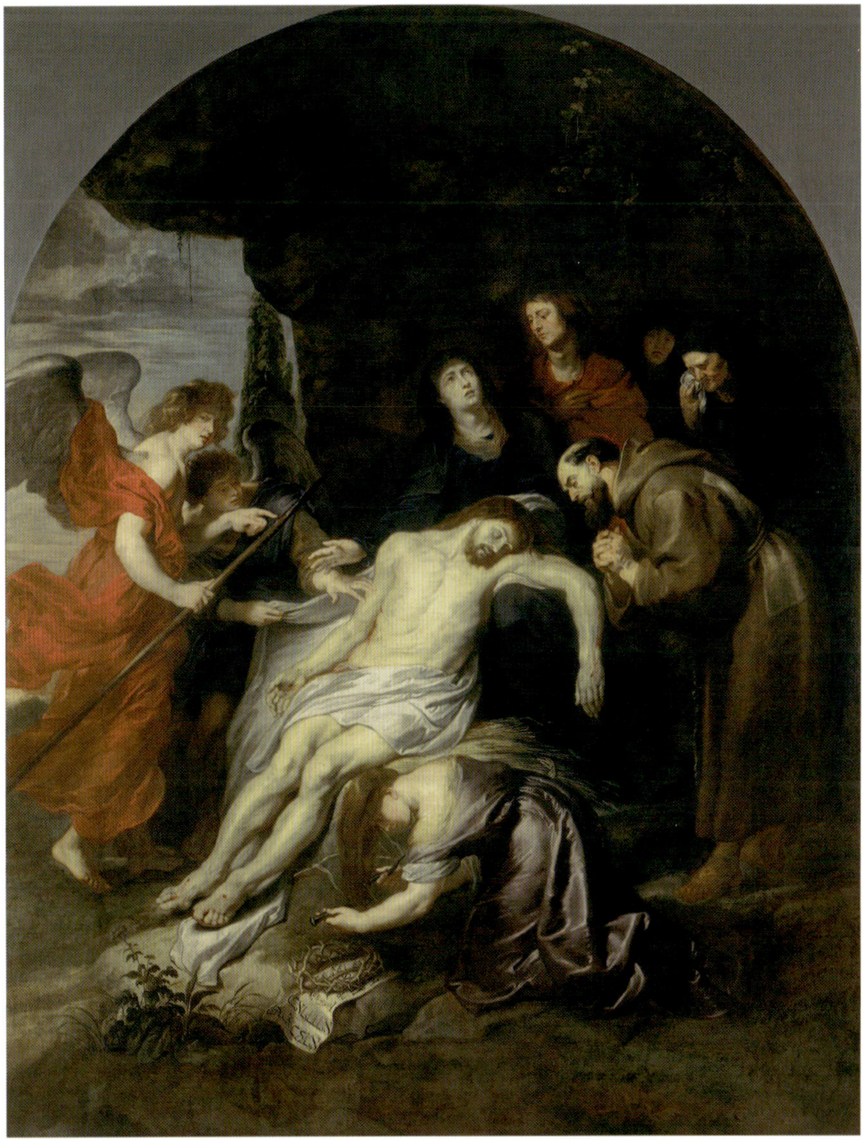

14a
Peter Paul Rubens
The Lamentation with Saint Francis
Brussels, Royal Museums of Fine Arts of Belgium

The panel was painted in 1618, at the height of the Counter Reformation. The references to the Eucharist – the Counter Reformation theme par excellence – are legion here. The straw and particularly the ears of corn on the Stone of Salvation, refer to the bread that is Christ, the breaking of the bread at the Last Supper, and by extension to the Eucharist and the suffering of Christ – and in a typical Counter Reformation way, to salvation. However, it goes further than merely a Eucharistic meaning. Mary lifts up the shroud and shows Christ's dead body. This is an *Ave, verum corpus* and refers directly to the Eucharist in which the body of Christ is shown to the faithful in the form of bread. This idea of 'showing' and the Eucharistic act of the Virgin parallels with the Birth of Christ and the Adoration of the Magi. In both cases Mary fulfils the same Eucharistic act: to show the body of Christ. On the left side panel she shows, as mentioned, the Child. Moreover, showing the dead body contains an inherent reference to the Resurrection, which is very striking in the context of an epitaph piece, and is why the different meanings seem to be interlaced.[20]

Various authors disagree on the iconographical meaning of this triptych. In my opinion one meaning does not necessarily exclude another, and it seems plausible that the three layers of meaning are coexistent in this panel. These 'layers' can be directly linked to the context in situ, for which the work was destined. Firstly, the *Lamentation* was a well-known composition within the Passion iconography for the audience of common worshippers, for whom the tradition of the burial ritual was familiar too. Secondly, to the commissioners this epitaph contained a particularly subtle reference to the resurrection and the union of loved ones. Lastly, there are numerous references to the Eucharist which entirely harmonise with Counter Reformation ideas. Again, Rubens confirmed that he was not only *the* painter of the Counter Reformation, but also a true *pictor doctus*.

PAUL HUVENNE

20 Judson 2000, p. 224; with thanks to Dr Hans Devisscher.

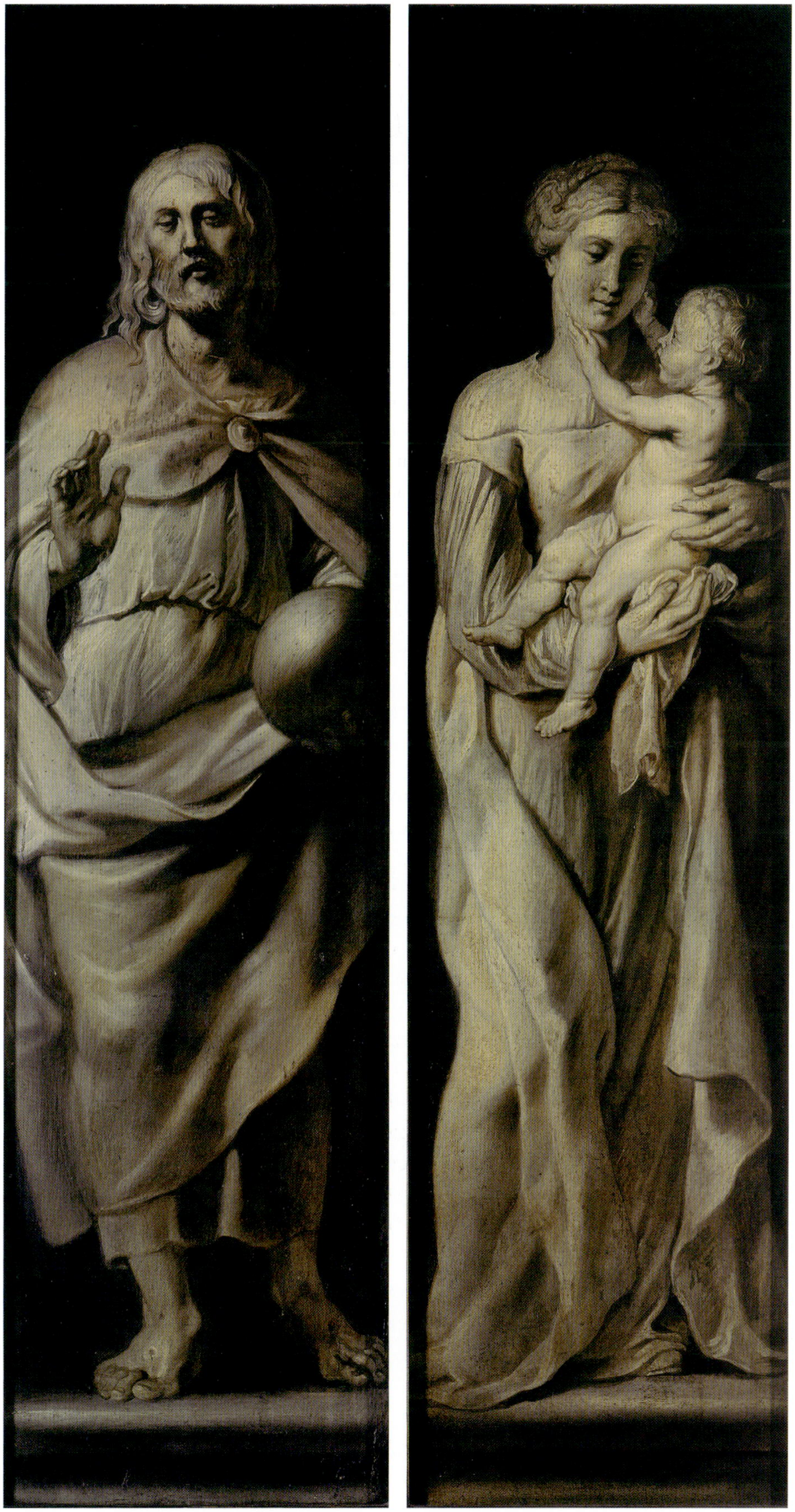

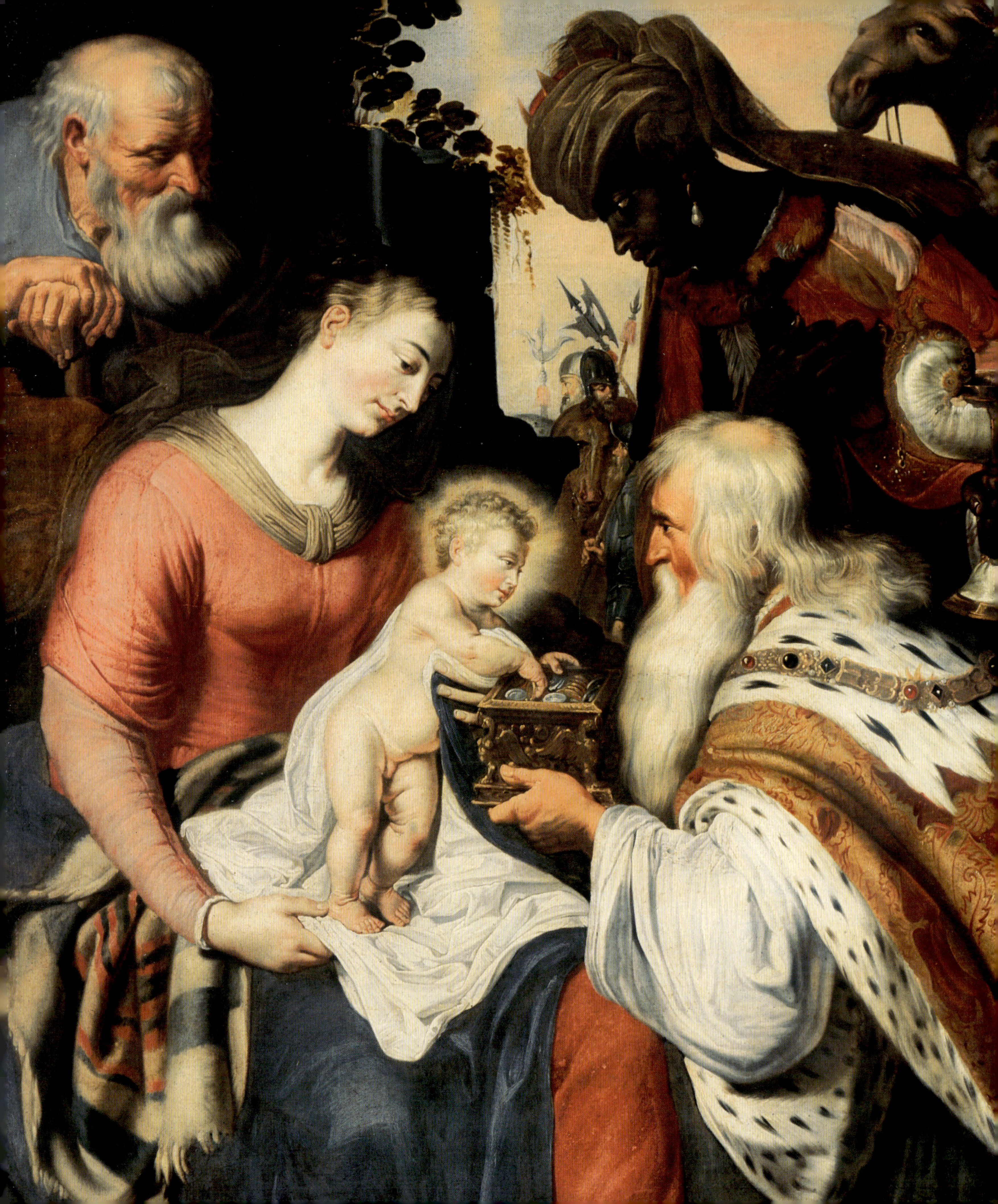

15 Altarpiece of the Tailors

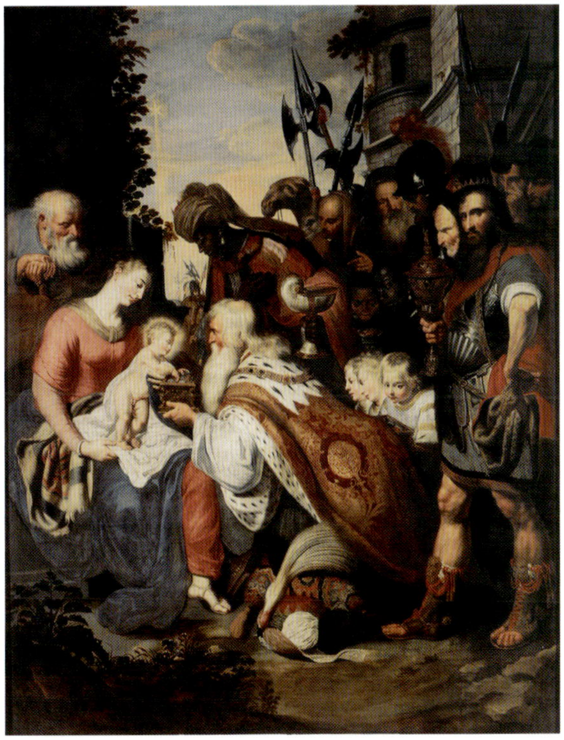

Artus Wolffort

Antwerp 1581–Antwerp 1642

The Adoration of the Magi

c. 1615–1620?

Oil on canvas
266 x 192 cm

Unsigned

Antwerp, Koninklijk Museum voor Schone Kunsten, inv. 439

Provenance: Altar of the Tailors in the Antwerp cathedral; transferred in 1798 to the École Centrale des Deux-Nèthes in the abolished Discalced Monastery; from then until 1811 in the Academy in the Exchange building; then transferred to the Museum in the former Friars Minor Monastery; foundational holding of the museum.

Bibliography: *Beschrijvinge 1751*, p. 6 (13) (as Pieter van Mol)
Mensaert 1763, p. 234
Descamps 1769, p. 147
Van der Sanden 1771, II, pp. 344, 347
Kerken van Antwerpen 1774, p. 19 (as Pieter van Mol)
Van Lerius 1841, p. 17
Rooses 1879, p. 504
Van den Branden 1883, pp. 765–766
Prims 1938–1939, XII, pp. 334–338
Van Brabant 1974, pp. 69, 233
Vervaet 1976, pp. 238–239
Vlieghe 1977, pp. 103–104
Baudouin 1993, p. 220
Grieten & Bungeneers 1996, p. 369

This altarpiece showing *The Adoration of the Magi* originally stood in the chapel of the Tailors, one of Antwerp's privileged crafts.[1] We have no information about a possible commission by the Tailors: documentation on this subject has not been found, but early sources[2] tell us something about these 'three kings'. On a ground plan of the cathedral from 1703 is handwritten in the first chapel on the right in the ambulatory: '3 king, theodatus delmont' (fig. 20).[3] Although that leaves room for doubt about the identification of the panel, de Wit writes in his *Kerken van Antwerpen:* 'From here one enters the ambulatory, where the first altarpiece at the right hand, the Tailors' *Adoration of the Three Kings* is by Petrus van Mol.'[4] While the attribution may be incorrect, the source does provide information about the original location of the work,[5] which is important because it also tells us more about the status of the craft. There was probably a hierarchy in the positioning of craft and guild altars in relation to the high altar, which was, as it were, 'protected' by (the altars of) the armed guilds.[6] The altars of the crafts that were (in) directly related to the preaching of the faith were located in the chapels of the ambulatory encircling the choir. The Tailors belonged to that group because they were responsible for the religious garments worn by priests and deacons.

If it seems strange that the Tailors did not choose a depiction of their patron, Saint Cornelius, this might be connected to the decree of the Third Synod of the Diocese of Antwerp, from 1610, which prescribed that on the centre panel of an altarpiece, only Christ, Mary, or a scene from the New Testament might to be displayed.[7] Another more financially pragmatic reason may be that no specific new commission was made for an *Adoration of the Magi*. The structure of the canvas, with several attached pieces, may indicate that an existing painting was adapted to the wishes of the Tailors and transformed into an altarpiece.[8] The existence of different versions of the composition – which are all by the same hand and, contrary to the painting discussed here, of a horizontal format – argues in favour of this hypothesis. These horizontal paintings may have been intended for bourgeois interiors, as it is known that Wolffort also painted for the open market.[9] Although this is far from certain, it would not be surprising at all for the Tailors to start from an existing piece. The Old Clothes' Merchants, a 'subdivision' of the Tailors,

1 *Inventaris 1925*, pp. 22, 23, 51.
2 Papebrochius 1695, V, pp. 340–358; Descamps 1769, pp. 146–147; *Kerken van Antwerpen 1774*, p. 19.
3 Van den Nieuwenhuizen 1962B, p. 71.
4 *Kerken van Antwerpen 1774*, p. 19.
5 Grieten & Bungeneers 1996, p. 369.
6 See the contribution of Ria Fabri in this publication.
7 Vervaet 1976, p. 201.
8 Vervaet 1976, pp. 238 –239.
9 Vlieghe 1990, p. 887.

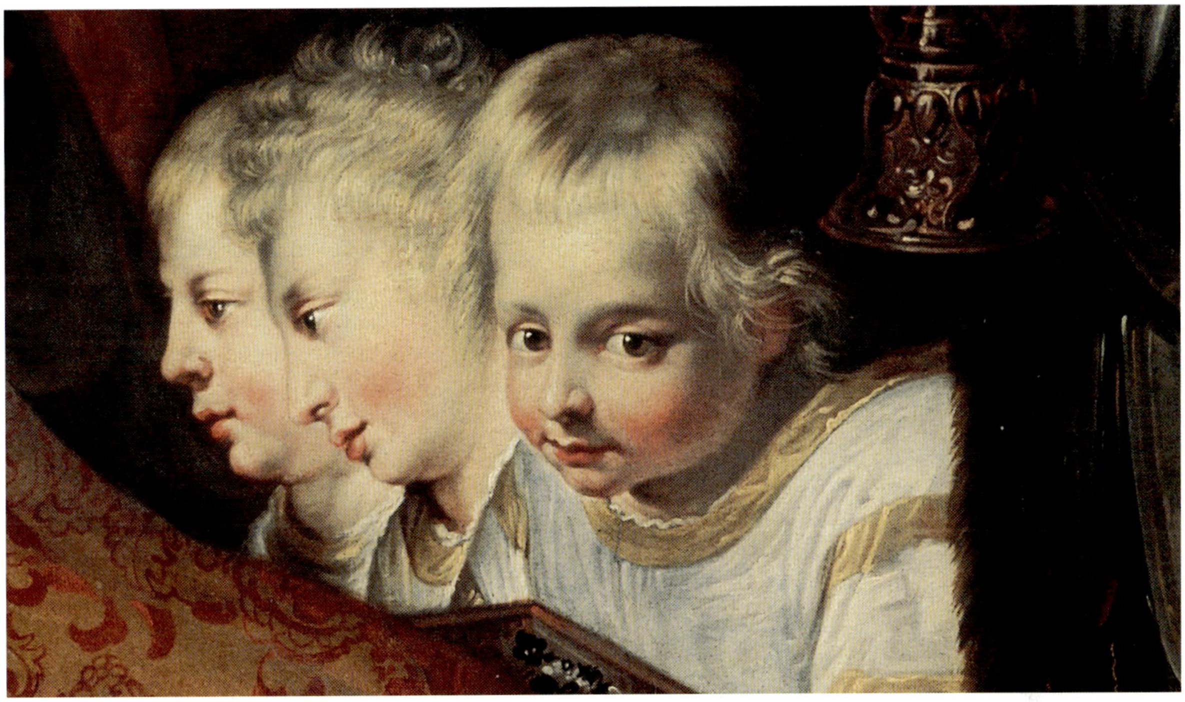

were the only party privileged to buy paintings at public sales and thus they regulated the second hand market.[10] They therefore had a good understanding of the availability of second hand paintings.

Although the Tailors could not choose to show their patron saint, the theme of *The Adoration of the Magi* offered other opportunities. Guilds and crafts often preferred a subject that was linked to their activities. This adoration scene shows exotic figures with appropriate clothing and rich draperies in luxurious fabrics, which obviously fitted very well with the Tailors' core business. The oldest magus, Melchior, has put his flamboyant head covering aside to hand the gold to the Child. His mantle of gold brocade trimmed with ermine fur stands in vivid contrast with the plain fabrics of Mary's robe and the modest travelling blanket on her lap. The naked Child rises from the opened winding sheet to receive the gifts. Balthazar, the Moorish king, has one hand on his heart and in the other he holds a beautifully decorated shell with myrrh. His mantle, decorated with feathers, is another demonstration of the artist's sense of the exotic. Caspar, the third magus, with the ciborium of incense in his hands looks self-confidently at the spectator. In his case, too, ample attention was given to the rendering of fabrics and materials. The star and the camels clearly refer to the biblical story. The cherubic, rosy-cheeked boys may be partly hidden behind Melchior's back, but their gleaming white tunics are clearly outlined against the dark background. The face of the child looking at the spectator can also be found in another work by Wolffort: in a series of apostles he looks over Saint Matthew's shoulder.[11] The head of the oldest magus, too, is a recognised motif in Wolffort's repertoire.

This *Adoration of the Magi* is now attributed to Artus Wolffort. After thorough research, Hans Vlieghe convincingly attributed the work to this master in 1977. It is interesting to see how the artist used and re-used an own repertoire of visual material. Among the features Vlieghe identified in the artist's oeuvre, the aforementioned heads played a major role in attributing the work convincingly to Artus Wolffort.[12] In stylistic terms, Wolffort's oeuvre demonstrates an early and a late period. The differences are clearly recognisable in popular depictions of *The Adoration of the Magi*, for example. The painting in the Koninklijk Museum voor Schone Kunsten is characterised by a strong linear quality, an angular pattern of folds in the draperies, attention to the rendering of fabrics, and a generally rigid and artificial composition. Therefore this work should be dated c. 1615–1620, rather than c. 1640, as was previously proposed.[13] In Wolffort's later period his figures

10 Van der Stighelen & Vermeylen 2006, p. 196.
11 Vlieghe 1977, p. 104.
12 Ibidem.
13 Documentation Ludwig Burchard, Rubenianum, Antwerp.

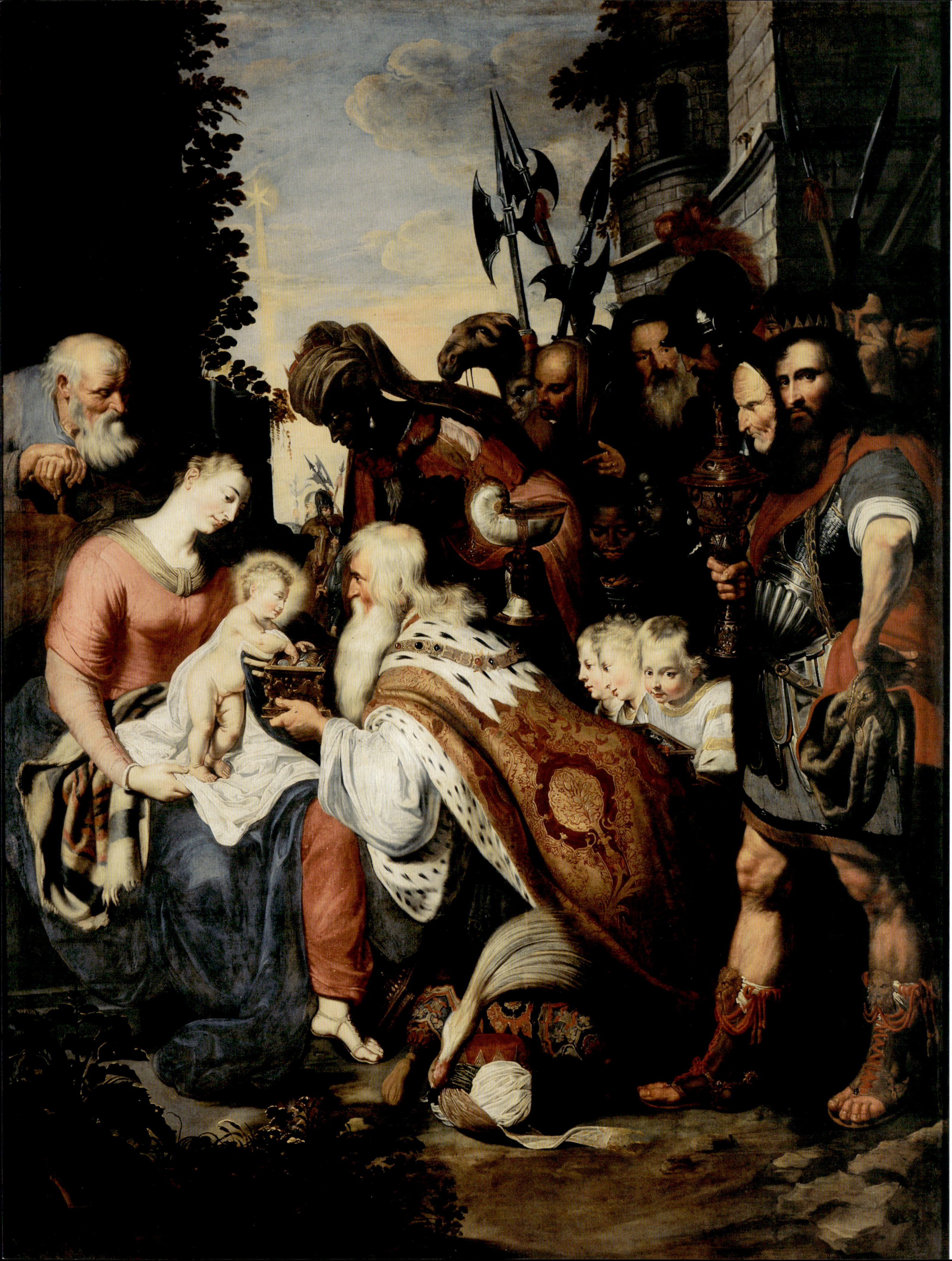

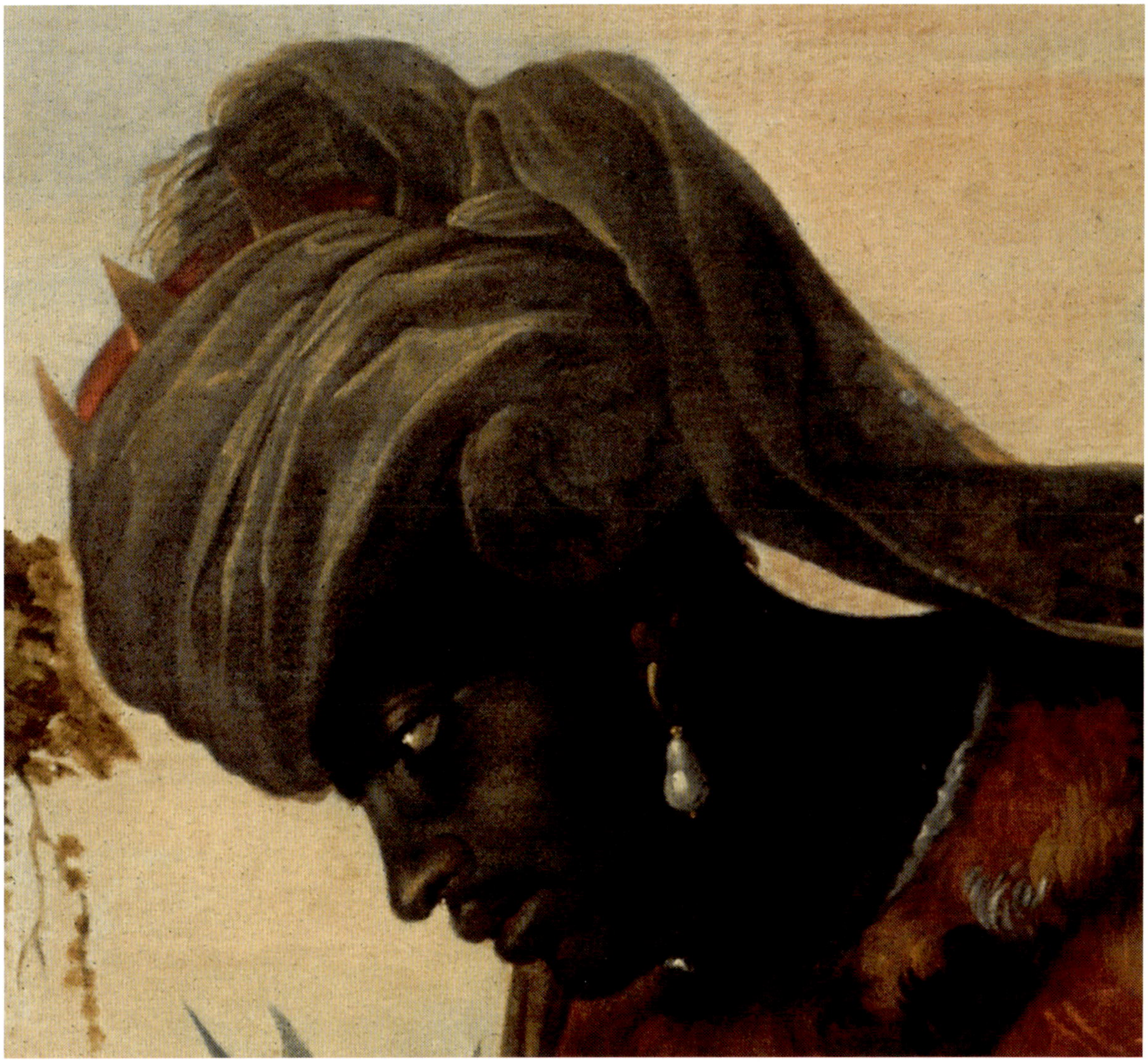

are depicted more plastically and the composition becomes more dynamic. Clearly, the influence of Rubens has something to do with this.[14]

In early art historiography the work was erroneously attributed to Deodatus del Monte and later to Wolffort's apprentices Pieter van Lint and Pieter van Mol.[15] Descamps, too, attributed the painting to the latter. 'The first Chapel on the downside of the Choir, belonging to the Tailors, is decorated with a quite rich marble Altar, with a painting by Pierre van Mol, representing the Adoration of the Magi. This apprentice-painter of Rubens copied the composition from the works of his Master. All is well coloured, but the shadows tend to be rather black.'[16] Sources from before the French Revolution may not always prove correct in relation to attributions, but they offer clear insight on contemporary reception of the work.

PRISCA VALKENEERS

14 Vlieghe 1981, p. 83; Vervaet 1976, p. 238.
15 Grieten & Bungeneers 1996, p. 369; Vlieghe 1990, p. 887.
16 Descamps 1769, pp. 146–147.

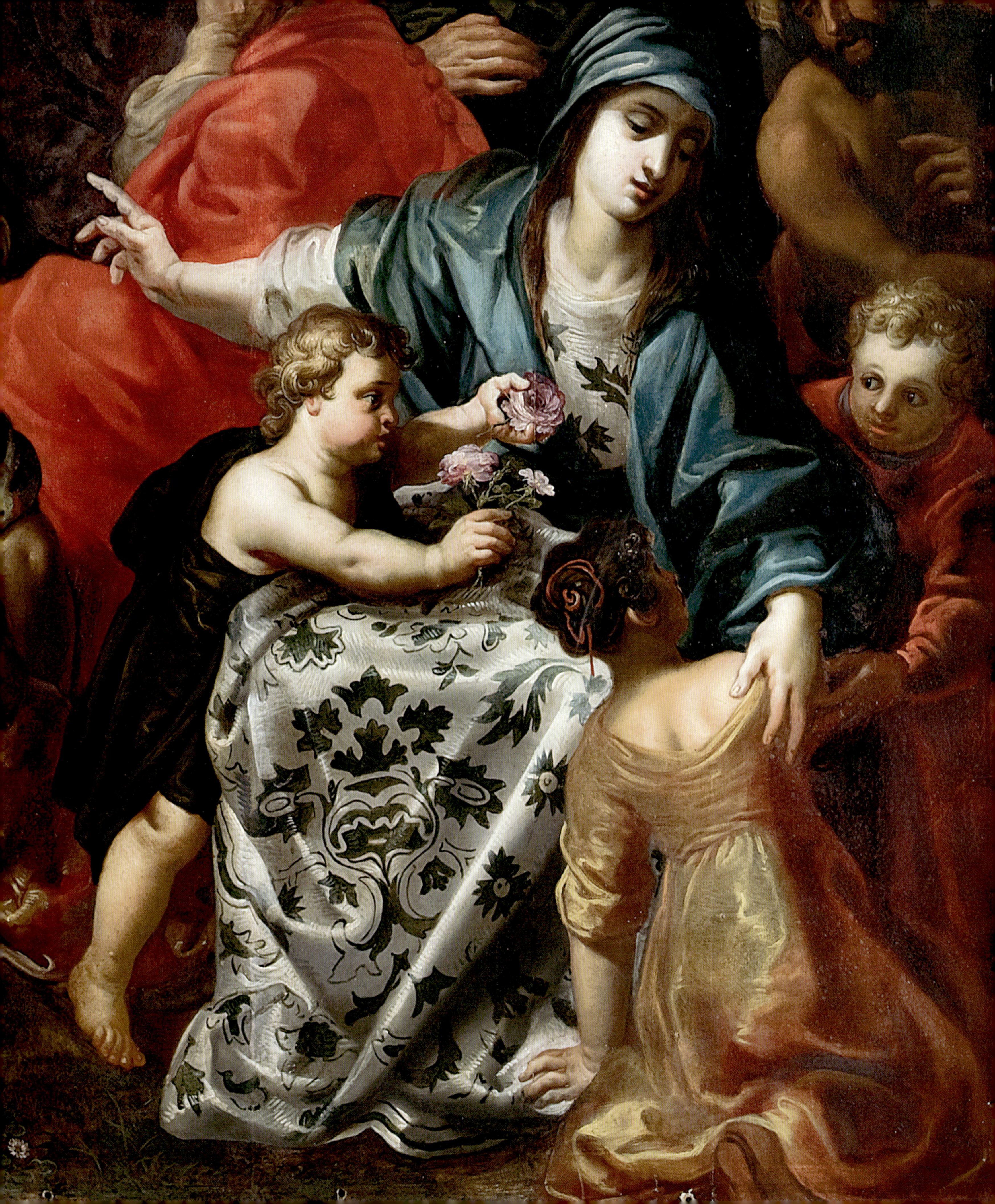

16 Altarpiece of the Cabinetmakers

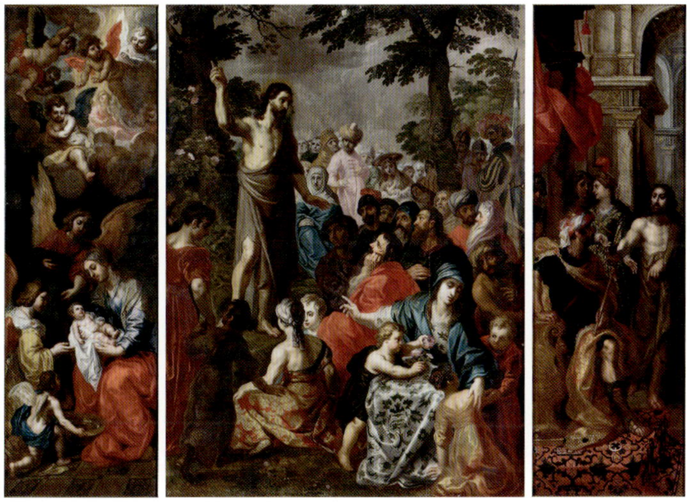

Hendrik van Balen

Antwerp 1573–Antwerp 1632

Saint John Preaching in the Wilderness

c. 1622

Oil on panel
centre panel: 270 x 201 cm
side panels: 270 x 85 cm

Unsigned

Centre panel: Antwerp, Koninklijk Museum voor Schone Kunsten, inv. 365
Side panels: Antwerp, Cathedral of Our Lady, inv. 954

Provenance: commissioned by the Cabinetmakers' craft; placed on the craft altar in the Antwerp cathedral in 1620–1622; transferred in 1798 to the École Centrale des Deux-Nèthes in the abolished Discalced Monastery; from 1802 to 1890 the centre panel was kept in the Museum in the former Friars Minor Monastery; foundational holding of the museum; until 2008 on long-term loan to Saint John's Church in Borgerhout (Antwerp); the side panels were returned to the Church of Our Lady in the early 19th century.

Bibliography: Papebrochius, 1695, V, p. 346
De Wit 1748, p. 23
Beschrijvinghe... 1751, p. 9 (14)
Mensaert 1763, p. 238
Descamps 1769, p. 150
Van Lerius 1841, p. 21
Bürger 1862, p. 71
Van den Branden 1883, p. 464
Piot 1883, p. 93
Van Herck 1951, p. 43
Van den Nieuwenhuizen 1957, pp. 48–49
Van Brabant 1974, pp. 83 and 221
Vervaet 1976, pp. 234–235
Larsen 1985, p. 62
Baudouin 1993, pp. 210–211
Grieten & Bungeneers 1996, pp. 406–407
Werche 2004, pp. 218–219

John the Baptist in the role of superpreacher: this was the theme the Antwerp Cabinetmakers chose for the centre panel of their new altarpiece in the Antwerp cathedral. More than a century after they had commissioned a *Lamentation* from Quinten Matsys (cat. 1) the deans of the craft, c. 1620–1622, sought a fashionable and contemporary work by the renowned Antwerp painter Hendrik van Balen. On the centre panel, a somewhat manneristically attenuated and youthful saint John addresses a varied crowd. He reinforces his words with raised right hand and extended index finger. He stands on a small prominence in a rather vague forest landscape somewhere in the Jordan region (Luke 3, 1–17).

In the lower right corner, an imposing seated woman with children points to John as he preaches, immediately attracting the attention. She leads, as it were, the spectator's gaze to the painting's main figure who towers behind her back at an angle. Clustered in a semicircle around John, are mostly male listeners, young and old, citizens and Roman or contemporary soldiers. Just as the Gospel text states (Luke 3, 10–14), they seem to question him. With varying attention they look at John, the forerunner of Christ. Some fix their gaze on an arm or part of his clothing. Others just look him over. Their interaction is minimal. However, John seems to have a special bond with a bearded old man, possibly a Pharisee, who wears the Hebrew word 'Yahweh' on his head covering. Is this a reference to the Gospel text in which John speaks in a threatening tone to the Pharisees and urges them to conversion? (Luke 3, 7–9; Matthew 3, 7–9; John 1, 24–25) Did van Balen deliberately paint such a variety of glances and eye contacts to make visible the varying effect of John's words on his heterogeneous audience?

To create depth, van Balen worked with as many as four receding planes. He also let the figures become ever smaller towards the back. Indeed, a soft funnel perspective leads our gaze to John, the main figure on the centre panel. The subtle chiaroscuro effect also contributes to the suggestion of depth.

As a theme for the left side panel, Hendrik van Balen chose the first bath of the infant Jesus. Mary, his caring mother, is assisted by a series of helpful angels of different sizes. Could the small bath be a prefiguration of the later Baptism of Christ by John?[1] As on the centre panel, the right panel shows an episode from the later life of John. The Baptist reprimands Herod in his sumptuous palace for the adultery with his sister-in-law. The woman herself and a companion, standing within hearing distance, react disapprovingly to the reprimand. The exterior panels show the craft's patron saints: John the Baptist to the left and John the Evangelist to the right, both depicted on a small podium and painted in grisaille.

In this triptych the attractive style of Hendrik van Balen is clearly recognisable – he was not labelled 'virtuoso' by his contemporaries for nothing.[2] His technical abilities in the use of highlights and soft chiaroscuro in contrast with vivid sparkling colour

1 Grieten & Bungeneers 1996, p. 407.
2 Werche 2004, p. 21.

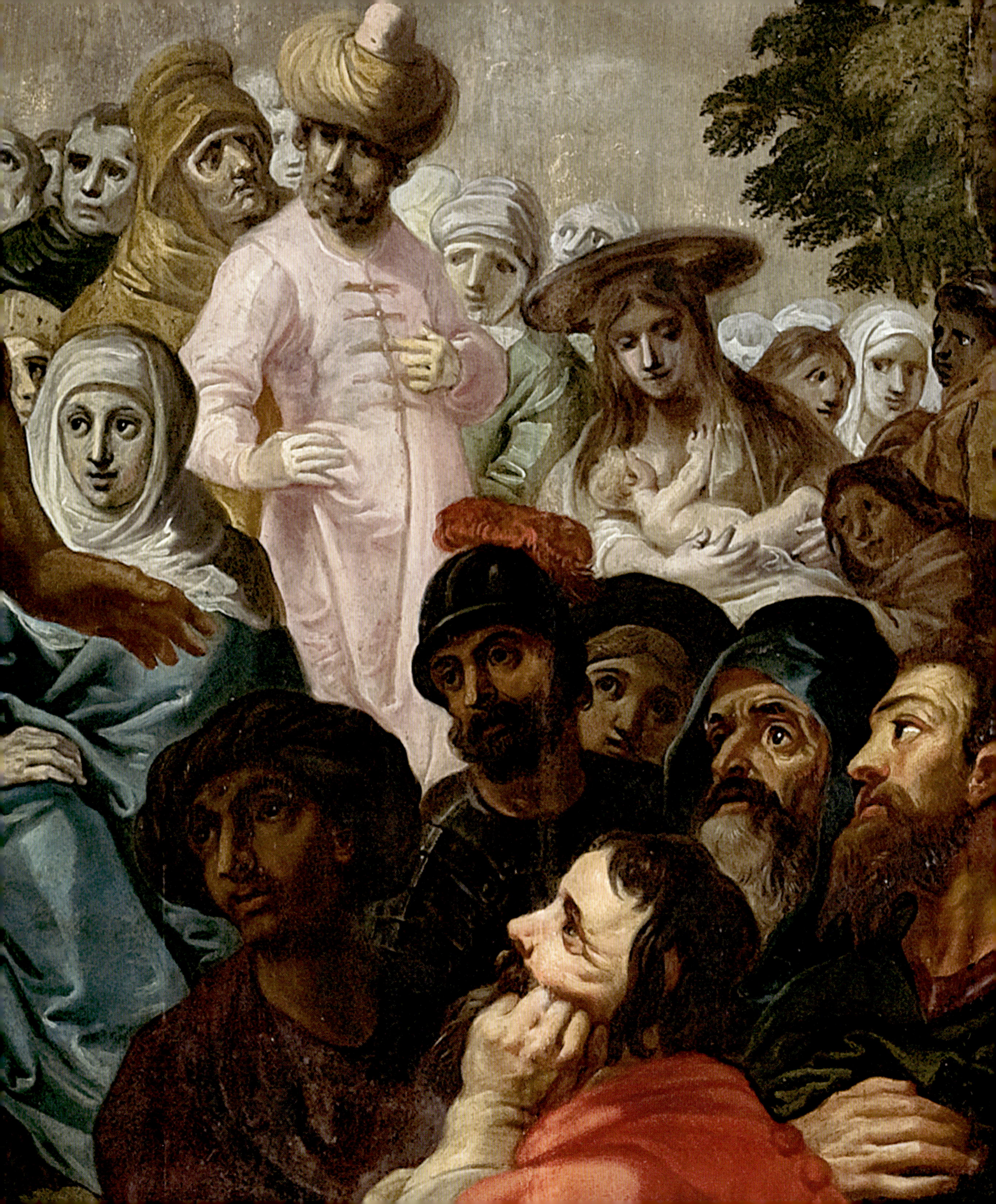

schemes are particularly attractive. Certainly on the centre panel, these technical *tours de force* are clearly present.

As a renowned painter of small panels and of mythological figures in small size, van Balen took on a significant challenge in working to a large scale. With a meticulous brush technique and strong sense of detail – as in the contemporary textiles, the contemporary and historicised costumes, and the women's hairstyles and jewellery – van Balen knew how to seduce his contemporaries as well as connoisseurs and potential patrons. The same brush technique can be seen in the side panels, where much attention was paid to attributes as the child's umbilical bandage, the precious metalwork, the rug, and the architecture. All this obviously contributes to a true-to-life representation.

In contrast with the aforementioned stands the fluent brush stroke *alla prima* in which the anonymous crowd and the fluttering angels are painted, in the background of the centre panel. Did Hendrik van Balen perhaps have the landscape executed by a colleague? The trees, plants, and flowers may reveal another trained hand. The brush strokes for the foliage are rhythmically accentuated and each brush touch is clearly discernable. Brown, yellow, and green ochres offer a somewhat cooler palette. Two stands of trees enclose, as it were, a clearing in the forest. The group of trees on the left, especially, is embellished with bushes of eglantine and, in the foreground, with red clover, daisies, moss, and various kinds of grass. Whether a symbolical meaning should be attached to the rose or peony the child in the right foreground holds in his hands is unclear, but it is certainly possible. In the 17th century is was common for artists, each with his own speciality, to collaborate on a painting. Van Balen repeatedly called on painters like Joos de Momper and Jan I Brueghel, according to documents that exist on the subject.[3]

Hendrik van Balen was a skilful painter of large altarpieces, as is shown here. These works – which he painted chiefly after 1620 – are characterised by a refined colour palette. Beside soft skin tones, he used warm ochre-yellows, crimson and scarlet, alternating with clear blue tones of ultramarine and azurite. Moreover, the warm reds are evenly divided over the three panels. Blended colours like pink, beige-grey, and diverse greens, going from verdigris to green earth, mountain- and moss-green, enhance the colouristic appeal of the work. Daring colour combinations of orange and blue-grey in the angels' wings on the left panel, confer a playful effect on the scene. With a brushful of creamy white paint he often heightens the colour planes to accentuate the decorative pattern of folds. From the richness of colours van Balen used in this triptych it may be assumed that he had many pigments at his disposal. This is confirmed by an inventory made of the property of his widow, six years after the death of the painter. There were still pigments in the house, such as 'a small box of cobalt blue pigment, boxes with ultramarine, and a small box of Florentine lacker'.[4]

Where did van Balen get his inspiration for the different motifs of this altarpiece? In both his religious and profane work, related elements can be found. Thus the strongly highlit figures in the lower left corner, both the standing woman and the foremost seated woman, already occurred in *Moses and Joshua* (Utrecht, Sint-Catharijneconvent, inv. 102).[5] In two other representations of the Preaching of John, dating from c. 1608 (present whereabouts unknown) and c. 1620 (present whereabouts unknown), crowds of packed personages were also used – even in very similar clothing – and they also display a seated woman in the same pose as the one here in the bottom right.[6] The same female figure can also be found in *The Rape of Europa* (Vienna, Kunsthistorisches Museum, inv. 814).

In the Kupferstichkabinett of the Staatliche Museum in Berlin keeps a drawing in pen in brown pen is kept, whose composition is almost identical to that of the left panel.[7] The sheet (fig. 16a) is entitled *The birth of the Virgin*. Might this not be *The first Bath of the Infant Jesus*? Perhaps it was a sketch for the left panel of the triptych discussed here. Possibly van Balen proposed several such sketches to the deans of the craft for approval. Other preliminary sketches or drawings for this triptych, as far as is known, do not survive. This drawing, however, may allow us to look over van Balen's shoulder – unless it is a *Birth of the Virgin*. If so, did van Balen use an existing composition for the left panel?

3 Ertz 1979, pp. 12 and 472: Werche 1997, pp. 67–74.
4 Duverger 1984–2004, IV, pp. 204–205. On the use of pigments, see Fabri 2009.
5 Dirkse 1984, pp. 1–2.
6 Werche 2004, p. 141; Jost 1963, p. 117 and Díaz Padrón 1993, pp. 408–409.
7 *Catalogue Berlin 1931*, no. 5720. Unnoticed in Werche 2004, pp. 225 and 485.

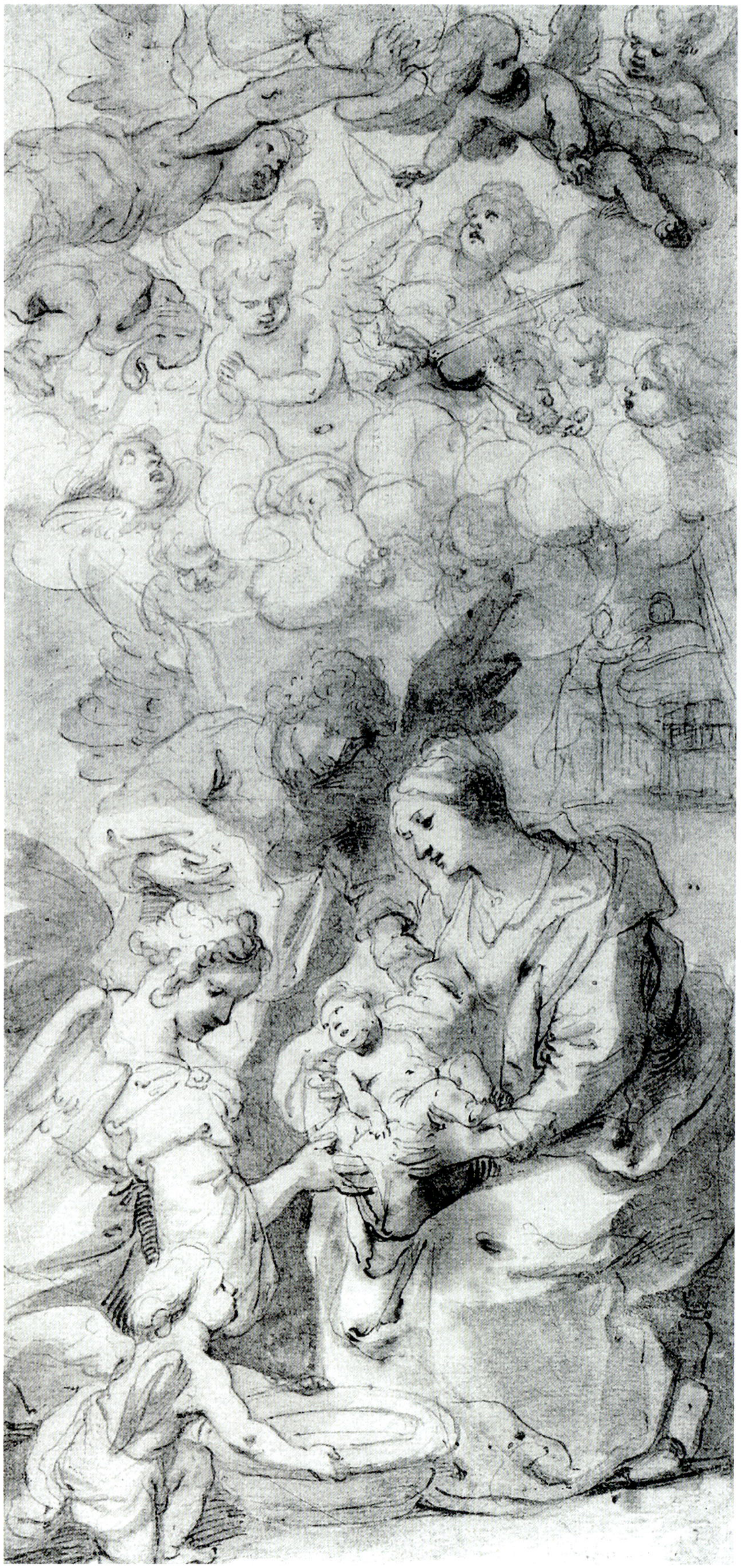

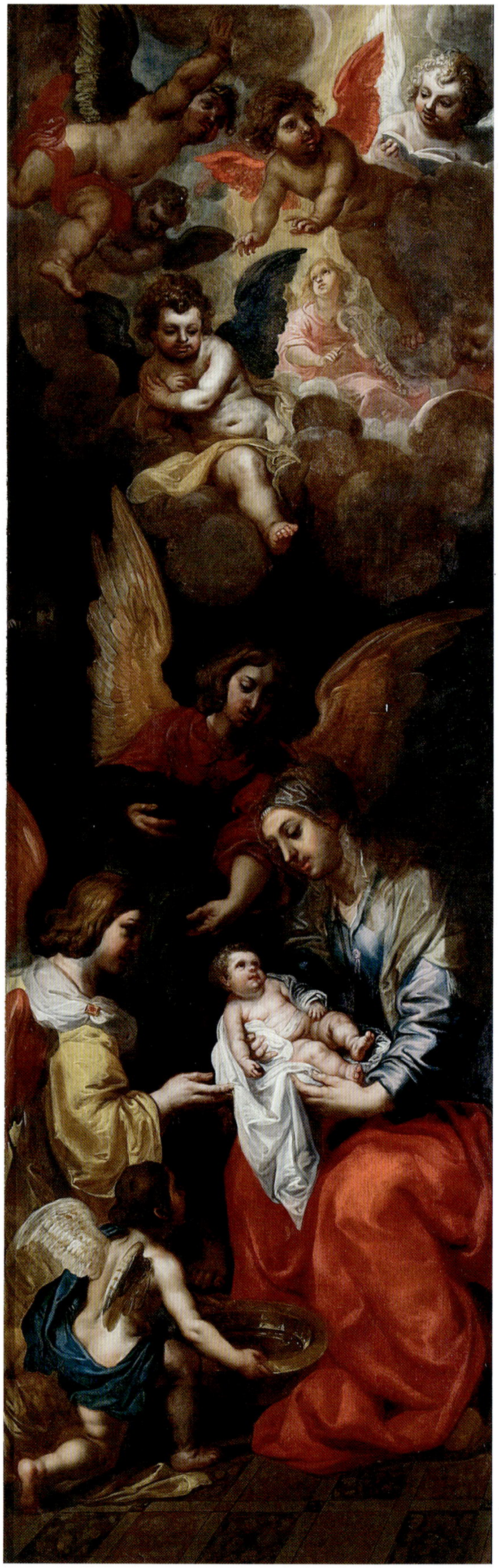

16a
Hendrik van Balen · *The First Bath of the Infant Jesus* · drawing · Berlin, Staatliche Museen, Kupferstichkabinett

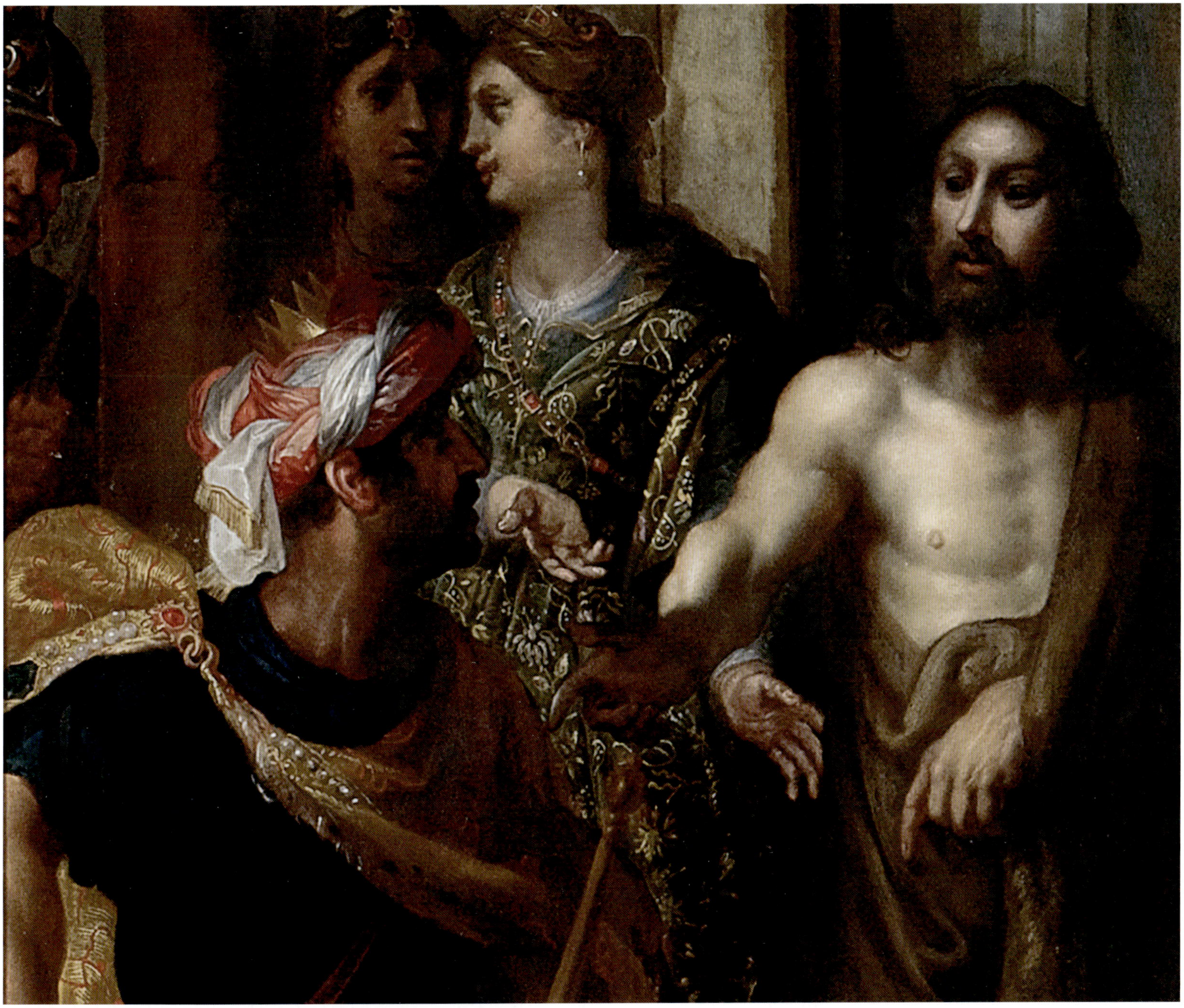

To what extent is van Balen indebted to Antwerp's most prominent baroque artist, Peter Paul Rubens, like so many of his contemporaries? Vividly gesticulating figures and tormented expressions, or furious movements, are not his forte. Rather, he had his own style.[8] Borrowings from the work of friends and colleagues, who were often occasional collaborators, were common to him. It was probably from Jan I Brueghel that he borrowed the schematically painted figures in the background who create the extra depth, along with the classic Turkish straw hat worn by one of the ladies.[9] In the oeuvre of Frans II Francken, the background figures are often treated in the same way. His slightly older colleague Adam van Noort, in his turn, inspired van Balen for the pose of Preaching John. The rich and subtle colour palette was probably influenced by Anthony van Dyck, who was one of his pupils.[10]

8 Werche 2004, p. 53.
9 Woollett & van Suchtelen 2006, p. 189; Kaveler 1999, p. 180.
10 Van de Velde 1996, p. 107.

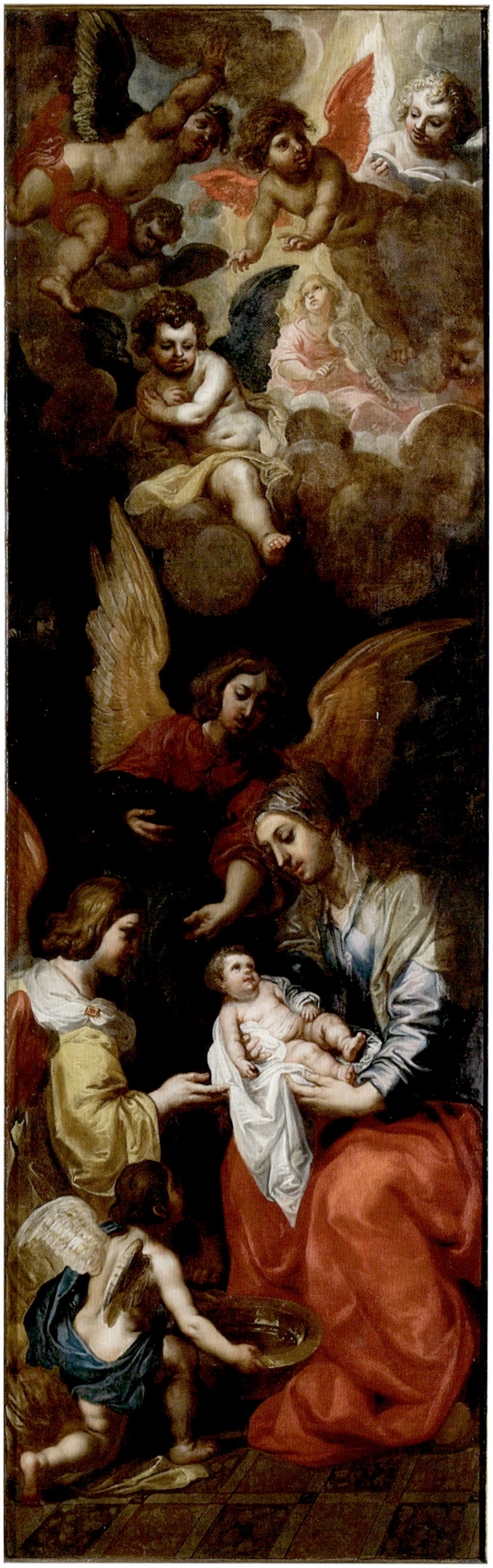

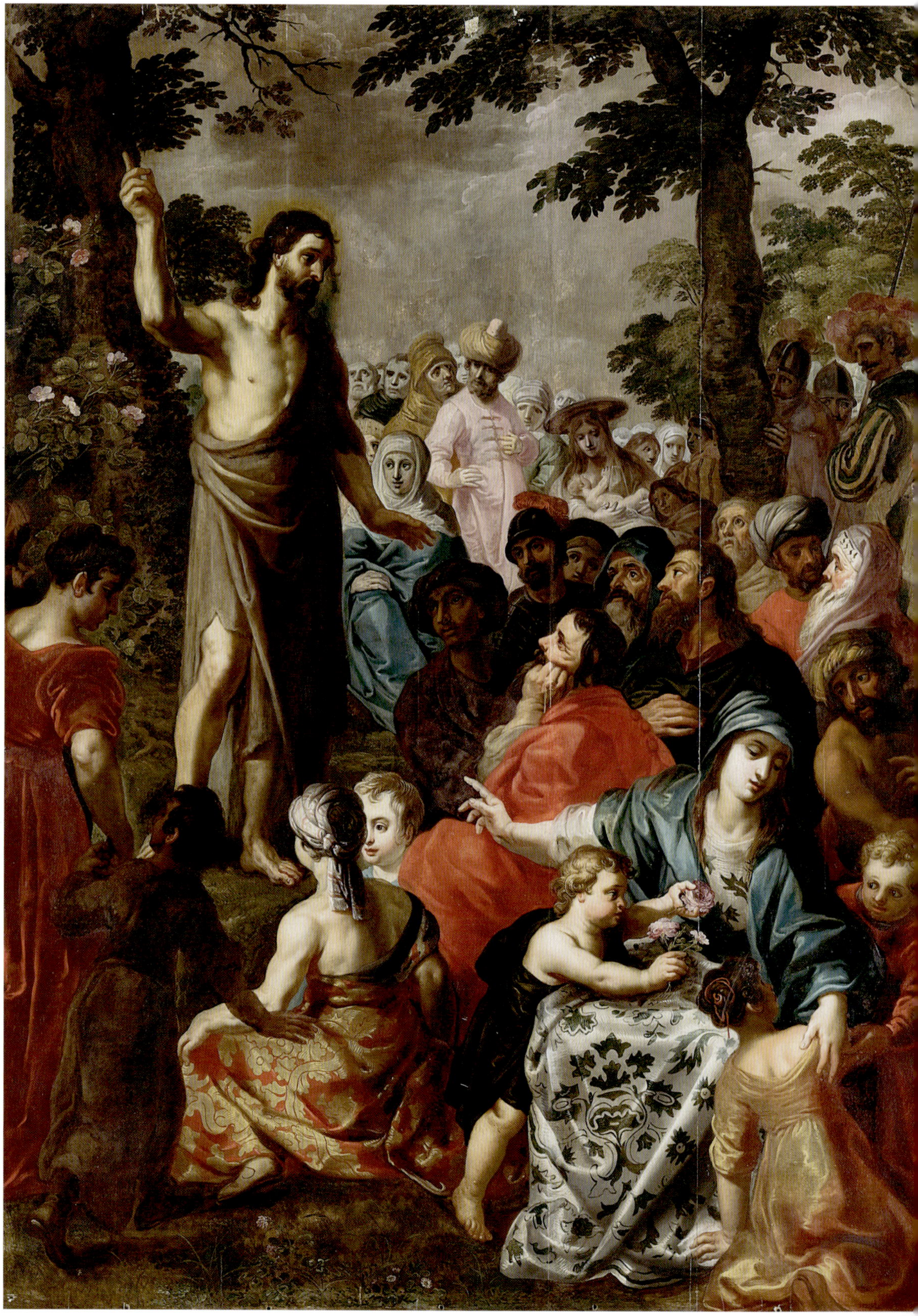

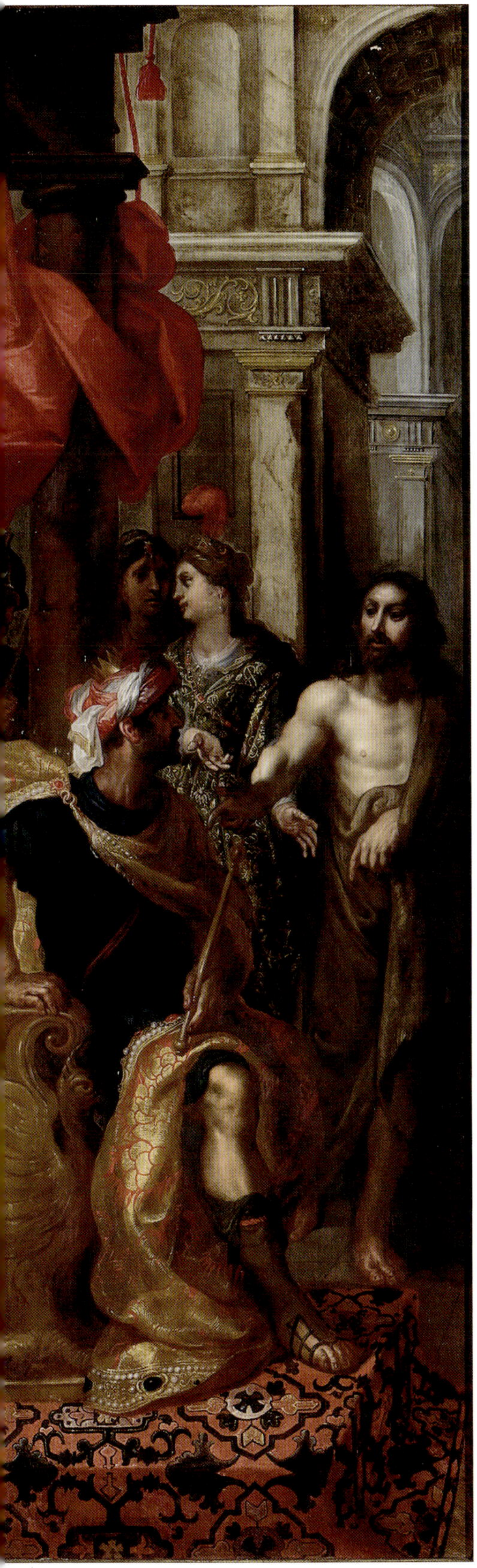

Contracts between van Balen and the Cabinetmakers do not survive. Nonetheless, we can be almost certain that the theme of the altarpiece was determined in consultation with the patrons and in agreement with the scholastics or other learned ecclesiastical functionaries. Precisely why the Preaching of John was chosen, may be inferred through a metaphorical reading of the subject. Could one find an explanation for the theme in the Antwerp Cabinetmakers' authority and privileges? As we know, the privileges within the wood-processing craft were very strictly separated. Cabinetmakers in the 17th century were allowed to make – beside profane furniture – pulpits, confessional boxes, and altars. In other words, by constructing religious furniture, they partly enabled the clergy to preach the Word of God, organise conversions, and perform Mass sacrifices. Thus, the cabinetmakers effectively contributed to the preaching of the faith. A metaphorical comparison with John's life's work could apply here. Moreover, that John the Baptist is accompanied by John the Evangelist on the exterior panels, could mean that the Evangelist, through writing down the deeds of the Baptist, also contributed to the Preaching in his way.

As a *pictor doctus*, van Balen certainly had a lot of books at his disposal.[11] He obviously used them effectively in the conception and finishing of this triptych. Did he learn from the book *Itinerarium Sacrae Scripturae*[12] how to catch the atmosphere of the story? Or perhaps the illustrated book by Giorgium Straubium[13] on clothing lies at the root of the strikingly immaculate clothing of the different figures. Publications on architecture, which were well represented on his book shelves, undoubtedly served as an example for the architecture of Herod's palace. Thus, the Dorian order of the pilasters with triglyphs and beads were borrowed from the work of Vignola from 1619,[14] and the circular trails from the fourth book of Palladio's *Quattro Libri dell'Architettura* from 1570,[15] which precisely treats the construction of temples. Whether van Balen also thought of the *Architectura* by Hans and Paul Vredeman de Vries – published in The Hague in 1607 – on the use of the Doric order, will never be known. In this work, the order is linked

11 Duverger 1984–2004, IV, pp. 209–211.
12 Bunting 1611.
13 Straubium 1600.
14 Vignola 1617.
15 Palladio 1616.

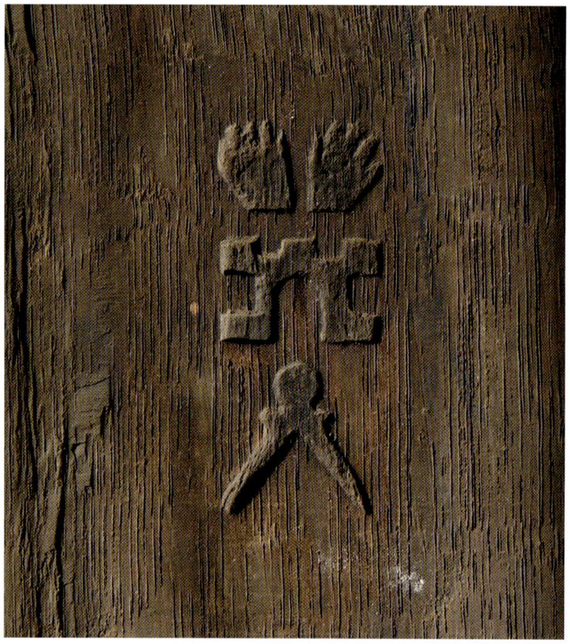

16b
Unidentified hallmark on the back of the centre panel

to the sense of *auditus,* or hearing, which certainly applies to the content of this scene.

Beside books, van Balen probably also used all sorts of other aids for his paintings. By analogy with what is known from inventories of contemporary painters, he had a red wax and stone 'anatomy' at his disposal in his atelier, or a human figure who could serve as an example. Could the 28 heads or plaster heads of men, women, and children, which lay around in his house, have served as models for painting his many figures? Four feet and eight hands from the same source material would likewise have proven useful for drawing all the figures.[16]

On the back of the centre panel, a schematic fortress and hands, a typical Antwerp hallmark, can be recognised (fig. 16b). The mark is accompanied by a pair of compasses that strongly resemble those of the Brussels mark. Could this be a yet-unidentified mark of some Antwerp panel maker?[17] Both marks seem to have been applied with the same iron, which is rather unusual and even militates against its authenticity. Also striking is the presence of the same marks on the frame of *The Holy Family,* a triptych van Balen painted in 1622 for Filip Heemsen and his wife – which is also kept in the collection of the Cathedral.[18] From 1617 onwards there was an obligation to apply Antwerp marks on the painting frames. This obligation, however, was scantily observed. Whether this mark on the frame is original, remains very much an open question.[19]

RIA FABRI

16 Duverger 1984–2004, IV, p. 208.
17 Van Damme 1990, pp. 193–236; Wadum 1998, pp. 179–198.
18 Grieten & Bungeneers 1996, p. 408; Bruyns 2009.

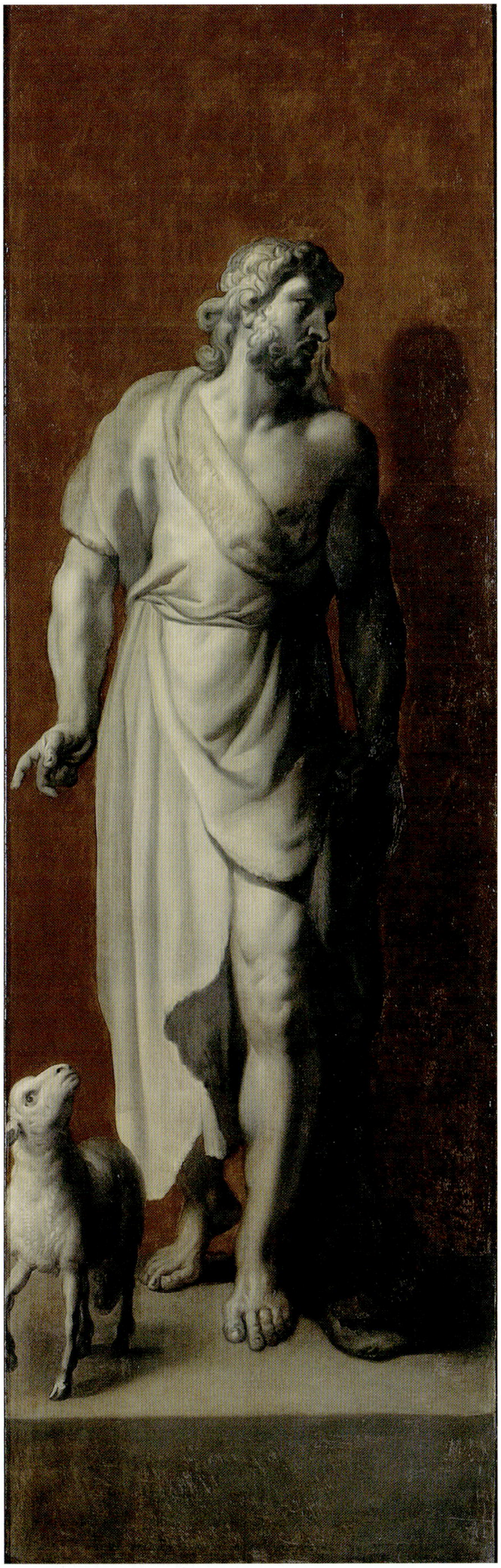
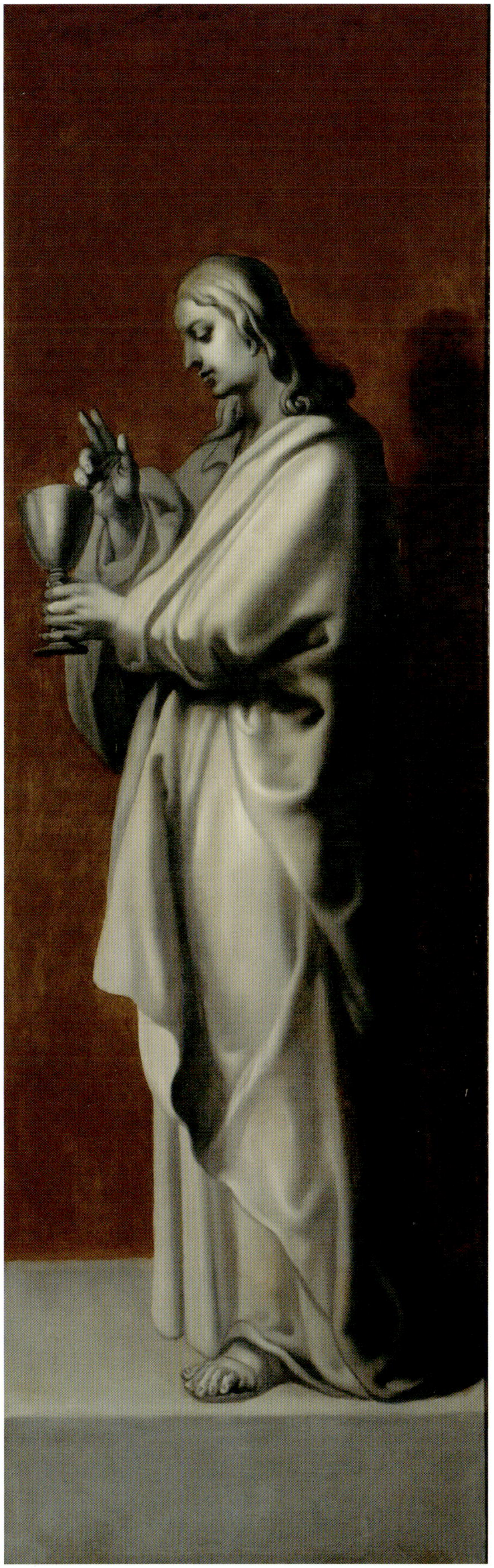

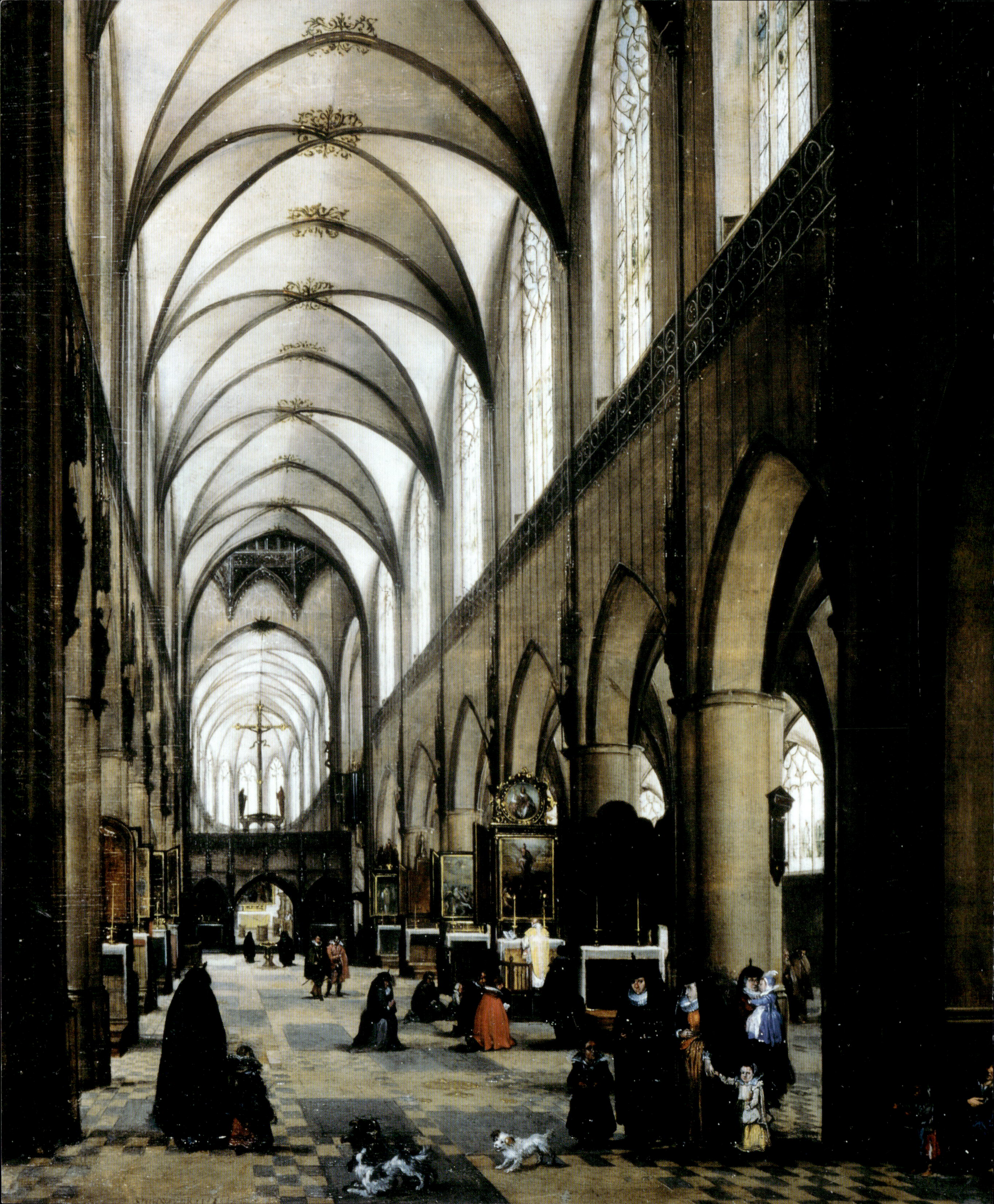

'Images are the books of the ignorant' [1]

Some Iconographical Notes on the of Antwerp Altarpieces

MARCEL GIELIS

Many triptychs in our churches and museums originate from the altars of benefices that were established to have Masses celebrated, to comfort the souls of their founders. The Church of Our Lady in Antwerp was richly provided with such altarpieces. It is more or less characteristic of the 'great merchant city of Antwerp' that the financing of the Church of Our Lady's building project was handled with a strong sense of commerce.[2] In the competitive desire of many guilds to acquire their own altars, the church fabric saw an opportunity to finance the church building. Thus they financed the construction of the pillars through guilds and crafts that sought to erect their altars against them. The iconography of the altarpieces of guilds and crafts was often closely linked to the specific history of the association concerned, along with the specific professional activities of their members.

The Altar of the Cabinetmakers

The earliest altarpiece of this exhibition is *The Lamentation* – or the so-called 'Nood Gods'[3] – by Quinten Metsijs (cat. 1). Concerning the identification of several persons in the painting, some additions may be proposed.

According to the four Gospels the deposition from the cross was undertaken by Joseph of Arimathea (Matthew 27: 57; Mark 15: 43; Luke 23: 50–51, and John 19: 38). According to the Gospel of John, he was assisted by Nicodemus (John 19: 39). According to the oral tradition of Scripture, two other Marys were present at the crucifixion and the entombment beside the Virgin and Mary Magdalene: Mary Cleophas and Mary Salome, both daughters of Saint Anne and therefore (half) sisters of the Virgin (Matthew 27: 55–56 and 61; Mark 15: 40–41, and 47; John 19: 25). As in many other paintings these personages are depicted on Metsijs' *Lamentation*. Beside these seven, another man and woman are present who cannot be easily identified (leaving aside the figures inside the grave and on Mount Golgotha). Some authors have suggested these might be a manservant and a womanservant. For the woman another hypothesis might be suggested: it is possible that Metsijs learned of the humanist criticism of the identification of (Mary) Salome (see Mark) with the mother of Zebedee's sons (see Matthew)[4] and that he therefore regarded these women – whom he still identified with each other in his *Holy Kinship of Saint Anne*, painted for Saint Peter's Church in Louvain, but now in the Royal Museums of Fine Arts in Brussels (fig. 1c) – as two separate figures, in such a way that not four, but five, ladies are present at the Lamentation.

In the 17th century the Cabinetmakers commissioned a new altarpiece from Hendrik van Balen (cat. 16). The exterior panels show both Saints John, the craft's patron saints. Yet, the attention mainly focuses on John the Baptist, as is clearly shown in the centre

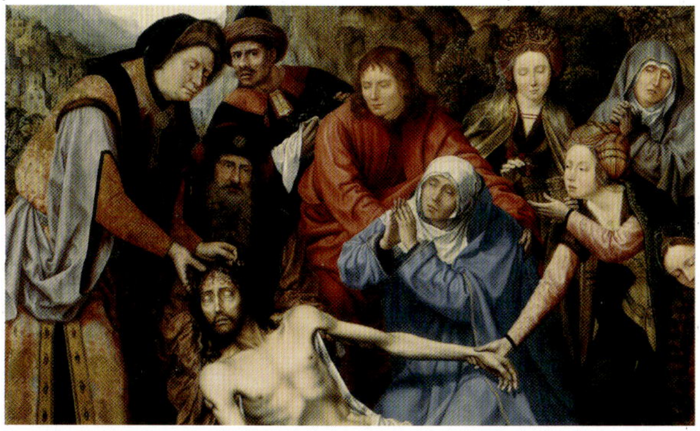

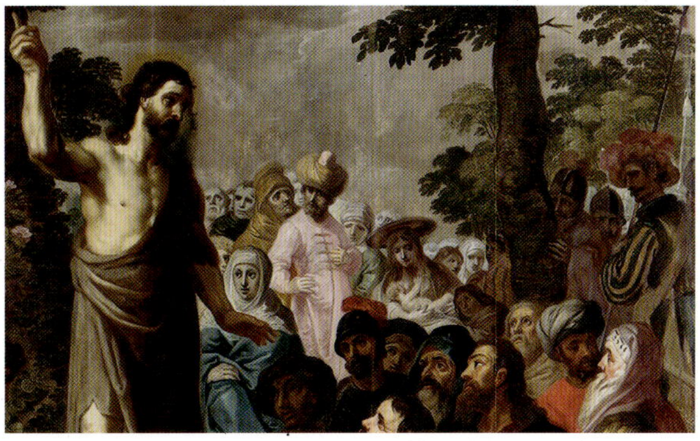

1 Quod legentibus scriptura, hoc idiotis praestat pictura (Gregory the Great, *Epistula ad Serenum Massiliensem episcopum*, in *Patrologia Latina*, LXXVII, col. 1128 C).

2 Vroom 1983.

3 The title 'Nood Gods' was originally used for Christ's agony in the Garden of Olives, but was also used for the *Pietà*.

4 Massaut 1974.

45
Hendrik I van Steenwijck · *Interior View of the Antwerp Cathedral of Our Lady* · 1583 (or 1593) · Budapest, Szépművészeti Múzeum

panel with a depiction of the *Preaching of John the Baptist*. In the depiction of John the Evangelist on the triptych's exterior, his attribute – a chalice – refers to the first torture he magnificently overcame, which preceded his torture in boiling oil. According to the legend, the priest Aristodemus would have made John drink the poisoned cup after the devastation of the Temple of Artemis in Ephesus.[5] John made the sign of the cross over this cup (or chalice), the poison left the cup in the shape of a snake or dragon – as is clearly visible in Metsijs' painting (cat. 1) – and John emptied the cup without experiencing any harm.[6]

The Altarpiece of the Schoolmasters

The Schoolmasters (cat. 6), the Wine Taverners (cat. 9) and the Fishmongers (cat. 4) – as early as the 16th century – chose subjects from the New Testament that were clearly linked to their various crafts. Nonetheless, some motifs on their altarpieces, such as the saints' figures, require further explanation.

The reason for Elia's presence on the right panel of the Schoolmasters' altar (cat. 6) is not immediately obvious, but it can easily be explained. According to medieval typological exegesis, Elia is a prefiguration of Christ. More specifically, the story of the widow of Zarephath was linked to the story of Martha, Mary and Lazarus (Luke 10: 38–42; John 11: 1–12, 11). The depiction of Elia in the house of the widow of Zarephath with the Miracle with the Oil on the right panel is therefore a pendant to what was originally shown on the left panel, notably Christ in the house of Martha and Mary. Moreover, the Schoolmasters shared their altar with the Soap Boilers, who made extensive use of oil for their professional activities. That may be why the scene of the Miracle with the Oil, unlike that of Christ's visit to Mary and Martha, survives (see cat. 6).

The presence of the four evangelists with their symbols, on the exterior panels of the altarpiece, can also be easily explained: the evangelists are indeed pre-eminently teachers.

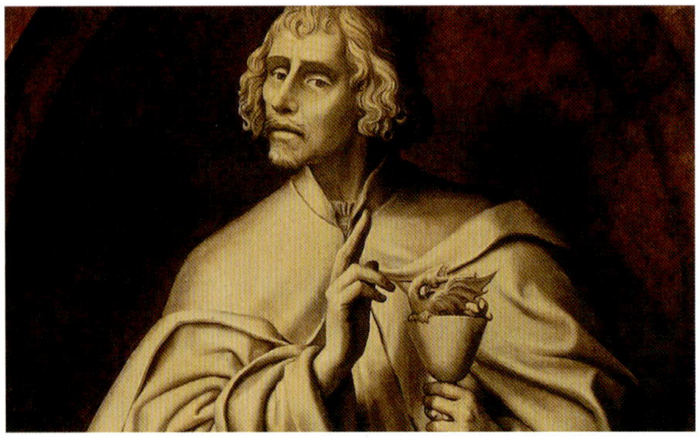

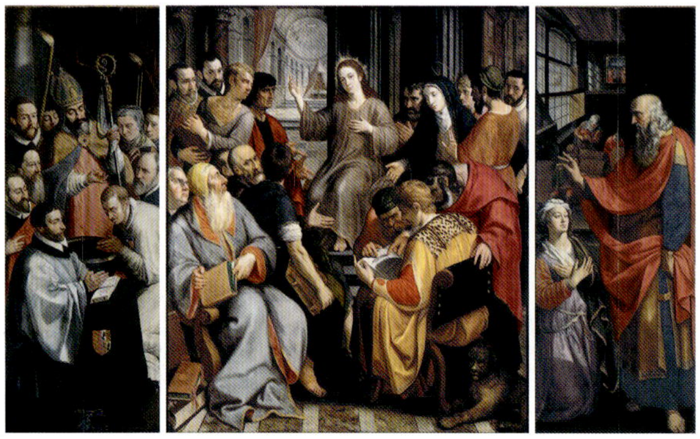

The Altarpiece of the Fishmongers

The triptych of the Fishmongers (cat. 4) is a very complex and extremely interesting painting. The different Gospels are combined in such a way that quite a special interpretation of the stories emerges. On the two predella panels, two episodes from the calling of the first disciples are depicted. In the Gospel of Luke the calling of the apostles and the miraculous draught of fishes are linked to each other (Luke 5: 1–11). Matthew and Mark only tell the story of the calling, but in more detail than Luke (Matthew 4: 18–22; Mark 1: 16–20). They are the only ones to mention the name of Peter's brother, Andrew, and they tell separately of the calling of James and John, the sons of Zebedee. With Luke, the emphasis lies on Peter; Andrew is not mentioned and Zebedee's sons only in passing, as companions of Simon Peter.

In one of the predella panels Peter kneels before Christ after the miraculous draught of fishes and confesses that he is a sinner. His companions haul aboard the nets, which begin to tear, and fill the boats with an abundance of fish until the vessels almost sink. The second man in Peter's boat is his brother Andrew (he does not appear in Luke, but in Matthew 4: 18 and Mark 1: 16), while Zebedee and his sons James and John sit in the other boat.

In the other predella panel, the sequel of the story is told, as we can read in Matthew and Mark: after Christ said to Peter and Andrew that he would make them Fishers of men, he also called Zebedee's sons, who abandoned their father and their boat, and followed Christ. James, who is apparently regarded as the patron saint of the craft, receives more attention here than John. He is depicted at the centre and kneels before Christ while John is still clambering from the boat.[7] Although John was also a fisherman, his later activities attracted many other patronages to him. He was apparently less suited as a patron for the Fishmongers. On the lost centre panel of the predella, both the crucifixion and Peter's walk on water may have been depicted (Matthew 14: 22–33, especially 14: 28–31; in the parallel text, Mark 6: 45–52, and also in John 6: 16–21, Christ walks alone over the lake).

The triptych's exterior right panel shows Saint Philip. Almost certainly, this is intended to represent the apostle (Matthew 10: 3; Mark 3: 18; Luke 6: 14; Acts 1: 13) about whom we learn some details in the Gospel of John (John 1: 43–51; 6: 7; 12: 20–22 and 14: 8–11). He was called a day after Peter and brought Nathaniel to Christ; he played a role in the multiplication of the loaves; he established contact between the Greek speakers and Christ; and he asked Christ to 'Show us the Father', upon which Christ made his famous statement 'Who sees me, sees the Father' etc. Philip is also the main character in the story of the baptism of the eunuch of the Queen of Ethiopia (Acts 8: 26–40), but this Philip is more likely to be the deacon (Acts 6: 5) than the apostle. The two figures are often confused.[8] On this altarpiece, too,

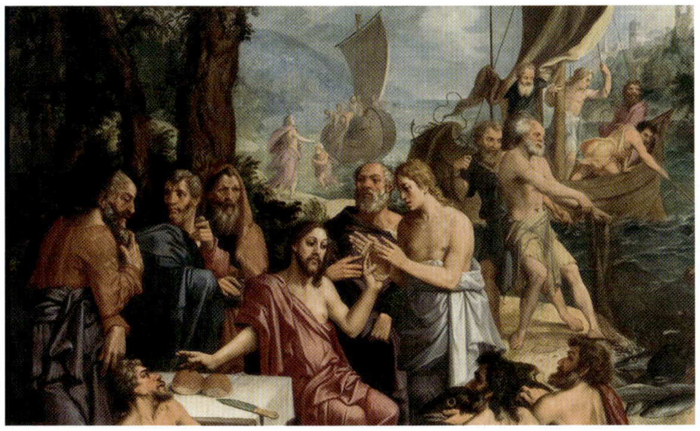

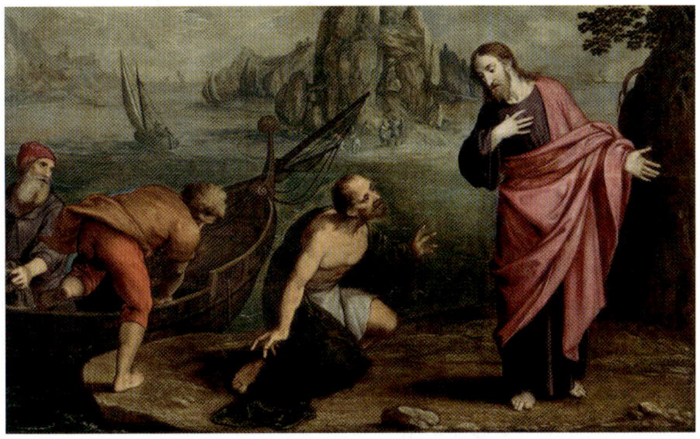

5 De Voragine (ed. Benz) 1997, pp. 69–70.
6 Keller 1975, p. 283; Goosen 1992, p. 127.
7 Compare to what happened under the pulpit of Saint Andrew's in Antwerp: here the church patron stands at the centre, while in this scene usually Peter is in the foreground.
8 De Voragine (ed. Benz) 1997, pp. 337–339, indeed discusses the apostle and the deacon together, but warns against this confusion.

this happens. Both Philips are at least combined with each other. Indeed, on the interior of the same panel the *Baptism of the Ethiopian Eunuch by Saint Philip* is depicted (fig. 4c). The right panel, currently kept in the Monastery of Saint Ghislain, is dedicated to James, the first apostle who died through torture (Acts 12: 2). On the interior, his decapitation by order of Herod is depicted; on the exterior he is 'portrayed' by analogy with the representation of Philip on the right panel. This image, however, has been lost through planing the panel down.[9]

The triptych's centre panel, which is kept in the cathedral, bears the title *Miraculous Draught*, but in some sources it is mentioned as the *Multiplication of the Loaves and Fishes.*[10] Although the arrival and the unloading of the boat in the right background can be linked to the story of the miraculous draught of fishes according to Luke, and this in connection with the calling of the first disciples, it is more probable that the centre panel contains the scene of Jesus' third appearance after the crucifixion as told in the Gospel of John (John 21: 1–14). In it, both the draught of a huge mass of fish and a walk by Peter through (not over) the lake is told. It is also possible that the story of the miraculous draught and that of the miraculous multiplication – not only of the loaves, but also of the fishes – were combined.

For synoptists, the story of the first multiplication of loaves (Matthew 14: 13–21; Mark 6: 32–44; Luke 9: 10–17) very generally states that there were five loaves and two fish on hand. John, however, elaborately describes where these loaves and fishes came from (John 6: 1–15). Here the apostles Philip and Andrew play a role. Philip answers Christ's request for bread: '200 denarii worth of bread is not enough for each one in this crowd to have a bite!' (John 6: 7). Andrew brings the boy with the five loaves and the two fish to Christ. The offering of the fishes is not explicitly described anywhere in the Gospels, but it could have been moved into the foreground to serve the needs of the Fishmongers' craft. That the bread is already on the table in the painting, tallies well with the synoptic story of the second multiplication of loaves (Mark 8: 1–10 and Matthew 15: 32–39).

If reminiscences can be found of the story of the multiplication of the loaves on the centre panel, the scene in the centre background apparently depicts the third appearance of Christ, as described in the Gospel of John (John 21: 1–14). The story of an appearance on a mountain in Galilee, too, at the end of the Gospel of Matthew, may tally with the scene on the Fishmongers' altarpiece. Nonetheless, it is more probable that the third appearance was the source of inspiration here. From the beach, the resurrected Christ commands his disciples in the fishing boats to cast the net to the right of the boat, resulting in another miraculous draught, at which Christ is recognised by his disciples, and Peter wades to him through the water. Subsequently, Christ,

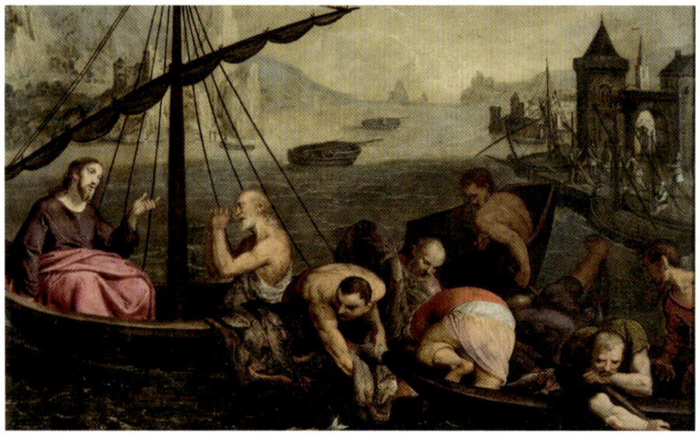

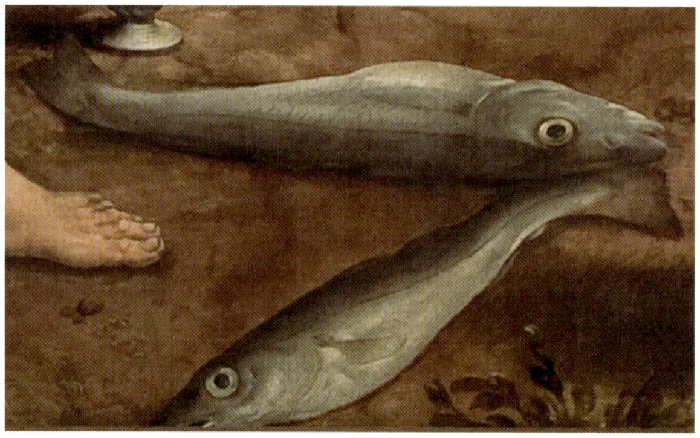

who asks them to bring some of their catch to him, takes a meal with bread and fish, on the shore with his disciples.

The Altarpiece of the Wine Taverners
The theme of the wedding at Cana (John 2: 1–12) obviously suits the Wine Taverners well (cat. 9). Balaam was a prophet who by order of the King of the Moabites had to curse the people of Israel, but after the miracle of the speaking ass blessed them, so that they would successfully invade Canaan (Numbers: 22–24). This story was interpreted by the Wine Taverners in relation to the idea that the Promised Land, shown in the giant bunch of grapes that the scouts brought with them from Canaan, not only abounds with milk and honey, but also with wine.

The Altarpiece of the Smiths
The Smiths originally had Frans Francken make an altarpiece about *Saint Eligius* (cat. 7). Eligius is widely regarded as the patron of the smiths, and today also of the metalworkers. The fact that a representation of the Acts of Mercy was chosen instead of miracles, probably coincides with the moralisation of the saints' image in the Counter Reformation and a more critical approach to miracles under the influence of humanism. On the exterior panels, Eligius can be seen as a smith (which explains his patronage) and as a bishop; on the interior panels he is only shown as a bishop.

The Altarpiece of the Guild of Saint Luke
Saint Luke's guild chose a depiction of *Saint Luke Painting the Virgin* for the centre panel of its altarpiece by Maerten de Vos (cat. 10). On the two surviving predella scenes, too, episodes from Luke's life occur. The content of the side panels is more debatable. Presumably, the exterior was chosen for the four evangelists because Luke, the guild's patron saint, was an evangelist. On the left panel the *Preaching of Saint Luke* is shown, which entirely conforms to expectations. On the right panel an episode from the life of Paul is depicted: *Saint Paul before Felix, Governor of Caesarea*.[11] If this initially seems a strange subject choice, it can be explained perfectly: Luke, who is not only the author of the third Gospel, but also of the *Acts*, was a companion and collaborator of Paul (Colossians 4: 14). The scene depicted here (Acts 24) is described between two passages written in the 'we' form, which therefore narrate events at which both Luke and Paul were present (Acts 16: 10–40; 20: 5–21, 8; and 27: 1–28, 16). It is therefore likely that Luke was also present at the event shown here. The inscription for this scene seems to be: 'Lucas est mecum solus'. This quotation from a letter by Paul (2 Timothy 4: 11) may indicate that the painting should be interpreted as a scene from the life of Luke and that Paul is, in a way, shown as his teacher here.

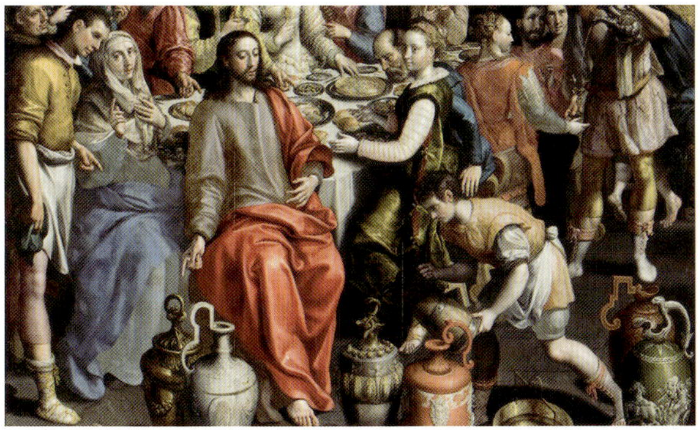

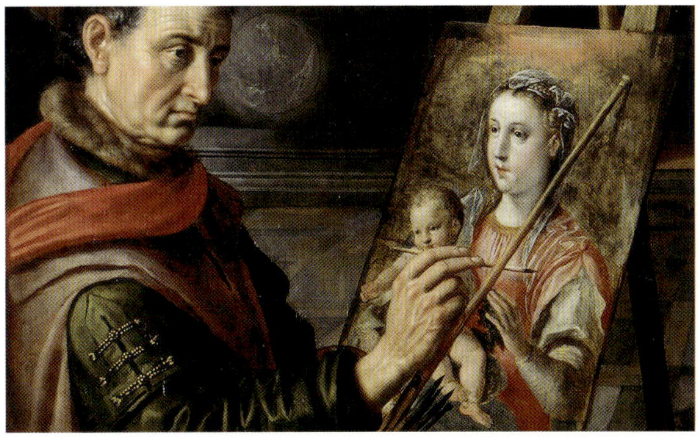

9 Philip and Jacob used to be celebrated on the same day, 1 May; they were therefore discussed in de Voragine (ed. Benz) 1997, pp. 337–349 one after the other.
10 For example on the website of the Koninklijk Instituut voor het Kunstpatrimonium / Institut royal du patrimoine artistique (www.kikirpa.be), cliché number: M203630.
11 In the catalogue note on the altar of Saint Luke's guild (cat. 10), a different iconographical explanation is given for this scene.

The Altarpiece of the Fencers

For the altar tables of some associations, the iconography is very clearly determined by the 'legend' of their generally acknowledged patron saint. As is shown above, this was certainly the case for the Painters and the Smiths, who respectively had Saint Luke and Saint Eligius as their patrons, but it also applies to the Fencers and the Arquebusiers – two armoured guilds who put themselves under the protection of Saints Michael and Christopher.

The Fencers' patron is in fact not a saint, but the archangel Michael, who leads the celestial armies. The theme of the *Fall of the Rebel Angels*, as depicted on the centre panel of Frans Floris' altarpiece for the Fencers' guild (cat. 3), was not borrowed from the Bible, but from exegesis. Basing himself on all sorts of texts (Job; Isaiah 14:12; Daniel; sayings by Christ; particularly the Apocalypse), Augustine, among others, in his *De Civitate Dei*, situated the creation of the angels between the creation of heaven and earth (Genesis 1) and that of man (Genesis 2). One third of the angels would later rebel, led by Lucifer, but would be defeated by the angels who remained faithful to God. The rebellious angels wanted to be God's equals. It is sometimes said that the motive for their rebellion was jealousy of the first humans – more specifically the fact that humans can have love and sexual relationships. The archangel Michael is often depicted with a shield inscribed with the Latin translation of his name 'Quis ut Deus' (Who is as God?). He symbolises the 'Strength of God' (another translation of his name), and nothing or no-one is a match for him. Floris' representation looks firmly based on the twelfth chapter of Revelation: the main devil is depicted as a seven-headed monster and in the lower left background the Woman robed with the sun and her child can be seen. According to tradition, Our Lady – as the Immaculate Conception – was predicted in paradise.

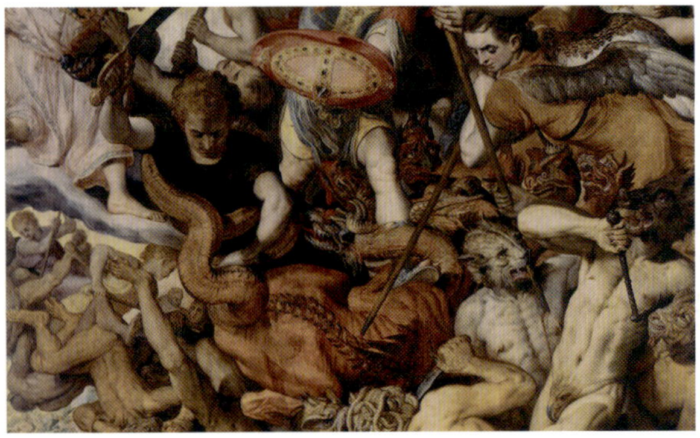

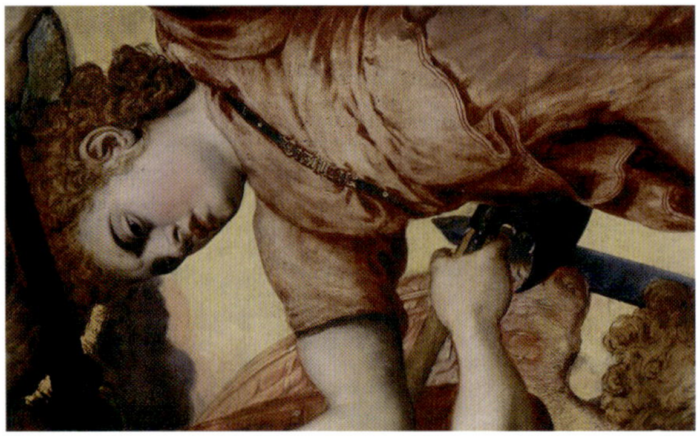

The Altarpiece of the Almoners

The explanation for the altarpiece that Barend van Orley painted at the beginning of the 16th century for the Almoners of the Table of the Holy Spirit, the *Last Judgement with the Seven Acts of Mercy* (cat. 2), can be found in Matthew 25: 31–46. The Almoners must have taken to heart Christ's words 'anything you did for one of my brothers here, however humble, you did for me'.[12] At the Last Judgement, all people and particularly the almoners will be examined for this. There has been some debate about the figures shown in the funeral scene in the centre panel: are these Luther and Melanchthon? It is known that Barend van Orley cherished reformatory sympathies: he was among those who had to appear before Nicolaas Coppin's inquisition court in 1527.[13]

Ambrosius Francken's *Descent of the Holy Spirit* (cat. 13) is often linked to the Almoners. There is no known documentation in support of this, but there is a plausible iconographical explanation for the possible relation between this painting and the almoners. The biblical story that underlies it, occurred during the first Whitsun after Christ's death on the cross (Acts 2: 1–4). All the apostles, who are listed name by name, remained in a 'room upstairs ... together with the women, the Virgin, Mother of Christ, and his brothers' (who according to this text are different than the twelve apostles) (Acts 1: 13–14). In this painting it is shown how the Holy Spirit, in the form of tongues of fire, descended on Mary and the apostles. The relationship between the Holy Spirit and poor relief is determined by the liturgy (and the underlying theology): in the order for Whitsun, *Veni Sancte Spiritus*, the Holy Spirit is praised as *pater pauperum*. Moreover, Whitsun is fifty days after Easter and is not only the feast of the Holy Spirit, but also the feast of the Law, the Ten Commandments, which were passed fifty days after the Exodus (Pasha Feast) on Mount Sinai. And this Law can be summarised as a commandment of love, of which poor relief, symbolised by the alms, virtually constitutes the most important aspect.

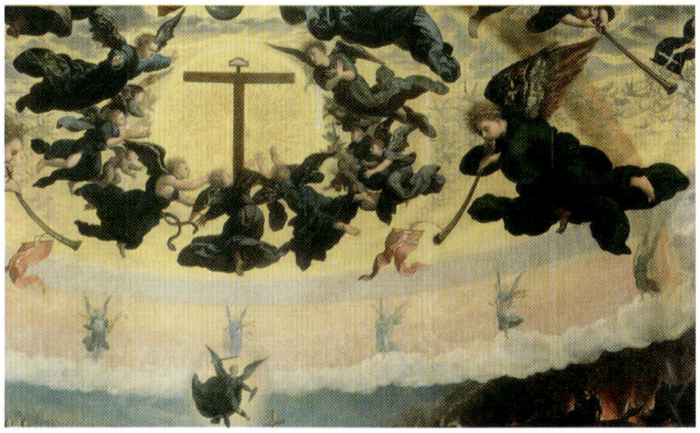

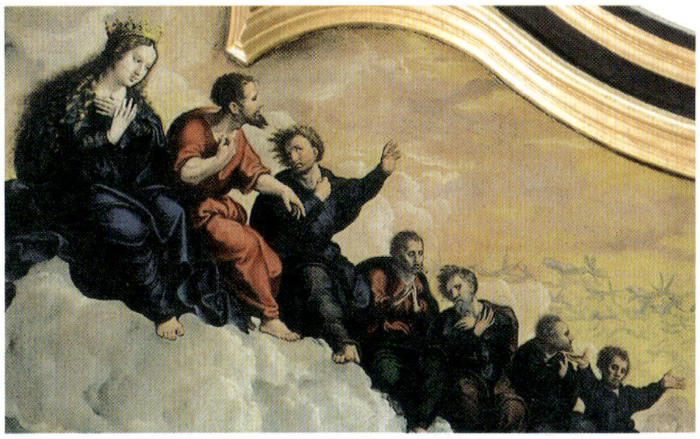

12 Wikenhauser 1932.
13 Gielis 2006.

Bibliography

Abbreviations

DAA Diocesaan Archief Antwerpen [Archives of the Diocese of Antwerp]

GA Gilden en Ambachten [Guilds and Crafts]

KAA Kathedraalarchief Antwerpen [Archives of the cathedral of Antwerp]

KCML Koninklijke Commissie voor Monumenten en Landschappen [Royal Commission of Monuments and Sites]

SAA Stadsarchief Antwerpen [Archives of the City of Antwerp]

Aerts et al. 1990
W. Aerts et al., 'De binnenrestauratie van kruisbeuk en koor van de Onze-Lieve-Vrouwekathedraal te Antwerpen. Een nieuwe interdisciplinaire aanpak', *M&L* [Monumenten en landschappen], V, 1990, pp. 12–37.

Aerts 1993A
W. Aerts (ed.), *The Cathedral of Our Lady in Antwerp*, Antwerp, 1993.

Aerts 1993B
W. Aerts, 'The restoration. The restoration of the Church and the South Tower', in W. Aerts (ed.), *The Cathedral of Our Lady in Antwerp*, Antwerp, 1993, pp. 356–383.

Aerts 1994
W. Aerts, 'De neogotiek in de Antwerpse Onze-Lieve-Vrouwekerk (1830–1850)', in J. Van Cleven & F. Van Tyghem, *Neogotiek in België* (cat. exh. Ghent, Bijlokemuseum), Tielt, 1994, pp. 84–89.

Aerts & De Ceulaer 1993
W. Aerts & R. De Ceulaer, 'Art Heritage. The Nineteenth and Twentieth Centuries', in W. Aerts (ed.), *The Cathedral of Our Lady in Antwerp*, Antwerp, 1993, pp. 281–303.

Aerts & Grieten 1993
W. Aerts & S. Grieten, 'Art Heritage. The Period 1794-1830', in W. Aerts (ed.), *The Cathedral of Our Lady in Antwerp*, Antwerp, 1993, pp. 267–279.

Ainsworth 2006
M.W. Ainsworth, 'Romanism as a Catalyst for Change in Bernard van Orley's Workshop', in M.A. Faries (ed.), *Making and Marketing - Studies of the Painting Process in Fifteenth- and Sixteenth-Century Netherlandish Workshops*, Louvain, 2006, pp. 99–118.

Amsterdam 1939
Bijbelsche Kunst, Rijksmuseum, Amsterdam, 1939.

Antwerp 1946
De Antwerpsche gilden en Ambachten in Rubens' tijd, cat. exh. Antwerp, Museum Vleeshuis, 1946.

Antwerp 2002
D. Christiaens, *Museum Maagdenhuis - Een selectie uit het kunstpatrimonium van het OCMW Antwerpen*, Antwerp, 2002.

Antwerp 2005
Rockox' huis volgeboekt. De bibliotheek van de Antwerpse burgemeester en kunstverzamelaar Nicolaas Rockox [1560–1640] (cat. exh. Antwerp, Rockoxhuis), Antwerp, 2005.

Baisier 2008
C. Baisier, *De documentaire waarde van de kerkinterieurs van de Antwerpse School in de Spaanse Tijd (1585–1713)*, unpublished doctoral dissertation, K.U.Leuven, 2008.

Barnes, De Poorter, Millar & Vey 2004
S. Barnes, N. De Poorter, O. Millar & H. Vey, *Van Dyck. A Complete Catalogue of the Paintings*, New Haven-London, 2004.

Baudouin 1972
F. Baudouin, 'Altars and Altarpieces before 1620', in J.R. Martin, *Rubens before 1620*, Princeton, 1972, pp. 45–91.

Baudouin 1977A
F. Baudouin, *Pietro Paulo Rubens*, Antwerp, 1977.

Baudouin 1977B
F. Baudouin, *Nicolaas Rockox, 'vriendt ende patroon' van Peter Paul Rubens*, Culturele brochurereeks, Kredietbank, Brussels, 1977 (published in English as [F. Baudouin], 'Nicolaas Rockox, Friend and patron of Peter Paul Rubens', in *Rubens in Context. Liber Memorialis Frans Baudouin*, Antwerp, 2005, pp. 67–103).

Baudouin 1977C
F. Baudouin, 'Rubens en de antieke kunst', *Hermeneus*, III, 1977, pp. 158–175 (also published in English, in [F. Baudouin], *Rubens in Context. Liber Memorialis Frans Baudouin*, Antwerp, 2005, pp. 105–123).

Baudouin 1978
F. Baudouin, 'De Kruisafneming van Rubens, één van de zeven Trofeeën van de Belgische kunst, *Antwerpen*, XXIV, 1978, pp. 122–126.

Baudouin 1984
F. Baudouin, '1585: de val van Antwerpen. Ook een belangrijke datum voor de kunstgeschiedenis der Nederlanden', in *Willem van Oranje 1584–1984. Herdenking door de Koninklijke Academiën van België. Brussel, 12 oktober 1984*, [Brussels], [1984], pp. 94–95 (offprint).

Baudouin 1989
F. Baudouin, 'Iconografie en stijlontwikkeling in de godsdienstige schilderkunst te Antwerpen in de zeventiende eeuw', in *Antwerpen in de XVIIe eeuw* (*Genootschap voor Antwerpse Geschiedenis*, IV), Antwerp, 1989, pp. 329–364.

Baudouin 1993
F. Baudouin, 'Art Heritage. The Seventeenth and Eighteenth Centuries', in W. Aerts (ed.), *The Cathedral of Our Lady in Antwerp*, Antwerp, 1993, pp. 205–259.

Belkin 1998
K. Belkin, *Rubens* (*Art & Ideas*), London, 1998.

Bellori 1672
P. Bellori, *Le Vite de' Pittori Scultori e Architetti Moderni*, Rome, 1672.

Benesch 1925
O. Benesch, 'Werk van Maerten de Vos', *Onze Kunst*, XXII, 1925, pp. 59–64.

Berbie 1756
G. Berbie, *Beschryvinge van de bezonderste schilderyen ende autaeren, glazen, beeldhouweryen ende andere rariteyten dewelke te zien zijn in de kerken, kloosters ende andere plaetsen binnen Antwerpen...*, Antwerp, 1756.

Berbie 1774A
G. Berbie, *Beschryvinge der bezonderste werken van de schilder-konste, en de beeldhouwers, nu ter tijd zynde in de kerken, kloosters, ende openbaere plaetsen der Stad Antwerpen, in 't licht gegeve tot profyt der Reyzers*, Antwerp, 1774.

Berbie 1774B
G. Berbie, *Description des principaux ouvrages de Peinture et Sculpture; actuellement existans dans les Eglises, Couvens, & lieux publics de la Ville d'Anvers...*, Antwerp, 1774.

Bergmans 1998
A. Bergmans, *Middeleeuwse muurschilderingen in de negentiende eeuw. Studie en inventaris van middeleeuwse muurschilderingen in Belgische kerken* (KADOC-Artes 2), Louvain, 1998.

Beschrijvinge 1751
Beschrijvinge van de gedenckweirdigste Schilderyen, die te sien syn in de Kercken van verschijde Steden van Vlaenderen, Brabant & waer by oock gevoeght is op sommige plaetsen de beschryvinge van de Schilderijen, die binnen in de Abdijen, en andere Kloosters, als oock in de Stadshuysen, Landtshuysen ende Gildehuijsen bevonden worden. Opgesteld tot wegbwijser der konstminnende personen, 1751, E. Duverger & L. van Biervliet (eds.), *Beschrijvinge: een eerste nederlandstalige gids voor kunstminnaars in Brabant en Vlaanderen (1751–1753). Inleiding en tekst (Facultés universitaires Saint-Louis. Studiecentrum 18de-eeuwse Zuidnederlandse Letterkunde, Cahier 17)*, Brussels, 1998.

Beschryvinge 1756
Beschryvinge van de bezonderste schilderyen ende autaeren, glazen, beeldhouweryen ende andere rariteyten dewelke te zien zijn in de kerken, kloosters ende andere plaetsen binnen Antwerpen, van al de oudste ende fameusste Meesters by een vergadert door de principaelste Liefhebbers, Antwerp, 1756.

Bialostocki 1964
J. Bialostocki, 'The Descent from the Cross in Works by Peter Paul Rubens and his Studio', *The Art Bulletin*, XLVI, 4, 1964, pp. 511–524.

Blockmans 1953
F. Blockmans, 'Het vroegste officiële ambachtswezen te Antwerpen', *Bijdragen voor de geschiedenis der Nederlanden*, VIII, 1953, pp. 161–201.

Bochius 1595
Johannes Bochius, *Descriptio publicae gratulationis, spectaculorum et ludorum, in adventu [...] Ernesti archiducis Austriae* [...], Antwerp, Officina Plantiniana, 1595.

Boespflug 1996
F. Boespflug, *J. Molanus, Traité des saintes images* (reprint), Paris, 1996.

Boon 1992
K.G. Boon, *The Netherlandish and German Drawings of the XVth and XVIth centuries of the Frits Lugt Collection*, Paris, 1992.

Borromeus 1577
C. Borromeus, *Institutiones Fabricae et Supellectis Ecclesiasticae*, Rome, 1577.

Bouwen aan de bouwgeschiedenis 1994
Bouwen aan de bouwgeschiedenis. Recent onderzoek naar de bouwchronologie van de Antwerpse Onze-Lieve-Vrouwekathedraal, cat. exh. Antwerp, 1994.

Braman-Buchan 1975
M. Braman-Buchan, *The Paintings by Peter Aertsen*, PhD dissertation University of New York, 1975.

Braun 1924
J. Braun, *Der christliche Altar in seiner geschichtlichen Entwicklung*, Munich, 1924, 2 vols.

Briels 1980
J. Briels, 'Amator Pictoriae Artis. De Antwerpse kunstverzamelaar Peeter Stevens (1590–1688) en zijn Constkamer', *Jaarboek Koninklijk Museum voor Schone Kunsten Antwerpen*, 1980, pp. 137–201.

Brising 1909
H. Brising, *Quinten Metsys, essai sur l'origine de l'italianisme dans l'art des Pays Bas*, Uppsala, 1909, pp. 26–31.

Bruyn 1966
J. Bruyn, 'Niet lange Pier maar Cleen Hansken', *Bulletin Boymans-van Beuningen*, XVII, 1966, pp. 2–12, 39.

Bruyns 2009
E. Bruyns, *Les cadres dans la peinture des Pays-Bas méridionaux au 17e siècle*, unpublished doctoral dissertation, UCL, Louvain-la-Neuve, 2009.

Bulletin 1962
P. Coremans et al, 'La Descente de Crois de Rubens. Etude préalable au traitement', *Bulletin Institut Royal du Patrimoine Artistique / Koninklijk Instituut voor het Kuntpatrimonium*, V, 1962, pp. 4–187.

Bungeneers 1993
J. Bungeneers, 'The History of the Building. The Romanesque Church of Our Lady', in W. Aerts (ed.), *The Cathedral of Our Lady in Antwerp*, Antwerp, 1993, pp. 103–106.

Bunting 1611
J. Bunting, *Itinerarium Sacrae Scripturae, Dat is: Het Reys-boeck der Heyliger Schrift in twee deelen onderscheyden*, Arnhem, 1611.

Bürger 1862
W. Bürger, *Musée d'Anvers*, Brussels-Leipzig-Ghent, 1862.

Büttner 2003
N. Büttner, 'Wie war Meister "Gielesz"? Der Vertrag über das Dortmunder Retabel und die Werkstattpraxis in Antwerpen', in B. Welzel, T. Lentes & H. Schlie (eds.), *Das 'Goldene Wunder' in der Dortmunder Petrikirche. Bildgebrauch und Bildproduktion im Mittelalter*, Bielefeld, 2003, pp. 57–76.

Buyle 1990
M. Buyle, 'Een hemel vol sterren. De conservering van een 15de-eeuwse gewelfschildering in de Onze-Lieve-Vrouwekathedraal te Antwerpen', *M&L* [Monumenten en landschappen], IX, 1, 1990, pp 12–24.

Capretti 1995
E. Capretti, 'Tipologie fiorentine di altari agli albori della Controriforma: un'indagine attraverso i disegni', in A. Forlani Tempesti (ed.), *Altari e immagini nello spazio ecclesiale. Progetti e realizzazioni fra Firenze e Bologna nell'età della Controriforma*, Florence, 1995, pp. 71–87.

Casteels 1961
M. Casteels, De *beeldhouwers de Nole te Kamerijk, te Utrecht en te Antwerpen (Verhandelingen van de Koninklijke Academie voor Wetenschappen, Letteren en Schone Kunsten van België. Klasse der Schone Kunsten*, 16), Brussels, 1961.

Catalogue Antwerp 1988
Koninklijk Museum voor Schone Kunsten, Antwerpen. Catalogus Schilderkunst Oude Meesters, Antwerp, 1988.

Catalogue Berlin 1931
E. Bock & J. Rosenberg (eds.), *Staatliche Museen zu Berlin. Die Zeichnungen alter Meister im Kupferstich Kabinett. Die Niederländischen Meister. Beschreibendes Verzeichnis sämtlicheer Zeichnungen mit 220 Lichtdrucktafeln*, 2 vols., Frankfurt, 1931.

Claes, Claes & Vyncke 2002
J. Claes, A. Claes & K. Vyncke, *Sanctus. Meer dan 500 heiligen herkennen*, Louvain, 2002.

Cuttler 1968
C. Cuttler, *Northern Painting - from Pucelle to Bruegel : fourteenth, fifteenth, and sixteenth centuries*, New York, 1968.

Dacos 1987
N. Dacos, 'Autour de Bernard van Orley, Peeter de Kempeneer et son compagnon', *Revue de l'art*, LXXV, 1987, pp. 17–28.

Dacos & Meijer 1995
N. Dacos & B. Meijer (eds.), *Fiamminghi a Roma. 1508–1608: artistes des Pays-Bas et de la principauté de Liège à Rome à la Renaissance* (cat. exh., Brussels, Palais des Beaux-Arts / [Rome, Palazzo delle Esposizioni, 1995], Ghent, 1995.

Dambruyne 1997
J. Dambruyne, 'Rijkdom, materiële cultuur en sociaal aanzien. De bezitspatronen en investeringsstrategieën van de Gentse ambachten omstreeks 1540', in C. Lis & H. Soly (eds.), *Werelden van verschil. Ambachtsgilden in de lage landen*, Brussels, 1997, pp. 151–212.

Dambruyne 2002
J. Dambruyne, *Corporatieve middengroepen. Aspiraties, relaties en transformaties in de 16de-eeuwse Gentse ambachtswereld*, Ghent, 2002.

Dambruyne 2006
J. Dambruyne, 'Representation and investment strategies in the early modern guild world. A comparison between the south and the north of the Low Countries', in I.A. Gadd & P. Wallis (eds.), *Guilds and associations in Europe, 900–1900*, London, 2006.

David 1622A
J. David, *Den Blom-hof der Kerckelicken Cerimonien Begrijpende de Serimonien inden kerckelijcken dienst ende uyt-reycken der H.H. Sacramenten ghebruyck worden*, Antwerp, 1622.

David 1622B
J. David, *Den Cruythof der Kerckelicken Traditien ende Cerimonien begrijpende in Vragen ende Antwoorden dat aengaet de besondere hoochtijden, feestdagen ende beelden der heyligen*, Antwerp, 1622.

De Bettignies 1868
Ch. De Bettignies, 'Compte-rendu de l'excursion du cercle archéologique à Saint-Ghislain', *Annales du Cercle Archéologique de Mons*, VII, 1867.

De Blaauw 1997
S. De Blaauw, 'Das Hochaltarretabel in Rom bis zum frühen 16. Jahrhundert: das Altarbild als Kategorie der liturgischen Anlage', *Mededelingen van het Nederlands Instituut te Rome*, LV, 55, 1996 (1997), pp. 83–110.

De Bosque 1975
A. de Bosque, *Quentin Metsys*, Brussels, 1975.

De Bosschere 1907
J. De Bosschere, *Quinten Metsys. Collection des grands artistes des Pays Bas*, Brussels, 1907.

De Ceulaer 1993
R. De Ceulaer, 'The History of the Building. Restoration in the Nineteenth and Twentieth Centuries, in W. Aerts (ed.), *The Cathedral of Our Lady in Antwerp*, Antwerp, 1993, pp. 143–157.

Deceulaer 2001
H. Deceulaer, *Pluriforme patronen en een verschillende snit. Sociaal-economische, institutionele en culturele transformaties in de kledingsector in Antwerpen, Brussel en Gent, 1585–1800*, Amsterdam, 2001.

De Groote 1967
H.V.L. De Groote, 'De zestiende-eeuwse Antwerpse schoolmeesters', *Bijdragen tot de Geschiedenis*, L, 1967, pp. 179–318.

Delvingt 2002
A. Delvingt, 'Une oeuvre retrouvée de Hans van den Elburcht, franc-maître à Anvers en 1536', *Oud-Holland*, CXV, 3–4, 2002, pp. 167–186.

De Munck 2007A
B. De Munck, *Technologies of Learning. Apprenticeship in Antwerp from the 15th century to the end of the ancien régime*, Turnhout, 2007.

De Munck 2007B
B. De Munck, 'La qualité du corporatisme. Stratégies économiques et symboliques des corporations anversoises du XVe siècle à leur abolition', *Revue d'histoire moderne et contemporaine*, LIV, 1, 2007, pp. 116–144.

De Munck 2008
B. De Munck, 'Skills, trust and changing consumer preferences. The decline of Antwerp's craft guilds from the perspective of the product market, ca. 1500–ca. 1800', *International Review of Social History*, LIII, 2, 2008, pp. 197–233.

Denhaene 1990
G. Denhaene, *Lambert Lombard. Renaissance en humanisme te Luik*, Antwerp, 1990.

Denhaene 2006
G. Denhaene (ed.), *Lambert Lombard. Peintre de la renaissance Liège 1505/06–1566. Essais interdisciplinaires et catalogue de l'exposition* (*Institut Royal du Patrimoine Artistique. Scienta Artis*, 3), Brussels, 2006.

De Piles 1699 [1725]
[R. de Piles], *Beknopt verhaal van het leven der vermaardste schilders, met aanmerkingen over hunne werken : benevens een schets van een volmaakt schilder, een verhandeling van de kennisse der tekeningen en schilderyen, en van de nuttigheit der printen / in 't Frans beschreven ... Roger de Piles; en nu in 't Nederduits vertaalt door J. Verhoek*, Amsterdam, 1725.

De Poorter 1970
N. De Poorter, 'De kunstwerken van het Antwerpse Barbiers- en Chirurgijnsambacht', *Liber memorialis. 350 jaar collegium medicum Antverpiense. 25 jaar geneeskundige dagen van Antwerpen*, Antwerp, 1970, pp. 123–136.

Descamps 1769
J.-B. Descamps, *Voyage pittoresque de la Flandre et du Brabant*, Paris, 1769.

De Vlaamsche School 1875
'Over het witten der Antwerpsche hoofdkerk', *De Vlaamsche School*, 1875, pp. 104–105.

De Voragine (ed. Benz) 1997
Jacobus de Voragine, *Die Legenda aurea*, aus dem Lateinischen übersetzt von Richard Benz, Lizenzausgabe [12. Aufl.] für die Wissenschaftliche Buchgesellschaft, Darmstadt: Wissenschaftliche Buchgesellschaft, 1997 (original edition: Heidelberg: Verlag Lambert Schneider, 1955).

Dhanens 1948
E. Dhanens, 'Jan van Roome alias van Brussels, schilder', *Gentse Bijdragen tot de Kunstgeschiedenis*, XI, 1945–1948, pp. 41–146.

d'Hulst & Vandenven 1989
R.-A. d'Hulst & M. Vandenven, *Rubens: The Old Testament* (*Corpus Rubenianum Ludwig Burchard*, III), London-New York, 1989.

Díaz Padrón 1993
M. Díaz Padrón, 'Una tabla de la predicación de San Juan Bautista de H. van Balen atribuida a Adam van Noort en la colección de Hartveld (Nueva York)', *Archivo Español de Arte*, 264, 1993, pp. 408–409.

Dijkstra et al. 2002
J. Dijkstra, P.P.W.M. Dirkse & A.E.A.M. Smits, *De schilderijen van het Museum Catharijneconvent*, Utrecht, 2002.

Dirkse 1984
P. Dirkse, 'Nieuwe Aanwinsten', *Catharijnebrief. Mededelingen van de Vereniging van de Vrienden van het Museum Het Catharijneconvent te Utrecht*, 5, 1984, pp. 1–2.

Donnet 1924 (1887)
F. Donnet, *Notice historique sur la chapelle du T.S. Sacrément en l'église cathédrale d'Anvers, Antwerp*, 1924 (1887).

Doutrepont 1937
A. Doutrepont, 'Martin De Vos et l'entrée triomphale de l'archiduc Ernest d'Autriche à Anvers en 1594', *Bulletin de l'Institut Historique Belge de Rome*, XVIII, 1937, pp. 125–197.

Duverger 1984–2004
E. Duverger, *Antwerpse Kunstinventarissen uit de zeventiende eeuw* (*Fontes Historiae Artis Neerlandicae*, I), 13 vols., Brussels, 1984–2004.

Duverger & Van Biervliet 1998
E. Duverger & L. Van Biervliet, *Beschrijvinge : een eerste nederlandstalige gids voor kunstminnaars in Brabant en Vlaanderen (1751–1753). Inleiding en tekst* (*Facultés universitaires Saint-Louis. Studiecentrum 18de-eeuwse Zuidnederlandse Letterkunde, Cahier 17*), Brussels, 1998.

Eisler 1967
C. Eisler, 'Rubens' Uses of the Northern Past. The Michiels Triptych and its Sources', *Bulletin Koninklijke Musea voor Schone Kunsten van België*, XVI, 1967, pp. 43–78.

Epstein 1998
S.R. Epstein, 'Craft guilds, apprenticeship, and technological change in pre-industrial Europe', *Journal of Economic History*, LVIII, 3, 1998, pp. 684–713.

Ertz 1979
K. Ertz, *Jan Breughel der Ältere 1568–1625: Die Gemälde mit kritischem Oeuvrekatalog*, Cologne, 1979.

Evers 1942
H.G. Evers, *Peter Paul Rubens*, Munich, 1942.

Fabri 2009
R. Fabri, 'Eenen ramenant van verf ende pinselen: some aspects of the materials used by seventeenth-century cabinet painters in Antwerp', in J. Kirby (ed.), *European Trade in Artists' Materials*, London, (forthcoming).

Farmer 1981
J.D. Farmer, *Bernard van Orley of Brussels*, Ann Arbor (MI), 1981.

[FGV] 1743
[F.G.V.], *Antwerpsch chronykje in het welk zeer veele en elders te vergeefsch gezogte geschiedenissen sedert den jare 1500 tot het jaar 1574 [...] door F.G.V. [...] in 't licht gebracht*, Leyden, 1743.

Filedt Kok 2006
J.P. Filedt Kok, *De heilige Lucas tekent en schildert de Madonna. Rede uitgesproken bij de aanvaarding van het ambt van hoogleraar atelierpraktijken en materieel-technisch kunsthistorisch onderzoek aan de Universiteit van Amsterdam op 6 december 2005*, Amsterdam, 2006.

Freedberg 1976
D. Freedberg, 'The Representation of Martyrdoms during The Early Counter-Reformation in Antwerp', *The Burlington Magazine*, CXVIII, 1976, pp. 128–138.

Freedberg 1984
D. Freedberg, *Rubens: The Life of Christ after the Passion* (*Corpus Rubenianum Ludwig Burchard*, VII), London-Oxford-New York, 1984.

Freedberg 1988
D. Freedberg, *Iconoclasm and Painting in the revolt of the Netherlands 1566–1609*, New York, 1988.

Freedberg 1992
D. Freedberg, 'Kunst und Gegenreformation in den südlichen Niederlanden, 1560–1660', in E. Mai & H. Vlieghe (eds.), *Von Bruegel bis Rubens. Das goldene Jahrhundert der flämischen Malerei* (cat. exh. Cologne, Wallraf-Richartz-Museum), Cologne, 1992, pp. 55–70.

Freedberg 1993
D. Freedberg, 'Schilderkunst en Contrareformatie ten tijde van Rubens', in P. Sutton, *The Age of Rubens* (cat. exh. Boston, Museum of Fine Arts; Toledo (Ohio), Toledo Museum of Art, 1993–1994), Ghent-Amsterdam, 1993, pp. 131–146.

Friedländer 1924–1937
M.J. Friedländer, *Die Altniederländische Malerei*, Berlin-Leyden, 1924–1937.

Friedländer 1967–1976
M.J. Friedländer, *Early Netherlandish Painting*, traduit par H. Norden, Leyden-Brussels, 1967–1976.

Gabriëls 1930
J. Gabriëls, *Een Kempisch schildersgeslacht. De Francken's. Bijdrage tot de Geschiedenis van het Nederlands Romanisme*, Hoogstraten, 1930.

Geudens 1891A
E. Geudens 'Le "Jugement dernier et les sept oeuvres de misericorde" par Bernard van Orley (1490–1541) – Notice', *Bulletin de l'Académie Royale d'Archéologie de Belgique*, sér. 4, 2, 1891, pp. 126–131.

Geudens 1891B
E. Geudens, *Het hoofdambacht der meerseniers (godsdienst en kunstzin)*, I, Antwerp, 1891.

Genaille 1954
R. Genaille, 'L'œuvre de Pieter Aertsen', *Gazette des Beaux-Arts*, XLIV, 1954, pp. 265–288.

Génard 1856
P. Génard, *Notices des oeuvres d'art qui ornent l'église Notre-Dame à Anvers*, Antwerp, 1867 (1856).

Génard 1863
P. Génard, 'Bescheeden rakende Quinten Massys', *De Vlaemsche School*, XI, 1863, pp. 126–127.

Génard 1868
P. Génard, 'Bescheeden rakende de schilderij "De Nood Gods", Quinten Massijs', *De Vlaemsche School*, XIV, 1868, pp. 50–52.

Ghijs 1988
I. Ghijs, *De Antwerpse magistraat in een laat-humanistische en contra-reformatorische periode: 1585–1621. Een institutionele, sociaal-economische en culturele analyse*, unpublished dissertation K.U.Leuven, 1988, 2 vols.

Gielis 2006
G. Gielis, '*In gratia recipimus*'. *Een studie over Nicolaas Coppin (ca. 1476–1535) en de inquisitie in de Nederlanden*, unpublished dissertation K.U. Leuven, 2006.

Glen 1977
T.L. Glen, *Rubens and the Counter Reformation; Studies in Religious Paintings between 1609 and 1620*, Ph.D. thesis, Princeton University, Princeton, NJ, 1975 (Outstanding Dissertations in the Fine Arts, Garland), New York-London, 1977.

Goetschalckx 1929
P.J. Goetschalckx, *Geschiedenis der Kanunniken van O.L.V. Kapittel te Antwerpen (1585–1700), Antwerp*, 1929.

Goosen 1992
L. Goosen, *Van Andreas tot Zacheüs: thema's uit het Nieuwe Testament en de apocriefe literatuur in religie en kunsten*, Nijmegen, 1992.

Grieten 1994
S. Grieten, 'Een heilige verbeeld. Iconografie en ideologische recuperatie van de heilige Begga', *Jaarboek Koninklijk Museum voor Schone Kunsten Antwerpen*, 1994, pp. 89–183.

Grieten 1995
S. Grieten., 'Reconstructie van het altaarstuk van het Antwerpse Meerseniersambacht. Nieuwe gegevens over Otto van Veen, Erasmus II Quellinus en Balthazar Beschey', *Jaarboek Koninklijk Museum voor Schone Kunsten*, 1995, pp. 135–158.

Grieten 1997
S. Grieten, 'De altaartuinen van de Kuipers in de Onze-Lieve-Vrouwekathedraal van Antwerpen', *Jaarboek Cornelis Floris*, 1997, pp. 18–29

Grieten & Bungeneers 1996
S. Grieten & J. Bungeneers (eds.), *De Onze-Lieve-Vrouwekathedraal van Antwerpen. Kunstpatrimonium van het Ancien Régime (Inventaris van het Kunstpatrimonium van de Provincie Antwerpen, 3)*, Turnhout, 1996.

Grieten et al. 1996
S. Grieten, M. Mees, L. Van Damme & L. Van Langendonck, *Een venster op de hemel. De glasramen van de Onze-Lieve-Vrouwekathedraal van Antwerpen, Antwerp*, 1996.

Gustafsson 1987
B. Gustafsson, 'The rise and economic behaviour of medieval craft guilds', *Scandinavian Economic History Review*, XXXV, 1987, pp. 1–40.

Hand 2004
J.O. Hand, *Joos Van Cleve: the Complete Paintings*, New Haven-London, 2004.

Held 1931
J.S. Held, *Dürers Wirkung auf die niederländische Kunst seiner Zeit*, The Hague, 1931.

Held 1996
J. Held, 'Carolus Scribanius's Observations on Art in Antwerp', *Journal of the Warburg and Courtauld Institutes*, LXV, 1996, pp. 174–204.

Hendrikman 1998
L. Hendrikman, 'Meester van het H. Bloed', in M.P.J. Martens (ed.), *Brugge en de Renaissance: van Memling tot Pourbus, II: notities*, Ghent-Bruges, 1998, pp. 50–58.

Hendrikman 2002
L.I. Hendrikman, 'Verknipte interpretatie - Rafaels invloed op het oeuvre van Bernard van Orley heroverwogen', in H.Th. van Veen, V. Schmidt & J. Keizer (eds.), *Polyptiek - Een veelluik van Groninger bijdragen aan de kunstgeschiedenis*, Zwolle, 2002, pp. 83–90.

Hendrikman 2009A
L.I. Hendrikman, 'The Last Judgement and the Burial of the dead', in J.P. Filedt Kok, J. Bikker et. al., *Catalogue Netherlandish paintings in the Rijksmuseum – artists born before 1500* (online catalogue: http://www.rijksmuseum.nl/early-netherlandish-paintings)

Hendrikman 2009B
L.I. Hendrikman, 'Bernard van Orley', in J.P. Filedt Kok, J. Bikker et. al., *Catalogue Netherlandish paintings in the Rijksmuseum – artists born before 1500* (online catalogue: http://www.rijksmuseum.nl/early-netherlandish-paintings)

Hermans 1992
G. Hermans, *De Gilde van Onze-Lieve-Vrouw-Lof in de Antwerpse Onze-Lieve-Vrouwekathedraal*, unpublished dissertation K.U.Leuven, 1992.

Herremans 2007
Valérie Herremans, '*eenen loffelycken ende hoffelycken aultaer*'. *Retabelplastiek in de Zuidelijke Nederlanden ca. 1585–1685*, unpublished doctoral dissertation, Vrije Universiteit Brussel, 2007.

Hessels 1887
J.H. Hessels, *Abrahami Ortelii ... Epistulae*, Canterbury, 1887.

Honnis 1984
M. Honnis, *Saint-Ghislain. Choses et autres du passé. Histoire, folklore, souvenirs*, Saint-Ghislain, 1984.

Hoogewerff 1912
G.J. Hoogewerff, *Nederlandsche Schilders in Italie in de XVIe eeuw: de geschiedenis van het Romanisme*, Utrecht, 1912.

Hoogewerff 1941–1942
G.J. Hoogewerff, *De Noord-Nederlandse Schilderkunst*, 5 vols., The Hague, 1936–1947.

Höper 2001
C. Höper, *Raffael und die Folgen. Das Kunstwerk im Zeitalter seiner graphischen Reproduzierbarkeit* (cat. exh. Stuttgart, Graphischen Sammlung der Staatsgalerie), Stuttgart, 2001.

Houbraken 1718–1721
A. Houbraken, *De groote schouburgh der Nederlantsche konstschilders en schilderessen*, 2 vols., The Hague, 1718–1721.

Hubala 1971
E. Hubala, 'Rubens und Michelangelo; eine Bemerkung zum Christus der Antwerpener Kreuzabnahme van 1611–1612', *Nordelbingen*, XL, 1971, pp. 64–76.

Humfrey 1993
P. Humfrey, *The Altarpiece in Renaissance Venice*, New Haven-London, 1993.

Huvenne 1984
P. Huvenne, *Pieter Pourbus, meester-schilder, 1524–1584* (cat. exh. Bruges, Memlingmuseum), Brussels, 1984.

Huvenne 1993
P. Huvenne, 'De kruisafneming van Rubens in de Onze-Lieve-Vrouwekathedraal van Antwerpen', *Openbaar Kunstbezit in Vlaanderen*, 1993, pp. 2–19.

Inventaris 1925
Inventaris van het archief van gilden en ambachten, Antwerp, 1925.

Jacobs 2000
M. Jacobs, 'De ambachten in Brabant en Mechelen (12de eeuw–1795)', in R. Van Uytven, Cl. Bruneel, H. Coppens & B. Augustyn (eds.), *De gewestelijke en lokale overheidsinstellingen in Brabant en Mechelen tot 1795*, II, Brussels, 2000, pp. 558–624.

Jaffé 1958
M. Jaffé, 'Un chef d'œuvre mieux connu', *L'oeil*, 43–44, 1958, pp. 15–20, 80.

Jaffé 1972
M. Jaffé, 'Rubens's "Le Christ à la Paille" reconsidered', *Apollo*, N.S., XCV, 1972, pp. 107–114.

Jansen & Van Herck 1943
A. Jansen & C. Van Herck, 'De Antwerpsche beeldhouwers Colyns de Nole', *Koninklijke Oudheidkundige kring van Antwerpen*, XIX, 1943, pp. 1–73.

Jansen & Van Herck 1944–1945
A. Jansen & C. Van Herck, 'De Van den Eynde's. Antwerpsche bouwmeesters en beeldhouwers uit de XVIIe eeuw', *Jaarboek Oudheidkundige Kring van Antwerpen*, XX–XXI, 1944–1945, pp. 5–90.

Jansen & Van Herck 1949
A. Jansen & C. Van Herck,' Archief in beeld. De nog bestaande kerken van Antwerpen', *Tijdschrift voor geschiedenis en folklore*, XII, 1949, pp. 57–107.

Janssens, Marčsik, De Meyere & Hänsch 1993
P. Janssens, A. Marčsik, C. De Meyere & C. Hänsch, 'Underneath the Cathedral. The Antropological and Palaeopathological Investigation', in W. Aerts (ed.), *The Cathedral of Our Lady in Antwerp*, Antwerp, 1993, pp. 338–343.

Jezler 2007
P. Jezler, *Himmel; Hölle, Fegefeuer, Das Jenseits im Mittelalter*, Zürich, 2007.

Jost 1963
I. Jost, 'Hendrick van Balen d.Ä. Versuch einer Chronologie der Werken aus den ersten zwei Jahrzehnten des Siebzehnten Jahrhunderts unter besonderer Berücksichtigung der Kabinettbilder', *Nederlands Kunsthistorisch Jaarboek*, XIV, 1963, pp. 83–128.

Judson 2000
J.R. Judson, *Rubens: The Passion of Christ* (*Corpus Rubenianum Ludwig Burchard*, VI), Turnhout, 2000.

Jürgens 1956
R. Jürgens, *Die Entwicklung des Barockaltars in Rom*, doctoral dissertation, Universität Hamburg, 1956.

Kavaler 1999
E. Kavaler, *Pieter Bruegel: Parables of Order and Enterprise*, Cambridge, 1999.

Keller 1975
H.L. Keller, *Reclams Lexikon der Heiligen und der biblischen Gestalten: Legende und Darstellung in der bildenden Kunst*, 3e ed., Stuttgart, 1975.

Kerken van Antwerpen 1774
(J. De Wit), J. De Bosschere, *De kerken van Antwerpen. Schilderijen, beeldhouwwerken, geschilderde glasramen enz. in de 18de eeuw beschreven door Jacobus De Wit (1774)*, (*Uitgaven der Antwerpsche Bibliophilen*, no. 25), Antwerp-The Hague, 1910, 2 vols.
Kirschbaum & Braunfels 1968–1976
E. Kirschbaum & W. Braunfels, *Lexikon der christlichen Ikonographie*, VII, Rome-Freiburg, 1968–1976.

Klein 1933
D. Klein, *St. Lukas als Maler der Madonna. Ikonographie der Lukas-Madonna*, Berlin, 1933.

Kloek 1990A
W. Kloek, 'Pieter Aertsen en het probleem van het samenstellen van zijn oeuvre', *Pieter Aertsen (Nederlands Kunsthistorisch Jaarboek)* XL, 1989.

Kloek 1990B
W. Kloek, 'De tekeningen van Pieter Aertsen en Joachim Beuckelaer', *Pieter Aertsen (Nederlands Kunsthistorisch Jaarboek)* XL, 1989.

Kraut 1986
G. Kraut, *Lukas malt die Madonna. Zeugnisse zum künstlerischen Selbstverständnis in der Malerei*, Worms, 1986.

Kultermann 1990
U. Kultermann, *Geschichte der Kunstgeschichte. Der Weg einer Wissenschaft*, Munich, 1990.

Lambrechts & Sosson 1994
P. Lambrechts & J.-P. Sosson (eds.), *Les métiers au Moyen Age. Aspects économiques et sociaux*, Louvain-La-Neuve, 1994.

Lammertse 1994
F. Lammertse, 'Hansje van Elburg. The Baptism of the eunuch', in *Van Eyck to Bruegel. Dutch and Flemish Painting in the Collection of the Museum Boymans-van Beuningen*, Rotterdam, 1994, pp. 390–395, no. 93.

Lampson 1956
D. Lampson, *Les Effigies des Peintres célèbres des Pays-Bas*, ed. J. Puraye, Bruges, 1956.

Landau & Parshall 1994
D. Landau & P.W. Parshall, *The Renaissance Print 1470–1550*, New Haven-London, 1994.

Larsen 1985
E. Larsen, *17th Century Flemish Painting*, Freren, 1985.

Lavalleye 1943
J. Lavalleye, 'Le style du peintre Bernard van Orley', in C. Dessart, *Bernard van Orley 1488–1541*, Brussels, 1943, pp. 43–70.

Lawrence 1984
C. Lawrence, 'The iconology of Rubens's "Miraculous draft of fishes" triptych', *Simiolus. Netherlands Quarterly for the History of Art*, XIV, 1984, pp. 25–35.

Leurs & Philippen 1938
S. Leurs & L.J.M. Philippen, *De kathedrale kerk van O.L.V. te Antwerpen (Ars Belgica, 9)*, Antwerp, 1938.

Lis & Soly 1994
C. Lis & H. Soly (eds.), *Werken volgens de regels. Ambachten in Brabant en Vlaanderen, 1500–1800*, Brussels, 1994.

Lis & Soly 1997
C. Lis & H. Soly (eds.), *Werelden van verschil. Ambachtsgilden in de lage landen*, Brussels, 1997.

Lis et al. 2006
C. Lis, J. Lucassen, M. Prak & H. Soly, H. (eds.), *Guilds in the early modern Low Countries. Work, power and representation,* London, 2006.

Lynch 2003
K.A. Lynch, *Individuals, families, and communities in Europe, 1200–1800. The urban foundation of Western society,* Cambridge, 2003.

Lynch 2004
K.A. Lynch, 'Behavioral regulation in the city: families, religious associations, and the role of poor relief', in Herman Roodenburg & Pieter Spierenburg (eds.), *Social control in Europe, Volume 1, 1500–1800*, Columbus, 2004, pp. 200–219.

Manderyck 1992
M. Manderyck, 'Rubens' schilderijen in de herinrichting van de Kathedraal', in R.-A. d'Hulst et al., *De Kruisoprichting van Pieter Paul Rubens,* Brussels, 1992, pp. 127–144.

Manderyck 1999
M. Manderyck, 'De binnenrestauratie van de O.-L.-Vrouwekathedraal van Antwerpen', in *Negentiende-eeuwse restauratiepraktijk en actuele monumentenzorg. Handelingen van het Nederlands-Vlaams symposium, Leuven 13–14 september 1996.* KADOC-Artes 3, 1999, pp. 188–201.

Marinus 1993
M.J. Marinus, 'People and Institutions In the Church of Our Lady. The Bishops and their Cathedral. 1559–1794', in W. Aerts (ed.), *The Cathedral of Our Lady in Antwerp*, Antwerp, 1993, pp. 39–59.

Marinus 1995
M.J. Marinus, *De Contrareformatie te Antwerpen (1585–1676), Antwerp,* 1995.

Marnef 1996
G. Marnef, *Antwerp in the age of Reformation: underground Protestantism in a commercial metropolis, 1550–1577*, Baltimore, 1996.

Martin 1968
J.R. Martin, *The Ceiling Paintings for the Jesuit Church in Antwerp* (*Corpus Rubenianum Ludwig Burchard*, I), Brussels, 1968.

Martin 1969
J.R. Martin, *The Antwerp Altarpieces*, New York, 1969.

Massaut 1974
J.-P. Massaut, *Critique et tradition à la veille de la Réforme en France: étude suivie de textes inédits traduits et annotés*, Paris, 1974.

Materieel-wetenschappelijk onderzoek 1989
Materieel-wetenschappelijk onderzoek van muur- en gewelfschilderingen in koor en kruisbeuk van de Onze-Lieve-Vrouwekathedraal te Antwerpen, unpublished research report, Antwerp, 1989. [Archief Vlaamse Overheid, Onroerend Erfgoed Antwerpen A/0192.]

Meganck 1998
T. Meganck, *De kerkelijke architectuur van Wensel Cobergher (1557/61–1634) in het licht van zijn verblijf te Rome* (*Verhandelingen van de Koninklijke Academie voor Wetenschappen, Letteren en Schone Kunsten van België*, 60), Brussels, 1998.

Meijer 1999
B.W. Meijer, 'Flemish and Dutch Artists in Venetian Workshops: The Case of Jacopo Tintoretto', in *Renaissance Venice and the North. Crosscurrents in the time of Dürer, Bellini and Titian* (cat. exh. Venice, Palazzo Grassi), London, 1999, pp. 133–143.

Mensaert 1763
G.P. Mensaert, *Le peintre amateur et curieux ou Description générale des tableaux des plus habiles maîtres, qui font l'ornement des églises, couvents, abbayes, prieurés & cabinets particuliers dans l'étendue des Pays-Bas autrichiens*, Brussels, 1763.

Mertens & Torfs 1845–1853
F. Mertens & K. Torfs, *Geschiedenis van Antwerpen sedert de stichting der stad tot onze tyden,* 8 vols., Antwerp, 1845–1853.

Meul 1994
V. Meul, 'Joseph Schadde, academicus en historiserend bouwmeester in de tweede helft van de 19de eeuw', *M&L* [Monumenten en landschappen], XIII, 6, 1994, pp. 4–61.

Meyssens 1649
Jean Meyssens, *Images des divers hommes d'esprit*, 1649.

Molanus 1570
J. Molanus, *De picturis et imaginibus sacris liber unus*, Louvain, 1570.

Monballieu 1977
A. Monballieu, 'M.I. Van Bree en de restauratie van Rubens' Schilderijen in het Museum van Antwerpen', *Jaarboek Koninklijk Museum voor Schone Kunsten Antwerpen*, 1977, pp. 325–359.

Müller-Hofstede 1957
J. Müller-Hofstede, 'Zum Werke des Otto Van Veen, 1590–1600', *Bulletin Musées royaux des Beaux-Arts de Belgique*, VI, 1957, pp. 127–174.
Musée central 1801
Notice des tableaux exposées dans la galerie du Musée, Paris, 1801.
Les noces de Cana de Véronèse 1992–1993
Les noces de Cana de Véronèse. Une oeuvre et sa restauration (cat. exh. Paris, Musée du Louvre, 1992–1993), Paris, 1992.
O'Malley 2005
M. O' Malley, *The business of art, contracts and the commissioning process in Renaissance Italy*, New Haven, 2005.
Op de Beeck 1978
R. Op de Beeck, *De Gilde van Onze-Lieve Vrouwe-Lof in de kathedraal van Antwerpen*, Antwerp, 1978.
Oost, Bungeneers, Veeckman, Ervynck & Sorber 1993
T. Oost, J. Bungeneers, J. Veeckman, A. Ervynck & F. Sorber, 'Underneath the Cathedral. Archaeological Investigation of the Site during Restoration', in W. Aerts (ed.), *The Cathedral of Our Lady in Antwerp*, Antwerp, 1993, pp. 304–337.
Oudt register 1336–1439
Oudt register mette berderen. 1336–1439, published in *Antwerpsch Archievenblad*, XXVI, [1912], pp. 429–433.
Palladio 1616
A. Palladio, *I Quattro Libri dell' Architettura*, Venice, 1616.
Papebrochius 1845–1853
D. Papebrochius, *Annales Antverpienses ab urbe condita ad annum 1700 collecti ex ipsius civitaits monumentis*, Antwerp, 7 vols., 1845–1853.
Paradisus musicus 1977
Paradisus musicus. Muziek en Samenleving in Rubens' Tijd, cat. exh. Antwerp, 1977.
Passavant 1833
J.D. Passavant, *Kunstreise durch England und Belgien, nebst einem Bericht über den Bau des Domthurms zu Frankfurt*, Frankfurt, 1833.
Peeters 1996
N. Peeters, 'De Maagschap van de Heilige Anna', in D. Allard (ed.), *S.O.S. Oude schilderijen*, Brussels, 1996, pp. 95–100.
Peeters 1999A
N. Peeters, 'Marked for the Market? Continuity, collaboration and the mechanics of artistic production of history painting in the Francken-workshops in Counter-Reformation Antwerp', *Kunst voor de Markt (Nederlands Kunsthistorisch Jaarboek*, L), 1999, pp. 59–80.
Peeters 1999B
N. Peeters, 'Brothers in art: Hieronymus and Frans Francken I and their family: portraits and crypto-portraits in the second half of the sixteenth century', in E. Griffey (ed.), *Crossways. Envisioning self and status, Self representation in the Low Countries 1400–1700*, London, 1999, pp. 80–102.
Peeters 2000A
N. Peeters, *Tussen continuïteit en vernieuwing. De bijdrage van Frans en Ambrosius Francken I, en de jonge generatie Francken, tot de historieschilderkunst te Antwerpen ca. 1570–1620*, unpublished dissertation, Vrije Universiteit Brussel, 2000.
Peeters 2000B
N. Peeters, 'Het leven van Christus en de H. Maagd. Een triptiek met dubbele luiken van Frans I Francken', in A. Balis, R. Hoozee, M.P.J. Martens & P. van Haute (eds.), *200 jaar verzamelen. Collectieboek Museum voor Schone Kunsten*, Ghent, 2000, pp. 72–74.
Peeters 2001
N. Peeters, 'Frivol ende absurd': het altaarstuk voor het Herentalse Brouwersambacht door Frans Francken I (1603)', *Historisch Jaarboek van Herentals*, XI, 2001, pp. 5–34.
Peeters 2003
N. Peeters, 'Frans I and Ambrosius I Francken, painters of the metropolis Antwerp, and their altarpieces in the years just after the fall of Antwerp (1585–1589)', *Jaarboek van het Koninklijk Museum voor Schone Kunsten van Antwerpen*, 2003, pp. 69–91.
Peeters 2005
N. Peeters, 'A Corporate Image? The Saint Luke's Altarpiece for the Cathedral of Our Lady in Antwerp (1589–1602)', in A. Balis et al. (ed.) *Florissant. Bijdragen tot de kunstgeschiedenis der Nederlanden (15de–17de eeuw). Liber Amicorum Carl Van de Velde*, Brussels, 2005, pp. 239–253.
Peeters 2007
N. Peeters, 'Painter's workshops and assistants in Netherlandish imagery (mid-fifteenth to early seventeenth century)', in N. Peeters (ed.), *Invisible hands? The role and status of the painter's journeyman in the Low Countries c. 1450–c. 1650*, Louvain, 2007, pp. 51–65.
Peeters 2008A
N. Peeters, 'Den "Quaden tyt"? The career of the young Antwerp artist Ambrosius Francken before 1585', *Oud Holland*, CXXI, 2008.
Peeters 2008B
N. Peeters, '"Painters pencells move not without that musicke". Prices of Southern Netherlandish painted altarpieces between 1585 and 1650', in A. Tummers & K. Jonckheere (eds.), *Art Market and connoisseurship, A closer look at paintings by Rembrandt, Rubens and their contemporaries*, Amsterdam, 2008, pp. 97–124.
Peeters 2009A
N. Peeters, 'Resilience and enterprise: the Francken-brothers in the years between the Iconoclasm and the Spanish Fury (1566–1576)', in H. Verougstraete (ed.), *Le dessin sous-jacent colloque XVI*, Louvain, fortcoming (2009).
Peeters 2009B
N. Peeters, 'The guild of Saint Luke and the painter's profession in Antwerp between ca. 1560 and 1585: some social and economic insights', *The artist in the Early Modern Netherlands (Nederlands Kunsthistorisch Jaarboek*, LIX), 2008, forthcoming (2009).
Peeters 2009C
N. Peeters, 'Wedding at Cana (workshop of Marten de Vos (1532–1603), 1597', in G. Koppel (ed.), *Catalogue of the collection of the Tallinn Art Museums*, forthcoming (2009).
Philippen 1940
L.J.M. Philippen, *De drie Laatste Oordeels schilderijen der Aalmoezenierskamer te Antwerpen, Bestuurlijk Verslag*, Antwerp, 1940.
Poffé 1895
E. Poffé, *De gilde der Antwerpsche schoolmeesters van bij haar ontstaan tot aan hare afschaffing*, Antwerp, 1895.
Prims 1927–1949
F. Prims, *Geschiedenis van Antwerpen*, 10 parts, 28 vols., Antwerp, 1927–1949.
Prims 1937
F. Prims, 'Het corporatisme der XVe eeuw', *Antwerpiensia*, X, 1936 [Antwerp, 1937], pp. 66–74, no. 8.
Prims 1938–1939
F. Prims, 'Altaarstudien', *Antwerpiensia*, XII, 1938 [Antwerp, 1939], pp. 285–339; XIII, 1939 [Antwerp, 1940], pp. 278–445.
Prims 1939A
F. Prims, 'De statuten van de Antwerpsche Lakengilde in het begin der 16de eeuw', *Verslagen en Mededeelingen van de Koninklijke Vlaamsche Academie*, 1939, pp. 19–46.
Prims 1939B
F. Prims, 'Cultuurwaarden en cultuurtekorten te Antwerpen in de eerste helft van de XVIe eeuw', *Verslagen en Mededeelingen der Koninklijke Vlaamsche Academie van Wetenschappen, Letteren en Schoone kunsten van België, Klasse der Letteren en der Morele en Staatkundige Wetenschappen*, 1939, p. 30.
Prims 1940
F. Prims, 'Locale kerkgeschiedenissen en de kerkhistorische studiën', *Collectanea Mechliniensia*, XXIX, 1940, p. 27.
Prims 1951
F. Prims, 'Quinten Matsys, een onbegrepen meteoor', *Antwerpiensia*, XXII, 1951, pp. 160–163.
Putnam 1993
R.D. Putnam, *Making Democracy Work. Civic Traditions in Modern Italy*, Princeton, 1993.
Puype & De Gryse 2006
J.P. Puype & P. De Gryse, *Viertalig Lexicon van de gevestwapens*, Brussels, 2006.
Réau 1958
L. Réau, *Iconographie de l'art chrétien, 3. Iconographie des saints*, II, Paris, 1958.
Restauratie 1989
W. Aerts et al., *De restauratie van de Onze-Lieve-Vrouwekathedraal te Antwerpen, 1965–1983. 1984–1989, Antwerp*, 1989.
Reynolds 1781
M. Mount, *Sir Joshua Reynolds, A Journey to Flanders and Holland in the Year 1781*, Cambridge, 1996.
Riegel 1895
H. Riegel, 'Rubens-Beiträge, Der Altar des Christ à la Paille Antwerpen', *Repertorium für Kunstwissenschaft*, 1895, pp. 18–22.

Rombouts & Van Lerius 1864–1872
Ph. Rombouts & Th. Van Lerius, *De Liggeren en andere historische archieven der Antwerpsche Sint Lucasgilde*, 2 vols., Antwerp-The Hague, 1864–1872.

Rombouts & Van Lerius 1961
P. Rombouts & T. Van Lerius, *De Liggeren en andere historische archieven der Antwerpsche Sint-Lucasgilde [...]*, 2 vols., Amsterdam, 1961 (new edtion of Antwerp- The Hague 1864–1876).

Roosen-Runge 1940
H. Roosen-Runge, 'Die Gestaltung der Farbe bei Quinten Metsys', *Münchener Beiträge zur Kunstgeschichte*, VI, 1940, pp. 125–144, 171–176, 182–183.

Rooses 1879
M. Rooses, *Geschiedenis van de Antwerpsche Schilderschool*, Antwerp, 1879.

Rooses 1886–1892
M. Rooses, *L'oeuvre de P.P. Rubens. Histoire et desciption de ses tableaux et dessins*, Antwerp, 1886–1892.

Sandrart 1675
J. von Sandrart *Academia todesca della architectura, scultura & pittura: oder Teutsche Academie der Edlen Bau- Bild- und Mahlerey-Künste*, Neurenberg, 1675.

Schnackenburg 1996
B. Schnackenburg, *Gemäldegalerie Alte Meister Kassel. Gesamtkatalog*, Kassel, 1996.

Scholliers 1956
E. Scholliers, 'Vrije en onvrije arbeiders voornamelijk te Antwerpen in de 16de eeuw', *Bijdragen tot de Geschiedenis der Nederlanden*, The Hague, XI, 1956, pp. 285–322.

Schone Kunsten in Antwerpen 1976
Schone Kunsten in Antwerpen, cat. exh. Antwerp, 1976.

Schopenhauer 1831
J. Schopenhauer, *Ausflug an den Niederrhein und nach Belgien im Jahr 1828*, II, Leipzig, 1831.

Silver 1984
L. Silver, *The Paintings of Quinten Massys with Catalogue Raisonné*, Oxford, 1984.

Smith 1829–1842
J. Smith, *A Catalogue Raisonné of the Works of the most eminent Dutch, Flemish and French Painters; in which is included a short Biographical Notice of the Artists, with a copious Description of their principal Pictures ...*, 9 vols., London, 1829–1842.

Soil De Moriamé 1931
E.J. Soil De Moriamé, *Inventaire des objets d'art et d'antiquité existants dans les édifices publics des communes de l'arrondissement judiciaire de Mons*, Charleroi, 1931.

Straubium 1600
G. Straubium, *Icones quibus Habitus omnium fere Mundi Gentium virili, tam mulieri sexui*, Sankt-Gallen, 1600.

Strauss 1980
W.L. Strauss (ed.), *Albrecht Dürer. Woodcuts and Wood Blocks*, New York, 1980.

Stynen 1998
H. Synen, *De onvoltooid verleden tijd. Een geschiedenis van de monumenten- en landschapszorg in België 1835–1940*, Brussels, 1998.

Stynen & Derks 1973–1974
J. Stynen & G. Derks, *Nota betreffende de vordering der restauratiewerken op 19 mei 1973* en *Overzicht van de vordering der restauratiewerken tijdens de periode van mei 1973 tot oktober 1974*, unpublished note 1974 (KCML A/0192).

Theunissens 1892
L. Theunissens, *Aanteekeningen van Jan Peter van Dyck kerksluiter en opperluider der Kathedraal van Antwerpen over geschiedkundige en wetenswaardige voorvallen dezer kerk betreffende, in den troebelen tijd (16 september 1782 tot 2 december 1804)*, 1892.

Thijs 1987A
A. Thijs, 'De contrareformatie en het economisch transformatieproces te Antwerpen', *Bijdragen tot de geschiedenis*, LXX, 1987, pp. 97–124.

Thijs 1987B
A. Thijs , *Van 'werkwinkel' tot 'fabriek'. De textielnijverheid te Antwerpen (einde 15de–begin 19de eeuw)*, Brussels, 1997.

Thijs 1990
A. Thijs, *Van geuzenstad tot katholiek bolwerk. Maatschappelijke betekenis van de Kerk in contrareformatorisch Antwerpen*, Turnhout, 1990.

Thijs 1993
A. Thijs, *Antwerpen internationaal uitgeverscentrum van devotieprenten, 17de–19de eeuw (Miscellanea Neerlandica, 7)*, Louvain, 1993.

Thijs 1997
A. Thijs (1997), 'Religieuze rituelen in het emancipatieproces van Vlaamse en Brabantse handwerksgezellen (zestiende–negentiende eeuw), in C. Lis & H. Soly (eds.), *Werelden van verschil. Ambachtsgilden in de lage landen*, Brussels, 1997, pp. 231–281.

Thijs 2006
A. Thijs, 'Religion and social structure: religious rituals in pre-industrial trade associations in the Low Countries', in C. Lis, J. Lucassen, M. Prak & H. Soly, H. (eds.), *Guilds in the early modern Low Countries. Work, power and representation*, London, 2006, pp. 157–173.

Tondreau & Huvelle 1982
L. Tondreau & J. Huvelle, 'Inventaire et description du mobilier de l'ancien Hôpital Sainte-Elisabeth à Saint-Ghislain', *Annales du Cercle archéologique de Saint-Ghislain et de la région*, III, 1982, pp. 227–228.

Van Brabant 1972
J. Van Brabant, *Onze-Lieve-Vrouwkathedraal van Antwerpen. Grootste gotische kerk der Nederlanden*, Antwerp, 1972.

Van Brabant 1974
J. Van Brabant, *Rampspoed en Restauratie. Bijdrage tot de geschiedenis van de uitrusting en restauratie der Onze-Lieve-Vrouwekathedraal van Antwerpen*, Antwerp, 1974.

Van Bueren 2007
T. Van Bueren, *Leven na de dood. Gedenken in de late Middeleeuwen*, Utrecht, 2007.

Van Damme 1985
J. Van Damme, *Bijdrage tot de studie van de Antwerpse schrijnwerkers, hun ambacht en hun werk tijdens het corporatief stelsel*, unpublished dissertation, K.U.Leuven, 1985.

Van Damme 1990
J. Van Damme, 'De Antwerpse tafereelmakers en hun merken. Identificatie en betekenis', *Jaarboek Koninklijk Museum voor Schone Kunsten Antwerpen*, 1990, pp. 193–236.

Van den Branden 1883
F.J. van den Branden, *Geschiedenis der Antwerpsche Schilderschool*, Antwerp, 1883.

Vandenbroeck 1981
P. Vandenbroeck, *Rondom plechtige intredes en feestelijke stadsversieringen: Antwerpen, 1594–1599–1635*, cat. exh. Antwerp, 1981.

Van den Nieuwenhuizen 1957
J. Van den Nieuwenhuizen, *Gids voor de kathedraal van Antwerpen*, Antwerp, 1957.

Van den Nieuwenhuizen 1962A
J. Van den Nieuwenhuizen, 'La descente de croix de Rubens. Etude préalable au traitement. Histoire matérielle', *Bulletin van het Koninklijk Instituut voor het Kunstpatrimonium*, V, 1962, pp. 27–85.

Van den Nieuwenhuizen 1962B
J. Van den Nieuwenhuizen, 'Antwerpse schilderijen te Parijs (1794–1815)', *Antwerpen*, VIII, 1962, pp. 66–83.

Van den Nieuwenhuizen 1993
J. Van den Nieuwenhuizen, 'People and Institutions in the Church of Our Lady. The Period 1124–1559', in W. Aerts (ed.), *The Cathedral of Our Lady in Antwerp*, Antwerp, 1993, pp. 23–38.

Van den Nieuwenhuizen 2000
J. Van den Nieuwenhuizen, 'Bestuursinstellingen van de stad Antwerpen (12de eeuw–1795)', in *De gewestelijke en lokale overheden in Brabant en Mechelen tot 1795*, II, Brussels, 2000, pp. 467–469.

Van der Meulen 1994
M. Van der Meulen, *Rubens: Copies after the Antique* (*Corpus Rubenianum Ludwig Burchard*, XXIII), 3 vols., London, 1994.

Van der Sanden 1781
J. Van der Sanden, *Oud Konst-toneel van Antwerpen* [manuscript], [1781]. Antwerp, Stadsarchief, Privilegiekamer, PK 171–173.

Van der Stighelen & Vermeylen 2006
K. Van der Stighelen & F. Vermeylen, 'The Antwerp Guild of Saint Luke and the Marketing of Paintings, 1400–1700', in N. De Marchi & H. Van Miegroet, *Mapping Markets for Paintings in Europe*, Turnhout, 2006, pp. 189–208.

Van der Stock 1998
J. Van der Stock, *Painting Images in Antwerp. The Introduction of Printmaking in a city, Fifteenth Century to 1585*, Rotterdam, 1998.

Van der Straelen 1770–1819
J.F. & J.B. van der Straelen, *De Kronijk van Antwerpen 1770–1819*, éd. A. Van Berendocks & J. Rylant, 8 vols, Antwerp, 1929–1936.

Van de Velde 1971
C. Van de Velde; 'Maarten de Vos, De bruiloft te Cana', *Openbaar Kunstbezit in Vlaanderen*, IX, 1971, no. 14.

Van de Velde 1975a
C. Van de Velde, *Frans Floris (1519/20–1570), Leven en werken (Verhandelingen van de Koninklijke Academie voor Wetenschappen, Letteren en Schone Kunsten van België. Klasse der Schone Kunsten*, 30), 2 vols., Brussels, 1975.

Van de Velde 1975b
C. Van de Velde, 'Rubens' Hemelvaart van Maria in de Kathedraal te Antwerpen', *Jaarboek Koninklijk Museum voor Schone Kunsten Antwerpen*, 1975, pp. 250–260.

Van de Velde 1993a
C. Van de Velde, 'The Art Heritage. The Sixteenth Century', in W. Aerts (ed.), *The Cathedral of Our Lady in Antwerp*, Antwerp, 1993, pp. 177–203.

Van de Velde 1993b
C. Van de Velde, 'De Coxcies uit de Onze-Lieve-Vrouwekerk van Antwerpen', *Handelingen van de Koninklijke Kring voor Oudheidkunde, Letteren en Kunst van Mechelen*, XCVI, 1993, pp. 193–214.

Van de Velde 1996
C. Van de Velde, 'Hendrik van Balen', in *The Dictionary of Art*, III, London, 1996, pp. 107–108.

Van de Velde 2005
C. Van de Velde, 'Frans Floris en de Italiaanse Schilderkunst', in N. Dacos & C. Dulière (eds.), *Italia Belgica. La Fondation nationale Princesse Marie-José et les relations artistiques entre la Belgique et l'Italie*, Brussels-Rome, 2005, pp. 149–162.

Van Dyck 1993
L. Van Dijck, 'De architecturale en monumentale polychromie in hoogkoor en vieringtoren in de Onze-Lieve-Vrouwekathedraal te Antwerpen', *M&L* [Monumenten en landschappen], XII, 2, 1993, pp. 10–21.

Van Even 1846
E. Van Even, *Notice biographique sur le peintre Quinten Metsys de Louvan*, Louvain, 1846.

Van Even 1870
E. Van Even, *L'ancienne école de peinture de Louvain*, Brussels, 1870.

Van Gerwen 1977
C. Van Gerwen, *De neogotische beeldhouwkunst in de Onze-Lieve-Vrouwekathedraal van Antwerpen*, Antwerp-Deventer, 1977.

Van Herck 1951
C. Van Herck, 'Het meubilair van de Antwerpse O.L.Vrouwekerk', *Jaarboek Antwerpens Oudheidkundige Kring*, XXIV–XV, 1951, pp. 37–56.

Van Langendonck 1988
L. Van Langendonck, *Onze-Lieve-Vrouwekathedraal te Antwerpen. Historisch onderzoek van muur- en gewelfschilderingen in koor en kruisbeuk,* Antwerp, 1988.

Van Langendonck 1989
L. Van Langendonck, *Historisch onderzoek van het hoogaltaar, de tochtportalen en het koorgestoelte in de Onze-Lieve-Vrouwekathedraal van Antwerpen*, unpublished note, 1989, (KCML A/0192).

Van Langendonck 1993
L. Van Langendonck, 'The History of the Building. The History of the Construction', in W. Aerts (ed.), *The Cathedral of Our Lady in Antwerp*, Antwerp, 1993, pp. 107–122.

Van Leemputten 1993
R. Van Leemputten, 'The History of the Building. The Restoration of the North Tower', in W. Aerts (ed.), *The Cathedral of Our Lady in Antwerp*, Antwerp, 1993, pp. 347–355.

Van Lerius 1841
Th. Van Lerius, *Notre-Dame d'Anvers, avant la seconde invasion française en 1794*, Antwerp, 1841.

Van Lerius 1851
T. Van Lerius, *Notice sur le catalogue du Musée d'Anvers*, Ghent, 1851.

Van Lerius 1855
T. Van Lerius, *Notice des oeuvres d'art de l'église paroissiale et ci-devant insigne collégiale de St. Jacques à Anvers*, Borgerhout, 1855.

Van Lerius 1871
T. Van Lerius, *Tableau des oeuvres d'art anciennes et modernes, dont l'église de St. Jacques à Anvers a été enrichi depuis une trentaine d'années*, Antwerp, 1871.

Van Mander 1604
K. van Mander, *Het Schilder-Boeck*, Haarlem, 1604.

Van Mander-Miedema 1994–1999
H. Miedema, *Karel van Mander, lives of the illustrious Netherlandish and German painters*, 6 vols., Doornspijk, 1994–1999.

Van Puyvelde 1963
L. Van Puyvelde, 'Het altaarstuk van het Ambacht van de Visverkopers te Antwerpen', *Bulletin Koninklijke Musea voor Schone Kunsten van België*, XII, 1963, pp. 35–30.

Van Rossum 1876
J.R. Van Rossum, 'Kerkelijke plechtigheden in de St. Salvatorskerk te Utrecht', *Archief voor de Geschiedenis van het Aartsbisdom Utrecht. Bijdragen*, III, Utrecht, 1876, pp. 109–259.

Van Vloten 1874
[J. van Vloten], *Nederlands schilderkunst van de 14e tot de 18e eeuw - voor het Nederlandsche volk geschetst door J. van Vloten*, Amsterdam, 1874.

Vergara et al. 2004
A. Vergara et al., *Rubens: The Adoration of the Magi*, Madrid, 2004.

Verleysen 2001
F. Verleysen, '"Pretense Confrerieën"? Devotie als communicatie in de Antwerpse corporatieve wereld na 1585', *Tijdschrift voor sociale geschiedenis*, 27:2, 2001, pp. 153–171.

Vervaet 1976
J. Vervaet, 'Catalogus van de altaarstukken van gilden en ambachten uit de Onze-Lieve-Vrouwkerk te Antwerpen en bewaard in het Koninklijk Museum', *Jaarboek Koninklijk Museum voor Schone Kunsten Antwerpen*, 1976, pp. 197–244.

Verzameling 1856
Verzameling der Graf- en Gedenkschriften van de provincie Antwerpen, Antwerp, 1856–1873, 7 vols, vol. 1: *Antwerpen. Cathedrale kerk, Antwerp*, 1856.

Vickers 1981
M. Vickers, 'A new Source for Rubens's Descent from the Cross in Antwerpen', *Pantheon*, XXXIX, 1981, pp. 140–142.

Vignola 1617
G.B. da Vignola, *Regola delle cinque Ordini d' Architettura*, Amsterdam, 1617.

Vlieghe 1972
H. Vlieghe, *Gaspar de Crayer, sa vie et ses oeuvres (Monographies du Nationaal Centrum voor de Plastische Kunsten van de 16e en de 17e eeuw*, IV), Brussels, 1972.

Vlieghe 1973
H. Vlieghe, 'Het altaar van de Jonge Handboog in de Onze-Lieve-Vrouwkerk te Antwerpen', in *Album amicorum J.G. Van Gelder*, The Hague, 1973, pp. 342–346.

Vlieghe 1977
H. Vlieghe, 'Zwischen van Veen und Rubens: Artus Wolffort (1581–1641), ein vergessener Antwerpener Maler', *Wallraf-Richartz-Jahrbuch,* XXXIX, 1977, pp. 93–135.

Vlieghe 1979
H. Vlieghe, 'De leerpraktijk van een jonge schilder: het notitieboekje van Pieter van Lint in het Institut Néerlandais te Parijs', *Jaarboek Koninklijk Museum voor Schone Kunsten te Antwerpen*, 1979, pp. 249–281.

Vlieghe 1981
H. Vlieghe, 'Nog wat over Wolffort, zijn atelier en Van Lint', in *Feestbundel bij de opening van het Kolveniershof en het Rubenianum*, Antwerp, 1981, pp. 83–87.

Vlieghe 1990
H. Vlieghe, 'Wolffort (Wolffaert), Artus, schilder', *Nationaal Biografisch Woordenboek*, XIII, Brussels, 1990, pp. 885–889.

Von Baldass 1944
L. von Baldass, 'Die Entwicklung des Bernart van Orley', *Jahrbuch der kunsthistorischen Sammlungen in Wien,* XIII, 1944, pp. 141–191.

Von Einem 1968
H. von Einem, 'Rubens's "Kreuzabnahme" in der Antwerpener Kathedrale', *Festschrift fur Leo Brandt*, Cologne, 1968, pp. 541–557.

Vroom 1983
W.H. Vroom, *De Onze-Lieve-Vrouwekerk te Antwerpen. De financiering van de bouw tot de beeldenstorm*, Antwerp, 1983.

Waagen 1862
G. Waagen, *Handbuch der Geschichte der Malerei*, Stuttgart, 1862.

Wadum 1998
J. Wadum, 'The Antwerp Brand on Paintings on Panels', in E. Hermens, *Looking Through Paintings: The Study of Painting Techniques and Materials in Support of Art Historical Research* (*Leids Kunsthistorisch Jaarboek*, XI), 1998, pp, 179–198.

Wauters 1892
A. Wauters, *Bernart van Orley,* Paris, 1892.

Wauters 1902
A.J. Wauters, *Les van Orley, Valentin, Bernard Pierre Richard, Jean – cinq notices biographiques*, Brussels, 1902.

Werche 1997
B. Werche, 'Die Zusammenarbeit von Jan Brueghel d. Ä. und Hendrik van Balen', in *Pieter Brueghel der Jüngere-Jan Brueghel der Ältere. Flämische Malerei um 1600. Tradition und Fortschritt* (cat. exh. Kulturstiftung Ruhr Villa Hügel Essen), Lingen, 1997, pp. 67–74.

Werche 2004
B. Werche, *Hendrick van Balen (1575–1632) Ein Antwerpener Kabinettbildmaler der Rubenszeit* (*Pictura Nova*, VII), 2 vols., Turnhout, 2004.

Wescher 1935
P. Wescher, 'Jan van Elburcht, ein vergessener Maler des 16. Jahrhunderts', *Oud Holland*, LII, 1935, pp. 127–129.

Whinney 1968
M. Whinney, *Early Flemish Painting*, London-Glasgow, 1968.

Wikenhauser 1932
A. Wikenhauser, 'Die Liebeswerke in dem Gerichtsgemälde Mt. 25,31–46', *Biblische Zeitschrift*, XX, 1932, pp. 366–377.

Winkler 1924
F. Winkler, *Die altniederländische Malerei 1400–1600*, Berlin, 1924.

Woollett & Van Suchtelen 2006
A. Woollett & A. van Suchtelen, *Rubens en Breughel een artistieke vriendschap* (cat. exh. The Hague, Mauritshuis), Zwolle, 2006.

Wuyts 1991
L. Wuyts, 'Bij de iconografie van twee Rubensschilderijen: De Bewening van Christus en Christus op het stro', *Jaarboek van het Koninklijk Museum voor Schone Kunsten Antwerpen*, 1991, pp. 61–86.

Wuyts 1996
L. Wuyts, 'Christus op het stro, Enkele bedenkingen bij het epitaphium van Jan Michielsen', *Kwintet,* XXX, 1996, pp. 18–23.

Wyffels 1951
C. Wyffels, *De oorsprong der ambachten in Vlaanderen en Brabant* (*Verhandelingen van de Koninklijke Vlaamse Academie voor Wetenschappen, Letteren en Schone Kunsten van België*, 12), Brussels, 1951.

Woollett 2004
A. Woollett, *The Altarpiece in Antwerp, 1554–1615: painting and the militia guilds*, Columbia University, New York, 2004.

Zuntz 1929
D. Zuntz, *Frans Floris. Ein Beitrag zur Geschichte der Niederländischen Kunst im 16. Jahrhundert*, Straatsburg, 1929.

Zweite 1980
A. Zweite, *Marten de Vos als Maler. Ein Beitrag zur Geschichte der Antwerpener Malerei in der zweiten Hälfte des 16. Jahrhunderts*, Berlin, 1980.

Index

Page numbers in italic refer to the illustrations

Biographies

Willem Aerts ❧ Master in Art History. Also graduated in Monuments and Sites Conservation. Head of the Section of Cultural Heritage (Department of Culture) of Antwerp Province, and in 2007–2008 Acting Departmental Head of Culture. Involved in the cathedral project since 1982. Under his aegis was published *The Cathedral of Our Lady in Antwerp,* Fonds Mercator, Antwerp, 1993.

Claire Baisier ❧ Doctor in Art History. Consultant for religious heritage and coordinator of Monumental Churches in Antwerp. She is an advisor on conservation and management of the cultural heritage in churches, develops projects for public functioning and establishes long-term policies on Antwerp's church heritage, more specifically for the five monumental churches.

Stef Binst ❧ Civil engineer-architect, graduated in Monuments and Sites Conservation. Associate of the Department of Infrastructure of Antwerp Province. From 2001 responsible for the coordination of restoration works on the Cathedral of Our Lady.

Bert De Munck ❧ Doctor in History. Lecturer of Social-Economic Modern History, History, and Social Studies in the Department of History, Antwerp University; also associate of the Centre for Urban History in the same department. Main research field concerns the history of crafts and professional education, social life and capital, and the circulation of technical knowledge. He is also coordinator of the journal *Stadsgeschiedenis.*

Ria Fabri ❧ Doctor in Art History. Curator of Antwerp Cathedral, member of the special academic staff of Antwerp University (Department of History) and of the Antwerp Provincial Commission for History.

Marcel Gielis ❧ Studied history and philosophy; doctor in Theology at Tilburg University. Professor at the Faculty of Catholic Theology at Tilburg University. Member of the Antwerp Provincial Commission for History.

Stefaan Grieten ❧ Master in Art History. Scientific assistant associated to the Section of Cultural Heritage (Department of Culture) of the Antwerp Provincial Executive and in this capacity the author and editor-in-chief of the inventory of the art patrimony of the Cathedral of Our Lady (Brepols, 1996).

Lars Hendrikman ❧ Studied art history at Groningen State University, specialising in early-Dutch art and material research. Afterwards he was an associate of the same university as a lecturer and scientific assistant. He collaborated on several exhibitions about early-Dutch art. Since 2006 he has been the curator of the Bonnefanten Museum in Maastricht. He is finishing a doctoral thesis on Bernard van Orley.

Valérie Herremans ❧ Doctor in Art History. Scientific assistant at the Antwerp Koninklijk Museum voor Schone Kunsten.

Paul Huvenne ❧ Doctor in Art History. Administrator-General of the Antwerp Koninklijk Museum voor Schone Kunsten. Under his supervision the museum realised exhibitions such as *Anthony van Dyck* (1999), *Fatal Women* (2003), and *Prayers and portraits: unfolding the Netherlandish diptych* (2007). From 1984 to 1997 he administrated the Rubens House in Antwerp.

Madeleine Manderyck ❧ Master in Art History, assistant-director at the Flemish Community, Agency of Environmental Planning · Heritage.

Maximiliaan P.J. Martens ❧ PhD at the University of California, Santa Barbara, 1992, Professor of Fine Arts in the Netherlands from the 14th to the 16th century at Ghent University. He researches the social-economic and material aspects of artistic production.

Natasja Peeters ❧ Doctor in Art History. She has published on art and the socio-economical position of the artist in the 16th century. Since 2006 curator of the art collection of the Musée royal de l'Armée et d'Histoire militaire in Brussels.

Prisca Valkeneers ❧ Master in Art History, scientific assistant at the Antwerp Centrum voor de Vlaamse Kunst van de 16de en de 17de eeuw (Rubenianum) and the Antwerp Koninklijk Museum voor Schone Kunsten.

Jos Van den Nieuwenhuizen ❧ Doctor in History. Honorary City Archivist of Antwerp and archivist of the Antwerp cathedral archives.

Carl Van de Velde ❧ Doctor in Art History. Emeritus professor at the Brussels University (VUB). He specialises in Flemish art in the 16th and 17th centuries and has produced authoritative research to the life and work of Frans Floris. He works as an editor for the *Corpus Rubenianum Ludwig Burchard,* published by the Centrum voor de Vlaamse Kunst van de 16de en de 17de eeuw.

Nico Van Hout ❧ Doctor in Art History. Curator and exhibition maker, associate of the Antwerp Koninklijk Museum voor Schone Kunsten.

Christine Van Mulders ❧ Master in Art History and assistant to the Department of Collection Research of the Antwerp Koninklijk Museum voor Schone Kunsten. Coordinator of the research project on the works of Peter Paul Rubens belonging to the collection of the Royal Museum.

Paul Van Remoortere ❧ Doctor in Law. Chairman of the Church Council of the Cathedral of Our Lady in Antwerp.

Colophon

This exhibition is organised by De Kathedraal vzw on demand of the church fabric of the Cathedral of Our Lady in Antwerp.
Its members are Paul Van Remoortere (Chairman), Philippe Michiels (Secretary), Frank Verhaegen (Treasurer), Elisabeth Berger, Ria Fabri, Hubert Hellraeth, Luc Leytens, Stefan Van Tricht, Canon Wilfried Verhaert, and Christian Devos (President).

The exhibition is organised to mark the occasion of the commemoration of the creation of the Diocese of Antwerp in 1559. It is realised in part thanks to the collaboration with the Antwerp Koninklijk Museum voor Schone Kunsten with Dr Paul Huvenne as its administrator-general.

Honorary committee Monsignor Johan Bonny, Bishop of Antwerp
Dean Canon Louis De Belder and the members of the Cathedral Chapter
Canon Wilfried Verhaert, Cathedral Priest, and the Priests Paul Smets and Tim De Mey
Luc Vannerum, President of the Chapel of the Blessed Sacrament
Jean-Marie De Meulder, President of the Chapel of 'Onze-Lieve-Vrouw-lof' (Praise of Our Lady)

Scientific Committee Willem Aerts, Dr Claire Baisier, Yolande Deckers, Dr Ria Fabri, Prof. Dr Marcel Gielis, Dr Paul Huvenne (president), Lizet Klaassen, Madeleine Manderyck, Rudi Mannaerts, Dr Marie Juliette Marinus, Hans Nieuwdorp, Dr Jos Van den Nieuwenhuizen and Dr Nico Van Hout

Organisation Committee Yolande Deckers, Christian Devos, Dr Ria Fabri, Dr Paul Huvenne, An Teyssen, Dr Nico Van Hout and Paul Van Remoortere (president)

Curators Dr Ria Fabri and Dr Nico Van Hout

Exhibition Coordinator An Teyssen

Exhibition Design Koen Van Synghel

Translation Filip Lagey & Perette Elizabeth Michelli

Editing Dr Hans Devisscher

Catalogue Design Frederik Hulstaert

Photography The photographs were provided by the museums and the owners themselves, by the Institut Royal du Patrimoine artistique, Lukas · Art in Flanders and the Province of Antwerp

Image Editing & Processing Blondé Communication

Publishers De Kathedraal vzw & BAI Publishers

Printing Blondé Printing

Acknowledgements	Erfgoedbibliotheek Hendrik Conscience, Antwerp Rubenianum, Antwerp (Hilde Bogaerts, Vivianne Verbraeken) Ruusbroecgenootschap, University of Antwerp (Erna Van Looveren) FelixArchief (City Archives), Antwerp
Frontispiece	Quinten Metsijs, *The Lamentation,* 1509–1511, centre panel [detail]
Frontispiece catalogue	Frans II Francken, *Christ among the Scribes,* 1587, centre panel [detail]
Cover	Pieter Paul Rubens, *The Descent of the Cross,* 1611–1614, right side panel [detail]
Back cover	Quinten Metsijs, *The Lamentation,* 1509–1511, centre panel [detail]
Legal deposit	D/2009/5751/16
ISBN	9789085865377

Printed in Belgium